Vinson Synan and Amos Yong, together with a veritable who's who of Pentecostal scholars from Europe and North America, have provided an invaluable service to anyone interested in both historical and up-to-the-minute reporting on the state of Spirit-empowered Christianity today. This fourth volume of *Global Renewal Christianity* offers sober correction to Pentecostal-Charismatic triumphalists who would imagine an exaggerated success in Europe based on spectacular revivals in Latin America, sub-Saharan Africa, and East Asia. At the same time the stories it tells of Spirit-led heroes of the past and of present-day church planters—both native European and immigrant—offer real evidence for hope that while calling on others, God will not pass Europe and North America by.

—Joseph Castleberry, EdD
President, Northwest University
Author, *The New Pilgrims: How Immigrants Are Renewing America's Faith and Values*

A most fascinating book on Pentecostal and Charismatic movements in the Western world. It provides valuable reflections of the past, careful analysis of the present, and challenging perspectives for the future. A helpful guide to understand Spirit-empowered Christianity in the twenty-first century.

—Cornelis van der Laan, PhD
Emeritus Professor for Pentecostal Studies
Vrije Universiteit Amsterdam

This volume provides a state-of-the-art account of what is taking place in the renewal movements across Europe and North America. As such, it is the new starting point for understanding contemporary developments in the renewal churches and the key theological issues at stake for the renewal movements in these areas of the world. It also provides a catalyst and foundation for an ongoing conversation for what the future holds for the European and North American renewal churches and their theological trajectories.

—Steven M. Studebaker, PhD
Associate Professor of Historical and Systematic Theology, Howard and Shirley Bentall Chair in Evangelical Thought, McMaster Divinity College, Hamilton, Ontario

This volume of *Global Renewal Christianity* gathers together critical analyses of European and North American scholars on the work of the Holy Spirit in their countries in the so-called global North. Spirit-filled preaching reached the hearts of people despite state oppression in Eastern Europe, the Nazi regime in Italy, the opposition of national traditions toward Roma people, and the cynicism of contemporary global market-driven European and North American pluralistic cultures. An international team of Pentecostal scholars and scholars of Pentecostalism call for theological reflection on the rise of the Pentecostal movement and future challenges in the mission of the church. The book is an invaluable addition to the history and theology of the Pentecostal church over the last century plus.

—Tatiana Gorbacheva
Professor of Christian Counseling, Eurasian Theological Seminary, Moscow
Head of the Education Department, Russian Union of Christians of Evangelical Faith

Vinson Synan and Amos Yong have prodigiously enriched the fast-growing field of Pentecostal studies with their magisterial multipart survey of Spirit-empowered movements across the globe. This volume on Europe and North America focuses on the two continents that have historically attracted the most academic attention where Pentecostal and renewalist Christianity are concerned, yet it manages to offer consistently fresh and often surprising perspectives on those continents. It does so by allotting proportionally more space than usual to less well-known countries and regions within them and by interlacing this commendably diverse national and regional survey with stimulating and sometimes provocative essays on more transnational themes, such as women and Pentecostalism in Europe, Pentecostal origins within and beyond North America, and the globalization of Oneness Pentecostalism. The contributors write to a consistently high standard, and the result is a truly comprehensive text that will serve theologians, sociologists of religion, and others very well for many years to come.

—Rev. Dr. David Hilborn
Principal, St. John's School of Mission
Nottingham, United Kingdom

VOLUME FOUR

EUROPE AND NORTH AMERICA

GLOBAL RENEWAL Christianity

VINSON SYNAN

and

AMOS YONG

EDITORS

CHARISMA HOUSE

Most Charisma House Book Group products are available at special quantity discounts for bulk purchase for sales promotions, premiums, fund-raising, and educational needs. For details, write Charisma House Book Group, 600 Rinehart Road, Lake Mary, Florida 32746, or telephone (407) 333-0600.

Global Renewal Christianity: Spirit-Empowered Movements Past, Present, and Future, Volume 4: Europe and North America by Vinson Synan and Amos Yong, Editors
Published by Charisma House
Charisma Media/Charisma House Book Group
600 Rinehart Road
Lake Mary, Florida 32746
www.charismahouse.com

Cover design by Lisa Rae McClure
Design Director: Justin Evans

Visit the Empowered21 website at http://empowered21.com/.

Library of Congress Cataloging-in-Publication Data:
An application to register this book for cataloging has been submitted to the Library of Congress.
International Standard Book Number: 978-1-62998-943-3
E-book ISBN: 978-1-62998-944-0

17 18 19 20 21 — 9 8 7 6 5 4 3 2 1
Printed in Canada

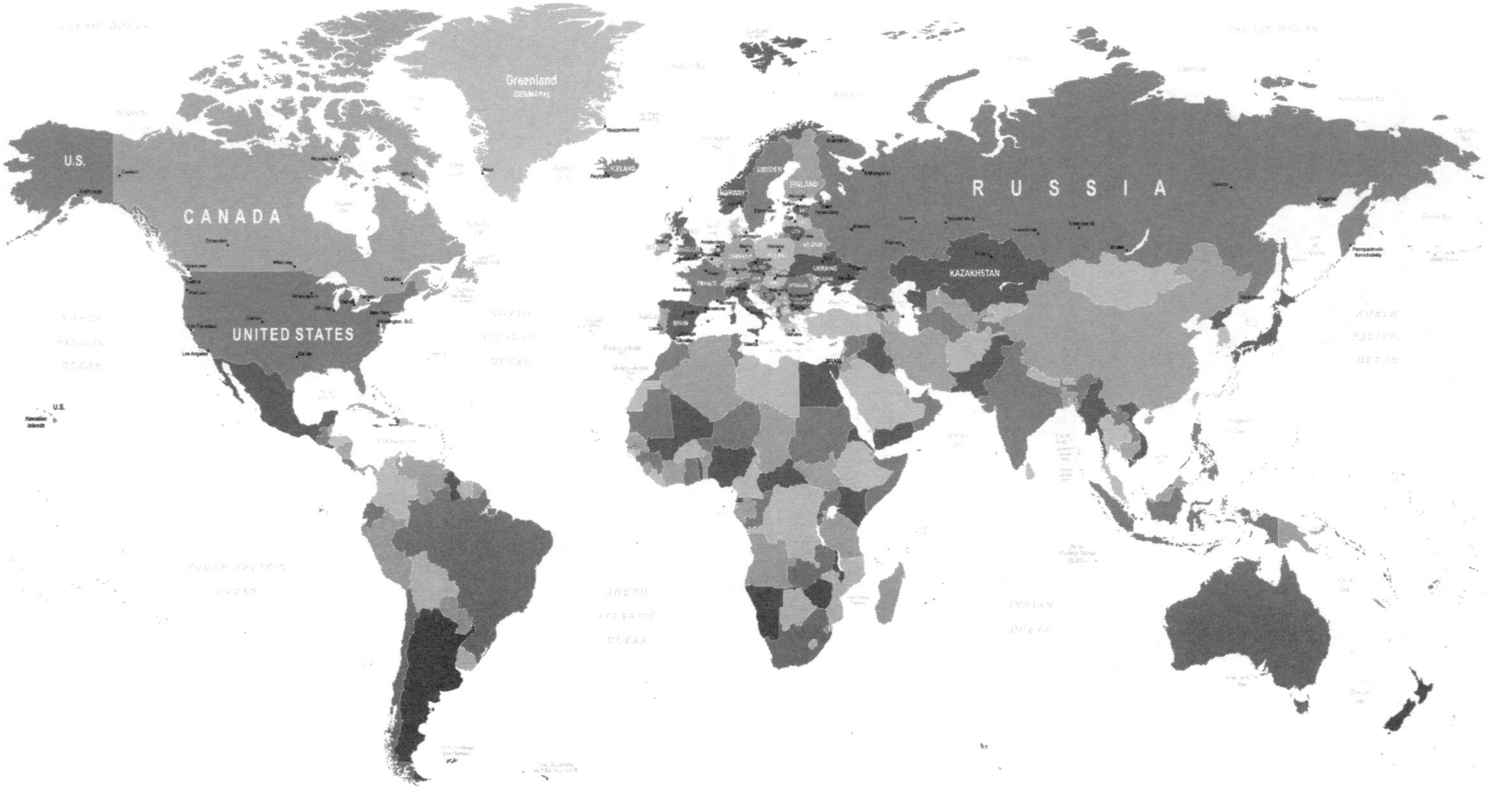
U.S.
CANADA
Greenland
ICELAND
UNITED STATES
SWEDEN
FINLAND
UKRAINE
RUSSIA
KAZAKHSTAN

Contents

Part III
Northern Europe

Part IV
North America and Global Theological Topics

Foreword

THE WORK OF the Holy Spirit around the world in our lifetime is changing the face of global Christianity. The prayer movements from across Asia, to worship in Africa and Latin America, to church revitalization in Europe and North America and the masses being evangelized daily worldwide give evidence that a significant spiritual shift has taken place. At the heart of this shift are millions of Spirit-empowered believers. This volume of exceptional scholarly analysis, one of four on the global Spirit-empowered movement, helps bring definition, understanding, and depth to the dynamic work that God is doing today.

Spirit-empowered, or renewalist, Christianity continues to expand exponentially. As this growth takes place, the depth of the movement and a clear twenty-first-century hermeneutic must also grow. Isaiah 54:2 provides prophetic encouragement for this increased depth by stating, "Enlarge the place of your tent, and let them stretch out the curtains of your habitations; spare not, lengthen your cords, and strengthen your stakes" (MEV).

As the tent of Spirit-empowered Christianity grows, the stakes of theological understanding must also deepen. This will allow the movement to withstand the twenty-first-century storms that will rage against us while sheltering those believers in this ever-enlarging tent.

Empowered21 is committed to serving the broad spectrum of Spirit-empowered Christianity including Pentecostals, Charismatics, and every subsequent wave of Holy Spirit expression in the body of Christ. It is with deep gratitude to our editors, Dr. Vinson Synan and Dr. Amos Yong, that we publish this exciting volume of essays with the hope that God will use this work to indeed "deepen our stakes" for the exciting days ahead.

My prayer is that as you absorb this material, God's presence will overshadow you so you may personally experience the Holy Spirit, who is moving globally today.

Serving a movement, empowering a generation,

—Dr. William M. Wilson
President of Oral Roberts University
Global Cochair of Empowered21

Foreword

In his vision, John the Revelator saw "a great multitude which no one could count, from all nations and tribes and peoples and tongues, standing before the throne and before the Lamb, clothed with white robes, with palm branches in their hands. They cried out with a loud voice: 'Salvation belongs to our God who sits on the throne, and to the Lamb!'" (Rev. 7:9–10, MEV).

What was for John a revelation of the end times is increasingly for us a picture of the present. No longer is it possible—if, in fact, it ever was!—for Western Christians to speak of the faith of Jesus Christ as a European and North American faith. Instead, we must speak of global Christianity, for the faith has gone out from Jerusalem to the ends of the earth (Acts 1:8).

In the last one hundred years, global Pentecostalism has been used by God to advance the good news of the kingdom of God within every nation, tribe, people, and language. The volume you are reading is proof of that. It is one of four volumes assaying the past, present, and future of global Pentecostalism.

I said that John's end-times vision is "increasingly" a picture of the present for us, but that adverb reminds us that there is still work to do. May God use this scholarly volume to inform and inspire a new generation of Spirit-empowered leaders to take the good news about His Son into every global nook and cranny, so that today's unreached may become tomorrow's white-robed, palm-waving praisers of Jesus Christ! Then, and only then, will John's vision be realized in full.

—Dr. George O. Wood
General Superintendent of the Assemblies of God (USA)
Chairman of the World Assemblies of God Fellowship
Global Cochair of Empowered21

Series Preface

THE EMPOWERED21 MOVEMENT had its origin in a vision given to Robert Fisher concerning a fitting celebration of the centennial of the Azusa Street revival that began in 1906. To plan for the event, Fisher organized the Center for Spiritual Renewal in 2000 in Cleveland, Tennessee. Unfortunately he passed away before the event took place, and his friend Billy Wilson was asked to complete the plans for the celebration and lead the conference. The celebration, which met in the Staples Center in Los Angeles in April of 2006, was a resounding success as more than fifty thousand persons attended the various events that were celebrated in several Los Angeles venues.

After the Azusa Street celebration in 2006, the center began a connection with Oral Roberts University (ORU) when Wilson and his friend Mart Green were chosen to lead the Board of Trustees of the university. From this association came a vision for another meeting on the campus of ORU. Although the meeting was under the auspices of ORU, the Center for Spiritual Renewal was chosen to administer the event. Called the "Global Congress on Holy Spirit Empowerment," the Tulsa meeting drew ten thousand persons to the campus in April 2010.

In preparing for the Tulsa meeting, Mart Green and his associates conducted a broad ranging survey of the young people of the next generation to find out what term best described the Pentecostal/Charismatic renewal in their minds. In the end the word *empowered* won out over the terms "Pentecostal," "Charismatic," or "full gospel." Also, since everyone wanted to look toward the future instead of the past, the numeral 21 was added, referring to the twenty-first century. Thus the term "Empowered21" (or E21) was born.

The vision statement of Empowered21 is powerful and pointed: "That every person on earth would have an authentic encounter with Jesus Christ through the Power and Presence of the Holy Spirit…by Pentecost 2033." Its mission statement proclaims that: "Empowered21 will help shape the future of the Global Spirit Empowered movement throughout the world by focusing on crucial issues facing the movement and connecting generations for intergenerational blessing and impartation." Thus the major focus is on what is called the "Nextgen" (next generation) in order to continue the "spiritual grace" of the Pentecostal/Charismatic renewal into future generations. Underlining all the efforts of this vision is a prayer for a "fresh outpouring of the Holy Spirit in the twenty-first century." These themes have permeated all the events and planning sessions of E21 from the beginning.

At the early years of the E21 movement Wilson led seventeen unique "conversations" with some five hundred church leaders and scholars from fifty-four nations and fifteen universities with the goal of answering the questions "What does it mean to be Spirit empowered in the twenty-first century?" and "What steps can be taken to engage new generations in the Spirit-filled experience?" Armed with the wealth of knowledge from these conversations, E21 conducted two major events on university campuses. The first was the aforementioned Global Congress on Holy Spirit Empowerment, which drew ten thousand persons to Oral Roberts University in April 2010 where 210 workshops produced a futuristic book edited by Vinson Synan titled *Spirit-Empowered Christianity in the 21st Century* (Charisma House, 2011). The second was a meeting at Regent University in 2012 in conjunction with the Society for Pentecostal Studies, which emphasized the "convergence" of Spirit-empowered generations and movements. More than five hundred leaders registered for this event.

During this time the E21 movement was organized on an international scale with a global cabinet and eleven regional cabinets around the world. Included in these groups were leaders from most of the Pentecostal and Charismatic movements in the world. The first global gathering after the American events at ORU and Regent University was the E21 Asia Congress held in Jakarta, Indonesia, in October 2011, which drew some fifteen thousand persons.

Other plans for the future include worldwide celebrations on Pentecost Sunday each year to celebrate the birthday of the church and the outpouring of the Holy Spirit in the Upper Room (Acts 2). On Pentecost Sunday 2012 many thousands gathered in local celebrations around the world. Totally ecumenical, the vision is to see Pentecost Sunday rise to the level of Easter and Christmas as great days to make a common witness to the world.

An important part of the E21 vision has been to gather scholars from around the world to study the past, present, and future of the Empowered movements on every continent and from as many nations as possible. To accomplish this goal, three meetings convened before the final one in Jerusalem in 2015. One was held in Oxford, England, in 2012 under the leadership of Dr. Harold Hunter. Another took place in Sydney, Australia, in 2013, where the focus was on Asia. Vinson Synan and Amos Yong directed this latter consultation and those that followed. The third meeting was in Quito, Ecuador, in 2014, where the focus was on Latin America. The last meeting of scholars was in Jerusalem in 2015 in the culminating congress where thousands of people gathered for one of the largest Christian meetings held in the Holy Land in modern times. Here the scholars read papers focusing on Africa, North America, and Europe.

In the end, four volumes of the papers read in these gatherings will be published and edited by Synan and Yong. They will be on Asia, Africa, Latin America, Europe, and North America, and will be published by Charisma House in Lake Mary, Florida. Many of the papers published in these volumes were initially presented in the above-mentioned conferences and consultations, but not all. Those who could not attend the conferences or consultations were invited to write specifically for the project. Most of the chapters across the volumes were intended thus to be read, although a few were written to be presented and heard and have retained their oral character (which will be easily identifiable as such in what follows). In all cases, scholars with a PhD or its equivalent and a recognized publication record were invited, although in a good number of cases our first choices were not able to participate because of other commitments or circumstances. In most cases, scholars are also personal participants in Pentecostal, Charismatic, or renewal movements, although again, not all. In any of the latter cases, of course, authors were invited because of their recognized capacity to present and discuss Pentecostal/Charismatic movements with sympathetic objectivity.

This mix of both confessional Pentecostal/Charismatic "insiders" and "outsiders" may result for some readers in a certain sense of unevenness as they move from chapter to chapter in each volume. Some writers write more from a first-person perspective, while others remain more distant. A few approached their task more pastorally, while many more academically, in overall orientation. Last but not least, many of the latter remain more descriptive in their approach while others are more normative with regard to the theology, practice, and mission of Spirit-empowered churches and communities. The editors hope that such a combination of voices, stances, and dispositions will introduce readers to the broad spectrum of Pentecostal/Charismatic scholarship. "Outsiders" might come to appreciate the animating concerns of Pentecostal/Charismatic scholars who are in touch with pastoral and ecclesial realities and challenges, while readers who are lay and ecclesial leaders, pastors, and bureaucrats (used here descriptively rather than pejoratively) in the Spirit-empowered renewal movement worldwide may perhaps also glean something useful from their academic colleagues.

The editors are hopeful that these volumes will be of wide-ranging benefit to readers from both of these domains in part because of the conceptual layout for the project. The task presented to each of the invitees was to write about the history and theology of Pentecostal/Charismatic or renewal movements in a specified region or country. With this, some assessment of theological orientation and development was expected, as well as analyses of opportunities and challenges lying ahead of these movements, especially on the theological front. Most chapters in these volumes follow this general format, although not all.

The Empowered21 movement, under the able leadership of Billy Wilson and the many worldwide leadership groups that he has gathered, seems poised to bring more coordination to all the Spirit-filled Pentecostal and Charismatic movements in the world to a level that has not been seen heretofore. In the long run, it is hoped that this set of books produced by these scholars will be a permanent and important milestone in the history and theology of the Empowered21 movement from the vantage point of the middle of the second decade of the twenty-first century.

Acknowledgments

MANY FRIENDS CONTRIBUTED to making this book a reality. First we thank the E21 leadership team whose vision brought this and the other books in the series into being. They include Billy Wilson, Mart Green, Ossie Mills, Assif Reid, Robin Cole, Gloria Smith, Alyssa Beard, Kristin Towles-Esparza, and their colleagues. Also special thanks are due to Tessie DeVore and Charisma House, publisher of the book, and to Mike Schatz, Debbie Marrie, Margarita Henry, Jackie Criche, and others for their help with the publication process. Adrienne Gaines has been an incredibly efficient editor to work with at Charisma through the entire project. We will miss working with her.

This European and North American volume owes much to the leaders of Empowered21 who provided facilities and support for the scholars to meet in the Pais Arena in Jerusalem as part of the Jerusalem 2015 Empowered Global Congress. Special thanks go to Ossie Mills for site planning and Assif Reid for overseeing the scholar's track. We are grateful also to Dr. Kathleen Reid Martinez and Dr. Eric Newberg of Oral Roberts University who co-chaired the track. Hoon Jung, Amos Yong's graduate assistant, helped with the index. Above all, thanks to the authors of the following pages whose excellent research and writing made this important book such a great contribution to the study of current Spirit-empowered movements.

Contributors

Rakel Ystebø Alegre (PhD candidate, Regent University School of Divinity) is academic dean at Substans Bible School, Bergen, Norway, and assistant professor of history and theology at the Norwegian School of Leadership and Theology, Oslo, Norway.

Jan-Åke Alvarsson (PhD, Uppsala University) is professor of cultural anthropology, Uppsala University, Uppsala, Sweden.

Miroslav Atanasov (PhD, Asbury Theological Seminary) is lecturer of intercultural studies, academic writing, and English at Renmin University of China, Beijing, China.

Ciprian Balaban (PhD, Babeş-Bolyai University) is lecturer in church history at Institutul Teologic Penticostal, Bucharest, Romania.

Lewis Brogdon (PhD, Regent University) is assistant professor of religion at Claflin University, Orangeburg, South Carolina.

Corneliu Constantineanu (PhD, University of Leeds) is professor of New Testament studies at Aurel Vlaicu University, Arad, Romania.

Pamela M. S. Holmes (PhD, University of Toronto) is in ministry in the United Church of Canada and formerly taught in the areas of theology, spirituality, ministry, and ethics at the School of Religion, Queen's University, Kingston, Ontario.

Tonny Jacobsen (DMin, University of Wales) is pastor of the Pentecostal Church, Vejle, Denmark.

William K. Kay (DD, Nottingham University) is professor of theology at Glyndŵr University, Wrexham, Wales.

Miriam (Mimi) A. Kelly (PhD, St. Patrick's College) is a lecturer of Pentecostal/Charismatic history and Irish church history at Irish Bible Institute, Dublin, Ireland.

Wojciech Kowalewski (PhD, University of Wales) is president of Golden Apple Institute, Wrocław, Poland.

Torsten Löfstedt (PhD, University of California, Berkeley) is associate professor in the Study of Religions at Linnaeus University, Växjö and Kalmar, Sweden.

Frank D. Macchia (DTh, University of Basel) is associate director of the Centre for Pentecostal and Charismatic Studies at Bangor University, Wales, and professor of Christian theology at Vanguard University, Costa Mesa, California.

Paolo Mauriello (MA, University of Salerno) is professor of faith and communication at the Facoltà Pentecostale di Teologia e Studi Religiosi, Aversa, Italy.

Michael J. McClymond (PhD, University of Chicago) is Clarence Louis and Irene Steber Professor of Theological Studies at St. Louis University, St. Louis, Missouri.

Carmine Napolitano (MA, University of Naples Federico II and University of Rome Tor Vergata) is professor of history and theology of the Pentecostal movement at the Facoltà Pentecostale di Teologia e Studi Religiosi, Aversa, Italy.

Eric N. Newberg (PhD, Regent University) is professor of theological and historical studies at Oral Roberts University, Tulsa, Oklahoma.

Raymond Pfister (Diplôme de Docteur de Théologie Protestante [PhD equivalent], University of Strasbourg) is senior tutor in biblical theology, church history, and messianic Judaism at King's Evangelical Divinity School, United Kingdom.

Jean-Daniel Plüss (PhD, Catholic University of Leuven) is chair of the European Pentecostal Charismatic Research Association and engaged in various ecumenical dialogues involving Pentecostals.

David A. Reed (PhD, Boston University) is professor emeritus of pastoral theology and research professor at Wycliffe College, University of Toronto, Canada, and president of Kairos International University, Irvine, California.

Calvin L. Smith (PhD, University of Birmingham) is principal of King's Evangelical Divinity School, Kent, United Kingdom.

Gottfried Sommer (PhD, Evangelische Theologische Faculteit) is pastor of a Church of God congregation in Rottweil, Germany, and a guest lecturer in historical and systematical theology at the Martin Bucer Seminary in Hamburg, Germany.

Vinson Synan (PhD, University of Georgia) is interim dean of the School of Theology and Mission at Oral Roberts University, Tulsa, Oklahoma.

Karl Inge Tangen (PhD, Norwegian School of Theology) is principal of the Norwegian School of Leadership and Theology, Oslo, Norway.

Amos Yong (PhD, Boston University) is professor of theology and mission at Fuller Theological Seminary, Pasadena, California.

Adrian Yuen (PhD, Walden University) is general superintendent of His Highest Praise International network of churches.

Huibert H. Zegwaart (MTh, Catholic University of Louvain) is professor of systematic theology at Windesheim University of Applied Sciences, Zwolle and Amsterdam, The Netherlands.

Introduction

"Back" to the West: Possibilities and Challenges for Pentecostal Histories and Theologies in the Twenty-First Century

Vinson Synan and Amos Yong

As the fourth and concluding volume of *Global Renewal Christianity*, this introductory chapter looks "back to the West" in two ways: in light of the preceding three volumes focused on renewal movements in the majority world and in light of the much-discussed contemporary shift of the center of Christianity to the Global South. Following the overarching structure of the essays in all of the volumes that provided both historical and theological perspectives on renewal Christianity in various regions and countries of the world, we will proceed historically first and then more theologically second. In both parts of the following introductory reflection, we will ask: What are the possibilities and challenges for Pentecostal historiography and theological methodology, always in light of both senses of looking "back to the West," but also to provide the reader of this present work with orientation to the chapters to come.

One caveat before continuing: This volume, part of the series *Global Renewal Christianity: Spirit-Empowered Movements Past, Present, and Future*, was conceived to review the status of the empowered movements in North America and Europe in the first decade of the twentieth century and to discern theological currents and developments. As with the other volumes, the discussions are by no means exhaustive. Even though they are divided primarily by nations (within regions) and include some chapters devoted to larger-scale theological analyses, there are innumerable lacunae, even according to the organizational categories deployed. Arguably, marginal perspectives remain underdeveloped, even as we have attempted to be as attentive as possible to the growing edges of scholarship on the global movement. Precisely for this reason, then, the following at least highlights what else needs to be done, even in light of the state-of-the-question research and assessments that are found in this volume and its companion texts.

Possibilities and Challenges for Pentecostal Histories

We utilize here in this first section the standard Pentecostal historiographical framework related to the classical, Charismatic, and "third wave" streams for two reasons.[1] First, it will orient us toward the content of this book, particularly when the chapters in part 4 on North America are prioritized. Second, recounting this standard historiography will provide opportunities to compare and contrast with Pentecostal historiography in global perspective, precisely what has been accomplished in the other three volumes of this series.

Pentecostal Roots: North America and Europe

The modern classical Pentecostal movement with a clearly defined theology had its first beginnings in a small Bible school in Topeka, Kansas, led by Charles Fox Parham.[2] A former Methodist pastor turned evangelist and teacher, Parham established Bethel Bible School in Topeka in 1900. Here he taught his students that a tremendous revival would come at the turn of the century that would herald the second coming of Christ. On January 1, 1900, the first day of the new century, a student, Agnes Ozman, spoke in tongues, to the astonishment of Parham and the student body. This experience led to Parham's teaching that speaking in tongues was the "Bible evidence" of the Pentecostal baptism in the Holy

Spirit.[3] For four years, Parham and his students held revivals in towns and cities from Kansas to Texas, where utterances in tongues drew multitudes of curious onlookers to his meetings. After establishing another Bible school in Houston, Texas, by 1905 his movement attracted thousands of followers.

One of the students in Houston, William J. Seymour, a black man, then took the Pentecostal message to Los Angeles in 1906, where a revival broke out in a tumbledown mission on Azusa Street. This meeting, which continued unabated for over three years, became one of the most notable and influential revivals in Christian history.[4] People came from all over the world to attend the services that went on three times a day, seven days a week. Here it was said, "The color line was washed away in the Blood," as blacks and whites, among others, worshipped together under the leadership of the black pastor.[5]

Spurred on by articles written by Azusa Street onlooker Frank Bartleman in the Holiness press, visitors came to Azusa Street, spoke in tongues, and went out as Pentecostal pilgrims throughout America and to the far reaches of the world.[6] American pilgrims included G. B. Cashwell, Charles H. Mason, and William H. Durham. Pilgrims who took the Pentecostal message abroad included A. G. Garr (India), C. J. McIntosh (China), Mary Rumsey (Korea), Thomas Ball Barratt (Europe), Daniel Berg and Gunnar Vingren (Brazil), Willis Hoover (Chile), Ivan Voronaev (Russia), and Luigi Francescon (Italy). One argument is that the Azusa Street Mission became the mother church and prototype for Pentecostal churches throughout the world.

Under the pioneering ministries of many of these Pentecostal missionaries, Pentecostal revivals were ignited in many parts of the world. Yet it is also the case that around the beginning of the twentieth century, several Pentecostal outbreaks occurred outside of North America, in Korea, India, and other places, with the appearance of such charismatic phenomena as speaking in tongues, prophecies, healings, and exorcisms, apparently without any Western Pentecostal missionary influence. Because of these charismatic outbreaks and the worldwide growth of these movements, one could speak of the new century as "the century of the Holy Spirit."[7]

Yet there has also been another argument regarding Pentecostal origins that hence has not privileged the North American revivals and suggested instead a polycentric model of the beginnings of this renewal movement.[8] From this perspective, Pentecostalism grew out of multiple revival centers, and Western missionaries hence arrived to connect these movements that, in turn, were able to exert greater influence than if they had remained isolated. The chapters in part 4 of this book attempt to adjudicate various aspects of these matters. Regardless of the final verdict, as we will note momentarily, in time Pentecostalism gained millions of converts during the twentieth century. Among the nations that saw the greatest growth were Chile, Brazil, Argentina, Korea, South Africa, and China.

In turning now to European Pentecostalism, the focus of the first three parts of this volume, we note the movement there took early root through the efforts of several Pentecostal pioneers.[9] Many look on Thomas Ball Barratt as the father of Pentecostalism in Northern and Western Europe. His first meetings in Christiania (now Oslo), Norway, in 1907 were followed by his efforts to spread the movement to Sweden with Lewi Pethrus, to Germany with Jonathan Paul, and to England with Alexander Boddy, an Anglican priest. Boddy made major contributions to the movement with his annual Whitsuntide conferences in Sunderland, England, and the publication of his magazine *Confidence*, which made Pentecostalism more acceptable in England and other European nations. In Eastern Europe, the movement began with the ministry of Ivan Voronaev in Odessa in 1922, who planted some 350 Pentecostal churches in Russia and several other Slavic nations. He was martyred by the Communists later, after serving a long prison sentence for preaching the gospel. In southern Europe, a dynamic movement was pioneered by Luigi Francescon, an Italian immigrant to the United States who founded strong Pentecostal churches not only in Italy but also in Brazil and Argentina.

Europe later was the scene of pioneering Pentecostal ecumenism through the efforts of the South African David du Plessis, who organized the first Pentecostal World Conference in Zurich in 1947. He was later to be known as "Mr. Pentecost" due to his leading ecumenical role during the Charismatic movement in the mainline churches in the 1970s and 1980s.[10] In England, a pioneering Pentecostal journalist and Bible teacher, Donald Gee, spread news of the fast-growing Pentecostal movements of the world in his influential magazine *World Pentecost*.

As three-fourths of this book demonstrates, European Pentecostals spoke in many tongues, literally. These Pentecostals also sent out missionaries to the ends of the earth.[11] Ironically, there is a sense in which these Western Pentecostal missionaries brought as much of their own culture with them as they did the gospel to those they evangelized.[12] In fact, they did this not just in what we now call the Global South, but also vis-à-vis the indigenous peoples of Europe and North America.[13] It has been in part for this reason that Pentecostalism has not taken off especially within Native American communities, although this is gradually changing, including among the Roma in the European continent.[14]

Latter Rain, neo-Pentecostalism, and the Catholic Charismatic Renewal

In the late 1940s and early 1950s, a new wave of revival swept the Pentecostal movement from a local revival centered at Sharon Bible School in Saskatchewan, Alberta, Canada. Known as the "New Order of the Latter Rain," this movement represented a renewal of charismatic gifts, such as prophecy and the interpretation of tongues as well as singing in the Spirit. In the end, the Pentecostal denominations largely rejected the revival because of perceived excesses that included the bestowal of specific gifts by the laying on of hands and a teaching called "manifest sons," where some claimed that they would never die.[15]

This movement also coincided with the beginnings of the healing revivals that began in 1948. In the following years, such men as

Oral Roberts, William Branham, T. L. Osborn, and Tommy Hicks led large crusades that spilled over to many nations as these men and others began to conduct these same kinds of meetings overseas. These crusades led to the expansion of Pentecostal churches in many nations of the world.[16]

By the 1950s, laymen were joining in the revivalistic fervor that was engulfing the entire movement. In 1951, Demos Shakarian, a millionaire dairyman from Los Angeles, started the Full Gospel Business Men's Fellowship International (FGBMFI). Although women and preachers could attend and even speak at Shakarian's events, they could not be voting members of the organization. By the 1960s and 1970s over four thousand chapters were operating all over the world, and at its height, about four million persons attended Full Gospel events each month. This Pentecostal laymen's revival brought people from all denominations to hotels and restaurants for salvation and healing meetings. Called by Oral Roberts "God's Ballroom Saints," the Full Gospel Business Men's Fellowship helped fuel the international growth of Pentecostalism.[17]

Before 1960, Pentecostal revivalism in North America was confined mainly to Pentecostal churches coming out of the Azusa Street revival. Often scorned by the mainline churches with scathing attacks by fundamentalist and Holiness leaders, the movement grew rapidly and eventually entered the major American churches. The first neo-Pentecostal to make national news was Father Dennis Bennett of Van Nuys, California. An Episcopalian, he identified with the Pentecostals when he confessed to speaking in tongues in 1960. In the next few years, Pentecostalism entered most of the mainline churches. Some leaders were Gerald Derstine (Mennonite), Larry Christenson (Lutheran), Brick Bradford (Presbyterian), Howard Conatser and Pat Robertson (Baptist), and Tommy Tyson (Methodist). By 1965, these neo-Pentecostals adopted the label *Charismatic* and achieved at least some measure of approval of their ecclesiastical leaders and remained in their denominations.

In Europe, all the Reformation Protestant churches experienced Pentecostal renewals just as their co-religionists had experienced in the United States and Canada.[18] When we consider that from the earliest days of the twentieth century, Pentecostal leaders wrote of a threefold revival heritage that included the Lutheran Reformation, emphasizing justification by faith, and the Wesleyan evangelical revival, emphasizing entire sanctification, these developments may not be as surprising. It may have been precisely this ecumenical configuration of modern Pentecostalism that eventually not only accommodated but also perhaps precipitated Charismatic Renewal across the Christian traditions.[19]

In 1967, another wave of Pentecostal revival suddenly erupted in the Roman Catholic Church to the surprise of everyone, including the Pentecostals. Although there had always been Charismatics in the Catholic mystical tradition, no one expected that a Pentecostal spirituality would break out in the Church. In calling the Vatican II Council in Rome, which lasted from 1962–1965, Pope John XIII called on every Catholic in the world to pray daily for the Lord to "renew [His] wonders in this our day as by a new Pentecost." Debates in the Council recognized the presence of many "charisms" (gifts) in the Church and called for spiritual renewal that would "open the windows of the church" for fresh winds of the Spirit.[20]

Only two years after the Council ended, a Charismatic movement began in Duquesne University in Pittsburgh among theology students and professors. From Duquesne, the movement moved at first to Notre Dame University and the University of Michigan before spreading to the grass roots across America. Instead of adopting Pentecostal revival techniques, the Catholic renewal made use of prayer meetings and days of renewal in local parishes and Charismatic communities. Conferences at Notre Dame in 1972 and 1973 brought the movement to the attention of the Vatican. The movement soon spread to over one hundred nations of the world.[21]

By 1976, Pope Paul VI approved the renewal and appointed Leon Joseph Cardinal Suenens of Belgium to serve as his liaison to the burgeoning movement.[22] Working with Suenens was the American Benedictine monk and scholar Kilian McDonnell, whose books and articles paved the way for acceptance of the movement by the

Vatican.[23] The Charismatic Renewal among Catholics grew fastest in Latin America and Asia. By the year 2015, estimates were that globally over 180 million Catholics were involved in the movement.[24]

Part of the result of the renewal movement across mainline Protestant and Roman Catholic traditions has been the Pentecostalization of world Christianity.[25] Across the majority world today, while some classical Pentecostal churches are looking and sounding less and less like Pentecostals, others are taking on that mantle. In addition, these historic churches and traditions are influencing Pentecostal theology and practice, in particular by expanding the classical Pentecostal understanding of mission and evangelism to include attentiveness to social realities, consideration of social justice, and engagement in the social sphere.[26]

Late twentieth- and early twenty-first-century developments

As the twentieth century drew to a close, two major revivals broke out in local churches in North America that had reverberations around the world. The first one began in a Vineyard church in Toronto in 1994. The Vineyard movement had begun in California, led by John Wimber, who became famous as a teacher at Fuller Theological Seminary from 1975 to 1985. In the Airport Vineyard Church in Toronto, an extended revival broke out that drew thousands of visitors from all over the world. The pastor, John Arnott, saw his church explode in numbers as curious visitors came to the service that continued six nights a week. In addition to such Pentecostal manifestations as tongues and prophecy, many people at Toronto experienced unusual manifestations, such as falling down, laughing in the Spirit, and roaring like lions. These unusual religious phenomena were soon dubbed the "Toronto Blessing." After Wimber investigated the revival, he characterized them as "exotic manifestations" and in 1996 excommunicated the congregation from the Vineyard fellowship. After this, Arnott then formed his own denomination.[27]

Another revival began in 1995 in the city of Brownsville, Florida, near the port city of Pensacola. This time the revival broke out in a local Assemblies of God church. As in Toronto, multitudes attended the services in Brownsville. Before the revival began to ebb, over two million people had attended at least one service in the Brownsville church, and over one thousand students who were converted in the revival have trained as young ministers at its Bible college. Unlike the Toronto revival, the Assemblies of God denomination decided to oversee the meetings and keep the church and the school within the denominational system. Both the Toronto and Brownsville revivals were highly publicized and caused many other revivals to begin in churches around the world.[28]

Part of the result of these revivals was the transformation of religion, particularly in North America, into what some have called a postdenominational landscape.[29] Independent, nondenominational, and other congregational forms of churches are emerging, most of which are Pentecostal or Charismatic in spirituality, without seeking formal ecclesiastical affiliations. Yet new networks are forming and developing, many connected to so-called apostolic leaders,[30] with others related to unique "brands," including music and worship phenomena like Jesus Culture and Hillsong.[31] This means that world Pentecostalism is continually being transformed, and now the "movement" is growing not only via traditional missionary efforts but also telecommunicatively, by way of mass media in a digital age.[32]

At the very end of the century, some of the largest Pentecostal revivalist crusades in history were taking place in Africa under the ministry of the German Pentecostal evangelist Reinhard Bonnke. Going to Lesotho, South Africa, as a conventional missionary in 1967, Bonnke soon became dissatisfied with the meager results of his ministry. Therefore, in 1975 he rented a large stadium in Botswana, where he began one of the most noteworthy evangelistic ministries in the history of Christianity. Traveling throughout Africa with a tent seating 34,000, Bonnke saw hundreds of thousands of conversions in his crusades. By 1990, he abandoned the tent and began to preach in the open air. He soon began to draw enormous crowds, even surpassing the records set by Billy Graham.[33]

Perhaps the largest such crusade took place in Lagos, Nigeria, in the year 2000. In one service, it was reported that 1.6 million people attended, with over 1 million people converted. In addition to Bonnke, other Pentecostal evangelists, such as the American Benny Hinn, regularly drew crowds of more than 500,000 people in India and Africa. This helped the Pentecostals build megacongregations around the world. One of these, the Yoido Full Gospel Church pastored by David Yonggi Cho in Seoul, South Korea, claimed over 700,000 members by 2000, making it the largest local church in Christian history.[34] Pentecostal movements thus have grown from being comprised of tiny groups of highly persecuted Christians in the beginning to now being one of the fastest-growing renewal movements in history. At this writing, the empowered movements, all together, are second only to the Roman Catholic Church in size and number some 644 million people throughout the world.[35]

Those who consider themselves part of this global renewal movement no doubt are expectant of even further growth. Simultaneously, there are also signs that renewal Christianity is plateauing in various places, not least in North America and the Korean contexts. In the former, it is the immigration of Hispanics that is sustaining renewal growth, and that particularly among Roman Catholic Charismatics. Earlier forms of Pentecostal triumphalism and elitism are now being tempered.[36] Are these indicators of theological developments as we move further into the second Pentecostal century?

Possibilities and Challenges for Pentecostal Theologies

In the rest of this introduction, we focus on theological trajectories of contemporary Pentecostalism in light of the achievements in this volume particularly, but yet against the backdrop of the four-volume series as a whole. What are the theological challenges and opportunities as a whole? We will begin in Europe and move to Anglo-America, partly following the structure of this book, and conclude with overarching considerations in light of developments in Pentecostal academia as these have unfolded to the present.

Pentecostal and post-Pentecostal theologies: European lenses

We included the chapter on Pentecostalism in the Middle East here in this book, although not without reservations, since such developments could easily have been accorded space within the context of the volume on Asia and Oceania, even as the chapter on Pentecostal-Charismatic Christianity in Egypt, in the Africa book, also touches on important issues in this context. The challenge is that there is insufficient research and scholarly documentation of renewal trends in these countries, even though there is significant Pentecostal presence and activity across this region. There is no doubt that the status of Israel in Pentecostal eschatology occludes many of the important theological issues that need to be discussed.[37] Pentecostal scholars like Calvin Smith are beginning to address these complex matters,[38] but there is much more work that needs to be done. It is not just a matter of comprehending better the challenges related to working for peace in the Middle East, although that ought to remain a priority on any agenda related to Pentecostal theology in the next generation.[39] The difficulties attend to theological questions of ecclesiology, specifically how to understand the church in relationship to Israel,[40] and of biblical hermeneutics and interpretation, especially how to read the Hebrew Bible (for Pentecostals, the Old Testament) in the twenty-first century.[41]

The chapters in this book on Pentecostalism in Eastern Europe obviously press for consideration of what a post-Communist Pentecostal and Charismatic theological project might look like. Before 1989, of course, as many of these chapters unfold, Pentecostal theological thinking in this context of persecution and martyrdom focused, understandably, on themes of suffering for the witness of the gospel. Further, the questions focused on survival in a socialist context. In an increasingly global but not definitively post-socialist environment, however, dispensationalist eschatologies identifying the Antichrist in relationship to Communist figures and realities are no longer plausible. Most immediately, Pentecostals are rejoicing at their newly experienced religious freedom, particularly for the purposes of witness and evangelism. But how else might Pentecostal theological thinking develop in this context?

A large part of the unexplored set of questions here pertains to how to consider the relationship between Eastern Orthodoxy and the global Pentecostal movement. Much of Eastern Europe remains Orthodox in overall religious character. Historically, Orthodox communions have felt threatened by Pentecostal proselytism in these regions.[42] Thus, building theological bridges between both traditions is a priority.[43] Pentecostals have to begin to understand the depth of the Orthodox theological tradition, and Orthodox Christians also ought to query if the "new kids on the block" might have something important to retrieve from the biblical and patristic traditions for contemporary Christian life. Beyond becoming reacquainted with each other, there is potential for theological synthesis to occur, particularly in calling on the strong pneumatological and Trinitarian emphases in both traditions and their spiritualities. How, for instance, might a Pentecostal-Orthodox convergence inform Christian thought and practice in a post-Communist global context that is struggling to understand the contemporary neoliberal economy in biblical and sustainable terms?[44] Might Pentecostal and Orthodox resources combine to present a substantive theological imagination that can engage and perhaps intervene in these matters? We invite readers to interact with the chapters in part 1 of this volume with questions such as these in mind.

In turning now to the northern and western European contexts, we are led to ask about the shape of what might be considered as post-Pentecostal forms of theology. Three lines of inquiry regarding Pentecostal theology as post-Western, postcolonial, and post-Enlightenment suggest themselves when reading the middle two parts of this book. As will become clear, the *post*-designations in these three directions are indicative that Pentecostal theology might itself undergo drastic reformation. Will it even be recognizable as such?

We can take up this matter first by considering Pentecostalism in Europe (not to mention North America) as being transformed in the twenty-first century primarily by migration.[45] Yet clearly these Pentecostal migrants, especially those from Africa, are not content to merely assimilate into European culture; rather, they desire to re-evangelize an obviously secularized European continent.[46] There are certainly many missiological issues for consideration in this context. How are the increasingly intensifying Pentecostal evangelistic and mission practices on the European front going to impact and transform the continent? How will such mission energies interact with similar trends among Muslim immigrants across Europe?[47] But from the missiological to the theological: How ought Pentecostal scholars and theologians think about the racial and ethnic diversification of Europe in light of these developments?[48] What will Europe look like going forward? Will a post-Western Europe look like the Europe of old? These are big questions, but Pentecostal academics ought to be engaged in these matters from their own theological perspective.

The dynamics of such "reverse mission" from the "rest" back to the European West suggest that the next generation of Pentecostal theology will need to be attentive also to trends in postcolonial studies. Postcolonial perspectives are registering themselves increasingly across the theological landscape, insisting that subaltern and other indigenous and local voices be heard in Christian scholarship. Pentecostal studies is primed for such postcolonial interface, not only given the predominance of renewal vitality in the majority world, but also given the role played by women and youth in these contexts. The challenge, however, is for Pentecostal scholars to engage the current center of gravity for Pentecostal theological work, which lies in the Western academy, even while honing in creatively on Global South sensibilities and commitments. Pentecostal scholars are beginning to pursue such postcolonial vantage points not only in reconsidering classical Pentecostal topics but also in articulating Pentecostal missiological approaches chastened of colonial presumptions.[49] Such research and rethinking is relevant not just for Western European and Anglo-American Pentecostal scholarship but also when applied to the post-1989 situation on the Eastern European front.[50]

The postcolonial horizon, however, is also interwoven with what can be identified as a post-Enlightenment theological methodology. If the Western and European Enlightenment bequeathed to modernity a discursive rationality that has fed the advance of modern science and technology, if not also spawned the scientism that insists on a reductionistic materialist and naturalist worldview, then the emergence of the postcolonial has brought with it the formulation of an alternative epistemological stance, one that does not minimize rational discursivity but that understands cognition not merely in intellectualist terms.[51] Pentecostals within their primarily oral cultural milieu and predominantly embodied and affective orientation to the world have never been tempted by the Enlightenment's definition of universal reason.[52] While not denigrating linear thinking, Pentecostals are as comfortable with dreams and visions, with the divine manifesting in and through embodied expressions such as tongues, healings, active worship, and dance.[53] Pentecostal "reverse mission" initiatives in the global context of the twenty-first century will require the movement's theologians to be diligently at work on these epistemological and methodological fronts in ways that bring Enlightenment rationality into dialogue with indigenous perspectives from around the world.

The West to the rest? American resilience and initiatives

Much that has been said so far about Pentecostal theology in European perspective applies also when considered within the North American frame of reference.[54] However, three additional *post*-perspectives loom large west of the Atlantic. In the following, we consider post-Christendom, postsecular, and postmodern forms of the emerging Pentecostal theological conversation.

First, the peculiar separation of church and state in the history of the United States has shaped Pentecostal political theology no less than it has Christian thinking about the political world in the last two centuries. Simultaneously, if not also ironically, many North American Pentecostals, much less Christian thinkers, have assumed that the state, so understood, is working out of a divinely intended framework and that such constitutional separation is uniquely Christian in its inspiration. While the merits of such a political theological point of view can be argued, how this translates into political practice has been increasingly muddled since 1965, when immigration was opened up, globalization ensued, and transnational relations complexified. In the current context, freedom of religion relates not only to Christianity but to the diversity and plurality of religious traditions now found not only across the Anglo-American world but also on the "old" continent. The point is that although "Christendom" was officially left behind with the founding of the American republic, in practice the "Christian" character of its form of government was thoroughly interwoven with the American way of life. In the present ferment, then, Pentecostal theology will need to be intentionally post-Christian in approach, not only to disentangle itself from an uncritical Americanism,[55] but also to move forward with the recognition that any theological program founded on the many tongues of the Day of Pentecost narrative will need to include, not ignore or overlook, the many voices and perspectives in a pluralistic world.[56]

Second, then, the emergence of many religious perspectives in the public square, even in the West, not to mention the United States, means that we no longer live in a merely secularized world. Rather, what is emerging is a postsecular public space, one in which secular values and perspectives are not absent but instead mixed in, however convolutedly, with religious sensitivities and commitments. Pentecostal scholars will need to factor into their analyses such postsecular realities and vantage points.[57] From a more robustly theological angle, however, the questions are deeply challenging: How to live faithfully in a postsecular time wherein there are a multiplicity of religious options in the public square that are yet all serving under the one deity of mammon? Put another way, in a post-1989 world, nation-states are less important in a postsecular domain governed by the neoliberal market economy. In this global economic context, Pentecostal theologians need to be asking about what it means to be *homo economicus*—fundamentally economic creatures—governed by the so-called invisible hand of the market.[58] If Pentecostal theologians continue to fight among themselves and with others about religious pluralism, they will lose the war to the late modern capitalist regime. The point is that contemporary Pentecostal thinking about the public square in postsecular terms will need to proceed in an interdisciplinary mode, in conversation with political theologians, globalization theorists, and economists of religion, no less than with theologians of the religions.[59]

Post-Christendom and postsecular approaches work alongside postmodern sensibilities and efforts. Pentecostals are already beginning to engage this perspective,[60] as complex as is the discussion because the notion of the *postmodern* is subject to so many different understandings. While each strand of the multifaceted postmodern conversation needs to be engaged, our interests are driven primarily by the concern that the West's encountering the "rest" and the arrival of the "rest" here in the West require that Pentecostal theologians come to grips with modern science and its challenges. The issue here is not that Pentecostals should buy into the so-called mainstream science or the "consensus" around evolution[61] but that these matters need to be engaged. Part of the challenge is that the "enchanted" cosmologies of the majority world—which include a populated "middle level" between God and humanity filled with innumerable spirit beings and other nondivine and nonhuman creatures—blames evil spirits for poverty rather than taking on political corruption, engaging in sociopolitical and economic development initiatives, or integrating modern medicine into a more holistic frame.[62] The point here is that the postmodern spirituality is open again to the many spirits, but we need more disciplined theological reflection about this pluralistic cosmology even as this can be facilitated by a more vigorous consideration of theology in relationship to modern science.[63] Pentecostal theology needs to get beyond the natural-supernatural binary, itself bequeathed by

Enlightenment thinking, in order to reconsider how the spiritual is interrelated with, not disparate from, human materiality, community, and history. Such an allegedly postmodern insight, one could argue, is closer to the spirituality of the biblical authors than is the modern dichotomy between the material and spiritual worlds.[64]

The point here is that Western and North American Pentecostals can no longer do their theological work apart from their colleagues in the Southern Hemisphere. Such collaboration involves mutual and reciprocal learning and interrogation. We cannot assume that any group holds a privileged perspective in this contemporary period. So if the first generation of Pentecostal and Charismatic believers founded Bible schools, colleges, and universities to deepen the historical and theological understandings of the movements, the most recent generation has seen the formation of theological and academic societies that are globally interrelated. Since the founding of the Society for Pentecostal Studies in 1970, a veritable number of scholarly groups have appeared, many with their own conferences, journals, and book series, thus perpetuating the global Pentecostal theological conversation. The following highlights the West meeting the "rest" and vice versa:

- The European Pentecostal Theological Association and its *Journal of the European Pentecostal Theological Association*
- The Pentecostal-Charismatic Theological Inquiry International and its *Cyberjournal for Pentecostal-Charismatic Research* (intermittent more recently)
- The Asian Pentecostal Society and its *Asian Journal of Pentecostal Studies*
- The Canadian Pentecostal Research Network and its *Canadian Journal of Pentecostal-Charismatic Christianity*

- The European Research Network on Global Pentecostalism (GloPent), which developed an informal relationship with *PentecoStudies: An Interdisciplinary Journal for Research on the Pentecostal and Charismatic Movements*

In addition to the above, there are regional centers for Pentecostal studies that have emerged, including the Centre for Pentecostal Theology at the Pentecostal Theological Seminary in Cleveland, Tennessee, that initiated the *Journal of Pentecostal Theology* in the early 1990s, with its Journal of Pentecostal Theology Supplement books series; the Centre for Pentecostal and Charismatic Studies at the University of Birmingham, United Kingdom, that initiated and remains connected with, among other initiatives, the Global Pentecostal and Charismatic Studies book series published by Brill; and the Center for Renewal Studies at Regent University in Virginia Beach, Virginia, with its *Renewal Dynamics* blog and, as an offshoot (since both editors began at, but are no longer affiliated with, the institution), the CHARIS: Christianity and Renewal—Interdisciplinary Studies book series published by Palgrave Macmillan. Alongside these are two other book series: the Asbury Theological Seminary Series in World Christian Revitalization Movements—Pentecostal and Charismatic Studies section, published by Emeth Press, and the Pentecostal Manifestos series published by William B. Eerdmans (which is winding down as of the time of this writing). Each of these represent global Pentecostal theological discussions, reflecting where Western and non-Western perspectives meet and cross-fertilize.

Overarching theological matters: going away, or which way?

We conclude our introduction with comments on three important theological topics: eschatology, pneumatology, and theology proper, or the doctrine of God. Each arena is fraught with opportunities and challenges. Global conversation, both within Pentecostal scholarly communities and engaging with ecumenical voices outside the movement, will be requisite for advancing the discussion into the middle of the present century.

First, as many of the following essays highlight, there is the issue of Pentecostal eschatology. How is the Pentecostal theological community going to grapple with the dispensationalist emphasis prominent at the popular and lay levels on the rapture of the church as motivating Christian and Pentecostal mission over the last century[65] but which is less plausible in the present time? This question is, of course, not unique to Pentecostalism, since the delay of the Parousia is one that Christians across the ecumenical spectrum have had to engage for the last two thousand years. Promising trajectories are those charted by Pentecostal theologians who are not captive to the dispensational framework,[66] an incongruous alliance considering that dispensationalist schemes have often denied the ongoing validity of the charismata. The way forward is reconceiving biblical eschatology in terms of the Spirit being poured out on all flesh "in the last days" (Acts 2:17, MEV) without embracing a dispensational escapism. How Pentecostal theologians, not to mention churches, grapple with this important matter will be central for Pentecostal mission and its capacity to engage with important global issues in the twenty-first century.

Second, then, and clearly, Pentecostal pneumatology will need to be reconfigured. Up until now, much effort has been expended to shore up the Pentecostal doctrine of glossolalia as initial physical evidence of Spirit baptism, as well as to argue for the ongoing relevance of the charismatic gifts, especially healings and exorcisms being among the more "spectacular." Yet the future for Pentecostal pneumatology, not to mention Pentecostal theology, spirituality, and practice, may lie less in these emphases than in the capacity to integrate its pneumatological commitments into a Christocentric and Trinitarian theological vision.[67] The goal here is not focusing on the Spirit and the gifts for their own sake but revitalizing Christian thinking across the theological spectrum and empowering Christian living "in the Spirit." The latter means that the Spirit-filled life involves, not extinguishes, the life of the mind,[68] so that a robustly Pentecostal theology for the twenty-first century will be one that is pneumatologically Christocentric and Trinitarian in every respect.

Last but not least, a fully Trinitarian Pentecostal theology for the next century, if not the third millennium, will need to include, not dismiss, the Oneness Pentecostal point of view. As David A. Reed's chapter in this volume shows—not to mention other discussions of the Oneness perspective in the other books in this series—the unity of the Godhead is nonnegotiable for a biblical monotheism in any age. The question is how to be informed by such Oneness commitments while also yet bringing this witness into the ecumenical conversation. There are deep ecumenical issues to be adjudicated on this front, but these are as missiologically and ecclesiologically relevant as they are of theological import.[69] In many respects, how Pentecostal theologians—Oneness and Trinitarian alike—engage with one another on this matter will be indicative of how far Pentecostal theology will make its mark in the wider ecumenical arena moving forward. Any incapacity to listen to and learn from each other in this intra-Pentecostal area will inhibit contribution to the wider discussion.

As the preceding hints at, and as the next few hundred pages unfold, there is much to be optimistic about, even as there are undeniable challenges ahead. Pentecostal theology will need to mature while not losing its distinctive voice. Can this happen? The possibilities are charted in this and its companion books. Welcome to the conversation of and amidst global renewal Christianity.

Part I
Israel and Eastern Europe

Chapter 1

Diverse Contours of Pentecostalism in Israel/Palestine

Eric N. Newberg

THE PURPOSE OF this chapter is to analyze the contours of the Pentecostal presence in Israel/Palestine. The chapter is organized around three questions: Who are the Pentecostals in Israel/Palestine? How did they get there? And what are their attitudes toward the state of Israel?

At the outset, a definition of *Pentecostalism* is in order. It is generally accepted that Pentecostalism consists of a series of movements of renewal in the Holy Spirit emphasizing the practices of ecstatic speech, healing, prophecy, exorcism, and divine revelation through visions and dreams.[1] In his overview of global Pentecostalism for the Global Christian Forum in Istanbul in 2011, Cecil Mel Robeck observed that in spite of the diversity within Pentecostalism, its adherents share in common an identifiable type of spirituality that "recognizes that within the Divine-human encounter with God's Spirit, a profound transformation in the believer is possible."[2] In the region of Israel/Palestine, we find Pentecostal groups that share a common spirituality yet also exhibit diverse contours. The chapter will focus on three forms of Pentecostalism in Israel/Palestine, which I categorize as *Messianic*, *Palestinian*, and *African migrant*.

Who Are the Pentecostals in the Holy Land Today?

Pentecostals share the Christian space in the Holy Land with many other Christian groups.[3] Pentecostals occupy a small yet vital and growing sector of the Christian space in Israel/Palestine. A number of Pentecostal churches are active in Israel/Palestine. These include local branches of international denominations (the Assemblies of God, the Church of God, the Church of God of Prophecy), independent Charismatic ministries (Cornerstone, Voice of Healing, and Christ for the Nations), African Initiated Churches (Church of Pentecost, Resurrection Power, Living Bread Ministries International, the Beth-El Prayer Ministry), and churches founded in Israel (King of Kings Assembly, the charismatic Catholic Congregation, and Come and See). To illustrate the diverse contours of Pentecostalism in Israel/Palestine, I will share three personal observations, two of which are mine; the third is from Don Seeman.

My first experience relates to Kehilat ha'she al Har Zion (The Congregation of the Lamb on Mt. Zion), which meets on Saturdays in Christ Church in the Old City of Jerusalem. This congregation is led by Benjamin and Reuven Berger and is made up largely of Jewish followers of Jesus, many of whom were airlifted to Israel in the 1990s after the demise of the Soviet Union. Most had been believers in Jesus before immigrating to Israel, even though they made *aliyah* on the basis of Jewish parentage. It was readily apparent to me that the founding vision of this congregation was integrally tied to the restoration of the state of Israel. As with most Messianic congregations in Israel, the story of the Congregation of the Lamb on Mount Zion began when two Jewish brothers, Reuven and Benjamin Berger, the sons of an Orthodox religious family of Holocaust survivors from New York, had divine encounters with Jesus. After coming to faith, the Berger brothers left their yeshiva, bade farewell to family and friends, and followed the call of Jesus back home to Israel. "It was like the children of Jacob carrying the bones of Joseph back to the land," said Reuven. "It was a homecoming for us back to our land, our people and our God."[4] The Berger brothers trace the founding of their congregation back to Theodore Herzl's vision and work for the restoration of Israel in the late 1800s; the nineteenth-century Messianic rabbi Michael Solomon Alexander, who founded Christ Church; and Alfred Sawyer, the Anglican minister who invited the Berger brothers "to begin a Messianic Jewish congregation in Jerusalem in order to fulfill the vision of this church."[5]

My second experience relates to Immanuel Church, a thriving independent Arabic-speaking fellowship in Bethlehem led by Nihad and Salwa Salman. I attended Immanuel Church in the fall of 2002 with my friend Dan Simmons, then director of World Vision in Israel. Nihad Salman was originally affiliated with the Church of God and received his MDiv from the Church of God School of Theology in Cleveland, Tennessee, in 1991. He later withdrew from the Church of God. During the service at Bethlehem Bible College, I was impressed by the international flavor of Immanuel Church in two ways. First, I was offered an earphone for translation of the service into English or German. Second, a sizable delegation of the German Brethren took part in the service for the dedication of a local community outreach center they had funded. The worship at Immanuel Church was contemporary and upbeat, well suited to a congregation of mixed ages, with a large group of young adults. Pastor Salman's sermon concerned the key to peace between Israel and Palestine. He related stories of harrowing scenes of medical emergencies, impugning the injustice of the checkpoints that hindered his people from receiving care during medical emergencies. The point of his message was that the key to peace was not violent resistance but rather the Prince of Peace. He exhorted the congregation to look to Jesus as their leader, stating that He is the only true hope for peace in the Holy Land. Recently, Salman stated in an interview, "*He* is our peace in the midst of violence. If we are more open to what Christ really stood for, we will have more opportunities to share the gospel because of the oppression and violence."[6] He closed the service with a prayer for the congregation to be directed by Christ, the Prince of Peace. After the service, I was invited to join the German Brethren delegation for a barbecue and tour of the outreach center in Beit Jala.

The third experience relates to an event narrated by Don Seeman, associate professor of Jewish Studies at Emory University, in his essay, "Pentecostal Judaism and Ethiopian Israelis."[7] A few years ago, Seeman attended a circumcision ceremony for the eight-day-old son of Tadesse, a descendant of Ethiopian Jewish converts to Christianity. Seeman first met Tadesse in 1991, when Tadesse was a seven-year-old boy languishing in a transit camp in Addis Ababa after his family was excluded from the massive airlift that transported more than 14,000 Ethiopian Jews to Israel in the space of two days. In 1995, Tadesse's family finally made it to Israel on humanitarian grounds. Now Tadesse is among the 75,000 Ethiopian Jews living in Israel.[8] The Ethiopians were required by the government of Israel to matriculate in a Return to Judaism program, after which most located themselves along the Jewish continuum, from secular to Orthodox. Tadesse was different, though, because after the Return to Judaism program, he opted to identify with "a unique amalgam of Ethiopian Pentecostalism and Messianic Judaism."[9] Tadesse rented a trendy facility and hired an ultra-Orthodox *mohel* (circumcision expert) for the circumcision. In a Jewish context, circumcision is understood as the symbolic entrance of a child into the Abrahamic covenant. It is fundamentally a transaction of Jewish kinship by virtue of a child's birth to Jewish mother. As Seeman puts it:

> Tadesse, a believer in the Holy Spirit though he might be, chose to have his son inducted the same way other Israeli Jews are inducted into that fellowship, and only the choice of a name with some ambiguous New Testament resonances would have given that fact away to a few of the guests.[10]

Those guests were Tadesse's "family in Christ," whom he referred to as his brothers and sisters because of his spiritual relationships with them. Tadesse's biological family, siblings and cousins, were conspicuous by their absence. For Seeman, the contrast between Tadesse's "intense but easy intimacy with these 'brothers' and the absence of many of his birth kin made this circumcision terribly poignant"; he concludes, "Though most other Jews would disagree, Tadesse does not think that he has left Judaism so much as he realized that his Judaism is now mediated by Christ."[11]

The above three vignettes illustrate the diversity of three forms of Pentecostalism in Israel/Palestine. Now we turn to the question of origins.

How Did Pentecostals Get to Israel/Palestine?

Pentecostals arrived in what was then called Palestine very early in the history of the Pentecostal movement. Some of the first missionaries sent out from the Azusa Street revival went to Jerusalem. In its first ten years, the Pentecostal mission in Palestine gained a foothold in Jerusalem, due primarily to the efforts of pioneering missionaries Lucy Leatherman and Anna Elizabeth Brown. In the interwar period, the Pentecostal missionaries established a mission station in Jerusalem and expanded their territory into Transjordan, Syria, and Persia. The mission was severely tested and lost traction during the Arab revolt of 1936–1939, World War II, and the Partition Crisis of 1947. With the War of 1948, the Pentecostal missionaries fled from the field of battle, and their predominantly Arab clients were swept away in the Palestinian Diaspora. After 1948, the Church of God (Cleveland, Tennessee) established an active mission in the West Bank with stations in Bethlehem, the Mount of Olives, and the village of Aboud. Led by the indomitable Margaret Gaines (1931–) from 1964 to 1999, the Church of God succeeded in developing an indigenous leadership that continues to sustain a vital Palestinian Pentecostal presence in the West Bank.[12]

Lines of historical connection can be traced from the Pentecostal mission in Palestine to contemporary Pentecostalism in Israel/Palestine. The one who forged the connection between the Pentecostal mission in Palestine and Messianic Pentecostalism was Derek Prince (1915–2003). Prince's ministerial career spanned the Pentecostal and Charismatic movements.[13] In the early 1940s, Prince embarked on doctoral studies in classical philosophy at Cambridge University, specializing in Plato. During World War II, he enlisted with the Royal Army as a noncombatant. During his military training in Scarborough, England, he visited a small Elim Pentecostal church and was converted and baptized in the Holy Spirit. Shortly afterward he was shipped out to North Africa. During a leave in Palestine, he was baptized in the Jordan River by Saul Benjamin, a Pentecostal missionary whom Prince had met in Jerusalem.[14] After the war, Prince was assigned to a duty station in Palestine. In February 1946, he married a Danish Pentecostal missionary, Lydia Christensen, and collaborated in her work with orphan children in Jerusalem.[15] After his marriage to Christensen, Prince moved to Ramallah and shared in her ministry to the Arab population and in parenting her eight adopted daughters, of whom six were Jewish, one was Arab, and one was English. Her home served as a mission outpost and hospitality station for lonely British soldiers like Prince. Christensen ushered Prince into the circle of Pentecostal missionaries, from whom he imbibed philosemitism (love for the Jewish people).

As the tension mounted in Ramallah during the debate in the United Nations over the partition of Palestine, Prince and his family received death threats, which compelled them to relocate to Jerusalem at the end of 1947. After the British Mandate terminated in May 1948 and full-scale warfare ensued between five Arab nations and the state of Israel, the Pentecostal missionaries fled their posts and Prince was evacuated in the summer of 1948.[16] The Prince family landed in London, where Prince planted a Pentecostal church. Later the Princes relocated to Canada and then the United States, from which Derek launched an international teaching ministry. His influence on the global Charismatic movement was quite significant. Prince was a central figure in the shepherding movement.[17] Eventually he returned to Jerusalem with his second wife,

Ruth, and they built a home, dedicated as a place of intercession, fellowship, and the promotion of "understanding and reconciliation between Jews and Christians."[18] For the last twenty years of his life, Derek Prince divided his time between Fort Lauderdale, Florida, and Israel until his death on September 24, 2003, in Jerusalem.[19]

Derek Prince's international teaching ministry expanded widely in the 1970s. According to Stephen Mansfield, Prince's biographer, "[Prince's] chief theme in his later years was love for Israel."[20] According to Mansfield, Prince held replacement theology in disdain because of its complicity with anti-Semitism. Prince feared that Western Christians had not grasped the theological significance of the formation of the state of Israel. If they had, he believed that they would have renounced replacement theology and, in so doing, their admiration and support of Israel would have been more resolute. Furthermore, Mansfield writes, "The truth is that Derek understood the whole of his life in terms of Israel. . . . Asked on his deathbed what his last commission from God had been, he said hoarsely, 'To pray for the peace of Jerusalem.'"[21]

Another historical connection of importance in the roots of Messianic Pentecostalism is the confluence of the Charismatic movement and Messianic Judaism. The Messianic Jewish movement spawned congregations that observed the Jewish calendar and feasts, utilized Hebrew terminology, and adhered to a "Messianic theology" based on the premise that Jewish followers of Jesus are still Jewish. Messianic Jews therefore refer to themselves as "completed Jews." Peter Hocken sees the rise of Messianic Judaism as one of the major events marking the growth of the Pentecostal-Charismatic movement of the twentieth century.[22] He also views the Charismatic movement as a significant factor in the growth of Messianic Judaism, claiming that "Messianic Judaism is predominately charismatic."[23] Hocken's claims are substantiated by the findings of an important study of the Messianic congregations in Israel conducted by Kai Kjaer-Hansen and Bodil F. Skjott in 1999. This study found that there were eighty-one Israeli Messianic Jewish congregations and house groups in Israel and Palestine. Approximately six thousand people belong to these congregations, of whom about half are Jewish adults.[24] Although it is not widely known, many of the Israeli Messianic fellowships are charismatic in character; that is, speaking in tongues, prophesying, and healing prayer are regular occurrences. A good portion of the Russian Messianic congregations are Pentecostal, differentiating themselves as either the "quiet Russians," who prefer a traditional worship style, or "noisy Russians," who use a more expressive, Western-influenced charismatic style.[25] Other Charismatic congregations have been influenced by the Toronto blessing, which has caused division in Israel, as elsewhere.[26] Hocken offers an explanation of the charismatic element in Messianic Judaism: "In the wisdom of God it required the massive energy of this outpouring of the Spirit to make possible the creative interaction of Jewish forms of worship with the confession of Jesus as the Messiah."[27] Be that as it may, the emergence of Messianic Judaism faced the Christian community with crucial questions: What happened to the Jewish church of the origins? Can the Jewish roots of the church be restored?

These are exactly the questions that were crucial to the development of King of Kings Assembly in Jerusalem, a flagship example of Messianic Pentecostalism in Israel. The story of King of Kings began in August 1983, when Canadian Pentecostals Wayne and Ann Hilsden moved to Jerusalem to plant a church.[28] For years, the Jerusalem Christian Assembly, as it was first called, met at the YMCA on King David Street. In 1988, Hilsden decided that his congregation should be more closely identified with local Messianic Jewish believers in Jerusalem and Israel. To make this happen, the following changes would be required:

- A greater emphasis on the Jewish/Old Testament roots of their faith
- A worship style more suited to Jewish-Israeli culture
- An expression of the message of Yeshua (Jesus) in terms Israelis could relate to and understand

- A commitment to stand alongside the nation of Israel through prayer and practical support
- A deeper level of communication and cooperation with other Messianic communities in Israel and abroad

In keeping with this strategy, the original name Jerusalem Christian Assembly was changed to King of Kings Assembly, and a concerted effort was made to hire a Messianic believer to join the leadership team.

At this juncture, Hilsden teamed up with Ray Gannon, who for over twenty years had been involved in pioneering Messianic congregations and teaching in a number of Bible colleges. Gannon's primary task was training local leaders. As a result, King of Kings College was established in 1990. The college grew significantly and has become the main leadership training center for Messianic believers in Israel. From the beginning, Gannon was committed to transfer leadership of the college to local Israelis. This was accomplished when Ilan Zamir was appointed president. Subsequently, a board of local leaders was put in place, and local Israeli scholars were added to the faculty. In order to be a locally led ministry, the name was changed to Israel College of the Bible (ICB). Currently, the president of ICB is Erez Soref, who earned a doctorate in psychology and studied theology at Wheaton College. During his tenure at ICB, Soref has expanded the Israeli Hebrew programs of ICB and rearranged the academic structure.[29] Currently, the student body of ICB is 60 percent Jewish, 30 percent Arab, and 10 percent international. The vision of ICB is for Jews and Arabs to study the Word of God together in peace and unity, serving Jesus as one new man.[30]

In 2001, after a retreat in Galilee, Hilsden experienced a powerful encounter with the Holy Spirit, leading to dramatic expansions of the ministry of King of Kings. First, an abandoned movie theater in the heart of Jerusalem was purchased and renovated as a worship center, now known as The Pavilion. Second, the Jerusalem

Prayer Tower was established in 2006 in the Clal Building on the fourteenth floor, the highest floor of the building, strategically overlooking the city of Jerusalem. A third expansion was the Kings School of Media, begun in 2009 for the purpose of taking God's Word to the land of Israel through media. Shortly afterward, two churches were planted and a Messianic school of music and arts opened with more than one hundred students.

Now we turn our attention to the story of Palestinian Pentecostalism, the origin of which dates from the War of 1948. During the war, at least eight hundred thousand Palestinian people were caught in the crossfire between the Israeli forces and the five Arab nations that attempted to thwart the newly established state of Israel. In the crush of the Palestinian Diaspora, many refugees resorted to living in tents, in caves, and under trees out in the fields because there were no houses for them. The Suleiman family, formerly associated with Assemblies of God, fled from Jerusalem at the beginning of the war and settled in Bethlehem. They soon began holding services in their home. A Church of God (COG) missionary in the Middle East, D. B. Hatfield, explained the situation in a report to his American readership:

> We gathered people together and had services in Brother Suleiman's home. Many of the people who lived in Jerusalem before the trouble, live in Bethlehem now. There is a good opportunity to begin a work in Bethlehem, where at present there is no Pentecostal work but several Pentecostal people that need a place for worship.[31]

The political situation stabilized when jurisdiction over Bethlehem was transferred from the Egyptian army to the Hashemite Kingdom of Jordan. Hatfield came to Bethlehem and rented a building known as "the cave."[32] In this location, Hatfield says, the gospel was preached, the sick prayed for, sinners repented, and souls converted at an old-time altar. Hatfield proudly states, "The Church of God was now an established work in Bethlehem and located on the street of the Prophet David, beside David's well in Bethlehem."[33] By the summer of 1950, the COG church in Bethlehem had grown to one hundred in weekly attendance.

In 1953, George M. Kuttab (1922–2006), a native of Jerusalem and former pastor of the Nazarene Church in Zarka, Jordan, affiliated with the COG and assumed leadership of the congregations in Bethlehem, Beit Jala, and Beit Sahur.[34] In 1962, the COG purchased land on the Mount of Olives and a church was built, including a residential facility. Kuttab assumed primary leadership of the newly established COG church on the Mount of Olives, which until 1967 was located outside of Israel in the territory of the Hashemite Kingdom of Jordan. Kuttab was well suited for the Arab population in East Jerusalem. He proclaimed, "I am a Palestinian Christian."[35] He was known as a patriot of the Palestinian cause who would often speak out against the injustices done to the Palestinians.

In 1964, Margaret Gaines, a graduate of Lee College, arrived in Israel after serving ten years in Tunisia and two years in France as a COG missionary. The world missions board had decided that her "experience with Arabs in Tunisia and knowledge of Arabic would prove beneficial to the missionary endeavors in Jordan."[36] Early on in her ministry, Gaines started two churches. The first was in the village of Aboud, thirty-three miles northwest of Jerusalem. According to tradition, Aboud was the birthplace of the Old Testament prophet Obadiah.[37] Aboud had been an important Christian site with a population of forty thousand in the fifth century. Since then, its population decreased to three thousand, of which half were Christian and half were Muslim. The second church planted by Gaines was in Amman, Jordan, where she rented an apartment so she could itinerate back and forth.[38]

Political events placed a damper on the COG mission and exposed Gaines to many ordeals. In 1964, the Palestinian Liberation Organization (PLO) was founded by the Arab League with the purpose of waging an armed struggle for the liberation of Palestine.[39] By July, Jordan suspended its ties with the PLO, disavowing the PLO raids across Jordan into Israel, which nonetheless continued unabated. As a reprisal to these raids, on November 13, 1966, Israel launched a tank-and-aircraft attack on the Palestinian village of Sammu near Hebron, killing eighteen, wounding one hundred, and demolishing 130 houses, a school, a clinic, and a mosque. In retaliation, Gaines reports, the Muslim leaders called for a jihad, and civil defense measures were immediately undertaken: "We painted our car lights blue and taped our windows. Fear mixed with frenzied nationalism dominated our emotions. Everyone knew what was inevitable. No one knew when or how it would erupt."[40]

Provocation on both sides had led to a war that neither side wanted or planned for. Surprisingly, in a mere six days, Israel soundly defeated the armies of Egypt, Jordan, and Syria. In the process, the Israelis occupied the West Bank, East Jerusalem, Gaza, the Sinai Peninsula, and Golan Heights. For several years the mission benefited from a period of relative political stability in the West Bank. The installation of electricity in 1983 boosted the quality of life in Aboud. From this time on, the villagers were able to enjoy the conveniences of refrigerators, washing machines, televisions, and other household appliances. By this time, most of the people were sleeping on beds and relaxing on sofas and armchairs. Work in Israel, even at the minimum wage, allowed families to enjoy a sense of prosperity and relief from hardship. The population grew as young married couples settled in Aboud. Small two-room houses sprang up, and the streets were paved. The 1980s were, as Gaines puts it, "a time of real hope and contentment. Although it could not have been called an economic boom by any stretch of the connotation, the slight easing of dire poverty has birthed confidence in the future."[41]

In March 1999, Gaines retired and left the field.[42] She could take satisfaction in the fruit of her ministry. She had planned and secured funding for the construction of a Christian school and additions to the Church of God building in Aboud. The school's enrollment had increased from 32 to 121 between 1993 and 1999. Gaines understood well that many people contributed to the success of her missionary career. The women to whom she had passed the leadership baton were performing brilliantly. Led by the head administrator Suhaila, the faculty included Raika El Khoury, Somaya Issa, Miriam El Khoury, Rima Azar, Iftihar Salem, Layla Hameed, Hannie El Khoury, Senneh Shaheen, and Mary Mualem. The Department of Education held the principal and the teachers in high regard. As Gaines recalls, "The Aboud Elementary School is rated as superior in all the Occupied West Bank."[43] Gaines was confident in the local Pentecostal pastoral leadership she had developed, including Nihad and Salwa Salman, with whom the author conducted an interview during his sabbatical in Israel/Palestine.

The great surprise in my research for this chapter was the presence of African migrant Pentecostals in Israel. They found their way to Israel between the late 1980s and early 2000s and came mostly from Ghana, Kenya, and Nigeria. The purpose of their stay in Israel was to find work. The opportunity for migrant labor emerged as a result of the first Palestinian intifada (uprising) between 1987 and 1991. In response, the Israeli government retaliated by erecting checkpoints in order to control the movement of Palestinian workers into Israel. This resulted in a wholesale exclusion of noncitizen Palestinians in the West Bank and Gaza from working in Israel, and dramatic changes ensued in the Israeli labor market. Whereas Palestinians constituted 4.5 percent of the Israeli labor force in 1993 and migrant workers accounted for 1.6 percent, by 2000 the proportion of Palestinians had dropped to 3.3 percent and migrant workers had raised to 8.7 percent. By 2003, the number of migrant workers had increased to 10–12 percent of the labor force. About half of the migrant workers came to Israel as documented laborers, the other half as undocumented.[44] The number of government permits issued to employ overseas workers increased from 4,200 in 1990 to 9,600 in 1993 and then tenfold to 103,000 in 1996. By 2000, the Israeli economy had become heavily dependent on transnational workers.[45]

In the same period, other pathways were available for African migration to Israel, some legal and others illegal. Large numbers of Ethiopians came to Israel seeking asylum from political and military conflict, and others came under the right of *aliyah*. In addition, growing streams of undocumented migrants made their way to Israel by means of what Sarah Willen calls the "tourist loophole."[46] Given Israel's profound archaeological, biblical, and religious significance for multiple world religions, the Holy Land attracted pilgrims, some of whom extended the period of stay allowed by their tourist visas and slipped unnoticed into the Israeli economy as undocumented workers. This loophole facilitated the entry of tens of thousands of migrants from West Africa and other countries. The African migrant workers replaced the newly excluded low-paid, low-skilled Palestinian workers from the West Bank and Gaza by cleaning houses and offices, serving in restaurants and hotels, caring for children and the elderly, and performing other low-wage, physically demanding jobs.[47] The majority of the African migrant workers settled in the poor neighborhoods of Tel Aviv, especially around the old Central bus station, where they found relatively cheap housing, discount shops and food markets, good bus transportation to all parts of the city and country, and the company of other migrant workers, including Africans. There are no official statistics available for the number of African migrant workers in Israel. Estimates range from 10,000 to 14,000 at their peak at the end of the 1990s. Due to massive deportation in 2003–2004, the number dropped to between 4,000 and 8,000. Currently the number stands around 4,000. Yet there may be many more.[48]

Most African migrants to Israel joined a church made up of fellow Africans. These churches tended to be Pentecostal and/or affiliated with the African Initiated Church (AIC) movement. The Africans in Israel derive spiritual, social, economic, and political benefits from their churches. In fact, the African churches have become the center of the lively African community in Israel. At their peak, more than forty such congregations were meeting in the southern part of Tel Aviv. Theologically, the African churches in Israel can be identified with all three types of AIC churches: African-Ethiopian churches, Prophet Healing churches (also called spiritual or Zionist churches), and neo-Charismatic churches. Most of the Africans interviewed by Galia Sabar in her ethnological research described their churches as Pentecostal.[49] The African migrant churches emphasize the power and gifts of the Holy Spirit; the experience of the Holy Spirit in trances, healing, and deliverance; the existence of witches and spirits; narrative theology; and the prosperity gospel. As with Pentecostal churches worldwide, the services in these churches provide release and a feeling of community and togetherness. The churches function as an extended family in providing support for members by means of rites of passage for marriage and death. Most African churches maintain their connection with Africa by offering lectures and seminars on political issues in home countries. Church leaders assume a political role in lobbying for improved living conditions and legal status. The churches provide not only a sense of belonging but also practical assistance. Church members help new arrivals find housing and work; explain the bus routes; teach housecleaning skills; and share tips about wages, hours, work conditions, and how to get along with Israelis. Finally, the vitality of the African churches in a Jewish state with a small Christian minority augments the importance of the African churches.[50]

What Are the Attitudes of Pentecostals in Israel/Palestine Toward the State of Israel?

Pentecostals in Israel/Palestine hold different positions on the legitimacy of the state of Israel. We will begin with the attitude of Messianic Pentecostals by focusing on the International Christian Embassy Jerusalem (ICEJ), a pro-Israel organization founded in Israel. Because of its charismatic leanings and its sponsorship of an annual event that draws thousands of its supporters to Jerusalem from across the globe, many of whom are affiliated with Pentecostal and Charismatic churches, its story tells us a great deal about the philosemitism that is widely held in the Messianic Pentecostal congregations in Israel.

When in 1980 the Israeli Knesset proclaimed Jerusalem as the capital of Israel, most of the embassies and consulates in Jerusalem relocated to Tel Aviv in protest. In counterprotest, the ICEJ was created, with Johann Luckhoff as its administrative director and Jan van der Hoeven as its official spokesman. At a time when the Israeli government was besieged with worldwide criticism in the media, it welcomed the support of the ICEJ and helped in securing the ICEJ a suitable building in Jerusalem, which, as it turned out, was the former residence of the illustrious Jewish theologian Martin Buber. Besides sponsoring the annual Feast of Tabernacles event, which draws between five thousand and seven thousand attendees per year, the ICEJ raises funds for Jewish immigration and carries out benevolence programs for new Jewish immigrants. The ICEJ maintains branches in many countries.[51] The message of the ICEJ is philosemitism. Its overarching goals are to proclaim the message of Christian Zionism to the international Christian community and to convince Christians of their responsibility to comfort and support the state of Israel.[52]

Palestinian Pentecostals are not exclusively anti-Israel, but this is by far the majority point of view.[53] As noted above, directed by Margaret Gaines from 1964 to 1999, the COG mission achieved a contextualized ministry among the Palestinian Arabs in the West Bank. Gaines fully identified with the Palestinian Arab situation in relation to Israel. When once asked by an interviewer, "Sister Gaines, if I understand correctly, you are a missionary to Israel," she deftly replied, "To be more exact, I think we have to say that I am a missionary in Israel.... My address is Israel, but I am a missionary in a village on the occupied west bank of the Jordan."[54] In her autobiography, Gaines critiqued the Israeli settlement policy, specifically blaming Menachem Begin for not keeping his promise to freeze settlement construction after the Camp David Peace Accords in 1978. Nonetheless, Gaines recognized that both sides were at fault for escalating the violence that wreaked economic havoc on the economies of Israel and Palestine alike. Gaines summed up her critique by stating, "Unfortunately, Israel trusted in her military power and technology. She ignored the fact that the human spirit cannot be broken and that force breeds force."[55]

Gaines is opposed to the pro-Israel position of her host denomination, which has traditionally embraced a Christian Zionist stance.

The COG presently maintains a permanent department known as Ministry to Israel. Its website states: "For over 25 years the director of Ministry [to] Israel, Michael Utterback, has been involved in challenging Christians worldwide to this responsibility. However, this message is not exclusive to Ministry Israel, in fact the Holy Spirit has been speaking to believers in numerous nations around the world. Millions of Christians worldwide are now embracing the message of loving and supporting the nation of Israel."[56] The COG maintains no such department for ministry to the Palestinian people, which, as we shall see below, is a sore point with two protégés of Margaret Gaines. During my 2002 sabbatical in Jerusalem, I had a conversation with Nihad and Salwa (née Subhi) Salman in which they expressed their disappointment with the pro-Israel bias of the American COG. Nihad and Salwa credited Margaret Gaines not only for her ministry in Aboud, but also for introducing them to each other. After their marriage, they became co-pastors of the Bethlehem COG church. However, they eventually tired of what they perceived as the intractable Zionist bias of the COG leaders and pastors whom they guided on tours of the Holy Land. Nihad and Salwa complained, "The American missionaries in this region were busy within Israel, supporting ministry to Jews. They had forgotten about us." They were also bothered that Pentecostal tours would roll through Bethlehem to see the sights and then go back to Israel to go to church and meet pastors. "It is as if we didn't exist," Nihad and Salwa said. Eventually Nihad and Salwa left the COG and in September 1999 established Immanuel Evangelical Church, an independent church plant in Bethlehem that has grown to more than sixty families and two hundred fifty people. Immanuel Church has in turn planted two more churches in Ramleh and Haifa, and has opened two Christian bookstores, one in Bethlehem and the other in Haifa. With the sponsorship of World Vision and the German Brethren, Immanuel Evangelical Church has constructed an outreach center in Beit Jala with a vision for evangelization through compassion and caring for the community. It is noteworthy that the church planted by the Salmans flourished after their disengagement from the COG. The success of Immanuel Evangelical Church represents a gain for the Palestinian Christian presence in the Holy Land and a loss for the COG.

The African migrant Pentecostals occupy a middle position. Over time, they developed an ambivalent attitude toward Israel due to harsh treatment by the immigration police. Initially the Africans harbored a sense of belonging in Israel, since it was the Holy Land. As devout Christians, they felt entitled to remain in Israel. Hence, they made a distinction between the Holy Land and the modern state of Israel. Beginning in 2000, African Pentecostal sermons took a turn, criticizing Israeli government policy toward migrant workers, particularly the practice of deportation of those who were undocumented. The stepped-up deportation of undocumented Africans in 2002 greatly soured the attitudes of African migrant Pentecostals. According to the immigration police website, by 2004, 123,000 foreign workers had left Israel, including 50,000 by expulsion. The impact of the mass deportation campaign of Africans in Israel was severe. Without a work permit or visa, Africans could not feel safe going to church and moving around in public. One by one, African churches were closed down, either because their pastors left voluntarily or were deported, and church members were afraid to come to the meetings. Some of the remaining pastors held services in their homes and thus kept out of sight of the immigration police. As a result, Africans came to view the government of Israel as violating their human rights and freedom of religion.[57]

Conclusion

Israel/Palestine is a land beset with intractable conflict. Yet we can conclude, based on our findings, that this region is also a place in which, in the midst of armed struggle, diverse peoples continue to experience divine-human encounter with God's Spirit and profound transformation, evidencing the commonplace indications of Pentecostalism spirituality.

Chapter 2

Pentecostals and Charismatics in Russia, Ukraine, and Other Post-Soviet States: History and Future Prospects

Torsten Löfstedt

THE PENTECOSTAL/CHARISMATIC MOVEMENT is the third-largest religious movement in Russia after the Russian Orthodox Church and Islam and the third-largest in Belarus after the Russian Orthodox Church and the Roman Catholic Church. It continues to gain in members and significance in Russia, Ukraine, and Belarus and in some other post-Soviet states. In the countries of the former Soviet Union, members of this movement refer to themselves as "Christians of evangelical faith" rather than as Pentecostals, a term that has negative associations for many in these countries.[1] Because they have fraternal relations with Pentecostal churches in other countries (such as the Assemblies of God and the Church of God), I will generally refer to them as Pentecostals in this article. In this article, I will focus on the Pentecostal movement in Russia and Ukraine, as they are numerically largest, but will also make references to the movement in other countries. Pentecostals in Russia, Ukraine, Belarus, and other parts of the former Soviet Union have a shared history and continue to have close ties.[2]

Historical Overview

The Pentecostal movement first came to the western parts of the Russian Empire (including today's Finland and Ukraine) before the Russian Revolution. In the interwar years, emigrants returning from the United States brought the Pentecostal movement to the eastern parts of the newly independent state of Poland, areas that today belong to Ukraine and Belarus.

One of the most important Pentecostal pioneers was Ivan Voronaev (born 1885), a Russian who emigrated to the United States in 1912, received baptism in the Holy Spirit, and returned as a missionary to the Soviet Union in 1921, in part sponsored by the Assemblies of God. He established the All-Ukrainian Union of Christians of the Evangelical Faith-Pentecostals in Odessa in 1926, and the following year he founded a larger national union in order to spread the Pentecostal movement throughout the Soviet Union. In the early years, Pentecostals focused primarily on bringing the message to other Protestants but not the Orthodox. Fletcher explains, "As a rule, missionaries of the new movement worked initially through the local Baptist or Evangelical Christian churches, seeking to work as a sort of Wesleyan movement of revival from within."[3] It may seem strange that this Pentecostal union was successfully founded during the Soviet era. During the civil war that began shortly after the Russian Revolution and during the period of the New Economic Policy from 1923 to 1927, Protestants had considerable religious freedom. The Communist Party opposed all religion, but it considered the Russian Orthodox Church to be its main enemy because of its close connections to the tsarist regime. By supporting Protestant churches, the Communists hoped to weaken support for the Russian Orthodox Church.[4] Boiter writes that Vladimir Lenin himself "argued that the Party must exploit religious conflicts, aiding the side likely to add most to the revolutionary cause."[5]

The Pentecostal movement grew in the first ten years after the Russian Revolution but was forced to cease its activities when the Russian Soviet Federative Socialist Republic promulgated the Laws on Religious Associations on April 8, 1929, which with slight emendations was in force until 1990. This law made unregistered religious activity a criminal offense.[6] In 1930, Voronaev was arrested;

he died in the Soviet gulag at some point in the 1930s. Other leaders of the Pentecostal movement were arrested repeatedly, and some of them were also killed by Soviet authorities.

Another important Pentecostal pioneer was the Russian-German missionary Gustav Schmidt (1891–1958), who was born in a German settlement in what today is Ukraine, and what at that time was located in Volynia, in the Russian Empire. He moved to Germany in 1905, then emigrated to the United States and studied theology at Rochester Bible Training School from 1915 to 1919.[7] Supported by the Assemblies of God, Schmidt worked in Poland from 1920 to 1925, and after that he made the free city of Danzig (today's Gdansk) the center of his activities. In 1930, he founded a Bible school there, which trained preachers from many parts of eastern Europe. Thanks in large part to Schmidt's ministry, the Pentecostal movement grew quickly in Poland, especially in the newly acquired eastern parts of that country, where the majority of the population was either Ukrainian or Belarusian. Gustav Schmidt, his Polish-German colleague Arthur Bergholz, and other Pentecostal leaders sought to create a larger union that would coordinate evangelistic activity in all parts of Poland. Many Pentecostal congregations joined together as the Union of Christians of Evangelical Faith of Poland on May 5, 1929.[8] The Pentecostal movement flourished in eastern Poland in the years leading up to the Second World War; in 1931, the All-Polish union counted some 12,000 members, and by 1937 it had an excess of 21,500 members.[9] When the lands that today comprise the western parts of Belarus and Ukraine were annexed by the Soviet Union in 1939, the number of Pentecostals in that country increased substantially.

In August 1945, the Pentecostal churches in the Union of Soviet Socialist Republics (USSR) were forced to join other Protestant denominations in the Union of Evangelical Christians-Baptists, which was closely watched by the state; the union forbade glossolalia and other characteristic forms of Pentecostal spirituality. Those congregations that did not register were disbanded and forced to operate illegally in secret. Within a year, most Pentecostal congregations in Russia had left the union and preferred to operate as unregistered, and therefore illegal, congregations.[10] In the Ukraine, the situation was slightly different. Like other religious movements, the Pentecostal movement was suppressed during much of the Soviet era, but it remained especially strong in Ukraine, like many other Christian denominations. Wanner notes that at the time the Soviet Union came to an end, "approximately 350,000 officially registered Pentecostals, or half of the total in the Soviet Union, resided in Soviet Ukraine."[11]

The religious situation in the Soviet Union changed suddenly when Mikhail Gorbachev, general secretary of the Communist Party of the USSR, launched his programs of *perestroika* and *glasnost* (openness) and in 1988 encouraged the celebration of the millennium of Russian Christianity. Pentecostal leaders from Russia, Belarus, and Ukraine took advantage of the new openness and succeeded in reestablishing the Union of Christians of Evangelical Faith, the Pentecostal union founded by Voronaev, on May 23, 1989.[12]

While many of the congregations that joined together to form the Union of Christians of Evangelical Faith dated back to Voronaev's time, much of the subsequent growth of the Pentecostal movement was the result of activities of missionaries from outside Russia proper. Foreign missionaries had begun coming in larger numbers already in the *glasnost* era, but their numbers increased rapidly beginning in 1989 and continued to grow after the promulgation of the new Soviet law On the Freedom of Conscience and Religious Organizations on October 9, 1990, and the breakup of the Soviet Union on December 26, 1991. In the early 1990s, the former Soviet Union was the trendy place to be for Western and Korean mission organizations.[13] Elliott and Corrado estimate that more than 5,000 Western missionaries as well as 557 Korean missionaries served in the former Soviet Union in 1996.[14] Big-name Pentecostal and Charismatic preachers from the United States, Sweden, and Germany went on preaching tours in Russia and other parts of the former USSR.[15] Some of them, like the Swedish Ulf Ekman, started long-term evangelization projects (Ekman's Russia Inland Mission claims to have founded over one thousand congregations in the former Soviet Union). Much of the hard work of building up these new congregations was carried out by missionaries from Ukraine and Belarus, however.[16]

Current Situation

The total population of the Russian Federation was estimated to be about 142.5 million in 2014.[17] The Russian Federation is a multiethnic state. The largest ethnic group is the Russians, making up approximately 80 percent of the population, but it is also home of more than one hundred other indigenous people, some of which are quite large (the Tatars, for example, number more than five million). As the result of seventy years of Soviet rule, most people in Russia do not practice any religion. In 2006, Russian sociologists Filatov and Lunkin estimated that the number who practice a religion is between twelve and twenty-four million. Of these, three to fifteen million are active in the Russian Orthodox Church, not more than three million are active Muslims (these were mainly people belonging to one of Russia's many ethnic minorities with Muslim background, such as Tatars and Chechens), while active Protestants number more than 1.5 million.[18] It is difficult to say how many Pentecostals and Charismatics there are in Russia, as not all congregations are officially registered. The Pentecostal movement has grown quickly since the Soviet era. In an article from 2014, Lunkin estimates that there are close to three million Protestants in Russia, of which more than half are Pentecostals.[19]

Most Pentecostals in Russia are affiliated with one of two large organizations, the Russian Church of Christians of Evangelical Faith (RCCEF), headed by Bishop Eduard Grabovenko and including close to two thousand congregations,[20] and the Russian Association of Christians of Evangelical Faith (RACEF), headed by Bishop Sergei Ryakhovsky, with close to eighteen hundred congregations.[21] Some are represented by the smaller United Church of Christians of the Evangelical Faith, with which close to five hundred "unregistered" Pentecostal congregations are affiliated.[22] RCCEF is, organizationally speaking, a more centralized organization, while RACEF consists of approximately twenty smaller denominations with considerable independence that affiliated with this organization for legal reasons. There are no significant theological differences between these organizations; Bishop Grabovenko, the head of RCCEF, was earlier affiliated with RACEF. The Pentecostal movement is strongest in the Urals, Siberia, and especially in the Far East and is weaker in central Russia, where the Russian Orthodox Church is better established.[23]

Even though they do not consider themselves believers, most ethnic Russians identify culturally with Russian Orthodoxy.[24] The Russian Orthodox Church has become a marker of ethnic Russian identity and has been given advantages over other Christian denominations. It is considered a traditional religion, together with Buddhism, Judaism, and Islam, while other Christian denominations have second-rate status. Pentecostals, in particular, are often labeled sectarians, and local government administrators often hinder new congregations from being registered.[25]

Ukraine has a population of approximately forty-four million (2014).[26] In western Ukraine, people in general speak Ukrainian, while in the east the Russian language is more common. Most understand both languages. Compared to Russians, Ukrainians are much more religiously active. The overwhelming majority of Ukrainians belong to one of the country's competing Orthodox churches.[27] There is no single Orthodox church that commands the adherence of the majority of the population, and unlike the situation in Russia, there is no established religion in Ukraine.[28] In fact, as Wanner notes, "From the start a commitment to religious pluralism was incorporated into the very idea of the post-Soviet Ukrainian nation."[29] Pentecostal and Charismatic churches operate freely in Ukraine (except in areas under rebel control). Although Evangelical Christians are still numerically few, they are growing and have a significant impact on Ukrainian religious and political life.[30] There were more than 4,400 Pentecostal or Charismatic congregations in Ukraine before the outbreak of war in 2014,[31] and according to Allan Anderson, Ukraine has "the highest number of Pentecostals in any European nation."[32] Pentecostals in Ukraine belong to many different denominations, the two largest of which are the All-Ukraine Union of Christians of the Evangelical Faith–Pentecostals[33] and the Union of the Free Churches of Christians of Evangelical Faith of Ukraine.[34] Charismatic Christians and other Evangelicals have been associated with movements toward greater transparency and democracy in government and with the turn toward Europe.

Belarus is considerably smaller than Russia and Ukraine, with an estimated population in 2014 of 9.6 million.[35] Most have Russian as their native language. The Belarusian Orthodox Church (part of the Moscow Patriarchate) is the largest religious denomination in Belarus (including, in some counts, approximately 80 percent of the population), but compared to Catholics and Protestants they are not very active. In fact, approximately half of the population in Belarus consider themselves atheists;[36] this number includes many who see themselves as culturally Orthodox. Thus, president Alaksandr Lukashenka has referred to himself as an "Orthodox atheist" and supports the Orthodox Church. Approximately 14 percent of the population belongs to the Roman Catholic Church, which is especially strong in western Belarus.[37] Roman Catholics have had considerable political influence; the first leaders of post-Soviet Belarus were Catholics.[38] Protestants make up about 2 percent of the population. Pentecostals are the largest Protestant denomination in Belarus; according to Łatyszonek, together with the Baptists they make up 90 percent of the country's Protestants. In Belarus, almost all Pentecostals belong to the same organization, the United Church of Christians of the Evangelical Faith in the Republic of Belarus, headed by Bishop Sergei Tsvor,[39] which includes more than four hundred congregations located all across the country.[40] The Pentecostal union maintains close ties with Pentecostals in neighboring countries. Belarusian Pentecostals are not especially active politically, but since the Maidan uprising in

Ukraine, the Belarusian government has kept an extra-close eye on its Pentecostals. As is the case in Russia, Pentecostals are often considered sectarians in Belarus. Considering that the Roman Catholic Church attracts more than a tenth of the country's population, however, the Orthodox Church is not likely to succeed in reserving special status for itself, as it has done in Russia, and for this reason the future for Pentecostal churches in Belarus is rather bright as long as Belarus remains independent.

Repercussions of the War in Eastern Ukraine

The religious situation in Ukraine has changed rapidly as a result of the loss of Crimea to Russia and the rebellion in eastern Ukraine that began in 2014. Up until the conflict with Russian separatists began, the Pentecostal movement had been quite strong in the industrialized cities of southeastern Ukraine. According to statistics from 2004 (the latest I have found that divide up the number of congregations by region), there were more Protestant congregations (615) than Orthodox congregations (556) in the Donetsk region.[41] The Charismatic Word of Life movement had been especially successful in the Donbass region of southeastern Ukraine, with a megachurch and Bible school in Donetsk.

Today the situation is different. More than a million people have fled from southeastern Ukraine, mainly to other parts of Ukraine and to Russia. In rebel-controlled areas of southeastern Ukraine, there have been some cases of violence directed against Pentecostals, most notably in Sloviansk, where four members of the Pentecostal church were murdered by Russian separatists on June 8, 2014.[42] In Donetsk, the Charismatic Word of Life megachurch was seized by pro-Russian rebels on August 13, 2014. Many buildings in Donetsk had been abandoned, but the church was still operating; the rebels' decision to seize the church was likely motivated not only by the building's high standards, but also by their dislike of Evangelicals.[43] Rebels in eastern Ukraine identify with the Russian language and the Russian Orthodox Church. Their negative view of Evangelicals was strengthened when the democratically elected president Viktor Yanukovych was deposed and Oleksandr Turchynov, who was known to be an active member of an Evangelical church, was installed as interim president (he served February 21–June 7, 2014). As rebels have advanced in eastern Ukraine, hundreds of thousands have fled. As a result, Pentecostal churches in that part of the country have closed, and their members have sought shelter among Pentecostals in other parts of Ukraine or Russia.[44]

It is often the case that people become more interested in spiritual matters in times of political and economic uncertainty, and this is likely to be the case here too. Assuming Ukraine remains independent, it is likely that an increasing proportion of the Ukrainian population will turn away from the Moscow Patriarchate, as it will be tainted by association with the rebels in eastern Ukraine who identify themselves as specifically Russian and Orthodox.[45] While most will affiliate with the Kiev Patriarchate, some may turn to Pentecostal and other Evangelical churches, perhaps not always for spiritual reasons.

Whereas in the past, Russian speakers and Ukrainian speakers worshipped together without difficulty, some Pentecostal congregations in Ukraine have now split along linguistic lines.[46] In the past, Evangelical Christians in all parts of the Soviet Union were first and foremost Christians. Regardless of whether they spoke Russian or Ukrainian at home, if they had access to Scripture at all, it was in the Russian translation from the 1800s, as that was usually the only one available. The state was officially atheistic, and Evangelical Christians supported one another wherever they were. Now that the Soviet Union is no more and the Russian Federation threatens the independence of smaller post-Soviet states, Christians in the region have to decide if their primary loyalties are religious or ethnic. The choice is not always easy to make.

The conflict in Ukraine also puts Pentecostal churches in Russia in a difficult situation. Historically, Russian Pentecostals have had close ties to Ukraine. Many Pentecostal congregations in Russia, including some of the largest megachurches, were founded by missionaries from Ukraine, and many are still headed by men born in Ukraine.[47] As tensions between Russia and Ukraine grow, Russian Pentecostal leaders are put under increasing scrutiny, and they have to be very careful about what they say.[48] Some do their best to make sure their allegiance to the Russian state is clear. Bishop Ryakhovsky, the head of RACEF, visited the Crimea shortly after that area was annexed by Russia in order to tie the Pentecostal churches there to his denomination, thereby giving his tacit acknowledgement of Russia's claim to the province.[49] Others don't take a stand on the conflict itself but try to help those who have suffered as a result. The Ukrainian-born head of a megachurch in Izhevsk, Bishop Pavel Zhelnovakov, has publicized on the church's homepage that they are welcoming Russian refugees from Ukraine to stay in their church.

As a result of the war, Pentecostals in Russia cannot maintain as close contacts with churches and theological institutions in other countries as they did earlier. In the past, Russian Evangelicals would often go to study theology in Ukraine, where there were several strong theological institutions serving not only Evangelicals from Ukraine but also students from other parts of the former Soviet Union.[50] At least one of these has shut down as a result of the war (Donetsk Christian University was taken over by rebels in July 2014), but other theological institutions in Ukraine remain strong. Should Ukraine continue to ally itself more strongly with the West, however, it is likely that Russian citizens will not be able to freely cross the border. This means that Pentecostal or Evangelical theological institutions in Russia must be strengthened. Ukrainians who wish to serve as missionaries in Russia will also face increasing obstacles.[51]

Under Vladimir Putin the Russian government and Russian media have become increasingly antagonistic toward the West. This has affected how Pentecostals profile themselves. Poplavsky noted that unlike what was the case in the 1990s, in the first decade of the twenty-first century, the Pentecostal churches in the Tyumen region in western Siberia have avoided mentioning any connections they may have had to Western churches or missionaries because of the negative attention this attracted from Russian nationalists.[52] These anti-Western tendencies on the part of the Russian authorities have only been strengthened by the conflict in Ukraine; pastors who have contacts with Western churches are treated by government officials as though they are agents of the West.[53]

Centrally related to the war, many of the post-Soviet states are experiencing an economic downturn. Pentecostals in these areas have years of experience helping those who are on the margins of society. Their work with alcohol and drug rehabilitation, with rehabilitation of former prisoners, and with children in orphanages are generally looked upon positively, even by those who are otherwise suspicious of them; thus, this period of economic uncertainty may also be a time when Pentecostals might grow in influence. The economic and political uncertainty has also encouraged many Evangelicals to move west, however. Hundreds of thousands of Evangelicals have moved to the West since the breakup of the Soviet Union, especially from Ukraine.[54] While their wish to escape economic uncertainty and persecution is understandable, the Pentecostal movement has been weakened, both because congregations have lost leaders and active members and because they give the impression of not being concerned about the welfare of their nations.

Missions

As was mentioned, Russia is a multiethnic state. Many of its indigenous peoples have no background in Christianity. From 1929 to 1990, Christian missions were forbidden by law in the USSR, but after Russia became independent, missionaries quickly sought out the various peoples. Pentecostal congregations have been established among many of Russia's aboriginal nations and other ethnic minorities.[55] In some areas, such as among the Tuva and Buryats in Siberia, Pentecostals have been quite successful. Pentecostals are less likely to be associated with Russian imperialism than are representatives of the Russian Orthodox Church.[56] Russian-speaking Pentecostals are also active in the predominantly Muslim post-Soviet states of central Asia, where there are still sizable Russian minorities (although their number is continually going down). While there have been successful attempts at establishing Christianity in some areas (such as Kyrgyzstan), in recent years the attitude toward Pentecostals in central Asia has become increasingly hostile.

Although Christianity was first established in the areas that would become Russia, Belarus, and Ukraine over a thousand years ago, most people in Russia and Belarus claim not to believe in God, and their knowledge of Christianity is minimal. Pentecostals are aware of the challenges facing them. The leading Pentecostal congregation (RCCEF) is actively trying to reach all of Russia in its evangelization campaign "One Year for Jesus" launched in 2011: "Our goal is to reach every community in Russia by mobilizing 20 teams of Christian volunteers who are willing to dedicate at least one year of their lives to evangelism in all parts of Russia, from Kamchatka to Kaliningrad. Ultimately, we would like for each team to reach 50 towns/villages per month, for 10 months each year, over 10 year period of time, which equals 100,000 villages/towns."[57]

Russian Pentecostals are energetic evangelists, but the task before them is difficult. In the Soviet era, Pentecostals were often accused of belonging to a dangerous sect (even being accused of child sacrifice),[58] and in many areas they are still labeled sectarian.[59] This makes it hard to make inroads. Unfortunately, Pentecostals in the post-Soviet states have certain traits that might be considered sectarian. The leading Pentecostal denominations are strictly hierarchical, which makes them effective but also provides temptations to abuse power. There is also a widespread tendency toward legalism and a focus on outwardly visible sins among Pentecostals in the post-Soviet states.[60] It is not uncommon that people who drink alcohol or smoke are not allowed to be members of Pentecostal churches. On the positive side, this means that Pentecostal congregations are tightly knit communities, but in the long run this judgmental attitude is unhealthy. When focus is put on visible sins, invisible sins that affect the life of the church as a whole, such as intrigues, hard-heartedness, or greed, are often neglected. Perhaps because of their rigorous attitudes, the Pentecostal and Charismatic movements are still only of marginal importance in many parts of Russia and Belarus.[61]

To counteract the sect label, it is important that Pentecostals in Russia seek to work together with other Christian denominations, and this they do on both national and regional levels. Cooperation with other Protestants and Roman Catholics has been rather successful, but they are often snubbed by the Russian Orthodox Church. While Pentecostal leaders do not characterize the Russian Orthodox Church as their enemy,[62] the Orthodox tend to see Pentecostals as dangerous sectarians of foreign origin.

Education

While there will always be those who hold on to their prejudices concerning Pentecostals, one way that Pentecostals may improve their image is if more local church leaders get access to a well-rounded theological education, offering deeper knowledge of other Christian traditions. Pentecostals in the Soviet era were denied access to higher education, and given the Soviet disciplines of "scientific materialism" and "scientific atheism," it is not surprising that some developed distrust for higher education. Older pastors often lack formal theological education, and while many younger pastors received a basic theological education in the theological seminaries and Bible schools that were founded in the 1990s, the education that was offered there was often not perceived as relevant.[63]

Theological education is important. In the urban centers of the post-Soviet states, people are generally well educated. Pastors need to be well educated as well if they are to win their respect.[64] There will always be members of the congregation who have theological questions; if pastors are unwilling to give serious thought to such questions, these members may seek answers elsewhere and eventually leave the church. To meet this need for education, it is not necessary to found more seminaries but to improve those that exist and to make further education for pastors available through distance courses.

There is also a continuing need for translations of solid but accessible Evangelical theology. To avoid being labeled a foreign import, Pentecostals in the post-Soviet states must also become more active in developing their own theology. Kuropatkina notes that they are "very dependent on their foreign brothers in faith" and that "their basic theological concepts as well as their practical theology come from the writings of American spiritual leaders."[65] It is especially important to develop theologies that interact with the best that Russian Orthodoxy and Roman Catholicism have to offer.[66] A deeper understanding of other Christian theological traditions would contribute to better relations with other denominations and thus make it easier for Pentecostals to be accepted in society at large. More importantly, it would further deepen their relationship to Christ and to members of His body who happen to worship Him in a different manner.

Chapter 3

The Pentecostal Church of Poland: A Historical Analysis and Current Missional Development

Wojciech Kowalewski

THE QUESTION OF the identity of the church and its mission in many different forms has always been central in the Christian global missionary movement. But the age of uniform theological, methodological, and structural mission has come to an end, and the cultural transformations of the last century have affected people all over the world, thus calling for a redefinition of Christian mission in various societies, cultures, and geographical areas. The societies of East-Central Europe are historically characterized as "the lands between," the lands between the empires of the West and Russia on the East.[1] This region has always been in the center of different struggles and varied influences and constantly under pressure between the East and the West. In many ways, this description applies to Poland, which geographically was always in the heart of Europe and historically has been oppressed many times. It is a place where rival cultures and philosophies have clashed in most forceful ways and the tensions of the European drama have asserted themselves on the living body of this nation.

Year 2015 marks the 105th anniversary of the Pentecostal presence in Poland. According to statistical data from 2010, there were 21,834 believers who associated themselves with the Pentecostal Church of Poland.[2] Within the Polish religious landscape, this gives

Pentecostals a minority status, with just over two hundred churches in the thirty-eight million population. Nevertheless, the Pentecostal Church of Poland represents the second-largest Protestant group in this nation.

The term *Pentecostal movement* is used with different meanings in Poland and absorbs various expressions of faith, from classical Pentecostalism to the Charismatic Renewal movements and current neo-Pentecostal networks.[3] This provides methodological problems, in terms of presenting unified perspectives and scholarly classifications that would be representative of all Pentecostal and Charismatic movements present in Poland.[4] Another problematic issue, from a researcher's perspective, is a considerable gap in terms of academic studies available concerning the Pentecostal movement in Poland. Zbigniew Pasek, professor of religious studies and sociologist of religion who published several academic books on various aspects of Pentecostalism, points out that the diversity of churches, the cultural mosaic in terms of spirituality, and the various expressions of faith present within that movement make it hard to generalize distinctive marks of that phenomenon that all scholars can agree on.[5] There is no doubt, however, that the Pentecostal and Charismatic movement continues to grow and influences not only Protestant churches and organizations, but also the predominant Roman Catholic Church, through the Catholic Charismatic Renewal.[6] In this chapter, however, we will focus mainly on the Pentecostal Church of Poland, which is the largest Pentecostal denomination in this nation. First, we will outline the history of the Pentecostal movement in Poland, then point to some theological issues that are critical in this region, and conclude with opportunities for missional growth.

Historical Outline of the Pentecostal Church of Poland

The history of the Pentecostal movement on Polish soil can be generally divided into four periods: the pioneering period (1910–1939), the Second World War crisis (1939–1945), the Communist regime period (1945–1988), and the post-Communist era (after 1989). We will outline some of the main characteristics for each of these epochs.[7]

When the Pentecostal movement emerged at the beginning of the twentieth century, the territory of Poland was divided into three different parts under the rule of Austria, Prussia, and Russia. Therefore, the beginnings of Pentecostal presence and missional activity came from different directions and formed their own associations. The first Pentecostals in Poland were Germans involved in the renewal movement within the Lutheran Church in the Eastern part of the German Empire. The first Pentecostal conference organized by them in the Lower Silesia region gathered in December 1909, and in 1910 they had already started a congregation in Wroclaw, while at the same time several groups sympathizing with the Pentecostal ideals emerged in other cities, like Brzeg, Głogów, Oława, Nysa, and Opole.[8] Two Lutheran ministers propagated the influence of neopietistic spirituality among Poles in the Śląsk Cieszyński region: Jan Pindor (1852–1924) and Karol Kulisz (1873–1940).[9] The latter formed the Christian Fellowship in Cieszyn, which developed contacts with German Pentecostal churches in Lower Silesia. As a result of this relationship, some members began cultivating charismatic spirituality and eventually were excommunicated by the Lutheran Church. On July 15, 1910, the group under the leadership of Jan Kajfosz legally registered under the name Bund für Entschiedenes Christentum (Alliance for Committed Christianity).[10] This alliance planted new churches and at its peak consisted of about two thousand members. Theologically, they represented the more moderate wing of Pentecostalism and emphasized the need for spiritual conversion and the baptism in the Holy Spirit but with no necessary expression of spiritual gifts as a sign of that. They are also known for publishing *Głos prawdy* (The voice of truth) and *Śpiewnik pielgrzyma* (The pilgrim's hymnbook); the latter was arguably the most important Evangelical hymnbook of the twentieth century available in the Polish language.[11]

The growth of Pentecostalism in the central and eastern part of Poland emerged from a different direction after the First World War ended and the country regained its independence. The first Pentecostal initiatives in this region came with a wave of emigrants from America and Canada, as well as other missionaries (mainly Germans) who began their evangelistic work here in the 1920s. As a result of this, many Pentecostal churches and initiatives grew dynamically. Finally, in May 1929, Artur Bergholc, pastor of the church in Łódź, led the formation of a denomination called the Evangelical Faith Christian Association (Church) in Stara Czołnica.[12] Its membership included not only Poles but also Ukrainians, Belarusians, Russians, and Germans. Theologically, they represented classical Pentecostal views with an emphasis on baptism in the Holy Spirit and the practice of charismatic spirituality, as well as a strong emphasis on the sanctification of believers.[13] The Bible Institute in Gdansk, founded in 1930 by Gustav Herbert Schmidt (1891–1958), Assemblies of God missionary to Poland, played a significant role in training pastors and missionaries and became an international center, propagating Pentecostal teaching throughout this region. Over five hundred students went through the theological formation there until the institute was forced to close by the Nazis in 1938.[14] The Evangelical Faith Christian Association had about three hundred churches and about twenty-five thousand members in 1939, when the Second World War began.[15]

During the war, both the Alliance for Committed Christianity and the Evangelical Faith Christian Association were banned by the Nazis. Many Pentecostal leaders and believers were arrested, sent to concentration camps, or forced to leave the country, all of which combined to stop the dynamic growth of the movement for years to come. Also as a result of the change of the borders after the war, Polish Pentecostals got much smaller and divided between Poland, Russia, and Czechoslovakia.

Under the influence of the Communist authorities in May 1947, the United Evangelical Church was created, which was meant to unite several Evangelical denominations, two of which were

Pentecostal in character: the Alliance for Committed Christianity and the Evangelical Faith Christian Association.[16] Although they officially joined together under the umbrella of the United Evangelical Church, and even as some other Evangelical denominations, like the Union of Churches of Christ and Union of Free Christians, were forced by the Office of Religious Affairs to join them, the differences both in theology and spiritual practice remained. Therefore, there were tensions within that church organization and no signs of a unified vision for what was meant to be the United Evangelical Church. Hence, the Evangelical Faith Christian Association decided to separate itself in 1956 and aimed to function independently, but the authorities did not legalize it and eventually forced them to rejoin the United Evangelical Church in 1959. Some Pentecostal churches, although persecuted by the Communists, chose to take the risk and function independently and often underground. The United Evangelical Church existed until the late 1980s, when the Solidarity movement grew stronger and the sociopolitical situation begun to change. In 1987, the Pentecostals left the United Evangelical Church and formed the Pentecostal Church of Poland during a council held on May 22 in Warsaw that was later legally confirmed on February 1, 1988.[17] This started a new phase in the history of Polish Pentecostalism and formed the largest Pentecostal denomination in this country. At this time, the Church consisted of about ten thousand members and eighty-two churches.[18] Not all Pentecostal groups joined the new denomination, and some formed their own associations—for example, the Evangelical Faith Christian Church, initially with seven churches in that network, or the Church of God in Christ (an independent Charismatic group not connected with the Church of God in Christ that originated in the United States) that formed its own denominational structures in Poland.

There is no doubt that the events that took place in Poland in 1989 initiated a massive transformation in every aspect of that nation's life. Since the collapse of Communism, Polish society (along with other societies in the region) has experienced a process of rapid change. The demise of the monolithic system and the emergence of new institutional structures gave rise to new opportunities and considerable liberties, suppressed "from above" in the previous epoch. The transformational challenges were also based on the fact that never before had there been an attempt to reorganize the economic, political, and social structures simultaneously.[19] Needless to say, such a sea change was associated with high social costs, the development of new lifestyles, and the emergence of new value systems, as well as new conflicts of interest. This sociopolitical transformation opened new opportunities for the Pentecostal Church of Poland to function freely and develop its own evangelistic and social ministries. This was confirmed even further when on February 10, 1997, the Polish parliament passed legislation that officially stabilized the relationship between the Pentecostal Church of Poland and the state, with all the rights and privileges pertaining thereto.[20] This allowed the church to legally register and run its own missions, foundations, schools, and social ministries that provided broad opportunities for missional engagement with the society. Internationally, the Pentecostal Church of Poland is a member of World Assemblies of God Fellowship and Pentecostal European Fellowship.[21]

Theological Directions and Dynamics of Charismatic Spirituality

In view of the preceding historical outline of the Pentecostal movement in Poland, we will now briefly point to some theological aspects that are significant in shaping Pentecostal identity and praxis. The Declaration of Faith of the Pentecostal Church of Poland includes eight key articles that shape Pentecostal belief and practice:

- The Word of God, which is infallible and inspired by the Holy Spirit, the only norm for faith and life
- One God in three persons of the Father, Son, and Holy Spirit

- The only begotten sonship of Jesus Christ, born of the Virgin Mary, crucified for the sin of the world, raised bodily from the dead, ascended to heaven and will return in glory
- The reconciliation with God through repentance and faith in the gospel
- The baptism in the Holy Spirit, experiencing the fullness of the Holy Spirit and His gifts
- One church, holy, universal, and apostolic
- Healing of the sick as the sign of grace and the power of God
- Resurrection and eternal life[22]

Polish Pentecostals, like other Evangelicals, point to the importance of the Word of God, need for personal justification, regeneration, and new birth on the basis of faith in the power of Jesus's sacrifice, which is to be followed by the process of sanctification in a believer's life. What distinguishes Pentecostals from other denominations is their emphasis on the experience of the baptism in the Holy Spirit and the practice of spiritual gifts. Some theologians even say that the Pentecostal movement adds a fifth postulate to the sixteenth-century Reformation—*sola experientia*, since experiencing the Spirit is a fundamental part of its identity.[23] Polish Pentecostals make a clear distinction between conversion and the baptism in the Holy Spirit leading to experiencing spiritual gifts. The gift of speaking in tongues is often perceived as a sign of the baptism in the Holy Spirit but not dogmatized as compulsory in the Polish context.[24] All Pentecostals pay attention to pneumatology and strongly believe that experiencing the Holy Spirit is a vital part of Christian existence and witness to the world. It is believed that the Holy Spirit is the source of God's power, not only in terms of individual experience in a believer's life, but also in the church, being united by the Spirit.[25]

Marek Kamiński, current bishop of the Pentecostal Church of Poland, uses the biblical metaphors of the desert and the journey to the Promised Land to illustrate the position of the Pentecostal Church in this nation as he envisions it. He points out that in a nation where Pentecostals are a small minority, which includes only 0.057 percent of the population, one of the priorities of the church should be renewed teaching on the role of the anointing of the Holy Spirit:

> Our churches should be a place of teaching and experiencing the baptism in the Holy Spirit, fervent prayers, atmosphere permeated with glory and activity of the Spirit, manifestations of the gifts and the fruit of the Holy Spirit and as a result of this rapid evangelization.[26]

He also concludes that fear and silence are two major factors limiting the growth of Pentecostal spirituality in the churches.[27] These emphases point to the importance of the connection between the practice of charismatic spirituality and its impact on actual church growth. The research on this theme conducted by Margaret Poloma in the Assemblies of God in the United States and later by William K. Kay in the United Kingdom is the model for a similar study by Oliwier Cieślar in Poland.[28] The study clearly confirms there is a significant correlation between the numbers of members publicly exercising spiritual gifts with growth in attendance.[29] At the same time, the research revealed that almost half of local congregations are low in charismatic activity. Cieślar concluded that although the baptism in the Holy Spirit is an important part of Polish Pentecostal theology, many believers treat it as a one-time event without following public manifestations.[30] This provides an important agenda for practical theology and a pastoral task to inspire the churches in the praxis of charisma that affects every aspect of church life and growth.

On the other hand, one of the challenges facing Polish Pentecostalism from a theological perspective is uncritical reception of Charismatic waves that come from different parts of the world. Wojciech Włoch, leader of the Church of God in Poland and author of several academic publications on the history of the Pentecostal movement, observes that Polish Charismatic churches follow global trends, like the spiritual warfare movement, faith movement, and third-wave movement, and are affected by them.[31] Reception of those movements is usually connected with revivalistic theology of expectation and hope for rapid spiritual change in the nation. In the 1990s, some Pentecostals got engaged with spiritual warfare beliefs and practices that soon involved other Charismatic groups and independent Charismatic congregations throughout the nation. They put great emphasis on intercessory prayer and spiritual mapping and developed particular strategies for spiritual warfare on the national and international level, including the "Movement of Intercessors for Poland" in 1999.[32] The methodology and approach of the movement caused a lot of controversy within the Pentecostal Church of Poland and eventually resulted in group leaders sympathizing with the intercessors leaving for another denomination. The network is still active, works interdenominationally, and has changed the name to Poland for Jesus.[33]

One of the problems facing Pentecostals is the lack of theological approach to charismatic phenomena that often results in uncritical reception of experience apart from critical self-understanding and biblical reflection. Such naiveté is often connected with a suspicious attitude of some Pentecostals toward academia and theological discourse in general, interpreted sometimes in terms of human wisdom versus God's wisdom.[34] However, over the last decade there is a growing interest in the study of Pentecostalism and, as a result, a growing number of academic studies and publications connected to this theme have appeared. A great example of this is the monograph of a Pentecostal scholar, Andrzej Migda, entitled *Mistycyzm Pentekostalny w Polsce* (Pentecostal mysticism in Poland), which defines charismatic experience in broader terms of phenomenology of religion, psychology of religion, and biblical theology.[35] In this volume, the author researches the mystical practices and beliefs present in Polish churches, examines the practice of spiritual gifts by Pentecostals, and analyzes the level of community activity in relation to collective religious experience bearing traces of mysticism.[36]

Another area that requires more reflection in the Polish context is Pentecostal ecclesiology. Piotr Karaś points to this need for defining distinctive Pentecostal ecclesiology in an ecumenical context. In his lecture entitled "Kościół w mocy Ducha: Eklezjologia Pentekostalna wobec wyzwań ekumenicznych" (The church in power of the Spirit: Pentecostal ecclesiology in the light of ecumenical challenges), Karaś examines various implications of "the full gospel church," "the church as a charismatic community," "the church as evangelizing community," and "progressive Pentecostalism" by emphasizing the need for integration of social responsibility with evangelism from an ecclesiological perspective.[37] Pneumatological ecclesiology, which seems to be the most representative by the Pentecostal churches, points to the importance of building unity in the body of Christ on the basis of empowerment of the Holy Spirit and provides an important area for theological development. The task of defining and promoting Pentecostal ecclesiology remains a challenge that requires deeper theological reflection and elaboration and is closely related to investing in leadership development. With new views of neoapostolic networks and prophetic movements, it is even more important to clarify the biblical and theological bases for spiritual leadership in the church.[38]

This is where the Pentecostal institution Wyższa Szkoła Teologiczno-Społeczna (Theological-Social School) in Warsaw has played and continues to play a significant role in shaping future leaders of the Pentecostal movement in the region. The educational offerings of the school include not only a bachelor of arts in theology program, but also courses of study in counseling, coaching and mentoring, and social communication, among other topics in their School of Mission, School of Leaders, and the John Godson Political-Social School.[39] The school also organizes academic conferences and invites scholars working in various fields and disciplines, representing a range of church traditions, to present their research in order to further the discussion from Evangelical and Pentecostal perspectives.

A good example of such a conference was the one organized in partnership with the Baptist Theological Seminary in April 2014 entitled "Trudne sprawy Ewangelikalizmu Polskiego" (Difficult issues in Polish Evangelicalism), which addressed issues such as marriage and divorce, in vitro fertilization, psychomanipulation, gender issues and homosexuality, church and unity, and attitudes to Roman Catholics, all from an Evangelical and Pentecostal perspective. These are the issues that are being discussed in the wider society but often are not addressed theologically in the churches. There are many other difficult topics that the church has had to face since the fall of Communism that require theological and missional engagement.[40] What is at stake is how the church will respond to these needs and whether this will have a deep and lasting social and cultural impact.

Missional Engagement With Contemporary Society

The critical issue facing the church in the post-Communist era is closely associated with the search for a relevant missional theology in light of the multidimensional transformations within post-Communist society. Surely, doing theology cannot mean the simple transfer of theological ideas and systems from elsewhere that is not suited to a particular context. In other words, what is important for missional theology is to move from being a theology that is influenced by its context to being a genuinely contextual theology that is able to self-consciously reflect on and engage the historical and cultural factors that have shaped its particular expression of faith and to discern the deepest issues behind the narratives, customs, and traditions of these faith communities.[41] The purpose of it is not to affirm a sectarian syndrome or minority mentality or escape into romantic views of history and the church but rather the rediscovery of its true identity and mission. Furthermore, such an approach will necessarily include and explore elements of that identity that need to be critically evaluated in light of transformations taking place within broader culture. Contextual theology, by definition, seeks contextual relevance and as such does not claim to be universal but rather attempts to express the truth of Christianity in a way that is suited to the thought patterns and cultural specifics of a particular context. This is important for the future of the church and cannot be ignored.

During an interdenominational academic conference in Warsaw in 2004 on the challenges of contemporary mission, Pentecostal theologian Edward Czajko presented a paper entitled "Mission of the Church From the Perspective of Enthusiastic Christianity," where he outlined key elements of Pentecostal understanding of mission.[42] The initial point of reflection on mission starts with a conviction that God is "a centrifugal Being," the One who sends and is the source of all mission.[43] This conviction is crucial and is based on a Trinitarian understanding of God, who is the foundation of mission, and therefore if mission is to be true to its identity, it needs to be rooted in the *missio Dei* (mission of God),[44] in the sense that the church is missionary in its nature and as such always needs to be connected to its source in order to fulfill its role in this world. Since the church is "a commissioned community," the mission of the church in Pentecostal understanding should be viewed as fourfold: "mission of worshipping God," "mission as offering prayers to God," "mission of social care," and "an evangelistic mission."[45]

The first aspect of mission as worship is evident in Pentecostal spirituality and often becomes a distinguishing mark, with its emphasis on freedom in the Spirit that is expressed through corporate worship, enthusiastic prayers, dancing, and preaching that points to the transforming power of God. All of these activities are expressions of living faith and empower believers to participate in evangelism to the world. However, it is very important to emphasize in the teaching and practice of the church that worship is not just about emotional expression of devotion to God but that "the worshipping believer should prove the quality of his or her discipleship by having a high level of moral life, which is particularly motivated by eschatological awareness."[46] The second important aspect of mission is intercessory and thanksgiving prayer, as distinguished from the act of worship.[47] Pentecostals put great emphasis on this aspect and therefore designate special time for prayer during their worship services and organize special prayer meetings, prayer ministries, and conferences focusing on various issues, like healing and intercession for the nation. This should be viewed as part of the missional responsibility of the church for the world.

The third aspect of mission emphasized by Pentecostals is related to social responsibility and care for the world.[48] The process of transformation in a post-Communist context, of integration into the European Union, and of globalization have informed the emergence of new worldviews, perspectives, values, and lifestyles largely dominated by a consumerist outlook. Thus, growing inequality of wealth and opportunity, coupled with a sense of meaninglessness and alienation of the so-called "losers" of society, are often expressed in the post-Communist discourse in terms of *loss* and *change*. Given this situation, there is a growing awareness of social responsibility issues among Polish Pentecostals. Questions about Christian social and political involvement come to the forefront of present discussions, which points to a new openness to the development of a social theology.[49] While Protestant social thought at first glance does not seem as developed as that of their Roman Catholic counterparts, it nevertheless provides many significant insights for contemporary discussion. Pentecostal scholar of political sciences Tomasz Debowski points to the importance of social involvement of Evangelical churches, along with some challenges and opportunities associated with that, and provides practical examples of Protestant social doctrine deeply rooted in moral values that are relevant to the struggles the Polish nation is facing today.[50] Similarly, Piotr Karaś, Pentecostal pastor and scholar, has examined the social activities of Evangelical churches in Poland in light of social-work theory, legislative initiatives, and theological prerogatives.[51] He concludes that it is important to the church to become an open and transformational community that integrates evangelism with social activities in the world.[52] Therefore, there is a growing number of Pentecostal charities, foundations, and educational initiatives, examples of which are New Hope Mission and Teen Challenge Mission, among many others, that seek to integrate evangelism and social witness.

The fourth basic aspect of a Pentecostal understanding of mission is evangelism.[53] The bishop of the Pentecostal Church of Poland, Marek Kamiński, emphasizes the great need for intentional evangelism in society and calls for churches to get involved, starting with fasting and prayer, organizing evangelistic teams on a local level, and working together to fulfill this vision.[54] Most exegetes today agree that the ministry of Jesus as described in the Gospels focused on announcing and demonstrating the reign of God and was generally centered on "the good news of the kingdom."[55] Such understanding of the gospel calls for manifestations of God's love through word and deed and integration of loving service with a proclamation that is not triumphalistic but rooted in solidarity with the hurting world. All too often, this kingdom dimension of the gospel is neglected in contemporary practices of evangelism. Limited understanding of the gospel or preoccupation with a narrow scope of evangelistic activities affects not only the practice of evangelism but also its perception by the wider community. Therefore, it becomes necessary to reflect on evangelism in the light of the holistic content of the gospel.

Thus, the crucial theological task is to find a way of relating the radical message of God's reign with the Christian community and of relating it to the real issues facing people today. Given this, it becomes clear that according to the whole gospel, both in word and life, proclamation and discipleship, personal renewal and community, each completes the other. Thus, the news that the church shares can become good news only when it reflects the true, life-giving gospel of Jesus Christ, which is concerned with holistic renewal, is theologically rooted in the commitment to God's reign, is closely linked with solidarity with the hurting world, and is reflected in responsible stewardship and service.

Chapter 4

"Not by Might, nor by Power, but by My Spirit": Pentecostalism in Romania

Corneliu Constantineanu and Ciprian Balaban

After a rather timid beginning at the end of the First World War and despite difficult times of persecution and marginalization in the decades of the Communist regime, the Romanian Pentecostal Church has developed to become, currently, the fourth-largest Christian denomination in Romania and is the only church in the context of central and Eastern Europe to have had significant growth in various respects in the last ten years. Beyond numerical expansion, the Church has also made progress with regard to several other areas, such as foreign missions; education; economic, social, and political engagement; as well as Roma Christianity. There are, of course, many challenges facing Pentecostals in the present, and there are signs that they are not shying away from but rather beginning to tackle them.

This chapter presents, in the first part, the origins and the development of the Pentecostal churches in Romania reflecting particularly the difficult history in their initial years, the persecutions and struggles under the Communist regime, as well as a brief account of the years of transition after 1989. Since not much has been written about the history of Romanian Pentecostalism, the first part will be more extensive. In the second part, we will highlight specific features of Romanian Pentecostalism, particularly its contribution to the economic development of local communities, advances in education, and unique mission impetus in the region. We conclude with some of the specific challenges Romanian Pentecostals need to respond to.

History and Development

The Pentecostal movement in Romania has had a continuous development since the beginning. This numerical growth began in the interwar period, continued during the Communist time despite severe challenges, and has surged after the revolution of 1989. In the census of 2011 over 360,000 inhabitants of Romania declared themselves Pentecostals.

The beginnings, in the midst of persecution and controversy (1922–1938)

When the first Pentecostals arrived in Romania depends on the sources consulted. Some indications are that the first Pentecostals appeared in Bucovina (the northwestern region of Romania) in the years 1908, 1911, and 1918.[1] A second, more credible perspective is that a group of Pentecostals appeared in either 1919 or 1921[2] amongst the Germans living in the county of Sibiu. However, the group that most influenced the spread of Pentecostalism throughout all of Romania appeared in the year 1922 in a town named Păuliş in the western region, located today in the county of Arad.[3] The initiators of this group were Gheorghe and Persida Bradin, who found out about the Pentecostal faith through people who had visited the United States and kept in touch with Pavel Budean, a Romanian with status in the United States, who at the time was also a Pentecostal evangelist.[4] In 1922, Persida Bradin was miraculously healed of tuberculosis and dropsy, illnesses from which she suffered for nearly three years.[5] Then the following year, the Bradin couple, together with other believers, experienced the baptism of the Holy Spirit.[6]

At the end of the year 1924, when the Pentecostal group from Arad numbered around fifty people, they submitted to the government their first petition for official recognition of the Pentecostal confession. They received a negative response, published in a national press article, which, ironically, contributed to the spread of Pentecostalism throughout Romania. Following that press article, Bradin received many letters and even visits from people unknown to him who were interested about the new faith.[7] Many other requests for official recognition were filed in the following years to the Romanian Ministry of Religious Affairs, but to no avail.[8]

In 1929, considering the large number of Pentecostal believers that appeared in the eastern part of the country, in the area of Galați–Brăila, a new strategy for obtaining state recognition bore a different title, avoiding the use of the term *Pentecostal*. This group later became known as the Apostolic Church of God under a different leadership and another center unfamiliar to the ministry, so that the Pentecostal churches throughout the country could adhere to this association if it received recognition.[9] Once the ministry discovered the ties between the Apostolic Church and that of the Pentecostals, recognition was withheld and the apostolic houses of prayer were ordered to be closed.[10]

The Pentecostal believers in this period were heavily persecuted. There were many cases in which believers were caught at gatherings for prayer and were either fined, beaten, or arrested by the police.[11] Three martyrs who died due to the brutal beatings deserve mention. Mihai Olaru and Partenie Pera from Lipova were arrested by the police as leaders of the Pentecostal group in Şoimoş. They were both beaten with chains so badly on the soles of their feet that after five weeks of excruciating pain, Pera died, leaving behind his wife and two children. The officer that beat him to death had been investigated and judged at the tribunal in Arad and was initially fined with 1,000 lei, though, according to Gheorghe Bradin, the officer was promoted in rank from sergeant to major.[12] Gavril Cârstian from Bilca, county of Suceava, died in 1935 from being beaten inhumanely by police officers. He was the central leader of the Pentecostals in northern Moldova and Bucovina.[13] We learn about another martyr whose identity is unknown from the Pentecostal magazine *Cuvântul adevărului* [The word of truth] that states that he died in December 1936 while being held captive in prison for his faith.[14]

During this period of time, despite hardships and persecutions, the number of Pentecostal believers and communities grew significantly. Gheorghe Bradin has suggested a correlation between persecution and the increase in numbers: "Every beating, wound, fine, mockery, prison, etc., which has been applied to us due to the fact that we serve the Lord, has been the seed for the thousands of members which form today's Apostolic Church of God."[15] The official statistics from 1931 submitted to the Ministry of Public Instruction and Religious Affairs show 169 Apostolic (Pentecostal) communities and a total of 3,560 minor and major members. However, due to the obstacles placed for the registration of the believers, the statistics were incomplete.[16] Another statistic from the second semester of 1938 presents the following details about Pentecostals: a total of 7,270 people, from which 6,069 were from rural areas and 1,174 were from urban areas; 3,669 were male and 3,601 female.[17]

Between 1931–1938, the number of believers doubled, even amidst doctrinal controversy. In 1929, some leaders of the Pentecostal movement in Romania fell under the influence of a Hungarian missionary, Ianos Lerch, who belonged to the organization Misiunea Penticostala pentru Estul Europei (The Pentecostal Mission for Eastern Europe), with their headquarters at Danzig (today's Gdansk, Poland). In 1930, the superintendent of that mission, Gustav Schmidt (who was also of Hungarian origin, his first name being Augustin Covacs) visited Romania, where he met with Gheorghe Bradin in Timisoara and proposed cooperation, but Bradin refused, for they did not practice foot-washing during the Lord's Supper, nor did they prohibit the consumption of alcoholic beverages. Several important Romanian Pentecostal leaders, such as Ion Bododel, Eugen Bodor, and Alexandru Isbaşa, sided with Gustav Schmidt, and this created deep tensions within the Pentecostal movement so that in December 1931 or January 1932, the church split into two groups.[18] Disputes between both groups on foot-washing can be seen in their magazines.[19] Though there were some efforts to reconcile, they were but ephemeral (until 1950, when the Communist authorities centralized these groups—see below).[20]

Growth in the context of disintegration (1938–1945)

Persecutions intensified in 1937–1938 when many believers were arrested. In April 1937, the publication of *Cuvântul Adevărului* was forbidden. Probably the ban had something to do with the March 1937 issue, which spoke of the aforementioned Pentecostal believer who died while imprisoned for his faith.[21] In this context, Gheorghe Bradin, the primary leader of the Pentecostals in Romania, received an offer of partnership from Alexandru (Sandor) Szaday, who presented himself as a representative of the Independent Baptist Association, which had received recognition from the Ministry of Religious Affairs, but the number of members that belonged to this association was very small. Alexandru Szaday proposed to Bradin that the Pentecostals register with this association but keep their Pentecostal beliefs.[22] The joining of the Pentecostals with the Independent Baptist Association was made official at the conference organized in Luna de Sus, county of Cluj, on August 14–15, 1938.[23]

The cooperation between Gheorghe Bradin and Sandor Szaday transformed into a violent dispute shortly after.[24] In an article published in 1947, Bradin testified that collaborating with Szaday was one of his biggest mistakes.[25] After this, Bradin contacted Iosif Iacob, from the commune of Zam, district Ilia, region Hunedoara, who at that time was the branch president of the Baptist denomination in Arad. Through the registration of a large number of Pentecostal believers within the Baptist denomination, they were able to evade the intense persecution.[26] Yet there were Pentecostal believers who did not agree with this relationship, for they saw it as compromising their distinctives.[27]

In December 1942, through the law decree number 927/28, the Baptist, Adventist, and Evangelical confessions were outlawed, for it was considered that their ties with the United States and England threatened Romania's national unity. The authorities even ordered the deportation of all the "sectarians" to Transnistria.[28] After the First World War, many of these believers from either Moldova or Bucovina were condemned to twenty-five years of manual labor because they would not convert to the Orthodox faith,[29] which at that time was identified with Romanian nationality.[30]

Yet during the war years, while the Pentecostal movement was going through a reconfiguration of identity, the number of Pentecostal believers doubled. After the end of the war, in 1945, when religious denominations were given freedom to organize themselves in Romania, there were approximately fifteen thousand Pentecostal believers.[31]

Provisional freedom and three Pentecostal groups (1945–1948)

Starting in 1945, when the Pentecostals in Romania were reorganizing, three Pentecostal associations received provisional recognition from the state: the primary Biserica lui Dumnezeu Apostolica Penticostala (Pentecostal Apostolic Church of God), a second group with the same name but with Crestini Botezati cu Duhul Sfant (Christians Baptized With the Holy Spirit) added at the end—these separated in 1931 over the practice of foot-washing—and Ucenicii Domnului Isus Hristos (Disciples of the Lord Jesus Christ). This last group appears to have evolved from a community founded in Bucharest in the year 1933 by Eugen Bodor, the leader of the Christians Baptized With the Holy Spirit, which had been taken over in the year 1934 by Ioan Danciu, the leader of the Pentecostal Apostolic Church of God.[32]

In 1945, the members of the Pentecostal Apostolic Church of God (Arad) were located near the provinces of Crişana and Transylvania; the members of the association Christians Baptized With the Holy Spirit were situated in Banat and Bucovina; while the majority of the Disciples of the Lord Jesus Christ were positioned in Bucharest. From 1945 until 1950, the number of Pentecostals in Romania grew from fifteen thousand to approximately thirty thousand people.[33]

Pentecostal Church under the Communist regime (1948–1989)

In 1950, the Communist authorities officially merged the three Pentecostal groups.[34] This centralization, following the Soviet model, was followed by the establishment of the Federatia Cultelor

Evanghelice (Federation of Evangelical Denominations) as an umbrella organization of the four evangelical denominations: Pentecostal, Baptist, Evangelical, and Adventist.[35]

The forced unification of the Pentecostal groups in Romania, as well as the federalization of the Evangelical denominations, were the first steps taken by the Communist regime to limit religious freedom. With the official recognition of the Pentecostal denomination in Romania in 1950 came an initial article of restriction: Pentecostals could "not hold ties to any organization outside the borders of the country."[36] The freedoms that disturbed the Communist power—such as the scope of the Pentecostal denomination, references to Sunday school, the missionary activity of the preachers, etc.—were revoked in this statute.[37] Likewise, for easier control, the number of regional branches was reduced from seventeen to five, and in the 1960s to as low as three.[38] The confession of faith of the Pentecostal denomination in Romania was considered so dangerous to the Communist regime that they restricted its publication. During the time of the Communist dictatorship in Romania, the Pentecostal confession of faith was published only once, and even then in a disguised manner, in a manual for pastors.[39]

During the Communist regime, the authorities involved themselves in the internal activities of the Pentecostal movement, seeking control over its confession and even attempting its dissolution.[40] This was realized, in part, through the so-called "empowered religious issues," which represented the Department of Religious Affairs on the field,[41] and through "collaboration" between the *Securitate* (Secret Police), pastors, and church attendees. Members were led to believe that the Secret Police knew everything that was happening, which instilled fear and moderate enthusiasm.[42]

In addition, the Ministry of Religious Affairs and the Department of Religious Affairs in 1958 sought to standardize religious services and eliminate charismatic manifestations. Even some of the songs that were sung were troubling to the Communist regime, especially those that referred to the Lord Jesus as King (in Romania, the monarchy was abolished by the Communist regime on December 30,

1947) or that called believers to arms for God (because these kept alive memories of the anti-Communist army's resistance). Songs that had a pronounced eschatological character or that made direct reference to the baptism of the Holy Spirit were censored. A series of songs taken out of Pentecostal hymnbooks in 1952 were reintroduced in the 1970 edition, of course after being modified so that it would be more acceptable to the Communist regime.[43]

At the time, the appearance of a Pentecostal religious magazine was postponed a few years, even though the Ministry of Religious Affairs in 1951 saw how the state could benefit from such: "This denomination has mystical religious practices and through understanding the religious services, there would be a possibility of controlling and leading to an even greater extent the religious practice of this denomination."[44] When the Pentecostals finally obtained approval to publish *Buletinul cultului Penticostal* (The bulletin of the Pentecostal denomination), state propaganda was evident from the first issue (September 1953), a compromise that made possible the reappearance of the magazine after six years of interdiction. The politicization of the magazine represented attempts by the state to brainwash Pentecostal believers through the exaltation of the Communist regime. Not a single issue of the Pentecostal newsletter escaped the infusion of Communist propaganda. On occasions, whole issues would be destroyed and a heavily sanitized version reprinted.[45]

The Communist power was implicitly active in the structural configuration of the Pentecostal denomination. Those who were not grateful for the Communist achievements were marginalized, as was the case with the second Pentecostal congress in 1956, when through the actions of the Secret Police the old executive committee was removed except for Gheorghe Bradin.[46] Likewise, the Communist regime limited religious services to being held only on Saturday night or Sunday morning. Once a month, they were also permitted to gather for a religious service on Thursday night (for the Lord's Supper). Another measure taken by the Communists to reduce the rate of growth within the Evangelical confessions was the assigning of smaller communities to larger ones within close proximity. This resulted in the abolition of many congregations due to the annexation of these by the larger churches, which created overcrowded churches and decreased the number of pastors.[47]

During the Communist regime, there existed some situations in which Pentecostals were subjugated to direct persecution for religious proselytism, illegal religious activities, and Bible trafficking with other religious publications. For example, Ioan Jiloveanu died after being beaten by the agents of the Secret Police in 1948.[48] In 1959, Pavel Ciuci from Picleu, who was well known for his charismatic gifts, was sentenced to six years of prison because of his activities as a Pentecostal dissident.[49] Eugen Bodor was condemned at the end of 1961 to five years at a correctional prison, with a three-year correctional ban and the confiscation of his belongings, because he edited *Studiu Biblic despre darurile Duhului Sfant* (Bible study about the gifts of the Holy Spirit).[50] Constantin Caraman was condemned in 1963, together with Vasile Gaşpar, to three years in prison and the confiscation of all their goods, for they were caught participating at an illegal gathering in the house of Nicolae Tudorache.[51] Constantin Caraman, Constantin Tarnavschi, Victor Răscol, and Cornel Mihai were retained and arrested for four months between October 1971 and February 1972 due to involvement in an illegal Bible study organized at Buşteni in the summer of 1970 and the illegal trafficking of Christian literature.[52] The Christian musician and composer Iacob Alecu, from Sibiu, was condemned in 1972 to eight years in prison because of his protests against the lack of freedom present at the time in Romania.[53] Vasile Răscol was arrested in the summer of 1974 for using his personal vehicle to transport smuggled Bibles; he was sentenced to two years in prison, and his automobile was confiscated.[54] Constantin Caraman was retained on April 3, 1977, together with the Baptists Iosif Ţon, Pavel Nicolescu, Radu Dumitrescu, Aurelian Popescu, and Evangelical Silviu Cioată, for signing the "Cultele neoprotestante si drepturile omului in Romania" (The neo-Protestant denominations and human rights in Romania). Due to the pressure exerted by the West, in a short period of time, the six signatories were released.

Until 1989, the United Nations Commission on Human Rights had to ask the Romanian Department of Religious Affairs about the fate of Constantin Caraman.[55] Viorel Lăcătuş, Ioan Samu, and Francisc Paris, leaders of the church Filidelfia from Mediaş, were condemned on November 6, 1978, to six months in prison because they participated in the religious services in the Pentecostal communities of Lugoj and Timişoara.[56] The Secret Police was concerned that after these communities received authorization to operate on October 27, 1977, after four years of insistence, they grew from five families to 468 people in only eight months.[57] Ioan Toader from Ploieşti was condemned in 1981 to five years of detention for the illegal distribution of Bibles and Christian literature.[58] There were many situations in which believers were marginalized at their workplaces, and in some cases even their children were expelled from school.[59]

Between 1970–1980, the rapid growth of Pentecostal believers made it more difficult to obtain authorization for opening and operating churches. Some churches were even demolished, as was the case with the churches in Câmpia Tuzii, Bisriţa, and even Bucharest (one located on Crângaşi Street, whose pastor, Pavel Bochian, at that time was the president of the Pentecostal denomination). The rationale for demolition was the rezoning of cities.[60] However, even in this situation it was possible to open *Seminarul Teologic Penticostal* (Pentecostal Theological College) in 1976 in Bucharest, the first to offer a three-year degree.

During the Communist era, the activities of the Pentecostals were especially monitored by the Department of Religious Affairs because they had the largest-growing rate of converts among all denominations, approximately two or even three times more than other Evangelical confessions, which also had growth rates that concerned the old regime.[61] If in 1950 there were approximately thirty thousand Pentecostal believers, in 1989 the number rose to up to three hundred thousand people. These came from approximately 1,100 churches, of which 800 were authorized and 300 unauthorized (illegal).[62]

The road to freedom (1989–2015)

After the revolution of December 1989, Romania became a democratic country. The illegal churches received authorization, new churches were built, and new foundations appeared within the country, which carried out humanitarian work among many people in need. There was also established the first Pentecostal mission societies with both internal and foreign mission foci. Within Romania, there was a priority for the southern part of the country, where the number of Evangelicals was very low, and in the areas of the southeast, where there were a large number of Islamic communities.

The Pentecostal education system also evolved during this period. Thus, the *Semiarual Teologic Penticostal*, which had been founded in 1976, became now a four-year, university-level college. The name was changed to *Institutul Teologic Penticostal din Bucuresti* (Pentecostal Theological Institute in Bucharest) in 1992, and it received full governmental accreditation as an institution of higher education in 2008. Many other Bible schools and general educational institutions were also founded.

An official 1992 survey showed some 220,033 registered Pentecostals,[63] and ten years later, growth rates of over 60 percent pushed that number up to 330,486 registered believers.[64] The growth of the Pentecostal believers continued in the next decade, and the official national census in 2011 registered 362,314 Pentecostals and some three thousand churches. These figures place the Pentecostal denomination as the fourth-largest in the country, after the Orthodox, Roman Catholic, and Reformed Churches.[65] Even though in terms of absolute figures this may not look spectacular (compared with some other nations from the Southern Hemisphere), for central and Eastern Europe it is remarkable. Already some years ago, seeing the great potential of the Romanian Evangelical churches in general and of Pentecostals in particular, Peter Kuzmic, the Croatian Pentecostal scholar, called Romania "the Korea of Europe."[66]

Some Specific Features of Romanian Pentecostalism

Romanian Pentecostal numerical growth is all the more noteworthy, as no unified vision or strategy for development exists at the level of national denominational leadership. This is perhaps because national-level leaders continue to serve as full-time pastors of their local church—many times as the only pastor of the congregation—so have little time or energy to devote to denominational matters. Yet there are local and regional initiatives, and in what follows, we highlight a few of these.

Foreign missions and education

If Romania has benefited greatly from the work of foreign missionaries, in recent decades there has emerged a unique, totally Romanian mission agency, the Agenția Penticostală de Misiune Externă (APME, or the Pentecostal Agency for Foreign Mission), which has sent missionaries across the world. APME currently has fifty-five long-term missionaries in twenty-one countries across three continents, most of which serve in Islamic contexts. There are an additional fifteen to twenty mission candidates, already trained, in the process of being approved by APME who will begin their mission work soon.[67] Ninety-nine percent of the agency's budget comes from Romanian churches and believers. With less than ten years in existence, a passionate and visionary team, led by Gheorghe Rițisan, has developed a clear strategy for foreign missions. From the beginning, the goal of APME was to mobilize Romanian churches for missions and "to facilitate the process of recruiting, training, sending and supporting Romanian missionaries, especially among unreached ethnic groups."[68] It order to be effective in its mission, APME has established its own mission school, Centrul Roman de Studii Transculturale (Romanian Center for Transcultural Studies), where cross-cultural mission candidates are properly trained and equipped. With its coherent and dynamic strategy, as well as its significant partnerships, APME has become an inspiring model of missions for other national churches in the region and even around the world.[69]

When it comes to education, it is not surprising to note that Pentecostals in general have been associated with a rather low view of the intellectual life and even with a strong anti-intellectualism. Historically, many gifted young men and women have been discouraged in their pursuit of higher education, and thus many genuine gifts for the intellectual and academic life of the church have been lost. Yet in this context, Romanian Pentecostals have emphasized education. With freedom from the Communist dictatorship since 1989, many schools opened at all levels to offer education within a Christian ethos.[70] As of 2013, the Romanian Pentecostal Church had the following educational institutions, all accredited by the Romanian government, or Ministry of Education:

- Two university-level Pentecostal colleges, with a total of 35 faculty members and 272 students
- Thirty Pentecostal Bible schools (of two years) in each of the nine denominational districts, with 198 teachers, 2,649 students, and over 16,848 alumni; these are the only programs that are not accredited from the present list
- Two post-high-school professional colleges, with 734 students
- Nine high schools, with 227 professors and 4,337 enrolled students
- Eight gymnasium schools
- Eight primary-level schools
- Forty kindergartens, with 119 instructors and 1,401 children

All told, the Romanian Pentecostal Church has ninety-nine educational institutions with a total of 9,393 students and over 579 professors, lecturers, and instructors. In addition, there is a fast-growing community of young Pentecostal professionals in all levels and areas of social, economical, political, administrative, and educational sectors, an excellent illustration of the shift in understanding and appreciation of the importance of education. It is also not an overstatement to say that the Pentecostal Theological Institute in Bucharest, with its fourteen full-time faculty, all Romanians with completed PhDs and academic rankings from full professors to lecturers, is one of the strongest Pentecostal theological schools in Europe.[71] There is, of course, much more to be done, in terms of advanced research and specific Pentecostal theology, but with its young and well-trained faculty, the school is also on the right track toward advanced research and theology.

Public engagement: economic, social, and political issues

Pentecostals have been rather known for their lack of concern for public engagement, and Romania is no exception to this rule. During the Communist regime, when the atheist rulers realized they could not eliminate religion, they attempted to limit religious manifestations exclusively to the church and private life. Believers also were unconcerned, as long as they were allowed to meet and worship God in their churches. However, over the years, Pentecostals have developed a renewed commitment to witness publicly to the lordship of Christ. Several new developments in the economic, social, and political sectors of Romanian society are underway.

Thus, in Romania there is a strong and growing community of Pentecostal businesspeople, some of whom have made significant contributions to the local and national economy. MG-Tec Group is a group of some fourteen companies owned by Ioan Tecar, a Pentecostal believer from Dej, that engages mostly in the production and distribution of building materials and provides retail sales of heavy trucks, hotel, and storage services. The company has a total of 1,213 employees and an annual turnover of some 145 million euro.[72] ATP Exodus is owned by Romanian Pentecostal Mircea Cirt from Baia Mare and offers a complex range of goods and services for vehicles, specializing in sales and service of Mercedes-Benz, Mazda, Opel, and MAN, with a used-car division and sale of spare parts for trucks. ATP Exodus is one of Romania's market leaders for accessories and spare parts for commercial vehicles, with a network of thirty-three national and ten international branches (in Bulgaria, Serbia, and Hungary). The company has a team of over 800 employees and an annual turnover of some 40 million euro.[73] Last but not least, Marelbo Prod-Com SRL, a family business and shoe factory owned by Aurel Bob, a Pentecostal believer from Vicovu-de-Sus, has over 200 employees, an annual turnover of some 10 million euro, and over forty stores throughout the country.[74] Marelbo offers job opportunities for several villages in the area, and together with similar companies of Pentecostal believers in the region has substantially contributed to the economic development of that area. The list could continue, even as we note that these Pentecostal businesspeople are involved in and support financially many local churches and Christian organizations.

Pentecostal churches and organizations are also engaged in the social area. There are many examples of churches and even individual believers who felt compelled to respond to the social needs arising, particularly after the abrupt change from a totalitarian regime to a free democracy. The following highlights a particular aspect of this work that came especially as a response to the plight of the abandoned orphans in Romania. The state of affairs regarding the situation of children in the former Communist context is dramatic. According to a recent UNICEF report, some fifteen thousand children are being abandoned annually in the former Communist countries.[75]

No one can forget the disturbing images of the orphans and institutionalized children in Romania made public immediately after the collapse of Communism in 1989. Twenty-five years later, there unfortunately remains far too many stories of child abandonment and street children, not to mention the plight of Roma (Gypsy) children or the tragedy of the so-called "eurorphans," the hundreds of thousands of children left behind by their parents, who migrated for work in Europe. There is still a perception that the state institutions are able to handle appropriately the plight of such children, and this is contrary to the evidence that such institutionalization is against the children's interest and well-being. It is in response to such urgency that many Pentecostal churches and individuals have begun to act on behalf of children in Romania, and thus many homes and centers have been established to feed, care, educate, and offer a future to these children. Corina Caba, a Pentecostal young woman from Oradea, is a remarkable example, as she opened her own apartment for destitute children. The apartment soon became too small to host so many children in need of help, and she founded Hope House Family Center in Oradea for these abandoned children.[76] Corina is just one of many people in Romania who offers a shelter and home to children at risk.[77]

Centrul Crestin pentru Reintegrare Sociala Onisim (the Christian Center for Social Reintegration Onisim) in Bistrița is another social initiative by Pentecostal believers offered to those who have served time in prison and need to be reintegrated into society. There are only five such centers in the country, and the Onisim center has many stories of people changed and transformed. Beyond social reintegration, people who have passed through the center have gone on to effect positive change in their communities. The center's significant impact led to its making the headline of a national newspaper in Romania.[78]

One comment about Pentecostal and politics ought to be made. If Pentecostals were primarily known for their intense, private spirituality and their lack of political engagement, in the last two decades the situation in Romania has changed. Thus, Pentecostal believers are running for and gaining seats in the Romanian parliament (some ten of them over the last fifteen years). Also, at the local levels there are many villages, towns, and even big cities in Romania where Pentecostals hold political and administrative positions, from counselors to city mayors. There was even a strong Pentecostal contribution to form a Christian democratic political party in an attempt to bring a specific Christian alternative to the governance of the country.[79]

Roma/Gypsy Christianity in Romania

A brief note about Roma/Gypsy Christianity, another significant feature of Romanian Pentecostalism, is appropriate. Even though this phenomenon has never been thoroughly researched throughout Eastern Europe,[80] it deserves to be mentioned, as Romania has the largest Roma population in central and Eastern Europe and, arguably, the largest number of Roma Christians, with the fastest growth rate. There are many individual Roma Christians in the Romanian Pentecostal churches, individual Roma churches within the existing Pentecostal denomination, and many independent churches, including, for example, the Christian Union of Roma Pentecostals in Romania (with some two hundred churches). In addition, there is a large number of small, independent Roma churches in villages and towns across the country. The most renowned place in Romania is Toflea (a village known for much violence and Mafia gangs), where a particular Christian movement among the Gypsies began in the early 1990s. From the testimonies of radical transformation of the lives of the first Roma converts, a large number of Roma followed—there was, for example, a single baptismal service in 2002 in which over six hundred Gypsies were baptized—and now some 90 percent of the village are Christians and attend the local Pentecostal church, which numbers well over one thousand members.[81]

There are, of course, other testimonies of entire Gypsy villages in Romania that converted to Christianity (such as Ramnicelu, Valea Rece, and Tecuci). A few years ago, *The Economist* ran the story of mass conversion among the Roma people in Ramnicelu and how this phenomenon brought significant and visible changes to the community:

> Typically Romani girls drop out of school when they marry. But the director of the schools in Râmnicelu says that girls are now attending classes, and that the boys are better behaved. Locals say the conversions have helped them understand the value of education. Field-officers from the National Agency

> for Roma attest that conversions have reduced violence, criminality and alcoholism in other parts of the country.[82]

Scholars of Romanian Christianity should watch developments in this area.

Evangelistic outreach and church life

If one asks why the Romanian Pentecostal Church is the only one to register growth in the last decade, part of the answer may be found in her evangelistic zeal and outreach efforts. Indeed, there is a special effort in all Pentecostal churches to organize at least a full week of evangelistic meetings every year, and the lay believers contribute a great deal to these events. There are also many public evangelistic meetings in stadiums, sports halls, and even big tents on the streets. There are many gifted singers and music teams as well as an increasing number of excellent Pentecostal preachers and evangelists who are traveling the country for these events. The experience of transformed lives has not only motivated testimonies but also attracted others.

Similarly, many larger Pentecostal churches are organizing evangelistic outreaches and church plants in the villages around them. One outstanding example is given by the Elim Pentecostal Church in Timisoara, one of the largest Pentecostal churches in Europe, which has currently no less than thirty-three church plants in the villages around Timisoara.[83] Another example of a particularly influential youth movement that attracts many young people is Fundatia Peniel (Peniel Foundation), which is focused on the young generation. There are thousands of younger people who attend its national, regional, and international meetings every year, and many are converted through this ministry.[84]

Pentecostal growth cannot be understood without reference to Pentecostal church life. Church services in Romanian Pentecostalism still last for three hours on Sunday morning and two hours on Sunday afternoon, and these include a full hour that is devoted to intense, fervent, intercessory prayer. Many people find that attractive, as they have the chance to bring all their concerns, hopes, and aspirations to God with the entire community. Every single church service also includes prayer for healing and deliverance, and many people are deeply touched. And there is also the element of poetry in Romanian Pentecostal church services. It would be rare for a church service to exclude the recitation of poetry. These are powerful, inspiring moments for the church attendees, as poets have unique gifts to evoke new possibilities and imaginatively envision the new creation in faith. These may be some of the reasons why people visit and join the church.

Conclusion: Further Challenges for the Romanian Pentecostal Church

For all the preceding, a good Pentecostal would ultimately say whatever was accomplished was done "not by might, nor by power, but by my Spirit." This is, indeed, one of the conclusions of the most comprehensive work on the history of Pentecostalism in Romania (two volumes, with a total of over 1,300 pages), written by historian Valeriu Andreescu: "We emphasize once more that the development of Pentecostalism in Romania was due and is still due to the work of the gifts of the Holy Spirit."[85]

If we have mentioned primarily some positive aspects and opportunities for the Romanian Pentecostal church, this should not be understood as the whole story. There are, of course, many further challenges to which Pentecostals need to respond. To mention only a few of the most important ones, note that the Romanian Pentecostal Church is rather isolated from the worldwide Pentecostal family and so there is an urgent need for stronger international connections, interactions, and partnerships. Another challenge is the need for solid, biblically grounded foundations for holistic engagement in the public life. Yes, there are a few good examples of public engagement (mentioned above), but these are still far too few compared with the potential for public contribution that the Romanian Pentecostal church has. Along the same lines, there is the challenge of developing a specifically Pentecostal way of reflection and theologizing, bringing to the fore the particular contribution that Pentecostals can make to Christian theology, spirituality, and mission. Higher degrees and more specialized research in this area are needed.[86] Finally, there is a need to continue to search for the best alternative in the leadership structure of the denomination in order to allow more time and space for strategic planning and development. There are many leaders in the denomination who think that those who are in higher authority positions in the denomination ought to be relieved of their duties/roles as local pastors to be able to devote more time to the actual vision, mission, and ministry of the Pentecostal denomination. There was actually such a proposal presented and discussed (eventually heavily debated) at the last national congress of the denomination in 2014, but it was eventually rejected. However, there are good signs that in the near future, this decision might be implemented and so we will see a more coherent strategy for Pentecostal development.

Chapter 5

The Pentecostal Movement in Austria and Hungary: History of Migration, Wars, and Challenges

Miroslav Atanasov

THE PENTECOSTAL MOVEMENT in Austria and Hungary began at a crucial time in history as their powerful political union, known as the Austro-Hungarian Empire, collapsed and split in two at the end of the First World War. The Spirit-filled faith was then affected strongly by migration and the other major events of the twentieth century. There are some significant differences in the two contexts, especially during the Cold War period, when Austria remained predominantly in the Western sphere of influence while Hungary was forced into the Communist camp as a client state of the Soviet Union. To this day, Pentecostalism does not have a strong presence among the religious groups in those countries. It is currently overshadowed by the predominant Catholicism and challenged by the post-Christian era of European culture. This chapter discusses Austria and Hungary in turn, and each section concludes with an assessment of the theological opportunities and challenges facing the Pentecostal movements in these countries in their second century.[1]

AUSTRIA

The Pentecostal movement in Austria began with the arrival of Swedish missionaries in Vienna in the 1920s—Alwin Christensson, Georg Steen, Elisabeth Phil, and Elof Hannsson-Rytterfeldt—sent by the Filadelfiaforsamlingen Church in Stockholm.[2] For some time, that mission received support from Erwin Lorenz in Germany. As a result of these early efforts, two vibrant congregations were formed: the Freie Christengemeinde "Philadelphia" and the Freie Christengemeinde "Salem."[3] One of them was known as the Halbgasse Church,[4] dating back to 1924, which is considered to be the first Pentecostal church in Austria. The building of a synagogue was used for a long time for the worship services of that congregation. These two churches were banned from conducting services in 1936 but were able to restart operations two years later "after the 'Anschluss' under the auspices of the 'Volksmission entschiedener Christen' of Karl Fix."[5]

The Swiss Pentecostal Mission Society also began work in Austria in the 1920s through the efforts of Josef Enzinger, a native Austrian who had converted to Pentecostalism while living in Wadenswil, Switzerland. Enzinger decided to go back to his hometown of Fuschl, Salzkammergut, Austria, to carry the faith and establish churches there. The new congregation initially experienced persecution from the Catholic Church and was restricted in its activities after 1936 by the National Socialist government. In order to escape these continuing outside pressures, it integrated into the Baptist Church in 1938.[6]

The Pentecostal Church in Austria was very small until after the end of World War II. Then the movement saw growth because of the many refugees who came from the German-speaking parts of Yugoslavia,[7] as well as from other East European nations. A revival broke out with their arrival, and the Pentecostal movement experienced significant increase, which necessitated some restructuring.

On December 14, 1946, an important meeting of twenty-six ministers in Sattledt took place; they came together to officially organize the Pentecostal movement in Austria under the name Freie Christengemeinde (Free Christian Fellowship). The actual name of the group reflected the influence of the many German-speaking immigrants from Yugoslavia, Hungary, and Romania. The delegates to the meeting decided to divide Austria into five regions and elected a national elders' council. They also began publication of a national periodical called *Die letzte stunde/lebensbotschaft*

(Last-hour message of life), and by 1948 there were about 1,800 members in the Austrian Pentecostal movement.[8]

In the 1950s the movement experienced a significant decline due to a major emigration wave, as many of those East European refugees departed for (mostly) Canada, but also the United States. Therefore, between 1952 and 1955 the Pentecostal movement was reduced to several hundred as about two-thirds of its constituents left Austria.

The movement experienced growth again in the 1970s through the assistance of missionaries who came from the Scandinavian countries, the United States, Great Britain, and Holland. By the time of its fiftieth anniversary, the Austrian Pentecostal movement had about forty churches and two thousand members. During the Communist times in Eastern Europe, Vienna served as the main hub for missionaries working in the closed countries, and they would use it as a home base. Because of the proximity, they would travel from there into Yugoslavia, Romania, Hungary, Bulgaria, and the other Eastern European countries. There were also some missionaries based in Graz and other cities, but most of them lived in Vienna.

The Church of God in Austria was started as a result of the fact that many Romanians sought asylum there in the 1980s. Superintendent Lambert DeLong and Moses Gaode, who was at the time studying at the European Bible Seminary in Rudersberg, contacted the Romanian believers living in the refugee camps. As a result, a Romanian church was started in Vienna in 1984; that church became strong and grew to about five hundred members. After the collapse of Communism, the Pentecostal movement in Austria continued to grow in the 1990s because of the steady influx of Romanian believers. By 1997, the Romanian Church of God in Austria became the strongest Pentecostal group in Austria "with thirteen churches and well over 2,000 believers. In 2009 that group was reported to have 6,000 followers in about 20 congregations."[9] There are now some really large Romanian Pentecostal churches there. This makes the Romanian churches associated with the Church of God a significant portion of the total number of the Pentecostal movement's adherents in Austria. Currently, about eight thousand in Austria identify themselves as Pentecostals; they worship in approximately seventy-five congregations. Their official name is Freie Christengemeinde-Pfingstgemeinde Oesterreich (Free Christian Pentecostal Congregations of Austria).[10] This group is associated with the Assemblies of God.

In 2013, the Free Pentecostals group came under the umbrella of the Austrian Free Churches, which also include the Baptist Union, the Federation of Evangelical churches, the Elaea-Christian communities, and the Mennonite Free Church. The reason they came together under that covering from all over Austria was that they needed to have 0.2 percent of the total population to seek recognition from the government as an official church.[11] Such status offers certain social and economic privileges to the movement and its members as follows:

1. Good official standing with the government and improved legal and tax status
2. State-funded religious education for members' children in the school system
3. Ease of obtaining residency permits for foreign missionaries
4. Availability of government-funded radio and TV programming

One local church that is worthy of notice is the Vienna Christian Center, the largest and best-known congregation in the Austrian capital. The main service is in English, as they minister primarily to foreign expatriates and have been very effective in reaching them. Their other congregations include Filipino, English African, Spanish (Latino), Iranian, and German-speaking ones where local Austrians can come and worship. In the last decade they have added Romanian, Ethiopian, Chinese, and French branches (mostly French Africans).

The Pentecostals in Austria are in fact the largest Evangelical group in the country. The movement clearly has some theological opportunities in the Austrian context. Many local people may look very satisfied on the outside but feel quite empty on the inside. The factors that attract Austrian nationals to the Pentecostal churches are:

1. The personal relationships built with members
2. The vibrancy and liveliness of the services
3. The love and care many feel in the Pentecostal churches
4. The new life and true relationship with Jesus Christ they find there

The movement also faces certain theological challenges that can be identified and summarized as follows:

1. *Relevancy.* The Pentecostal churches in Austria have always been fairly small and conservative. This makes them somewhat irrelevant to the younger generations. Many local Austrian congregations are somewhat stagnant trying to hold on to what they have. They need to find new ways to engage the youth.
2. *Evangelism.* The Austrian Pentecostals need to find ways and inspiration to become true evangelistic centers instead of simple culture clubs. Even though there are no major ethnic minorities in Austria, the Pentecostal believers can look for ways to engage the Muslim groups of Turkish immigrants and Bosnian refugees who have recently settled in the country. They are reaching out to minister among the Gypsies in Hungary and can look for other opportunities for both evangelistic and social outreach, which can promote growth in the movement.
3. *Indigenous leadership.* The involvement of Scandinavian Pentecostal missionaries has been impressive and quite effective in the Austrian work.

There are many Norwegian, Swedish, and especially Finnish missionaries and church leaders. Only about half of the present-day leaders in the movement are Austrians, and the other half non-Austrians. Therefore, many Austrians have foreign pastors. The membership, however, consists mostly of Austrians, even though there are many internationals in those congregations as well. There is clearly a leadership vacuum in Austrian Pentecostalism, and some of the university students who get converted and discipled by campus ministries can help fill that void.

4. *Stewardship teaching.* Talking about money and relating the biblical principles of stewardship can be a challenge because of the 3 percent official state tax taken from members of both the Roman Catholic and the Lutheran churches in Austria. This causes teaching on money to have some negative connotations. From an economic point of view, certainly the 3 percent tax required by the official state churches[12] is less than the tithe, which the Pentecostals encourage. Therefore, when the Pentecostal churches instruct on biblical financial principles, they should take those contextual factors into account.

5. *Catholicism.* The Roman Catholic Church is a major factor in Austrian society. Many believe that to be Austrian is to be Catholic. Austrians cannot hold dual church membership, so a person needs to change their membership after baptism. Their status in society is not promoted by joining nonconformist churches, and this can be a social hindrance to many. Some fear losing certain legal privileges, like burial rights in Catholic cemeteries or the opportunity to become godparents to the children of Catholic relatives.[13]

   Most people in Austria are agnostics or atheists

in practice, while the Catholic churches are mostly empty.[14] The distaste for and disillusionment from organized religion due to their previous experiences with the Catholic Church can be both an opportunity and a challenge for Pentecostal outreach. The Charismatic Renewal among some of the Austrian Catholics is also encouraging and can serve as a good point of contact and dialogue. Two important scholars that have associations with the Austrian Catholic Charismatic movement are Father Peter Hocken and Dr. Norbert Baumert.

6. *Humanism*. Many Austrians are hindered from joining the Pentecostal churches because of the philosophy of secular humanism. They feel that they should do what is best for them and what feels good; therefore, not much place is given to discussions of values outside of secular humanism. Often Austrians do not feel like they need anything, which deprives them of the need or strong motivation for converting to the Pentecostal faith. The work with young people is challenging because to them, anyone who claims to have authority or exclusive truth can be labeled as intolerant. There is a prevalent idea of cultural relativism among Austrian youth, and they prefer the New Age worldview or postmodernism.

Hungary

Hungary was dedicated for political reasons to the Virgin Mary and brought into the Catholic Church by the apostolic king Saint Steven. Then later, the Calvinists and Lutherans had a great impact there during the Ottoman times and their number reached over two million. The first laws in Europe allowing freedom of religion were adopted in Transylvania, east of the Ottoman Empire at this time. After that period was over, the Catholics started a counter-Reformation and the Protestants lost ground. There was a spiritual hunger in the Reformed churches, also inspired by the Welsh revival, and many came together for prayer and Bible reading. Baptist missionaries arrived in 1846, and one of them baptized ten thousand people. A great spiritual harvest was also reaped by the Nazarene, Methodist, and Holiness churches. The first Pentecostals came from these groups, and the new movement began after Hungary's heavy losses in the First World War.

Pentecostalism came to Hungary in the so-called Christian era (1921–1939), when the country enjoyed a brief period of independence.[15] Even though the movement was officially established in 1928, there were several groups with reported Pentecostal experiences much earlier:

1. In 1913, there was Gy Kallay, a lady in the city of Bekescsaba, holding services with some Quakers; they had lively worship and believed in healing through divine power.

2. In 1924, there was a group known as the Mission of Pitvaros in the Viharsarok region. It consisted of about twenty-five to thirty former Baptists who learned of the Holy Spirit baptism from the Apostolic Faith Mission literature. Then, after receiving Spirit baptism, they held services in the house of Paul Tazar, next to the Baptist church. The newly formed congregation had contacts with the Portland mission and then joined the Pentecostal Union in 1928.[16]

3. A group of Hungarians converted to the faith and received Spirit baptism in a prison camp in Russia during World War I. They were active in ministry after their return to Hungary. One of them was Istvan Sipos from Morichida, who together with Istvan Sebestyen contacted Jacob Bechtold, leader of the Church of God (Anderson, Indiana); that church

was already experiencing Pentecostal outpourings in several cities. Another one of those former prisoners was Pal Ondruc; Ondruc and other fellow former prisoners preached and planted fellowships, but their work was sporadic and somewhat isolated. The group was called the "footwashers" and later joined the official Pentecostal movement.

4. A group of Hungarian believers converted to the movement in the United States and even established Hungarian Pentecostal churches there. By 1921, several of them went back home to Darany, Hungary, and the first Pentecostal church building was erected there in 1923. They worked with the Szalai family, a member of which was Jozsefine Szalai (Mama Joo), a woman on fire for God with very authentic faith.[17]
5. Johann (John) Lerch was a returnee from America who planted a church in 1923 among the German community in Gyonk, Tolna County. Benjamin Schilling also came from Berlin and ministered in that area along with Lerch. Lerch was a tentmaker who spoke good German, English, and Hungarian and believed in developing indigenous churches.

The 1920s were a time of crisis in the country, and a significant percentage of the Hungarian population immigrated to the United States. One of those immigrants was Imre (Ernest) Mihok; he converted to Pentecostalism under the ministry of the American Assemblies of God, and since the denomination did not have an Eastern Europe policy at the time, he returned to Hungary on his own to spread his newfound faith. Mihok came from Detroit, Michigan, and began working in Hungary in 1926. He started worship services in Bakonycsernye on Easter and preached to a Baptist group interested in Spirit baptism. He had to leave Hungary in the summer of 1926[18] but came back again in 1933 with financial support from Joseph Wahenmacher, a Hungarian Gypsy violin player and pastor in Milwaukee, Wisconsin. Mihok's ministry and publication activities had a great impact on the movement in his native Hungary and also on Slovenia, where his wife, Mary, was from.

Ferenc David Raroha heard the Pentecostal message from Mihok and decided to return to Hungary from the United States in 1927. He and his wife were very excited and enthusiastic about assisting the work of spreading the message to their people. They were involved in church planting and started several congregations and also became leaders of the Kispest church near Budapest. The Rarohas were very influential in the movement's development.[19] They bought a printing press and started the publication of *Apostolic Faith*, which became the Hungarian Pentecostal movement's magazine. They also organized the newly planted congregations into a denomination. The name of that first organization was Magyarorszagi Istengyulekezetek (Hungarian Churches of God, not related to Cleveland, Tennessee), established at a conference February 5–9, 1928. The headquarters of the organization at that time was located at the house of Istvan Sebestyen at 6 Villany Street at Kispest. Gyorgy Farago was the first chairman of the movement.[20] At that conference, eight congregations were present and signed a constitution for the organization. The network of churches experienced growth under the leadership of the Raroha family. A year later, the group had fifteen congregations, and the following, twenty. By 1932, the group reached seventy local churches and changed its name to Alliance of Churches of God in Hungary. The leaders selected for the organization at the time were Istvan Siroky, Jozsef Tomi, and Jozsef Fabian. Around the same time, the Rarohas were "banned from the country and forced to return to the US."[21] Their support for the Hungarian work continued from America. The Pentecostal movement, still relatively young at the time, underwent tremendous persecution in the mid-1930s; that caused tension, which led to an eventual breakup.[22]

After Raroha left for good in 1935, the Hungarian movement split into three groups (the names here were given to me by my informants):

1. *Evangelical Christians*, led by Istvan Siroky. They were characterized as good, prayerful, and sincere believers, albeit with anti-intellectualist tendencies.
2. *Pentecostal Church*. The leader was Jozsef Tomi, an intellectual and good communicator who spoke English and German and played music. This group was considered smart, sophisticated, and in touch with the cultural environment. It was the only one out of the three branches that founded and maintained an orphanage.
3. *Original Christians*, led by Mrs. Sarkany. They were influenced by a prophetic movement from Voivodina and overemphasized the use of prophecies.

The country became openly Fascist in 1939, and the Teleki government limited the freedom of assembling and abolished religious cults, like the Pentecostals, because they were declared a threat to state security. The Baptists, Methodists, and Lutherans helped the persecuted Pentecostal churches from that time until the end of the Second World War. In spite of the fact that most churches were often visited by state agents and informers and some pastors were even arrested and tried, salvations, healings, and spiritual revivals continued to take place. Even though the tyrants could not hinder the revival,[23] there were certain consequences for the young movement, and the three above-mentioned factions had to look for cover; Jozsef Tomi's group went under the umbrella of the Baptist and Lutheran churches, and most of Siroky's group went underground. The third one—the prophetic wing—stopped having meetings, dispersed, and eventually lost its Pentecostal identity due to fear of persecution.

Georg Steen, son-in-law of Benjamin Shilling, a former missionary to Austria, came to Hungary in 1948 and tried to bring the three groups together. There were prophecies that if they did not unite, the consequences would be harsh. The first and second groups agreed to reunite, at least unofficially, but the third refused.

There was a spiritual harvest in the movement during Communism, according to some local informants, cited by Lange. Some of the testimonies of older Pentecostal Hungarians testify that faith expressions of ecstasy provided useful compensation for people who are in lack of material goods. Pastor Horvath's sermons affirmed the fact that in the period after the Second World War, poverty caused people to convert to the faith and look for spiritual influences. During the war, many people were able to overcome the rough condition of life and lack of sufficient nutrition through their Christian faith. Many who immigrated to the United States wanted to make money and return home, but those who converted to Pentecostalism during their migration struggles brought home the faith. Poverty and the political powerlessness during the Communist period were certainly important reasons for the conversion of many Hungarians in the villages of the south and central part of the country.[24]

After the end of World War II, Hungary remained in the shadow of the Soviet Union under the puppet Communist government of Mátyás Rákosi, who came to power in 1948. Even though there were restrictions for all religious groups, the main pressure was actually on the four historical churches: Orthodox, Catholic, Calvinist, and Lutheran. The Catholic schools were nationalized and a number of priests imprisoned, especially those involved in political opposition.[25] In order to ostracize the historical churches, the government was actually giving some freedom to the Pentecostals and other small free churches.

Interestingly enough, the later János Kádár regime was different from countries like Russia, Romania, and Bulgaria because Hungary was used as the most presentable place in the Eastern Bloc. After 1953, there were certain changes in policy by which the government tried to divide and weaken the historical churches. In regard to the Spirit-filled leaders, the government's persecution was indirect: they were not promoted on their jobs[26] and could not send their children to universities. The government was especially strict with pastors who got involved in anti-Communist activities. There were a few underground Pentecostal groups during Communism, but most were official. Things did tighten up after the uprising of 1956, and the church had to be careful, but the economic challenges were more serious at that time than the political ones for the movement. The efforts of the government to centralize various institutions were a challenge to nonconformist churches; they made the Pentecostals unite artificially and form hierarchical structures, which hindered the movement's spontaneity and organic development.

In 1962, two major groups, the Evangelical Christians and the Pentecostal Church, were united under the name of Fellowship of Evangelical Pentecostals, and the differences between them gradually disappeared. The churches were organized into four districts and overseen by a seven-member central committee.

In 1970, the movement established contacts with Swedish and Norwegian Pentecostals, and the headquarters building of the movement was built with Swedish money. The first Assemblies of God missionary for Eastern Europe, Bob Mackish, was appointed in 1968 and worked out of Vienna. In 1974, the Free Christian Church received the Spirit baptism, experienced growth, and impacted the nation's spiritual life; recently it joined the International Pentecostal Holiness Church.

The new freedom that came to Hungary in 1990 brought numerous opportunities for Pentecostals to organize crusades, publish books, use national media, and undertake various evangelistic and social activities.[27] After the collapse of the Communist regime, the church in Hungary experienced revival with many conversions, healings, and manifestations of spiritual gifts. The State Office for Church Affairs was eliminated, and new legislation made it possible for newer church groups to be organized legally and for existing underground ones to be officially registered. Prior to that time, there were ten official denominations besides the historic churches. In 2011, there were more than one hundred officially registered denominations in Hungary, a number of which were Pentecostal or Charismatic.[28] The number of registered denominations was limited to fourteen (about half of them non-Christian) by the Orban government in 2012. All the other groups had to change their status to nongovernmental organizations (NGOs) which deprives them of major privileges but does not limit their freedom to worship.[29]

The new wave of emotional and physical manifestations caused some controversy and division within the Pentecostal movement because many could not accept them as works of the Spirit. One particularly interesting group that is currently strong in Hungary—the Faith Church in Budapest—became closely aligned with the Faith Movement. Between the years 1995 and 1998, it conducted a total of 152 services in the Budapest Sports Hall, and the average attendance was around ten thousand people. In those three years, they baptized 6,800 people. After the year 2000, their growth slowed down and they experienced some fragmentation, which is unfortunately a characteristic phenomenon in Pentecostal/Charismatic movements.[30]

The Faith Church, under the leadership of pastor Sandor Nemeth, may have been the only group that was adequately prepared for the changes and took full advantage of them. They only had about two thousand members during the Communist period and were totally underground. They were connected, however, with the newly formed liberal parties, which gave them political influence in the transition period. Currently, the Faith Church claims about sixty thousand to seventy thousand adherents in the whole country. They major on big meetings, mainly targeting businesspeople with resources, and are less interested in social outreach. They currently have an accredited institute and over 50 percent ownership in a TV station. They once even had two members in the Hungarian parliament, and although presently are less interested in politics, their voice continues to be influential. They are openly pro-Israel and used to be critical of the Orban[31] government. In spite of this, they got their registered-church status under the recent legislative reform. For various reasons, the Faith Church has little fellowship with the classic Pentecostals in Hungary.

Dan and Rose Smith, a missionary family that returned from Albania in 1997, revived the work of the Hungarian Church of God and reorganized it. Since then, they have been planting churches around the country that are part of the Church of God International.[32]

Today the majority of the Pentecostal movement is part of the Magyar Pünkösdi Egyház (Hungarian Pentecostal Church), which is one of the fourteen registered denominations in the country. "Two thirds of the members are women; the predominant age group is 20 to 40 years."[33] According to current statistics, the Pentecostals in Hungary have 146 churches or preaching points and about ten thousand members. That number consists of four thousand classic Pentecostals, which is actually the same as the figure given by Raroha in 1929. The others that come under this umbrella are the Free Christians, Charismatic Baptists, Charismatic Nazarenes, Charismatic Calvinists, the Latter-Day movement (not Mormons), and the Pentecostal Gypsy Churches. There are some Charismatic Calvinist clergy in the Hungarian Pentecostal Church, as well. The last census in the country from 2011 showed that most churches do not have a serious base to impact Hungarian society and actually have fewer followers than they had thought previously: Catholics (39 percent), Reformed (11.6 percent), Evangelicals (2.2 percent), and Orthodox (0.1 percent).[34]

Several theological opportunities and challenges should be lifted up in the context of the Hungarian Pentecostal movement:

1. *Context awareness.* Since Hungary is primarily a secularist society, the Pentecostals need to find new ways to engage the general population of the country, which is not as open now as it was after the changes in 1989. Rev. Simonfalvi, a fourth-generation Hungarian Pentecostal minister, scholar, and former church executive, regrets the fact that the movement lost its momentum of the early years and missed many good opportunities for growth and expansion. Church leaders need to be aware of political and social changes and adapt their mission approaches accordingly. For example, when the Pentecostals came first to Hungary, the country was an agrarian society and there were some large churches in the villages. The leaders of the movement, however, did not show foresight when the Communist-forced industrialization process caused the urbanization of

Hungarian society. Thus, many Pentecostal youth moved to the cities and, having no Spirit-filled churches to attend, either became Baptists or left the Christian faith completely. There are still about nineteen major cities in Hungary without Pentecostal churches at present. The Adventists and the Faith Church were smarter in their approach by focusing on the cities in the country from the beginning.

Often there were unbalanced and sectarian approaches in the past, like overemphasizing tongues over other things. That overemphasis caused the next generation to neglect spiritual gifts altogether. Many young people today are not Spirit-filled but have turned to the prosperity churches.

2. *Education.* In the beginning, the Pentecostal movement in Hungary was, like in most other places, somewhat anti-intellectual; the main emphasis was on the Holy Spirit baptism with the evidence of tongues, and that caused an attitude of spiritual arrogance. There was no serious discipleship, and pastors were often poorly chosen because there weren't enough mature believers who were up to the calling. The churches were not trained in evangelism or biblical financial principles.

The first pastoral and theological training opportunities were organized in the 1970s. In late 1991, the Pünkösdi Teológiai Főiskola (Pentecostal Theological College) was organized and then recognized by the Hungarian government. The major problem today is that, because of accreditation requirements, 70 percent of the professors in it are non-Pentecostals because there are no Pentecostals with doctorates. As a result, the Pentecostal ministers who study there certainly have a challenge in maintaining their identity.

Some in the church realize it needs to invest in the college's future, first of all in finding scholarships for key teachers with a Pentecostal identity to get their PhDs. They need to offer academically solid courses on theology, Pentecostal spirituality, spiritual gifts, Old and New Testament exegesis, servant leadership, church planting, team ministry, and counseling. The training there should also be adapted to the local situation and contextualized in order to meet the challenges and needs of the Hungarian movement's ministry.

3. *Social agenda.* The Hungarian movement has had a good record of active engagement in regard to the social needs in their context and yet have much to learn from the so-called "progressive" branch of world Pentecostalism.[35] Since their country has been relatively poor in their recent history, many Hungarian believers are sensitive to the needy in their society. They know that mission starts when the saints leave the church building.

   At a time when most Pentecostal leaders were afraid to take initiative, one courageous woman went to the minister of culture of the Communist government of János Kádár and sought official license to open a rehabilitation center for drug addicts. That is how Elizabeth Simonfalvi Fabian, wife of Reverend Attila Fabian,[36] with little outside support started Teen Challenge in 1985 in Dunaharaszti. She also found a castle where a home for the elderly was opened up. These ministries have been developed and expanded in Hungary.

   The churches are indeed the best institutions to assist in alleviating poverty in any society, because, unlike nongovernmental organizations, they are strongly rooted in the local communities and can thus bring about lasting change. There are certainly enough people with resources among the Hungarian Pentecostals who can support their churches' social activities.

The work with the Roma (Gypsies) has been an interesting phenomenon in the Hungarian Pentecostal movement. The churches take both government and nongovernment money to do social work with the Roma (as they are called). The Pentecostal movement has been the most effective one in Hungary for reaching the Roma with the gospel, and the Spirit-filled people among them are proportionally much higher than among other groups. There are still a number of areas in which the Hungarian Roma believers have room to grow, like taking creative initiative, discipleship, balanced ethnic identity, self-motivation, education, and indigenous leadership.[37] However, the Spirit movement among the Roma, considered outcasts of society, is very impressive in Hungary, as it has been all over the world.

Conclusion

The Pentecostal movement in Austria and Hungary developed in the context of turbulent historical changes and some of the monumental events of the twentieth century. Even though the number of Spirit-filled believers in these countries is not high in proportion to the general population, they are very much present there. They face a variety of theological challenges and practical needs, both internally and externally; they should strive for better-quality ministry education and leadership development; they must seek new ways to engage their contexts through relevant methods of evangelism and social outreach; they ought to find creative means to stand for truth in the face of historical religious traditions and secularist post-Christian societies. Perhaps the emerging generation of Pentecostals will produce scholars who will discover the ways and useful paradigms to do just that.

Part II
Western Europe

Chapter 6

Pentecostalism in Italy: Origins, Developments, and Future Challenges

Carmine Napolitano and Paolo Mauriello

THE FOLLOWING OVERVIEW discussion of Italian Pentecostalism is divided into three sections, following the indicators given in the chapter subtitle.

THE ORIGINS

Among those who had the Pentecostal experience at Azusa Street (Los Angeles), there was William H. Durham (1873–1912), a Baptist pastor from Chicago who returned to his hometown, where at the time he was taking care of a church called North Avenue Mission. Thanks to his work, the Pentecostal message spread across the American Midwest and was received by the leaders of the churches that later would be called the Pentecostal Assemblies of Canada. Durham is crucial for the origins of the Italian Pentecostal movement; in fact, his presence and his work in Chicago link him directly to the pioneers of Italian Pentecostalism.[1]

At the end of the nineteenth century, Italy was affected by a great wave of migration that involved many Evangelicals who moved abroad in groups, especially to the United States and South America. They came from different parts of Italy, and once they arrived in the overseas countries, they established cohesive and fervent communities that grew rapidly, thanks to their energetic evangelistic work. In the United States, between 1901 and 1921, this phenomenon led to the founding of hundreds of Evangelical communities of Italian language that were influential. The first churches founded were the Italian Baptist Church in Buffalo, New York (1890), and the Presbyterian Church of Chicago (1892).[2] The birth of the Italian Pentecostal movement is related to the events of this second community.

Among the members of the newly founded Church of Chicago was Luigi Francescon (1866–1964), an immigrant from the province of Udine who arrived in the United States in 1890 and there became an Evangelical. A few years later, Francescon began helping the congregation alongside Waldensian pastor Filippo Grill. In 1900, a group of people from Tuscany joined the Presbyterian Church of Chicago. They had become Evangelical through the evangelistic work of Giuseppe P. Beretta, who came from the Free Methodist Church. In Chicago, two liturgical expressions that were later adopted by the Italian Pentecostal Churches were practiced: 1) a form of worship that included spontaneous prayers and 2) the practice of the "testimony" (that is, the narration of experiences related to their own faith). The congregation also formed the conviction that pastors had to be unpaid, and this later came to characterize the Italian Pentecostal Church. (In fact, to this day many churches have strong convictions that the ministry must be exercised without receiving a salary.) The Tuscans did not ask to be admitted as members of the church, and this circumstance, together with the different liturgical conceptions, prompted the group to leave the church in 1903 when the church council, taking advantage of the pastor's absence, tried to impose the official ideas of the community on them.[3]

Francescon was gripped by the spontaneity that characterized the liturgical expressions of this group and kept contact with it, partly because he and Beretta had the same job and often met. In the meanwhile, he and other church members had been nurturing the belief that infant baptism (practiced by the Presbyterian Church) did not conform to the teaching of the New Testament, and thus they opted for adult baptism. Francescon talked of this to Beretta, who after some hesitation was baptized by an American Christian belonging to the Brethren Church, and then, in his turn, baptized

Francescon and his friends. The two groups merged and opened another room for public worship on Grand Avenue in Chicago, which at that time was the heart of the Italian city suburb. The following year (1904) in this new small community a dispute flared up between Francescon and other church members about the significance of Sunday rest. In Francescon's opinion, the Sunday rest had to be observed in a strict way according to the model of the Jewish Sabbath, but the majority of the community did not share this position. So Francescon left the group, choosing instead to meet and worship with a few others mostly in private houses.

This situation went on until 1907, when Francescon came into contact with Durham's mission on North Avenue. Durham had recently returned from the Azusa Street revival in Los Angeles, and Francescon was caught up by the Pentecostal experience. Francescon reinitiated contact with the group that he had left and urged them to attend the meetings led by Durham. After a few months, the whole community received the Pentecostal experience, and so it became the first Pentecostal church in Italian.[4] Once the dispute on the Sunday rest was solved, Francescon returned to guide the church at Grand Avenue and became committed to reaching all the Italian immigrants with the revival, even to the homeland. Apparently he was encouraged in this by Durham.[5] From this emerged a pattern of missionization among Italians near and far that was soon adopted by other Pentecostal churches. Francescon and other members of his church first visited other Italian communities in the United States and then traveled to South America (especially Brazil and Argentina), often relying on family ties that offered valuable logistical support to missionary activities. In a few years, dozens of Pentecostal communities in the Italian language were founded out of these ventures.[6]

From this missionary action sprang also the journeys that brought the Pentecostal message to Italy. How and when this happened is not very clear, since all the historical references that we have are derived from oral traditions and not supported by documentary sources, with the exception of the autobiographies of the protagonists. However, this tradition is fairly unanimous in fixing the date of the first Italian encounter with Pentecostalism in 1908. In the month of April of that year, four people without an official charge came from the United States to spread the Pentecostal word to their motherland, albeit with poor results. However, at the end of that year, Giacomo Lombardi (1862–1934), sent by the church in Chicago, began the official mission. Once he arrived in Italy, he tried to spread the Pentecostal message among Evangelicals, but after some strong opposition he decided to connect personally only with those willing to listen. It is from these friendships that the first Pentecostal group in Italy was established. From 1910 onward, Lombardi and other members of the Chicago church would regularly come to Italy to spread the Pentecostal message, relying mainly on relatives and acquaintances. This missionary activity led to an initial spreading of Pentecostalism in various Italian regions so that a list held by the Ministry of the Interior dating back to 1929 reported the presence of Pentecostals in some one hundred fifty locations, with no fewer than twenty-five places of worship open to the public.[7]

Developments

In the 1930s, the Pentecostal movement faced the opposition of the Fascist government. The slender recognition granted to the pastor of the church in Rome (1931), Ettore Strappaveccia, on the basis of the 1929 law on "allowed cults" was questioned a few years later (on April 9, 1935) with the infamous circular "Buffarini Guidi," widely considered as the most religiously intolerant piece of legislation enacted in Italy after the unification of the peninsula.[8] This circular suppressed religious freedom based on racial reasons, even before the approval of the racial laws against the Jews (1938).[9] In fact, it argued that the Pentecostal churches were "developing religious practices contrary to the social order and harmful to the psychological and physical integrity of the race."[10] For the Pentecostals, this act initiated a period of persecution that lasted until 1943 (when Italy signed the armistice with the Allied forces on September 8, 1943),[11] although the damage persisted far beyond, until it was finally abolished in 1955.[12]

The secrecy to which the Pentecostals were forced, at least for a large majority of them, caused the breaking off of relations between the churches with foreign contacts and made much more difficult the sharing and exchange of ideas. Relationships developed with the conferences in the late 1920s were curtailed, and this led to silos that exacerbated divergences within the movement. Such differences were bound to become deeper, in part due to the isolation of the churches during the 1930s, when there was little possibility of confrontation, and in part because of what was happening in the United States among the Italian churches that undoubtedly was to affect the course of events in Italy. From the persecution, the movement in Italy became deeply unorganized. A division emerged during this time between a more conservative wing and another more moderate one that was open to institutional innovation.[13] The former coalesced around some individuals who were considered prominent personalities and gathered into a number of strictly congregational churches, later called *zaccardiane*, that were closed to any outside influences and interactions.[14]

It is in this historical context that we must set the unprecedented visit of Pope Francis on July 28, 2014, to the evangelical Church of the Reconciliation in Caserta, pastored by Giovanni Traettino, that claims to be a Pentecostal church, although many traditional Pentecostals would question such an association. On that occasion, Pope Francis apologized for the past persecution of Pentecostals by Catholics under Italy's Fascist regime, but the great majority of the Italian Pentecostal leaders remained wary. It is significant what the Pope said: "Among those who persecuted and denounced Pentecostals, almost as if they were crazy people trying to ruin the race, there were also Catholics, I am the pastor of Catholics, and I ask your forgiveness for those Catholic brothers and sisters who did not know and were tempted by the devil."[15] We will come back to this when speaking of the ecumenical challenge.

The year 1946 was to be a watershed in the history of the Italian Pentecostal movement. A conference was held in Rome from August 28 to September 1 that laid the foundations for the institutional organization of the movement in Italy. Three factors pushed in this direction and drew together even the most hesitant people: first, the need to manage the funds of collections coming from the US churches in order to help the needy after the war; second, the news from the United States about legal recognition for all churches set in motion by the Christian Churches of North America; and third, the boost of the Italian government linked to the promise of legal recognition if the movement was to be organized in such a way as to become a reliable institutional partner.[16] It had been about forty years since Pentecostalism had reached Italy, and the 1946 gathering was only the fifth such conference of Pentecostal believers, but it turned out to be decisive for the future of the movement. Representatives of Pentecostal foreign organizations, such as Henry Ness (Assemblies of God) and Herman A. Parli (Swiss churches), were present, as well as Nicolò Di Gregorio (Church of Chicago), who had worked closely with Francescon. The preamble of the minutes of the conference highlights the fact that

> their presence, besides from being useful for practical reasons, has been particularly significant from a moral point of view, because with their presence we have had implicitly the adhesion of the many brotherhoods they represent. It has been possible to express with moved voice the heartfelt thanks of the brotherhoods of Italy for what has been done by the Church of the United States and of Switzerland to help the brothers of this nation spiritually and materially, both in a private way and, above all, through the "Missionary Committee and Fund of Mercy."[17]

On this basis, the following year in Naples the great majority of the Italian Pentecostal churches adopted the name Assemblies of God in Italy and in doing so affiliated with the American Assemblies of God.[18]

This consolidation of the Pentecostal movement in Italy led to the rise of several currents. At least five groups were identifiable by the end of the 1950s. The largest was the Assemblies of God in Italy (ADI), followed by the Christian Pentecostal Congregations grouped mainly in the southeast of Sicily. The other three were miniscule in comparison:

the *zaccardiane* communities, another group in the Valle del Sele (in Campania), and a set of independent and isolated communities of congregationalist inspiration. The majority of these declined being incorporated into the ADI, but the Sicilian congregations and, to a lesser extent, the churches of the Valle del Sele, developed a network that could be considered a real alternative to the ADI.[19]

Despite the small number of churches, the Pentecostal Congregations came together on January 23, 1958, in Vittoria (Ragusa) with the intent of restoring the original form of Communion, accepting as the basis of their fellowship the confession of faith ratified at Niagara Falls in 1927.[20] Their point of reference, therefore, remained the Church of Chicago and its leader, Luigi Francescon. They opted for a system of collegial pastorates both within individual churches as well as in large meetings.[21] The *zaccardiane* churches were similarly inspired, although they were characterized by an irreducible aversion to any form of connection (except those guaranteed by the historical leaders) and by a rather sectarian notion of interpersonal and social relations, so much so that they were given from the other Pentecostals the nickname of "the Most Holy." The churches of the Valle del Sele, on the other hand, were heavily influenced by the thought of Giuseppe Petrelli (1876–1957), regarded as the most important early Italian Pentecostal theologian, allegedly filtered through his disciples and others who often misunderstood or misrepresented his ideas.[22]

The Present Situation and Future Challenges

The current situation of the Pentecostal world in Italy is quite fluid. Over the past three decades, the Pentecostal movement in Italy has grown in all its streams and is one of the biggest, numerically speaking, among Western European countries. Its expansion is also linked to the phenomenon of urbanization that arose in the second half of the twentieth century, which pushed people from the countryside to the city, so today it is not uncommon to find Pentecostal churches in big cities with thousands of adherents. In recent times there has been a repositioning of many Pentecostal churches, giving rise to the Federation of Pentecostal Churches (FCP, founded in 2000), that defines the Italian Pentecostal world more clearly. The FCP brings together churches and movements at local, national, and regional levels. However, this organization represents only a part of the movement in Italy, the other being the Assemblies of God in Italy. Together they represent 80 percent of Italian Pentecostals.

In addition to these two large networks, other smaller, completely independent circuits total about two hundred fifty thousand people.[23] A separate world is further constituted by the Pentecostal churches of immigrants in the north, who are deemed to have already reached about one hundred thousand and probably already passed (in size) the Italian Pentecostal Churches in that region, but because they are often closed groups, it is difficult to get reliable data. The most numerous ethnic communities among these churches are the Romanian, Chinese, Nigerian, Brazilian, and Ghanaian communities.[24] The Italian Pentecostal world is somehow cut off from the major international circuits, even though it is probably among the most numerous in the European Union. This relative isolation derives in part from the traditional distrust toward foreign movements (as in the past the Italian Pentecostal churches have suffered from the initiatives of foreign movements) and in part to the low level of education that only in recent years has increased, thanks to a generation of pastors more attentive to their need to be more informed about happenings around the world. The FCP has joined the Pentecostal European Fellowship and has started several projects, including the creation of the Faculty of Theology and Religious Studies, whose academic courses are accredited by public universities abroad and recognized as suitable for further study by some Italian universities.[25]

In the last twenty years, Pentecostal churches have developed creative ministerial and missional initiatives. Some of these have been managed by churches or parachurch agencies and multiplied, especially voluntary organizations or agencies of social promotion, and grown in many directions: from drug rehabilitation (which seems to be a privileged area of engagement for Pentecostals)[26] to the commitment in prisons and hospitals to the distribution of food to the needy to missionary engagement abroad among troubled populations. Many initiatives are not even counted because they are closely intertwined with the life of the local churches and neither professionalized nor advertised. In other cases, Pentecostals are individually engaged in large organizations, such as the Association of Voluntary Italian Blood Donors, the Association of Voluntary Italian Hospital Staff, or the Italian Red Cross. All this implies that the social commitment of Pentecostals in Italy is higher than what has been perceived, but this is due also to the fact that often the parties concerned do not seek publicity for their efforts but live out their commitment as part of the mission to which they feel called as Christians.[27]

In Italy, the attitude of Pentecostals toward politics has been shaped by the hostility that the Fascist state before and the first republican governments after had shown toward them. This explains why, in the aftermath of the Allies landing in Sicily (when the war was not yet over), the churches were finally able to meet again and resume their relations after fifteen years of isolation. Inserted between the various provisions of a conference held in 1944 in Raffadali in the province of Agrigento, they took a stance on commitment to and engagement with a political party "because it is our duty to resist the evil, not within the parties, but in the light of the word of God."[28] This attitude has accompanied the Pentecostals to this day. In this perspective, any profession of partylessness does not imply an apolitical attitude; instead, it signifies the stance that injustice (evil) has to be fought with the Word of God, that is, with the announcement of the gospel that transforms the conscience, rather than merely ideologically or politically. In line with the theology of revival, it is stated that it is the change of the individual that can transform society, but this can happen only by the work of the gospel. Today, Pentecostals and Charismatics worldwide believe such and on this basis justify their (political) actions, adding that the preaching of the gospel is not possible without the work of the Holy Spirit.

Immediately after the war, Pentecostals settled almost completely in the southern rural and mountainous part of the country, with a few on the outskirts of the big cities of the north. The members of the churches were mostly peasants and artisans, and many of them emigrated abroad or to the north. Hence, the small churches of the city suburbs began to grow, thanks to this interior immigration phenomenon with a social composition distinctively marked by the working class. Walter Hollenweger, a careful scholar who in those years was doing research in Italy, documented the electoral orientation of the Pentecostals, who seemed locked in their churches and disinterested in what was happening around them.[29] Perhaps for this reason they were perceived as Protestant and accused of Communism, according to a cliché that was applied to other Evangelicals; paradoxically, the latter believed that Pentecostal spirituality derived from Catholicism.

In the last thirty years, there have been complex and dynamic developments. Pentecostals have increased greatly in number and are the greater Evangelical component, of whom the immigrants represent a third. At least 70 percent is concentrated in big cities, which is a significant change compared to the prior generations. The phenomenon of urbanization has also changed significantly the sociocultural matrix, which, to oversimplify, we could say has passed from the peasant and working class to the small middle class with a gradual increase in average education. This framework is also reflected in the attitude toward politics that, given the numbers, can only be pluralistic and open to a much more diverse set of electoral choices. Over the last years, different Pentecostal circles are working to create a stronger political consciousness pointing to party identity, and a small number of Pentecostals are engaged with the administration of public affairs in some local authorities. On this matter there is a vivid debate and a confrontation that passes through various occasions and circumstances. The entry of a Pentecostal into parliament a few years ago for the first time in the history of the republic and the path charted by such for future generations will surely prompt ongoing reevaluation and discussion of such matters.[30]

The Italian Pentecostal churches generally recognize the importance of the ecumenical movement but do not adhere to or interact with the official ecumenical bodies.[31] This lack of involvement is motivated by widespread uncertainty about the aims of the ecumenical movement. In particular, Pentecostals are skeptical to take a path that seems to them oriented to safeguard the interests of the ecclesiastical institutions at the expense of a path that reflects what they consider to be the biblical teaching about Christian unity. They have a cautious attitude toward the ecumenical movement also because they can see the danger of a political-diplomatic drift, which, ultimately, tends to limit the freedom of evangelization. The character of Pentecostalism as a movement of revival and mission undermines for them any form of identification dependent on territorial and ecclesiastical confession, especially those they consider typical of Roman Catholicism, Orthodoxy, or, in different forms, some Protestant churches in Europe. Pentecostal churches, having already very often suffered discrimination, persecution, and restrictions to their freedom of mission, fear that there might be a potential and arbitrary misuse of the ecumenical dialogue to limit their freedom of evangelization and conversion or to make such dependent on the consent of the religious denomination of the nominal majority in the area.

The relationships with other Evangelical churches have not always been friendly. Only in recent years and under the unifying pressure of the Federation of Pentecostal Churches something has changed. One of the most striking and interesting results was the dialogue with the Waldensian and Methodist churches that has produced interesting documents.[32] This experience has stimulated the emergence of a formal dialogue with the Union of Baptist Churches and with Adventist churches. The growth of the relationships between the historical Evangelical churches and the Federation of Pentecostal Churches culminated with the mutual inclusion of observer members in their respective federal assemblies.[33] Among the Pentecostal churches, there are many that believe that today there is no basis for starting a dialogue with the Roman Catholic Church. This is because there are still tense relationships in many local communities and also because of a certain instrumentalization that has been made in past years of some local attempts of dialogue, where it was given the impression that there were no more differences between Pentecostals and Catholics. However, they are aware that for many years there have been official dialogues between the Roman Catholic Church and members of the international Pentecostal world. For them, nonetheless, they are distant experiences that often do not take into account the Italian situation and have frequently led to the rise of suspicion and discontent in Italy.[34]

We already mentioned the visit of Pope Francis to the Charismatic church of the Reconciliation in Caserta on July 28, 2014. Most Pentecostal churches, even though they appreciated the Pope's declaration, did not like the fact that such a statement was done in a Charismatic church. Unlike in English-speaking countries, the term *charismatic* in Italy has almost exclusively Catholic (rather than Evangelical) connotations, and since the Pentecostal movement has had no official relationship with the Roman Catholic Church, with very few exceptions, this term has been viewed with suspicion. To make matters worse, the Church of the Reconciliation has cultivated relationships with some official Catholic Charismatic circles, which has by and large been avoided by the rest of the Pentecostal world in Italy. In any case, the president of the FCP, Remo Cristallo, in an interview tried to explain the position of classical Pentecostals on the matter. He stressed the importance of the words of the Pope but acknowledged that it would have been better to address them to those Pentecostals who suffered that persecution.[35] It should be noted that among Pentecostals, there are different views on this issue and some churches are historically and theologically sensitive to it, hoping that sooner or later there will be the possibility of serious interaction with the Catholic Church. This is certainly one of the most important future challenges that the Pentecostal Church in Italy will have to face, especially during the pontificate of Pope Francis, who can count on the sympathies of some Pentecostals and many neo-Pentecostals, especially in South and North America.

Most Pentecostal churches in Italy keep classical positions. The neo-Pentecostal churches are the minority and are more prevalent among immigrants. However, this presence has fostered interchanges and in some cases has introduced innovations on both the liturgical and organizational level. We will see what the future holds.

Chapter 7

Swiss Pentecostals: A Journey Between Corporate Identity and Christian Unity

Jean-Daniel Plüss

In a way, the beginnings of the Pentecostal movement in Switzerland can be likened to the historic Day of Pentecost, when the disciples of Jesus were filled with the Holy Spirit and understood the 120 praising God in a variety of languages. I do not say this primarily because the Swiss people are a conglomerate of three different cultures—German, French, and Italian—but because early Pentecostal groups in Switzerland were also influenced by people who were communicating in English—British English, that is. It may well be that this multilingual context shaped Swiss Pentecostalism to be more flexible in practice and more international in outlook than its sister movements in the neighboring countries.

The experience of a new Pentecost was brought to Zurich in the early days of August 1907 by two Norwegian missionaries that had been sent by Thomas Ball Barratt, the Methodist pastor who had shared news about the Azusa Street revival with his congregation in Oslo on the second day of Christmas 1906. He had experienced his baptism in the Holy Spirit after reading issues of *Apostolic Faith* and corresponded with the people at Azusa Street.

Revivalist and Holiness circles had been praying for a new infilling by the Holy Spirit for some years. They had read the writings of Andrew Murray and others that spoke about a baptism in the Holy Spirit. The reports about the Welsh revival in 1904–1905 had only raised the expectations of the seekers in continental Europe. The news that a group of Christians had been experiencing this blessing from above spread quickly, and Zurich became a meeting point for a number of international missionaries and church leaders.[1] Switzerland was ideally located to welcome visitors from various European countries.

This situation was facilitated by the fact that the first pastor of the Pentecostal congregation in Zurich was an Anglican minister, C. E. D. de Labillière. The first Swiss Pentecostal pastor, Anton Reuss, had been raised in England, and T. B. Barratt, who visited Zurich twice in 1908 and then again in 1910, was English born. The three gentlemen not only had a common experience of the Holy Spirit; they also communicated fluently with each other and shared common cultural values. They understood each other, whether they were raised Anglican, Methodist, or Reformed.

Early Pentecostal congregations could also be found in French-speaking parts of the country,[2] and contacts existed with Italian Pentecostals.[3] In 1910, an international conference took place in Zurich with the participation of various European Pentecostal leaders.[4] As a result, Swiss Pentecostalism developed in a way that was not dominated by a single culture, as was, for instance, the case in Germany and later in France and Italy. Swiss Pentecostals had an openness and freedom to receive pastoral and theological insights. In 1913, at a time when other Pentecostal groups had already begun to be defensive toward other churches, Swiss Pentecostals still nurtured an ecumenical outlook. Seven years after the first meetings had begun, the Pentecostal pastors of Zurich and St. Gall wrote an open letter inviting all Christian churches to participate in the blessing that came from the Holy Spirit.[5] The gift of God was for everyone and could be received in any place where the name of Jesus Christ was called upon.

The beginning of the Great War restricted international travel, and the continental postal system was truncated. This naturally led to a preoccupation with their own assemblies. In the early 1920s, however, Smith Wigglesworth came to evangelize Switzerland on several occasions. He traveled to the German- as well as the French-speaking parts, and as a result the number of Pentecostal gatherings greatly increased. He also spoke to the pastors of the larger congregations and encouraged them to establish a mission society. It was founded in 1921 under the name Swiss Pentecostal Mission Society, which immediately began to prepare, send, and support missionaries (Schweizerische Pfingstmissionsgesellschaft).[6] Note that these churches were still independent and not yet a denomination.

Developments in the 1930s

During the early years of the 1930s, the ministry of a number of British evangelists had a visible impact on Switzerland. The ministries of Stephen Jeffreys and Douglas Scott deserve special mention. Surprisingly, Douglas Scott had received the invitation to preach in western Switzerland by a group of Reformed pastors who had been open to the Pentecostal revival.[7] Stephen Jeffreys was invited by Pentecostals and ministered in various cities with outstanding results. The Swiss were receptive to the fourfold gospel message, which emphasizes that Jesus saves, heals, baptizes, and comes again.

Up to then, the Pentecostal assemblies were all independent, although they enjoyed strong contacts and various levels of cooperation. Since 1909, they had published a common magazine and organized regional conferences. They coordinated the visits of traveling ministers and collaborated in matters pertaining to missionary activities. In 1932, their magazine, called *Die Verheissung des Vaters* (The promise of the Father), began to publish a common statement of faith.[8] Shortly thereafter, the pastor of Zurich, P. Richard Ruff, introduced the idea that the churches affiliated with the missions society could group as a denomination. In 1935, the Swiss Pentecostal Mission (Schweizerische Pfingstmission) was founded as a cooperation of churches. Although some churches hesitated because they felt that too much organization would stifle the work of the Holy Spirit, it soon became apparent that this new-found association brought a sense of identity to the movement.

Other Pentecostal churches also founded organizations at that time.[9] This development was inevitable and facilitated such things as mutually accepted ordination standards, membership certificates, national conferences, and coordinated youth programs. But it also led the churches to have a preoccupation with themselves. Perhaps this was the reason that a time of slow growth or stagnation began. This situation was exacerbated by the fact that the first leader of the Swiss Pentecostal Mission, P. Richard Ruff, who was a talented and charismatic pastor, was forced out of office due to a moral failure. His successor, Karl Schneider, was strongly tied to the Holiness tradition, and a more conservative period began. To that, one might add that Swiss Pentecostals experienced the Second World War in insular neutrality. What impact would the six dark years have on them?

Demands on Unity and Organization

In 1946, Swiss Pentecostals that were associated with their major denominations were grateful for having survived the war without too much suffering. Their brothers and sisters in the surrounding nations were facing a different situation. The leadership of the Swiss Pentecostal Mission felt obliged to do something on behalf of their friends abroad. Two practical consequences can be mentioned.

During a Communion service, Leonhard Steiner felt led by God to call for an international conference and began preparations for what would eventually be the first Pentecostal World Conference in Zurich in 1947. One of the major reasons was to coordinate help for Pentecostals in the war-torn areas of Europe. In fact, an international bureau for relief work in Europe was organized at the Pentecostal church in Basel as a result of this gathering. Help poured in from four continents.[10] In reviewing the events of the conference in Zurich, Donald Gee reflected on the fact that although there was unity in the Spirit, there was much conscientious discussion of which particular ways Pentecostals should unite in order to help the destitute with food and clothing.[11] The Swiss, together with the British and American Pentecostals, had experienced some form of organized collaboration as being helpful. On the other side were the Scandinavians, who felt that every church should be autonomous. They argued from their understanding of churches in the New Testament and were influenced by Baptist ecclesiology. Furthermore, they were skeptical whether the human tendency to govern would be sufficiently sensitive to the leading of the Holy Spirit. Even with regard to coordinating missionary activities on Pentecostal mission fields so that overlap and unnecessary competition could be avoided, they would only go as far as supporting the publication of an international magazine that would inform what Pentecostal missionaries were doing. As a result, the magazine *Pentecost* was commissioned.[12]

Another consequence of Pentecostal involvement beyond the Swiss border was related to the fact that German Pentecostals were very fragmented after the war. Not only was there a mix of organized and independent churches, but some Christians claimed that the German Pentecostals were chaotic, fragmented, and sometimes working against each other.[13] Karl Schneider and Leonhard Steiner from the Swiss Pentecostal Mission felt that some form of unity was essential to the Christian witness in Germany. With the help of the North American Assemblies of God, they participated in a conference in Stuttgart in 1948. The official purpose of this meeting was the production of a Pentecostal hymnal for all German-speaking areas of Europe. In fact, this conference led to the beginning of an alliance of German Pentecostal churches, which has fruitfully developed to the present day.

Exercises Toward Unity

If a rapprochement of Pentecostal churches was possible in Germany, how about developing a partnership among the different Pentecostal churches in Switzerland? As mentioned before, various groups had developed in different regions of the country and at different times. As these churches began to spread, a certain amount of competition ensued. One group considered itself more spiritual; the other was larger in size; the third saw itself as more relevant in society; the fourth was happy to be under a central leadership.[14] The Swiss Pentecostal movement had grown to about five thousand members by the end of the 1950s.[15] In spite of their differences, many of which had arisen naturally, were they not baptized in the same Spirit into one body (1 Cor. 12:13)? Had they not the same Lord and the same calling (Eph. 4:4–5)? Did not Jesus pray for unity so that others may believe (John 17:21)? It was time to talk together.

The largest Pentecostal church in Switzerland was in Zurich. Its pastor, Karl Schneider, called a meeting of pastors from the various groups in 1958. There was agreement in principle that contacts had to be intensified, open communication encouraged, and cooperation in certain areas could be possible. As a result, the pastors of three German-speaking Pentecostal denominations would begin to gather yearly for unity conferences. French-speaking Pentecostals, participants from other groups, and international guests were usually present as well. The 1960s and 1970s saw collaboration in printing a common magazine, the establishment of a common Bible school, and cooperation in youth ministry.[16] In 1973, an Alliance of Pentecostal Churches in Switzerland was formed. It looked as if endeavors toward unity were making progress. Many church members were optimistic that more than cooperation was possible. Meetings continued to be held, but in 1983 it became apparent that a fusion of the three major German-speaking Pentecostal groups would not be possible.

What were the reasons for such a failure? Theologically speaking, there was much agreement, and even in ecclesiological matters one could probably have found common ground. However, different administrative systems, the role of various properties, and other vested interests proved to be stumbling blocks. In other words, it was material aspects and differences in personalities among the leadership that stood in the way of a merger. Ironically, as one of the denominations got into big financial trouble, a merger between the Swiss Pentecostal Mission and the Freie Christengemeinden did take place in the mid-1990s. One wonders: Was the failure to unite indicative of a problem or simply a sign of pragmatic realities and the state of human nature?

Surprised by the Charismatic Renewal and Neo-Pentecostal Churches

Just about the time when merger discussions were in full swing, there was the beginning of the Jesus People movement. Pentecostals in Switzerland were surprised by the fact that young people were suddenly interested in attending church. Hippies and intellectuals came to a living relationship with Jesus and joined in worship. Up to then, Pentecostal churches were rather traditional. They paid attention to dress codes and hair length. Church music was played in a classical style and with acoustic instruments only. In a matter of months, however, the Pentecostals learned to sing to a new tune. There was a shift from externals to more substantial issues. Not style or appearance were essential, but the content of the gospel and the incarnation of faith.

Another paradigm shift happened when the Charismatic Renewal began to make waves in Europe. Suddenly Pentecostals were challenged to acknowledge that Catholics and Protestants could be Spirit-baptized without leaving their church and changing their doctrine. They were praying for the healing of sick people, and some would get restored to health. Lewi Pethrus, the eminent leader of the Swedish Pentecostal movement, was quoted in the Swiss magazine *Wort und Geist* as saying, "The outpouring of the Spirit or the so called charismatic wave among Christians from different churches continues unabatedly. I am fully convinced that this is a work of God."[17] The question of unity in the Spirit was raised, crossing theological convictions. In the following year, Leonhard Steiner, pastor of the Pentecostal Mission in Basel, visited the second meeting of the Roman Catholic–Pentecostal dialogue in Rome. Although he raised questions with regard to the reformability of the Roman Catholic Church, he conceded, "I was filled with amazement, praise and gratitude about the worldwide move of the Spirit in all churches, across all human barriers."[18]

In the 1980s, it became apparent that the Reformed churches in Switzerland did not receive the Charismatic Renewal with the same openness as Catholic communities. Swiss Pentecostals adopted a more differentiated attitude with regard to Charismatics. Nevertheless, it had become apparent that God has His people in all churches.

The arrival of neo-Pentecostal[19] churches in the 1990s brought the discussion on Christian unity into new focus. Whereas Evangelicals in Switzerland had been opposed or hesitant to adopt Pentecostal ways of worship and doctrine for the most part of the twentieth century, new independent churches began to sing and worship like their Pentecostal neighbors. Suddenly it became normal to raise one's hands in worship and to pray publicly for people who were ill or in need of help. Some new independent churches would not call themselves Pentecostal, but the experience of being baptized in the Spirit and the practice of prophetic speech had become acceptable in their circles.

This "charismatization" of Evangelical churches had a series of effects on Pentecostals. First of all, ancient animosities were falling away. Pentecostal practices were no longer considered to be sectarian or even demonic. Second, religious distinctives were no longer a reason why one would belong to one particular church. Many Pentecostals no longer felt the need to remain committed to their church. A transfer to another church seemed easy, and doctrinal differences did not seem to be significant between classical and neo-Pentecostal groups. A third aspect that arose was that there was new strength in numbers. Societal issues could be addressed together in fresh strength. There was a sense of unity in purpose. However, the charismatization of other churches brought along a challenge to the Pentecostal groups. How was their identity expressed, now that external markers, like speaking in tongues or the practice of charisms, were no longer powerful reminders of identity? What other factors building identity were there—language, nationality, or culture?

These questions were quickly tested as the influx of migrants to Swiss society sharply increased. Initially, migrant workers and their families came from Roman Catholic regions of southern Europe. Then came the labor force from Eastern Europe; many of them were formally Muslims. In either case, this was seen as an opportunity to evangelize these *Gastarbeiters* (guest workers). Pentecostal churches in the larger urban centers began to offer services in Italian, Spanish, and Serbo-Croatian.[20] But from the 1980s on, the labor force and refugees came also in sizable numbers from Latin America, Africa, and Asia. As a result, an internationalization of the churches took place. Again, whatever one understood by Pentecostal identity had to be redefined.

Reflections on Pentecostal Identity and Christian Unity

What kind of development can one see with regard to an understanding of Christian unity and Pentecostal identity after one hundred years of Pentecostal history in Switzerland? And if there has been a development in the appreciation of these two ideas, what would that possibly imply for the future of these congregations and their national headquarters?

Pentecostal identity

The first leaders of European Pentecostalism and the early Swiss Pentecostals especially had experienced the work of the Holy Spirit across cultural, linguistic, and ecclesial barriers. This fact helped them to seek their identity beyond that which is usual with humankind. As part of a new Christian movement, they were tolerant of a variety of theological opinions as long as the focus was on the work of Jesus Christ, the ministry of the Holy Spirit, and the coming kingdom of God. Who could speak against obvious blessings given by the Spirit of God? The indwelling presence of God would surely bring identity.

It was only in the 1930s that Swiss Pentecostals found a new form of identity as they began to be part of newly founded denominations.

At the same time, the Pentecostal leaders wanted to preserve the Pentecostal heritage of the former generation and were conservative in approach. Having roots in the Holiness Movement, they emphasized moral values that were associated with being filled by the Holy Spirit. This view led to a certain amount of legalism and introspection.

The unity conferences in the 1960s and 1970s among Swiss Pentecostal churches indicated that spiritual unity would benefit from structural identity. At that time the various denominations established themselves and acquired hotels and retreat centers in order to symbolize and promote their identity within Switzerland.[21] One can notice a development in the expression of identity. First, it was enough to be baptized in the Spirit; then membership in a national organization was the norm and the observance of certain moral mores. Later, buildings provided additional means of identification.

The advent of the Charismatic Renewal and independent and neo-Pentecostal churches opened the horizon. Identification with significant others and their ideas could also be found outside a particular group or fellowship of churches. Self-reflection was no longer limited to a particular context. The contours of Pentecostal identity could be defined in a variety of ways. This impression was exacerbated when Pentecostal congregations were enriched by the spiritual life of Christian migrant communities, provided they worshipped together.

Another way of looking at the issue of Pentecostal identity is by considering religious perception from a pedagogical point of view—that is, by studying the way people perceive their religious experiences and appropriate their faith. Three significant areas of religious perception in Pentecostal church services can be mentioned: their worship, the practice of giving testimony, and the custom of praying for the sick and spiritually needy.[22] These played a significant role in the identity formation of the believer. The fact that the same elements can now be found in neo-Pentecostal churches means that there is little left for classical Pentecostals to call their own. Other Christians have also been empowered by the Holy Spirit, worship in a fashion formerly attributed to Pentecostals only now common in many churches, and also tell stories of God's graceful intervention in their lives and pray for others to be healed in Jesus's name. Nonetheless, what no one can take away from classical Pentecostals in Switzerland is their particular history. If their members are aware of their roots, they have reason to find and appreciate their particular identity. To that, of course, one should add a sense of identity that is attributed to the work of Jesus Christ and the indwelling of God's Holy Spirit.

Christian unity

The desire for Christian unity runs like a red thread through the history of Swiss Pentecostals, especially those of the largest denomination, the Swiss Pentecostal Mission. As we have seen, their particular context during the early years of the twentieth century and their international network was a felicitous blend of unity in diversity. Swiss Pentecostals were part of a group that favored Pentecostal unity during the international conference in Stockholm in 1939.[23] Their special situation after World War II allowed them to be a catalyst in order to foster unity among Pentecostals in Europe and worldwide through the organization of the first Pentecostal World Conference in Zurich in 1947. The same was true due to the Swiss participation at the Stuttgart conference in 1948.

For about twenty-five years, Swiss Pentecostals were seriously working on ways to bring more unity with regard to their respective groups. In all these endeavors, it became obvious that there are two types of unity: organizational and spiritual. As it turned out, it was not possible to merge the two. Some were concerned about abandoning their organizational structures that had given them some sense of identity. It was easier to agree on some form of confessional unity. That is probably the reason why all major Pentecostal groups became members of the Evangelical Alliance of Switzerland, as well as the Federation of Free Churches in Switzerland and have been actively involved on the highest level.[24]

Identity and unity

By means of a conclusion to this reflection, the question may be raised if the desire to maintain a particular identity makes Christian unity difficult, if not impossible. This query has, of course, major consequences with regard to ecumenical discussions and activities. One could also ask the other way around: Has the history of the ecumenical movement shown that unity in Christ can only be achieved partially, based on basic confessional agreements, finding the lowest common denominator? What would the role of Pentecostals be if this quest would continue? Could the efforts of Swiss Pentecostals serve as an illustration for future activities toward greater Christian unity and ecumenical collaboration without the loss of a denomination's particular identity?

First of all, there is a general responsibility toward Christian unity. The worldwide Pentecostal movement is a bit more than one hundred years old. During that time, the number of Christian denominations has risen from about 1,600 to 41,000.[25] The proliferation of independent churches and denominations is, to a large extent, the result of Pentecostal missionary activities and church splits. It would seem appropriate if Pentecostals would be especially conscious of the need for moving toward greater unity. In the case of Swiss Pentecostals, this awareness has been with the movement throughout its history. They interpreted the work of the Holy Spirit as one that could not be divided but rather was bringing believers together and preparing them for the day of Christ's return. Efforts were made and some success was achieved. It became also apparent that structural unity, although desirable, has so far not been easy to attain. However, there were some pragmatic developments toward unity and general confessional agreement.

Second, the World Council of Churches does not aim to become a superchurch. It is aware that denominational and confessional identities are important. Nevertheless, Christian unity is to be more than spiritual unity. One way of working toward more tangible unity is expressed by the notion of "spiritual ecumenism."[26] A principle argument that is raised therein claims that every church has gifts worthy of sharing. Accordingly, Pentecostals have gifts that should be shared with the other Christian churches. The sharing of such graces is a way of engaging in evangelization, the revitalization of churches. Such an approach is close to the heart of many Pentecostals. The history of Swiss Pentecostals has illustrated that this sharing may start among Pentecostal groups and then extend to other churches.

Finally, the intense discussions with regard to structural unity among Pentecostals in the twentieth century had shown that a viable alternative is to create fellowships rather than organizations. In that way, many Pentecostal denominations, Swiss ones included, could maintain their identity and at the same time reach out with the right hand of fellowship (Gal. 2:9). There seems to be a tendency among some historic churches to move in the same direction.[27] Seen from that vantage point, the failure of Swiss Pentecostal churches to merge was not that bad after all. It has been an exercise toward increasing fellowship by means of sharing gifts while keeping one's identity. The open letter written in 1913 by the pastors of the Pentecostal churches in Zurich and St. Gall still rings true today. The gift of God in Christ and through the Holy Spirit is for everyone.

Chapter 8

Pentecostalism in Germany: Historical and Theological Perspectives

Gottfried Sommer

THIS CHAPTER IS divided into four sections. The first three are more historical, on the early years of Pentecostalism in Germany, on the Third Reich and its aftermath, and on the emergence of the association of the Arbeitsgemeinschaft der Christengemeinden in Deutschland (Free Pentecostal Churches), later called BFP. The final section briefly considers some theological issues.

THE HISTORICAL ESTABLISHMENT OF GERMAN PENTECOSTAL FELLOWSHIPS

We begin our discussion with the pietist background, discuss the emergence of the movement and the Berlin Declaration of 1909, and then give an overview of the various Pentecostal fellowships.

The Pietistic movement within the state church as the "cradle" of the German Pentecostal movement

In Germany, the newly forming Pentecostal movement faced a peculiar situation. It "saw itself as a direct continuation of the previous development of the Pietist Fellowship movement (Gemeinschaftsbewegung)."[1] One has to keep in mind that with the exception of the Anabaptist movements, "free churches" were a relatively recent phenomenon in Germany. The history of Protestantism in Germany by and large was the same as the history of Lutheran or Reformed state churches, while the Pietist Conventicles can be seen as an early form of a free church. The Gemeinschaftsbewegung (Pietistic Fellowship movement) within the German state church was founded as a consequence of the German revival movement in the nineteenth century and was an umbrella organization of Christians who wanted to implement Luther's vision of the *Ecclesiola in ecclesia*, the little congregation of the believers within the church, without leaving the established state churches.

It was Emil Meyer (1869–1850), leader of the "beach mission" in Hamburg, who in 1907 visited the church of Thomas Ball Barratt (1862–1940) in Christiania (today called Oslo) and brought Pentecostalism from Azusa Street to Europe. In the same year, Meyer invited two women, Dagmar Gregersen and Agnes Thelle,[2] to visit with a group of friends of the growing Pentecostal movement in his house in Hamburg to share their testimony of speaking in tongues. Other international guests had been present there, like Barratt, Alexander Boddy (1854–1930), Cecil Polhill (1860–1938), and Gerrit Polman (1868–1932), among others.[3]

Kassel and the Berlin Declaration of 1909

At Meyer's mission, traveling evangelist Heinrich Dallmeyer (1870–1925), from Kassel, who was connected with the fellowship movement, met the Norwegian women, received the baptism in the Holy Spirit, was healed from a physical disease, and became fascinated by their gift of speaking in tongues. He invited the women to hold meetings with him in Kassel. Pentecostal manifestations attracted attention:

> Reports varied about the degree of chaos, uncontrolled manifestations, and how often the meetings got out of control.... It was reported that uncontrolled screaming and shouting in the meetings could be heard all over the district in which the meeting was held. Finally, government officials and police ordered the meetings to be stopped and public order to be restored.[4]

Yet from another perspective, the first two weeks of the meetings were conducted in a rather sober and orderly manner.[5] "The meetings continued over the course of the following days like before, the only difference was that more and more people were baptized in the Holy Spirit and received the gift of speaking in tongues and prophecy."[6] Renowned leaders of the Gnadauer Verband, as the organization of the Pietistic fellowship movement, went to Kassel to see firsthand what was going on. Elias Schrenk (1831–1913) visited Kassel during the second week of the meetings. He gave an account of what he saw:

> Brethren! I was ordered to come to Kassel with the intention to end the movement. But I could not do this service to my brethren. This movement is from God. For fifty years I have been waiting for the gifts of the Spirit, and I am pleased, that the Lord answers in our times. This movement will continue.[7]

By August 1907, "the reports and reviews from the Gnadauer Verband, the Evangelical Alliance and other Holiness people were in general affirmative and positive."[8] It is important to note that the early opponents of the German Pentecostal movement were not cessationists, as the influence of Johann Christoph Blumhardt (1805–1880) then still lingered on. Ironically, such noncessationism included those who sought to practice exorcism and "drive out the Pentecostal Spirit."[9]

In September 1909, Walter Michaelis (1866–1953), who was the bishop (Präses) of the Gnadauer Verband, and General Georg von Viehbahn (1840–1915), the representative for the Evangelical Alliance, invited leaders of the Gemeinschaftsbewegung, the Alliance, and Free churches to Berlin. On September 15, sixty of these met there to debate the issues, and a response was drafted.[10] After nineteen hours, the Berliner Erklärung (Berlin Declaration) was finalized and signed by fifty-six of the sixty representatives. Conspicuously, none of the leaders of the newly emerging Pentecostal movement were invited to explain or straighten out any misunderstandings or respond to the accusations. Obviously, there was no interest in resolving the conflict.[11] The main points of the declaration were:[12]

1. The so-called "Pentecostal movement" is not from above but from below. It has many manifestations in common with spiritism. Demons are sent by Satan to deceive Christians.
2. The evil spirits' primary entry point are prophecies, which gradually seek to replace Scripture. What makes matters worse: these prophetic words are given mainly by women, who usurp authority over men.
3. The doctrines promulgated by the so-called revival—of a second blessing, sanctification, and perfection—are rejected.
4. Pastor Jonathan Paul (1853–1931) is the main leader of this movement and its unbiblical teachings.
5. There was only one Pentecost, that witnessed to in the Bible.

Two weeks after the Berlin Declaration, the Second Pentecostal conference took place in Mülheim. A counterstatement, Die Mülheimer Erklärung (Mülheim Declaration), was published that attempted to correct the misrepresentations and criticisms of the Berlin document.[13] Yet even "attempts at mediation by the 'neutrals' [within the Gnadauer Verband] were without effect."[14] The Gnadauer Verband was determined not to cooperate with the "tongues movement."

The establishment of various German Pentecostal fellowships

The Pentecostal conferences of 1909 and 1910 drew unprecedented numbers of people (1,700 and 2,500, respectively) from Germany, Switzerland, the Netherlands, Hungary, and even Russia. In 1914, the emerging Pentecostal movement incorporated as the Christlicher Gemeinschaftsverband GmbH Mülheim (Mülheim Association of Christian Fellowships). Also in 1914, Paul and five others published the first modern German-language translation of the New Testament, the first "and so far the only Pentecostal group which had done so."[15] The motivation for this translation was the longing for a New Testament in a contemporary language.[16]

The new movement, called in the first decades the German Pentecostal movement, did not consider itself a new church or denomination but a transdenominational initiative empowered by the Holy Spirit. This was made clear in a statement that Jonathan Paul and Carl Octavius Voget (1874–1936) issued through a main gathering of elders, the Hauptbrüdertag, that took place between April 3–7, 1922: "We do not see it as our task to create a new denomination. We do, however, regret that we have been forced to create independent [groups and fellowships] in certain places due to the circumstances."[17]

Nevertheless the strong ties to the Protestant state churches persisted, which inhibited the development of a genuine Pentecostal theology. Doctrines regarding baptism, ecclesiology, Holy Scripture, and eschatology remained close to that found in the Reformational confessions of the Protestant state church. On the other hand, the movement was influential practically. Over the years, Pentecostal spirituality was promoted by significant members of the clergy from the state church, and several state church societies and fellowships took on a Pentecostal character, including the practice of the gifts of the Spirit.[18]

The most important reason for the rise of actual denominations and congregations independent of the state church—that is, of free churches—was the particular pneumatology connected to the belief in the initial sign that distinguished the Pentecostal movement. The Mühlheim Association, on the other hand, maintained another position:

> We know that through the fruits we can see with whom we are dealing (Matt. 7:16). The fruit of the Spirit (Gal. 5:22) therefore is the main issue. This is found [in the person] where the Spirit of God has made His home. In no way do we desire to elevate speaking in tongues beyond what Scripture teaches.[19]

All independent Pentecostal denominations and congregations in Germany were of the same opinion regarding believer's baptism, whereas the leader of the Mühlheim Association, pastor Jonathan Paul, sought to overcome the debate about baptism with his treatise "Baptism in Its Most Complete Sense."[20] His thesis was that the baptism proclaimed by Jesus and the apostles was the baptism in the Holy Spirit. Yet most Pentecostals felt strongly about adult baptism and were unconvinced by Paul's advocacy of the contrary. Wilhelm Kowalski, one of the most important leaders of the independent Pentecostal churches in East Prussia, described it as a day of mourning when he read the tract by Voget and Paul in which both men defended infant baptism.[21]

The importance of the local congregation in particular was emphasized by the Pentecostal free churches, in contrast to the Mühlheim Association and its model of working within the Protestant state church. The independent circles wanted to have local churches with local leadership, which is only responsible to the exalted Lord (1 Pet. 5:1–4), and a private municipal budget.[22] This emerging congregational Pentecostal model included neither the Christen-Gemeinden Elim (Elim Christian Community), which were affiliated to Zeltmission Berlin-Lichterfelde e.V. and its authoritative leader Heinrich Vietheer (1883–1968), nor the Gemeinde Gottes (Church of God, Cleveland, Tennessee). Later, individual churches were regarded as inseparably linked with the church movement and its central leadership.[23] So in the first half of the twentieth century, Pentecostalism in Germany was organized in three church models: a Pietist, inner church type; a congregational form; and a centralized episcopal version.

Although few of the founders of the free Pentecostal churches would have admitted to following personal and emotional motivations for leaving sound and stable organizations and "starting up shop alone," some confessed to having received visions or hearing the voice of God calling them to new beginnings. For example, in 1934, even after the beginnings of the Nazi dictatorship, Karl Fix (1897–1969) started his own revival meetings in Berlin. He was prompted to do so when someone had a clear inner picture during prayer that Fix should start a church in the northeast of Berlin, where the poorest of the poor lived.[24]

Marie Primmer (1873–?), upon whose initiative the Missionsgemeinde Entschiedener Christen Weckhof e.V (Mission Congregation of Committed Christians) was founded, received a similar calling to Germany. In 1925, she had a vision. Jesus came to her riding on a white horse, nodding in a friendly manner toward her and saying gently, "My child, go to Germany. I will be with you!"[25] She persuaded a sister in Christ to wait for confirmation from God for her, and when this was given, she promptly traveled to Germany within a year and contributed her services to the founding of a church.

It is remarkable that in the first decades of the worldwide Pentecostal movement, the influence of the Assemblies of God, the largest and most significant Pentecostal church in the United States, on the German Pentecostal groups was relatively minor. Of special importance for the German Pentecostal groups was the Russian and Eastern European Mission (EEM), which emanated only indirectly from the Assemblies of God. It had been founded in the spring of 1927 by the American Paul Bernhard Peterson (1895–1978), and he had worked together closely and over many years with the Department for Foreign Missions of the Assemblies of God until that relationship ended in 1940.[26] Gustav Herbert Schmidt (1891–1958), who had worked before as a missionary in Poland, was sent to Eastern Europe in order to establish a headquarters for the EEM. On March 2, 1930, he inaugurated the Danzig Instytut Biblijny and served as president there until Nicholas Nikoloff (1900–1964) took over this task in 1935.[27] The language of instruction was German,[28] and some of its graduates were later leaders of German Pentecostal churches.

The German emigrant to the United States Hermann Lauster (1901–1964) joined the Church of God there in Cleveland, Tennessee, and was sent as its missionary back to Germany. Because of the centralized structure of the Church of God, the Gemeinde Gottes (Church of God) in Germany stayed closely connected with the

American mother organization. However, due to the war, this relationship only made a difference after 1945.

Another reinforcement from the United States was the manufacturer Ludwig (Luis) Graf (1861–1935), who, however, had grown up in Germany. In 1911, he was visiting Germany and felt called to evangelize there. In 1913, he worked together with the evangelist Maria Woodworth-Etter (1844–1924).[29] During the war, he was director of a larger charity for German children. Through this contact, he came to Germany in 1922 and evangelized in the Margraviate of Brandenburg (German: Mark Brandenburg), in Silesia (today Poland), Leipzig, Halle, Hamburg, and Altona.[30] In 1924, his ministry was reported to have led to approximately four thousand conversions.[31] From these examples it should be clear that the Pentecostal movement in Germany, as a free church movement, has been influenced by American Pentecostalism but cannot be understood merely as a product of American itinerant preachers.

As soon as the first Pentecostal movements had sprung up in Sweden, they got active in exterior missions. In 1938, the Pentecostal missionary society in Sweden had grown to become the largest missionary society of Sweden, with more than two hundred Swedish Pentecostal missionaries.[32] When one surveys the different volumes of the magazine *Der Feste Grund* (The solid ground), which had been started by Benjamin Schilling (1865–1930), what stands out is the influence of the Swedish Mission in the German churches, which is shown by the many sermons they preached in free Pentecostal churches. Most significant were Swedish missionaries like Georg Steen (ca. 1892–?) and Thure Roos (?–1934). Steen, the son-in-law of Benjamin Schilling, was not only editor of *Der Feste Grund* for several years, but also led the church at the Küstriner Platz (Berlin-Friedrichshain) and at times also the Tabor-church. The founder of the German Elim movement, Heinrich Vietheer (1883–1968), took over the German Pentecostal magazine *Glaubensherold* (Herald of faith) from two Swedish missionaries, Ivar Eriksson and Margarete Clasen in Kiel, in order to entrust it to the editorial leadership of Hermann Dittert (1896–1988), a German.[33] Also, the Bible courses in the Elim congregation in Lauter (Saxony, Germany) were conducted according to the Swedish model.[34] What was striking is that after Vietheer had founded his own free church, the Elim movement, the connection to the Swedish missionaries is no longer mentioned. Characteristic of the Swedish Pentecostal understanding of church was a strict congregationalism, which was to become formative for a large part of the German Pentecostal movement.

Roughly the same groups that made efforts at unification had already existed in 1939 as separate organizations.[35] These were the Zionsgemeinden (Zion churches) under the leadership of Heinrich Wohlfahrt; the Deutsche Volksmission (German Peoples Mission) under Karl Fix; the Internationale Volksmission (International People's Mission) under Paula Gassner (1906–1981); the Erweckungsmission Deutschland (Revival Mission Germany) in Berlin under Bruno Bartknecht; the nonorganized, which were connected through the magazine *Der Feste Grund,* edited by Erwin Lorenz (1906–1985); and the Freier Pfingstverein Weckhof (Free Pentecostal Union Weckhof) under Georg Breuninger. In addition to these, the Missionsfreunde Velbert (Friends of Missions Velbert) were especially known for their mission activity abroad.

The Situation During the Third Reich

The following sketches developments during and after the era of National Socialism and the Second World War.

The position of the various Pentecostal fellowships concerning National Socialism

There were different Pentecostal groups during the time of National Socialism (NS), and they cannot all be subsumed under a single category regarding their views with respect to the Jewish question and the Nazi regime. Gerhard Krüger (1914–1987), one of the pioneers of Pentecostalism in the time of rebuilding of postwar Germany, said: "Many Pentecostals have soiled themselves with Hitler."[36] Pentecostal groups and individual churches that were not large enough to be acknowledged by the Nazi government had to go underground, including all the churches that have been connected through the journal *Der Feste Grund*. Hermann Lauster (1901–1964), the founder of the Church of God in Germany, began 1937 with evangelization in Stuttgart and was arrested because he called officers of the Gestapo "Hitler-gangsters." Already on March 23, 1938, meetings in Krehwinkel and Asperglen had been forbidden because neighbors complained to the authorities because of loud prayers and singing. From August 22, 1938, until March 16, 1939, he was detained in the concentration camp Welzheim,[37] but after a global prayer initiative of the international Church of God (Cleveland, Tennessee) movement, he was set free.[38] Others, like those in the Elim congregations, united with the Baptists in 1937. In 1942, Baptist and Elim churches united with some churches of the Brethren movement to become the Bund Evangelisch-Freikirchlicher Gemeinden (BEFG, or Association of Evangelical Free Churches in Germany).

A German Nationalist mind-set with negative consequences can be found among the Mülheim Association and the Elim movement. For instance, Emil Meyer, who originally brought Pentecostalism to Germany and worked as an independent Pentecostal preacher and author, prophesied that all Jews must first immigrate to Egypt in order to learn to work there, because they have forgotten to do so and only exploited their host nations.[39] His views refute the myth of the Pentecostals being only "innocent victims."[40] There are few historical records or accounts of Pentecostals actively helping the persecuted Jews[41] and even fewer prophetic voices from those times that spoke out on behalf of the Jews. The following extract by Fritz Voll (1930–), an eyewitness, who later did much for Jewish-Christian relations, tells us something about Pentecostal fears and provides a window into some of the factors that led them to be more silent than outspoken about the Nazis:

> The night of November 9, 1938, left a deep impression in my memory. I was eight years old, and it was the first time that I saw a house fire. It was also the first time that

> I consciously felt a discrepancy between a comforting and positive Nazi propaganda we heard and read every day and a very nasty reality, a reality of death and destruction that would unfold quite openly. That night we woke up to loud noises on our narrow one-way street, the Georg-Buchholz-Strasse in Arnswalde, Germany, and saw the synagogue diagonally opposite our house in flames. We had actually never noticed that the building was a synagogue.... Did the synagogue have to burn to be noticed as the place of Jewish worship and learning?... I also heard from my parents that the synagogue had been torched as an act of violence against the Jews. I overheard them whispering to each other that the persecution of the Jews would only be the beginning. Next in line would be the "true" Christians.... It was only in the late seventies, when my parents were in their mid-seventies that I once heard my father say regretfully: "Why did we not save a single Jewish life?"[42]

The following article of the constitution of the Mülheim Association is a revision that was made in compliance with the Nuremberg laws of 1936, which dealt with euthanasia and the elimination of Jews from Germany. It came into effect on October 13, 1938, only twenty-seven days before Kristallnacht, November 9–10, when the Nazis carried out a series of coordinated attacks on Jews in their homes, businesses, and synagogues:

> With thankfulness to God we confess that we are, according to his providence, members of the German people. The dependence on God and the mind of Jesus Christ enable us to stand with our people (Volk) with body and life, with possessions and blood. The energetic support of all public endeavors of the People's Welfare system is to us the duty of our Christian conscience. We honor and accept the nation's leadership and government. In sincerity we promise all loyalty and every obedience, which we are indebted to render together with all Christians to our earthly authorities according to God's

> will and the word and spirit of our Lord, Mark 12:17; Romans 13:1-7; 1 Tim. 2:1-4; 1 Peter. 2:13-17.... In the race laws we see a divinely willed and biblically founded endeavor to purify and to keep pure the people (Volk) from mixture with alien races. The leading-out of the Jews from the community of our people, as also from other peoples, is for us a process according to divine providence and divine will.[43]

The Mühlheim Association formulated in 1991 a formal and official declaration of repentance concerning its behavior in the time of NS under the title Erklärung des Hauptbrüdertages des Mülheimer Verbandes von 1991 zur Stellung des Mülheimer Verbandes während der Zeit des Nationalsozialismus (Declaration of the Main Committee of Elders in 1991 Concerning the Position of the Mülheim Association in the Time of National Socialism).[44] There was no other statement formulated by Pentecostal circles in Germany because the only other group that was known to have supported the government at that time, the Elim movement, was part of the German Baptist movement then.

Resurrection of the German Pentecostal movements after World War II

After May 1951, the so-called Mülheimer Gemeinschaftsverband (Mühlheim Association of Pentecostal Churches) was completely forbidden in the areas of East Germany (the later German Democratic Republic, or GDR). Some Pentecostals fled to the West. The total number of members in West Germany was then about twenty-five thousand.[45] The remainder of the Elim movement in Western Germany could be seen as a rather unified group, due to the former firm leadership of Heinrich Vietheer. Even under the umbrella of the BEFG, together with Baptist and Brethren churches, he had basically kept the same structure and connections.

Especially in light of the former atrocities that had been committed under the command of the NS movement in Germany and which had become visible in its extent only after the end of the war,

Christians in the United States realized how important it was to reach Germany with the gospel.[46] It was now perceived that after the end of the war, there was another open door in Germany.[47] Next to Gustav Kinderman, the field secretary of the Assemblies of God in Europe, it was especially C. W. Loenser (1893–1969), the leader of the German branch of the Assemblies of God, who raised awareness regarding the importance of mission to Germany again. Being strongly focused, he was able to mobilize people and raise money to support the Pentecostal movement in Germany.[48] Concerning evangelization in Germany, the former Hollywood photographer Hal Herman (1906–2003) played an important role, and he also served in the Assemblies of God.[49] Pastor Hans R. Waldvogel (1893–1969) from Ridgewood Pentecostal Church in Brooklyn, New York, went as an evangelist to Germany and filled his tents and was known nearly everywhere (including by pastor Wilhelm Busch and Billy Graham) and valued as such.[50] A missionary of the Pentecostal Assemblies of Canada, Willard Cantelon (1916–1999), and his wife came to Germany in 1951 and took over the responsibility for raising funds for the construction of the Beröa Bible School in Erzhausen (about thirty minutes south of Frankfurt/Main), and they produced a film under the title *Germany's Destiny*.[51]

In order to transmit the urgently needed food and supplies to the suffering Pentecostal churches in Germany after the war, the Swedish Pentecostal movement used the Swedish Red Cross (among others), so Swedish missionaries came in Red Cross uniforms and brought relief aid to the needy in Germany. Entire shiploads of aid were sent to Germany[52]—not only food and clothes collected by the Swedish churches, but also entire wooden church buildings. Swedish missionaries who came to Germany after the war not only served as pastors of churches, but also as teachers of Bible courses and later as staff at the Bible school of the new group of Pentecostal churches.[53]

The Gathering of Free Pentecostal Churches and Formation of the Arbeitsgemeinschaft der Christengemeinden in Deutschland (ACD)

This section discusses the consolidation of the ACD and the Seminary Beröa and other denominational developments.

The way to unity

The impulses from the Pentecostal World Conferences in Zurich (1947) and, later, Paris (1949), which focused on unity within the Pentecostal movement, resonated in German Pentecostal circles. On May 13–14, 1947, representatives of the so-called free Pentecostal churches gathered in Stuttgart (southwest Germany).[54] From August 10–13, 1948, also in Stuttgart, a first Unity Conference took place at which representatives of almost all so-called free Pentecostal churches, including the Elim churches and the Mülheim Association, were present.[55] The decision was made here first that the different free Pentecostal fellowships were to unify. For that purpose, at another conference, from September 21–23, 1948, a preliminary working group called Free Pentecostal Churches was founded.[56] At a conference from October 8–12, 1951, of the Pentecostal Elim Church in Hamburg-Barmbek, of which we have only a very short record of proceedings, a new consolidation between these free Pentecostal groups occurred.[57] In discussing whether the association was to continue as it had started, it was agreed: "God's Spirit worked agreement among all the brothers present, so that they agreed that the cooperation should continue and that it should complete the duties which they had received from the Lord."[58]

Already at the second Unity Conference in Mülheim, from April 26–29, 1949, the Vereinigte Pfingstgemeinden in Deutschland (Association of Pentecostal Churches in Germany) was founded, which included the Mülheim Association and the Free Pentecostal Churches.[59] However, this connection did not last long. In contrast to the successful unification of the Free Pentecostal Churches, the differences between this group and the Mühlheim Association were too large. After the registration of the Free Pentecostal Churches under the name Arbeitsgemeinschaft der Christengemeinden in Deutschland e.V. (ACD, or Association of Christian Churches in Germany, registered group) in 1954, this group and the Mülheim Association worked independently but in "peaceful coexistence" with each other.[60]

From the beginning of the discussions, the nascent ACD sought to be an organic fellowship of congregations but yet not in any way as would undermine congregational autonomy.[61] Hence, even with its official registration and recognition (e.V.), the congregationalist principle, which Erwin Lorenz was very committed to his whole life, was not to be tampered with. So, on March 19, 1954, the ACD e.V. was established.[62]

The seminary Beröa and other denominational developments

In 1951, the Assemblies of God in Stuttgart bought a centrally located building, which had room for up to forty students, in which those called by God to become pastors, evangelists, or teachers could be prepared for service.[63] Although at first the faculty was comprised of foreigners, the goal was one day to have the leadership completely in German hands.[64] Since the Mülheim Association didn't see the soil prepared enough for unity yet, the representatives of the Free Pentecostal Churches, which later founded the ACD, left the seminary alone. Yet the school outgrew the building in Stuttgart, and a new property was bought in Erzhausen, near Darmstadt, in the fall of 1954.[65] With this move, the Bible school changed its name, following the biblical Bereans in Acts 17, which it carries until today: Beröa.

The following highlights the history of the Bund Freikirchlicher Pfingstgemeinden (BFP, or Free Pentecostal Churches).[66] The official name was agreed upon at the seventieth national conference of the ACD in Velbert in May 1982. The organization later also included (since 1988) the Volksmission Entschiedener Christen (VMeC, or

Mission of Born-Again Christians)[67] and (since 2008) the Gemeinde der Christen Ecclesia (Congregations of the Ecclesia).[68] In 1991, after the unification of the two Germanies, the Elim Gemeinden Ost (Elim Congregations of the Former East Germany), which were in Eastern Germany united with the Baptists during the Communist time, was integrated into the BFP after leaving their association with the Baptist and Brethren churches.[69]

As the BFP also accepted congregations from other cultures and languages, they put some basic guidelines in place to nurture fellowship and relationships. As of the time of writing of this chapter, there are 13 congregations from other European nations, 31 congregations from Asian nations (of which 17 are Korean), 131 congregations from Central and West African backgrounds, 2 congregations with North American backgrounds, and 3 congregations with Latin American backgrounds.[70]

At many of these conferences discussing the unity of the Pentecostal movement, the Church of God was never discussed. The Church of God (Cleveland, Tennessee) is the second-largest Caucasian Pentecostal movement in the United States and mostly was active in Germany in the region of Wurttemberg. This lack of relationship is due to the fact that the Church of God founder in Germany, Hermann Lauster, had a very exclusive understanding of Christian faith. For him, his denomination was *the* Church of God, and whoever wanted the full blessing should join it.[71] Therefore, the option of working together was never explored. Of course in the last decades, the situation has changed and there have been talks even for unification between the German Church of God and the BFP, but because of the international structure of the Church of God, this has not happened.

A Few Theological Perspectives

In 1996, in a joint declaration of the Deutsche Evangelische Allianz (DEA, or German Protestant Alliance) and the presidium of the

BFP in Kassel,[72] the following was iterated, representing a kind of "evangelicalization" of the BFP:

1. The BFP holds as the basis of faith the confession of the DEA.
2. In the spirit of and with the DEA, the works of the Holy Spirit, including His role and His gifts, ought no longer be considered as referring to different levels of salvation. The gifts of the Holy Spirit are recognized for Christian service, but their presence is not to be considered as signs of any form of superior Christian identity. In regard to speaking in tongues, the order, as found in 1 Corinthians 14, are agreed on and committed to. Besides requests for physical healing, it is important to express through counseling and preaching that God also can bless and can glorify Himself in times of illness.
3. Since manifestations such as "slain in the Spirit" have brought confusion and dissension, these should not be found in the context of events under the DEA.
4. Both organizations wish to work together in the future and are committed to conversations that can clarify their positions and enhance their cooperation.

In this context, it should be mentioned that in 2009, after one hundred years, there appeared also the Gemeinsame Erklärung des Evangelischen Gnadauer Gemeinschaftsverbandes und des Mülheimer Verbandes Freikirchlich-Evangelischer Gemeinden zur 'Berliner Erklärung' von 1909 (A joint declaration of the Evangelical Gnadenauer Association and of the Mühlheim Association of Evangelical Free Churches in regards to the Berlin Declaration of 1909), which acknowledged that in both the Berlin Declaration and the Mülheimer Declaration a serious spiritual struggle to prevent damage to the church of Christ could be seen. "These historical documents (the historical Berlin Declaration of 1909 and the response from the Mülheim Association in the same year) had, however, no meaning for the present cooperation with each other. We know that Jesus Christ is working in each of the movements."[73]

What is emerging among a new generation of Pentecostal theologians in Germany are historical pieces that show the contexts of individual churches or organizations and that express the movement's development in its various parts and as a whole.[74] Included among these is a dissertation about a Charismatic revival movement in Farther Pomerania (Germany, part of Prussia then, and Poland after the Second World War) starting in 1820, which led to the founding of a free church and that highlights aspects of German revivalism in the nineteenth century in connection with the Pietism behind the modern Pentecostal movement.[75] On the topic of missiology, Paul Clark, missionary of the Assemblies of God in Germany, has written about Pentecostal church planting in Germany between 1945 and 2005.[76] The statistical material that he delivers is not to be underestimated and ought to generate much more research. For instance, of the five hundred churches planted between 1945 and 2005, only forty-six were planted by foreign missionaries. Clark's data reveals the indigenous character of the German-speaking Pentecostal churches.

It should also be mentioned that thirty-six BFP churches have their roots in former Charismatic groups of other churches. A dissertation about this topic from a practical or pastoral theological perspective provides case studies of such pastoral, ministerial, and mission initiatives.[77] Much more work needs to be done to explore the history and theology of German Pentecostalism and to explicate their relevance for the present and future of German Pentecostal churches in particular and for the global renewal movement in general.

Chapter 9

Dutch Pentecostalism and Eschatology: Consequences of Tapping Into an Eschatologically Charged Religious Matrix

Huibert H. Zegwaart

THE HISTORICAL ORIGINS of the Pentecostal movement in the Netherlands have been extensively researched by Cornelius van der Laan.[1] In *De spade regen* he gives an adequate account of its historical roots, sketching the conversion of a Salvation Army officer, Gerrit Roelof Polman, and his wife, Wilhelmine Blekkink. The couple experienced the baptism in the Spirit and embraced the conviction that this baptism constitutes an experience distinct from conversion.[2] Since the historical connections between the Azusa Street revival and the genesis of the Pentecostal movement in Holland is well attested, this chapter will focus on some other aspects of the religious matrix of Dutch Pentecostalism.[3] The eschatological expectations that can be found there are treated in this chapter. First, I will trace some ups and downs of eschatological fervor and then describe some theological positions it gave rise to.[4] Finally, I will outline some theological challenges that need to be tackled in the near future.

The Religious Context in Which Pentecostalism Arrived in the Netherlands

Van der Laan provides his readers with a brief account of the history of the Netherlands. Devoting a single paragraph to the seventeenth and eighteenth centuries, he focuses on the nineteenth century, in which the country became an independent nation-state (1813). In a few pages he treats the changing state-church relationships, the changing political landscape, the genesis of the working classes, and the increasing secularization.[5] His cursory overview leads up to a brief description of a characteristic that was peculiar to Dutch society during a large part of the twentieth century, namely the division along socioreligious boundaries (*verzuiling*).[6] More extensively, he describes the precursors of the Pentecostal movement, identifying five movements that exerted considerable influence on the budding Pentecostal movement in the early twentieth century, namely the Salvation Army, the Christian Apostolic Church in Zion (founded by A. J. Dowie), the healing movement, the Holiness Movement, and the revival in Wales.[7] Some of these precursors possessed a profound and intense eschatological fervor that cohered well with two core teachings of the fourfold gospel proclaimed by the Pentecostals: Jesus as the coming King and the outpouring of the Spirit in the so-called latter days.[8]

Little did the pioneers of the Dutch Pentecostal movement suspect that the end-time movement they were part of would still be around in the twenty-first century. They lived with the strong conviction that Jesus's second coming was imminent. The outpouring of the Spirit was itself a sign of that. This is hardly surprising in view of their literal reading of Peter's sermon on the Day of Pentecost, with its strong eschatological overtones: "It will be in the last days that I will pour out my Spirit upon all flesh" (cf. Acts 2:16–17). They combined this prophetic verse with the passage about the "early and the latter rain" (cf. James 5:7–8). Theirs was the conviction that the fulfillment of Joel's prophecy, cited by Peter, was the "early rain," while the outpouring of the Spirit that they who lived in the last days experienced was, in fact, the "latter rain." Polman's writings as well as other early Pentecostal authors are brimming with references to this idea.

A Historical Overview of Imminent (Apocalyptic) Eschatology

Before treating the ups and downs of Pentecostalism's eschatological sentiments, we must take a closer look at apocalyptic eschatology's ups and downs in the history of Christianity. Jesus preached the coming of God's kingdom—already a profoundly eschatological notion at that time.[9] On the one side, Jesus's ministry implied the breaking in of an eschatological reality into present existence; on the other hand, its full realization was still unrealized.[10] This state of affairs gave rise to both the realized and futuristic conceptions of eschatology. However, already in the first century the church's kerygma loses the apocalyptic flavor[11] that many modern exegetes find in Jesus's message.[12] As the Second Coming is delayed and eschatological fervor diminishes, the historical and cosmological aspects recede into the background. The focus then comes to fall primarily on questions pertaining to personal eschatology.[13]

Subsequent to Constantine's conversion (AD 313), this tendency becomes even more pronounced. By then, the many cosmological aspects of so many Jewish apocalypses (wisdom elements, such as calendar issues, and heavenly journeys) have largely vanished from Christian apocalyptic thought. The void is filled with speculations concerning the nature and the time at which the Millennium will come (Rev. 20:1–6). In effect, Christ's coming becomes synonymous with the end of history as we know it or, worse, the end of the world, hence the panic at various severe historical crises throughout the Middle Ages and later times. In some of these, the eschatology found in the Scriptures combined with apocalyptic modes of thinking to form an intense spirituality. This potent mix sometimes gave rise to political action on the part of those who strove to overturn the status quo.[14] Mainstream Christianity usually quenched these revolutionary apocalyptic movements, preferring more quietist types of eschatology that generally focus on personal salvation. After Constantine, then, when the persecuted Christian minority gradually became Christendom and the dominating political power, the conviction grew that God's kingdom had become a historical reality at last. No longer were the apocalyptic-eschatological passages in Scripture interpreted literally. Instead, they were explained with the help of the allegorical method, which is eminently suited to the often vivid images found in apocalyptic texts.[15]

Many centuries later, the optimistic spirit of the nineteenth century gave rise to a tendency to adopt a non-eschatological interpretation of the Christian message as a whole. The thought that culture (almost a synonym for Christianity) steered humankind in the direction of God's kingdom was widely held in academic theology. Education, economic development, discoveries, and inventions—all of this would, when guided by the light of the gospel, bring about God's kingdom. In German theology, this train of thought is usually called *Kulturprotestantismus*.[16] Important representatives of this school were Albrecht Ritschl and Ernst Troeltsch, who propagated a *Vermittlungstheologie*, i.e., a theology serving as an interface between the biblical message and the modern world.[17] Yet, around the turn of the century, Johannes Weiss and Albert Schweitzer concluded that Jesus's own message, instead of being an interface, was highly confrontational due to its (apocalyptic) eschatological character and, hence, was very unlike the German theology at the time.[18] In the aftermath of the Great War (1914–1918), their contention became (more) widespread, and a renewed interest in eschatology resulted.[19]

Now, before we get ahead of ourselves, we should return to the early half of the nineteenth century. In Britain, groups of religious dissenters embraced the eschatological motifs that had been neglected by the theological and religious establishment. England, which was rapidly industrializing, saw a great divide emerging between a wealthy elite and a large proletariat of industrial laborers that existed in poverty and unhealthy living conditions. If the adage that "social ferment arises when people can imagine a better life" contains a kernel of truth, then the masses of Britain (as well as in other European nations with similar circumstances) were ready to embrace any message that would engender hope. In this climate, the futurist eschatology of John Nelson Darby (1800–1882) found a favorable hearing,[20] which (for different reasons) also became popular in Holiness circles in the United States. The American Holiness Movement is, of course, an important element of the matrix that gave birth not just to American but also to Dutch Pentecostalism, and from which both inherited their eschatology.[21]

The Impact of Premillennialism on (Early) Pentecostalism

A number of early Pentecostal leaders formerly belonged to religious groups that firmly held some apocalyptically colored eschatological convictions. Especially the influence of Darby's premillennialism strongly influenced the Anglo-American Holiness Movement, the *Scofield Reference Bible* (1909) being its most effective vehicle.[22] This reference source was widely used by Pentecostal preachers and authors.

The story of how Darby's premillennialism replaced the postmillennialistic views of the American Holiness Movement, which at first taught that Christ's return would take place at the end of the Millennium, has been told at length by Ernest Sandeen.[23] Due to a number of disappointing events in the United States (notably the Civil War), this last eschatological paradigm quickly lost its appeal. The conception in which Christ would return at the beginning of the Millennium was actively promoted and increasingly gained credibility. The new teaching asserted that during the Millennium, Christ would reign on behalf of God the Father. Yet before Christ's second coming, a number of events (the "signs of the times") would have to take place. Among these, the following stand out: the preaching of the gospel throughout the world, the restoration of Israel, the rebuilding of the temple, and the coming of Antichrist, culminating in the Great Tribulation. This, of course, is the short version of the eschatological scenario; details are added according to one's persuasion. In general, it is fair to say that the more detailed the scenarios of future events, the greater the disagreement among the Bible expositors. Often in premillennialism this leads to an inordinate preoccupation with end-time charts. One of the major points of contention is the moment of the Rapture, the gathering up into heaven of the saints living at some juncture of end-time events. The big question, then, is: Will it take place seven years before Christ's (public) Parousia or halfway through the Great Tribulation? Darby taught that it will occur before the rule of Antichrist and the period of God's wrath—that is, before the Great Tribulation.[24] For him this constituted the end of the New Testament era because at that point God will resume His original design with the people of Israel. According to Darby and many in his wake, Israel is the central player in the drama of the so-called end times.[25]

Partly due to the influence of the periodical of the Maranatha movement, *Het Zoeklicht*, which Johannes de Heer (1866–1961)[26] published from 1919 onward, many Dutch Pentecostals of an earlier generation strongly held these views. Today, Dutch Pentecostals—insofar as they still concern themselves with these issues—would subscribe to one of the end-time scenarios outlined above. There are, however, dissenting views. In the following paragraphs I will first recount the views of two pioneering figures and in the subsequent paragraph I will examine some alternative voices within the Dutch Pentecostalism.[27]

Diversity in Eschatological Views Within Dutch Pentecostalism

Many of the early Dutch Pentecostal leaders came from circles that were profoundly influenced by Darbyist eschatology, with or without its corollary, dispensationalism. This is the case with both Polman and Margaretha A. Alt.[28] Both of these pioneers may be regarded as representatives of "old Pentecostalism."[29] Gerrit R. Polman (1868–1932), the founder of the movement in Holland, together with his wife, Wilhelmine Blekkink, had lived for some time in Zion City near Chicago (Dowie's settlement and headquarters). Margaretha A. Alt (1883–1962),[30] who pioneered over a dozen congregations in the Dutch Indies before returning to Holland, was a former Seventh Day Baptist.[31] Both of them adhered to premillennialism, expecting the speedy return of Jesus. Yet neither of them set a date for the awaited Parousia.[32]

Polman named the periodical he published from 1908 onward *Spade regen* (Latter rain), a title bristling with eschatological overtones. The second issue of the periodical (August 1908) opens with an exposition by A. B. Simpson in which this expression is explained. In it, Simpson identifies recent revivals with the eschatological outpouring of the Spirit that would precede the Second Coming, a theme that regularly recurs in *Spade Regen*. By and large, Polman seems to follow Darby in his eschatological teachings.[33] Interestingly, Polman links the expectation of Christ's speedy return to being filled with God's Spirit. He attributes the prevailing lack of interest in the return of Christ to spiritual dryness and even a grieving of the Spirit—in short, to not being filled with the Spirit.[34] This point is underscored by a reference to the image of the wise and the foolish maidens (Matt. 25:1–13). World War I and its aftermath brought about an intensification of end-time expectations. The Bolshevik revolution in Russia, the British Mandate in Palestine, the creation of the League of Nations, and other global events were interpreted as signs of Christ's imminent coming. Although Polman expressly rejected the practice of date-setting, he nevertheless wrote in 1925 that he had not expected the Lord to tarry so long.[35]

The name of Margaretha Alt's periodical, *Gouden schoven* (Golden sheaves), contains a reference to the expected harvest of souls preceding the return of Christ. This is not surprising, seeing that her *Bijbelstudie voor zelfonderricht* is permeated with dispensationalist eschatology.[36] This shows particularly in her treatment of the Book of Revelation. John's Apocalypse, she holds, must be explained as literally as possible. She does this particularly from chapter 4 onward—that is, those chapters that in her understanding contain revelations concerning the time subsequent to the church's rapture. In line with Darby, she asserts that between Revelation 3 and 4, there is a clear division, whereby the preceding chapters deal with the church of all times. The Great Tribulation, then, to which "the saints" will be subjected from chapter 4 onward applies not to the Spirit-filled believers of the true church of the latter days. They are new converts. Moreover, the seven churches to which the letters in chapters 2 and 3 are addressed are a typological prophecy concerning the different periods of the church's existence between Christ's ascension and His Parousia.[37] Thus, Ephesus represents the years AD 50 to 100, in which the church loses her first love. Similarly, Smyrna represents the period in which the church is persecuted (100–310); Pergamum represents the period in which church and state merge (311–600); Thyatira signifies the full blooming of power (600–1500); Sardes represents the period in which Protestantism comes about and later becomes a dead religion (1500–1800); Philadelphia, to the contrary, represents the true church of the end times (1800 until the Rapture); and Laodicea, finally, represents the false church of the end times (1800 until the Parousia). This dichotomy between these last two "churches" clearly stands out in her book—a sharp distinction between the true church, symbolized by the "wise maidens" in the parable of Matthew 25 whose lamps are filled with oil and who have a jar with oil in reserve, and the other Christians, the "foolish maidens," whose lamps are burning but who lack a backup container. Christ, "*moesje*," Alt believes, will return in secret "to gather His own unto Himself" (cf. 1 Thess. 4:13–18). Then, seven years later, after the Great Tribulation, He will return in public, the Parousia. As there are two returns of the Lord, so there will be two resurrections, one for the believers and one for those whose names are not written in the Book of Life (cf. Rev. 20:15). The latter will—after the last Judgment—die a second death.[38]

In line with the Pentecostal pioneers, some more publications may be noted. When in 1967 the Broederschap van Pinkstergemeenten, the oldest Pentecostal denomination in the country, was reorganized, it aligned itself with the American Assemblies of God.[39] For the occasion, a new brochure was published in which the denomination presented itself. Its title, "Het zal zijn in de laatste dagen,"[40] pointed to a self-understanding in which pneumatology is paired to eschatology. This is confirmed by looking at the statement of faith, which was drawn upon the insistence of the new American partner and was an adaptation of the "Fundamental Truths" of the Assemblies of God.[41] Of the fourteen articles in the Dutch version, no less than four deal with eschatology.[42] Article 11 contains a statement on the future plight of the church; article 12 speaks about the millennial reign of Christ; article 13 pertains to the Last Judgment; and article 14 deals with the new heavens and the new earth. The denomination's leading eschatologist, Wim Embregts, set forth the classical position in several publications, most importantly in his commentary on the Book of Revelation.[43] Though this book is thorough and shies away from extreme views, the author is quite dismissive of any alternative reading of John's Apocalypse. True to his tradition, he never speculates about a date for the Second Coming, but the inclusion of newspaper clippings clearly suggests that the days in which the readers are living are, in fact, the last days.[44] Indeed, the author proves to be a staunch adherent of premillennialism and pretribulationism positions. The Book of Revelation is interpreted in a strictly linear fashion, while the Bible as a whole is read literally. Moreover, whenever biblical texts seem to paint a different picture of the future, the author takes recourse to a harmonizing approach in which the different sequences of events are placed on a continuous timeline.

Dissenting Views

Pentecostalism is far from theologically homogeneous. It is hardly possible to find a theological subject about which exists broad doctrinal consensus. Eschatology is not an exception.

Elisabeth Hoekendijk-La Rivière

In the late 1950s, a new Pentecostal movement emerged: *Stromen van Kracht*.[45] It held another position concerning the Lord's return. According to the movement's most influential writer, Elisabeth Hoekendijk-La Rivière,[46] the Bible teaches only one return of Jesus, before the Millennium but after the Great Tribulation. Hence, the church will live through this period of ordeals, which is conceived of as an intensification of present oppression and a period of testing and sifting the believers. It will become clear just then who the truly faithful believers are. During this period, the church will learn what it means to remain faithful under extreme pressure. Spirit baptism is necessary in order to cope with the Great Tribulation. However, as the Bible says, those days will be shortened on account of the faithful.

Jo van den Brink

Another influential writer, J. E. van den Brink, representing *Kracht van Omhoog*,[47] yet another brand of Dutch Pentecostalism, sets forth his views on eschatology in a commentary on the Book of Revelation called *De gemeente in de eindtijd*. His expositions of the text are much more symbolic than is common practice within Dutch Pentecostalism. The apocalypse, he asserts, sheds light on that which takes place in heavenly places, the unseen world. Hence, the only way to arrive at a correct understanding is to proceed spiritually—that is, with knowledge of the spirit world.[48] His hermeneutical key to unlocking the hidden meaning in biblical texts is the movement's own particular teaching concerning the heavenly kingdom.[49] Central to this highly dualistic teaching is the battle between God's forces and the satanic and demonic forces that rages in heavenly spheres. The fact that this teaching is finally being taught is itself a sign of the last times.[50] His book may be dealing with the final days, but the polarity he poses does not so much move along the horizontal axis (present versus future), but much more along the vertical axis (opposing earthly and heavenly realities).[51] Also singular is his assertion that the future only begins with the breaking of the seventh seal (Rev. 8:1). There the wise are separated from the foolish maidens.[52] Everything that is written prior to Revelation 8 must be explained as figurative characterizations of historical events. His "spiritual exposition" concerns the "walk of Christians in the heavenly spheres"[53]—the "high road," as his followers were fond of saying. Of God's Spirit he says that it is "the power that stems from the unseen world,"[54] which Christians need in order to maintain themselves in the last days. Believers are not to be raptured to heaven. To the contrary, the church (i.e., the sons of God) is the elite that will be victorious in the final struggle and is only then gathered unto God in heaven.[55] Also unique is his assertion that the Great Tribulation differs from all kind of oppression since the beginning of time. It differs in terms of intensity, but above all as it consists of a direct assault by evil spirits.[56] In van den Brink's view, the apocalypse relates in images how the true church reaches perfection, whereas the "false church, Babylon (treacherous Jerusalem), crumbles under the attacks of the forces of darkness, which she cannot withstand. Believers have to leave this false church."[57] Nevertheless, he refuses to identify the false church with any existing denomination, claiming that the influence of "Babylon" is found in many groups and churches. "Whoever qualifies a denomination as 'false' will immediately discover that there are still many real children of God in it. Whoever qualifies a church as 'true', will find out that in its midst are nominal Christians and hypocrites."[58]

Mystic and even gnostic tendencies may be discerned in van den Brink's approach, as said knowledge of the spiritual world is crucial not just for understanding the Book of Revelation properly but for being a Christian. Moreover, being inhabitants of the heavenly realm, believers are called to wage war there against the demonic forces.[59]

Huib Zegwaart

Even though I belong to the classical Pentecostal tradition, my position on eschatology can be construed as a dissenting voice. Toward the end of the 1980s, I wrote an article about the theological significance for Pentecostals of millennial beliefs.[60] In it I waged a battle on two fronts—first, against those British preachers who dismiss millennialism as theological ballast, and second, against literalist understandings (with dispensationalist leanings). Positively, I pleaded for a real appreciation of apocalypse as a literary genre. Through a phenomenological and historical analysis of the function of eschatological images, we can reclaim them as sources for proclamation and celebration. Eschatological images engender hope and provide a sense of direction for Christian (socio-ethical) activity in the world. And they tell us that God crowns history with His Messianic kingdom and remains faithful to His promises not just to Israel, but to His creation itself. This plea, I fear, is thirty years later still relevant, since it went largely unheeded.[61]

Recession of Eschatological Fervor?

Since the 1980s—as Jean-Jacques Suurmond noted[62]—eschatological fervor within Dutch Pentecostalism is waning, becoming relatively silent on the topic of the imminent return of Christ. This, of course, begs the question: Now what? If the speedy return of Christ belongs to the core of Pentecostal spirituality, as D. William Faupel maintains, what will this development entail for the future of Pentecostalism, for the development of its identity?[63]

Several strategies spring to mind. First, one may attempt to rekindle eschatological fervor. This was done in 1993, when *Parakleet* published an article by George O. Wood on eschatology.[64] In it Wood sought to reiterate the classic Pentecostal conviction that Christ's second coming is closely related to world evangelism. In this approach, the marginalization of eschatology is resisted, but whether this is effective is open to questioning. In my view, attempting that too often entails the risk of losing one's credibility when the Parousia fails to actually take place.

Second, one might accept the marginalization of eschatology as a fact. As we saw, this happened before, and that process seems somewhat inevitable. If that is indeed the case, several things may happen, or can be done:

- Eschatological fervor is replaced by other concerns, be it church growth programs, trends in worship, a greater stress on the charismata, or, in some Pentecostal circles in the Netherlands, the ministry of deliverance from demonic forces. This builds on historical precedents in both *Stromen van Kracht* and especially *Kracht van Omhoog*.

- Eschatological fervor is stronger or weaker according to the felt presence of disconcerting situations arising in world politics. This builds on the fact that the eschatological texts in Scripture are given a heightened or lessened relevance as the situation demands.
- A deeper meaning in overtly (apocalyptic) eschatological passages in Scripture can be brought out through allegorical interpretation. In this way, texts relating to the temporal axis are interpreted along the spatial axis.[65] In that case, one could easily move in the direction of a gnosticizing reinterpretation of eschatological texts and theological themes.
- Eschatological motifs in both Scripture and Christian theology are theologically grappled with in a manner not unlike that of Jürgen Moltmann, Wolfhart Pannenberg, or Friedrich-Wilhelm Marquardt. From my earlier publication, it should be obvious that this alternative is what I prefer.[66] However, since this approach entails serious intellectual work, there is a possible tension with the character of Pentecostalism as an emo-religion.

In Conclusion

Eschatology (including its apocalyptic flavor) remains an integral part of the Bible. As a consequence, its place in a biblically oriented theology is assured, while it can be dormant on the level of the lived faith of believers in a particular time frame or part of the world. Yet since it is also so deeply ingrained in the fabric of the Pentecostal faith, there is a risk leaving it at that. On balance, it seems to me that engaging in creative theological work and, hence, with Pentecostal identity, will be the best option for the future of the global Pentecostal movement…should the Lord tarry.

Chapter 10

Pentecostalism in France: A Multiform and Ecumenical Movement of the Spirit?[1]

Raymond Pfister

THE HISTORICAL ROOTS of the French Pentecostal movements are manifold yet primarily Protestant and European. To be mentioned are the more distant, at times overlooked, Catholic roots of the French mystical tradition (sixteenth to seventeenth centuries)[2] that emphasized both the importance of experience with God and prayer life. A significant French Protestant prophetic movement lasted from 1688 to at least 1715, with several hundreds of French prophets in the Cévennes region in southern France.

The major figure among the forerunners of European Pentecostalism—not only in German speaking countries, but also in France—is the "father of Pietism" Philipp Jacob Spener (1635–1705), born and educated in Alsace. Best known for his classic work *Pia Desideria* (1675), he made a major contribution to the reorientation of theological thinking within Protestantism. During the seventeenth and eighteenth centuries, Pietism started as an inner-church movement with its own organization within the German Lutheran Church. In many ways it can be seen as a forerunner of the modern Evangelical-Charismatic movement, as it promoted both an individual experience of faith (through conversion/new birth) and a renewal of community life (through committed small circles of believers, the *collegia pietatis*).[3]

More recently, French Pentecostalism is variously indebted to

Wesleyan thought for its focus on Scripture as the rule of faith, as well as individual aspects of its treatment of salvation (*Ordo Salutis*), entire sanctification (Christian perfection), and baptism in the Holy Spirit.[4]

Pentecostal Protestantism: Pieces of a Complex Jigsaw Puzzle

Defining itself as a movement of the Spirit, Pentecostalism has developed into a complex and open-ended phenomenon without definite boundaries. During its century-long history, Protestant Pentecostalism in France has undergone significant changes, moving away from national, rather monolithic structures (until 1968, it was almost exclusively identified with one single denomination: the Assemblies of God) to an extraordinary diversity of congregations, denominations, and networks, more and more global in character, yet certainly not without tensions. The following traces these developments, including in charismatic, neo-Pentecostal, and Oneness directions.

Internal growth: French Assemblies of God/Gypsy Mission

The Pentecostal experience of Spirit baptism and charismatic gifts within French Protestantism was initially hoping to bring new spiritual fervor to all Protestant churches, be they multitudinist (e.g., Reformed churches) or professing (e.g., Baptist churches) in character. Historically, the immediate background of the story of French Protestant Pentecostalism[5] is located in the British Isles and is to be understood against the background of British Holiness-Keswick spirituality ("higher life") and British Pentecostal missionary fervor. Early Pentecostal Anglican pioneer Alexander Boddy (1854–1930) visited France in October 1909. He shared about the Pentecostal message on the subject of "full salvation, including the Baptism of the Holy Ghost with Signs."[6] This led eventually to the invitation of other preachers from England, in particular healing evangelist Smith Wigglesworth (1859–1947) in the early 1920s. Most significant was the ministry of Pentecostal pioneer Douglas Scott (1900–1967), whose essential contribution led to the birth of the Assemblies of God in France.

Founded in 1932 in Le Havre, the Assemblées de Dieu de France (hereafter ADD for French Assemblies of God) became quickly a significant, homegrown evangelistic and missionary-minded movement. Within a few decades, a story of unparalleled growth made them the main representative of Protestant Pentecostalism in France. Intense evangelistic meetings and healing missions coupled with church-planting initiatives occurred in the northwestern and southeastern parts of France. Emerging leaders included individuals from various European and denominational backgrounds. For example, Pierre Nicolle was French and Baptist, Christo Domoutchief was Romanian and Orthodox, and Ove Falg was Danish and Lutheran. Those developments received international recognition, as witnessed by the Second Pentecostal World Conference organized by David du Plessis (1905–1987), which met in Paris in 1949. With no formal organic link with their American or British counterparts, the ADD has always remained a strongly autonomous movement.

Despite internal divisions and external opposition, the ADD has remained a strong lay missionary movement. It has established 428 local churches (2014)[7] under the leadership of nearly 480 pastors. There are no official Pentecostal statistics for France,[8] but according to some estimation the ADD has about 42,000 members (baptized by immersion) and reaches altogether between 100,000 and 120,000 people.[9]

Doctrinally, conservative evangelical theology has been largely adopted, while mostly confined to its fundamentalist expression, dispensationalism, and its particular focus on dispensational premillennialism with its pretribulation Rapture postulate. It has allowed for a number of minor modifications to that system of interpretation in order to accommodate its Pentecostal experience and reading of the Book of Acts. It usually advocates a two-stage understanding of salvation: conversion and Spirit baptism, with glossolalia as accompanying "initial sign."

The ADD maintains various national ministries (e.g., media, children, youth, family, home missions). Its foreign missions department involves over forty missionaries on various mission fields, mostly in French-speaking West Africa. While its activities led to continuing growth, the emergence of other Pentecostal and Pentecostal-like denominations[10]—partly in the form of divisions and separations—happened for various reasons (e.g., doctrinal disagreements, moral shortcomings, leadership conflicts, rejection of monolithic denominationalism, call for more pluralism and diversity).

The French Gypsy Pentecostal revival that started in Brittany in the early 1950s is still today the most important form of "ethnic Pentecostalism" in France.[11] It traces its roots to the ministry of French ADD pastor Clément Le Cossec (1921–2001), who became the *gadjo*[12] founder of the Evangelical Gypsy Mission of France (also called Life and Light Mission). The newly born Gypsy mission became most naturally an integral part of the French ADD until 1968. That year, the French Pentecostal Gypsies decided to establish their own autonomous organization in order to meet the needs of their historical and cultural specificity often exposed to discrimination and rejection in French society. Although they have kept their own cultural identity, the Pentecostal Gypsies remain in many ways, in doctrine and in practice, a typical expression of French Protestant Pentecostalism, very similar to the ADD.

According to Pastor Zanellato, coordinator of the Gypsies and Travellers International Evangelical Fellowship (GATIEF), there are about 140,000 baptized adult members (about one-third of the Gypsy population in France) and 1,460 preachers/pastors (2006).[13] This would make the Pentecostal Gypsies the strongest Pentecostal church in France. About thirty missionaries are at work in Eastern Europe, Russia, Central Asia, and India. Even though they remain a nomadic people, there are 221 Gypsy congregations listed in major French towns and cities.

Sociological as well as ecumenical reasons explain its membership of the Fédération Protestante de France (hereafter FPF for French Protestant Federation) since 1975. It has helped give a new sense of personal belonging and acceptance to people who are treated as second-class citizens because of a lifestyle that is colliding with the habitus of sedentary life. Cooperation with the French authorities has helped with organizing specific and temporary events, some of which are large conferences ("conventions") that gather hundreds, if not thousands, of caravans.[14] There is a strong emphasis on conversion and healing, evangelism, church planting, and leadership training, but also on musical discourse and social justice.

External growth (direct UK/US links): Apostolic Church, Church of God, Elim Pentecostal Churches, and Foursquare Church

First established in Britain in 1916 by Daniel P. Williams (1882–1947) as a result of the Welsh revival (1904–1905), the Apostolic Church started in France in 1925, which makes it chronologically the first Protestant Pentecostal denomination. It was also the first Pentecostal denomination to join the FPF in 1972. Early missionary work included sending Welsh evangelist Thomas Roberts (1902–1983) to France in 1926. They now have a total of twenty-six congregations in France reaching between 2,200 and 2,500 people.[15]

The Church of God, with international headquarters in Cleveland, Tennessee, is one of the largest and oldest Pentecostal denominations in the world (1886). It was first established in France with the help of French pastor André Weber (1929–), a relative of Pentecostal pioneer Pierre Nicolle (ADD). He established the Eglise de Dieu en France in 1959, with headquarters in Troyes (Aube). However, the denomination first came to France by way of Germany through the ministry of Hermann Lauster (1901–1964), a German-born immigrant who returned to his homeland in September 1936 after having experienced the baptism of the Holy Spirit while living in the United States. It was only in 1957 that Lauster expanded his evangelistic ministry beyond southern Germany into the French province of Alsace.

Churches would be founded mostly in rural areas until 1982, when a strategic change was implemented in favor of an expansion into larger cities, mostly in the metropolis of greater Paris. Today, the Church of God has a total of seventeen congregations in France reaching about 1,400 people in their worship services. Unlike the ADD, it is not a national autonomous movement, as its leadership remains accountable to an international executive council of the Church of God located in the United States.

Founded in the United States in 1923 by Aimee S. McPherson (1890–1944), the International Church of the Foursquare Gospel did not become established in France until the 1980s. Founded in 1983 without lasting success, it was not until a relaunch in 1994 that Foursquare actually developed its work in France. In 2014, a total of thirty-two congregations reach altogether 2,162 people (including 1,391 members).[16]

The Elim Pentecostal Church is a large British Pentecostal denomination founded by George Jeffreys (1889–1962) in 1915. His evangelistic ministry abroad brought about an inner-church movement called Union de Réveil (Revival Society) in the 1930s in the Swiss Reformed Church. But most of the participants opted for a new Pentecostal church with a congregational structure not linked to the British Elim Churches. In 1935, Geneva became the birthplace of the first Eglise Evangélique de Réveil (Revival Evangelical Church). The French branch started only in 1957 in Villeurbanne (Rhône-Alps region) and counts today nineteen congregations reaching possibly over 2,000 people.

It is only in more recent years (since the late 1990s) that four French Elim churches have become associated with the British Elim Churches. Kensington Temple London City Church, one of the largest Elim churches in England, has had for a number of years an ongoing missionary interest in France. As part of their network, they started in the suburbs of the French capital the Temple de Paris (2003).

The Union des Eglises évangéliques de Réveil, the Union des Eglises évangéliques Elim de France, and the Union des Églises Protestantes Foursquare France have all become full members of the FPF.

The inner-church renewal: United Protestant Church (Reformed-Lutheran) and Baptist churches

Did the modern Charismatic movement follow chronologically a so-called first-wave Pentecostal movement? This is usually considered to be an established fact in much of Pentecostal historiography. How accurate is such a paradigm? Walter Hollenweger points out that there existed in France "a very old and highly indigenous charismatic movement" at least thirty years before its North American counterpart.[17]

It was within the French Reformed Church that Louis Dallière (1897–1976) became a key leader of the Pentecostal movement in France. It was in 1930, when listening to British evangelist Douglas Scott, that he came into contact with the Pentecostal message and experience. He welcomed this new Pentecostal renewal in his parish of Charmes-sur-Rhône (Ardèche) and encouraged his colleagues to do the same, hoping that it would bring about a revival within the French Reformed Church. He met great opposition, especially from French revivalists and fundamentalists, while trying to make a case through various writings for the theological and ecclesiological orthodoxy of the movement.

Both the national and regional synods of the Reformed Church in France were challenged by increased tensions over the Pentecostal views, particularly the one on believer's baptism by immersion. In Dallière, the French Charismatic movement had found a most talented theologian who was able to articulate with depth and breadth the manifold dimensions and ramifications of Pentecostal spirituality.

Soon after World War II, Dallière's ministry would concentrate on the Prayer Union movement (Union de Prière, formed in 1946) based in Charmes. Thomas Roberts left the Apostolic Church and became the pastor of an independent Reformed church in Paris in 1936. With his friend Louis Dallière, he became involved with the Union de Prière. But he was also associated with La Porte Ouverte (The Open Door), founded as a free Bible school in 1956 by missionary Albert Burkhardt (1911–1999). It became a Charismatic mission agency as well as an ecumenical retreat center, offering seminars and conferences to Evangelical Protestants and an increasing number of Catholics. La Porte Ouverte hosted the first interdenominational Charismatic convention in 1971 with David du Plessis, J. Rodman Williams (US Presbyterian theologian), Albert de Monléon (French Catholic/Dominican priest), and Kilian McDonnell (US Catholic/Benedictine priest).

From 1963, Roberts felt particularly called to a traveling ministry while being very involved in the organization of major Charismatic conferences in various French cities. In the 1970s, along with other key Charismatic leaders, he spoke to thousands of Christians at many Charismatic and ecumenical gatherings, particularly those at the Centre Chrétien in Ganières (Gard), a retreat center promoting evangelism and Christian unity. The most significant event during those years was the "Pentecost Over Europe" gathering (1982), the first major European Charismatic conference, held in Strasbourg, one of Europe's capitals, with some twenty thousand participants.

Already in the nineteenth century, the early developments of the Baptist churches in northern France were greatly impacted by the teaching of Edward Irving (1792–1834), founder of the Catholic Apostolic Church. Between 1830 and 1850, his views on charismatic gifts (including glossolalia and prophecy) and an eschatological apocalyptic-oriented ecumenism were very successful.

In the twentieth century, when the Pentecostal message reached the Baptist churches in the 1930s, some joined the ADD while others remained within their denominations. The Charismatic movement in French Baptist churches would progressively have an impact on many of their congregations (40–50 percent).

Pastor Jules Thobois (1922–2004), along with some other young Baptists ministers, was instrumental in a revival in Northern France lasting into the 1960s. Thobois experienced Spirit baptism in 1947. Already in 1952, the French Baptist Federation adopted an official resolution allowing Charismatic teaching and practice in their midst.

After having been a Baptist pastor in various churches, Jules

Thobois succeeded Thomas Roberts in 1963. In only two decades, the congregation grew from some eighty members (early 1970s) to over eight hundred (late 1980s), plus another few hundred in five daughter congregations. After a visit to Pastor Yonggi Cho's megachurch in Seoul (1980), Thobois successfully translated the Korean Pentecostal model of church growth through house cells into the French context. The success story of the congregation, now called Communauté du Point du Jour, gave it a national standing and reputation as a vital element of the French Protestant Charismatic movement.

The neo-Pentecostal/neo-Charismatic churches

It was in the second half of the twentieth century, mostly in the 1980s and 1990s, that a large number of Charismatic churches came into existence. Some were all-new ventures, while others merely redefined their identity and affiliation. That happened for a number of reasons: (1) missionary and evangelistic projects of independent neo-Pentecostal or neo-Charismatic churches from denominations based in Africa, Asia, and North and South America; (2) divisions, exclusions, or defections from earlier Protestant Pentecostal churches (mostly from the ADD); (3) strategic development of those new neo-Pentecostal or neo-Charismatic churches; and (4) personal initiatives.

Most significant among those newer churches is the Fédération des Églises du Plein Évangile en Francophonie (FEPEF, or Federation of Full Gospel Churches of France). From the 1960s onward, pastors from different Pentecostal/Charismatic churches across France came together in order to build relationships. Well aware of their differences, they shared a common aspiration: to be enriched by way of a spiritual and fraternal covenant. What was at first an informal fellowship of pastors became eventually the FEPEF.[18] There are ninety congregations in France with approximatively eight thousand active members. It is particularly noteworthy that more than a quarter of them are part of a megachurch found in the agglomeration of Mulhouse (Alsace): Porte Ouverte Chrétienne

(Christian Open Door), the largest autochthonous Pentecostal congregation in France.

The Communion des Églises de l'Espace Francophone is a native Charismatic church-planting movement, mostly located in the southwest of France, that developed during the 1980s and 1990s. Various specialized ministries (training, worship, and mission) were established during those years. Church leadership has both a local (pastors, elders, and deacons) and a regional (apostolic teams) dimension. Their activities include involvement in community projects fighting poverty and oppression (e.g., food-bank network, work among refugees, and asylum seekers). They count a total membership of about one thousand members in forty congregations.

In the 1990s, pastor-evangelist Vincent Esterman started a Charismatic contemporary church-planting movement that eventually became the Union d'Assemblées Protestantes en Mission. They have now twenty-four congregations with about fifteen hundred members. Past president pastor Georges Michel has been the general secretary of the FPF since July 2014.

That the history of Pentecostalism is characterized by a succession of differentiation (moving apart) and rapprochement (moving closer) is clearly illustrated by the story of a great many (mostly smaller) congregations. A large number of Pentecostal and Charismatic churches are independent, meaning they remain either without any particular affiliation or are only loosely linked to a network of churches.[19] French sociologist Jean-Paul Willaime estimates that a new worship place is opened every eleventh day in France.[20]

An unconventional chapter: Oneness Pentecostalism

The United Pentecostal Church (UPC) is a US Oneness Pentecostal denomination formed in 1945. Many doctrinal beliefs (e.g., Spirit baptism, with speaking in tongues as the initial sign) and standards of behavior (e.g., modesty expressed in strict rules of conduct and dress code) held by the UPC reflect the North American Holiness-Pentecostal tradition of the early twentieth century. Established in France since 1979, the Fédération des Églises Pentecôtistes Unies de

France has twelve churches, twenty-eight licensed ministers, a Bible school, and over one thousand constituents (2004).[21] The distinctive doctrines of the UPC include a non-Trinitarian view of God and a water baptismal practice "in the name of Jesus," which is seen as the only correct formula (based on Acts 10:48). In the absence of dialogue with Trinitarian Pentecostalism in France, isolation has prevailed and differences have remained largely unresolved.

Roman Catholic Pentecostalism: The Other side of the (Same) Coin

It may come as a surprise, but Catholic Pentecostalism in France is overwhelmingly stronger than all of the Protestant Pentecostal and Charismatic churches put together. According to the statistics published by Barrett and Johnson in 2002, the Catholic Charismatic Renewal (CCR) could represent over 80 percent of French Pentecostalism. The date of its origins may be traced to 1971, when two Catholics among two hundred Protestants attended the first interconfessional Charismatic convention sponsored by the Union de Prière de Charmes, a Charismatic expression within the Reformed Church. In 1973, the pendulum was swinging as Charismatic ecumenism reached new peaks: Catholics grew from one-third (two hundred Catholics alongside four hundred Protestants in July at La Porte Ouverte) to over half of the participants (in November at Viviers, Ardèche). After that, Catholics became dominant, with a movement and momentum of their own, as witnessed by the Charismatic convention at Lyon (1977), which had only one hundred Protestants and ten thousand Catholics.[22]

Protestant Pentecostals were caught by surprise and reacted at first with mixed feelings of caution and confidence. As they kept observing developments within the CCR, they shared what they saw as the "hopes and limitations of the Charismatic movement."[23] As articulated by Le Cossec, there was real hope in "an ecumenism of the Spirit" that would lead to the creation of "an ecumenical Pentecostal movement" with new structures between churches with different confessions. But there was also concern that the Charismatic experience might not, as anticipated, promote a return to biblical teaching.[24] Protestant Pentecostals thought of themselves as the historical expression of Pentecostalism, and they expressed hope that the Holy Spirit would transform Charismatic Catholics into some kind of Protestant Catholics who would turn their back on Catholic dogma and tradition. Instead, the Roman Catholic Church was welcoming the charismatic work of the Holy Spirit by promoting the road of integration, leaving Protestant Pentecostals and Charismatics interpreting such move as repossession.[25] While Catholic Pentecostals were encouraged to see the charismatic structure of the Church in the context of a "Catholic theological culture," Protestant Pentecostals adopted biblical fundamentalism and dispensational hermeneutics together with a revivalist framework for their theology and praxis. It is no secret that the Catholic Charismatic movement is indebted to Protestantism. When in 1974 French Catholic theologian René Laurentin wrote his own introduction about the CCR, it was noticeably entitled *Pentecôtisme chez les Catholiques*, which would be translated in its English edition as *Catholic Pentecostalism* (1977).[26] As has come to be recognized, however, Pentecostalism could not be a mere uncritical import from Protestantism.

The designation *Pentecostal* will be *peu à peu* left to Protestant Pentecostals who first introduced the term before taking full ownership. In France, *Pentecostal* became almost synonymous with *Assemblies of God*.

By 1974, the spread of the Catholic Charismatic movement in France had already produced a great variety of covenant communities with phenomenal growth, established in (mostly) university towns and cities. For example, the Emmanuel community (1972) in Paris, with its evangelistic orientation, had grown from five to five hundred within a year and by 1986 had expanded to six other European countries and four African countries, reaching altogether three thousand members, while the Community of the Beatitudes in Cordes-sur-Ciel (Tarn) was now present on five continents (including nine other European countries) and became particularly renowned for its healing ministry. The Chemin Neuf Community grew out of a prayer group in Lyon (1973) and became known for its ecumenical commitment. It currently has around two thousand members in over thirty countries. Many of the new communities share a threefold renewed interest in Judaism and Israel, in Greek patristic and Orthodox theology/spirituality, and in an ecumenical vision for unity and reconciliation. Jeunesse Lumière (Youth Light) was founded in 1984 by Fr. Daniel-Ange as an International Catholic School of Prayer and Evangelism in southern France.

Despite a certain reluctance at first by the French episcopacy, the formal canonical recognition of many French Charismatic communities by the Vatican will allow their founders to integrate with the ecclesial hierarchy by becoming either deacons (if married) or priests (if single). With well over one thousand registered Charismatic prayer groups in France (1996), CCR has had undeniably a real impact on Catholic parish life, with one-third of its priests now belonging to the Charismatic Renewal legacy.[27]

Messianic Judaism: The Challenge of Non-Pagan Origins of the Church

Jews have been for centuries an ethnic minority in a Gentile-dominated, called-out-of-paganism Christian church that got accustomed to dissonant relationships with its Jewish roots. Jewish believers in Jesus who identify themselves with a Jewish identity and lifestyle are referred to as Messianic Jews. They are predominantly Pentecostal-Charismatic in orientation.

The modern Messianic Jewish movement in France was founded by Paul Ghennassia (1923–2011), a Sephardi Jew from Algeria.[28] Following his Pentecostal experience in 1953, Ghennassia worked with the French Assemblies of God (from 1958 to 1964). When he moved to Paris, he established the Messianic Witness to the People of Israel and, soon after, the Messianic congregation El Bethel (both in 1964).[29]

Other Messianic congregations were founded in French cities with larger Jewish populations, like Marseille, Lyon, Toulouse, and Strasbourg. Their leaders are usually referred to as rabbis or Messianic pastors. They usually hold on to a dual identity of Jew and Christian while making clear that any Jew who becomes a believer in Jesus does not give up his Jewishness or convert to another religion. In order to reach the half million Jewish population in France, the third-largest Jewish community in the world,[30] many Messianic Jews maintain their credibility by keeping a safe distance from Christian churches where various forms of "replacement theology," in which the promises God made to national Israel must be spiritualized in favor of the church, are still prevalent.

The Alliance Francophone des Juifs Messianiques, the French branch of the International Messianic Jewish Alliance, is led by Jacques Elbaz, a French Pentecostal missionary pastor in Israel (affiliated with the ADD) and director of the Francophone Bible Institute in Jerusalem.[31]

What impact will Messianic Jews have on the future of Christian theology? The significance of Messianic Judaism is primarily theological and should not be overshadowed by less impressive statistics. A rediscovery of the Jewishness of the gospel and its implicit eschatology (i.e., awaiting reconciliation and restoration for all of creation) cannot be underestimated. Hocken points out, in particular, three levels of challenges that Gentile (non-Jewish) believers in Jesus have to face if they are going to take seriously the implications of Messianic Jews for the life of the church: (1) respecting their existence means giving up replacement thinking and teaching; (2) respecting their identity means giving up a view of the church that is only Gentile and does not allow it to be joined to a truly Jewish entity; (3) respecting their history means turning away from an attitude of arrogance and embracing a spirit of repentance toward deeply rooted anti-Jewish attitudes.[32]

Multiethnic Pentecostalism: Challenges From a Global Perspective

Immigrants from Francophone Africa and the French Caribbean as well as newcomers from Asia and Latin America have generated a new Christian presence among French-speaking Protestants and Catholics. During the last two decades of the twentieth century, a whole new phenomenon of (mostly) Pentecostal congregations emerged largely unrelated to previous developments of (Protestant or Catholic) Pentecostalism in France. Most of them strongly stress the importance of the Holy Spirit and charismatic gifts, but also deliverance from evil spirits and some form of prosperity. There has been an explosion of churches in urban areas, in particular in the suburbs of Paris, gathering over ten thousand people in their services.[33] The number of African churches in greater Paris is estimated between 250 and 400.[34] They are not necessarily affiliated with an explicit Pentecostal denomination or network.[35]

Two multiethnic megachurches, both located in the Paris metropolitan area, are reaching people in the thousands (mostly Caribbean and African). The largest is Charisma Eglise Chrétienne, with five weekly services and two thousand home groups. Charisma Christian Church is today the largest Christian church in France.[36] Even though their worship services are clearly demonstrating a contemporary, upbeat, and youthful Pentecostal worship style, they define themselves as part of the Evangelical (rather than the Pentecostal) movement.[37] In 1987, a Portuguese pastor couple, Nuno and Natalie Pedro, arrived in France (with an Assemblies of God background and training) and founded the church four years later. Since 2002, they have been establishing new congregations in major cities in France (e.g., Lyon, Marseille, Bordeaux, Strasbourg, and Nantes) and abroad—over seventy new church plants in less than ten years. Their church Bible school, Charisma School of Power, offers a two-year training program to three hundred students. Structured in seventy departments, they offer social services and various other activities related to arts, media, and spiritual exercises.

Paris Christian Centre is another Pentecostal megachurch, founded in the mid-1980s by Indian Pentecostal pastor Selvaraj Rajiah (1952–2011), who first came to Europe to follow a four-year training program at the International Apostolic Bible College in Kolding, Denmark. The congregation, since 2012, is under the leadership of his French widow, Dorothée Rajiah. Self-defined as a Protestant church,[38] it is growing by means of home groups, training programs, and lively worship services.[39]

Among the many Pentecostal immigrant churches established in France since the 1980s, there is the Church of Pentecost in France, with a little over a thousand members. About fifteen congregations located in an urban context, a third of which is in the Paris metropolitan area, are primarily made up of English-speaking Ghanaian migrants who find a renewed sense of community and orientation when facing relative precariousness and instability and yet help with legal and cultural issues of integration. Since 1994, worship services in French are aimed more specifically at French-speaking Africans.[40]

Latin American Pentecostalism is represented by the Universal Church of the Kingdom of God (Igreja Universal do Reino de Deus), a Brazil-based Pentecostal church founded by Edir Macedo in 1977, whose prosperity message is aiming at both spiritual and material well-being, including healing and deliverance (exorcisms). They have been officially established in France since 1992. They have had little success with the native French population and instead are massively joined by migrants, especially Portuguese, Brazilian, and West African.[41]

It is among the African Initiated Churches that one finds the greatest challenge of non-Western inculturation of the church in France. The Nigerian-based Celestial Church of Christ[42] was established in France in 1974 as Eglise du Christianisme Céleste. It is probably the most popular independent Pentecostal church in West Africa, a prophetic church with a complex and elaborate structure. It is mostly in greater Paris that about twenty-five congregations serve as a support community and recruit not only Nigerians, but also people from a diverse ethno-national background. By adopting a cosmology that seems to be in substantial agreement with the traditional religious worldview of the Yoruba, a West African ethnic group,[43] it seems difficult for their particular theology and liturgy to fit into the patterns produced by Western Pentecostalism and Christianity.

The Place of Pentecostalism in Today's French Religious Landscape[44]

The actual use or nonuse of the label *Pentecostal* or *Charismatic* is, in itself, not necessarily indicative of Pentecostal reality. Since French Pentecostal churches do not necessarily or explicitly describe themselves as Pentecostal (or even Charismatic), it has become increasingly difficult to identify them in today's French religious landscape. Pentecostalism in France (with around 1.8 million participants, meaning congregations and communities having adopted Pentecostal-Charismatic practices) is most certainly a multiform and ecumenical movement of the Spirit that includes not only the various expressions of Protestant Pentecostalism (narrower scope), but also Catholic Pentecostalism (extended scope) as well as Messianic Judaism, African Initiated Churches, and Oneness Pentecostalism (marginal scope). Today, Pentecostalism in France needs to be recognized as a Roman Catholic reality (with over one million participants) just as much as a Protestant reality (about half a million).

Historically, terms like *Protestant*, *Pentecostal*, and *Evangelical* have never been synonymous. Some Evangelicals have traditionally been anti-Pentecostal and hostile to its (supposedly or real) *Solus Spiritus* driftings,[45] just as much as some Pentecostals have long been anti-mainline church establishment (Roman Catholic and Protestant alike), and vice versa. By putting a strong emphasis on the visible, voluntary assembly of believers and the priesthood of all believers, a growing number of French Pentecostal denominations are led to see themselves as historically linked to the left wing of the Reformation (Anabaptists). They have chosen to refer to themselves only as Protestant and/or Evangelical and not as Pentecostal, a term that was often the source of past tensions that seems to have kept strong sectarian connotations in French society. At least ten Pentecostal denominations have joined the FPF[46] since the 1970s, but for organizational and theological reasons, the ADD has not (yet) made that step, and such possibility remains a debated question within and without. For some of the African churches, adopting a French Protestant identity has become a major strategic development in order to achieve their objectives of greater integration in the French landscape.

Gypsy pastor Steevo Demeter speaks about being "evangelical with a Pentecostal inclination."[47] It remains unclear how much inclination makes it Pentecostal. Even though it has positively affected many French Evangelicals, it is difficult to assess the impact of the "Pentecostalization" of Protestant Christianity in France. Statistical evidence remains incomplete, even disputed, but Fath suggests that 60 percent of all French Evangelicals are actually Pentecostal or Charismatic in their orientation.[48]

Theological Opportunities and Challenges for Pentecostalism in France

Global Pentecostalism has produced a growing number of theological seminaries in many countries all over the world, as well as a significant number of theologians (with an earned doctorate). This is not yet the case in France despite its otherwise major role in Europe and the world. As the following discussion shows, this lack of development in Pentecostal-Charismatic theological education might be directly linked with the fact that the ministry of the Spirit has generally not been understood as promoting Christian unity, particularly between Protestant Pentecostalism and Catholic Pentecostalism.

Pentecostal-Charismatic theological education in France

The vast majority of French Protestant Pentecostals became Evangelicals with a difference, and they continue to major on a pragmatic approach to mission while manifesting a distinct lack of interest in theological thinking and analysis. The opposite is true for Catholic Pentecostals, whose interest in the life of the Spirit soon benefited from major Catholic theological contributions in the field of pneumatology, such as French Dominican Yves Congar's magnum opus *I Believe in the Holy Spirit* (originally published in French in three volumes between 1979 and 1980).[49]

Because of their reluctance toward academic theological training and a professional clergy, Protestant Pentecostal and Charismatic churches in France have only developed praxis-oriented Bible institutes or discipleship training programs.

Since 1968, the ADD has a Bible school (now called Institut de Théologie Biblique, located south of Bordeaux since 1985) with a two-year program open to all Christians. Its single purpose is to offer discipleship training and prepare for Christian service. An additional third year is focused on vocational development and field experience. Since February 2014, the school serves also as headquarters for Global University France. This is a North American–based Christian university by distance learning in the Pentecostal tradition that offers its undergraduate programs also in French. However, it is a model of apprenticeship, based on learning on the job rather than formal biblical and theological training, which has since its beginnings defined the typical pathway for those entering the pastoral ministry. The Mission Évangélique des Tziganes de France also has its own Bible school with reportedly two hundred students every year.

There is no Pentecostal-Charismatic faculty of theology or (university-level) seminary in France. The crying absence of an autochthonous French Pentecostal-Charismatic theological education has led to a deficiency of native French literature in that area. Most books written are concerned about being practically relevant for church ministry and Christian life. A new generation of Pentecostal-Charismatic leaders has been educated in Protestant schools, foremost in evangelical theological faculties at Vaux-sur-Seine or Aix-en-Provence (Reformed-Evangelical), where they have acquired a Protestant and Evangelical identity and theology while maintaining a Pentecostal-Charismatic spirituality.

Pentecostal-Charismatic pneumatology and Christian unity in France

Pentecostals have been known more for speaking in tongues, prophesying, and praying for healing but less for their working toward visible Christian unity. Over the years, the Holy Spirit has been seen as promoting greater spontaneity in worship, promoting greater freedom of expression of human emotions, and advocating experimental free enterprise. However, the Holy Spirit is also a decisive actor of reconciliation among Christians in France.

This is witnessed, for example, by the formation of an Evangelical Council in France in 2010, the Conseil National des Evangéliques de France (CNEF), which is understood as a place of dialogue, reflection, teamwork, and prayer—a platform aiming to reinforce the visibility of and connections within the French Evangelical Protestant world while respecting its diversity. At this stage, Pentecostal diversity is expressed in three separate Pentecostal groupings within the CNEF: (1) the sole Assemblies of God, (2) Pentecostals and Charismatics (four denominations), and (3) three other Pentecostal denominations that are part of yet another mixed grouping with non-Pentecostal Evangelical churches, all of which have in common their affiliation with the FPF.[50]

Twenty-first-century France needs a new generation of Pentecostals with a Spirit-filled education with a positive understanding of tradition, not just their own. There is a need for an ecumenical Pentecostal-Charismatic theology of the Spirit *made in France* that will produce Christ-centered men and women of dialogue who are able to share and explore together the rich blessings of the life in the Spirit toward a new face of Christianity in France tomorrow.

Chapter 11

History, Nature, and Challenges of Spanish Pentecostalism

Calvin L. Smith

A GREAT DEAL HAS been written about the explosion of Pentecostalism in Spain's former colonies in Latin America. Indeed, so substantial is this body of interdisciplinary research that arguably Latin American Pentecostalism has contributed to the emergence of Pentecostal studies within the theological academy.[1] Yet despite this wave of Pentecostalism sweeping across Spanish America, detailed scholarly treatments of Spanish Pentecostalism are far less forthcoming. Much of what is known of the movement comes from hagiographic or anecdotal sources. It is only in recent years that a handful of scholars have begun to pay attention to Spanish Pentecostalism and to explore the extent to which the movement's expressions and penetration there echo those in its former colonies.

Severe circumstances were faced by Spain's Evangelicals during the last quarter of the twentieth century.[2] Churches were few and far between, while *obras* (works or ministries) tended to be small and pioneering in nature. Fellowships grew painfully slow, American and British missionaries came and went, unable to cope with a hard and resistant land, while fierce Catholic opposition strongly resisted Protestant penetration.

Yet in just a few decades following the death of Franco in late 1975, everything changed for Spain's Pentecostals. The movement has grown steadily, organizing and establishing itself to create numerous (and some large, by European standards) active churches up and down the country. Pentecostals have also established wide, strong networks, while successful political engagement on social and religious issues has culminated in marches involving many thousands of Pentecostals in Spain's capital, Madrid, with mainstream political parties actively courting Pentecostal support. Add to this a vibrant and uniquely Gypsy Pentecostal movement, together with a major influx of Latin American migrant workers forging their own version of Pentecostalism, as well as the rise of ex-pat-driven international Charismatic fellowships and it is clear something substantial and significant is now taking place in Spain (albeit far from the scale of that in her former colonies).

Thus, the purpose of this chapter, which consists of two parts, is to survey and explore this shift. Part 1 offers a historical survey of Spanish Pentecostalism, tracing in broad brushstrokes the rise and development of the movement from earliest inception through to the present. This survey serves as a backdrop for the second part of the chapter, which moves on to identify and discuss in greater depth several key issues, trends, and challenges facing Spanish Pentecostalism. My concluding remarks reflect upon where Spanish Pentecostalism goes from here.

History, Nature, and Distribution of Spanish Pentecostalism

By 1492 the Catholic monarchs (Ferdinand and Isabella) had secured Spain's reconquest and unification of the Iberian Peninsula after wrestling it back from Muslim control. Significantly, their strong Catholic rule, together with the role of the Spanish Inquisition in rooting out doctrinal impurity following the reconquest, as well as Spain's perception of itself as a bulwark of medieval Catholicism, severely hampered any Protestant penetration of the peninsula for hundreds of years. It was only when Spain underwent a period of political liberalization in the mid-nineteenth century, leading to a progressive constitution that paved the way for greater religious freedom, that Protestants from northern Europe began to arrive in the country.

British Protestants especially were keen to establish Spanish missions, and a British presence in Gibraltar provided them with a distinct strategic advantage over their Protestant rivals.[3] Aside from Bible colporteurs and roaming preachers (notably the fascinating autobiographical account of George Borrow describing his travels across Spain, during which he distributed some 14,000 copies of the Bible),[4] in the latter stages of the nineteenth century the Brethren and Baptists were particularly active in establishing works in Spain.[5] Yet the strong Catholic identity of the country continued to make Protestant work there extremely difficult.

A Pentecostal presence on the Iberian Peninsula came much later. Indeed, although Pentecostal missionaries began establishing works all over the world even during the movement's early stages, Pentecostalism only arrived in Spain in the 1920s. Several Pentecostal researchers identify the first work with Swedish missionaries in Gijón on the north coast in 1923.[6] Antonio Rodriguez, later one of Spain's leading Pentecostal ministers, who would go on to have an important role within the movement's history in Spain, attended this first Pentecostal church.[7] Fellow Swedish missionaries shortly thereafter established a work in Madrid in 1927.[8] A Swedish missionary presence has continued to exist in Spain since that time, initially concentrating in the northern region, where it was first established.[9] Interestingly, the wife of a Spanish evangelist closely associated with these early Pentecostal fellowships tailored shirts for the dictator Franco himself.[10]

In 1930, another Pentecostal fellowship was established in Ronda, Malaga (to the south, near Gibraltar), by British and American missionaries.[11] From 1933, this new fellowship was assisted by the British Elim missionary George Thomas and his wife, Maud.[12] They had earlier become involved in an early Elim work among Spanish immigrants to Wales, which likely contributed to their involvement in future Spanish-speaking work. In 1926 they travelled to

Mexico, then worked for some time with Mexican students at a Bible college in San Diego before returning to Europe to work in Ronda.[13] It seems by the mid-1930s these three fellowships in Gijón, Madrid, and Ronda were the only Pentecostal works in the whole of Iberian Spain[14] (though it is claimed two American women missionaries visited and sowed the seeds of the Assemblies of God in the Canaries in 1930).[15] Later in that decade, the Church of God may have established its first presence in Spain in 1937.[16]

Yet the violent Spanish Civil War (1936–1939) that brought the Catholic and Fascist-leaning military dictator Francisco Franco to power meant that the tiny Pentecostal existence in Spain was precarious, marked by persecution, political violence, and missionaries leaving the country.[17] The Elim missionary George Thomas was forced to flee and, together with other British nationals, was evacuated by the British Navy to Gibraltar. He returned some months later to find his home and possessions safe, but the church had been ransacked by Republican troops (there would be no further Spanish Elim work until the early 1980s).[18] Meanwhile, the Swedish Pentecostal missionaries in Gijon were so hassled by various militias that they were forced to return to Sweden, leaving the work in the care of the Spanish until circumstances changed.[19] Thus, the Pentecostal historian Vinson Synan notes a modest Pentecostal presence and very slow growth until after the Second World War.[20]

Several works were established by Spanish Pentecostals following the Civil War—for example, the congregation begun in La Coruña in 1946 by two families, one Spanish, the other Cuban.[21] Also notable is a work established in the 1950s in Oviedo, Asturias, by an Evangelical Spaniard, Ramón Blanco. While it appears he was not Pentecostal, nonetheless Blanco (together with the pastor who replaced him, Rubén Fernández) was instrumental in shaping the life and future Charismatic ministry of Constantino Justo, who was saved under Blanco's ministry in 1961.[22] Justo later studied at the International Bible Training Institute in West Sussex (United Kingdom) before establishing important Pentecostal and Charismatic works in Murcia and Alicante. Justo, who worked with several British missionaries in that region, went on to work in radio ministry, even during the latter stages of the Franco regime. His radio (and some television) ministry went on to grow considerably after the death of the dictator and represents an important aspect of Spain's Pentecostal and Charismatic history. His son now pastors one of the largest Charismatic churches in the Torrevieja area. Also significant about Blanco's ministry from a Pentecostal perspective was that it appeared to have received backing from American Pentecostal Sidney Correll's ministry.[23] Certainly, the Corrells established a ministry in Spain "long before air travel was the normal mode of transportation."[24]

The next significant wave of Pentecostalism in Spain was during the 1950s and 1960s, which was a period of predominantly North American and English influence.[25] North American–established works included those of Kenneth and Martha McIntyre in Barcelona (1952); Mexican American missionaries José and Carmen Aldapa in Seville (1966); Anthony and Rita Giordino in Valencia (1967); and Roberto Goitía, a Puerto Rican, who opened a church in Vigo (1969).[26] Also arriving in the 1960s was the Apostolic American Daniel del Vecchio, to Malaga in 1964.[27] His work would bring groups of American youth over to assist with the work, and some of those churches continue to this day.[28] Also down in Malaga in the 1960s and 1970s, a missionary also recalls an important work by an American Oneness missionary (name unknown).[29] Yet several of these works aside, by the early 1970s, the bulk of the North American Pentecostal presence centered in and around Madrid, Spain's capital, as well as in Barcelona, the second-largest city, together with the central and northern regions of Spain.

Meanwhile, the British missionaries focused their efforts predominantly along the Mediterranean coast, from Almeria in the south, northward past Valencia, to eventually include Castellón. The main figures behind the emergence of this Mediterranean Pentecostal presence were Gordon and Margaret Burgess. A sailor in the British Navy during the 1950s, Gordon recalls a fascination with Spain as a mysterious and closed land whenever he sailed past, en route to Gibraltar. Undergoing a Pentecostal experience several years later after leaving the navy, he felt a call to Spain and allied himself with several British Assemblies of God pastors also interested in establishing some kind of work in Spain (their efforts were unofficial, as at that time the British Assemblies of God would not permit missions work in Europe). Burgess toured the United Kingdom, raising support within this network, before the couple left for Spain with their young son in 1961. They pioneered works, first in the city of Almeria (in the region of Andalucía), then Murcia, before moving to the seaside fishing town of Aguilas (in the province of Murcia) and later establishing a church in the city of Alicante. They worked closely with Constantino Justo, establishing the first Pentecostal works in this region. Other British missionaries later joined Burgess, and eventually additional works were established in Valencia and Castellón. This group also established its own Pentecostal mission covering this region, which was led by Burgess, which in the late 1960s was formally brought under the auspices of the British Assemblies of God.[30] At age eighty-seven, Burgess continues to minister in Spain to this day (his wife died in 2010) and considers Spain his home.

Another British Pentecostal pioneer was Colin Warner, who engaged in short-term missions in Almería in the early 1960s. Later a well-known figure in the British Assemblies of God (and until his recent retirement a personal colleague), Warner faced difficulties obtaining permission to work in Almería. This was because the local population sided with the Republicans during the Civil War, earning foreigners mixing with them the unwelcome attention of the regime's paramilitary Guardia Civil. With further missionary efforts being disrupted over visa issues, Warner explored other means of visiting the region. Almería's arid climate and desert terrain led to it becoming a filming location for the "spaghetti Westerns" (a genre that launched the film careers of, among others, Clint Eastwood, who filmed there). Problems in Jordan with the filming of Horizon Pictures' *Lawrence of Arabia* meant it was filmed partly in Almería, giving Warner the opportunity to apply for a work visa and assist the film crew as someone who knew the area and spoke some Spanish. He recalls negotiating rented accommodation for the actor Alec Guinness and buying heating paraffin for film director David Lean, and he was even asked to be available as a stand-in for American actor Arthur Kennedy. However, Warner (who was shortly thereafter arrested by the authorities and after a few days in jail expelled from Spain) recalls, "The greatest fun I had was when I was asked to work with the Casting Director in the task of visiting surrounding villages and looking at groups of Spanish gypsies to recruit them to function as an army of Arabs."[31]

Various Pentecostals visiting Andalucía in the 1960s and 1970s, where there is a particularly strong *gitano* (Gypsy) presence, expressed considerable interest in the Gypsy people.[32] The activity and faith embraced by many of these Romani people mark an important—and separate—stage in the history of Spanish Pentecostalism. In neighboring France during the 1950s, a Pentecostal Gypsy revival began and was led by Clément Le Cossec (a non-Gypsy),[33] which attracted, among others, the participation of Pentecostal evangelist T. L. Osborn.[34] This revival eventually spilled over to northern Spain, in Balaguer, Lleida, during the mid-1960s, and Gordon Burgess recalls visiting a church led by a Swedish Pentecostal missionary in Lleida at that time. He describes how he and the Swedish pastor, at the invitation of a young man, a new Pentecostal convert returning from France, invited them to speak to a gathering of about a hundred Gypsies wanting to know more. Many accepted Christ that day, after which some went to Irun to share with others, after which "it took off like wildfire."[35]

Initially strongest in Spain's northern provinces, the new Pentecostal Gypsy denomination took the name Filadelfia and quickly surpassed in size that of the French Gypsy revival.[36] T. L. Osborn, as well as working with the French Gypsies, also became involved with Filadelfia in the 1960s, further contributing to the growth of the movement.[37] Pentecostal scholar Allan Anderson has noted that Filadelfia is now the largest Gypsy church in the world.[38] A 1988 source numbered Filadelfia at 1,500 preachers and 100,000 members (compared with the Assemblies of God's 70 churches and 3,000 to 5,000 members and the Church of God's 15 churches and 2,000 members).[39] By 2011, an obituary for Filadelfia's founder "El Emiliano," who was saved under Le Cossec's ministry, numbered the denomination at 1,000 fellowships, 3,000 pastors and workers, and 200,000 members.[40]

Moving on from Filadelfia, the 1960s and 1970s witnessed the establishment of various small indigenous plants by Spanish pastors and workers across the country.[41] Meanwhile, in the 1960s, charismatic expressions emerged within non-Pentecostal Protestant churches in Spain, which caused some tensions within those denominations. The 1970s also witnessed the arrival of various Latin American Pentecostal missionaries.[42] Yet growth was still hampered by a strong Catholic presence, together with limited religious freedom and scrutiny by the Franco regime.

However, the death of Franco in November 1978, marking the demise of a semi-Fascist military regime, a severely weakened Catholic Church, and the eventual emergence of democracy and new freedoms, would eventually contribute to burgeoning Evangelical, particularly Pentecostal and Charismatic, activity, which over the decades since has transformed the movement's presence in Spain. In 1979, one estimate put the number of Spanish Pentecostals at 50,000, rising to 85,000 by 1993.[43] By 2001, Pentecostals were the largest Protestant group in all of Spain.[44] Spain's Federation of Evangelical Religious Entities estimated in 2002 that there were 350,000 Evangelicals in Spain,[45] while in 2014 Spain's *El País* numbered Evangelicals at 400,000.[46] Various estimates and reports suggest Pentecostals represent the bulk of these. Gordon Burgess spoke of 400 Assemblies of God churches in Spain, including several in the north enjoying attendance of 1,000-plus worshippers, with many others across the country numbering 100–250 believers.[47] The decades following Franco's death also marked the rise of the Spanish Charismatic movement, numbering among them some of Spain's largest churches. Indeed, Charismatic growth has been so great in Spain that it has been suggested that Spanish Charismatics (many of them Roman Catholic Charismatics) outnumber Pentecostals by as much as thirty-five to one[48] (though given several statistical issues detailed below, this figure should be used with caution).

Also very important in the Spanish Pentecostal narrative is the huge influx of immigrants and their attendance in Pentecostal churches. Various international—mainly English-speaking—churches have been established to cater to the needs of believers among the hundreds of thousands of ex-pats who have settled permanently up and down Spain's sunny *costas*. But the most important external penetration, by far vis-à-vis Spanish Pentecostalism, is the arrival of multitudes of Latin American immigrant workers.[49] Many have brought their Pentecostal faith with them and have established many churches across Spain, while others have joined existing churches. The size and activity of this Latin American Pentecostal entity, which is discussed further below, represents a central aspect of Spanish Pentecostalism's more recent history.

Emerging Issues and Trends

A survey of Spanish Pentecostalism yields several issues and trends meriting further discussion. Particularly significant is the considerable political change and extension of religious freedom following Franco's death, which has transformed Pentecostal activity in Spain. During the Franco era, *Evangélicos* were regarded with suspicion, routinely watched, even oppressed.[50] Several missionaries recount various dealings and difficulties with the Guardia Civil.[51]

Meanwhile, the Catholic nature of the Franco regime contributed to a deep suspicion and abuse of non-Catholics, even as late as the 1970s.[52] Several missionaries to Spain prior to Franco's death recall strong Catholic opposition to Protestants, which was arguably reminiscent of the dark days faced by Pentecostals in Catholic Latin America prior to the 1960s. Such wariness of *Evangélicos* by everyday Spaniards also made evangelism extremely difficult. Converts often attended meetings secretly, fearful that such activity would be noted and recorded by the Guardia Civil.[53]

Yet today the situation for Spain's Evangelicals is completely different. Legal registration of churches is straightforward compared with Franco days. Radio ministry is abundant, churches buy property, ministries advertise freely, and believers enjoy considerable freedom. Neither do Pentecostals face any political obstacles compared with previous times. Indeed, Pentecostals—including Gypsy Pentecostals—are now openly courted by Spanish political parties.[54] Thus, today's Spanish Pentecostals and Charismatics are active, sharing their faith freely and openly, and participating in expressions of their faith without fear of intimidation or political involvement. Thus, one missionary who has lived through both the Franco and post-Franco eras observes how younger Spanish Pentecostals can hardly believe the stories of oppression they hear from an older generation.[55]

Another important issue in the Spanish Pentecostal narrative is its fragmented history and heterogeneous nature, which in turn raises several issues meriting further discussion. For example, the American and British missionary endeavors developed separately from each other, geographically, politically, and in terms of vision, theological emphasis, and praxis. When in the 1960s new legislation was passed concerning church registration, the Americans registered the name Assemblies of God, which meant the smaller, separate British Mediterranean presence (by this stage officially under the auspices of the British Assemblies of God) had to find an alternative name (Pentecostal Spanish Assemblies). When its leader, Gordon Burgess, offered to bring this entity under the American-led Assemblies of God in Spain and work under its leadership, the American Assemblies leader in Spain, Kenneth McIntyre, declined, noting the differences between it and the British Assemblies. Eventually the British mission was incorporated into the Spanish Assemblies of God some time after the work was indigenized.[56] To confuse matters further, a separate Assemblies of God was established in 1980 in the Spanish Canary Islands by Italo Frigoli, formerly a missionary in Madrid (later Frigoli and his wife moved to Chile and founded a church there).

Another separate expression of Spanish Pentecostalism is, of course, Filadelfia, further demonstrating the heterogeneous nature of the movement on the Iberian Peninsula. Filadelfia specifically sought to create a distinctly Gypsy theology and ecclesiology within a Pentecostal framework.[57] It also jealously guarded its role as evangelist and shepherd to the Gypsy people.[58]

Meanwhile, the heterogeneous nature of Spanish Pentecostalism is evident elsewhere. Spain has witnessed considerable Latin American missionary penetration in recent years (for example, from the Good Shepherd Church, Mexico, and the Pentecostal Church of God of Puerto Rico, among others).[59] But it is the huge influx of migrant workers from Latin America, estimated at 1.5 million in 2014,[60] that has particularly boosted Spanish Pentecostal numbers and had a huge impact on the size and nature of the movement in that country. Hundreds of new, predominantly Latin American churches have been established in recent years across Spain.[61] Echoing the situation in Latin America, where migration to large and hostile cities has led rural workers to seek solace within Pentecostal churches, so too in Spain have Latin American workers far away from home joined churches (many of them previously not practicing believers)[62] as a survival strategy. Others who were already believers have brought with them their own distinctly Latin American form of Pentecostalism. The result has been an explosion of Pentecostalism in Spain, exhibiting the style, methods, practice, and even vocabulary of Latin American Pentecostalism that is now being emulated by the Spaniards in those churches.[63]

Significantly, this large (and growing) Latin American expression of Pentecostalism belies the commonly held view that Spanish Pentecostalism is booming. It *is* growing rapidly, in the strict sense that the number of Pentecostals in Spain is rising, but not in the sense that this is a distinctly Spanish Pentecostal phenomenon among the indigenous population. To be sure, authentic Spanish expressions of Pentecostalism are growing, but it is ultimately an influx of Latin American Pentecostalism that has contributed most to recent Spanish Pentecostal growth.[64] Importantly, Gordon

Burgess observes how even now, in 2015, "there is still cultural resistance from native Spaniards; much of the growth has come from Latin American immigrants."[65]

Spaniards retain a proud Spanish history, Catholic religion, and culture, as well as a strong sense of class. Thus, while this characteristic came to the fore during the Franco days, as exhibited toward Evangelicals, despite years of post-Franco liberalization of laws and attitudes, Catholicism and this strong sense of Spanish culture remain deeply rooted in society. It has also shaped Spain's many festivals and social events that continue to be celebrated across Spain and shapes fundamental aspects of what it is to be Spanish. Thus Burgess's observation that "there is still cultural resistance by native Spaniards" continues to affect Evangelical efforts in Spain. For their part, many Pentecostals in Southern European countries are somewhat ascetic, rejecting some cultural events, pastimes, and activities, while an acute Spanish Pentecostal opposition toward Catholicism, which also extends to resisting ecumenical dialogue or collaboration with Catholic Charismatics,[66] further contributes to a Spanish perception of Evangelicals as an exogenous cultural force, and with it resistance. This would seem to be supported by the statistics. With an estimated Evangelical population of slightly under 1 percent of the total Spanish population, even if all of these were Pentecostals, clearly claims of a Spanish Pentecostal boom appear somewhat ambitious. That much of it (with the important exception of Filadelfia) is owed to an influx of Latin Americans as well as some ex-pat churches on the *costas* demonstrates even further how Spanish Pentecostalism is still, in some ways, being strongly resisted by the Spanish people.

Important, too, is how the *Evangélicos* are often regarded by Spaniards as low class, which is further exacerbated by the influx of lowly Latin American immigrant workers (many of whom are strongly Pentecostal), for which many of the indigenous population have little time. Thus, many largely Latin American Pentecostal churches have been eschewed by Spaniards so that in some, only lower-class Spaniards remain.[67] Consequently, unlike its peers in other countries whose adherents have gone on to enjoy social upward mobility, much of Spanish Pentecostalism remains the religion of the poor.

Concluding Remarks

Allan Anderson observes how, despite reaching Spain in the early 1920s, Spanish Pentecostalism "has grown slowly,"[68] and statistics detailed in this chapter confirm this observation. To be sure, there is important and accelerating growth—with, for example, the Assemblies of God superintendent Juan Carlos Escobar noting that the Spanish Assemblies of God has approximately doubled in size every decade up to 2010. Escobar also observes, "We have seen an incredible growth, it hasn't been explosive, but it has sustained," before going on to recognize and pay tribute to the important contribution of immigrants to the spreading of the gospel in Spain.[69]

So, what is next for Spanish Pentecostalism? The country's Assemblies of God has launched an initiative—Alcance 2020—with the aim of having one thousand fellowships across the country by 2020. The Gypsy Pentecostal work is flourishing, while the Latin American Pentecostal churches continue to enjoy remarkable growth that, if anything, appears to be accelerating. With Spain increasingly seen as an immigration destination rather than a country along an immigrant route, this important Latin American facet seems set to continue. Elsewhere, international ex-pat churches continue to be established along Spain's Mediterranean coasts to serve non-Spanish-speaking residents.

Perhaps a key question facing some of these disparate sectors of Spanish Pentecostalism is the combined effect they might achieve should they become less insular, working more closely together to reach the indigenous Spanish population. By the new millennium, some of the vibrant Gypsy churches had begun to attract British and other ex-pats living on the coast of Costas. I visited several Gypsy churches in Andalucía while on sabbatical in 2001–2002 where numerous British, French, and Dutch ex-pats were regular attendees. Thus, there seems no reason why the Gypsy movement, as well as the Latin American fellowships and the non-Spanish international churches, cannot look beyond their immediate constituency and engage in more concerted mission endeavors among the Spanish population.

Spain has been—and remains—a difficult land for Evangelicals, among them Pentecostals, to penetrate, leading the Spanish Assemblies of God superintendent Juan Carlos Escobar to describe the country as a cemetery for preachers, evangelists, and missionaries.[70] Thus, in many ways, Spain, unlike her former colonies, has strongly resisted Pentecostal penetration and continues to represent a challenge to Evangelicals in general. Yet recent Pentecostal and Charismatic growth suggests Spain may at last be turning this particular corner and may finally—albeit belatedly—be beginning to experience something of the religious phenomenon currently taking place across her former colonies.

Part III
Northern Europe

Chapter 12

Pentecostalism in Sweden and Finland

Jan-Åke Alvarsson

SWEDEN WAS PROBABLY the first country outside the North American continent to be reached by Pentecostalism—through the first missionary sent out directly from the Apostolic Faith Mission at 312 Azusa Street, Los Angeles, in July 1906. Pentecostalism was transferred to Finland only two years later. The relationship to the early forms of Pentecostal spirituality is thus obvious.

In 1956, Norwegian scholar Nils Bloch-Hoell dubbed Sweden "the most Pentecostalized country in the world,"[1] and in 2000 one of the major Swedish newspapers, *Expressen*, ranked Swedish Pentecostal leader Lewi Pethrus as one of the five most important people in Swedish society during the twentieth century—more important than even Olof Palme and Raoul Wallenberg.[2] Today, Finnish Pentecostalism sends out more missionaries per member than any other country. According to church historian David Bundy, Pentecostalism of Scandinavian origin has played a major role in the development of world Pentecostalism.[3]

Background

Scandinavian Pentecostalism, especially the Pentecostal and Charismatic movements in Finland, Norway, and Sweden, were early and influential offshoots of Azusa Street Pentecostalism. In many respects, however, the Nordic movements were—and still are—different from the ones in North America, and often also from those in the rest of Europe. There are typical idiosyncrasies due to the history and culture of the region that characterize them theologically as well as in praxis.

The historical interconnectedness also makes it logical to treat Sweden and Finland in a single account. They were one and the same country from around the twelfth century up until 1809. They share the same languages, Finnish and Swedish.[4] Thus proximity and interconnectedness have marked the region in several ways.

When Pentecostalism, as we define it today, came to Scandinavia in late 1906, first to Sweden and a month later to Norway, this region was nothing like a *tabula rasa* in a religious sense. It was well prepared for the advent of Pentecostalism through massive influence from Pietism, Methodism, and the Holiness and Baptist movements. A tradition of revivalism, a discourse on baptism in the Holy Spirit,[5] and the talk about the "imminent return of Jesus" were all there already, especially in Sweden.[6]

Early History of the Incipient Movement

Several Swedes were present at the 1906 Bonnie Brae meetings in Los Angeles, prior to the Azusa Street movement.[7] The one who became essential for the development of Pentecostalism in Scandinavia was Andrew G. Johnson (Ek), a Swedish immigrant with no connection to the established churches in his home country.[8] Johnson experienced his conversion in California in 1904 and received his baptism in the Holy Spirit during the time at Bonnie Brae.

Johnson participated in the Azusa Street movement but soon left it as a missionary in July 1906. As a participant in a "missionary band," he traveled across the United States to New York. In September, at the Christian Alliance Home, he met with another key-figure-to-be in Scandinavian Pentecostalism, Thomas Ball Barratt. According to Johnson, some of the zeal emanating from the Azusa movement was transferred to this British-Norwegian Methodist.[9] Later, Barratt also established contact with the Azusa Mission via letters.

Before any of the Azusa Street participants reached Europe, the news of the revival was spread via periodicals. The first report to be published in Europe may have been that of Swedish *Närkesbladet* (*The Närke paper*), in Örebro, on September 18, 1906, entitled "What Is Happening?"

Just about two months after the first report, on November 16, the first "eyewitness" arrived in Scandinavia when Andrew G. Johnson disembarked in Gothenburg and proceeded to Skövde. There he started to spread the Pentecostal revivalist news. On December 15, Johnson wrote his first report back to his "home base" at Azusa Street from the humble work in Skövde.[10] Less than a month later, through an invitation from Rev. John Ongman, Johnson was instrumental in establishing Örebro as a first center of Pentecostalism in Sweden.

When the Norwegians celebrated Little Christmas (*lillejul*), in December 1906, T. B. Barratt returned from New York. Unlike the other Scandinavian American witnesses with few contacts left in the region, his return was well prepared. Barratt had used his own periodical, *The City Post*, to transmit every move and every impression from his trip to the United States. Now he started Pentecostal meetings at Torvgaten 7 in Christiana.

In Sweden, John Ongman of the Örebro Filadelfia congregation acted as gatekeeper for Johnson. He is often forgotten in mainline church history, but he was a mature preacher with a large network that opened up for the new impulses from the United States. Through Ongman and his voluntary staff of young men and especially women, the Azusa Street movement could spread much more rapidly in the region than what otherwise would have been possible.

In a mere few months, the Pentecostal message was spread not only to Örebro, but also to Stockholm, Gothenburg, and a number of other places, all over Sweden. When Johnson moved to Sweden's second-largest city, Gothenburg, in mid-1907 and started work at Torghallen (a building known in English as the market hall), the focal point of the "New Revival" in Sweden also shifted from Örebro to Gothenburg. This was marked by the appearance of two new Pentecostal hymnbooks, *Glory Songbook* and *Voice of the Turtle Dove* (*Turturduvans röst*), as well as a periodical, *Glöd från altaret*

(Embers from the altar). The latter was a typically Scandinavian enterprise. Student Algot Gustafsson and Pastor T. B. Barratt from Norway joined forces in starting something entirely Pentecostal.

In 1907, Andrew Johnson traveled incessantly in the Nordic countries, using Gothenburg as his home base, to spread the spirit of Pentecostalism. That same year, one of the first groups of missionaries left the Apostolic Faith Mission at Azusa Street for China. Four out of seven were Swedes: Adolph and Linda Johnson and Ellen and Gustaf Lundgren. Just a couple of months later, restless Andrew G. Johnson left the work in Gothenburg and also embarked for China.

Through the influence of Johnson's disciple Carl Widmark from Skövde, the previously independent Betania congregation in Adelöv became the first church in Sweden to officially adhere to Pentecostalism. The concept of independent congregations, later a hallmark of Swedish Pentecostalism, was naturally a facilitating factor in the process. The following year there were two more Pentecostal congregations in the country: the Betel church in Skärhamn and the Salem church in Luleå.

At the request of many evangelists, especially women, John Ongman initiated a training school for missionaries in 1908, the Örebro Missionsskola (Örebro Mission School). In due course, this developed into a three-year theological seminary—open to women[11]—probably one of the first Pentecostal higher-education centers in the world. As Ongman allowed women to enter and encouraged them to preach, many women evangelists gathered in Örebro. Because of the numbers and the controversy about women preachers, they were called *Ongmansystrar* (Ongman sisters), initially used as a derogatory term but later used by the "sisters" themselves.

The same year, in 1908, Pentecostalism caught fire in Finland. Women evangelists and, probably, "Ongman sisters" Greta Andersson and Anna Blom, went from Sweden to Vaasa in Finland. There they associated with the Fria Missionen (Free Mission).[12] Revival spread rapidly around Vaasa, and around a dozen people experienced Holy Spirit baptism before the revival abruptly ended in 1909 with a tragedy. A preacher tried to walk out on the water in the Spirit and drowned.

The 1910s

In 1910, a group of Spirit-filled believers started the seventh Baptist congregation of Stockholm. It took the name Filadelfia, after Ongman's church in Örebro, and became the new center for Pentecostals-to-be in the Swedish capital.

In 1911, Pekka Brofeldt founded the journal *Toivon tähti* (Star of hope) in Finland.[13] This successively associated with Pentecostalism and came to support the "free direction" of Finnish Pentecostalism. The same year, two Swedish missionaries, Daniel Berg and Gunnar Vingren, left the United States for Brazil to start an Apostolic Faith Mission there, later called Assambléias de Deus.[14] In 1911, *The Apostolic Faith* briefly appeared on the Swedish scene, first in Malmö and later in Gothenburg, initiated by Norwegian David Grov.[15] For a short time, the journal was published also in Swedish under the name of *Den Apostoliska tron*.

In 1911, the pastor of the Filadelfia congregation of Stockholm, Emil Valdemar Olsson, left his position.[16] The Filadelfia Church then called young pastor Lewi Pethrus to become its leader.[17] That same year, the second Swedish Pentecostal periodical was founded by two influential preachers, Olov Leonard Björk and Carl Hedeen, called *Brudgummens röst* (The voice of the Bridegroom). Lewi Pethrus was invited to join the editorial committee, possibly as a youth representative.

This year was the breakthrough of not only Pethrus in Sweden, but also of Pentecostalism in Finland. For some time Laestadian groups in Helsinki had invited T. B. Barratt to come, but he could not make it until the autumn of 1911.[18] Apart from visiting the group in Helsinki, he also went to the YMCA in Kuopio and the Methodist Church in Viipuri. He also visited St. Petersburg, Tampere, and Turku. At the end of the year, Norwegian American Gerhard Olsen Smidt arrived in Helsinki from the United States and the city experienced a revival. Another place that was touched through Barratt and Smidt was the city of Tampere. From this year, there was a rapid diffusion of Pentecostalism. Before 1914, Pentecostal work was established in virtually all parts of Finland.

The first Finnish midsummer meetings were organized by Pekka Brofeldt in 1911 at Juankoski and in 1912 in Lempäälä and Tampere. During these meetings, Baptist influence in Pentecostalism became increasingly obvious, and many participants were rebaptized.[19] In the summer of 1912, Joseph H. King from the Pentecostal Holiness Church in the United States and Carl Hedeen from Sweden visited and preached in Finland. *Ristin voitto* (The victory of the cross) was published in Finnish,[20] and the first Finnish Pentecostal missionary, Emil Danielsson, was sent out to Kenya.[21]

In Sweden, the first entirely Pentecostal book, *Jesus kommer* (Jesus is coming), by Lewi Pethrus, appeared. As the Baptist editorial refused to publish it, this also meant the emergence of a Pentecostal editorial or publisher, the Förlaget Filadelfia. Two years later it produced a new Pentecostal hymnbook, *Tones of Victory* (*Segertoner*). In due course, this hymnbook became the most frequently used in the movement.

In 1912, the initial Swedish Pentecostal prayer group in Skövde left the Baptist Elim congregation and thus also the Baptist movement. The year after, in 1913, the success of the Stockholm Filadelfia Church increased the tension between the "new movement" and the orthodox Baptists. While Ongman and the Örebro Mission remained within the Baptist movement, Stockholm Filadelfia was expelled and subsequently remained outside the movement.

In 1914, the Bible study gathering in Lahti assembled some five hundred people, and the ones responsible for teaching were Gerhard Olsen Smidt, Pekka Brofeldt, and Frank Bartleman from Los Angeles. The preachers who were present formed a "Veljesliitto" (Pentecostal Alliance of Brethren), which somehow symbolized the formation of a distinct Pentecostal movement in Finland.

At the end of 1914, Smidt left Finland because of the First World War.[22] In 1915 to 1916, because of the political turmoil, public meetings were forbidden for, among others, Pentecostals. The reason stated was that some Russian seamen had refused to enter military service and that Pentecostal hymnbooks had been found on a Russian war ship. These books proved to be from the Russian Pentecostal Church in Helsinki. Churches were closed, for example, in Helsinki, Viipuri, Turku, Tampere, and Oulu. Meetings were held behind closed doors up until the Russian Revolution of 1917.

In 1915, after a conflict with John Ongman, Lewi Pethrus complemented the five-week Bible school in Örebro with one in Filadelfia, Stockholm. This was done to open up a Bible school that was clearly separated from the Baptist movement. Later the same year, Pethrus started a new Pentecostal periodical, *Evangelii härold* (The gospel herald). For almost eight decades, this was to be the most influential Pentecostal journal in Scandinavia.[23]

In May 1915, the first Pentecostal congregation in Finland was founded (it took the name Siloam in 1922) when a group of members was excluded from the Baptist congregation in Helsinki. Albert Kervinen became the leader of the new congregation. In Sweden, the first Bible Study Week was held at Korsberga, southeast of Skövde, and the first yearbook was published in Stockholm under the name of *Julens härold* (The Christmas herald). In 1918, the third Swedish Bible Study Week was held in Kölingared, a location that still hosts the largest Swedish Pentecostal summer conference (nowadays called Nyhemsveckan).

The following year, in 1919, the participants of "the Week" published the Declaration of Kölingared, officially a refusal of cooperation with the established churches and, indirectly, in fact a declaration of a new Pentecostal denomination. The statement also confirmed the first major split among the Swedish Pentecostals. Lewi Pethrus, together with ninety-seven other men and five women, signed it. John Ongman, O. L. Björk, Carl Hedeen, and several other early leaders within Pentecostalism were notably absent.

At the same conference, in 1919, Danish couple Anna Larssen Bjørner and Sigurd Bjørner were baptized. They now returned to Denmark with a more overt Baptist agenda and started the Evangelieforsamlingen (Gospel Congregation) in Hellerup.

During the same year, in 1919, there was a major split in the Finnish Pentecostal movement over open or closed Communion and about "congregationalism," the question of whether congregations should be united in a central organization or just loosely united in some kind of imaginary association.[24] One direction was more universal, called the Helluntaiystävät (Pentecostal Friends),[25] which saw the believers as belonging to a more universal church, not a local one, and practiced informal fellowship. The other direction, inspired by Sweden,[26] was called the Helluntaiherätys (Pentecostal Revival) and insisted on clearly defined, local congregations. In the 1920s, the two groups were of equal size but, successively, the Pentecostal revival grew stronger. In the late 1930s this constituted the largest denomination, with ninety congregations and some twenty thousand members.

Into the Next Generation

In the beginning of 1920, Barratt and Pethrus were invited by the Bjørners to an early Scandinavian Pentecostal Conference in Copenhagen. There they discussed foreign missions, among other things a mission to Africa, resulting in an invitation to Gunnerius Tollefsen to come and talk about missions in Stockholm. A year later, Tollefsen, together with Swede Axel B. Lindgren, led the first Scandinavian expedition into eastern Belgian Congo. This resulted in the establishment of the first Norwegian mission in the country in 1924.[27] Only in 1930 were the Swedes able to join in.

In 1920, Gerhard Olsen Smidt was back in Finland, this time not as a leader but as a coworker. He helped in founding the Filadelfia Church in Helsinki. In only four years it grew to the size of five hundred members.

Healing has been a pivotal point of interest and an important means of attention from the outside for the Nordic Pentecostal movements. By April 1921, British healing evangelist Smith Wigglesworth visited Sweden for public healing campaigns.[28] Ten years later, Wigglesworth had big meetings in Helsinki,[29] and in 1949 and 1950, North American healing evangelists William Freeman and William Branham also visited Scandinavia for similar events.[30]

As a consequence of the healing campaign in 1921, Swedish writer and publicist Sven Lidman joined the Swedish Pentecostal movement, something that caused headlines in many Swedish newspapers. Just like the Bjørners, he was baptized at a Kölingared Week. A mere year later, he was the editor of *The Gospel Herald* and transformed it into a successful journal. At the height of its popularity in 1945, some 72,500 copies were printed of each edition.

In Finland, a short Bible course was held in Kuopio in 1922, and the first one-month Bible school was held in the Helsinki Filadelfia Church in 1926. Teachers were Lewi Pethrus, Anton Magnusson, Väinö Pfaler, Akseli Puhakainen, and Pekka Brofeldt.[31] Other teachers included, in 1931, Donald Gee from Great Britain, and in 1936, K. E. Abraham and K. C. Cherian from the Indian Pentecostal Church.[32] In the 1940s, a few weeks' Bible courses were held regularly in churches all over the country.

In 1923, Anders Petter Franklin transferred from the Swedish Alliance Mission to the Pentecostal movement in Sweden. He quickly became the leading man in overseas missions. In 1924, he became the leader of the Swedish Free Mission, an attempt to organize Pentecostal missionary work. This was accompanied by the Högsby School for Missionaries, founded in February 1922.[33]

In 1925, Gerhard Olsen Smidt left the Helsinki church, and Eino Manninen became the first pastor.[34] In Stockholm, Einar Ekberg was called to become the first fully employed church singer of the Pentecostal movement. His career included extended time in the United States, hundreds of recordings, and two hundred of his own compositions. He is probably the most noted church singer of all time in Sweden.

In Finland, in 1926, the administration behind *Ristin Voitto*, considered to be the official Pentecostal journal since 1922, was reorganized as a publishing firm. The year after, in 1927, the Suomen

Vapaa Ulkolähetys (Finnish Free Foreign Mission) was founded. Yet another year later, in 1928, there was a split of Finnish Pentecostalism into two branches, one Finnish-speaking and one Swedish-speaking. The main congregation in Helsinki was split into two, according to the mother tongue of the members. The Finnish-speaking members founded a congregation called Saalem, while the Swedish-speaking retained the name Filadelfia for their new assembly.

The year of 1929 saw changes in mission organization in Scandinavia. In Sweden, Pethrus clashed with Franklin and closed down the Swedish Free Mission. In Norway, Barratt withdrew from the missionary organization in Oslo, and in Finland the Finnish Free Foreign Mission (FFFM) was suspended.[35] Instead, all three movements went back to basics: foreign mission should be carried out by local congregations without the intervention of a centralized missionary organization.

Simultaneously, the movements were consolidating. In Finland, the Pentecostal movement surpassed 10,000 members, and in Sweden it reached almost 35,000. In Stockholm, the Filadelfia congregation, under Lewi Pethrus, constructed the largest church building in northern Europe. On November 1, 1930, the new building was inaugurated in the presence of many European leaders of Pentecostalism.

In 1932, after twenty years of Pentecostalism in Finland, the summer conference organized by the Pentecostal churches in Helsinki came to be called the (Annual) Pentecostal Conference. As from 1939, these have been national events. For the first time in 1963, and then regularly since 1983, the summer conferences have been hosted by the Finnish Pentecostal Bible Institute, now known as Iso Kirja Education and Conference Centre, in Keuruu. The conference may gather some thirty thousand people, which makes it the largest annual Pentecostal conference in Europe.

In the year of global depression, in 1933, the social work of Filadelfia Stockholm reached its climax. Long lines of poor and needy awaited food and support at the new Filadelfia Church. The year after, in 1934, the first Preachers' Conference was held in

Stockholm. This quickly became the ideological and theological meeting point of the leaders of the movement.

In 1938, the Saalem Pentecostal congregation inaugurated its own church building in Helsinki, Finland, and in 1939 the European leaders met for the first European Pentecostal Conference in Stockholm. This has often been seen as a precursor of the Pentecostal World Conferences and was initially intended to be one, but the Second World War impeded that idea.

In 1942, the Filadelfia Church of Stockholm started the Rörstrand Folk High School. This was later transferred to Kaggeholm Castle, which the movement bought in 1944. In 1943, the first Missionary Conference was held in Alingsås, in southern Sweden. The focus there was on how to reinforce foreign missions. In 1944, at the Kölingared Week, the call was for "100 new missionaries and 10 million kronors to missionary work."[36]

In 1945, Lewi Pethrus founded the first Pentecostal daily newspaper, the *Dagen*. This was done to make way for a Pentecostal voice in Swedish society and to fight rationalism and secularization. The following year, the first Nordic Pentecostal Conference was held in Helsinki. The same year there was an attempt to unify the Baptist Pentecostal movements of Sweden with the Unity Conference in Örebro. The initiative failed.

In 1948, the twenty-seven-year-long cooperation between Lewi Pethrus and Sven Lidman ended in a public schism, and Lidman left the Filadelfia Church. The main reason for the split was an increasing division regarding vision. Lidman wanted more of the early Pentecostal spirituality, while Pethrus wanted to make a mark on secular society. Also in 1948, there was an attempt to reorganize the Finnish Free Foreign Mission to make the Finnish mission initiatives more effective.

The Second Half of the Twentieth Century

In 1950, the Renovation Revival (Förnyelseväckelsen) impacted the Swedish Pentecostal movement. Tears, public confessions, and reconciliation marked the movement. Young evangelist Algot Niklasson was the informal head figure, and Stockholm and Jönköping were two of the cities most affected.[37]

In 1952, the first Finnish Bible Institute was founded at Paimio. In 1959, it was moved to Katinala, on the road between Helsinki and Tampere. For several decades, Bible courses were held there, lasting from a few weeks to a few months, and the focus was on equipping the students to evangelize. The Bible Institute moved to Keuruu in 1990, and all educational ministries set up headquarters here. The area got the name Iso Kirja (Big Book). In 1994, a bachelor of arts program in theology was offered in cooperation with Global University, and in 1999 a master of arts program was added.

In 1955, IBRA radio was founded by the Swedish Pentecostal movement in response to alleged discrimination of the movement on the Swedish radio. Almost from the start, the Norwegian Pentecostal movement joined forces. Later Denmark and Finland also became collaborators. The first broadcasting center was found in Tanger, Morocco. Very soon IBRA[38] transmitted in a variety of languages over four continents.

The same year, the fourth Pentecostal World Conference, and the first one to be held in Scandinavia, was celebrated in Stockholm. It was estimated that some 20,000 to 25,000 people from thirty-five countries participated in the conference. Naturally, IBRA transmitted news and commentary on the event.

In 1957, preacher Åge Samuelsen left the Norwegian Pentecostal movement and started Maran Ata. He was influenced by American healing evangelists like William Branham and A. A. Allen. Soon Norwegian descendant Arne Imsen, in opposition to Lewi Pethrus and the Swedish Pentecostal movement, joined forces with Samuelsen, and a Swedish branch, called Maranata, was formed. These initiatives were founded in reaction to the default Pentecostal position prohibiting involvement in commercial enterprises and in society. The Maran Ata people wanted a revolution, to go back to Pentecostal basics, back to a free spirit and free expressions. In the

1960s they had considerable success, but the revival split and waned with the end of the decade.

In 1958, there was a notable shift of leaders in the Stockholm Filadelfia congregation. Lewi Pethrus was replaced by former missionary to France Willis Säwe. This was not only difficult for the congregation, but it was a challenge both to the two leaders and to the Pentecostal movement. As a matter of fact, Pethrus changed his ideological position on a number of issues.

The year after the shift saw the first "free" initiative by Pethrus. He started the Lewi Pethrus Foundation for Philanthropic Activities.[39] Former alcoholic Erik Edin was entrusted the leadership. In 1978 the foundation acquired the former dancing palace Nalen and made it the center of activities.

The 1960s signified a decade of turmoil in Finnish Pentecostalism. First, following a general line of emigration, thousands of Pentecostals moved to Sweden, Australia, or Canada.[40] A new split in Finnish Pentecostalism also occurred in the 1960s when Vilho Soininen started Vapaa Helluntaiherätys (The Free Pentecostal Movement). Not until 1985, and after considerable negotiation, did reintegration with the main Pentecostal movement take place.

In 1964, seventy-year-old Lewi Pethrus founded the Kristen Demokratisk Samling (Swedish Christian Democratic Party). He did not act as the first party leader, however, but in an effort to broaden the base for the party entrusted its leadership to a priest in the Swedish Lutheran church, Birger Ekstedt. It was not until the Charismatic son of a Pentecostal preacher, Alf Svensson, took over the leadership in 1973, however, that the party attracted a more varied following. In the 1990s, it was the fourth-largest political party in Sweden, according to the number of members. The party formed part of the government and was given three ministerial posts in the 1991 Swedish government, and again three ministerial posts in the 2006 government.

In 1965, Petrus Hammarberg of the Swedish Pentecostal Mission founded the PMU InterLife.[41] He did so, with the explicit support from several mission leaders, to be able to distribute state funds for development through missionaries and mission projects. The same type of organization, and cooperation with the respective governments, were taken on by the Norwegian PYM and the Finnish FFFM. Over the years, the three agencies together have distributed millions of dollars to the third world.

In 1969, a new series of European Pentecostal Conferences was initiated at Nyhem, Sweden. This was a reaction to the conferences initiated by the European Pentecostal Fellowship in 1966. Lewi Pethrus wanted to see more edifying conferences, open also to the "free" Pentecostal movements. Under the leadership of Swiss Jakob Zopfi, the European Pentecostal Conferences have met every three years, notably often in the Nordic countries: apart from Nyhem in 1969, also in Hamar (Norway) in 1975, in Helsinki in 1981, in Jönköping (Sweden) in 1991, in Helsinki again in 2000, and in Oslo in 2007.

In the 1970s, revivalist preacher Niilo Yli-Vainio led a wave of renewal within the traditional Pentecostal movements of Finland, Sweden, and Norway. Until his untimely death in 1981, he incessantly preached and evangelized all over the Nordic countries and beyond. His ministry was marked by healings, signs, and sermons displaying a typically Pentecostal zeal.

Another wave of renewal, especially among young people, came through the Jesus movement, an offshoot of Christianized hippie culture from California. Lonnie Frisbee and a group of his followers visited Scandinavia in 1971. A Jesus movement community was founded in Gothenburg the same year. In 1972, to the surprise of many, Lewi Pethrus invited a group of Jesus people to the Nyhem Week.

Outside the Pentecostal movements, waves of Charismatic Renewal reached Scandinavia through Catholics and Lutherans. The Charismatic Renewal led to a reevaluation of ecumenical positions. Pentecostals, not always with official support from their denominations, participated in the World Council of Churches in Uppsala in 1968, in the ecumenical G-72 conference in Gothenburg (also known as the Gothenburg-1972 meeting), as well as in the Karisma-72 arranged in Stockholm. Somewhat later, the Charismatic movements within the mainline churches became established in

Scandinavia. A precursor of the Oasis movement (the Charismatic movement within the Lutheran churches) was the 1977 Minister's Conference in Oslo. The Oase (Oasis) movement proper started in Kristiansand in 1980 and in Sweden in 1983.

Ecumenical exchange and transdenominational contacts came to question the hard Nordic opposition against education for Pentecostal preachers. In 1971, the Pentecostal congregation in Gävle started a one-year Bible school. The initiative lasted for ten years. It was followed by other initiatives, including a one-year course in Filadelfia, Stockholm. The folk high schools of the Pentecostal movements grew as a response. In Sweden, the Mariannelund folk high school came as an addition in 1972, Viebäck in 1979, and Dalkarlså in 1991.

But the Bible schools of the folk high schools were not enough for the growing interest in theological education. In 1981, a two-year "pastors' education" was started in Stockholm, in the suburb of Bromma. Not until 1999, however, was there a formal initiative in Sweden to start higher education in theology. That year the Pentecostal Theological Seminary (PTS) of Sweden was founded.

The missionary zeal was strong in all the Nordic countries. In spite of being a smaller movement, Finland successively increased its number of missionaries. At the end of 1976, the numbers had risen to 220 Finnish-speaking and 30 Swedish-speaking Pentecostal missionaries in more than twenty countries.[42] The Swedish Pentecostal movement reached its peak with regard to missionaries in 1983, with around 1,000 missionaries in some one hundred countries.[43]

In 1977, the commercial nature of the Swedish Pentecostal movement became more emphasized with the inauguration of the Dagen-huset (Dagen building) in Stockholm. In this company-style building, several branches of the movement were gathered: the *Dagen* newspaper, an editorial firm, a record company, a bank, an insurance company, and the like. For many years this was the official façade of the movement.

In 1980, Wasti Feldt-Johansson became the first woman to officially pastor a Pentecostal congregation in Sweden. This marked the end of a long process, from the profusion of women evangelists and board leaders of the early twentieth century to the weeding out of all women in leading positions during the 1940s through 1960s and again the promotion of women leaders in the 1980s. The first women elders in the "modern era" in Sweden were consecrated in 1988 in the congregation of Sollentuna. Not until 1996 did the Stockholm Filadelfia open up for women elders.

In 1980, the Bjärka-Säby castle in southern Sweden, with a prominent heritage from the New Evangelical movement, was donated to the Pentecostal congregation of Linköping. Through the leadership of Peter Halldorf, this rapidly developed into an ecumenical center for retreats, summer meetings, and the like. Today it houses the only Pentecostal monastery in the Nordic countries.

In 1983, the IBRA was supplemented with the start of a television company, TV-Inter. This was a Swedish initiative, but, as in many other projects, other Scandinavian countries came to share the vision. The Norwegian Pentecostal movement joined forces with the Swedes in 1991. From this date, several successful TV programs were produced, first in Denmark in 1984, and later in Norway, Germany, Austria, Russia, the Baltics, Romania, and the Middle East. In Scandinavia, several popular programs, televised on Swedish television, have been produced.

In 1983, Livets Ord (Word of Life), a Charismatic faith movement in Uppsala, was founded by Lutheran priest Ulf Ekman. He soon attracted a large following and started European conferences that gathered an increasing number of people. The Livets Ord Bible School attracted young people from all over Scandinavia, especially from Norway. In 1987, the Livets Ord movement also reached Norway officially through Jan Hagen, who founded his Elihu congregation that year. In 1989, the Södermalm congregation in Stockholm left the Pentecostal movement and joined Livets Ord.

With the institutionalization of the Swedish Pentecostal movement, several new entities were added. In 1984 the Pentecostal Information Centre, today Pentecostal Archives and Research, was founded, and in 1987 the PMU Missionary Institute was added as an agency for documentation, evaluation, and research on Pentecostal missionary initiatives. In 1991, the Pingstförsamlingarnas handikappverksamhet (PHV, or Pentecostal Agency for Assistance to the Disabled) was started to assist the congregations in their activities for people with disabilities.

In 1993, the Swedish Pentecostal movement started a new line of development when it inaugurated the PMU InterLife building at Flemingsberg, southern Stockholm. That very year, however, the Pentecostal house periodical, *The Gospel Herald*, was discontinued, giving way to an ecumenical initiative, *Petrus*.

In 1995, the first Nordic mission program was launched, *Aktion Ibrahim*. This program united efforts by IBRA, TV-Inter, and individual missionary initiatives to promote Christianity in the Middle East. The center of activities was placed in Cyprus.

In 1999, a new periodical was founded, probably as a result of the absence of *The Gospel Herald*. The periodical concentrated on information about and for the Pentecostal movement. In conformity with computer language, it was called *Pingst.nu*.

The Turn of the Millennium

On December 8, 2001, the first national assembly ever of the Swedish Pentecostal movement convened in Stockholm. That very year, the PMU InterLife building at Flemingsberg was enlarged to also house the new direction of the Pingst Fria Församlingar i samverkan, which represented a formalization of the Pentecostal movement. In 2003, these two agencies, together with IBRA and other Pentecostal agencies, moved into this center, often referred to as the Pingsthuset (Pentecostal building). In 2004, the denomination became official.[44]

In Finland, the Pentecostal movement has built its overall structural cooperation on associations, big events, and pastors' conferences. There has been an association behind all main branches of cooperation, like education, publishing, missions, and the like.

Thus, it was not until 2002 that the Pentecostal Church of Finland was officially established.

In the first decade of the new millennium, several so-called "migrant churches" of Pentecostal origin were established in Scandinavia. One of them was the Redeemed Christian Church of God from Nigeria, first founded in Luleå by Tillarh Mukasa and now present in around twenty cities in Sweden. Others included initiatives from Ghana and South Korea. In many ways these migrant churches were representative of the new social situation of Scandinavia. While the traditional Pentecostal churches were stagnating, or even diminishing, these churches featured growth and enthusiasm.

Some Analytical Conclusions

The Nordic Pentecostal movement has its roots in Pietism, Methodism, and the Baptist movement. Apart from indirect influences through the Azusa Street revival, it resembled the Holiness Movement but also differed on a number of points, especially in pneumatology. Initially, Nordic Pentecostalism was heavily influenced by popular movements that reinforced Baptist democratic tendencies and congregational commitments.

All through Scandinavia we see how periodicals made way for Pentecostalism—for example, the *Swedish Tribune* in Sweden and the *Star of Hope* in Finland. We also see the importance of gatekeepers, such as John Ongman in Sweden.

A first interdenominational phase, from 1906 to around 1910, was characterized by open borders and mutual bliss and joy. After this period, the Methodists and the Salvation Army somehow managed to domesticate Pentecostalism, especially in Sweden, while the Baptists instead came to expel the infidels.[45] This is the period when the first denominational Pentecostal congregations were formed,[46] often as a direct response to Baptist disdain.

During a second phase, with an increasing focus on foreign mission during the 1910s, we see the sending out of missionaries from all countries in Scandinavia (except Iceland). We see the formation of missionary organizations and more efficient evangelization. In the decades to come, however, we see a backlash over increasing organization. Almost simultaneously, in the late 1920s and early 1930s, we see a return to "free" congregations and splits in Norway, Sweden, and Finland.

The movements in Scandinavia have always been loosely organized, marked by New Testament ideals and congregationalism. Instead of strong central organizations, the movements have been united through the voices of periodicals and discussions at conferences, the biggest one being the summer conference in Finland.

Pastors' education has, in general, been limited to the four- to five-week Bible schools: the Ongman one in Örebro, Sweden, started as far back as 1891; the one in Stockholm in 1915; the one in Helsinki in 1926; and so on.[47] These initiatives were originally intended for women as well as for men. These Bible schools were complemented by folk high schools, especially for missionaries. The Örebro Mission School is probably one of the oldest long-term educational organizations with Pentecostal roots in the world. Today, theological schools at the university level are available in Norway, Finland, and Sweden.

Pentecostalism in Scandinavia was early compared to the rest of the world, and it developed rapidly up until the 1970s. Something happened after the 1950s, however. In spite of several renewal efforts, the Scandinavian Pentecostal movements lagged behind the development in the rest of the world. Even though the Swedish movement surpassed 100,000 members in the 1970s, the other movements did not increase as expected. In Finland, there are some 3,000 members in the Swedish-speaking churches and some 46,000 in the Finnish-speaking ones. In Sweden, there are now less than 100,000 Pentecostals and neo-Pentecostals altogether. This situation should prompt immediate reflection on the part of the leaders. Why did the Nordic countries fall out of line?[48]

Chapter 13

Pentecostal Movements in Norway

Karl Inge Tangen

In 1906, Thomas Ball Barratt returned to the capital of Norway eager to share his testimony of being "baptised with the Holy Spirit and fire." The distinguished English-Norwegian Methodist pastor preached, danced, and spoke in tongues in the Spirit.[1] His testimony had an immediate effect in Christiania (now Oslo). In the following weeks people were experiencing visions and dreams, healings and exorcisms, shivering and laughter in the Spirit, and, of course, inspired speech in terms of tongues and prophecy. The meetings under the "guidance of the Spirit" became front-page news in the local newspapers, and as a result the police had to regulate the queue on the outside.[2]

Barratt was later asked to resign from his responsibilities in the Methodist Church but was welcomed by Erik Andersen Norquelle, who led an independent holiness congregation called the Free Friends in Torvgaten 7. In the next months, this simple venue attracted revival-hungry pilgrims from all parts of Europe.[3] Barratt was also invited to preach in a number of European countries and became an apostolic father figure for several European Pentecostal movements.[4] The Pentecostal fire was spread through Spirit-filled people who established friendships with one another and traveled to and from emerging Pentecostal centers and conferences. Christian magazines like Barratt's publication *Byposten*, later *Korsets seier* (The victory of the cross), played an important role. The spread of the Pentecostal gospel also offered a new interpretive frame for people who already experienced the Spirit in a similar way. Ida Bertea Seehus received the gift of tongues in solitary prayer in 1905. Her husband, who was a Baptist pastor in Skien, was initially skeptical, but as reports from Barratt's experience reached them, Carl Magnus Seehuus did a systematic Bible study and concluded that tongues was a valid spiritual gift. The next year, he and his wife found themselves in a blazing revival that not only included Spirit baptisms and supernatural charismatic gifts, but also radical conversions.[5] As a result, the church split, and Europe's first Pentecostal assembly was established in April 1908.

Pentecostalism in Norway 1910–1940: Expansion and Empowering Institutionalization

Yet in Norway the movement continued to see itself not as a new denomination but rather as a revival movement that had a message for the whole church.[6] Barratt, who strongly believed in alliance ecumenism, did not start an official Pentecostal church before 1916, although a loosely organized assembly had existed since 1910. In 1919, the church adopted a more or less Baptist form of ecclesiology, requiring believer's baptism as a requirement for membership. The formation of the Filadelfia Church came as a result of rejection from established denominations, a growing need for order in the revival, and theological impulses from Barratt's Baptist-Pentecostal friends, like Lewi Pethrus and John Ongman. This new way of organizing churches led to a decisive separation between Barratt and his former benefactor, Erik Andersen Nordquelle, who promoted a more organic ecclesiology without membership and preferred to speak about the infilling of the Spirit.[7]

It was nevertheless the more organized Pentecostal movement that grew the most during the 1920s and 1930s.[8] Tor Edvin Dahl and Jon-Willy Rudolph suggest that the five-week annual Bible course that Barratt established in 1919 contributed significantly to this growth.[9] Through these courses, Barratt was able to transform working-class "Sunday evangelists" into travelling agents of a movement "for the people by the people." These agents were loaded not only with the Bible, but also with the magazine *Korsets Seier* and the hymnbook *Maranata*, which was published in 1911. According to Nils Bloch-Hoell, *Maranata* included both songs that stirred revivalist emotions and more classical doctrinal hymns.[10] The hymnbook also included new re-creations of popular music of that time.[11]

The Bible school students were trained in both Pentecostal spirituality and in more general Christian dogma.[12] I will suggest that this, in sum, represented a sevenfold Scandinavian Pentecostal gospel. It began with a defense of the authority of Scripture as the foundation of general Christian faith; included the fivefold gospel of Jesus as Savior, Sanctifier, Healer, Baptizer in the Spirit, and coming King; and finally promoted a certain version of Baptist ecclesiology, including believer's baptism, as the biblical model of the church.[13] It is important to note that this theology was Christocentric. The doctrine of Spirit baptism may have separated Pentecostals from other Christians, but the Pentecostal vision was always missional and Christocentric. One would seek to be empowered to be witnesses for Christ so that people could be saved through the cross of Jesus. One might also add that both Wesleyan and Baptist views of sanctification seemed to exist side by side in the movement. This "peace" was probably grounded in the strong personal alliance between Barratt and Pethrus.[14]

The congregational structure of free, autonomous, and basically democratic churches also created opportunities for empowerment in the sense that people were enabled to act in relation to God and one another on their own terms. In some churches, like Filadelfia, women could also participate in the leadership meetings. There were also entrepreneurial female evangelists, like Alma Halse, who in 1933 left Aalesund to start a significant evangelistic and diaconal work in Finmark, where she built houses for the poor, started orphanages, and helped the sick. For this the Norwegian king later awarded her a decoration.[15] Possibilities for empowerment were even improved as the missionary societies of the Scandinavian

Pentecostal movements were dissolved in 1929 (and onward) and responsibilities for missionaries were handed over to the local churches.[16] However, it is worth noticing that Pentecostalism was not the only movement that offered "maximum participation." Some Baptists could, for instance, offer the same level of maximum participation. In order to explain the growth from 1919 to 1940, one must therefore also consider the nature of Pentecostal spirituality. During the 1920s and 1930s, there are numerous reports of both revivals and the establishing of new churches in *Korsets Seier*.[17]

Moreover, from the beginning, the Scandinavian Pentecostal movement demonstrated an extraordinary passion for mission. Barratt sent out missionaries before he established churches. Dagmar Gregersen (later Engstrøm) and Agnes Thelle were sent from Oslo to Germany, Switzerland, and Denmark in 1907. Likewise in Denmark, when the first Danish Pentecostal church, Eben Ezer in Lyngby, was founded on October 12, 1911, six missionaries were sent to China the same day. This passion for mission was initiated by the Pentecostal belief in a global revival before the return of Christ. It was sustained by trust in God as the supernatural provider of resources, and it was renewed by regular encounters with the Spirit. The shift to a local responsibility for missions in 1929 was not unproblematic, but it led to a massive expansion in the missionary work in the movement. In Norway in 1929, the young movement had twenty-three missionaries; only ten years later the number had increased to seventy-five.[18]

Consolidating Institutionalization, Charismatic Renewal, and Conflicts: 1940–1990

In 1940, Barratt died. Already in the late 1930s, there were those who claimed that the movement had become too static.[19] Bloch-Hoell sums up the process of institutionalization as follows:

> ...taking as its model Barratt's congregation, clearly shows how the evolution from uncontrolled ecstasy to controlled emotionalism, from spontaneity to organised evangelistic training and regular parish work, from enthusiastic interdenominationalism to Pentecostal doctrinalization. Evidence of this transformation process is the existence of new and radical Pentecostal assemblies outside of the accepted Pentecostal churches of Norway.[20]

Bloch-Hoell nevertheless observes that "once in a while" emotions flared up, especially in connection with healing services held by foreign "miracle preachers" like William Branham and William Freeman.[21]

While I am agreeing with Bloch-Hoell's main point, his description is too one-dimensional. Although the ministers that succeeded Barratt in Fialdelfia—Osvald Orlien and Erling Strøm—were pastoral teachers rather than revivalists, they managed to work not only with foreign but also Norwegian evangelists like Knut Pettersen into the 1970s. Moreover, if one looks at the Pentecostal movement as a whole, there were certainly churches that focused on revival. Oscar Halvorsen in Evangelisalen kept preaching about Spirit baptism, spiritual gifts, and healing, and the senior pastor in Tabernaklet Bergen, Kristian Heggelund, continued to see frequent healings.[22] In every church there were not only pastoral services at 11 a.m. every Sunday; there were also revival meetings in the evenings. Thus, although the pastoral dimension may have been dominant, the evangelistic dimension was not totally lost.

However, if established movements lose their capability to absorb good revivalist impulses, they may move, as Margaret Poloma suggests, into a crisis of overinstitutionalization.[23] Bloch-Hoell is therefore spot on when he focuses on the fact that radical new movements were established on the outside of the movement. In the early fifties, there were exciting reports of a "move of the Spirit" as conversions, healings, and Spirit baptisms were manifested through the vibrant preacher and songwriter Åge Samuelsen.[24] However, tensions with many Pentecostal churches arose, and in 1957 Samuelsen formed his own movement: Maranata-bevegelsen. Samuelsen went far in ridiculing others, and he struggled severely with certain character issues. As a consequence, Samuelsen also had to leave Maranata in 1967.[25] The movement served as a renewing force in terms of using more contemporary musical expressions. It was also characterized by a bold pursuit of charismatic gifts, including praying for the sick in public, which at the time was forbidden by Norwegian health authorities.

In the early 1960s, an even more powerful evangelist arose. Aril Edvardsen[26] was a bold visionary entrepreneur and a good organizer with a remarkable political talent. In 1960 he received a calling to become a world evangelist through national churches and national "witnesses." He immediately started to support indigenous evangelists with his own money. In the following year he published his first magazine; in 1963 he wrote his first book and started a publishing company. From 1965 he hosted an annual summer conference that within a few years would gather more people than the Pentecostal movement's own conference. His missionary work grew almost exponentially. Most Pentecostals saw Edvardsen as an agent of renewal, and until the late seventies he was considered a leader of a renewal movement within established Pentecostalism.

Yet Edvardsen's way of organizing his ministry around himself and his openness toward the Charismatic movement, including Charismatic Catholics, provoked a group of central leaders. These leaders tried to exclude Edvardsen from the movement during the annual preachers' conference in 1977. They lost the vote, but the intense debate that lasted from 1974 to 1977 created a deep division between traditional Pentecostals and more progressive Charismatic leaders. For many traditional churches, this meant that they lost touch with the more Charismatic and revivalist spirituality that was now manifested only in parts of the movement. Aril Edvardsen went on to build an international evangelistic ministry of huge proportions that also hosted peace conferences in many countries.[27]

However, after 1977, Edvardsen moved closer to mainline denominations, and his Charismatic theology became more moderate. In the following years, the renewal stream spread in different ways. In the early 1980s, many relatively independent Charismatic churches were planted outside the classical Pentecostal movement. This included the Fellowship movement, which accepted the authority of British apostles and prophets. The perhaps most influential Christian fellowship was initiated in 1982 in Bergen by Norvald Askeland, Kåre Kristing, and Erling Thu.[28] The International Church of the Foursquare Gospel established itself in Norway in 1982 as a church-planting mission by the American Greg Bretz. Although Bretz managed to recruit a team of very good pastors, this mission is still in progress. In 2015, there were two Foursquare churches in Norway.

Within the classic Pentecostal movement, there were only a few church-planting initiatives in this period. However, a lot of important diaconal ministries were launched. In the early seventies, Ole Bjørn Urne started the Ten Center. One of his coworkers, Leiv Holstad, established the interdenominational Marita foundation in 1984, which now provides several diaconal services, including drug rehabilitation. In 1983, Lise and Ludvig Karlsen established Evangeliesenteret, a foundation that cooperates closely with more traditional Pentecostal churches in order to help people struggling with drug and alcohol abuse. Since 1989, Evangeliesenteret has been acknowledged with a grant from the state budget. When Karlsen died in 2004, he received a state funeral.

The most powerful wave of church planting in the 1980s and 1990s was initiated by Åge Åleskjer when he established Grorud Kristne Senter (later Oslo Kristne Senter). Åleskjer was a former Pentecostal evangelist who had studied at Rhema Bible Traning Center in Tulsa, Oklahoma. The excellent communicator and visionary pastor was capable of building a new church that in a few years became Norway's largest free church. It was profoundly inspired by Billy Joe Daugherty's Victory Christian Church in Tulsa, and in the following years many other independent "faith churches" and even some Pentecostal churches were structured as pastor-led churches.[29] The even more entrepreneurial Envald Flåten established a Word of Faith church (Levende Ord) in Bergen in 1992. From 1992, Levende Ord was the fastest-growing church in Norway, until it imploded in 2006 when Flåten had to leave the church after an internal conflict. The most visible representative of the faith movement in 2015 is Jan Hanevold, who manages a large and at times controversial Satellite TV channel, Visjon Norge.

Charismatic Ecumenism and New Waves of Church Planting: 1990–2015

In the year 2000, two passionate leaders with roots in the faith movement, Stephan and Anne Christiansen, started the Jesus Church in Oslo. Anne and Stephan were already influential leaders among young Charismatic Christians since they had initiated two dynamic youth organizations, New Generation and Jesus Revolution. In 2004, the young couple surprised many independent Charismatics as they chose to join the classical Pentecostal movement. However, since 2005, many other free independent churches have joined the classical Pentecostal movement.

There are several reasons for the renaissance of the classical Pentecostal movement. From the 1990s and onward, it has become significantly more ecumenical. This process might have been initiated in 1986, when the Lutheran Oase movement was invited to the Filadelfia Church.[30] It accelerated during the early 1990s as David Østby and a new generation of leaders initiated a series of interdenominational conferences that included the "whole Evangelical-Pentecostal family."[31] In the late 1990s, Pentecostals intensified their participation in church-planting networks like DAWN and gave up their resistance to mainstream ecumenical forums. It is not without symbolic value that the current leader of the advisory board of the movement[32] comes from a church with a more open membership policy, in the sense that believer's baptism is no longer required.[33]

Another reason is that the classical Pentecostal movement has repented from the protectionist dogma of only one church in every city. This means that new church-planting initiatives no longer take place in opposition to traditional churches. The next generation of entrepreneurial church planters, like Jostein Krogedal (the INTRO churches) and Øystein Gjerme (the SALT churches), have therefore chosen to be associated with the movement from the beginning.

Thirdly, Gjerme and Krogedal represent a new generation of leadership in the movement that combines Pentecostal spirituality with more contemporary cultural expressions. The orientation toward contemporary language may also be seen in TV programs made by the television production company TV-Inter, which was established in 1992 and now produces programs for national television (TV 2).

Egil Svartdahl, who has been hosting a weekly Christian program on national television, became the senior pastor of the Filadelfia Church in 1995. He was able to facilitate seeker-sensitive services that attracted a lot of people. At the same time, he made space for younger Charismatic leaders, like Karl Inge Tangen, who was experiencing a Charismatic renewal in the church's Bible school and prayer ministry. As a result, Filadelfia became a church with different and yet relatively integrated Pentecostal "languages." The renewal of the church has continued under a new team of pastors led by Håkon Jahr. As a result, Barratt's old church has once more become the largest Charismatic church in Norway, with about 3,500 registered attendants. The church has also been a driving force behind the establishment of a Baptist-Pentecostal university college, the Norwegian School of Leadership and Theology, which was established in 2008.

The Charismatic Movement 1969–2015

So far, I have followed what is commonly called the classical Pentecostal movement in Norway.[34] There are, however, also renewal streams that mainly have their root in the international Charismatic movement. This revival was known and spread in Norway through different channels,[35] including Aril Edvardsen's summer conferences and Full Gospel Business Men meetings. Representatives from the Jesus movement that came to Norway in the early 1970s were also instrumental, in terms of introducing new forms of music and worship to a wider audience. Yet the public breakthrough of the movement came after a lunch meeting at Grand Hotel, Oslo, in 1970, where the Lutheran ministers Hans Jacob Frøen and Hans Christian Lier publically confessed that they spoke in tongues.

Frøen had actually been filled with the Spirit in 1938, but this experience was revitalized through interaction with his son, Evind, who had become a Christian in a meeting with the Pentecostal evangelist Emmanuel Minos. In the early 1970s, Frøen launched weekly renewal meetings in the Lutheran church in Oslo, as well as "deeper life conferences." He also spread Charismatic literature through his publishing company. His son, Eivind Frøen (and Øyvind Hofstad), also established a Norwegian branch of Youth With A Mission (YWAM) in 1971 that still serves as a vital missional organization that introduces Charismatic spirituality to young people from all denominations.[36]

The Charismatic Renewal also influenced a group of young leaders in the Lutheran state church (Church of Norway). In 1977, these leaders initiated the first "Holy Spirit seminar" that filled the largest venue of Indremisjonen (Lutheran Home Mission). These seminars evolved into the Oase movement, which from 1980 onward hosted both an annual leaders' conference and an open summer conference. The new generation of Charismatic theologians, like Tormod Engelsviken, nevertheless challenged classical Pentecostal theology. The Oase movement preferred to see the Charismatic experience as an infilling of the Spirit that actualized what God had already given through (infant) baptism. Moreover, although key leaders like Jan Gossner and Jens Petter Jørgensen spoke in tongues, they stated that the charismatic experience could emerge as a process and manifest through other spiritual gifts.[37]

Oase has been instrumental, in terms of spreading contemporary forms of worship music that perhaps has become the most central characteristic of ecumenical Charismatic Christianity.[38] Although the movement has not been able to create significant institutional changes in the Church of Norway, it continues to influence individual leaders as well as the laity within the larger body of Lutheran organizations. The summer conference gathers from three thousand to five thousand persons, and Charismatic and prophetic guest speakers that appear as controversial from a more traditional Evangelical perspective are regularly invited.[39] YWAM has also contributed to renewal of free church denominations by introducing international Charismatic ministries to the Norwegian context. In the late 1980s, teams from John Wimber's Vineyard churches introduced a new and more relaxed way of praying for the sick that was well received in many denominations.

From 1992, Vineyard started to plant churches in Norway.[40] The church in Oslo hosted both the Toronto renewal and prophets from Kansas City and grew rapidly until 1998. In 1997, the pastor of Oslo Vineyard was linked to a sensational conversion of a group of New Age believers, and some saw this as the beginning of the "end-time revival" often referred to by the prophets. However, in 1998, it seemed that the alternative spirituality of the group rather had influenced the pastor to the degree that his overseers in Vineyard encouraged him to resign. The church has recovered, and today ten Norwegian churches seek to realize Vineyard's original vision of congregations that combine Evangelical theology with Charismatic spirituality and social diaconal work.

The number of migrant churches has also increased rapidly in the last two decades. There are at least 250 migrant churches in Norway and about 100 in the Oslo area.[41] To what degree these churches are Pentecostal or Charismatic is not clear. However, a qualitative study shows that even churches that join the Baptist union see themselves as more Charismatic than Baptist.[42] One of the leading experts on migrant churches in Norway, Stian Eriksen, assumes that at least 50 percent of migrant churches in Norway are Charismatic in some sense of the word.[43]

A Short Historical and Theological Analysis

It is not possible to present an exhaustive analysis of the complex history of the Norwegian renewal movements within the scope of this chapter. However, it is possible to identify some key themes.

In terms of cultural orientation, Scandinavian Pentecostalism can be seen as a grassroots movement with ties to prior Pietistic and Free Church movements. It rose in opposition[44] to cultural Protestant and bourgeois knowledge regimes.[45] As such, it was led by notions of "Christ against the dominant culture" and "the church as the only hope of world." Yet, at the same time, they saw Christ as the transformer of men and culture. It is worth noticing that the movement grew the most when it was able to integrate evangelists who spoke the language of its context. At this point, I find Dahl and Rudolph's analysis very helpful.[46] The empowering institutionalization of the Norwegian Pentecostal movement in the 1920s and 1930s is very important in terms of understanding Pentecostalism as a movement of and for the people—in this case, the working class.[47]

It is also worth noticing that later Charismatic leaders, like Aril Edvardsen and Egil Svartdahl,[48] were able to connect to the culture of the middle class through new forms of language and media. I would argue this should not be easily dismissed as a kind of "Pentecostal pragmatism." Whether this should be regarded primarily as forms of adaptive pragmatism or as critical theological contextualization will remain unknown without further research. In terms of theological orientation, the Norwegian Pentecostal movement has historically been characterized by a unifying dream of building Bible-based and Christ-centered local churches modeled after the churches found in Acts. This corresponds to the wider Evangelical movement, and in particular with what James William McClendon Jr. calls "'the Baptist vision' of the church, summed up in the motto: 'The church now, is the primitive church.'"[49]

However, the overall orientation of the Norwegian Pentecostal movement has also been formed by more distinctive Pentecostal ideas. In its formative years, it emphasized transformational experiences, due to its Wesleyan heritage and the doctrine of the baptism in the Holy Spirit. Moreover, this has inspired the pursuit of spiritual gifts, including healing, prophecy, and speaking in tongues. In addition, the eschatological expectancy of the imminent return of Jesus inspired a significant and disproportionately large contribution to global missions.[50] One might ask, however, whether this sense of eschatological urgency has been lost in recent years. Possibly this is due to the failures of overly speculative eschatology, but it is also caused by influences from "relevant" Evangelical theology that focuses more on the life and service of Christians in this age than the events of the future.

The Charismatic movements in Norway have also made a significant impact on Pentecostal practices. They have brought new forms of Charismatic theology, introduced new cultural expressions, including forms of worship and music, and, most importantly, contributed to the revitalization of the Charismatic ecumenism that was central to the early Pentecostal movements. The story of Scandinavian Pentecostalism may demonstrate, as Terje Hegertun suggests, that Pentecostal-Charismatic spirituality is ecumenical in its fundamental orientation.[51] However, how the unity that flourished through personal alliances in the early days of the movement can find new and even more institutional forms today remains an important challenge for the future.

As this historical account demonstrates, Charismatic spirituality is not a static phenomenon, nor is it a phenomenon that can exist without some forms of empowering institutionalization. I would suggest that the story of Scandinavian Pentecostalism demonstrates that Charismatic spiritualty exists in an unavoidable tension between under- and overinstitutionalization. Both Bloch-Hoell and Margaret Poloma seem to suggest that there is a lack of ability to integrate renewal movements as a result of overinstitutionalization,[52] although it must be said that some ministries, like that of Samuelsen, may be impossible to integrate.[53] This study nevertheless suggests that Charismatic ministries might serve as sources of renewal, even from the outside-in movements, where power structures are sufficiently decentralized and fluid.

At this point, it might be useful to supplement these Weberian theories of institutionalization with a system theory that uses theological language. Somewhat simplified, I will suggest that there are at least three forms of spiritualty that have contributed to the growth of the Scandinavian renewal movements. The first system is a combination of *evangelistic* and *prophetic* ministries that have been able to make encounters with the Spirit available in a local language. However, since this kind of spirituality, by its charismatic nature, moves in waves, it needs to be stabilized by a second system that provides *teaching and pastoral care*. Pastors and teachers might provide leadership that keeps movements healthy over time, yet as the narrative above demonstrates, if some form of mutual subordination between the evangelistic and pastoral perspective is absent, both systems lose their dynamic.

Charismatic movements nevertheless depend on *missionary entrepreneurs* that may represent a third subsystem. This system initiates or reforms missional practices beyond cultural or geographical boundaries. Again, Weberian theory may be helpful. When Thomas Ball Barratt suggested that he has lived by the principle that one should "not wait for something to happen, but make it happen,"[54] he seems to express an entrepreneurial attitude that is deeply embedded in the Protestant ethics, which has fueled both Methodism and modern capitalism.[55] However, the testimony of Barratt's Spirit encounter also demonstrates that he submitted all his plans to God and surrendered to the Spirit's infilling and help. The most important factor behind the missionary capabilities of the Scandinavian Pentecostalism is, therefore, as I have argued above, its distinctive missional spirituality.

Future and Present Theological Challenges

I will suggest that the ecumenical renewal that seems to take place among Charismatics and Pentecostals is relatively fragile. In the wake of the Charismatic movements, there are many Charismatic spiritualties that have merged with other traditions. This creates hybrids between church culture and the late modern culture in which the world is imploding. The sociological forces of pluralism and fluidity in late modernity might also give shape to what appears as ecumenical openness. Pastors and members may now download all kinds of theological writings and podcasts on their tablets and computers. These works are influenced by interdenominational networks, as well as by secular philosophy. Norwegian Pentecostal leaders therefore face Charismatic leaders who convert to Catholicism,[56] as well as Pentecostals who are simultaneously influenced by elements of neo-Calvinistic theology, Greek-Orthodox spirituality, and versions of liberation theology.[57]

In this context, classic ecumenical questions may still be valid, but the more important question would be: Is it possible and desirable to develop a common theological identity that is robust and powerful enough to inspire coordinated missional action over time? In relation to Pentecostal history, this requires a double, and in part critical, hermeneutic. In my view, it is relatively easy to identify vital resources in the Pentecostal heritage that may contribute to the future: the love for the Bible that produced resistance to cultural Protestantism, the devotion of Barratt's Wesleyan Pentecostalism, the missional passion of early Pentecostals, and the different Charismatic theologies. Yet if Pentecostalism is future-oriented and determined to discern what the Spirit wants to do next, Pentecostal theologizing must also seek "innovation in the Spirit."

If Pentecostal theology is rooted in its spiritualties,[58] then academic theologians cannot undertake this kind of theological work in isolation. The theologians need to interact with ministerial gifts that can revitalize Pentecostal practices and nurture Pentecostal affections, like passion for God, and a sense of eschatological-missional urgency. This kind of interaction should be programmatic for any kind of theological reflection that seeks to move beyond what has been regarded as naïve Biblicism toward more sophisticated versions of constructive theologies, which still see the Bible as the ultimate norm of theology.[59]

Perhaps the toughest practical theological challenge for many pastors today is ethics, and, in particular, sexual ethics. Pastors find themselves under heavy pressure when it comes to questions of cohabitation, homosexuality, and extramarital sexuality of singles. It is difficult to address these questions in a social context where a traditional Christian perspective is one of the most politically incorrect positions that anyone can defend.[60] At the same time, it is also difficult for Pentecostal insiders who want to raise critical questions toward traditional positions. In this double silence, with no profound theological reflection, most church members are probably slowly and silently conforming to competing moral visions.

In order to face these and other moral challenges, Pentecostals must address several fundamental questions: How should we understand the normativity of the Bible? How should we perform the hermeneutical task of reading and applying Scripture in today's world? And finally, what is our moral vision of humanity, the church, and the good society?[61] As I see it, the best starting point would be to approach questions of normativity and hermeneutics from a critical realist perspective, embedded in the Pentecostal tradition.[62] Unlike cultural Protestantism, Pentecostal theology has roots and resources in the Anabaptist theology of discipleship, which offers real alternatives to cautious strategies of self-censorship and cultural conformity (including the Pentecostal alternative of the so-called pragmatic market adaptation).

However, such a discussion will inevitably face the narratives of the people that are at stake in the process and face the pain that comes with being different.[63] This implies that those who consider themselves to be traditionalists must ask self-critical questions in a spirit of authentic hospitality and genuine dialogue with those who are critical to traditional answers. Yet one must also dare to challenge the premises of other visions of the good society—for example, the more pansexual anthropology of certain versions of queer theology and feminism.[64] Doing this is undoubtedly a painful task that can begin in safe spaces in the church, but it can never end there. If Pentecostal churches want to model themselves on Acts, their theology must also be public.

The perhaps most fundamental problem that Pentecostalism faces, both in public and in ecclesial space, is that of cultural pluralism. Above I have suggested that not only the Pentecostal Charismatic movement as a whole, but also local churches like the Filadelfia Church, appear de facto as churches that express themselves through many sociocultural "languages." Fortunately, there are academic works that offer good resources for theological reflections on "one Spirit, with many tongues," as well as on the possibility of mutual hospitality in a late modern world.[65] Yet local Norwegian churches need to move beyond such general concepts and work out shared visions that may guide local practices.

Along with Phillip Jenkins, I hope that the growing number of migrant churches represents the next Christendom in Europe.[66] Yet Jenkins's hypothesis seems to overlooks the fact that most migrant churches fail to integrate youngsters, possibly due to their exposure to local versions of Western youth culture. For this reason, Pentecostals should seek to empower these young people to understand and present Christ in "new languages." This also implies that the new wave of ecumenical Charismatic Pentecostals must expand their horizons and seek forms of multiethnic cooperation that can serve the world to come. If Scandinavian Christians can model how one builds Bible-believing, Spirit-filled, and yet relevant and growing churches in a highly secularized part of the world, their future might become more important than their past.

Chapter 14

Pentecostal and Charismatic Movements in Denmark and Iceland

Tonny Jacobsen and Karl Inge Tangen

THIS CHAPTER FOCUSES on Danish Pentecostalism, with a brief glance at developments in Iceland and the Faroe Islands. Our approach is primarily historical, with discussion also of Charismatic Renewal in Denmark. We conclude with reflections on the challenges confronting Pentecostalism in this region.

THE "WILDFIRE OF THE SPIRIT," 1906–1910

The Pentecostal movement came to Denmark as revival-thirsty Danes traveled to T. B. Barratt's meetings in Christiania (later Oslo) and Norwegian Pentecostals traveled to Copenhagen during the spring of 1907. Bloch-Hoell nevertheless suggests that the movement was not established, in terms of a small community of friends with a distinct identity, until Barratt visited Copenhagen in June 1907.[1] The emerging Pentecostal movement in Copenhagen received a lot of attention, and resistance grew, partly because of the sensational conversion of the famous actress Anna Larssen. She received an infilling of the Spirit as Barratt laid hands on her and prayed for her in a house meeting in 1908.[2] Larrsen, who already had appeared in one the first Danish movies, later married (in 1912) the Pentecostal leader Sigurd Bjørner and became an important Scandinavian symbol of the transformative power of Pentecostalism.[3]

The case of Denmark may serve as an example of how the

Pentecostal fire was spread through Spirit-filled people who established friendships with one another and traveled to and from emerging Pentecostal centers and conferences. The spiritual wildfire of the young movement also was fueled by magazines like Barratt's publication *Byposten* and later *Korsets seier* (The victory of the cross), that was translated in part into Danish.

Denmark 1919–1924: Church Commencements and the Great Division

The first Pentecostal church, Eben Ezer, was founded on October 12, 1911, in Lyngby.[4] Yet the Danish Pentecostal movement remained relatively interdenominational until Anna Larssen Bjørner and Sigurd Bjørner were baptized in Sweden and established the church Evangeliehuset in Copenhagen after the Scandinavian congregational model of Barratt and Lewi Pethrus.[5] In terms of theology, the movement seems to have promoted the Scandinavian fourfold version of the Pentecostal gospel.[6]

Bjørner, nevertheless, sensed a lack of leadership in the relatively loosely coordinated emerging movement. In 1920 someone prophesied over him that he would do an apostolic work in Denmark. This prophecy was later confirmed by another prophecy he received when he visited the summer conference of the Apostolic Church in Wales in 1923. The following year, five brothers came over from Wales to clarify the apostolic mandate of Bjørner. Seven hundred participants from ten churches accepted this claim on February 6, 1924.[7] Yet Andreas Endersen and eight other churches with about two hundred members resisted the idea of an apostolic structure, with the support of Barratt, who saw the apostolic model as an "unbiblical Papal hierarchy in miniature."[8] In 1926, Endersen established the Elim Assembly in Copenhagen, a church that would come to represent the congregational Pentecostal movement.

The Apostolic Church 1924–2000: Modest Growth, Inner Tensions, and Decentralization

The Apostolic Church started ten new churches in the period of 1924–1934. During this period, Bjørner and his church in Copenhagen acted as the mother church for the developing communities of new Pentecostals. However, as new pastors demanded more authority and became more independent from the mother church, Bjørner sensed that the apostolic structure provided ground for overly authoritarian leadership on the local level. Anna Larssen Bjørner and her husband therefore left the movement in 1936 and became a part of the classical Pentecostal movement as they started a new church in Copenhagen called Evangelieforsamlingen. The movement nevertheless continued to experience a modest growth, and in 1949 there were forty churches with about two thousand members.

The movement was also able to start what would be a vital Bible college in Kolding in 1939, and to the time of writing, this school still attracts students from around the world and hosts a summer conference with around three thousand participants. According to Jacobsen, Jacobsen, and Ahonenen, the period from 1950 "was characterized by the construction activities as new church buildings were being erected."[9] They also observe that the movement was able to send out a relatively high number of missionaries. Yet within Denmark, the churches predominantly recruited people from within their own families. The movement had grown to 2,340 members in 1998.

Over the years the movement started questioning the apostolic structure that invested permanent authority in apostles and prophets.[10] The movement still believes in the fivefold ministry gifts described in Ephesians 4:11–12 but has in recent years sought to create a more "interdependent, dynamic and flexible structure."[11] As we shall see, this has also provided ground for a partial reunion with the more congregational Pentecostal movement.

Congregational Pentecostals 1924–2000: Modest Growth, Then Renewal

After the split in 1924, the churches that rejected Bjørner's apostolic mandate formed a distinct congregational identity through theological articles in the magazine *Maranata*. In the following years, this group grew moderately under the leadership of Endersen and H. P. Rosenvinge.[12] In the late thirties, there were about eight hundred members in the Elim Assembly, and the church seemed to function as a kind of mother church for other congregations under Endersen's visionary leadership. Yet there were also inner tensions, and in 1947, a group of people from the Elim Assembly established the Tabor Church, with Holger Pedersen and later Hans Friberg as pastors.

As in the Apostolic Church, most of the membership growth appears to have derived from within, and in 1974, there were twenty-four churches with 3,400 members.[13] However, from the seventies onward the movement started to grow more rapidly. Jacobsen, Jacobsen, and Ahonen identified at least three factors that contributed in this growth. First, Pentecostals opened up to the Charismatic Renewal and invited members of the Jesus movement into their churches. Second, the Jesus movement also helped the Pentecostals to regain its evangelistic vision and energy. Finally, pastor Alfred Lorenzen was a human catalyst for this renewal. One might add that Lorenzen, who became the pastor of the Elim Assembly in 1968, and Kurt Christensen, the pastor of Tabor Church, were able to bring the two churches closer together, leading to the creation of several joint initiatives.[14]

In addition, Lorenzen reshaped the practical theology of the Pentecostal movement in a way that made encounters with the Spirit available to a new generation of Pentecostals all over Scandinavia. He encouraged people to study the Bible regularly and wrote a highly inspirational book on prayer.[15] To a certain degree, Lorenzen was a classic "two-stage" or "Baptist Pentecostal," who made a clear distinction between "being born by the Spirit" and "being baptized in the Spirit," yet he also dared to modify earlier models of Spirit baptism. He suggested that people could have been baptized in the Spirit without speaking in tongues, though insisted that this gift was available to all Spirit-baptized persons.[16] Like many Charismatics, Lorenzen stressed the presence and availability of the Spirit, making it easier for people to receive the infilling.

At the same time he also resisted the idea that Spirit baptism or speaking in tongues was a kind of experiential peak of the Spirit empowerment and encounter. If this was to be the case, he argued, why do we manifest so little power in our churches?[17] Rather than looking on Spirit baptism as a goal, Christians should see it as an entrance into processes where they learn to walk with the Spirit and grow in both power and love. Although he rejected the idea of perfection, Lorenzen, like Barratt, emphasized the importance of deep devotion and submission of oneself to God. In this way, Lorenzen both integrated and challenged Wesleyan and Baptist models of Spirit baptism. Moreover, inspired by Paul's second letter to the Corinthians, Lorenzen described "walking in the Spirit" as a paradoxical experience of "power in weaknesses."[18] He could therefore openly speak about his failures and the hardships of ministry and at the same time insist that the church should believe God, take risks in the Spirit, and move in charismatic gifts.

Due to these factors, a new generation of Charismatic and entrepreneurial pastors emerged. These were heavily involved in church planting through the 1990s. It became evident that it was a very difficult task to plant new churches in one of the most secularized countries in the world,[19] yet those churches that survived were able to develop new and creative expressions of the church. During 1992–1993, four of Copenhagen's old Pentecostal congregations, including Elim and Tabor, merged into one church, Pinsekirken, led by Jarle Tangstad. In 1997, the church succeeded in buying an old school building in central Copenhagen containing fifteen thousand square meters of space.

This building was renamed Copenhagen Christian Culture Centre and includes and incorporates a large variety of facilities, as well as a large, 930-seat auditorium and several smaller meeting rooms. The Pentecostal Church defines itself as a church within the

Culture Centre. The Culture Centre, which is owned by the church, is open to different organizations that mediate art and different forms of popular culture. The church, however, preaches Christ and engages in charismatic practices, like praying for the sick. Tangen's recent study has documented that conversion of a broad spectrum of Danes has been facilitated amid the present form of Pentecostalism, including businessmen, Muslims, and people from the alternative religious movements.[20]

2000–2015: Evangelical and Charismatic Ecumenical Networks

Pinsekirken hosted in 2001 the first ecumenical event in Denmark, in which all Christian denominations gathered under one roof. In 2004, many, but not all, of the churches in the two traditional Pentecostal denominations established a new network, FrikirkeNet, that also incorporated some Baptist churches and a number of independent Evangelical churches. The network represents around one hundred churches and organizations. This includes the Vineyard church, which was established in Copenhagen in 1997. Vineyard presently numbers three churches that claim around 750 adherents.

The network coordinates international mission and domestic church planting, in addition to diaconal initiatives on an ad hoc basis. FrikirkeNet also functions as a resource for communicating with, and in, the public sphere. It is worth noting that the old Pentecostal denominations still thrive and that they still hold separate annual summer conferences in Kolding and Mariager. FrikirkeNet nevertheless hosts an annual leader and coworker national conference, as well as regional conferences.

Moreover, there are still a number of independent Charismatic churches on the outside of the network.[21] The largest of these is the newly planted Hillsong Church, which was established in Copenhagen in 2012. Currently the church mostly offers services in a combination of English and Danish, and the number of attendees has grown to six hundred in a short time. Moreover, as in Norway, there are many Charismatic migrant churches, particularly in Copenhagen.

The Charismatic Movement in Denmark

As in Norway, the Charismatic Renewal entered Denmark through different persons and ministries. Obviously, the Holiness revival and Pentecostal movement had influenced people from other denominations. H. P. Mollerup, who later founded the Danish Salvation Army, had a deep and powerful experience of being baptized in the Spirit already in 1905.[22] However, according to Stig Christensen, it was through the Jesus movement that visited Copenhagen in 1970 that the renewal became public.[23] Christensen notices that one of the hosts, Alfred Lorenzen, came to the realization that he, as a Pentecostal pastor, needed the renewal of unconventional young people in the churches. The Spirit fell on the younger generation of the Elim church, and in the next couple of years, several hundred young people were converted.

In the same year, a group of Danish Christians, including Michal Harry and his wife Svetlana, visited a renewal conference in Swanwick, England, where Michal Harper was preaching. Christensen saw the unselfish ministry of Harry as instrumental to the spread of the Charismatic movement in the following years. Harry and his friends were also introduced to the "Fountain Trust" and invited Cecil Cousen and Tom Smail to Denmark. The first large Charismatic conference was organized and held in Roskilde in 1975. The conference was marketed in terms of its theological purpose. The goal was to encourage

> Christians from all denominations to receive the power of the Holy Spirit so that Christ can be glorified by the manifestation of the fruit and power of the Spirit in their lives—in order to enrich their worship, strengthen their testimony, and make their fellowships deeper.[24]

Tom Smail was the main speaker, accompanied by Aril Edvardsen, Alfred Lorenzen, and the Catholic Charismatic leader Lars Messerschmidt.

The organizing committee was nevertheless more important. It consisted of a group of relatively young leaders, like Helge Pahus, who in the following years would bring the renewal to their local congregations. Pahus was part of a group of Lutheran priests, including Svend Boysen, Stig Christensen, and Hakon Bojsen, who had gathered the previous year to study the Acts of the Apostles. They reflected on what Acts meant for the contemporary church, and as a result they laid hands on one another and prayed for the power of the Spirit.[25] The renewal transformed several local churches in the late seventies,[26] despite the fact that the movement was ignored by liberal Lutherans and criticized by the more traditional, conservative Lutherans.

In the early eighties, a number of tragedies struck the movement, which included sectarian leadership and broken marriages.[27] Yet in 1985, Stig Christensen received a new vision through a series of dreams. With a group of Lutheran priests, he wanted to create Danish Oase, modeled after the Norwegian Oase. In the following years, these leaders and priests invited leaders and theologians from different older "low church" revivals to a number of conventions to discuss the possibility of initiating a network-based movement. However, because of theological differences, the attempt failed.

Particularly two points were critical in this process. Although the Lutheran Charismatics had developed a neo-Pentecostal theology, more conservative Lutherans felt that the Charismatic teaching was "a doctrine of Spirit baptism in disguise." Moreover, as confessional Lutherans, they were also concerned about the ecumenical openness of the Charismatics. Shortly thereafter, the Charismatic part of the different conventions founded Dansk Oase (Danish Oase). In the beginning, Dansk Oase mainly concentrated on conferences and seminars. However, after a merger in 2002 with another Danish organization, churches and communities could now become members of the movement. According to Levi Dørken, through gathering between three and four thousand participants in its summer conferences, the movement has "grown into an influential movement in the larger Danish church."[28]

Pentecostalism in the North Atlantic: The Faroe Islands and Iceland

In the beginning of the twentieth century, Pentecostalism also spread to the independent countries in the Danish sphere in the North Atlantic. The following briefly discusses developments on the Faroe Islands and the country of Iceland.

The Faroe Islands

In the early 1920s, when a Faroese woman, Petra Andersen, lost her husband in Norway, she found comfort in the spirituality of a local Pentecostal church. In 1924 she returned to the Faroe Islands and started prayer meetings in her home, and in one of these meetings she was baptized in the Holy Spirit. In 1936, Barratt visited this group of friends, and on July 21 of that year, the first Pentecostal church was established, called Evangeliehuset, in Torshavn. Another Pentecostal church was established in the capital city in 1972, called Filadelfia, presently led by Thomas Jacobsen.[29]

The Charismatic movement came to the Faroe Islands in the early 1970s through the ministry of Norwegian evangelist Eivind Frøen. The renewal also touched small congregations in the prayer houses of the Lutheran Home Mission. Part-time evangelists, and in particular song evangelists like Jógvan Lamhauge, who used more contemporary music than the classic hymns, seemed to have transformed the renewal into an Evangelical folk movement.

As people were saved and healed, the revival spread on the small island group, but it also met strong resistance from the central leaders of the Lutheran Home Mission. As a result, some of the Charismatics became Pentecostals, others started to build independent Charismatic churches, like the assembly of Hoyvik in Torshavn, whereas some chose to stay in the prayer houses of the Lutheran Church. The largest independent Charismatic church in the Faroe Islands, Kjeldan, is found on Eysteroy, led by Pauli and Jastrid Høj.[30]

Iceland

The Pentecostal fire touched Iceland through a local Icelander that encountered the movement in the United States. He started to preach and establish a group of friends in Reykjavik in 1918, but the group dissolved rather quickly.[31] In 1920, Barratt visited the big island, but the largest Pentecostal church, Filadelfia Reykjavik, was not founded until 1936.[32] The first blooming Pentecostal church was planted in the Westman Islands in 1924 by the Swedish-Norwegian missionary couple Signe and Erik Aasbø.[33] A remarkable Charismatic leader who was converted in this church, Einar Gislason, later became the senior pastor of Filadelfia Reykjavik. Under the leadership of Gislason and, later, Haflidi Kristinsson and Vördur Traustaso, the Pentecostal church grew to become the fourth-largest religious movement in the nation.[34]

As in Denmark and Norway, the Pentecostal movement has traditionally been heavily involved in missionary work in both Europe and Africa. These missionaries have acted as representatives of the Icelandic Church, sometimes in close affiliation with other Scandinavian churches. In 1973, the movement also set up a nonprofit organization, Samhjalp, after the model of the Swedish Levi Pethrus Foundation. Its mission to facilitate treatment for drug abusers and alcoholics has been recognized by the National Health Services of Iceland.

Challenges Before the Danish Pentecostal Churches

The Evangelical Pentecostal Charismatic churches in Denmark confront a number of challenges and opportunities when facing the future. Among the opportunities is the increasing openness to spirituality in Danish society at large as well as a growing awareness that Christianity is a significant cultural and personal resource.[35] This is reflected in the fact that Pentecostal churches are welcoming substantially more visitors, often nonchurched, to their services than, say, twenty years ago. Also, the growing numbers of immigrant churches are generally well received. Their ethos is often shaped by Charismatic Christianity, which they boldly express in their interaction with Danish society. On the intrachurch scene, churches are cooperating across denominational lines as never before.

Pentecostalism is, however, also facing a number of challenges, which we will limit to three main issues. The first concerns the vitality of its spirituality, the second the formation and development of its ethical stance, and the third regarding the influence of individualism in Pentecostal churches. Turning to spirituality, many Pentecostal churches have rethought the expression of their spirituality at church services. There is less emphasis on speaking in tongues in public and fewer spontaneous manifestations of tongues with interpretation in services compared to earlier days. Some churches would argue that tongues-speaking is for private devotion and smaller prayer meetings but not for public meetings. On the other hand, other gifts, such as healing and words of knowledge, perhaps receive greater emphasis than in former generations. These days, the singing of worship choruses is often the place to express personal and corporate spirituality.

This shift of emphasis is driven, to a large extent, by a desire to be more missional. In the past, many church members were reluctant to bring nonchurched friends (if they had any!) to their meetings for fear of "what might happen." Theologically and methodologically, this may be understood as influenced by the teachings of John Wimber and the Vineyard movement that have reshaped traditional Pentecostal practices. Other influences were a reaction to what was perceived as excesses of the Word of Faith movement in the 1990s and the pragmatic methodology of the seeker-sensitive church forms of American megachurches, such as Willow Creek and Saddleback Community Church.

As helpful as this is from our perspective, Pentecostals are concerned that they do not end up neglecting the power of divine encounters, revelation, visions, prophecy, and glossolalia. They fear that this does not happen due to changes of theology, but rather as a consequence of an overemphasis on being culturally acceptable and relevant. Many are convinced, however, that such cultural accommodations will be counterproductive, not the least for the next generation of Pentecostals, since Pentecostal spirituality has historically been one of the driving engines in the growth of the movement from ostracized groups of "fanatics" to its present size and influence.

The second challenge concerns how Pentecostals argue and live out their ethical convictions in society. This challenge is shared with the rest of Evangelical—and, to some extent, Catholic—Christianity in these countries. The Lutheran Church in Denmark claims 78 percent of Danes as members, yet Denmark has one of the lowest churchgoing rates in the Christian world.[36] The Lutheran Church is generally theologically liberal, and the majority of Lutheran vicars would hesitate to claim a particular Christian ethics in areas related to sexuality, abortion, and economics. Representative of the state of the issue, the Lutheran Church decided in 2013 to approve marriages of homosexual couples yet allows for individual pastors to refuse to conduct such ceremonies for reasons of conscience.

Pentecostals have traditionally been clear—at times legalistic—in their ethical standards. Yet with the pressure from a culture that moves increasingly further away from its Christian moorings and with the influx of new believers who have not grown up in a Christianized culture, Pentecostals are under pressure in their traditional ethical stances, especially when it comes to sexual ethics. This is felt in questions of cohabitation, homosexuality, and extramarital sexuality of singles, and Pentecostals have recently taken some flak from the gay lobby in some media cases that have generated some negative publicity.

It is generally felt by pastors and leaders that simply repeating the prohibitions will not do, especially not when done with a legalistic mindset. Some pastors have become defensive and keep a low profile on these contentious issues to avoid negative reactions. Others seek to find ways to advocate a biblical stance in the contemporary moral climate.

It may be helpful to learn from the catechumenate of the early church. According to the apostolic tradition, the church of the second and third centuries trained catechumens in a relational manner in Christian lifestyle over an extended period before baptism.[37] This formation not only was designed to transform those interested in the Christian faith away from unacceptable ways of life, but also was primarily an attempt to involve them in Christian ministry. This relational approach would need to be coupled with theological reflections on ethics that answer the *why* questions based on theological reasoning rather than selective proof-texting.

Turning to the issue of individualism, this is of course a major issue across the Western world. People tend to choose freedom over communalism and to approach a fellowship inquiring, How well does this fulfill my needs? Such an approach spawns a consumer mentality that people, unconsciously or not, bring into church life.

Pentecostals have traditionally valued individual revelation and personal Bible study. This has a number of positive consequences for personal spirituality, and it helps congregants trust God to "move mountains" against all odds. Yet, if such a stance of faith is not balanced with a robust vision of the Christian community, it exacerbates the individualism of the surrounding culture and even justifies such, inappropriately, using Christian vocabulary. That this is an issue is seen in the fact that Pentecostal churches and congregations are continuously dividing and fragmenting and that Pentecostal believers are prone to "church shopping," seeking out the latest "spiritual thing" in town. Sometimes their rhetoric gives them away when they turn the promises of God (often believed to be given to "we" and "us") into a mechanistic method of "how to receive your *personal* miracle."

The reshaped catechumenate mentioned earlier might help create a much-needed counterculture, since it is intensely relational and builds on personal accountability. If coupled with a robust theology of the biblical vision of the Christian community, Pentecostals might begin to understand and appreciate how intensely communal the biblical promises and callings actually are. On a leadership level, Danish Pentecostal churches and church leaders have in recent years built relationally based accountability structures that have helped remedy some of the negative consequences of their traditional emphasis on "free, independent churches."

Chapter 15

Pentecostalism in the United Kingdom: Retrospect and Prospect

William K. Kay

PENTECOSTALISM IN BRITAIN can be schematically considered as existing in four main stages, each with different social contexts and theological emphases. The first stage, from about 1908 until about 1915, concerns the disorganized beginning, arising out of the Welsh revival and the Sunderland conventions. The second concerns the long period after 1918 until the early 1950s that saw the establishment and growth of the classical Pentecostal denominations, which may be defined as those denominations that included within their founding documents a reference to baptism in the Spirit and spiritual gifts. There were three such denominations: the Apostolic Church founded in Wales in 1916 (but dating back slightly earlier), the Elim Pentecostal Church founded in Ireland in 1915 but later transferred to England, and the Assemblies of God founded in England in 1924. The third stage took place from the late 1960s and ran through until about the year 2000 and was marked by the appearance of the Charismatic movement, which, from 1970 onward, divided into two streams, one remaining within the framework of traditional churches (Anglican, Baptist, Methodist, and so on) and the other splitting off and pioneering radical neo-Pentecostal or independent Pentecostal congregations that eschewed the machinery of denominationalism and formulated themselves as networks. A fourth stage appears to be emerging in the twenty-first century. This is marked by further diversification that, on one hand, includes new, often African denominations planted primarily among the African Diaspora in Europe and, on the other, hybridized Pentecostal denominations that now contain within themselves mini-networks. The following four sections discuss each stage from social and theological perspectives, respectively.

Stage One: Beginnings

The periodisation of the twentieth century adopted here uses major chronological markers, like the First World War, and the step-change transitions within the church, such as the onset of the charismatic movement. We are interested primarily in the Pentecostal church and so examination of it must be given priority, but without taking background social change into account it is impossible to give a rounded picture of the church's development; internal or theological factors by themselves are insufficient. The following discussion aims to show the church grows and adjusts roughly in step with the society of which it is part.

Social

British society in the first part of the twentieth century was fundamentally stratified and showed vestiges of a landowning aristocracy, a trading or artisan middle class with increasing wealth and access to education and, below this, a large base of a less well-educated and poorer working class comprising rural and urban manual laborers.[1] Pentecostalism for the most part functioned within the working class that had affinities with trade unionism and, although Elim drew members who aspired to the middle class, the Assemblies of God was largely recruited from a literate working-class population that had either left school at the age of twelve or extended their skills through trade apprenticeships. Only a few gained night-school qualifications that opened the way to clerical jobs. Many of the women were in domestic service and possessed neither property nor pensions.

This was an almost entirely white United Kingdom without any obvious immigrant presence apart from the Irish, who were traditionally Roman Catholic. There were very few Caribbean, Asian, African, or other groups and therefore negligible numbers of Muslims, Hindus, Sikhs, or Buddhists. In short, British Pentecostalism began before the era of multiculturalism at a time when deference was commonplace and educational opportunity restricted. Of the first generation of members of the Assemblies of God, only one (C. L. Parker) was known to possess a university degree; in Elim, tertiary education was equally rare, and among the Apostolics it was nonexistent.

Very few people owned a car, but this did not prevent widespread travel because the rail network was extensive and reached to almost every corner of the British Isles. A huge number of people still labored on the land in farming occupations but, since the Industrial Revolution, many had moved into the cities to earn their wages in factories. One of the consequences of this was that the population was regimented by the working hours of the factory with the result that, when Pentecostal congregations came into being, their meetings needed to be timed to fit common shift patterns or the opening and closing of the factory gates.

Theological

The Welsh revival of 1904–1905 was not intrinsically Pentecostal, although a sprinkling of later accounts claims that speaking in tongues sometimes took place.[2] When the outpouring of the Spirit occurred in Sunderland, England, in 1907, a year after the Azusa Street revival began and indirectly connected with it, the first understandings of Spirit baptism were similar to those elsewhere: this was the restoration of spiritual gifts to the church and an indication of the long-desired latter rain. Although speaking with tongues was understood to be a sign of baptism in the Spirit by some preachers, this position was not dogmatically held and was, indeed, argued against by others.

We are fortunate to have extensive information about the

concerns of early British and European Pentecostals through shorthand notes taken during open discussions at the Sunderland conventions (1908–1914).[3] We also have the programs of those convention meetings and can see which topics were selected. In some instances we have printed versions of sermons.[4]

The data indicates a strong desire to understand the significance of the outpouring of the Holy Spirit. In many instances, the restoration of the Spirit to the church at the start of the twentieth century was deemed to be an eschatological sign of the end of the age. Questions were asked about how speaking with tongues and accompanying spiritual gifts might affect the life of the church as a whole. It was not clear whether some sections of the church—for instance, independent, nonconformist congregations—would accept the outpouring of the Spirit more readily than Methodists or Anglicans. After all, the convener of the Sunderland conventions, Alexander Boddy, was himself an Anglican vicar.[5] He and Cecil Polhill eventually came to believe the outpouring of the Spirit should permeate the existing churches without bringing new ones to birth.

Beyond this there were discussions about the role of women within ministry, since it was apparent that spiritual gifts were not distributed on the basis of gender. If women could prophesy or pray for the sick, then surely they could participate in other forms of ministry? And even if women did not formally hold ministerial positions, then surely they could contribute to open worship through prophetic utterance or by speaking in tongues or interpreting tongues? No formal theology was enunciated or agreed upon, and discussion at the level of anecdote does not read impressively today, although at the time it may have helped extend the range of what was acceptable.[6]

Discussion of healing was more systematic.[7] Boddy understood healing to be in the Atonement and therefore available to all Christians, and he also understood it to be conveyed through spiritual gifts. His concerns were primarily practical in that he accepted conventional medicine and the advice of doctors. He taught that there was a high road or a low road Christians might choose to take, the high road involving the repudiation of all medicine and the claiming of healing and health entirely by faith and the low road resorting to doctors and the medical profession.

Once the First World War broke out, pacifism was debated and opinion polarized. Boddy argued for the moral rightness of the defense of Belgium against German aggression, and others, like A. S. Booth-Clibborn, insisted Christians should never under any circumstances kill other human beings.[8] This was not essentially a matter of Pentecostal theology, but it separated the radicals from the more conformist Anglicans.[9] The social radicals were revealed as theological radicals. Eventually they founded the Assemblies of God and envisioned the future work of the Spirit as unfolding through specifically Pentecostal fellowships rather than through the revitalization of every Christian tradition.

One of the earliest contentious issues among Pentecostals concerned the status of New Testament prophecy. Was a prophetic utterance given in a congregation to be assigned canonical status? Nearly all Pentecostals said a resounding no, but one influential leader, William Hutchinson (1864–1928), argued the opposite. The Apostolic Church (in Wales), which broke away from him in about 1912, never thereafter accepted the canonical status of contemporary utterances, but it did recognize the authority of the apostles and prophets and allowed its churches to be ruled by this combination of ministries.[10] To prevent practical conflict, the ministries of apostles and prophets were heavily circumscribed by the Apostolic Church's written constitution, but, nevertheless, the connection between spiritual gifts and ministry gifts was overtly made. In the case of Hutchinson, who became an isolated figure, spiritual gifts were said to support the British Israel position, which, in this instance, took upon itself to identify the king of England with the descendants of King David.

The result of this episode was to ground the next stage of the Pentecostal theological development firmly in the exposition of Scripture, and Donald Gee was the prime exemplar of this tendency.

Stage Two: Consolidation

The growth and development of Pentecostal churches can be described using sociological theory. The theory assumes that at this stage they were "sectarian," which means they were effectively outside the mainstream of public life and protected from it by their own strict holiness codes. There is some truth in this, but it does not tell the whole story. On the contrary, the evangelistic zeal of Pentecostals took them out into society rather than into an isolationist enclave. Yet by standing on the margins of religious life in Britain in the 1930s, Pentecostals avoided the influence of liberal theology and the crisis of conscience that caused many other Christians to agonize over the worsening situation in Europe. While others wrung their hands, Pentecostals, often because they viewed events through their beliefs about the end of the age, thought they knew where they stood and so maintained their distinctive beliefs and values. They thought revivalism was the key to inter-church cooperation rather than the ecumenical negotiation favored by Anglicans.

Social

The mechanized warfare of 1914–1918 slaughtered thousands of young men with machine guns, shells, and poisonous gas. The survivors returned home, though many of them had been maimed or disabled during the conflict. Among the rich, the 1920s was an era of jazz and the Charleston, and, among the poor, a unionized struggle for the rights of workers led to a general strike in 1926 and then the stock market crash in 1929. There was no National Health Service in the 1920s, and mass entertainment was found in the music hall and in black-and-white movies. Television was unknown and radio still an expensive luxury. During the 1930s economic conditions gradually improved while, at the same time, the spectre of Fascist power grew in Germany, Italy, and Spain; across a fortified border, in Soviet Russia, grim Communism armed itself. The liberal elites of democracy were prepared to do almost anything to avoid another war—hence appeasement—and ignored the totalitarian cruelty perpetrated by Secret Police on the Russian population, including its Pentecostals.

In the 1920s and 1930s in Britain, Elim and the Assemblies of God grew steadily, often by hiring large halls and holding evangelistic healing crusades, but they stood outside the mainline churches and tended to be the objects of distaste or criticism. It is true, though, that accounts of miraculous healings were reported in the popular press more or less uncritically and sometimes sensationally and with photographs. The big circulation tabloids enjoyed razzamatazz, although some of them were prone to mistake divine healing for a type of spiritualism.[11]

When war came in 1939, crusades and campaigns were automatically reduced in size and scope because of the need for blackouts (i.e., curtaining to prevent light being seen by night bombers) and petrol rationing and, in any case, conscription sent young men and women abroad to fight. The Pentecostal churches continued through the six years of war and enjoyed unity within their own ranks. Although the Assemblies of God officially approved of pacifism in its constitutional statements, pastors avoided splitting their congregations on the issue by supporting any of their young people who put on uniform and joined the armed services.[12]

After the war the country was involved in a massive building program to repair bomb damage. The habit of churchgoing had been broken among those who had joined the military, but there were determined efforts to recapture the crusading days of the 1930s. These, however, largely failed in the sense that no Pentecostal evangelist gained a national profile. What happened was that Evangelicals joined together and supported the Billy Graham crusades that built in size and influence from the time of his first visit to the United Kingdom in 1947.[13]

Theological

Pentecostals had, when they founded their denominations, formulated their theological beliefs and written these down in statements of faith or "fundamental truths." To this extent, their theology was fixed and explicit. The work done following the meeting at Hot Springs, Arkansas, in 1914 had found its way across the Atlantic. British Assemblies of God held beliefs almost identical to those set down in the United States, although in Britain, Oneness Pentecostalism was almost unheard of. The British Assemblies of God statement of faith included a belief in the Bible, the Trinity, the Atonement, the premillennial second coming of Christ, and baptism in the Spirit evidenced by tongues and associated with the spiritual gifts of 1 Corinthians 12:8–10. Each of the statements was justified by references to biblical verses, although, in contrast with what happened in the United States, there was no lengthy discussion about the beliefs before their adoption. The issue that exercised the Pentecostals who became part of Assemblies of God concerned the autonomy of the local church. That is what mattered to them and what prevented the formation of the denomination at abortive conferences in 1920, 1921, and 1922.[14]

The Assemblies of God had been formed in 1924 out of various preexisting congregations, some of which had been ignited by the sparks of the Welsh revival. Others had become Pentecostal because their leaders had visited Sunderland. The Elim churches, by contrast, were brought about largely by the powerful ministry of George Jeffreys (1889–1962), who had gone to Ireland in 1915 and preached a series of campaigns and conventions, drawn around himself a group of young evangelists and pastors, and by 1920 founded a network of around fifteen lively congregations.[15] Jeffreys had been converted out of the Welsh revival and attended at least one of the Sunderland conventions. His message was one of Pentecostal baptism, healing, and conventional Evangelical salvation. Coming out of the religious subculture of Ireland, with its strong Protestant and anti-Catholic bias, Jeffreys had affirmed his belief in the Bible from cover to cover. During the summer of 1924, he had visited Canada and the United States and come into contact with the Foursquare movement of Aimee Semple McPherson. As a result (though acknowledgement of this is hard to discover), Jeffreys had incorporated the term *Foursquare* into the title of his organization.

Elim stood *foursquare* for Jesus as Savior, Healer, Baptizer in the Spirit, and soon-coming King. It stood *foursquare* on the Bible and, in relation to post-Enlightenment doubts about miracles and the authority of Scripture, Jeffreys's dismissive language had fundamentalistic overtones.[16] In many respects, the 1925 Elim statement of faith[17] was the same as that of the British Assemblies of God. But by the time Jeffreys published *The Miraculous Foursquare Gospel* in 1930 and *Healing Rays* in 1932, the doctrine of healing was located more explicitly in the work of the Spirit and in the name of Jesus than in the Atonement. Even so, Jeffreys could write "bodily healing is one of the present-day benefits of that atoning and redeeming work" before going on to quote James 5:14–15.[18]

Until 1919, the Apostolic Church officially operated through the medium of the Welsh language. In 1920, after spreading to England, Scotland, and Ireland, a statement of faith was published in English and composed of eleven Evangelical and Pentecostal tenets. They emphasized the unity of the Godhead and the Trinity, the "utter depravity" of human nature and the need for regeneration, the Virgin Birth, sinless life, resurrection, the abiding intercession of Christ, and His second coming and millennial reign. Regarding baptism in the Spirit, this was "for believers, with signs following." Gifts of the Spirit were for the comfort, edification, and building up of the church, and the sacraments of baptism by immersion and the Lord's Supper were enjoined upon believers. The Scriptures were given by divine inspiration and therefore authoritative. Church government was "by Apostles, prophets, evangelist, pastors, teachers, elders and deacons," and there was a possibility of falling from grace. Tithes and offerings were obligatory.[19]

Once the Pentecostal denominations had been founded in the United Kingdom, their theologies changed very little. There was a fleshing out of the doctrinal statements around which the denominations cohered. Donald Gee, for instance, wrote a series of articles in *Redemption Tidings*, which became books that remained in print for at least twenty years and which articulated a Pentecostal understanding of charismatic gifts and the ministry gifts of Ephesians 4.[20]

In this way, Pentecostal ecclesiology was made explicit at the local church level. At the denominational level, changes were constitutional and quasi-legal rather than theological, and the place where these changes were made was almost invariably the annual general conference that each denomination held for its own ministers.

The three denominations invested in ministerial and missionary training, and it is here that the underlying features of their theology can be most clearly seen. In the Assemblies of God, the teaching was focused almost exclusively on the Bible, and lecturers might go through each book of the Bible, expounding it in a way that might help students later give church Bible studies. The doctrines of sin and salvation were clearly taught and, added to these, Pentecostal distinctives of baptism in the Spirit were defended and expounded. In Elim, there was a kind of "Sunday school" feel to instructional material and a definite shunning of modernistic tendencies that included any accommodation with the doctrine of evolution or higher biblical criticism. What mattered to Pentecostals was the ability of their ministers and missionaries to preach and to declare the Word of the Lord. All the training involved practice in preaching, and much of the lecturing had a preaching ethos. If there was an implicit theology for preaching, it lay in the notion of the "anointing"—based very loosely on 1 John 2:27 or Acts 10:38—as a mysterious quality imparted by the Holy Spirit to some speakers and not to others.

There was a strong holiness code implicit in Pentecostal preaching. This might involve the forbidding of expensive clothes, jewelry, alcohol, attendance at sporting events, cinema-going, and even novel reading. On top of this, congregations were expected to tithe, although neither Assemblies of God nor Elim included obligatory giving within their tenets of faith. There is a sense, then, that Pentecostal theology was used to justify a style of living that might, by sociologists, have been dubbed sectarian and, by the young, as old-fashioned.

After 1945, there were discussions in denominational magazines about revival, evangelism, and gospel preaching. There were attempts to plant new congregations with the well-tried evangelistic methods of the past that included hiring halls and distributing advertising leaflets and posters. The results were positive but on a far smaller scale than had been achieved in the 1920s and 1930s. By inclination, Pentecostals were almost 100 percent Arminian, although prayer for revival led some writers and some preachers into a more Calvinistic position.

From the 1950s, immigration from the Caribbean brought many new arrivals who, receiving no welcome in the existing churches, founded their own New Testament Church of God, which, because of its connections with the Church of God (Cleveland, Tennessee), takes its doctrine from its conference in the United States and tends to focus on the socioeconomic condition of its members rather than wholesale evangelism. Its relationships with other Pentecostals and with Evangelicals through membership of the Evangelical Alliance has been good.[21]

Stage Three: The Charismatic Movement and Its Consequences

The Charismatic movement brought about ecclesiastical change through direct religious experience of the Holy Spirit. Ecclesiastical change was made easier by the loosening of society, the unbuckling of dutiful restriction, and the acceptance that, in some respects, "the world belonged to the young." Had the outpouring of the Spirit occurred when society was closed and buttoned down, the effects would have been less and the social forms created by the new Charismatic gifts would have been fewer. In short, as the following discussion shows, the connection between the Charismatic movement and social change was profound.

Social

The 1960s saw enormous social change. The generation born after 1945 was the first of the twentieth century that did not need to fight a war. Instead of depression and unemployment, there was prosperity and employment. The heightened tensions of the Cuban missile crisis in 1962 may have led to an attitude of fatalism. Instead of the prevailing sense of duty that marked the first half of the century, there was now a prevailing sense of self-expression that was found in music, drug-taking, and, by the end of the decade, sexual activity rendered irresponsible by the widespread availability of contraception.[22] In Britain, satire boomed, and the laughter was directed at the attitudes and values of the previous generation. Student riots on the campuses of Berkeley and Paris in 1968 were echoed to a lesser extent in Britain. There was an intergenerational shift of cultural power from the old elite to the new "celebrities." Added to this, legislative reform allowed abortion and homosexuality and forbade capital punishment.

This mix of cultural and social change inevitably impacted the Pentecostal churches, which now, more than ever, found themselves to be out of step and old-fashioned. Their old gospel services, their clothing, the language of their hymns, and, in many instances, their out-of-date buildings counted against them. When the Charismatic movement began with the outpouring of the Spirit on mainline denominations and when Anglican clergymen along with Baptists, Methodists, Salvationists, and others spoke in tongues, Pentecostals were aghast. They expected the new tongues-speakers to leave the mainline churches and join Pentecostal congregations, but this rarely happened. The aging leadership of the Pentecostal churches was unable to explain what was happening and at first questioned the validity of the spiritual experiences of those in the mainline churches. Only when it was too late did they realize what was happening, and by then Charismatic congregations were in action and some were beginning to attract new and wealthy, middle-class converts.[23]

But by the early 1970s there were those within the Charismatic movement who became restless. The movement itself left ancient ecclesiastical structures intact. There was no reform of the Catholic hierarchy, and the Anglican bishops continued to balance liberal, Evangelical, and Anglo-Catholic opinion in an attempt to hold their Church together. The radical Charismatics decided to branch out on their own and, although they might have joined Pentecostal denominations, were repelled by the plethora of bylaws and constitutional requirements that bogged down proceedings at Pentecostal general conferences. So the new radical Charismatics stressed the importance of relationships and formed their churches by reference to "relationship with an apostle." They detested committees, ballots, votes, and propositions. The new groups that came into existence were first called house churches and then new churches and finally became apostolic networks, acquiring, as they did so, property, shape, direction, and a mode of operation that centered round the recognition of the apostolic gifts of their leaders.[24]

During the late 1980s and 1990s, immigration to Britain from Commonwealth countries, especially from West Africa, resulted in a large flow of people to Britain, especially to parts of London.[25] Large Ghanaian and Nigerian churches were pioneered, bringing with them a strong emphasis upon the preaching of the gospel and, in many cases, a desire for the amelioration of the condition of the poor, many of whom were black, as well as a sensitivity to British politics and a suspicion of Islam based upon perceptions of the violent struggle between Christians and Muslims in West African territories.[26]

Theological

Although the Pentecostal movement influenced the Charismatic movement's understanding of spiritual gifts, the Charismatic movement influenced the Pentecostal movement in other ways. By and large, the Charismatics accepted Pentecostal exegesis of 1 Corinthians 12. What they brought to the table was a softening of the Pentecostal holiness position, or, to put this another way, Charismatics were better adapted to secular culture than Pentecostals. In respect of clothing, music, attendance at sporting events, and in any lingering sabbatarianism, Charismatics, with a strong doctrine of grace, simply overrode Pentecostal scruples.

These changes rested upon a reexamination of New Testament social teaching. Beyond this, the question of apostleship lingered.

In theory, Pentecostals had recognized the existence of apostles much earlier. The Apostolics had always accepted these ministries, and Elim, in the 1930s, had referred to George Jeffreys as an apostle. In the Assemblies of God, W. P. F. Burton (1886–1971), who went to the Congo in 1915, was widely regarded as an apostle because he planted a huge number of congregations where there had been none before.[27] So, seeing an apostle as a church planter was perfectly possible. But the new churches began to see apostles rather more broadly, as either a spiritual father or as a kind of church growth consultant. The meaning of the term was fluid and, when the shepherding movement arose, apostolic gifting was associated with potentially abusive authority.[28] The unresolved issue concerned the possible existence of apostles *within* a framework determined by a constitution.

Partly in response to these challenges, business sessions at the Assemblies of God and Elim conferences were streamlined. Debates about reforming the ancient fundamental truths were held, especially over belief in the premillennial second coming of Christ, the evidentiary role of tongues in Spirit baptism, and the precise notion of healing in the Atonement. Consequently, these distinctives were slackened but not abandoned.[29] The radical Charismatics were inclined to teach along amillennial lines: "Jesus is ruling now as much as He will be in the future," and this fostered a more triumphalist church than had been seen previously, since the fear of tribulation and the Antichrist had undoubtedly unsettled pre-war Pentecostals.[30]

Although there was no extended consideration of ecclesiology, the mushrooming of house groups within new Pentecostal congregations were influential and with the result that almost all growing congregations within Britain adopted the home-group system. This had the effect of creating a cohort of home-group leaders who functioned with indeterminate status, sometimes seen as biblically qualified elders and sometimes not. The theological topic of leadership moved up the agenda.[31]

Stage Four: Hybridization and Diversification

There were heightened expectations as the church approached the end of the first millennium and the year 1000, and the same thing happened as the church approached the end of the second millennium and the year 2000. In both cases, there were heady expectations of revival, of a biblical millennium, of special signs of the times and the return of Christ. Separate from such prophetic futures, non-religious analysts recognized the introduction of desktop computers was epoch-making and could be paralleled with the invention of the printing press or the Industrial Revolution. Over and above these changes were migration rate pressures as huge numbers of people moved from Africa into Europe or from the troubled Middle East to the more stable and traditionally Christian West. The word "globalization" became current, and Christians awoke to the opportunities it created while being concerned by the new challenges it posed.

Social

The most obvious social change of the 1990s in the first part of the twenty-first century concerned the extension of digital communication through the Internet. Social networks thrived and created a new sphere where public opinion could quickly be aroused or mobilized. Churches and denominations made their presence felt in this space along with thousands of other institutions and voices. Among these voices were those of the immigrant communities in Britain, the Muslim contingent being the most numerous and best organized politically. Gradually, too, with the rise of the new atheism—some of it a reaction against Islam—religious groups of *all* kinds found that their authority was challenged both in the media and in public debate. Some Christians felt themselves to be the butt of persecution.

The new social connectivity made an impact on the classical Pentecostal denominations in three ways. First, it made them less exclusive, because pastors or churches could now simultaneously belong to several groupings at once (to more than one network, as well as to their original denomination). Second, within the classical Pentecostal denominations, networks might be formed by creating a hybrid context (ministers might belong to a denomination but feel they owed loyalty to an apostolic figure within the denomination). Third, it allowed churches to attract new people by electronic means, including Facebook, texting, and chat rooms.

Theological

As the Pentecostal church in Britain faces the next part of the twenty-first century, the following theological issues appear important. *Secularization*, according to most statistical indices, is destroying vestigial religiosity.[32] Fewer young people believe in God than ever (perhaps a third of young people call themselves atheists), and many are ignorant of the basics of Christianity. Public expressions of the Christian faith in, for example, memorial services for the war dead or at Christmas appear to belong to the older generation. This begs questions about the need for rethinking the theology of Christianity within contemporary Britain and, perhaps, its need to engage in political debate.

Islam, while it is currently associated in the public mind with terrorism, is broadly tolerated and courted by politicians who want the Muslim vote. There is a willingness to accept Islamic ideas in some liberal quarters as an expression of the government policy of multiculturalism—that is, that all cultures should coexist equally. For the most part, the churches appear to know little about Islamic history or doctrine or, indeed, about any of the other religions on their doorstep or to command few of the tools of the Christian apologist. There are theological issues here which need addressing.

Christian *leadership* is expressed through a variety of models, some democratic and others not. Pentecostal churches may give room for debate and discussion as well as voting or, as in the case of the Assemblies of God, have transitioned to a form of government that is said to be apostolic but which bears close resemblance to those of hierarchical business organizations. Where there is democracy, there is accountability. Where there is no democracy, accountability is limited to the bare strictures of charity law. There is room for a biblical reexamination of leadership and a need for clarity about apostolicity.

The new black churches (e.g., the Redeemed Christian Church of God or Kingsway International Christian Centre) that have grown in major urban centers and which especially attract Nigerian or Ghanaian worshippers have impressed by their size, their vigor, and their comprehensive Pentecostal vision. Their worship is vibrant, and their all-night prayer meetings are impressive, but they face the challenge of *attracting the indigenous white populations* to their meetings if they are to grow further.[33]

Finally, Pentecostals, having shown sectarian attitudes in the past, are now more comfortable in *ecumenical settings*. Anglicans have learned from Pentecostals and adopted a number of their features (for instance, the Holy Spirit weekend in the Alpha Course)[34]; black Pentecostals in a number of parishes borrow Anglican church buildings. In any case, ecumenical collaboration in the face of secular pressure may drive future developments of Pentecostalism and its theology.

Chapter 16

The Origins and Development of the Assemblies of God in the Republic of Ireland: Exploring the Opportunities and Challenges That Pentecostalism Faces in the Island of "Saints and Scholars" in the Twenty-First Century

Miriam (Mimi) A. Kelly

THIS CHAPTER WILL endeavor to examine the current challenges and opportunities that the Assemblies of God faces in twenty-first-century Ireland. In order to address these questions adequately, it is essential to locate those questions in their historical and social context. To achieve our aim, the chapter will initially provide an overview of the religious and economic context in Ireland from the 1970s. Subsequently, the origins and development of the Assemblies of God in the Republic of Ireland will be examined and will take into account, as part of the exploration, the historical and theological significance and influence of the Charismatic Renewal on Pentecostalism in the Irish context. In the final section, I explore some of the challenges and opportunities facing the twenty-first-century Pentecostal/Charismatic community in the Republic of Ireland.

An Overview of the Religious and Economic Context in the Republic of Ireland From the 1970s

The religious context in Ireland, up until the late 1970s, was characterized by the high level of adherence to the Roman Catholic Church. During this era, more than 90 percent of the population identified themselves as members of the Catholic Church, and of those, more than six in ten attended Mass at least once a week.[1] The vast majority of Irish people were born, married, and buried within the Church, and they regarded their link to the Church as being important to their Irish identity. Religion was not merely a question of accepting certain beliefs and teachings; it was something that was actively practiced. Irish Catholics regularly received the sacraments and obeyed Roman Catholic teaching, and many accepted its definitions of what constituted good moral conduct. Arguably, it was for these reasons that Irish national identity was so closely tied to the Catholic Church; to be Irish was to be Catholic. Up until the late 1970s, the Roman Catholic Church had maintained dominance in the religious and moral spheres of Irish society.[2]

Gradually, since the 1980s, the influence of the Catholic Church has been eroded. Religious language, symbols, and rituals no longer frame Irish social life as they once did. The lives of many Irish Catholics are no longer lived within the framework of religious seasons and holy days; they "are becoming more Protestant—that is, devising their own spiritual and moral path to salvation—they are also becoming more secular."[3] The decline of the influence of the institutional church in the religious field has been matched by a gradual decline in its influence in other social fields. Since the 1980s, this is evident particularly in politics, education, health, social welfare, and the media. The clerical abuse scandals have also had a negative influence on the Irish nation, and although the majority of people still say they are Roman Catholic, a considerable number do not practice their religion and have distanced themselves from the institutional Church. Notwithstanding these trends, the term *a la carte* has been used to describe the new approach to religion in the Republic of Ireland. Today individuals are tending to pick and choose what they will accept and what teachings they will practice without any reference to the Church hierarchy or canon laws. The important thing to keep in mind is that *a la carte* Catholics are still loyal to the Church, even though they redefine the Church for themselves. "They retain the touchy-feely harmless bits of a belief but omit the rules that might actually impinge on one's life, such as those relating to sexual continence outside of marriage for example."[4]

In the past ten years, Ireland has undergone momentous changes, economically, socially, demographically, and in the religious landscape. In the space of approximately ten years, Ireland went from being the so-called Celtic Tiger economy of Europe to becoming a bankrupt nation. The monoculture that was so prevalent quickly changed to become a multicultural landscape; an island that had been known for its emigration was up until very recently an island that experienced substantial immigration. The total population stands at 4.5 million, with no less than 10 percent of the Irish population being perceived as the New Irish. The term *New Irish* is used to describe the diversity of people who have migrated into Ireland, in particular individuals from Eastern Europe, the African nations, and the Philippines. Into this broad context, the most recent census published in 2012[5] in the Republic of Ireland found that 84.2 percent of the Irish population (3.86 million) consider themselves Roman Catholic, while the second-fastest-growing religion in percentage terms is the Apostolic and Pentecostal community. This demographic change occurred during the economic boom years in the Republic of Ireland throughout 1999 and 2008, when an increasing number of migrants had come to live and work in the republic, principally when ten additional Eastern European countries became members of the European Union and cross-border travel was permitted without the need for working visas.[6] A significant number of these individuals were from Pentecostal/Charismatic and Apostolic backgrounds that have connected with local Christian communities or set up church communities where they now reside. One of the indigenous Pentecostal/Charismatic organizations is the Assemblies of God in Ireland (AGI). We will now explore the origins and development of the Assemblies of God in the Republic of Ireland.[7] As part of the data-gathering process, a number of one-to-one interviews were carried out with key individuals from the AGI, and the information is used in what follows.

The Origins of the Assemblies of God in Britain and Northern Ireland

Before focusing on the Republic of Ireland, some thought has to be given to the wider context within which the AGI has developed. The Assemblies of God in Great Britain and Ireland was founded in 1924 from independent Pentecostal congregations in the United Kingdom. (When Ireland is used in the title of this organization, it usually refers to Northern Ireland.) It was an attempt to bring together many of the scattered assemblies and fellowships into a loose federation, in part for the purpose of providing support for missionaries. A gathering was arranged at Aston, Birmingham, in 1924, which was attended by fourteen people. John Nelson Parr was elected as the chairman and assured those present that the autonomy of the local assembly would be strictly observed. Parr had in mind a British fellowship based on the pattern of the North American Assemblies of God.

The first conference of the Assemblies of God in Great Britain and Ireland was held in May 1924, and 37 congregations in England and 1 from Belfast joined immediately. Another 38 assemblies joined at Monmouth, Wales, in August of the same year. In 1946, there were 403 congregations; in 2014, no fewer than 600 churches from all over Britain are members of the Assemblies of God in Great Britain and Ireland.[8]

Up until 1983, there was no officially recognized indigenous independent Assemblies of God association in Ireland. Although attempts had been made to plant Pentecostal churches in the

Republic of Ireland since the 1940s, they had limited success. Perhaps an influencing factor for this was the geopolitical and religious context within Ireland, especially the tensions during the late 1960s onward. It appears that in the 1980s, there were just two Assemblies of God fellowships in the Republic of Ireland, one in Dundalk and the other in Dublin.[9]

The Origins of the Assemblies of God Ireland: 1980–2005

Rev. Gary Davidson, an Assemblies of God pastor from the United States, is one of the founding pastors of St. Mark's Pentecostal Church, located in the heart of Dublin, Ireland's capital city. He arrived in Ireland in May 1980 by invitation from the Irish region of the Assemblies of God in Great Britain and Ireland. Along with a number of other individuals, Rev. Davidson was instrumental in registering the first Irish Assemblies of God (IAOG) as a limited company and as a charity with the Irish Revenue Commissioners in 1983. The initial motivation for the setting up of this company was a practical one, namely that it would provide both legal and financial covering for its members.

With a growing membership, there was a need for a more structured and coordinated organization that had a national vision. The IAOG began to see the need to develop a national network connecting fellowships, churches, and groups from the whole of Ireland. This would serve as a resource for the growing number of churches planted around the republic and would foster a sense of interdependence and support among its members. During this growth period, the groundwork was laid for a new national organization to be founded. The primary purpose and vision statement of this new organization, which is named the Assemblies of God Ireland (again, AGI), is to give every man, woman, and child in Ireland the opportunity to understand the gospel. They want to provide a church where they can grow and develop in ministry for the glory of God.[10]

THE DEVELOPMENT OF THE ASSEMBLIES OF GOD IRELAND: 2005–2015

Individuals of the board of directors of the Assemblies of God Ireland met with a number of the key leaders of the Irish region of the Assemblies of God in Great Britain and Ireland. Initially it was envisioned that it would take ten years for the new organization to be up and running. However, after only three years of prayerful work and negotiations, the official launch of the newly named Assemblies of God Ireland was held in 2005 with approximately thirty churches from both Northern Ireland and the Republic of Ireland as members.[11] As far as one can ascertain, this was a historic event. It was the first time in Irish history that Pentecostal churches, groupings, and fellowships had come together in unity from both the Northern Ireland and the Republic of Ireland under one umbrella organization.

Furthermore, this unity in diversity is significant as, broadly speaking, in Pentecostal/Charismatic circles, the tone and character of the fellowships established in the south since the late 1980s appear to encompass a more informal approach to worship services. This is perhaps characteristic of the more unperturbed, easy-going way of life. The churches in the Republic of Ireland tend to reflect the lifestyle of the indigenous population, whereas, in general, services in Northern Ireland tend to be more formal in nature and more hierarchical in structure and may have a more reformed theology.[12]

The AGI had its own national training center, the Christ for Ireland Training Institute (in 2007, the college was renamed Carraig Eden Theological College [CETC]), and it provided training in ministry, theology, biblical studies, and pastoral placement. Students who registered were awarded degrees by the University of Wales, Bangor.[13] Unfortunately, due to the Irish economic collapse, the college was financially unsustainable and was forced to close. The students from the AGI college transferred to the Irish Bible Institute (IBI) in 2009. At present, IBI is the official college for the

AGI and has facilitated the Pentecostal/Charismatic community in Ireland by specifically designing modules to meet both their credentialing requirements and any students who have an interest in Irish Pentecostalism. Further evaluation regarding theological education in the AGI will be explored later.[14]

The Assemblies of God Ireland is a member of the General Council of the Assemblies of God, one of the largest Pentecostal fellowships of churches and organizations in the world. In 2015, there were approximately forty member churches located in the major cities and towns throughout Ireland. A considerable number of churches have multiethnic congregations; for example, St. Mark's Pentecostal Church, Dublin, presently has a congregation of members and adherents from no fewer than thirty nations. A significant number of these churches have individuals now in ministry who were involved in the Charismatic Renewal. We focus next on the historical and theological significance of the renewal movement in the development of the Pentecostal community in the Republic of Ireland.

The Significance of the Charismatic Renewal and the Irish Experience: 1970s–1980s[15]

The Charismatic movement had its roots in the United States in the 1960s and began to make inroads in the Irish Republic from the mid-1970s onward. Although having a similar emphasis to earlier Pentecostalism with regard to the gifts of the Holy Spirit, the Charismatic movement gradually developed within the more traditional denominations. Furthermore, a visit from the Reverend David Watson, an Anglican Charismatic clergyman to the YMCA, in the late 1970s added impetus to the new developments in Dublin.[16] Additionally, at a popular level, the pope's visit to Ireland in 1979 gave a strong boost to Roman Catholic morale, with over 2.5 million people attending at the seven venues of the pope's itinerary.[17]

The outbreak of Charismatic experience in the Roman Catholic Church in the republic was evident during this period.[18] Several large gatherings took place at the Quaker Friends Meeting House in Eustace Street, Dublin, at which various Pentecostal, Charismatic, Catholic, and Protestant people read the Scriptures and praised God together. The renewal spread across the country throughout the 1970s, with several "Life in the Spirit" seminars being organized in which the Spirit-filled Christian gospel was explained to people. As a result, thousands of individuals came into a personal and vibrant relationship with God and many were filled with, or baptized in, the Spirit.

However, after a few years, the Charismatic Renewal movement was drawn more closely under the control and authority of the Catholic hierarchy. Perhaps there was a growing concern among the Catholic Church's authority regarding the experiential and spontaneous nature of the new movement, which seemed to have little time for formal liturgy and ritual. Over time, thousands of individuals and families who had had a deep experience of God within the Charismatic Renewal now found their way into new Charismatic groupings; thus, a new situation emerged in Ireland in the 1980s and 1990s.

The full action of the Holy Spirit in bringing the Charismatic Renewal to Catholics in Ireland can never be fully recounted; however, the historical and theological significance of the Charismatic Renewal on the growth and development of the Pentecostal community is clearly evident. First, this growth is evident from the number of individuals and families who came from the Charismatic Renewal into the Pentecostal community, especially during the mid-1980s and early 1990s. These people were not only full of the Spirit, but the time spent in the Charismatic Renewal afforded an opportunity for people to become informed biblically and to have a good, solid foundation of the gospel and of the vital importance of having a personal relationship with the Lord. Second, a considerable number of these individuals are now senior leaders and pastors in the Pentecostal community, and from the data gathered from the one-to-one interviews, it became evident that several of their sons and daughters are also now involved in ministry. These individuals and their families have helped shape and influence the historical and theological development of the AGI and the wider Pentecostal community in Ireland. The Catholic Charismatic Renewal[19] is still very much alive and well in Ireland, with hundreds of prayer meetings taking place in villages and towns across the island.

Presently, although general erosion in the institutional church is occurring, the number of Pentecostal, Charismatic, and Evangelical Christians is on the rise. The growth comes from a number of sources. First, there came the beginning of what is called the "house church" movement. House churches can be characterized as independent groups or fellowships that meet in venues, such as private houses, schools, and hotels, for prayer, worship, Bible studies, and participative services. Perhaps the rise of these groups reflects Irish society's general drift away from established structure and authority. The strongest of these could be described as accessible, informal, relational, and charismatic. Some of these fellowships have developed structures and forms of leadership appropriate to the growing Christian communities.

Having explored the origins and the development of the AGI in Ireland, the Charismatic Renewal, and highlighting the historical and theological significance of the Charismatic Renewal movement on the development of the Pentecostal community in the republic, the final section explores some of the challenges and opportunities facing the twenty-first-century Pentecostal/Charismatic community in the Republic of Ireland.

Several interviews were carried out during the past year with senior members of the AGI and with pastors/leaders involved in ministry in other Pentecostal churches. The question posed was: What do you think are the challenges and opportunities that face the Pentecostal community in Ireland? The following is a summary of the respondents' thoughts.

Opportunities and Challenges

The rich diversity within the growing Pentecostal/Charismatic community in Ireland today provides a timely opportunity for all to work toward mutual understanding and enhanced cooperation in sharing the gospel. The New Irish or migrant-led Pentecostal and Charismatic communities are growing steadily in Ireland, and Abel Ugba, in his book *Shades of Belonging: African Pentecostals in Twenty-First-Century Ireland* (2009), has provided useful insights into these new churches regarding their theology, culture, customs, and sense of community. Some of the larger Pentecostal/Charismatic organizations in Ireland today are Christ Apostolic Church, Redeemed Christian Church of God, the Mountain of Fire and Miracle Ministry, and the Gospel Faith Mission.[20] It would be advantageous for further interaction to take place between the more established communities and the various newer Pentecostal organizations. The Republic of Ireland, relatively speaking, is very small in comparison to other countries, and Irish society needs to see and witness more cohesiveness within the wider Christian church so that the gospel can be proclaimed and lived out in unity within diversity.

Second, the values of equality and pluralism allow for the pursuit of spiritual experiences in a way that contrasts with the situation in the earlier part of twentieth-century Ireland. A significant number of people are looking for some type of spirituality. We have a wonderful, rich history of oral tradition in Ireland, and as the Pentecostal/Charismatic community comes together, there is an opportunity to tell people about the faith and about Jesus. The prevailing worldview of scientific materialism tends to discount spiritual experiences that are not outwardly observable and measurable. Nevertheless, people in wider Irish society are favorably disposed to people telling their stories, and the Pentecostal/Charismatic community has a wonderful opportunity through enhanced cooperation to share the gospel in the areas where they live. The lived-out social gospel is a powerful tool, and the AGI needs to be engaging in this type of evangelism. Irish history tells us that over the centuries, beginning with St. Patrick, the gospel reached into Irish society from AD 430 until his death. His example may provide a template for the AGI today.[21]

Since the economic downturn, Irish society has experienced huge fiscal problems, with the result that the unemployment rate stands at 11 percent. The social deprivation is tangible across the country; people and families are struggling to pay mortgages and pay for their children's education, and small rural and urban communities have been decimated. Irish society is crying out for help, and once again the opportunity to help, to support, and to live out the gospel is there for the Pentecostal/Charismatic community to actively engage.

The interim superintendent of the AGI, when asked about the challenges and opportunities that face the Pentecostal/Charismatic community in Ireland, suggests that the shifts in Irish society have created a massive spiritual hunger in the land. The leaders and individuals in the AGI are having conversations with people we never thought we would engage about life, about life matters, and about church and what that means. This present situation offers a timely opportunity for the Christian community to actively engage with people and share their testimonies with regard to the love of the Lord and to encourage people to see that He is the answer to their spiritual hunger.

One of the main challenges that faces the AGI is the lack of finances. So many of the proposed initiatives that will help support, train, and equip the various churches in the AGI are lacking the financial aid to carry out these programs. The financial crisis that has impacted Ireland and its economy over the past six years has had a significant effect on the AGI and its members. Churches around Ireland are struggling to pay their own pastors a living wage, and as a result there are little or no finances to advance necessary ongoing theological and pastoral education for the ministers already involved in ministry.

Another challenge for the AGI is the issue of how best to lead the movement at present and into the future. The first national leader has set the vision and identified three core pillars—raising up leaders, strengthening the local church, and planting churches—and now we need to create a new model of leadership for the AGI. The AGI is there to serve churches, and given the economic crisis, financing a superintendent whose primary role is to lead the AGI may not be a sustainable model in the Irish context. Over the next two years, the AGI hopes to craft a suitable template that will sustain the growing national movement and its leadership team.

In spite of the fiscal situation in Ireland, it is evident that the AGI are actively pursuing the education of their present and future leaders in a wide range of biblically and theologically focused courses. The formation of the School of Advanced Leadership Training (SALT) in 2012 is just one example of the commitment the AGI has toward further education. Additionally, in most AGI churches, there are various types of discipleship and internship programs. The challenge at the present time is for the AGI to actively engage more robustly with the validated IBI college and to use the resources that are readily available. The benefits of being partnered with IBI are manifold: students can avail themselves of wider theological perspectives, actively engage with students and staff from different faith expressions, and, crucially, have a more informed and rounded theological foundation that would be of benefit to their ministry in Ireland in the twenty-first century. Facilitating students to think for themselves and to be able to critique and evaluate diverse theological and biblical perspectives are core skills that need to be encouraged, and IBI has the resources to assist Pentecostal/Charismatic communities in this endeavor in Ireland.

A further challenge that became evident as a result of the research is that of women in leadership roles. The AGI theologically subscribes to advocating both women and men as pastors, teachers, and in leadership roles, yet the reality is that in only a few churches are there any women in senior leadership. As far as one can ascertain at present, there are no women on the general council of the AGI or women on the credentialing committee. Consequently, the challenge that faces the Pentecostal community is for a more conscious effort to discern, actively promote, and train young women into ministerial roles within the AGI. On a positive note, since its inception in 2012, SALT has had an equal number of men and women committed to the yearlong training, and a significant number of women are presently involved in children's ministry and pastoral ministry. Nevertheless, although this issue is perhaps a universal one, it needs to be addressed in a more direct and decisive manner in the present and for the future of the Pentecostal/Charismatic community in Ireland.

Addressing the Issues

Since its inception, the AGI has clearly achieved a considerable amount in respect to church planting, training up leaders, and strengthening the local churches, but much work still needs to be done. The theological challenges and opportunities outlined in this research will need to be kept in mind and at the forefront of the movement in the present, but also into the future.

The Republic of Ireland has a long Christian heritage dating back to the fifth century, and now, as we endeavor to live as Spirit-filled Christians in the twenty-first century, the movement needs to fully embrace the concept of unity in diversity, grapple with the significance of promoting and engaging with ongoing theological education, address the issue of women in leadership roles, formulate an appropriate template for the AGI leadership, and find new and creative ways to finance the movement. One of the ways to address these issues might be to engage with the global Pentecostal community and embrace its rich heritage and experience in these matters. Second, seeking outside assistance from experienced pastors, fundraisers, and women who are active in leadership roles in the republic may prove very insightful and be a support to the AGI leadership team in the present and into the future. Third, a genuine willingness and a desire to address these issues may involve a change in attitudes and perspectives, principally regarding furthering theological education, considering women in leadership, and working toward a deeper sense of connectedness with the wider Christian community. In addition, cultural mores that have been inculcated into the hearts and minds of individuals, such as having male-only priests, maybe an unconscious mind-set that the AGI has embraced and has not fully addressed or is even aware of; nevertheless, this is an issue that the AGI needs to acknowledge. The AGI celebrated its tenth anniversary in 2015, and while it would be beneficial to reflect upon its origins and development, more significantly it ought to be asking fundamental questions regarding the challenges that have been discussed here. This may prove beneficial to the Pentecostal community in the Republic of Ireland.

Conclusion

The essential prerequisite for the AGI in the twenty-first century is for the movement to stay relevant and connected through the leading of the Holy Spirit while promoting well-trained and theologically informed men and women leaders who can in turn mentor the present and future generations of Spirit-filled and renewed individuals to minister in the Republic of Ireland in the spirit of unity and mutual understanding. The present challenges and opportunities that face the Pentecostal movement are manifold, yet determination and a willingness to address the issues one by one will no doubt facilitate the AGI in strengthening its role in Irish society and as a result make a real contribution in spreading the Spirit-filled gospel across this nation in the twenty-first century.

Chapter 17

Women in Pentecostalism in Europe

Rakel Ystebø Alegre

When Pentecostalism came to Europe in 1906 and 1907, many women had the freedom to preach, teach, pray, and prophesy in public, and women proved essential for the expansion of the movement in its early years. They ministered in their churches and homes, traveled as evangelists and missionaries, and wrote extensively in Pentecostal publications. The experience of Spirit baptism was empowering, and as both men and women wished to be led by the Holy Spirit, it was important to not restrict the Spirit's work and influence—even if it came through a female vessel. As the years passed, however, the ministry of women was increasingly limited, especially because of an uneasiness concerning the right interpretation of Pauline passages on women's public ministry, but also as the result of increasing institutionalization. Several Pentecostal scholars have interpreted this dynamic within the framework of "Max Weber's conjecture that religion of the disprivileged classes is characterized by the tendency to allot equality to women initially, until the routinization and regimentation of community relationships sets in and the early practice recedes."[1] Another approach to this dynamic is the analysis of how Pentecostals' restorationist and pragmatic impulses affected women's opportunities to minister both positively and negatively, which resulted in mixed opportunities for women in the early decades of the movement.[2] In recent times, many of the formal restrictions on women in leadership have been removed, but Pentecostal women still experience barriers in entering the ministry—as can be seen in the case of Norwegian and Swedish Pentecostalism.

In this chapter, I will first demonstrate the prominent role of women in early northern and western European Pentecostalism and then look at some of the central Pentecostal leaders' views on women in ministry in the movement's first decades. Thereafter, I will focus on recent developments in the public ministry of women, choosing Norwegian and Swedish Pentecostalism as a case study. As will become apparent to those familiar with the topic, the trajectory of European Pentecostal women's opportunities in ministry has in several ways been parallel to the developments in North America,[3] of which much more research has been done, but it is also distinct because of particular national and ecclesial contexts.

The Role of Women in Early European Pentecostalism

The writing of Pentecostal history has demonstrated a "persistent gender bias," where the role of men has been emphasized and that of women downplayed.[4] The story is usually centered on the arrival or leadership of a man, as in the case of Lucy Farrow (1851–1911) and William Seymour (1870–1922), and the ministerial work of women is often uncredited, or at least disappears in the story of the great male leaders.[5] Some efforts have been done to correct this story by investigating the role of female leaders related to Azusa Street, the spread of early Pentecostalism through female evangelists and missionaries, and the great impact that women such as Maria Woodworth-Etter (1844–1924), Carrie Judd Montgomery (1858–1946), Pandita Ramabai (1858–1922), and Aimee Semple McPherson (1890–1944) had on the Pentecostal movement.[6] Telling the story of these women is an important task, not only to overcome the gender bias in Pentecostal historiography, but also because when the evidence of female leaders is left out, this may reinforce restrictive views of women's ministry today.

The common way to describe the beginnings of European

Pentecostalism is by tracing the story of Thomas Ball Barratt (1862–1940), "the apostle of Pentecostalism to Europe," and male leaders from other countries who directly or indirectly came into contact with Barratt and the Pentecostal revival in Oslo in 1907.[7] Lewi Pethrus (1844–1974) from Sweden, Alexander A. Boddy (1854–1930) from England, Jonathan Paul (1853–1931) from Germany, and Gerrit Polman (1868–1932) from the Netherlands were very important leaders of European Pentecostalism in its founding years. However, the focus on the role of these men may obscure the important role of women in the movement's beginnings in the countries they represent. To illustrate this point, we can look at the key role of women in leading Barratt to his Pentecostal conviction and experience and then highlight the story of some key female leaders in the spread and growth of early European Pentecostalism.

T. B. Barratt was a British-Norwegian Methodist minister who was in New York when he heard of the Azusa Street revival in 1906. Inspired by the periodical *The Apostolic Faith*, the testimonies of eyewitnesses he met in New York, and his own correspondence with Azusa Street, he started to fervently pray for his own Spirit baptism with tongues.[8] He was still seeking this experience when Lucy Leatherman (ca. 1870–1925), who had been baptized in the Spirit when Lucy Farrow laid hands on her at the revival at Azusa Street, arrived in New York in November 1906.[9] Barratt requested to talk to her and explained his feelings surrounding this in the following way in 1907:

> Calling on Mrs. L-, the wife of a physician, who had received her Pentecost, I conversed with her about the subject and requested her prayers. The Devil taunted me by saying: "The idea of a minister going to ask a woman to pray for him!" I bade him begone. She prayed with me and sent me to a meeting, conducted by a friend of hers.[10]

Maud Williams was leading the meetings she recommended, and there, on November 15, 1906, Barratt received the baptism in the

Spirit and started speaking in tongues while Lucy Leatherman and a Norwegian man prayed for him.[11] Thus, we see the key involvement of women in Barratt's experience of Spirit baptism, an experience that was decisive for his future Pentecostal ministry in Europe.

From the first days of the Pentecostal revival in Oslo in 1907, there were especially three Norwegian women who stood out as important leaders: Laura Barratt (1866–1951), Dagmar Gregersen (1881–1984), and Agnes Thelle (1876–1968). Barratt's wife, Laura, was a strong partner in ministry from the time they married in 1887. She assisted her husband in pastoral tasks, in leading meetings, and in editing and publishing the periodical *Byposten*, and she was often left in charge of the ministry when he was traveling abroad. Laura became an experienced preacher, was a leader in the women's temperance movement, was an active supporter of social work and reform, and was a great champion for women's right to minister.[12] In addition, she ministered to many of their national and international guests informally in their home. It is also likely that Laura greatly influenced Barratt's decision to endorse believer's baptism and be rebaptized in 1913.[13] When Barratt officially founded the Filadelfia Church in Oslo in 1916, Laura was on the board as deaconess, and though they worked in many ways as partners in the ministry, Laura is rarely recognized for her contribution.[14]

Dagmar Gregersen, a twenty-five-year-old teacher, and Agnes Thelle, a young milliner, were leading figures in early Norwegian Pentecostalism known for their evangelistic and prophetic ministries and especially for their messages in tongues. They made an impact on early European Pentecostalism when, in 1907, they set out on a five-month preaching tour, visiting Denmark, Germany, Switzerland, and England.[15] In several places, revivals broke out, and the meetings attracted large crowds. Their best-known meetings were those held in Germany. The German Holiness preacher Emil Meyer (1869–1950) met the women and heard them give messages in tongues when he visited Oslo in June 1907. Impressed by their ministry, he invited them to accompany him to Hamburg to preach there. While in Hamburg, they met the evangelist Heinrich

Dallmeyer (1870–1925), who invited them to minister with him in Kassel starting July 7, 1907.[16] The meeting campaign started well, and the women preached and gave messages in tongues, and several were baptized in the Spirit. However, soon some of the people attending started having excessive and hysterical manifestations, and Dallmeyer lost control over the meetings, which led visiting leaders to state that a foreign spirit had infiltrated the meetings. Contradicting messages in tongues were given, and when Dallmeyer would not take further control or discontinue the meetings, Gregersen and Thelle left Kassel in protest on July 25.[17] The following week, further chaos emerged in the meetings, and on August 2 they were discontinued by order of the police and city council of Kassel. The movement that started there was soon widely condemned and caused major difficulties for German Pentecostalism, but despite the Kassel event and mixed opinions about their ministry, Gregersen and Thelle are still viewed as key figures in the start and development of German Pentecostalism.[18] They also played an important role in Switzerland as the first preachers to bring the Pentecostal revival to the country.[19]

In 1908, Gregersen and Thelle represented Norwegian Pentecostals together with Laura Barratt at Alexander Boddy's first Pentecostal conference in Sunderland, and the three women were given several opportunities to speak.[20] Some of Gregersen's and Thelle's visions, prophetic messages, and testimonies were also published in the British Pentecostal periodical *Confidence* and thus distributed to a large audience.[21] After the conference, Gregesen and Thelle left for New York to train for missions at A. B. Simpson's Bible Institute, and in 1910 they became the first Norwegian Pentecostal missionaries when they left for Banda in India.[22] From that time, they were also leading in the expansion and organization of foreign missions from Norway.

Women also played a very important role in the beginnings of British Pentecostalism, as demonstrated by Diane Chapman in her research on women in the period 1907–1914,[23] though the story is often centered on the leadership of the Anglican vicar Alexander

Boddy and other male leaders. The first person associated with the Pentecostal revival to speak in tongues was Mrs. Catherine Price, which she did in early January 1907 in her home in Brixton, and the next night she gave a message in tongues with interpretation at a convention meeting in London.[24] Mrs. Price was leading a prayer group, and the meetings held with them after her Spirit baptism are considered the "first definitely Pentecostal meetings established in England."[25]

In March 1907, Alexander Boddy had been in Norway and seen the Pentecostal revival in Oslo, and since then he had insisted that T. B. Barratt come minister at his parish in Sunderland.[26] Barratt finally arrived the last day of August, and Mrs. Mary Boddy (1859–1928) was the first to be baptized in the Spirit and speak in tongues when Barratt prayed for her. Ten days later, on September 21, the Boddys' two teenage daughters, May (fifteen years old) and Janie (fourteen years old), were also baptized in the Spirit. Alexander Boddy did not speak in tongues for several months but widely distributed the testimonies of his wife and daughters.[27] Mrs. Boddy figures as a clear leader of the movement in Sunderland along with her husband and participated extensively in Pentecostal meetings and publications. Her ministry of laying on of hands for divine healing and Spirit baptism was especially strong, and well-known Pentecostal ministers, such as Smith Wigglesworth (1859–1947), Stanley Frodsham (1882–1969), and Gerrit Polman, were filled with the Spirit and spoke in tongues under her prayers.[28]

The Sunderland Convention led by Alexander Boddy and held once a year from 1908 to 1914 was an important center for European Pentecostalism and gathered leaders from many nations in Western and Northern Europe. In these conferences, women participated extensively as speakers and in discussions on different theological issues, and this demonstrates the freedom given to women as preachers, prophetesses, and teachers in the early years.[29] Other British women who impacted early Pentecostalism were Mrs. Lydia Walshaw (1854–1945), Eleanor Crisp (d. 1923), Polly Wigglesworth (1860–1913), and Christina Beruldsen (1885–1969).[30] The early openness to female ministers is likely connected to the Holiness Movement's and Keswick Convention's influences on many early Pentecostal leaders, such as Alexander Boddy. In the decades before the Pentecostal movement began, women such as Phoebe Palmer (1807–1874), Hannah Whitall Smith (1832–1911), Maria Woodworth-Etter (1844–1925), Catherine Booth (1829–1890), and Jessie Penn-Lewis (1861–1927) had paved the way for female ministers in Britain.[31]

The famous Danish actress Anna Larssen (1875–1955) had been working in theaters in Copenhagen since 1885 when she became a Christian in 1908. Later that same year, Barratt held Pentecostal meetings in the city, and on Sunday, December 13, 1908, Larssen was invited to dine with him and the widowed pastor's wife Mrs. Mollerup, with whom he was staying.[32] Here Barratt prayed for her and she was instantly baptized in the Spirit. After this event, Larssen states that she became a bold witness to her friends and colleagues and invited her colleagues to her house to hear Barratt preach.[33] Within a week, Anna Lewini (1876–1951), an actress who had been present, was also baptized in the Spirit. The news that both Larssen and Lewini had become Pentecostals caused a great uproar in Copenhagen, and even more so when they announced that they would leave the theater to serve God.[34] Larssen was thought to have suffered a mental breakdown and had to spend five weeks at a psychiatric institution for observation before she was released from her contract at the theater.[35]

Larssen now dedicated herself to preaching, writing articles in the movement's defense, and conducting readings of biblical dramatizations.[36] Her fame drew great audiences and gave her access to a variety of stages, as, for instance, when in 1913 she told her testimony in front of seven hundred students with the secular media reporting that it had a great effect on the audience.[37] In 1912, Larssen married Sigurd Bjørner (1875–1953), a Salvation Army officer, and together they became the most prominent leaders of the Danish Pentecostal movement. She served as evangelist and pastor, also preaching in Norway and Sweden, and is considered the most effective leader of the early Pentecostal movement in Denmark.[38]

The most important leaders in the birth and formative years of Dutch Pentecostalism were Gerrit and his wife, Wilhelmine Polman (1878–1961). They had a Salvation Army background, but in 1903 they went to Alexander Dowie's Zion City, Illinois, to study and returned to the Netherlands in 1906, where they started a prayer group in Amsterdam.[39] The group soon heard of the revival in Azusa Street and that Spirit baptism with tongues was occurring in Europe, as well, and on "October 29, 1907, Mrs. Polman was the first of the prayer circle to receive the baptism with the Holy Spirit in this way."[40] The Polmans later became appreciated speakers at international Pentecostal conferences in the following years and were often mentioned as a couple in early publications, indicating that Wilhelmine was considered an equal partner in their ministry.

The beginnings of Pentecostalism in Norway, Germany, Switzerland, England, Sweden, and Denmark were strongly interconnected, and as we have seen, several women were key figures in the movement's early years. Many more could have been mentioned, as, for example, the Swedish evangelists Greta Andersson and Anna Blom, who brought Pentecostalism to Vaasa in Finland,[41] or Mrs. Ada Esselbach-Whiting (1867–1927), who is believed to be the first Pentecostal witness in Belgium.[42] In many countries, the majority of Pentecostal missionaries and a large number of their evangelists in the early years were women,[43] with many female leaders ministering in informal settings, such as their homes. Often women were the first to be baptized in the Spirit and speak in tongues, and their testimonies, preaching and prophetic gifts, and the laying on of hands for Spirit baptism and healing were essential in the expansion of Pentecostalism. The many testimonies and letters signed by women and printed in periodicals such as *Confidence* further gives evidence of the active role of women in the early years. Highlighting the role and stories of these women may help us see how women "were not just peripheral but central to the narrative" of early European Pentecostalism.[44]

Early Pentecostal Leaders' Views on Women in Ministry

As early as 1907, the Pentecostals came under scrutiny for the role of female leaders and adherents, and several reports remarked derogatorily that the majority of those attending the Pentecostal meetings were women.[45] While much of the manifestations of the revival was attributed to the emotionalism of hysterical women, many also were critical of women's liberty to prophesy, preach, teach, and lead, and some argued that women were more prone than men to be led astray.[46] In Oslo, the faculty at the Norwegian Lutheran School of Theology attacked the Pentecostals for permitting women to preach, and there was pressure from society and other Christians to conform to established gender roles and to a restrictive interpretation of verses concerning women's public ministry.[47]

The role of women was contended also among some early European Pentecostals, who were divided on the issue. Their different perspectives were influenced by the diversity of ecclesial backgrounds and national contexts and disagreements as to how to understand the Pauline verses that seemed to restrict women's ministry. T. B. Barratt was Methodist and Alexander Boddy Anglican, and both were strongly influenced by the Holiness movement. Paul was Lutheran, Pethrus was Baptist, the Polmans had a Salvation Army background, and those who joined the movement in each nation also came from diverse backgrounds. All were to some extent influenced by their respective tradition's views on women in ministry, as well as their personal experiences.

At the last Sunderland Convention in 1914, the topic "A Woman's Place in the Church" was discussed, and several leaders, including Alexander Boddy, Jonathan Paul, Joseph Walshaw, and Mrs. Polman, participated. There was consensus that women should engage in public prophetic ministry, but opinions were divided as to the possibility of women having *authority* over men through leadership and teaching.[48] Jonathan Paul seemed especially determined to limit women's ministries in these areas and appealed to 1 Corinthians

11, 1 Corinthians 14:34, and 1 Timothy 2:11–12. Further arguments were made from Genesis 1 and the headship of man, as well as from existing cultural assumptions concerning women's nature and place in society.[49] Joseph Walshaw and Alexander Boddy, who both had wives that were very active in ministry, seemed content with the current liberty of women to minister in Pentecostal circles. Boddy especially endorsed couples in ministry, saying, "Where the husband and wife worked together in harmony there was little or no difficulty, for the two were one."[50] He also clearly endorsed women's freedom to preach, teach, and prophesy through giving them a platform in his conferences and his periodical, and though his Anglican Church did not ordain women at the time, he did seem to favor the continued public ministry of women.[51]

One of the early Pentecostal leaders to go furthest in his defense of women's right to minister was T. B. Barratt. In his book *Kvinnens stilling i menigheten* (Woman's position in the church) from 1933, Barratt argues extensively for an egalitarian view of men and women in ministry, addressing the verses that were seen as restrictive of women's ministry. The key verses for Barratt are Galatians 3:27–29, and his main arguments are that allowing women to participate in church leadership is biblical and that a *Spirit-filled* church will recognize the callings and gifts of the women and not limit their ministry.[52] Barratt states that Jesus brought full restoration to women, that Paul in reality wished to liberate and emancipate women, and that the ministries of Priscilla, Junia, Lydia, Phoebe, and Deborah demonstrate that women are free to preach, teach, and do apostolic work and are capable of leadership.[53] Their current work on the mission fields demonstrates this, as they fill many more roles than those of evangelists, deacons, and prophetesses.[54] Barratt also argued that 1 Corinthians 14:34 cannot be referring to public speaking but addresses chattering during the services, because in other verses Paul shows that women are to use their spiritual gifts, such as prophesying publicly, and when the Spirit constantly gives women the gift of prophecy it is evident that God does not intend them to be silent.[55] He also believed that they could teach and preach as long as they did so led by the Spirit and in humility, which should also be the case among men, and argued that 1 Timothy 2:11–12 only refers to teaching with a desire to *govern* or *suppress* men and that a strong emphasis on these verses does not take all of God's Word into account.[56] Further, he said that those who repress women and their gifts are sinning against the influence of the Holy Spirit and that if women are suppressed, both men and women suffer the consequences and the church is weakened.[57]

Barratt believed that full equality between men and women is the real model of the early church and the biblical ideal but that it sometimes is necessary to adapt to the gender norms of a local culture if the gospel of salvation is to have entrance there, which always is the most important consideration. Adapting to culture is also motivated by the desire to keep peace in the church and within society, but he made assurances that in the eyes of God there is no difference between men and women.[58] In his booklet, he indirectly argued that women may hold any leadership position in the church, such as those of elder, pastor, and apostle, without stating his endorsement of this with plain words. Using these titles may have felt too controversial, but his assistant pastor, Martin Ski, maintains that Barratt in his later years argued for full equality in ministry and that his book was not received well among Pentecostals in Norway.[59] Even though Barratt was the undisputed leader of Norwegian Pentecostalism from 1907 to 1940, he could not win over the majority of Pentecostal preachers for his views on women in ministry.

Women's Leadership in Norwegian and Swedish Pentecostalism

The Norwegian Pentecostal movement (NPM) and the Swedish Pentecostal movement (SPM) are congregationalist and loosely organized movements. They have not had a strong central organization, nor have they had binding teaching documents or national credentials, and the churches have been united mostly through periodicals and conferences.[60] The debate on women's ministry has taken place in this particular context and thus differs from that of many Pentecostal denominations in other countries. Both NPM and SPM have had many female missionaries, evangelists, prophetesses, preachers, and leaders, but women were usually excluded from pastoral positions and the boards of elders until recent times. Even though each church is independent and may decide if they wish to have female pastors or elders, most churches have adhered to the prevailing majority opinion on the issue at different times in the NPM and SPM.

When Barratt structured the leadership of his Pentecostal church Filadelfia in 1916, he organized the leadership group to include the main pastor, male elders, and female deaconesses.[61] However, when Barratt died in 1940, his leaders in Filadelfia started excluding women from leadership. The role of deaconesses was gradually reduced, and they were no longer allowed to participate in the board meetings, to Laura Barratt's great disappointment.[62] From this period, it seems that only men figured on the boards of NPM churches.[63] Lewi Pethrus, the most important leader of the SPM, was more restrictive in his views on women in ministry than Barratt and did not allow women to be senior pastors, elders, or teachers. The majority of pastors and preachers in the SPM shared his views and interpreted 1 Corinthians 11:3ff and 1 Timothy 2:9ff literally.[64]

From about the 1940s to the 1970s, there was a decline in Pentecostal women's public ministry and leadership positions in both countries,[65] though they continued to be very active on the mission fields, but in the late '70s and early '80s the debate on women's position in the church resurfaced in Pentecostal periodicals and conferences. In Sweden in 1978, Wasti Feldt (1929–2012) published the book *Kvinnan i frikyrkan* (Women in the free church), where she addressed the Pauline problem texts and argued in favor of female leadership. In 1980, she became the first woman to officially pastor an SPM church, but the issue of allowing female pastors was not discussed in the national conference until 1995.[66] The first female senior pastor to be consecrated in an NPM church was Marit Landrø (1941–) in 1993.[67]

In Norway, the debate on allowing women to be pastors and elders was ignited by the republication of Barratt's book on women in ministry in 1980 and the publication of the book *Kvinnen—fri til tjeneste?* (Woman—free to minister?) in 1984 by Ole-Georg Hoaas and Oddvar Tegnander. They argued sociologically, theologically, and exegetically for the full participation of women in leadership positions.[68] Thoralf Gilbrant (1919–2006), editor in chief of the Norwegian Pentecostal periodical *Korsets seier*, highly criticized this work, and in 1995 he published the book *"Her er ikke mann og kvinne"* ("There is neither male or female"), referring to Galatians 3:28. Here Gilbrant states that women can preach and be evangelists and deaconesses[69] but warns all church leaders against permitting women to be pastors, elders, or apostles or in authoritative teaching positions, since this would be against God's Word. These two books represent the poles of the recent debates in both Norway and Sweden, which mostly concerns the interpretation and application of the Pauline "problem verses" in the church today.

In Sweden, the first female elder in recent times was consecrated in 1988, and in 1996, the Filadelfia Church in Stockholm also opened up for female elders.[70] By the 1990s, some NPM churches had elected female elders, and in 1995 the issue was addressed at the preachers' conference. It was evident that opinions were divided, and no general recommendation was given, but from then on, more and more churches allowed for women to be elders and pastors. Filadelfia Oslo, the largest Pentecostal church in Norway and the congregation Barratt himself founded and led, decided to accept women as elders in 2007. Today many Pentecostal churches in Norway have women on the board of elders, and several also have female pastors, but due to the congregational structure, each church still decides their position on the issue.[71]

Though women in many NPM and SPM churches now face few formal or theological limitations, relatively few women occupy pastoral positions. A report from 2013 showed that the number of women pastors in the SPM was unchanged since 1994 and concluded that though the theological restrictions were removed, there were still barriers for women in entering pastoral ministry.[72] A debate concerning these barriers for women in ministry was sparked in Norway after the movement's national conference, Led (Lead), in February 2014. A young female preacher critiqued the conference and the NPM for the lack of female preachers and leaders.[73] Others followed up the critique and argued that it was a problem that the NPM was highly male-dominated and that women needed to be taken seriously and given more encouragement and opportunities.[74] Twenty-five-year-old Ingvild Ofte Arntsen suggested implementing gender quotas for conferences and boards to combat the current imbalance, which she believes is a result of culture and not theology, but this suggestion was met with mixed reactions.[75] However, the attention that this issue received by Pentecostal leaders and in Christian periodicals in 2014 and the beginnings of 2015 gives reason to believe that more conscious efforts to encourage and recruit women to preach and to be in leadership will be made in the future.[76] This dynamic, where women are allowed to hold pastoral and other leadership positions in Pentecostal denominations but where very few do so, can be witnessed in other European countries as well as in North America.[77] However, European Pentecostalism is so diverse in its origins, denominational structures, and different national, cultural, and historical contexts that the case of women in ministry in Norway and Sweden is not necessarily representative of Pentecostals in many other countries.[78]

Looking Toward the Future

Highlighting the role of women in the birth of the Pentecostal movement is an important aspect in looking for the way forward for Pentecostal women's ministry. It shows that women were and are *central* and not *peripheral* in the role of spreading the gospel and the Pentecostal message and that the mobilization of women for ministry will benefit the whole church. By consciously reinserting women in the historiography of the movement, one provides women today with role models and encourages Pentecostals to understand that men and women should work together also in public ministry for the effective expansion of the kingdom of God. However, as we have seen, Pentecostal women have faced, and still face today, different barriers that may discourage or limit their ministry. Some of these are theological or hermeneutical, and among Pentecostals in Norway, for example, there are still mixed views on what the biblical restrictions on women's public ministry are, which can create a sense of uneasiness for female ministers and in local churches.[79] Further biblical and theological work needs to be done among Pentecostals if more women are to feel at liberty to fill the positions of pastors and elders, for example. An interesting aspect of this is that T. B. Barratt, Norwegian Pentecostalism's greatest leader, could not convince many of his followers of his egalitarian view of men and women in ministry, but the movement he started now has begun to adopt his position. On the other hand, there are the dynamics of the "glass ceiling," which applies to women in both ecclesial and secular contexts.[80] Women do not only need to have theological acceptance to flourish in their ministry; they also need to be encouraged through role models, networking, training opportunities, leadership, speaking opportunities, and fair economic compensation for their work.[81] Finally, I believe the testimonies of early Pentecostal women can be of inspiration for Europeans and others. Anna Larssen (-Bjørner) gave testimony that the baptism in the Holy Spirit gave her *courage* to be a witness, and this *boldness* that the empowerment of the Spirit can give is an aspect of the Pentecostal heritage its women should revisit.

Part IV
North America and Global Theological Topics

Chapter 18

Canadian Pentecostals: Between a "Rock" (United States) and a "Hard Place" (Britain) Versus "Come Out From Among Them"

Pamela M. S. Holmes

When Canadian Pentecostalism emerged at the beginning of the twenty-first century, it found itself within a context where there was no real separation of church and state. Although Protestant (Anglican and then Scottish) clergy reserves had been abolished several decades later, the influence of the Church of England on Canadian ecclesial, political, and economic life was still significant.[1] Additionally, the Roman Catholic Church not only continued to provide social services within Quebec, but also was allocated national tax support for its separate (from public) school system throughout the country.[2] However, during the 1980s, under the guidance of prime minister Pierre Elliot Trudeau, about the same time as the maturing Canadian Pentecostal movement became more actively involved in the political realm, not only did Canada wrest its independence from England through the ratification of a distinctly Canadian constitution, but also it adopted a concurrent Charter of Rights and Freedoms in an American-style separation of church and state with its basis in Enlightenment rationality and liberal individualism.

Therefore, this chapter shall examine Canada's place as a country founded by an old empire, England, and influenced by a new empire, the United States of America, by comparing and contrasting the political and religious spheres of the three countries in order to argue that Canadian Pentecostalism's position as a "submodern" or early postmodern movement has a role to play in the ongoing formation of the dominion of Canada.

Historical Context

The United States of America was founded in 1776, when the Enlightenment's enthrallment with rationalism was in full swing. In contrast, "Canada had no enlightenment and very little eighteenth century [history as a nation]."[3] With its founding religious cultures being French Roman Catholic and British Anglican, Canada found it necessary to learn to accommodate diversity at least with its colonial and immigrant populations, if not its aboriginal peoples (with which it has had an admittedly horrid relationship). Rather than worrying about the pursuit of life, liberty, and happiness, as were the revolutionary writers of the Declaration of Independence in the United States in 1776, in 1867 the pragmatic Fathers of Canadian Confederation were looking to link together a vast, diverse, thinly spread people through building railways. While the United States was developing a national identity around the motto *E Pluribus Unum* (out of many, one), Canadians were striving to make sense of themselves as a nation *A mari usque ad mare* (from sea to sea). Part of that process of Canadian nation-building included blunting "the most menacing effects of the one situated immediately to their south" through the creation of a nation of people loyal to the Crown.[4]

As a result of this decidedly pragmatic and relatively unphilosophical approach to unity, groups within Canada, including religious ones, have enjoyed a much more British model of the relationship between church and state, whereby accommodation (not separation, as in the United States) is valued. As Canadian philosopher Charles Taylor quipped, "In a way, accommodating difference is what Canada is all about."[5] This included the Evangelical population. As sociologist Sam Reimer has pointed out, two of the biggest areas of differences between Evangelicals in Canada as compared to the United States involve political views and tolerance. While in the United States, religious and political conservatism oftentimes, although not always, go hand in hand, with many Evangelicals identifying themselves with the Republican Party, Canadian Evangelicals who share the same religious beliefs as their counterparts south of the border are much more tolerant and politically diverse. Reimer suggests this difference can be explained both theologically and historically by drawing on the work of historian Mark Noll. In the United States, an "optimistic postmillennialism, the Manichaean perception of the world as a battleground between good and evil, their moral absolutism, and their weak sense of institutional loyalty" fertilized the roots of evangelism, leading to political extremism. In contrast, in Canada, the "greater British influences, including deference to authority, the notion of responsible government, and the significant historical involvement of evangelicals in left-leaning politics" led to less extreme and polarized political involvement.[6]

However, it must not be thought that Canada replicated the British model. It did not. For example, in 1791, even before Canadian Confederation, a British parliamentary bill established that one-seventh of all lands (reserves) in Upper Canada had to be set aside for the use of Protestant (really only Anglican) clergy and church.[7] Even earlier, New France (later Lower Canada, now Quebec) and the Roman Catholic Church had been granted huge tracts of land (reserves) in exchange for providing educational and other social services. However, the abolishment of clergy reserves for the Anglican Church made it clear that England's establishmentarian approach would not be duplicated in Canada. Nor would the American separationist model or even the French's secular republicanism be adopted. Rather, Canada, even as it was disentangling itself from British practices, still kept a religious component in its formulating identity that included the idea of national churches, including Roman Catholicism.[8]

By the time of the Confederation in 1867, even though the

disestablishment of Anglican privilege had left the religious scene somewhat in disarray, the influence of religion remained in Canadian constitutional, social, economic, and political matters so much so that it was fair to depict Canada as fundamentally a religious nation, even a Christian one, with the goal of spreading this Christianity from "sea to sea."[9] Over the next forty years as Canada developed and expanded, "the consolidation of state, economy and religion went hand in hand," even as the population, 90 percent of which declared themselves to be Christian, doubled.[10] Even after the Second World War, it could be claimed that "the influence of organized religion in this country has never been stronger... even where emancipation from religious control has extended furthest a sharp limitation has been placed upon activity of a purely secular character."[11]

Recent Decades

By the 1960s, religion in Canada was in upheaval. Politically, partly in response to Quebecois nationalism and its striving for sovereignty through several failed referenda and accords,[12] the Canadian government published a controversial seven-volume *Report of the Royal Commission on Bilingualism and Biculturalism* intended to enshrine both French and English cultures as equal partners in Canada's founding.[13] However, the backlash from Canadians beyond these two groups led to the recognition of Canada as a multicultural mosaic.[14] By 1971, the federal government adopted a policy called "multiculturalism" and deemed it a good to be cultivated.[15] With Quebec and First Nations forming the context in which this pluralistic multiculturalism was adjudicated, religious diversity became intertwined with ethnicity or practice regarding how to live peacefully as diverse peoples.[16]

In terms of religious groups, up until the 1980s, Canadians could expect to be treated according to the prevailing British model of collective and communal accommodation. However, a move toward a more American style of individual rights emerged in 1982 when then prime minister Pierre Elliot Trudeau oversaw the signing of the new Constitution and its accompanying Charter of Rights and Freedom. No longer would groups be allocated rights, as was often the case in the traditional, collectivist, British approach, but rather, following the modern liberal and more American model, only individuals. Even though this new Constitution began with the words, "Whereas Canada is founded upon principles that recognize the supremacy of God and the rule of law,"[17] the Canadian state now had an obligation to make sure that individual rights and freedoms were legally upheld in spite of what any group, including religious ones, may want, decide, or believe.[18] This modern, liberal, American way of viewing the relationship between the church and the state as supposedly autonomous and separate spheres that can function without any influence on each other presupposed a dualistic bifurcation of the church as a place of private morality and belief and the state as a public forum comprised of presumably neutral political institutions where individual rights and freedoms are held in check.[19]

In spite of these changes, even as late as 1988 it could be confidently stated that Canada remained "a society where Christian traditions with historical roots in Britain and Western Europe dominated the demography of religious identity from Newfoundland to British Columbia."[20] Today Canada is officially a multicultural mosaic with religious pluralism as part of this ideology, with a British communal style of accommodation coupled with an American style emphasis on the rights and freedoms of individuals. Therefore, categories of *tolerance* and *accommodation* become legal terms for adjudicating relationships related to differences including such matters as sexual orientation, political dissent, and disabilities. However, when it comes to cultural differences that are indissolubly intertwined with religious differences, the practice becomes less clear and often conflictual, with tolerant accommodation easily set aside.[21] Nevertheless, as Janet R. Jakobsen has pointed out, "If religious differences block public participation—if the representation of a plurality of religious participants in the public sphere is not possible, for example—then the promise of democracy remains unfulfilled."[22] While the memories of religious warring, both recently (after the events of 9/11 in the United States) and in the distant past (during the Protestant Reformation, when religious wars were tearing apart Europe), may have made the longing and striving for secularism, with its supposedly religious free social space, an attractive option, such a space is, in reality, infused with oftentimes unrecognized or unacknowledged value systems. Within a modern liberal context such as the one currently functioning within Canada, religion becomes essentialized as "something that inheres in people rather than an arena for reasoned deliberation" and is, therefore and ironically, reductively marginalized by the same ideal of liberal tolerance that claims to be value-free.[23]

Canadian Pentecostalism

While Canadian Pentecostalism has undoubtedly benefited from the contributions of immigrants and settlers from throughout the world, as Michael Di Giacomo has pointed out,[24] in the opening years of the twentieth century, as it was emerging in Canada and formulating who and what it was, it was noticeably influenced by both the United States and Britain. For example, on the one hand, Ellen and James Hebden, the founders and leaders of what may have been the first Pentecostal mission in Canada, the Hebden Mission in Toronto, Ontario, were British immigrants.[25] A British Anglican vicar from Sutherland, England, who had become Pentecostal attempted to establish the movement in Canada by organizing as the Pentecostal Missionary Union but failed.[26] On the other hand, Robert E. McAlister, who was active in the early organization of the Pentecostal Assemblies of Canada, claims to have received his baptism in the Holy Ghost at the Azusa Street Mission in Los Angeles, California, before returning to Canada to minister.[27] A. H. Argue, a businessman from Winnipeg, Manitoba, who helped found Pentecostalism in the Prairie provinces, received his baptism at the Chicago Mission of William H. Durham.[28] Nevertheless, the strong

British influence on Canada generally as a British colony was bound to influence the fledgling Pentecostal movement that in 1911 had only 515 members.[29] Therefore, it should not be surprising to discover that Canadian Pentecostalism has developed in ways that, while similar to the United States and Britain, has also attempted to learn from both of those nations' experiences as it struggled to find its own path. For example, while Canadian "Christian values" does not lead to an identification with the religious Right and the late Jerry Falwell's "moral majority" to the same extent as it does in the United States,[30] Pentecostal David Mainse, the host of *700 Huntley Street* along with Baptist leaders such as Ken Campbell have brought together a type of moderate majority and Renaissance Canada. With Pentecostal Assemblies of Canada pastor Harry Faught spearheading the emergence of the Evangelical Fellowship of Canada (EFC) in 1964, which brought together Pentecostals and Evangelicals, a venue for political input was formed, including but not limited to government involvement in lotteries and the treatment of women in Canadian society.[31] During 1981, a concerted effort was made by the EFC to have God recognized in the new Canadian Constitution even though then prime minister Pierre Elliot Trudeau was quoted as saying that he didn't think "God gives a damn whether he was in the constitution or not."[32] Nevertheless, God was included.

While this undoubtedly encouraged these Pentecostal and Evangelical lobbyists, it also indicated that Canada would not be a secular state with a clear separation of church and state. Rather, religion and the state would continue to share this particular public space. When Pentecostal Brian Stiller assumed the directorship of the EFC, the political activities expanded to include such matters as child abuse, the arms race, poverty, the nature of human life in regards to abortion and euthanasia, and homosexuality, along with the expected topic of evangelism.[33] Significantly, in recognition of Canada's multiculturalism, the EFC regularly stated its Evangelical views in the form of "reasonable persuasion in this pluralistic context." At no time did it call for a return to a "'Christian Canada,' with no inappropriate appeals to special revelation per se, and no threats of political revenge by Evangelicals if their preferences were not met. (All this was in marked contrast to their counterparts south of the border)."[34] While it remains to be seen whether or not the EFC is able to continue this type of dialogue or will be drawn into an American-style culture war, "Stiller and his colleagues played by the rules of Canadian public discourse. They argued their views with civility and cogency, holding makers of public policy and opinion to the standards of the Canadian public sphere."[35]

Nevertheless, as Canadian Pentecostalism, whether on its own or in conjunction with such groups as the Evangelical Fellowship of Canada with its political involvements, seeks to engage more intentionally with the political and public realms, it needs to first recognize its own adoption of modern, American-style, Enlightenment rationality in order to discern what is life-bringing and what is oppressive.[36] Perhaps embracing what the late Gerald T. Sheppard, a Pentecostal and former instructor at Emmanuel College in Toronto, called its "submodern" status could assist with this task of self-critique. While the term *modernity* is admittedly highly contested,[37] Sheppard used the categories of "right and left wings of modernity" to explain Canadian Pentecostalism's relationship with modernity and its inability to neatly fit into a "conservative versus liberal" paradigm.[38] While Pentecostals are oftentimes lumped with the right wing of modernity within Canada, Sheppard has pointed out that this is a historical misconception. As Sheppard has pointed out, while Pentecostalism emerged within modernity, it nevertheless was "not invited as equal partners into the modernist debate."[39] However, it could also be argued that Pentecostalism was a type of "early postmodern" movement, in the sense of being critical of modernity.[40] While at the time of its emergence in the early years of the twentieth century Canadian Pentecostals considered the rest of the churches to be deeply entrenched in the modernist movement, they considered their own Pentecostal emphases and critiques evidence of a "Third Force" within Christianity.[41] Therefore, those who became Pentecostal often found it necessary to "come out" from other churches.[42] More recently, as a shift to postmodern thinking and practices has occurred within many churches, this separation from the churches has not been necessary and Charismatic movements *within* the churches were formed.

Whether labeled as a submodern or early-postmodern movement, Canadian Pentecostalism has particular insights it can bring to the public sphere as Canada continues to develop its multiculturalism. Pentecostal are suspicious of modernity and do not for a moment believe that any system, philosophical or otherwise, can know the truth, the whole truth, and nothing but the truth. Such knowledge is only the domain of the divine. On the one hand, Canadian Pentecostals in congregations with which I have had contact have been quick to renounce worldly ways and sinful principalities and powers and have been reluctant to affirm man's wisdom and human knowledge.[43] On the other hand, they have assumed that they are quite capable of living their everyday lives in a way that reflects their ongoing relationship of openness to God within that same world. On the one hand, Pentecostals encourage one another to be "in the world but not of the world." On the other hand, their communal gatherings are meant to empower and equip for service to the rest of the world of which they are a part.[44]

In addition, as an experientially expressed form of Christianity that emphasizes what are understood to be divine/human encounters, Pentecostalism is distinctly mystical and ecstatic. Rational reflection is not excluded but is secondary to experiences of a human encounter with the Spirit understood to empower people to live out their Christian faith in a transformative fashion.[45] Supernatural manifestations of the presence of God are expected and welcomed.[46] Therefore, fears are present of becoming too intellectual and replacing an emphasis on the experiential and mystical aspects of faith with the rational. Pentecostals understand themselves to have a mission to help all peoples of the world come to know God in Christ through the Spirit by their evangelistic efforts. The movement is from the personal and inward, both as individuals and as communities, to the outward and public, both personal and nonpersonal. The assumption is that only transformed people can change structures. Transformation of corporate evils into life-giving realities is understood to involve individuals and the spiritual realm. The movement is from the corporate church community—both people and structure—to the world at large, both people groups and structures.[47] For Pentecostals, social transformation is not a rational, altruistic exercise but a synergistic relationship between humanity and God that begins with mystical encounter.[48] Nevertheless, as Sam Reimer points out,[49] while Pentecostals may not be able to specifically state how their personal transformation translates into public action, they are convinced that it does.

Pentecostals are looking for indications of the Spirit's presence in everything—that is, indications of spiritual life, as it is often called, that can be practically experienced as appropriate and livable by anyone and everyone. This submodern or early-postmodern critique of modern society that is part and parcel of what Pentecostalism is about is significant and deserving of further investigation, particularly as it confronts and challenges Enlightenment-style rationality with its emphasis on the rights of individuals.

However, as Alistair MacIntyre has pointed out, while liberal individualism explicitly assumes that there is no overriding good, it implicitly makes rulings and laws based on some normative stance and assumptions of what constitutes the good that is used to discern between various preferences and choices. This unacknowledged, normative stance not only allows those who have the power to impose their political, legal, social, and cultural views and preferences on others; it also silences dissenting, "rival conceptions of the good in the public arena."[50] Oftentimes this normative stance within pluralistic, liberal democracies such as Canada includes the notion of tolerance. Even if we disagree with what others think or do or believe, we agree to disagree—we tolerate each other—in order to live together without oppressing one another. Unfortunately, what is overlooked is that this particular normative stance is based in a particular epistemology—that is, that of the Enlightenment and its beliefs about what constitutes reason and knowledge, which both reflected and legitimated the interests and concerns of white Western European elite males. As Kristen Deede Johnson explains it:

> Liberal invocations of tolerance have their roots in a very distinct epistemology, which includes a belief that through the use of reason all people can be unified around a body of common truths and morals, regardless of their other differences. The goal is a unity that can stand despite an independent of differences, so that "public" life engages only what is held in common, while "divisive" differences are left in the "private" sphere.[51]

Having an explicit debate about various conceptions of the good rather than letting an unvoiced, hidden assumption rule would be in keeping with the pluralistic ideology of Canada, whose history does not include the period of the Enlightenment.

Conclusion

Before he left the EFC in 1997, Stiller reminded us that it was not individual versus communal, not personal versus political, but rather both/and. As he stated in regard to the work of the EFC:

> The emphasis on revivalism—life in the Spirit—and evangelism—calling people to faith and repentance—must not be lost. The renewal of inner life and reaching out to others must remain on top of our agendas. Now as we add another, redemptionism—the calling of our culture to obedience—let us not be trapped.[52]

These communal and relational aspects of Canadian Pentecostalism have been reaffirmed in recently years by David Wells, the general superintendent of the Pentecostal Assemblies of Canada (PAOC). In a pamphlet entitled "What I See" published in 2008, Well encourages the PAOC to move from a denomination dominated by bureaucracy to an undenominational or post-denominational family bound together by mutual cooperation and a commitment to church growth rather than any particular Pentecostal history of theology.[53] The emphasis on the relational and communal even at the corporate level, rather than individual rights, is striking in a Pentecostal group that affirms the need for individual salvation and Spirit baptism.

Pentecostalism in Canada has not yet been thoroughly researched.[54] The data that is coming forth indicates that there are similarities with the United States, its large and powerful neighbor to the south, but also significant differences. One of the significant reasons for the differences from American Pentecostalism is the influence of Britain on the Canadian Pentecostal scene in its emergence. Recognizing and owning this British influence could assist in countering the drift toward individual rights and freedoms and encourage Canadian Pentecostals to continue considering the communal well-being of all within the multicultural mosaic that is Canada. In addition, if Canadian Pentecostals were to own their identity as a submodern or early-postmodern communal group, it could continue to exercise a significant challenge to the liberal individualism currently noted within its Charter of Rights and Freedom. As a result, Canadian Pentecostalism could be one of several partners seeking to move Canada to a truly pluralist public sphere.

Finally, while this chapter has focused on the similarities and differences between American and Canadian and British and Canadian cultures and Pentecostalism, factoring in the contributions of those Canadian Pentecostals from others parts of the world needs to occur.[55]

Come, Holy Spirit. We need You…

Chapter 19

The Pentecostal Movement in Hawaii

Adrian Yuen

THIS CHAPTER PROVIDES a historical overview of religious beginnings in the Hawaiian islands and the early influx of Pentecostalism. Hawaii's unique multicultural, ethnic, and religious diversity is discussed, as it impacts the spiritual culture of the islands and the assimilation of Hawaii's churches from mainland denominational origins into their identities. The prospects for the future of Pentecostalism in Hawaii are also presented.

INTRODUCTION

When Hawaii assumed its position as the fiftieth state of the United States in 1959, it emerged in strategic prominence because its location in the Pacific was a catalyst for world trade, travel, and military defense; it also acted as a pathway for world missions and the spread of the gospel in the Pacific and Asia. Amidst the chain of many small volcanic islands that span over 1,500 miles, Hawaii is comprised of eight main inhabitable islands located at the southernmost end of the archipelago. Starting with the largest, these are Hawaii, Maui, Oahu, Kauai, Molokai, Lanai, Niihau, and Kahoolawe. Honolulu, the state capital, is located on Oahu, which has a population of nearly 1 million people. The population of the entire state is close to 1.4 million people.[1]

Hawaii is "the melting pot of the Pacific," a phrase used to describe Hawaii's diversity and blend of ethnic groups, cultures, and religions. That diversity makes Hawaii one of the most multicultural societies on earth. Hawaii mostly comprises the following ethnic groups: 336,599 white; 197,497 Filipino; 185,502 Japanese; 80,337 Native Hawaiian; 53,963 Chinese (excluding Taiwanese); 24,203 Korean; 21,424 black or African American; 18,287 Samoan; 9,779 Vietnamese; 6,316 Marshallese; 4,830 Tongan; and 4,164 American Indian and Alaska Native.[2] However, these numbers do not take into account people who identify as being of more than one race, which inflates the numbers for each ethnicity by 60 percent. The ethnic distribution of the total population in Hawaii was, in 2007, reported as 55 percent Asian, 23 percent Anglo, 10 percent Hawaiian, 9 percent Hispanic, and 3 percent African American.[3]

The spiritual climate of the islands is mixed with different religious movements. About 13 percent of Hawaiians attend church regularly, much lower than the national average of 17 percent. The distribution of major denominations in Hawaii in 2009 indicated 7 percent of church adherents were Evangelical, 2 percent mainline Protestant, and 4 percent Catholic, with 87 percent of the population absent.[4] The state motto of Hawaii, "*Ua Mau Ke Ea o ka Aina i ka Pono*" (originally with "*Iesu Kristo*" added to the ending), means "The life of the land is perpetuated in righteousness (in Christ)." It suggests a strong spiritual sense born from its ancient heritage, intricately woven into the *tapa* (fabric) of its culture.

Early History

There are different perspectives on the religious history of Hawaii. One view purports that the first missionaries came from the continental United States in the early 1800s with the intention to convert the Hawaiian people to Christianity and take them away from what the missionaries considered pagan religious practices. The other view argues that the Polynesian Hawaiians arrived in Hawaii with a belief system acknowledging one God. The Hawaiians worshipped the "One Supreme God, who created the heavens and the earth," whom they called *I'o*. They called the first man *Atea*[5] and "possessed the concept of a Supreme Being named *Hika-po-loa* or *Oi-e,* the latter meaning, 'most excellent,' 'supreme.'"[6]

The Hawaiian people had a rich oral history that was passed down generationally by word of mouth, which indicates that the "ancient Hawaiians who discovered and settled Hawaii over 1,600 years ago, knew and worshipped the One True God."[7] However, around 1,300 years ago, Tahitian conquerors, led by the priest Pa'ao, overthrew the worship of the one true God and established the harsh bondage of the kapu system of sacred laws. For over 500 years, the people lived under severe repressive laws and the absolute power of the ruling class, which operated under conditions of isolation, fear, and oppression.[8] According to traditional Hawaiian belief, "Pa'ao instituted the severe religious observances which built up the power of the chiefs and priests" and put to death all of the old *kahunas*, or priests, which resulted in very little being known of this ancient triune God.[9]

In the late 1800s and early 1900s, several historians salvaged and recorded what was left of the ancient oral histories of the Polynesian people. King Kamehameha V appointed a historian by the name of Abraham Fornander, who arrived in Hawaii shortly after the missionaries, to record the ancient oral histories of the Polynesian people. Because his wife was an *ali'i* of Molokai, Fornander had an appreciation for the dying Hawaiian culture and felt it was being replaced by the missionaries' culture. With his extensive knowledge of the Hawaiian language and with the appointed assistance of the future king, David Kalakaua, and the future queen, Lili'uokalani, Fornander was allowed to hear the "sacred traditions of the deep past that were never recorded before."[10] Fornander's dedication resulted in the compilation of these historical accounts in a large collection that describes the ancient beginning of the Polynesians. The early Hawaiians did not have any written language prior to the one developed by the missionaries. Their legends and myths had many similarities to biblical stories. These ancient Hawaiian historical narratives reflected the "ancient accounts of the various other Polynesian peoples," such as the Samoans, Tahitians, Tongans, Marquesans, and

Maoris, who were all referred to as "very close cousins."[11] There are many similarities among the accounts of Polynesian peoples, which indicates that "they were common to the Polynesians before they separated and spread to their various islands."[12] It was discovered that the ancient Hawaiians at one time not only believed in and worshipped one god, named I'o, but also that I'o comprised of three entities: Kane, Ku, and Lono.[13] While Kikawa's position is not necessarily widely accepted by the Evangelical Christian community of the islands, his views are increasingly being welcomed by the general Christian populace in Hawaii.

The Life and Prayers of Henry Opukahaia

The arrival of the white man to Hawaii introduced different ideologies and material resources that created a difficult social, economic, political, and cultural transition. During this tumultuous time, just four months after the death of King Kamehameha, the malevolent and harsh kapu system, which had been created by the kahunas and consisted of supposedly sacred laws, was abolished. This left the Hawaiian kingdom in chaos and spiritual confusion.[14]

The winds of spiritual change and the indelible influence of the missionaries in Hawaii cannot be described without first speaking about the moving biography of a Hawaiian youth named Henry Opukahaia. He lived from 1793 to 1819 and was fondly and inspiringly remembered as the first Hawaiian Christian.[15] Opukahaia had a tragic childhood. At the age of ten, he watched his parents slaughtered in war.[16] After the death of his parents, Opukahaia was raised by his uncle, a high kahuna in the Hawaiian religion, and was apprenticed in the rituals of their ancient religion and in the knowledge of their gods.[17]

Attempting to escape the tragedies of the past, the orphan Opukahaia was offered passage on a ship by a sea captain sailing to New England and eventually ended up in Connecticut. Also known as Obookiah, he accepted the one true God and was tutored by missionaries in the gospel of Jesus Christ. Millard writes, "Opukahaia, who was nurtured at the school, was filled with thanksgiving to Almighty God and His people. He was moved by compassion and burdened for his Hawaiian people, who remained in the gross of darkness of a heathen and superstitious society."[18] It is believed that Henry became quite a scholar, equivalent to that of a PhD degree recipient, and was found weeping on the steps of Yale College, asking God to save his people and to send missionaries to the islands.[19] Opukahaia attended the Foreign Missions School in New Haven, where he became a missionary and traveled all over Connecticut, pleading for churches to send missionaries to his people. Sadly, after contracting an infectious disease, Opukahaia died at the age of twenty-six. However, his fervent prayers and impassioned pleas were answered when missionaries set sail to the Hawaiian Islands, then called the Sandwich Islands.[20]

The First Missionaries and the Great Awakening

The first missionary group, made up of seventeen people, landed on the Kona coast of the Big Island on April 4, 1820. There they sought an audience with King Liholiho with the intent to convert him and the monarchy to Christianity. In 1825, the wife of Kamehameha the Great, Queen Ka'ahumanu, and King Kamehameha the Great's son, King Liholiho, both accepted Christianity. Dr. Henry Boshard records the account of the first missionaries who came to Hawaii and started the famed Mokuaikaua Church.[21] Thought to have initiated one of the greatest revivals in history, the Congregational missionaries began to make new converts to Christianity, especially among the reigning monarchy.[22]

The gospel's message was slow to win the hearts of the Hawaiian people. It took time for the missionaries to learn the Hawaiian language, to create the Hawaiian alphabet (since there was no written language at that time), and to translate the Bible into Hawaiian. However, much later, from 1837 to 1850, a revival broke out in what came to be referred to as the Great Awakening. There were more

Christians "per capita in Hawaii than in the United States."[23] Haili Church in Hilo was the largest church in the world, with 7,000 members and up to 10,000 people during this time of spiritual awakening. As spiritual revival swept through the islands, it was estimated that out of a population of 71,019 people, 68,241 claimed to be Christians. The spiritual hunger of the people caused some to walk to church services from as far as sixty miles away.[24]

Titus Coan, the co-pastor of Haili Church in Hilo, records some of the great manifestations of God during the time of the Great Awakening. He mentions the multitudes of people attending his meetings, openly repenting and praying. Coan writes:

> A very large concourse [congregation] were seated on the grass and I was standing…preaching, "Repentance toward God and faith in the Lord Jesus." Of a sudden, a man who had been gazing with intense interest at the preacher, burst out in a fervent prayer, with streaming tears, saying, "Lord, have mercy on me. I am dead in sin." His weeping was so loud, and his trembling so great that the whole congregation was moved.[25]

Coan records the following: "Sabbath, July 1838, out of 3,000 new converts, 1,705 new believers were baptized and received communion into the church."[26]

The Great Awakening was short-lived, as some descendants of the missionaries who became merchants began to exploit the people for financial gain, land acquisition, and sexual purposes. During this time, the merchants engaged in immoral sexual activities with the native Hawaiians, introducing venereal diseases and causing thousands of Hawaiians to die. As a result of this catastrophic social interaction, it is estimated that of the 150,000 native Hawaiians populating the islands in the 1800s, there were only about 3,800 native Hawaiians left by the 1950s. The Hawaiian peoples became spiritually disillusioned with the white missionaries, which caused some of the Hawaiian people to return to their old pagan gods and ancient practices.[27]

The Twentieth Century

During the 1920s, Christian denominations in the United States sought to plant more churches and to evangelize in foreign countries.[28] The Pentecostal revival also led to the formation of new denominations and new churches.[29]

The Assemblies of God

On May 1, 1929, a little over a hundred years after the first missionaries came to the islands, the first Assemblies of God missionary, Bernice Proctor, arrived in Hawaii. She wrote to the General Council of the Assemblies of God regarding God's call to go to Hawaii and was informed that the church had no immediate plans to send missionaries.[30]

Ms. Proctor persisted and fulfilled God's call to the islands and arrived in Hilo on the Big Island without financial support from her denomination.[31] After three years in Hawaii, she established the Glad Tidings Church in Hilo, which was within walking distance of where the first revival outbreak at Haili Church occurred under the co-leadership of Titus Coan. It seems that the early Pentecostal missionaries who came to Hawaii, much like the first Congregational and Anglican missionaries that arrived in the 1800s, came with the specific vision of sharing the message of Jesus Christ to people they assumed were pagan in their religious practices.[32]

Later, out of the Glad Tidings Church came a Filipino church pastored by E. C. Liberato, who would later plant other Filipino churches under the name of Church of the First Born Assemblies, known more popularly in Hawaii as the Full Gospel Temple, located on Oahu.[33] In December 1938, Reverend Peter Funk and his wife heard the call of God to preach the gospel and came to Hawaii. He eventually became the first Hawaii district superintendent for the Assemblies of God in 1949, followed by Harold Headrick, Woodrow Yasuhara, and George Nagato.

The Assemblies of God has been a leader among churches in advancing the more traditional perspective of the Pentecostal movements in the islands. Today, the Assemblies of God has one hundred churches in Hawaii, with an estimated membership of 12,000.[34] The foreign missions department allowed the Hawaii field to develop on its own.[35] During the 1960s, the First Assembly of God and the Door of Faith Church in Honolulu were the two largest churches in the state of Hawaii.

Today, the First Assembly of God and King's Cathedral, pastored by Dr. James Marocco, are the two largest Assemblies of God churches in the islands. There are several King's Cathedral Chapels in Hawaii, with Dr. Marocco as the one pastor with many supporting ministers.[36] Dr. George Nagato, the district superintendent, attributes the success of the Hawaiian churches to their having biblical balance along with an emphasis on world missions. He believes that leadership training and maintaining a good relationship with his leaders are the keys to success in the church. In the last five to ten years, several of the local churches have undertaken church-planting enterprises.

The Pentecostal Holiness Church and Door of Faith Church

In 1936, Mildred Johnson arrived as the first missionary for the Pentecostal Holiness denomination on Oahu. After graduating from Holmes Bible and Missionary Institute in 1935, where she learned the teachings and life of faith, Johnson felt the call of God to the islands, where she immediately began a church in Honolulu.[37] Her story is filled with testimonies of many miracles, signs, and wonders. Mildred Johnson married Alexander Peter Brostek, a US army officer, and became Mildred Johnson Brostek. By 1940, however, she was no longer affiliated with the Pentecostal Holiness Church.[38]

In 1941, just prior to World War II, Mildred Brostek established the Door of Faith Church in Honolulu, which has since grown in church plants and membership. Brostek was considered by some as Hawaii's Aimee Semple McPherson or Hawaii's Kathryn Kuhlman because of the many signs and wonders that were present in her church services. Brostek was theologically Pentecostal and was quick to identify teachings she felt were not consistent with biblical or Pentecostal teachings. Barbara Tengan, whose parents became pastors of the Wailuku church, worked with Brostek after graduating from Southwestern Baptist Theological Seminary in 1971. Although Brostek believed strongly in spiritual training, she discouraged formal education of the level that Tengan had achieved. Tengan was the first leader of the church with an advanced degree in Christian ministry. Tengan recalls donors giving properties to the ministry of Mildred Brostek, which enabled it to spread throughout Hawaii and to foreign countries. At one time, Brostek's ministry had over seven hundred churches in the Philippines, as well as churches in Hong Kong, Indonesia, Okinawa, Paris, South Africa, and Canada.[39]

When Mildred Brostek passed away in 2005, controversy ensued within the Door of Faith Church that caused some delay in the transition. Peter Brostek, Mildred Johnson Brostek's son, was appointed the successor. Peter's administrative and business sense made him aware of some of the changes the Door of Faith Church needed in order to transition from a top-down structure to a bottom-up leadership model. The Door of Faith Church is adapting to its new restructuring. Although Mildred Brostek may not have transferred the leadership in a timely manner, her legacy inspired many people to serve in the body of Christ and in other churches outside of her own organization, including people like Urban and Sally Wong, who established the United Gospel Fellowship on Oahu.

Mildred Brostek summed up her call to the mission field with the following:

> In a few short years the mission walked out of the cradle and across these islands. We trained our workers with the good old fashioned doctrine of Holiness. The power of God and Heaven's special duty angels are still at work, and by His grace we shall press the battle until we reach the gates of heaven and answer the roll call with millions from the Isles and every country of the world.[40]

After Mildred Brostek departed from the Pentecostal Holiness Church, the organization underwent a period of transition. Later, John McCaul, a missionary and convert from one of Brostek's meetings, and his wife, Mae, moved to Hawaii and began the Good Shepherd Pentecostal Holiness Church on Oahu. The couple devoted their lives to the formation of the Pentecostal Holiness Church in the islands.

After nearly thirty years of ministry under the McCauls and one year with the interim pastor, Dale Parker, the Pentecostal Holiness evangelism director, Leon Stewart, contacted Dr. Adrian Yuen to oversee the work in Hawaii. Dr. Yuen immediately established the local vision by creating Redemption Academy, a Christian day school, and Redemption Bible College, which has trained hundreds of Christian leaders. During Dr. Yuen's tenure between 1978 and 2005, the Pentecostal Holiness Churches expanded throughout Hawaii and the Pacific Rim, reaching out to New Zealand, the Philippines, and Australia. In addition, Dr. Yuen opened up a Spanish church in Honolulu called Su Gran Alabanza (His Highest Praise), and he established Fijian and Filipino outreaches. In 2005, Adrian Yuen resigned from the Pentecostal Holiness Church and started His Highest Praise International, a network of churches and affiliates throughout Hawaii, Nevada, California, New Zealand, the Philippines, Thailand, and Australia. These developments are indicative of rifts that can emerge between mainland denominational organizations and emerging leadership in the islands as church leaders try to navigate between established structures and Hawaii's unique multicultural perspectives.

The Pentecostal Holiness Church's presence in Hawaii has continued to grow under the leadership of Bishop Greg Hood to a total of fifteen churches throughout Hawaii. The Spanish Pentecostal Holiness Church in Hawaii is the largest Spanish Pentecostal church in Hawaii. Pastor Brian Mauricio and his wife, Sonia, have been pastoring the church since the late 1980s.

The Church of God (Cleveland, Tennessee) and the Church of God of Prophecy

In 1937, Fred and Lucille Litton came to Hawaii as missionaries for the Church of God. Immediately upon their arrival, there was a revival lasting twenty-six months that gave birth to two churches for the Church of God organization.[41] The first Church of God missionaries preached at churches throughout the islands until their departure four years later.

Charles Conn observes, "The Hawaiian work has increasingly assumed the appearance of that on the American Mainland, encouraged by the influx of preachers and members from the continental States."[42] The Church of God in Hawaii has maintained a strong mainland denominational identity alongside its multicultural diversity. Today, the Church of God has twenty-six churches located on the islands, including several ethnic churches. The total number of adherents to the Church of God in Hawaii is about 2,600.[43]

According to Gary Langley, the current bishop of the Hawaii Churches of God of Prophecy:

> The first recorded mention of interest for an organized Church of God of Prophecy (COGOP) church in the Hawaiian Islands was started in the year of 1955 by a young minister named Raymond Pruitt, who had a desire to further his education and fulfill God's call upon his life. After Mr. Pruitt graduated from the University of Hawaii, the Church of God of Prophecy in the islands ceased to exist for a period of time.[44]

In 1963, Charles Lanter was appointed by the General Assembly of the Churches of God of Prophecy as the missions overseer of the Hawaiian Islands. A plan for church planting and church growth has been laid out by the current leadership in Hawaii and includes addressing the exclusive mind-set that has existed in the past, improving coordination in church planting, combining three congregations into one church on Oahu, and providing leadership training and coordination, especially for newer or younger leaders.

West Coast Influences

In the early years of Hawaii's Pentecostal history, the churches that established outreaches were organizationally based in the Midwest or in the southern United States and reflected a specific philosophy of ministry and eschatology. Missiologist and historian Gary B. McGee describes the "radical strategy" of Pentecostal missiology as involving

> a uniquely pneumatological approach to mission that affirmed a belief in the need for a subsequent spiritual empowerment that sent the recipient toward a destiny connected to the continuing redemptive mission of Jesus Christ. The empowerment was for the purpose of world evangelism and the soon return of Christ made it necessary to "work while it is day."[45]

The West Coast churches that impacted the islands did not fully embrace the traditional Pentecostal missiology.

Three church groups, described as movements, originating from the US West Coast have swept the religious scene in Hawaii: the Calvary Chapel Association, the Hope Chapel churches, and the New Hope churches. Although these groups believe in the soon return of Jesus Christ, they have adopted a broader view regarding the ministry of the Holy Spirit that deemphasizes traditional practices, such as speaking in tongues, outward weeping, being slain in the Spirit, and the preaching of hellfire and brimstone. The younger and newer churches are not necessarily identified as Pentecostal, although two of these church clusters are affiliated with the International Church of the Foursquare Gospel. In fact, some of these churches, despite having a strong Evangelical foundation, are considered by some traditional and classical Pentecostals to be "lite gospel," with the focus on seeker-sensitive worship experiences. The urgency of the times, preached in the traditional Pentecostal churches, emphasized the belief that Jesus was coming soon. The doctrine of salvation was hinged on the state of a person's spiritual life at the moment of Jesus's return or at that person's death. To the early Pentecostals, only the pure in heart would see God, especially in light of the Wesleyan influences on Pentecostal theology espoused by some mainland organizations. A shift from this mindset has created a different approach to nonbelievers, who are viewed as "the unchurched" or "pre-believers."

Calvary Chapel

Calvary Chapel in Hawaii is associated with the late Chuck Smith, the founder of Calvary Chapel in Costa Mesa, California, and the father of the Calvary Chapel movement, which has over 1,500 associated fellowships in the world. Smith began Calvary Chapel Costa Mesa in 1965 with just twenty-five people, and today it attracts about 25,000 people weekly.[46]

Chuck Smith writes, "As I started reading and studying the Word of God, I could not find the Scripture that said the primary purpose of the church is the evangelization of the world."[47] He continues, saying, "But, I did find in Ephesians that God has placed gifted men, apostles, evangelists, prophets, pastor-teachers for the perfection of the saints for the work of the ministry, the building up of the body of Christ." It is from this perspective that Smith and Calvary Chapel churches emphasize expository preaching through the Bible. He concludes, "I no longer preached evangelistic sermons per se, but began to teach the Word of God in a consistent way designed to produce growth within the believers."

Calvary Chapel Honolulu is pastored by Bill Stonebreaker, who came to Hawaii in the early 1970s and eventually began the North Shore Christian Fellowship. In a moving biography, Stonebreaker talks about his troubled past and his journey with God, which has led him to become the senior pastor of his current church near Pearl Harbor.[48]

Calvary Chapel, known for the biblical exposition style of its original founder Chuck Smith, has a strong emphasis on biblical teachings and calls for balance rather than emphasizing on the visible manifestations of the Holy Spirit. Calvary Chapel is a loosely knit organization of churches "in fellowship" with about twenty-four churches affiliated with this organization. Calvary Chapel owns a radio station in Honolulu and is selective of the speakers allowed on their radio programs—a reflection, perhaps, of its founder's caution regarding extreme teachings in the Christian community.

Hope Chapel

Ralph Moore, founder of the Hope Chapel churches throughout the world, now resides in Hawaii and emphasizes accepting people just as they are without any expectations or conditions. Discipleship is an important component of the church, and there are many small church groups at the Kaneohe Bay Church. Moore is also responsible for the planting of Hope Chapel Hermosa Beach in California and many other churches on six continents. There are over two thousand weekly attendees at the Kaneohe Church.

Hope Chapel is an organization that appeals to baby boomers and younger people. Recognizing that Moore and Hope Chapel churches are relevant for these times and are consistent with the vision of the Foursquare denomination, Reverend Doug Murren, pastor of Eastside Foursquare Church in Bellevue-Kirkland, Washington, believes that Foursquare churches have been developed in preparation for the baby boomers and later generations.

New Hope

New Hope churches were founded by Hawaiian-born Wayne Cordeiro, whose local cultural roots and life story have an immediate appeal to islanders. Pastor Wayne and his family moved to Oahu in 1995 after twelve years of ministering at New Hope Hilo. New Hope has established churches throughout Hawaii, in four other states, and in other parts of the world. New Hope, like Hope Chapel, is associated with the International Church of the Foursquare Gospel. The worship tends to include a seeker-sensitive approach and practical and relevant preaching. Cordeiro believes that the ministry of the church is encouraged through teamwork. He advocates a broader view on the gifts of the Holy Spirit to embrace the totality of the gifts, such as serving, tongues, leadership, mercy, and giving.[49] They are considered to be one of the fastest-growing churches in the United States.

Future of Pentecostalism in Hawaii

The Pentecostal movement in Hawaii has the potential to grow and expand on many levels. However, various considerations may impact these prospects.

First, as churches in Hawaii diverge from their mainland traditional and denominational ties to find relevance in the context of the islands' diversity, they are emerging with their unique identities and are appealing to the local people, those in the younger generation in particular. Growing exponentially in church plants and adherents, these contemporary churches, which have similarities to new apostolic churches that are emerging, have the potential to become megachurches.[50] As these churches become less dogmatic in their traditional or denominational stance, some may decry the lowering of personal standards, which were greatly emphasized in the early Pentecost movement. Others may feel the need to address the perceived mind-set of exclusivity, which projects a posture of isolation and hesitancy in networking with other churches.

Second, traditional and denominational boundaries have become more permeable in Hawaii as people increasingly interface with one another in this technological age. With the increased visibility of churches, people are experiencing the freedom to visit other churches and their venues while maintaining their church identity or affiliation. While Hawaii's Pentecostal church attendance in 2008 accounted for 25 percent of all denominations in Hawaii, future statistics may be less defined as some churches move away from requiring membership, due in part to the fluidity and transiency of movement exercised by adherents among churches.[51]

Third, Hawaii's diverse culture, along with the "spirit of aloha," perpetuates a tolerant disposition that may eventually find Pentecostal churches becoming more receptive to networking with one another in what is called *ho'olokahi*, or "coming together as one force." Although it is highly unlikely that these churches will reach a one-church ecumenicity, Pentecostal churches will assume a more blended identity. Churches in the past were influenced by their own denominational cultures, which gave them a sense of uniqueness and identity. Ironically, there is a growing polemical and apologetic caution among some churches and movements that may cause their leadership to hesitate in coming together.

Fourth, there is also a countermovement in Hawaii that transcends any religious institution. For Pentecostals, such is born in the heart of the human soul that hungers and thirsts after God and seeks to find relevance, theologically and perhaps even therapeutically, while trying to understand one's own life. Vinson Synan, drawing from Bishop Lesslie Newbigin, speaks of "three streams or three divisions of Christianity." The first stream is the importance of the "continuity, orthodoxy, and sacraments to the life of the church," the second stream emphasizes the "centrality of the scriptures and the importance of the proclaimed Word of God," and the third stream emphasizes the "present action of the Spirit in the church through the gifts of the Holy Spirit"; all of these streams converge into "one river" to produce a "unified Christian witness."[52] Perhaps one stream apart from the others will not quench the insatiable thirst for God, but rather drinking from the river created by the three streams working together. Hawaiian Pentecostals believe sound biblical doctrines based on the inerrant Word of God and the power and gifts of the Holy Spirit are essential for the church body to become a unified force.

As the people in Hawaii are stirred to take the gospel of Jesus Christ to the nations of their ethnic and cultural origins, denominational infrastructure will need to accommodate the spontaneous work of the Holy Spirit emphasized by Pentecostals. In order for this movement to translate into the lives of the individual believers, Pentecostals insist a personal spiritual transformation must occur and be based on the truth of the Word of God and the ministry of the Holy Spirit. This is for them consistent with the gospel writer's claim: "God is spirit, and his worshipers must worship in the Spirit and truth" (John 4:24, NIV).

Chapter 20

The Emergence of Prosperity and Blessing Theology: Black Pentecostalism in North America, 1980–2010

Lewis Brogdon

THE LAST TWO decades of the twentieth century and the first decade of the twenty-first century have been interesting times for African American Pentecostals. African American Pentecostals became major figures and forces behind many developments among African American churches, including the increased number of megachurches; the increased influence of televangelism; the practice of spiritual gifts, such as tongues and healing; the widespread use of praise and worship teams; the emergence of bishops in Baptist and nondenominational churches; and the shift from congregational revivals to multicongregational and multidenominational conferences. Pentecostalism has been the driving force behind these developments to the extent that one could argue that in three decades, it has transformed African American Christianity.

More precisely, the most significant development in African American Christianity has been the increasing prominence of *African American* nondenominational Pentecostalism. Beginning in the eighties and continuing into the first decade of the twenty-first century, the slow numerical and political decline of African American mainline and classical Pentecostal denominational churches on one hand and the growth of African American Word of Faith, neo-Pentecostal Baptist and nondenominational churches on the other has been noticeable. As congregations in the African Methodist Episcopal (AME) churches and Christian Methodist Episcopal (CME) churches, among others, have shrunk,[1] clergy in these churches have also lost ground as major leaders in the arena of national politics. Conversely, African American Pentecostal leaders have gained significant ground here. The last two presidents of the United States have been increasingly turning to nondenominational pastors of major churches for counsel and to spearhead initiatives. When Coretta Scott King, wife of the late Dr. Martin Luther King Jr., died, her funeral was not held at the historic Ebenezer Baptist Church where King pastored with his father but at New Birth Missionary Church, a neo-Pentecostal church that was a part of the Full Gospel Baptist Fellowship under Bishop Paul Morton. This church hosted the current president and three former presidents of the United States and many other dignitaries and celebrities. T. D. Jakes, a nondenominational pastor, gave the invocation at the inauguration of the first African American president, not the president of the National Baptist Convention or any sitting bishop in the AME or CME church. In many respects there has been a changing of the guard in the black church. African American nondenominational churches that were once relatively small have become large congregations with hundreds and sometimes thousands of members in a matter of a decade.

The Influence of African American Pentecostalism in the Black Church

What are the causes behind the increased prominence of Pentecostalism among African Americans? It is possible that its spirituality and message resonates with the diverse peoples that comprise the African American community. This community, though often spoken of in monolithic terms, is very heterogeneous. In the book *Disintegration*, Eugene Robinson argues that when talking about the black community, we need to nuance our descriptions because of the changes desegregation brought on. He argues that black America consists of the following:

> A mainstream middle class majority with a full ownership stake in American society; a large, an abandoned minority with less hope of escaping poverty and dysfunction than at any time since Reconstruction's crushing end; a small transcendent elite with such enormous wealth, power, and influence that even white folks have to genuflect; and two newly emergent groups—individuals of mixed race heritage and communities of recent black immigrants.[2]

Beyond nuancing our language and descriptions, this fourfold categorization is important because it recognizes both relatively successful African Americans as well as the large numbers of blacks who continue to face significant social and economic challenges. This is crucial when studying the impact of black religious movements on African Americans. Robinson's description of diverse peoples requires examinations of black churches to assess their impact among both groups. African American churches will have to develop, and have been developing, congregations and ministries that can respond to the needs of both groups.

During these three decades, African American nondenominational Pentecostals have been effective in responding to both middle class, relatively wealthy, and marginally poor African Americans, while African American mainline and classical Pentecostal denominational churches have been ineffective in ministering to this diverse group and have experienced stagnation, malaise, and loss of influence. Black Word of Faith, neo-Pentecostal, and nondenominational churches have experienced substantial growth, increased influence, and affluence. One of the reasons this distinct group of Pentecostals has been effective with African Americans is because of its theology of prosperity and blessing. These emergent churches have a theology that resonates with both groups.

Prosperity theology is a new form of theological discourse that not only offers hope for a better life but also provides a different way to frame the plight or condition of African Americans. The message of prosperity gave meaning to middle-class African Americans as well as a way to escape the curse of American racism for those still struggling to make it. And part of the story of the success of the neo-Charismatic movement in the black community lies in the fact that preachers and churches have laid out a path for well-to-do blacks to use their gifts for a higher purpose and to rebuild their lives after the bitter years of segregation. And it lays out a path for poor blacks to escape the prison of generational poverty. Prosperity theology gives African Americans a way to move from cursing to blessing and prosperity.

Prosperity theology rests on a belief that the world is fallen and under a curse. For prosperity teachers, the curse on creation goes back to the story of Adam and Eve's disobedience in the Garden of Eden and the curse of the Law that results from human disobedience in Deuteronomy 28. Humans are cursed because of the reign of sin in the world and cursed because they cannot comply with the obligations of the Law. This dual curse is the reason why there is suffering in the world: hate, violence, war, racism, poverty, and death. The good news that prosperity teachers bring is that this curse has been eradicated through the death and resurrection of Jesus Christ (see Genesis 3:1ff; Deuteronomy 28:1ff; Romans 5:1–11; Galatians 3:10–11, 13–14). In prosperity teaching, the curse has been reversed and now children of God live under the blessing.[3] Therefore, they feel compelled to help people transition from lives that are marred by curses of various kind to blessings. This theology provides a way for African Americans to give meaning to the suffering they experienced because of centuries of slavery and racism and offers hope that these evils do not have the final word over their lives.[4] What Jesus did on the cross and in the resurrection represents a turning point for them that is efficacious when they believe in Him.

Prosperity Preachers and the Historic Importance of Religion Among African Americans[5]

The curse of racism is real for African Americans, and the better one understands this experience, the better they'll understand why more black Americans are turning to this Pentecostal message.[6] Many of the problems confronting the African American community are a result of 246 years of institutionalized slavery, 99 years of legalized segregation, and 50-plus years of racial discrimination. This history of racism has influenced every facet of life for African Americans. In fact, African Americans continue to face struggles directly related to the unresolved issues of slavery and institutionalized racism.

One of the paradoxes in the African American community is the reality that in spite of the progress made since the civil rights movement, as a whole the African American community is still experiencing social decline on an unprecedented scale. We are witnessing devastating inequities and immense suffering. According to various studies, African Americans have higher and/or the highest rates of the following: depression, homicide, hypertension, heart disease, cancer, divorce, unemployment, poverty, HIV/AIDS, incarceration, and suicide. In fact, for African Americans ages fifteen to thirty-four, homicide and HIV/AIDS are the two leading causes of death. Today many African Americans live incredibly difficult lives, and too many are dying.

The popularity of the prosperity message among blacks was inevitable, given the current economic plight of African Americans on one hand and the historic importance of the church in the black community on the other hand. The long tradition of black preachers who speak to a range of existential issues affecting blacks; vibrant spiritualities that emphasizes worship, singing, prayer, and faith in a powerful God who can transcend human limitations; and ministries that seek to meet real needs in the here and now—all have been resources to blacks for centuries. This function of black religion is nothing new. Unless the discussion about African Americans in the prosperity movement considers the larger context of economic marginalization and the continuing importance of the church, they will continue to miss a significant factor as to why many are so drawn to the movement.

This message became so important because it spoke to their needs. For example, Creflo Dollar, a prominent pastor of World Changers Church in Atlanta, gave a very practical reason why he preaches prosperity:

> Most people who come to me their issue is I'm broke, I can't pay my bills. Don't tell me about a Jesus that won't help me get a better job. So by dealing with the Word showing them how to have a good attitude, how to get focused, how to operate in diligence, and how to discipline their lives, then you can change the way people think and live and have a better person at the end of the day.[7]

In light of the dire social conditions that many African Americans are facing, it is no wonder that large segments find promise in black prosperity-teaching churches. The opportunity to merge economics with faith is a promising combination for those who aspire to carve a brighter future for themselves and their respective families and communities. And this turn is rooted in a tradition of drawing on religion and faith to address inequities and injustices that goes back to the days of slavery. The church has occupied this central place because it gave disenfranchised people a sense of "somebodiness." And no one was probably more responsible for giving African Americans a sense of hope than the black preacher. Beginning in slave times, the black preacher would affirm the value of black existence and interpret their experiences in light of the Exodus event and the suffering of Jesus on the cross.

Black prosperity churches do this as well. I would contend that preachers like Creflo Dollar, Leroy Thompson, Eddie Long, and T. D. Jakes, who all preach aspects of prosperity teaching, are following a long line of African American ministers that seek to interpret the socioeconomic realities of black America in light of gospel.[8] Dollar, one of the most prominent neo-Charismatic pastors in America, believes that his message resonates with human need. He sees himself and his church as responding to people who can't pay their bills. And it would seem that he is not alone. African American Pentecostal preachers have been ministering among the poor and marginalized for over a century. Dollar, though a different kind of Pentecostal preacher, is standing in this tradition that has deep resonance with the poor. But there is more to his message of prosperity than money. In fact, he challenges the incorrect understanding of prosperity as only pertaining to money in one of his books on the subject:

> You see God is concerned with every aspect of your life.... Biblical prosperity is the ability to be in control of every circumstance and situation that occurs in your life. No matter what happens, whether financial, social, physical, marital, spiritual, or emotional, this type of prosperity enables you to maintain control in every situation.[9]

Dollar argues for what he refers to as "total life prosperity," a belief that maintains that God's anointing enables the faithful to handle every situation that life presents and proceed from it successfully. This message is drawing large numbers of African Americans into the neo-Charismatic stream of global Pentecostalism.

But there is more to this movement than the teachings and ministries of popular black preachers. Most studies of the prosperity movement focus entirely too much on preachers like Creflo Dollar, Fred Price, and T. D. Jakes while giving little or no attention to the contours of local preachers who teach variant forms of prosperity. It is important for scholars and students of this movement to study the systems of belief, congregations, and ministries that these Pentecostals construct to support their communities, and they need to do it in more contexts than just large megachurches in places like Atlanta, Dallas, and Los Angeles. Such an approach is largely missing in most studies of this movement. The prosperity movement is not just about large churches in big cities; it is also about poor people in rural communities who believe in God, want a better life, and are a part of the changes going on in the larger Pentecostal world.[10] It is about the poor black preachers who preach forms of this message to others in a similar situation. The movement is about the poor preaching to the poor about a better life. It is also about middle class blacks who have it better than the poor but are still a few paychecks away from poverty themselves. They want a better life, too, and they want preachers who resonate with their experience, needs, and desires. These mid- and lower-profile pastors preach prosperity as a way to model excellence and advancement. They may be poor, but they don't have to live and have the mentality of the poor. They reject mediocrity and victimization. For these people, the message of prosperity represents a better life. The resonance of this movement lies in the fact that even high-profile leaders like Jakes and Dollar intimately know the experience of poverty. Since God does not show favoritism, preachers and people alike expect God to bless them too. To this context I now turn because it is where I came from.[11]

Prosperity and Blessing Theology in Rural Contexts

From 1997 to 1999, I was a member of an African American nondenominational church in West Virginia, one of the five poorest states in the country, with an African American population of 3.6 percent.[12] Poverty is a major problem in the state, especially for black Americans, and its effects are widespread and varied, as 17.6 percent of people in the state live below the poverty line. In addition, this state ranks third-highest among states in fair to poor health status, fifteenth-highest with citizens with no health care access, and seventh-highest among states with people who cannot afford medical coverage.[13] Poverty touches almost every part of these people's lives. It is extremely difficult to make a good living in small towns like Bluefield, Welch, Princeton, and Beckley and in larger cities like Charleston and Huntington, all of which have higher concentrations of blacks than other parts of the state.

The pastor of Redeeming Life Christian Center (now Faith Center Church) preached prosperity to the middle class and poor blacks like myself. While I did not agree with all aspects of the message, it was empowering to hear this message. It was good news in a very depressing region in the country. We were not just told that God wants us to be rich or that money would drop out of heaven to us. We were taught that we are God's children, that it was not God's will for us to languish in poverty, and that we could have a better life. We didn't have to accept a miserable life but could have good things in this world. Our pastor modeled this lifestyle by living in a nice home and driving nice cars and taking care of his credit. More importantly, he used his blessings to help others. He would bless people with money, take people out for a dinner they couldn't afford, and lay before people like me an honest path out of poverty. We used the language of blessings and prosperity, and our understanding of them encompassed the spiritual and material aspects of life. This was a very radical message in this region because quite a few black churches taught that we shouldn't expect better in this life and that God wasn't concerned with such matters. They taught that worldly things pass away and that Christians should focus on spiritual blessings like salvation, a close walk with God, prayer, and a moral life. The pastors of these churches were very critical of what they perceived as a liberal and heretical church, often referred to as a cult by local Baptist and Pentecostal ministers.

This church grew rapidly and became one of the largest and most influential churches in the region. Redeeming Life Christian Center was one of the hybrid neo-Charismatic churches that were becoming increasingly popular in urban centers and rural communities nationwide. It is a part of the Pentecostal tradition but is not connected to a Pentecostal denomination. The pastor grew up in a United Holy Church in Anawalt, West Virginia, but attended

Rhema Bible Training College.[14] So his church is a unique blend of two traditions within the larger Pentecostal movement. This church was very dynamic and unique. A key part of the history of this movement was that increasing numbers of poor and marginalized blacks chose these churches with their Pentecostal spirituality to speak to their existential plight as well as to provide meaning and hope to their lives and communities. And this choice in some way was a rejection of traditional teachings in Baptist and Pentecostal denominational churches, which seemed resigned to tell blacks to accept their place in society and be faithful to God, who will bless them spiritually or eternally.

In the face of dire social conditions, many African Americans in this region found promise in this black church that espoused the prosperity doctrine because it offered five things that seem to connect with them in a deep way. The first is a God who cares about spiritual and material well-being. The second is a spirituality that emphasizes personal piety and social progress. Third is a faith that centralizes personal agency (autonomy and responsibility). Fourth is a belief in change and advancement in life as a result of faith in God and works in the world. Fifth is a holistic vision of salvation that encompasses forgiveness of sin and restoration to new life in this life and the next. These beliefs resonated with middle-class and poor blacks and drew them to prosperity churches with their rich Pentecostal spirituality.

What does this theology look like, and how is it different from more traditional black churches? Black prosperity churches like Redeeming Life Christian Center (again, now Faith Center Church) lay out a distinct vision of God and how it relates to their lives. This vision frames the context for worship practices, preaching, and the cultivation of faith in the lives of the people. Redeeming Life believes that God cares about matters of the Spirit, like prayer, worship, and reading Scripture. Material matters like finances, jobs, cars, schools, and where you live are just as important. God cares about every facet of your life, especially the existential plight of people in the southern West Virginia region. God cares about people who can't pay their bills. God cares about people who cannot afford health insurance. God cares how humiliating it feels to stand in line to apply for food stamps because you cannot afford to feed your own family. God cares about people who walk to work or to the store while people drive by in cars.

There are actually two particular theological streams of influence that converge in unique ways in prosperity churches: the existential focus in traditional black church thought and the Pentecostal emphasis on pneumatological immanence or the presence of the Holy Spirit.[15] This belief represents a redefining or amending of a traditional belief or core emphasis in black church thinking, which is a focus on existential or lived issues. Faith or theology in the black church invariably begins with existential or lived experience. This emphasis is seen most clearly in black preaching. Some of the most powerful sermons in the history of the black church focus on existential issues or dilemmas. Even the tradition of prophetic or justice preaching has the existential situation at its core. This preaching tradition continues in prosperity churches. In sermons, the pastor is careful to connect human need with the God who created them and cares for them. Often biblical stories like Hannah's prayer for a son in 1 Samuel, the widow of Zarephath in 1 Kings, or the woman with the flow of blood in Mark are used to illustrate God's concern for desperate human need and acute suffering. People in West Virginia have their life stories framed through the lens of those in Scripture who know what it is like to be in difficult situations. The difference between these neo-Charismatics and more traditional Baptists and Pentecostals is the belief that divine presence, once encountered in worship and active faith, means one's life can change. Why the difference? Because for them it is important that people know they can do something about their plight. This is why the pastor insists that things can get better in our lives. He fundamentally rejects a theology that assigns people to poverty and mediocrity. Christians (the pastor used the language of believers) should expect to see blessings because that is a natural result of the concern God has for His children. God wants better for them, too, and will work in and through them to make changes.

How does transformation happen in the lives of believers? Faith begins by encountering God in worship. The experience of divine presence during praise and worship is significant, taking up as much time in the worship service as preaching. If the faithful have not encountered and been touched by God, they have not really worshipped God. This Pentecostal belief and religious practice has undergone change with the proliferation of Charismatic and non-denominational churches. The encounter with the presence of God happens during praise and worship, not necessarily at the altar after the sermon, as tarrying continues to be a practice in black denominational Pentecostal churches. During this time there is a divine-human exchange. Praise leaders give parishioners space to pour their hearts out to God and to receive ministry from God. In worship, we expect God to touch us and strengthen us. There is a wide array of practices employed by people during praise and worship: people stand to reverence God, raise their hands, dance, walk around, sing, pray in tongues, weep, and bow. There are times when the pastor or one of the elders senses that people may need special prayer and the congregation is invited to the altar for intercession and a prophetic word. This can happen before or after the message. Both the vision of God put before the people and the communal experience of divine presence provides the ground for new possibilities in life.

Change occurs when believers act on their faith. African American faith teachers like Fred Brown, who studied at Rhema Bible Training College, maintain that faith is essential to change. But their understanding of faith is different than what traditional Baptist and Pentecostal pastors believe. These hybrid Pentecostals are not thinking about "the faith," as in the body of Christian beliefs, or "faith in God" as one who provides for the Atonement or redemption of the world. For these teachers, faith is what activates and makes operative in a person's life all that they believe God can and will do.[16] Brown studied under Kenneth Hagin at Rhema

Bible Training College but was influenced by Fred Price and was affiliated with his network Fellowship of Inner City Word of Faith Ministries while I was a member.

These teachings took on a different form in West Virginia. Brown stressed faith but did so by framing a believer's life as a story of faith with both ups and downs, but through it all as experiencing the faithfulness of God. One of his favorite scriptures was Romans 1:17, which says, "The righteousness of God is revealed from faith to faith" (MEV). This text accents the unfolding nature of the life of faith and was apropos for people whose lives were far from a finished product. The text he most often utilized to illustrate this was the story of the children of Israel in the Old Testament Books of Exodus, Numbers, and Joshua. This story documents their story from slavery in Egypt to freedom, independence, and blessing in the land of promise. This story that begins with a promise to Abraham in Genesis 12 functions as an overarching theme in his preaching. Whole sermon series were based on this story, and frequent allusions to this story were made to it. In one's life there is a trajectory from a life of difficulty or mediocrity before encountering God to a life of blessing and prosperity. This journey begins with salvation and being filled with the Holy Spirit, but it is not just salvific. God wants to do more than save souls and fill them with the power of the Spirit. God desires that they experience abundant life, a promise recorded in the Gospel of John. This means that the life of faith is a process that unfolds itself over time as we respond in faith to God and that areas of our lives such as our marriages, families, and finances should get better.

Brown emphasized the importance of individual initiative and responsibility. Because jobs were scarce and poverty was so widespread, there was a tendency among some blacks to resign themselves to a life of poverty and mediocrity. Some would not try to do better. They would not look for a job, accept a minimum-wage job, or even accept a temporary job. They would sit around and do nothing yet expect their life to change. He would not accept such reasoning and challenged it on numerous occasions. We had to do something and begin with what little we had. Two texts were instrumental in reinforcing this message: the parable of the mustard seed in Matthew and the story of Moses's call to return to Egypt and lead the Israelites out from slavery. One sermon emphasized the importance of utilizing "what's in your hand" to be the key to miracles and provision. For him, God starts where you are and with what you have. That is why it was important that in faith one puts his or her best foot forward. This consisted of simple acts, like applying for another job or taking a job that does not pay what we need or like to make ends meet. It could be taking two jobs for now or going back to school while working full time. That might be where you start, but if this act is done in faith that God has better things for you, some opportunity will come. On the other hand, not doing so was actually an act of unfaithfulness rooted in unbelief, doubting that God could change our situation. He preached that such responses were a form of what he termed "stinking thinking," a way of thinking that keeps marginalized people stuck in defeating cycles of poverty and underachievement. He emphasized this in a sermon on the Numbers 13 text where the spies returned back to Moses with an evil report. Ten of the spies perceived they could not defeat the giants in the land and so encouraged a large contingency of people to appoint another leader and return to Egypt. This was illustrative of an attitude Brown thought was counterproductive. An "I can't" or "we can't" attitude could nullify what God may want to do, and there was no room for "stinking thinking" at Redeeming Life because we, like Joshua and Caleb in Numbers 13, believed we could possess the promises of God.

Pastor Brown did not just expect people to try. Faith doesn't just wing it but instead takes actions that reflect an attitude of expectancy. I remember him saying, "The atmosphere of expectancy is the breeding ground for miracles." If we expected God to change our lives, then believers needed to commit to doing their best work in preparation for God's blessing. He emphasized this in three ways: by his insistence on excellence in life and ministry, by prosperity connections, and by stressing the importance of vision (what you see).

During my time at Redeeming Life, one of our emphases was that we were committed to being a church of excellence. Everything we set out to do was to be done in a spirit of excellence. This insistence came directly from the pastor, who strove for excellence in all areas of life. Excellence was demonstrated in a variety of ways: keeping the church clean and looking immaculate, doing good work when asked, going above what is expected or what people consider average or enough, and being organized in ministry and life tasks. In a culture that tempts people to accept mediocrity, excellence was our standard because it best reflects the God we represent. Prosperity connections is a different way of talking about communalism and good relationships. If you want to succeed in life, then you need to associate with people who are going somewhere. Pastor Brown made sure we were exposed to a steady dose of successful and ambitious leaders in ministry and business who were willing to pass on what they knew. These people would travel from Washington DC, Baltimore (Maryland), Charlotte (North Carolina), and Tulsa (Oklahoma) to Bluefield (West Virginia). For some people this was the first time they'd met a highly successful black person. He did this because he believed prosperity is dependent upon the people around you. People can either increase your capacity to prosper or decrease it. Furthermore, he took his calling very seriously because he believed our lives should be enriched by our association with him.

Vision was absolutely essential to a life of prosperity. Often we would hear him quote the text out of Proverbs, "Where there is no vision, the people perish" (Prov. 29:18, MEV). One of the primary roles of his preaching was to instill a vision of better things and higher expectations in the minds of the people. He worked hard to ensure that his people did not succumb to a poverty mentality that did not expect better in life. Stories and illustrations inundated his sermons. Sometimes he would use props, and always he would use humor. But people could not catch the vision without seeing things differently themselves. That is why Pastor Brown thought it was important for people in this region to travel and see a different side of the world. He wanted them to see that there was a different side of life and that a better life was possible for them. It was important for people to see that everybody in the world is not struggling and sad. So he found ways to expose the members of the church to the other side of life that he preached about in sermons. He would host conferences in places like Charlotte, North Carolina, in a nice hotel or even a nice local venue, perhaps a resort that people may not have known was there. On one occasion the church sponsored a trip to the Bahamas and took a large contingency of people outside the country for the first time. Doing this was a part of changing the mentality of the people and opening their minds to new possibilities. While people worked hard to come up with money for trips like this, even sacrificing money for other important and essential things, for many it was an investment in a better life. Pastor Brown knew this and used the institutional power and finances of the church to leverage opportunities for people, some of which were not even members of our church. Even smaller things, like fishing trips to the ocean or eating at a nice restaurant, were ways to sow seeds into the minds and lives of poor and disenfranchised people. Sitting in nice conference rooms or driving onto the grounds of a resort and being treated like a person of worth had a powerful effect on one's confidence and sense of self. The commitment to excellence, positive associations, and a vision of a better life instilled a sense of determination and focus to see the process and journey through, whether that meant going back to school or transitioning to a new profession.

Conclusion

The message and ministry of Fred Brown and Redeeming Life Christian Center in Bluefield, West Virginia, provide a compelling case study of what it means to do ministry in the black community in the latter part of the twentieth century and the challenges it faces. While not easy, he sought to lay before people a radical vision of a God who cares and is invested in changing things in their lives for the better. He rejected any belief that blacks were stuck in a system that they could not get out of. He firmly believed that they could do something about their situation. He rejected any narrative of victimization. Blacks could go from unemployed and poor to prosperous. The church was invested in living out this vision together. The prosperity gospel is thriving because Pentecostals are present in poor communities like Bluefield, West Virginia, and preach a message that refuses to victimize them but instead empowers them and gives them hope that they can do something about their situation. Today this church is still thriving and helping people deal with the challenges of life.

More African Americans are turning to nondenominational "Pentecostal-like" churches for their vibrant spirituality, their message of empowerment and hope, their communalism where people use their blessings to help others, and their visionary and dynamic leaders who lay out paths for them to move from cursing to blessing. This emphasis on prosperity has been a major development in African American religion, although for some it is not necessarily a good one. Just because more blacks attend these churches does not necessarily imply that they are making the black community better or remedying all the hurts enacted on blacks over centuries. In fact, during this three-decade period, black religious scholars and some mainline pastors were very critical of these churches and this message because they believed it did not help African Americans.[17] They critiqued prosperity theology because it was too capitalistic, too individualistic, too exploitative, and too unchristian to help marginalized people like African Americans. For them, the growing number of blacks in these Pentecostal churches was not a good development at all. Prosperity teachers heeded some of the critiques and ignored others, but there are signs that some aspects of this teaching were amended over time. The debate about this movement and its prominence among blacks will continue for years to come. But what these scholars and pastors miss is the broader assessment of these churches within the world of Pentecostalism, why and how its message speaks to them in ways mainline churches and their theologies do not.

The future of African American and possibly North American Pentecostalism may depend on what it does with prosperity theology, what new forms of prosperity teaching will emerge in the next decade, whether prosperity teaching will have a dramatic effect on issues of poverty and inequality in North America, and what role this message will have in strengthening or weakening the movement's emphasis on the work of the Holy Spirit. These questions will shape the future of Pentecostalism for years to come, particularly among marginalized people like the African American community.

Chapter 21

"I Will Pour Out of My Spirit Upon All Flesh": A Historical and Theological Meditation on Pentecostal Origins

Michael J. McClymond

LET ME BEGIN with a quotation: "Many charismatic gifts were reported... [and] I am thankful to the Lord, who is pleased to pour out His Spirit upon poor sinners without distinction of white or black, and rich or poor."[1] Where and when was this said, and who said it? In light of the phrase "without distinction of white or black," many might guess that the statement is somehow connected with the Azusa Street revival, thus spoken around 1906. Yet the quotation in fact comes from John Christian Arulappan, who said this regarding the Christian Pettah (village) revival, which took place in India during the 1860s, about a half-century before the much-better-known Azusa Street revival.

Let us consider another episode. A Christian minister has been asked to address a prestigious gathering of missionary leaders who oversee evangelization in far-flung regions of the globe. He tells them that their verbal message of salvation in Christ is not sufficient to meet the requirements of the missionary task and the challenge of the non-Christian world. There must also be a visible demonstration of God's power—through the healing of the sick and the casting out of demons. The mandate Jesus gave to His apostles—"Heal the sick, raise the dead, cleanse lepers, cast out demons" (Matt. 10:8, ESV)—did not end during the first century.

Might this be a story about John Wimber or C. Peter Wagner and their controversial teaching during the 1980s regarding so-called "power evangelism"?[2] On the contrary, this took place in 1824, when Edward Irving addressed the London Missionary Society with an address entitled "Missionaries After the Apostolical School."[3]

To give one more example: Picture a group of laypersons from a more traditional Christian church that begins to meet together in private homes, without clergy present, and where numerous people begin speaking in tongues. A number of women participants deliver powerful, prophetic messages that leave a lasting impact on their hearers. Meanwhile, the male church leaders denounce these gatherings as heretical because of the tongues-speaking that occurs and because women were claiming to be speaking under the power of the Holy Spirit. Where and when did this take place? Answer: This episode is not from the twentieth-century mainline Charismatic Renewal but from Finland in 1808–1809. In an article published in 2009, Jouko Ruohomäki provided documentation for the existence of a tradition of glossolalia and prophetic utterance that began in 1756 and lasted continuously in Finland for one hundred and fifty years prior to the beginnings of global Pentecostalism. This movement took place in a rural, rather than urban, region; it was concentrated among women rather than men; and the meetings generally took place with no clergy present. So perhaps it is not surprising if few people have heard of this movement. Ruohomäki's essay provides copious documentation, yet the literature is in Finnish—a language that few non-Finns can read.[4]

Examples could be multiplied. The three examples just given should be a warning to us that what we think we know about various Christian renewalist movements during the modern period is still fragmentary and incomplete. During the last fifteen to twenty years, new information has been recovered on such pre-1900 groups. Alongside the classical Pentecostals, mainline Charismatics, and neo-Pentecostals, we might also need to speak now of proto-Pentecostals or perhaps paleo-Pentecostals.[5]

Scholars of Pentecostalism in recent years have debated the issue of Pentecostal monogenesis (single origin) in contrast to the notion of Pentecostal polygenesis (multiple origins).[6] In what follows, I will first touch on historical and historiographic issues and then present a theological reflection on the possible meaning of the events we are discussing. I will argue two theses. First of all, on the historical level, I will examine some recent contributions to the discussion of origins by Allan Anderson, Michael Bergunder, Cecil Robeck, and Adam Stewart and suggest that the distance or discrepancy between so-called monogenetic and polygenetic views is neither sizable nor significant.[7] It is possible to acknowledge the contributions made in each point of view and to get the pieces to fit together. My second claim, more theological in nature, may sound paradoxical. I will argue that the claim of polygenesis does not diminish the significance of the Azusa Street revival but rather enhances it.

Pentecostal Origins: What Are the Claims and Arguments of Today?

An online Azusa Street revival documentary features a global map with a point of light breaking out in Los Angeles and sending rays from Los Angeles throughout the world.[8] This may be the simplest way of imagining a Pentecostal monogenesis, centered on Los Angeles. Yet the best-known scholar of the Azusa Street revival—Cecil Robeck—offers a more nuanced view than we see in the popular video. What is more, Robeck's account has shifted somewhat. In 1993, Robeck wrote, "Without wishing to be triumphalistic, the evidence gathered in all serious quests for origins of the modern Pentecostal movement appears inevitably to point to North America."[9] In 2013, Robeck conveyed less confidence regarding the centrality of Azusa Street: "While the Azusa Street Mission may not in the end be viewed as providing the primary genesis for the worldwide Pentecostal Movement, its contribution remains unsurpassed during the first decade."[10]

Robeck's reference to "the first decade" is worth emphasizing. His claim in the second quotation is that Azusa's dominance lasted over a decade, not over a century. In the next paragraph of the 2013 essay, Robeck wrote of "Azusa Street's unparalleled role in the establishment of global Pentecostalism." If we link these statements, then it seems that Robeck is asserting that Azusa Street played a prominent—and indeed unparalleled—role in the Pentecostal establishment over a decade's time. What was it, though, that had its "establishment" by 1916 or thereabouts? Clearly, this "establishment" did not include neo-Pentecostalism or the mainline Charismatic Renewal. What is more, the British Pentecostal churches had not established their international networks prior to 1916. Robeck appears to be referring to networks created through the efforts of the Azusa Street alumni—those Spirit-renewed through the meetings in Los Angeles.

In his major study on early Pentecostal mission and expansion, *Spreading Fires* (2007), Allan Anderson noted that Western Pentecostal missionaries by 1916 had settled in at least forty-two nations outside of North America and Europe.[11] A number of essential facts are not in dispute between Robeck and Anderson: (1) there was a remarkable expansion of Pentecostalism from 1906 to 1916, (2) more than forty countries were affected, and (3) the Azusa Street revival played a leading role in the establishment of these early Pentecostal churches. The pre-1916 churches were all so-called "classical Pentecostal" congregations, and so the global network that Robeck speaks of as being established, then, is not the global network of Spirit-filled or renewalist as it exists today.

In defending polygenesis in his 2014 essay, Adam Stewart made concessions to the monogenetic viewpoint, writing, "Nowhere do I claim that evidence of Pentecostalism's multiple points of origination means that there were not early centres of the movement that played especially important—and, in the case of Azusa Street, even predominant—roles in spreading the revival."[12] After demonstrating that both the Mukti revival in India and the Hebden revival in Toronto originated and developed without connection to the Azusa Street revival, Stewart conceded that Los Angeles was "predominant…in spreading the revival." Based on what Robeck wrote in 2013 and what Stewart argued in 2014, it is not clear that there is a major difference of views between them.

Stewart's essay suggested that the monogenetic viewpoint in the United States did not derive simply from American nationalism or church boosterism but also from theological presuppositions. Radical Evangelicals at the turn of the century had prayed for—and had come to expect—a new Pentecost for the church. Since the original Pentecost event *began in one place* and then *diffused in concentric circles*—as suggested by Acts 1:8, "in Jerusalem... Judea and Samaria... to the remotest part of the earth" (NASB)—would not the new Pentecost occur in a comparable way? Stewart thus offers a plausible explanation for how and why monogenetic ideas dominated early Pentecostal thinking about the Los Angeles revival.[13]

If the monogenesis view became dominant from an early date, then it was not held by all the early observers. Frank Bartleman famously declared, "The present world-wide revival was rocked in the cradle of little Wales. It was brought up in India, following; becoming full grown in Los Angeles later."[14] To belabor the obvious, Bartleman here thinks and speaks as a polygeneticist. The "present... revival" is said to be "world-wide" rather than local and denoted as singular rather than plural, suggesting that it was *one revival* occurring in *multiple locations*. Moreover, the quotation suggests that the revival had been developing and maturing—like a human being passing through multiple life stages. Bartleman mentioned Wales as the "cradle" of "world-wide revival." While for Bartleman Los Angeles represented the "full grown" revival, this was because the global revival had gained momentum after starting in Wales and moved on to India and California. Primary sources show that thrilling reports from the Welsh revival of 1904–1905 raised expectations for Christian revival in Korea, India, and Los Angeles. At least one author attempted a Wales-centered account of global Christian revivals in the early 1900s.[15] Yet the arguments against a Los Angeles–based monogenesis would apply also to a Wales-centered monogenesis. Each revival had a local coloring or flavoring, and none of them was exactly like any of the others.

If one of these revivals helped to spark revivals elsewhere, then the shifting character of the revivals weighs against the notion of a simple transference to new locations. The revivals in Korea and India stressed repentance and confession of sins; the Welsh revival highlighted communal singing; and in Chile many people had visionary experiences.[16] The revival in Los Angeles emphasized glossolalia. While it is possible to find many of the same phenomena in diverse locations, there was nonetheless a different blend of elements and so a different ethos from place to place. By analogy, we might conceive the international revivals in epidemiological terms, like a spreading virus—for Pentecostals, no doubt a "good infection" rather than bad. Yet this virus "mutated" over time, and the symptoms associated with "infection" changed accordingly.

Pentecostal Origins in India and Latin America

In Robeck's reckoning, a distinguishing trait of Azusa Street was the large-scale sending of missionaries—an impressive feature, indeed. Another diffusive center, almost concurrently, was the Mukti Mission in Pune, India. Allan Anderson's research shows that Mukti was not merely a local revival but also a mission-sending center. The Mukti revival lasted for a year and a half and resulted in 1,100 baptisms and the sending out of about seven hundred younger women into surrounding regions of India. As many as one hundred evangelists went out daily, sometimes remaining away from Mukti for a month at a time. Pandita Ramabai formed a Bible school of two hundred young women and "Praying Bands" tasked with the responsibility to evangelize. The Praying Bands spread the revival into regions of India surrounding Pune, and remarkable healings were reported.[17]

Why have the missionary efforts at the Mukti Mission not become better known? An obvious reason, as Anderson notes, is that "women played a more prominent role in the Indian revival than in the American one."[18] If truth be told, women's service in ministry has never—at any period of church history—received as much attention as men's. In that sense, the neglect of the Mukti Mission story in favor of the Los Angeles story follows a recurrent but regrettable pattern in Christian historiography. And there could be another factor. While Indians and Americans both missionized, Americans in 1906 had access to resources to travel further and to engage cultures in far-flung regions. Knowing what we now do about the Mukti Mission, it would be unfair to perpetuate the idea that American missionaries mattered while Indian missionaries did not. Throughout Africa and Asia, many congregations over the last two centuries were established not by white Western missionaries but by innumerable catechists and village evangelists whose names are now lost to us. God knows. So it is, therefore, to acknowledge that the Mukti Mission was a diffusive center in early Pentecostalism, as was the Azusa Street Mission.

In Latin America and Central America, the early spread of Pentecostalism followed a complex pattern largely independent of the Azusa Street Mission. Néstor Medina notes that

> Latina/o and Latin American expressions of Pentecostalism are not all offshoots of the revival at Azusa Street in 1906. It is important that we go beyond US centered views of the birth and dissemination of Pentecostalism in order to undercut notions of Manifest Destiny left over even in some expressions of US Latina/o Pentecostalism.[19]

In 1907, Gabriel García was among the first Pentecostal pioneers in Mexico who went to the small village of Tecupeto. Pentecostalism came to San Salvador through the efforts of the Canadian missionary Frederick Mebius, who became Pentecostal in 1911 and disaffiliated from the Central American Mission, under which he served since 1904.[20] The first active Pentecostals in Guatemala in 1916 were the independent Christian workers Charles Furman and Thomas Pullin. From 1921, Furman served the Primitive Methodist Church, and in 1932 he began to introduce Pentecostal practices. When he resigned, the churches he had led voted to leave with Furman and to affiliate with the Church of God (Cleveland, Tennessee). From the beginning, this movement encouraged indigenous leadership. In 1934, John Franklin of the Pentecostal Assemblies of Canada established a mission in Jutiapa. Converts to Guatemalan Pentecostalism generally came not from Catholicism but other Protestant churches.[21] The roots of Cuban Pentecostalism are likewise Canadian rather than US-based and go back to 1930.[22]

Moving southward to consider Brazil and Argentina, Paulo Ayres Mattos notes that the roots of Pentecostalism "have more to do with William Durham than with William Seymour."[23] It was not Seymour's Azusa Street Mission in Los Angeles that served as the diffusive center for southern Latin America, but rather William Durham's North Avenue Mission in Chicago, Illinois. Durham was a mentor to Luigi (Louis) Francescon, who preached the Pentecostal message to Italians in North America, Argentina, Brazil, and Italy. Moreover, Durham also guided Daniel Berg, who in 1910, with fellow Swedish-American Gunnar Vingren, established Pentecostalism in Belém in northern Brazil. Also worth mentioning is Durham's influence in the life of Aimee Semple McPherson, founder of the International Church of the Foursquare Gospel.[24] So Chicago ranks with Los Angeles and Pune, India, as another diffusive center, with special importance for Brazil and Argentina.

One of the unexpected links is between India and Chile. Paulo Ayres Mattos notes that Chilean Pentecostalism in its origins is wholly independent of North America and could be seen as a fruit of the Mukti Mission revival. The origins of the Chilean movement lie in the friendship of American missionary Minnie Abrams, serving in Pune, India, with her American friend in Valparaiso, Chile, Willis Hoover. Abrams and Hoover had met as students at the Chicago Training School for Home and Foreign Missions (another Chicago connection during the 1880s). As news of the Welsh revival of 1904–1905 raised hopes for spiritual awakening among those who were already seeking it in Los Angeles, the news of the India revival of 1905 reached Hoover by way of Abrams, and a revival happened in Chile by emulation of the prior revival in India.

The Culturalist and Discursive Turn: The Contribution of Michael Bergunder

Michael Bergunder employs a cultural studies perspective that treats Pentecostalism as a discursive practice. Some might regard the cultural studies perspective as arcane. Yet this approach can enrich the discussion of origins by providing heuristic tools.[25] Bergunder deflects attention from the question "When and where did Pentecostalism begin?" to one that concerns sociolinguistic practice: "When and where did people begin speaking about something that they called Pentecostalism?" The follow-up questions would be: "Who called it that? When did they call it that? And was their use of the term accepted or contested by other people?" Bergunder proposes that one begin with the prevalent terminology of the present time—what he calls the *synchronic perspective*—and then move backward in time for the *diachronic perspective* and look for a time when there was some rupture or break in linguistic practice. Pentecostal origins may be dated to the time of this rupture.

Now, if we return to the beginning of the twentieth century, where discussion on Pentecostal origins is mostly focused, we see interesting things happening with regard to the term *Pentecostal*. The church body incorporated as Pentecostal Church of the Nazarene by 1919 had dropped *Pentecostal* from its denominational name. Why? The answer seems obvious. When the denomination organized itself in 1907–1908, the word *Pentecostal* had a broader meaning, associated with an openness to the Holy Spirit. By 1919, though, the word had become fixed in a new way, so that the Nazarenes no longer felt that the term accurately described them.[26] Here we have a classic instance of Bergunder's discursive rupture.

What happens when we apply Bergunder's discursive analysis, starting from the present and moving into the past, as he has proposed? The results are intriguing. One finds a rupture in linguistic or discursive practice that has generally gone unnoticed and that occurred about fifteen to twenty years ago. I refer to the self-renaming of members of older Pentecostal churches no longer as simply *Pentecostal* but now as *classical Pentecostal*. The introduction and widespread use of the adjective *classical* is significant and may be as significant in its own way as the decision by the Church of the Nazarene to drop the word *Pentecostal* from its name.[27] By adding the adjective, those within this family of churches defined and distinguished themselves from others. With regard to mainline Charismatics and neo-Pentecostals, classicals feel both affinity and difference. The word *Pentecostal* is thus not a fixed term but a floating signifier. While the term *Charismatic* is a preferred term today, books and articles appearing around the 1970s often used the term *Catholic Pentecostal*. Like *classical Pentecostal*, this is another adjectivized identifier, yet in this case the use of the term did not last long and soon gave way to the term preferred now, *Catholic Charismatic*. To the question "When and where did Pentecostalism begin?," one might get behind the question by asking, "Which particular Pentecostalism are you asking about?"

Bergunder makes another basic point, which is that Pentecostalism, from its outset, was always conceived of and spoken of as a network of churches. Churches somehow separated or un-networked were never regarded in the full sense as Pentecostal. In scholarly literature, there have been ongoing terminological debates about the African Initiated Churches (AICs) and whether these should be considered as one ecclesial family under the Pentecostal umbrella or as being Pentecostal at all. A similar and seemingly unanswerable question concerns the unregistered house churches in China that mostly originated since the 1960s, practice spiritual gifts, and yet have no significant genealogical connection to Pentecostal churches outside China. Bergunder is correct: observers are not sure whether to call these Chinese churches Pentecostal. Apparently Spirit baptism, glossolalia, divine healing, and prophecy by themselves are not enough. Congregations practicing these spiritual gifts have to be networked with others acknowledged as Pentecostal to be regarded themselves as Pentecostal.[28]

Strikingly, Bergunder comments that the global network of churches that today are often just called Pentecostal originated no earlier than the 1970s and 1980s. So he claims that the quest for origins ought to take us back not to the first decade of the twentieth century but rather to the 1970s and 1980s. If it seems wildly plausible to claim that Pentecostalism in some sense is only thirty-five to forty-five years old, then let us remember the point above regarding classical Pentecostalism. In adding the adjective *classical*, members of older Pentecostal churches might implicitly be agreeing with Bergunder. From a discursive standpoint, there must be a reason that the adjective *classical* got added, and the timing of this change in linguistic practice tends to confirm Bergunder's claim of a global Pentecostalism thirty-five to forty-five years old.

Do Pentecostal origins really matter? Bergunder questions whether they do. He links the debate over origins to Walter Hollenweger and Allan Anderson and to what he calls *strategic essentialism*—an effort at identifying and promoting what is regarded as important in a religious tradition. Debates over the definition or meaning of a religious tradition often lead back to issues of origins. This has been the case with regard to Anabaptist and Evangelical origins, as noted above, and of course Roman Catholics and Orthodox Christians have for an entire millennium been debating the events of the church's first centuries. Walter Hollenweger's proposal of "black origins" for Pentecostalism during the 1970s has had wide repercussions for the academic study of Pentecostalism. Prior to Hollenweger, most scholars pointed to Charles Parham as Pentecostalism's founder, to glossolalia as Pentecostalism's distinctive practice, and to "initial evidence" as Pentecostalism's defining doctrine. Yet as Hollenweger's arguments began to prevail, attention shifted from Charles Parham, and, correspondingly, William Seymour emerged as the most widely acknowledged early leader of Pentecostalism. What is more, Seymour's notion of a racially and social inclusive, Spirit-filled community began to be seen as an innovative Pentecostal teaching that was just as important as glossolalia. Many have quoted Frank Bartleman: "The color line was washed away in the blood [i.e., the blood of Christ, or Jesus's atoning death]."[29]

Since the early 2000s, Allan Anderson has moved a step beyond Hollenweger. In Anderson's writings we find not simply "black origins" but "global origins," as Anderson offered new evidence for Charismatic or Spirit-centered movements occurring all around the world in the decades before and after the year 1900. The opening quotation from John Christian Arulappan comes from Anderson's research into this hitherto little-known figure. During the last decade or so, a surge of new studies has pointed in the direction of global origins. This trend seems likely to increase in the years ahead as new information comes to light.

From Black Origins and Global Origins to Inclusive Origins

For a purely historical inquirer, questions of Pentecostal origins might not matter. Yet such is not likely to be the case with one who self-identifies as a Pentecostal and participates in the life of the community. In reflecting theologically on origins, my suggestion is that those who are Pentecostals (in a broader sense) might need to shift from thinking simply of black origins or even of global origins and instead embrace what we might call "inclusive origins." What I am proposing does not contradict Hollenweger's or Anderson's insights. Yet I believe that it might be helpful to clarify the implicit theology of the black origins and global origins views. The message might be summed up in the word *inclusion*, perhaps with the added word *empowerment*. Putting them together, we might speak of *empowering inclusion* or *inclusive empowerment*.

In his excellent book on Latino Pentecostalism, Gastón Espinosa emphasizes that Seymour did not simply popularize Parham's message but "crafted his own message." Espinosa comments:

> [Seymour] taught that the outpouring of the Holy Spirit was ushering in a new age that made everyone level at the foot of the cross, regardless of race, class, and education. The Spirit...poured out spiritual gifts so that people could cross race, class, and nationality lines, spread the love of Christ to all nations, and usher in the Second Coming....Seymour's central message was not tongues or eschatology, but rather that...a regenerate person had to demonstrate their faith through brotherly love and the fruit of the Spirit manifest in how they treated their fellow man, irrespective of race or class.[30]

This interpretation finds support in Seymour's life and actions and concurs with the statement in the *Apostolic Faith* newsletter indicating that the evidence for baptism in the Holy Spirit was divine love.

Seymour in later life had second thoughts about appeals to tongues-speaking as evidence of Spirit baptism, and he concluded that tongues-speaking could not be considered an evidence of Spirit baptism unless accompanied by brotherly love and the fruit of the Spirit. He commented, "Wherever the doctrine of the Baptism of the Holy Spirit will only be known as the evidence of speaking in tongues, that will be an open door for witches and spiritualists, and free lovism...because all kinds of spirits can come in."[31] Seymour came to believe that external manifestations—including tongues—were not self-interpreting. One needed spiritual discernment to see if particular manifestations were genuinely from God.

What made Seymour great, in my view, and what magnifies the importance of the Azusa Street revival is that he, in his thinking, preaching, and writing, *made fully explicit what was implicit in the event of the Spirit's coming in power.* In effect, Seymour went back to the very beginning, to those opening words of explanation in the first-ever Christian sermon: "This is that which was spoken by the prophet Joel...'I will pour out of my Spirit upon all flesh'" (Acts 2:16–17, KJV). Unlike many contemporaries, Seymour did not simply examine and embrace the external manifestations. Instead, he grasped the underlying meaning of the manifestations and so was decades ahead of other observers in perceiving God's purpose of creating a socially inclusive community in racially and ethnically divided America. Some viewed the early Pentecostal revival as an end-times event, pointing to Jesus's speedy return. Others saw it as a mission movement, a prelude to global evangelization. Without denying either interpretation, Seymour—perhaps more than anyone else—perceived the revival as reflecting God's heart for unity and God's desire to break down every social barrier.

Consider some of the lesser-known cases of Spirit movements mentioned already. What might these cases have in common?

- Women from rural Finland spoke in tongues and shared prophetic messages with one another—despite opposition and denunciation from clergy and bishops.
- An Indian Christian—though discouraged from doing so by white Western missionaries—experienced speaking in tongues and noted how God was "pleased to pour out His Spirit upon poor sinners without distinction of white or black, and rich or poor."
- The most popular preacher in London allowed rural Scottish women speak in tongues in the midst of his fashionable congregation because he did not want to quench the Spirit's work—but then lost his church position.

Is the pattern becoming obvious? Let me include some other cases, not mentioned earlier, to make the point yet clearer:

- The very first manifestation of the Holy Spirit at the Azusa Street Mission occurred not among white or black Christians but among the impoverished Mexican laborers who were preparing the building for worship on April 13, 1906.

- The first reported healing at Azusa also happened among the Mexicans—arguably the most marginalized group of all—when a man with a club foot was said to be healed.[32]

- To consider early Evangelical revivals: some of the first reported Protestant spiritual awakenings (1590s–1630s) took place among persecuted Scottish Christians forced to worship outdoors because of church and state opposition.[33]

  This Scottish outdoor revival preaching and reception of the Lord's Supper became known as the "Holy Fair," and this was the starting point for the great Cane Ridge revival in Kentucky in 1802–1803.[34]

- The roots of the Evangelical awakening in England—according to the erudite British historian W. R. Ward—lay not in the activities of Wesley's Holy Club at Oxford University, but rather can be traced back genealogically to a gathering of persecuted Protestant children in German-speaking Silesia around 1700.[35]

  Turned out of their homes and their church buildings by Catholic authorities and exposed to the elements, a group of younger people began what became known as the "Children's Revival" when they refuse to stop praying and worshipping God. Eventually these children persuade the adults to join with them, and the spiritual impact of this revival—according to Professor Ward—may be traced into the early phases of the Evangelical revival in England.

- A group of mostly black Christians gathered in a former church building—at this time dilapidated and in use as a horse stable—and sought God's presence after their initial experiences of baptism in the Holy Spirit and glossolalia. In an age of horrific racial

> injustice and oppression of black Americans, the Azusa Street Mission welcomed all comers—regardless of race, ethnicity, gender, or religious background.

Above I proposed the paradoxical thesis that the claim of Pentecostal polygenesis does not diminish the significance of the Azusa Street revival but enhances it. Now we are in a position to see why. The message of Acts 2—which was Seymour's message—is encapsulated in the divine promise: "I will pour forth of my Spirit upon *all flesh*." The "all flesh" reference obviously cannot be limited to Los Angeles but includes the other places mentioned—Britain, Germany, Finland, India, Brazil, Chile, etc.—and still more localities and the cases that we perhaps do not yet know about. This is why it might be better to think and speak of *inclusive origins* rather than black origins—the story transpiring in Los Angeles—or global origins—a phrase suggesting a multiplicity of locations but not highlighting a shared theological meaning.

Azusa Street and the Coming(s) of the Spirit in Acts of the Apostles

We can deepen our insight in Pentecostal origins if we consider Acts of the Apostles as a polygenetic book—though it is not often read this way. In Acts, the Holy Spirit came among the Jews in Acts 2, the Samaritans in Acts 8, and the Gentiles in Acts 10. Moreover, there was a noteworthy difference between Acts 8 and Acts 10. In the case of the Samaritans, Philip the Evangelist had to call for Peter and John to come down from Jerusalem to Samaria to lay on hands so that the Samaritans might receive the Holy Spirit (Acts 8:14–17). In the case of Cornelius and the other Gentiles, however, Peter never had the opportunity to lay hands on them. Instead, the Spirit showed up in the middle of Peter's sermon and the text tells us that "the Holy Spirit fell upon all those who were listening to the message" (Acts 10:44, NASB). Shortly afterward, these Gentiles received water baptism, and yet the text does not stress the baptism with water. It was the sudden coming of the Spirit on the Gentiles—analogous to the Acts 2 coming—that left Peter and the other Jews "amazed" (v. 45, NASB).

Why this difference between Samaritans and Gentiles? The Samaritans were, so to speak, renegade Jews. They had tampered with the text of the Torah to affirm Mount Gerizim—in their own territory—as their center for worship rather than Mount Zion in Jerusalem. The Samaritans were also known for their religious syncretism—which is why Simon the Magician was having a major impact among them (Acts 8:9–11) at the time that Philip the Evangelist came to them to preach to them the true gospel. So the Spirit baptism of the Samaritans at the hands of the Apostles Peter and John was a sign that the Samaritans would be reconciled to God by first being reconciled to the Jewish people. Conversely, the Spirit baptism of Cornelius and the other Gentiles took place without any laying on of Jewish hands in order to signify that the Gentiles were *in direct relationship to the God of Abraham*, not an indirect relationship and not a relationship that would be mediated by the Jews as gatekeepers or rule-makers for Gentile believers.

If Cornelius had only received the Holy Spirit once Peter laid hands on him, then Cornelius would likely have been considered a prime candidate for circumcision and instruction in the Torah. The Apostle Paul's mission—allowing Gentiles to become Christians without first becoming Jews—might thus have been imperiled. What is more, if Paul's mission to the Gentiles as Gentiles had not been embraced by the earliest churches, then the Jerusalem Council of Acts 15 might never have happened, and Christianity could have ended up as a sect of Judaism rather than a culture-crossing, linguistically translational, and universally oriented missionary faith.[36]

Now let us turn to the twentieth-century story. Gaston Cashwell—a white man who came to the Azusa Street Mission from North Carolina—was at first put off when he arrived in Los Angeles and saw black men and women leading the meetings there. He returned to his hotel room, and Cashwell said that God began to deal with him, convicting and convincing him of his racism. He stated that he had to "crucify" his own racism to be in right relationship with God. After he repented of this sin, he was baptized in the Holy Spirit after he went back to the Azusa Street Mission and asked a young black man to lay on hands and pray for him.

What is the theological meaning here? The answer seems clear: Cashwell's racism was in direct contradiction to the racially and ethnically inclusive purpose that God sought to achieve. Cashwell had to repent of racism *before he could be included himself in the inclusive community.* The case of Gaston Cashwell can be seen as an indication that God sends the Holy Spirit in a way that conforms to God's purposes at a particular time and place. Cashwell did not receive the Holy Spirit until he repented of racism and had hands laid upon him by a young black man. Cashwell, in that sense, is like the Samaritans of Acts 8—he needed first to be reconciled to the reconciling community. On the other hand, Cashwell's experience was exceptional. What we usually see in the various global cases is that God sends the Spirit in a way that emphasizes that *each new community is in a direct relationship with God* and not in a relationship *mediated by another community.*

John Christian Arulappan went against the wishes of the local white missionaries, both in seeking to experience the charismatic gifts himself and in encouraging others to do likewise. The rural women of Finland in the 1700s and 1800s also went their own way, with little or no support from their clergy. No Lutheran clergyman laid hands on these Finns. So, too, in the other instances. Repeatedly in history we see a repetition of the Cornelius story rather than the Samaritan story. Speaking generally, God does not seem to be in the business of making sure that everyone reports to home base, stays connected to headquarters, and avoids taking new initiatives without advance approval. The whole of the Acts of the Apostles stands against such an interpretation of Christian life, ministry, and mission. The importance of what today's historians and missiologists call local or indigenous agency is inextricably interwoven into early Pentecostal narratives.

So we see that the theological argument against monogenesis is perhaps just as strong as the historical argument against it. Bluntly stated: This is not how God works. The Spirit came and comes "suddenly...from heaven" (Acts 2:2, NASB). The Holy Spirit is quite capable of arriving anywhere in the world without booking a connecting flight through Los Angeles. Of course, the same thing applies in all the other directions too. The Spirit does not need to stop in India—or in Wales—before getting to Los Angeles. *We might say that the Holy Spirit specializes in nonstop flights, in unexpected arrivals, in unanticipated delays, in flights through nasty weather (when it might seem better not to fly), and in flights arriving at tiny, out-of-the-way airstrips rather than major hubs.* A would-be air traffic controller is liable to throw up his hands in frustration when facing a Spirit pilot who does not follow directions from ground control. This pilot seems to get directions from somewhere else. Let's hope that some overzealous air traffic controller doesn't call in the military to shoot down "the crazy pilot in the rogue plane."

In concluding, let me suggest that today's Pentecostals should be wary about trying to explain the movements and activities, the whys and wherefores, of God's Spirit in the cities, nations, peoples, and places of the world. "The wind blows where it wishes" (John 3:8, NASB). Whenever one of us puts our finger at a spot on the globe and says, "This is the center of what God is doing today," or, "This was the epicenter of what God was doing," then the chances are that we will get it wrong. For Christian believers, the record of history should show us that God seeks to create inclusive community and that this divine purpose was already announced on the original Day of Pentecost: "I will pour out of my Spirit upon *all flesh*" (Acts 2:17, emphasis added). Spiritual discernment will always be a challenge in seeking to grasp what God might be saying and doing in the early twenty-first century. Yet I think we will not go too far astray if we keep our primary focus on God's intention to come in power on behalf of the poor, the weak, and the marginalized and, beginning with them, to establish a community that includes everyone else as well.

Chapter 22

God's Indwelling Spirit: Reflecting on the Theological Challenges of Pentecostalism

Frank D. Macchia

In 1906, William Seymour's *Apostolic Faith* paper contained a remark (most likely written by Seymour himself) that the Pentecostal movement "began among the colored people."[1] Walter Hollenweger took that simple insight to be key to Pentecostalism's ecumenical and theological challenge as a movement of Christian affirmation. Pentecostalism's penchant for orality, narrative, and holistic and inclusive communal participation is to be found in its black African roots.[2] Of course, more recent research in Pentecostalism has pointed to multiple origins of the movement. But one must still take seriously Seymour's conviction that something in the early 1900s had come together at the Apostolic Faith Mission at Azusa Street in Los Angeles that was quintessential for the larger movement.[3] Here was a movement that rose up from among those who mostly existed at the margins of society and church life but who felt empowered to point the larger church toward a renewal that was holistic (of body and soul), charismatic (inclusive, non-hierarchical), and missional (not institution-based, potentially ecumenical).[4]

The fact that the renewal arose largely from the margins of society and church life seemed fitting to Seymour. He continued, "God blessed several wash women with the Holy Ghost, who have been much used of him.... Since then, multitudes have come. God makes no difference in nationality. Ethiopians, Chinese, Indians, Mexicans, and other nationalities worship together."[5] Seymour (and others belonging to the mission) were convinced that spiritual renewal was profoundly communal and implicitly social in that barriers were overcome between gender, age, race, and tongue in order to form a fellowship in which the Spirit's gifting determined the dignity and direction of a person's life. Social constructs such as race or gender that were so influential in determining one's dignity and purpose in the larger society were being fundamentally subverted by the little Pentecostal missions that dotted the landscape of American religious life and elsewhere. They saw themselves as colonies of the Spirit from the kingdom yet to come with a mission to point people to Christ and, through Christ, to the reality of the new creation inaugurated in Him. They were becoming the dwelling place of the Spirit and, as such, witnesses to the love of God revealed in Jesus Christ. It is indeed possible from this core conviction to point to several theological challenges Pentecostals pose both to themselves and to the larger church world.

Starting With the Spirit

The Pentecostal movement celebrated the God near at hand who lives, breathes, and speaks through individual lives and communities, especially those who have no voice in the larger society. For guidance in understanding this experience of God, they turned to narratives of Scripture, but they did so in ways that accommodated a charismatically diverse community. Pentecostal theological method thus arguably starts with the third article of the Creed, the communal experience of the Spirit. Terry Cross wondered whether or not this place for the experience of the Spirit in theological method is in any way relevant to contemporary theology. He asked the question as to whether or not Pentecostals have anything to bring to the ecumenical meal that might make for heartier intake than mere "relish."[6] They will have nothing more to offer than relish if they depend on encyclopedic guides to doctrine, such as

P. C. Nelson's *Bible Doctrines*, written under the influence of mainstream fundamentalist Bible doctrines.[7] Of course, Cross had in mind a Pentecostal theology that reflected on the heartbeat of experience of God in the context of gifted communities of the Spirit dedicated to the performance of narratives that subvert the powers of this age.

Partly in response to his conversation with Pentecostals, Jürgen Moltmann wrote of the false dichotomy between a theology of revelation (proposed by Karl Barth) and a theology of experience (proposed by Friedrich Schleiermacher).[8] Of course, both Barth and Schleiermacher can arguably be shown to have been sensitive to the need to overcome such a dichotomy. Pentecostals may be said to have intuited this need as well. They read Scripture and bore witness without reservation from the vantage point of their experience of God, an experience that was communally diverse, oriented to the biblical narrative, and more or less consciously contextual. Gerald Sheppard noted that while fundamentalists and liberals were quarreling over what may or may not be proved concerning the historicity of biblical events (and, by extension, perhaps the factual veracity of biblical propositions), Pentecostals were preoccupied instead with discerning the life-transforming power of the biblical witness in real life experience and ministry. They saw their lives as part of that witness, as an extension of it in the world. Their entire lives were viewed in the glow of that blinding light. Sheppard thus was fond of referring to Pentecostals as "submodern" rather than modern in their hermeneutic.[9] Kenneth J. Archer has expanded on this thesis, showing that Pentecostals read Scripture from the margins, not well aware of the hermeneutical debates of the citadels of learning in North America or Europe. But their narrative reading of Scripture, in which God was dynamically and immediately present, was spiritually transformative, personally empowering, and praxis driven. If developed, their hermeneutical trajectory could stand on its own two feet as an alternative to the hermeneutical debates of which they were only vaguely aware.[10]

In fact, I would maintain that there is much in common in this trajectory with Karl Barth's hermeneutical revolution, in which the "finger" or Spirit of God stirs the biblical text so that it becomes a pool for healing and prophetic discernment.[11] The Bible within this Barthian revolution is a living measure of our faith and praxis, having both an objective source in the divine self-disclosure but also encountering us in transformative ways, enabling creative "performance" or living witness. There is therefore no theology of revelation without a theology of experience. Pentecostalism is not the only movement to have posed this challenge; liberation theologies have as well. But much to the denial of certain fundamentalist expressions of the Pentecostal movement today, Pentecostals did so at a time and with a force of grassroots influence that was unique.

Experience in theological method implies a question: Whose experience? Spiritual renewal seeks to be as inclusive as possible, especially among those whose voices are not well heard in the larger society. Those that others might consider less honorable are granted greater honor within the fellowship of the Holy Spirit (1 Cor. 12:23). If the church is the primary social base of theology, then broad charismatic participation in the discernment and praxis upon which theology reflects in the light of revelation and larger social context is vital. Seymour and others of the Azusa Street revival could not conceive of renewal unless it involved everyone gifted of the Spirit. The Spirit spoke with both the cries from the depth of the soul and the rhythms of bodily motion and surrender. They couldn't conceive of spiritual renewal apart from broad charismatic participation of the entire community of faith in which hierarchical systems stratified by social privilege were overcome and relegated to a bygone era, left behind by the era of the Spirit. Western dualisms and Eastern hierarchies are overcome within a notion of the Spirit of God as indwelling any and all human vessels and turning them into mediums of divine revelation. As Hans Küng showed us, defining ministry in the church should not begin with those uniquely gifted to the ministry of oversight but rather with the charismatic structure of the entire church, consisting of all believers.[12] Only then can the hierarchical institutionalization of the charismata be avoided. Veli-Matti Kärkkäinen has written of the significant contribution that Pentecostals have made to furthering this insight.[13] Highlighting the charismatic structure of the church may indeed be one of Pentecostalism's most significant challenges to the larger church.[14]

Discussing the conditions for human experience of God, however, involves recognition of how experience is mediated to us, not only through the biblical text and other religious symbols, but also through culturally inherited symbols. Peter Neumann notes that a stress on the immediacy of the divine presence can lead to a naïve confidence in the revelatory significance of Pentecostal experiences in worship. After all, not all Pentecostal testimonies are consistent with the gospel or are liberating. Experiences are mediated and open to critical scrutiny. But an emphasis on the mediated nature of Pentecostal experience can lead to skepticism about the revelatory relevance of Pentecostal experiences. Neumann opts for a "mediated immediacy," in which God is presumed to be present powerfully in revelatory moments of Pentecostal worship but the expressions are nevertheless subject to critical reflection and reappropriation.[15] As an example of such critical reflection, Pentecostal authors working in dialogue with feminist theology have pointed to the role of social construction in how the community of faith interacts creatively and critically with inherited understandings of issues like gender. Lisa Stephenson has proposed a theological method that starts with the third article of the Creed (the Holy Spirit) or, more specifically, with the spiritually gifted community that subverts oppressive constructs concerning gender and pushes for liberating ones.[16]

Liberating praxis within the community of faith provides the basis for the church's living witness in the world to God's inauguration of a new humanity in Christ. The marginalization and subordination of women in the church, therefore, have devastating consequences for the integrity of Pentecostal witness to Christ. Pentecostals who follow Evangelical complementarianism, in which women are fulfilled only as they complement sanctioned male leadership, fundamentally oppose the early direction of spiritual renewal within Pentecostalism, not to mention the direction of the gospel found within the pages of the New Testament (cf. Acts 2:17; Gal. 3:28). John Christopher Thomas has noted that if the Spirit working through the Gentiles was proof positive for the early church that God was no respecter of persons when it came to race, the same conclusion may be drawn today in the relationship in the church between men and women.[17] Using the hermeneutics suggested by Acts, Pentecostals may conclude on the basis of what the Spirit is doing through the lives of women today that the cause of Christ in the world today is meant to be gender inclusive. Regarding the issue of race, David Daniels has shown more clearly than anyone else how long black Pentecostals strove to keep alive the dream of a justly integrated Pentecostal witness to the new humanity inaugurated in Christ. Those struggles speak powerfully of how the *koinonia* of the Spirit pushes in the direction of a community shaped by the crucified and risen Christ as the point of reconciliation across social and cultural barriers.[18]

Of course, the boundaries between the church and the world are porous. The Spirit's work is not confined to the biblical text or even the community of faith when providing the necessary conditions for experiencing God and even for spiritual discernment on some level, as Amos Yong reminds us.[19] God wills by the Spirit to create analogues in the world of the liberating and just relationships within the community of faith. These analogues help to alleviate suffering, glorify the Creator, and create a context in which the preaching of the good news finds a meaningful point of contact. Indeed, all of humanity lives and has its being in God (Acts 17:28). Pauline statements about spiritual death due to sin (Eph. 2:1) is a potent reminder of how helpless we are to save ourselves apart from Christ. Such statements, however, should not be absolutized to mean that humanity outside of explicit faith in Christ has no spiritual sensitivity or discernment, no capacity whatever for experiencing God. The overall challenge of a Pentecostal theological method will be to work toward articulating a broadly based pneumatological imagination that is ultimately directed among the people of God toward the liberating truth of Jesus Christ in the world. Daniela Augustine has proposed a richly pneumatological and charismatic vision of the Spirit's desire to transform society.[20]

A stress on liberating discernment and praxis does ultimately require an equally strong emphasis on the way of Christ, the second article of the Creed. Otherwise, we lack objective guidance for the dynamic process involved in Christian discernment and witness. For example, speaking in tongues for Seymour was not merely an expression of human ecstasy in reaching for God. It was more than that. It was a sign of various peoples coming together across barriers of misunderstanding in order to form a united witness to the love of Christ. Implicit is a theological method that listens to many voices.[21] The church can detect secular analogues of the Spirit's work in breaking down barriers in the world because of the Spirit's witness to Christ within the community of faith. Charles Mason even viewed his first experience of speaking in tongues as a participation in the groaning of Jesus from the cross for the suffering of the world.[22] For Mason, the foretaste of liberty in the Spirit only leads to a yearning to see this liberty fundamentally free the entire suffering creation. Speaking in tongues for Seymour and Mason was not a mere shibboleth that marked some as filled with the Spirit as a privileged group. Tongues were ideally a sign of something the Spirit was doing throughout the world, a just and liberating reconciliation of people in Christ. Tongues functioned as a kind of sacrament of the divine presence to bring to expression groaning for the coming kingdom and a coming together across barriers in concrete witness to its reality dawning in our midst.[23]

Focus on Spirit Baptism

There was in fact a sharp Christological qualification of experiences in the Spirit that guided the direction of Pentecostal spirituality and theology. Donald Dayton's characterization of Pentecostal theology highlights a distinctive doctrinal *Gestalt* or convergence of doctrinal loci revolving around the work of Christ through the Spirit: salvation, sanctification, Spirit baptism, healing, and the coming kingdom. It seems clear from a reading of the early literature of the movement that the reception and fullness of the Spirit is the overwhelmingly dominant concern among these loci. The greatest Pentecostal point of emphasis is arguably the baptism in the Holy Spirit, not merely as an experience of empowerment, but more deeply and expansively as a root metaphor for our participation in God's self-impartation through Christ and in the Spirit. There are rich resources within this root metaphor for developing the conviction that all of the divine works are directed toward turning humanity—indeed, all of creation—into the dwelling place of God.[24]

If the baptism in the Spirit is the crown jewel of Pentecostal doctrines, one would do well to look at the distinct theological challenges posed by this metaphor. Early Pentecostals were taken with the process by which sinners become the dwelling place of the Holy Spirit and the vessel of the Spirit's work. Seymour described it this way: "The Lord has mercy on him for Christ's sake and puts eternal life in his soul, pardoning him of his sins, washing away his guilty pollution, and he stands before God justified as though he had never sinned"; then Seymour concludes that the presence of God works deeper to break the hold of original sin (which is entire sanctification, or the total surrender of the will to God). Only then is the person on the altar, ready for the fire of God to fall, which is the baptism in the Holy Spirit, "the free gift upon the sanctified, cleansed heart."[25] Spirit baptism for Seymour was Spirit empowerment and renewal precisely as an enhancement (or better expansion) of the sanctified life, turning it outward in the direction of empowered witness.

The dividing lines between conversion, sanctification, and Spirit baptism, however, were not always neatly drawn, even for Seymour. In fact, Seymour and others called Spirit baptism a total baptism in divine love with soteriological significance: "So when we get the baptism with the Holy Ghost we have overflowing love, we have rivers of salvation."[26] It is thus love that is the most basic sign of

Spirit baptism: "What is the real evidence that a man or woman has received the baptism with the Holy Ghost? Divine love, which is charity."[27] One author even finds the breaking down of barriers between different races as the clearest meaning of Spirit baptism.[28] The line between sanctification and Spirit baptism was thus at times blurred as well: "There is no difference in quality between the baptism with the Holy Ghost and sanctification. They are both holiness."[29] The variety does not stop here. Some implied that the blood of Christ does the converting and the cleansing, so the Holy Spirit does not arrive until Spirit baptism! Others argued that the Spirit enters the vessel to convert and to sanctify but does not come in fullness until Spirit baptism. The Wesleyan wing to the movement stressed how Spirit baptism is the gift bestowed upon the work of entire sanctification, while the more Reformed segment tended to disregard entire sanctification and simply add Spirit empowerment to one's initial conversion to Christ. Still others (the Oneness Pentecostals) viewed the initial arrival of the Spirit as the only arrival, namely, as the crowning moment of a complex conversion event involving faith, repentance, and water baptism in Jesus's name. For the Oneness Pentecostal, the arrival of the Spirit comes with both sanctification and Spirit empowerment.

Since the early years, differences between Wesleyan, Reformed, and Oneness options became more clearly defined because of the influence of denominations, especially in the United States. Yet global research into the variety of viewpoints worldwide today would certainly call up a diversity of options that would not be far removed from the colorful variety evident in the early years. So, when one asks about the Pentecostal doctrine of the baptism in the Holy Spirit, one could very well respond, Which one? None of this is meant to deny the popularity throughout Pentecostalism of the idea of subsequence or that the experience of the baptism in the Holy Spirit is distinct from one's incorporation into Christ by faith. Some version of this idea is the majority viewpoint. But it is by no means the only one, and there are variations of understanding even within it. In fact, the popular view may not be the one most suggested by the early theological direction of Pentecostal spirituality. David William Faupel has convincingly argued that the Christocentric focus of early Pentecostalism tends toward the Oneness view of Christian initiation.[30] If Christ embodies the total victory of God in the life of the new creation, as most Pentecostals believed, then receiving the Spirit cannot proceed substantively beyond the ontological change that is enacted and confirmed at baptism. Subsequent experiences can at most release into life or otherwise bring to outward visible fulfillment that which is already mysteriously hidden in Christ.

The doctrine of subsequence can have value in that it points to the need to strive for experiences of the Spirit in greater fullness and outward expression. Simon Chan has shown that Pentecostals have their own version of the ancient church's conviction that the life of the Spirit is realized among the people of God in stages, except in the ancient church this realization was sacramentally distinguished (baptism, confirmation, experiences of renewal during the celebration of the Lord's Supper). While not confining spiritual renewal to the sacraments, his suggestion is that Pentecostals come to appreciate the role of the sacramental life of the church in occasioning the landmarks in their journey to become the vessel of the Spirit's overflowing presence and ministry.[31] The Oneness Pentecostals have moved in this direction by locating baptism as the most likely place to receive the crowning moment of the Spirit's possession of a human vessel. Chris E. W. Green's work of a Pentecostal/pneumatological understanding of the Lord's Supper can help take us further in the direction of Chan's suggestion as well.[32]

Part of the challenge when seeking to substantiate the doctrine of subsequence from the New Testament, however, is the absence of any narrative or instruction that distinguishes two distinct stages (incorporation and Spirit filling) in one's reception of the Spirit. Partly in response to this challenge, Robert P. Menzies and Roger Stronstad have sought to use the well-accepted principle concerning the diversity of New Testament voices to posit a fundamental difference between Lukan and Pauline pneumatology. Briefly put, Luke's understanding of Spirit baptism is assumed to support the typically Jewish understanding of the Spirit as the Spirit of prophecy, blessing those already belonging to the covenant of the faithful with the capacity to bear prophetic witness. Paul, however, introduces a novel understanding of Spirit baptism as incorporation into Christ by faith. Though neither Paul nor Luke assume two distinct receptions of the Spirit, one may assume such a distinction by putting Paul and Luke together. Paul reveals the Spirit's work in incorporating us into Christ (1 Cor. 12:13) while Luke highlights the Spirit's subsequent work of empowering those already incorporated into Christ.[33] Of course, Luke also presents the Spirit's work as community forming, and Paul also finds it to be diversely charismatic. But the difference of emphasis between the two is informative.

The challenge here is to recognize that the difference of emphasis is informative not only in connecting Pentecostal pneumatology with a larger ecumenical audience but also in facilitating an intra-Pentecostal discussion on the experience of the Spirit. As we noted, there are differences among Pentecostal camps when it comes to how Spirit baptism is understood. One could propose on the basis of Stronstad's and Menzies's work that Spirit baptism is based in the incorporative work of the Spirit but finds empowering release or expression in the experience of Spirit filling and renewal. After all, though the gift of the experience is experienced in different dimensions, it is still one gift. But the subsequent experience of the Spirit is not equal to the first, for the subsequent experience merely releases in life the grace received through faith and baptism. Such an insight can bring Holiness, Reformed, and Oneness Pentecostals to the table in dialogue. From the vantage point of such conversations, Pentecostals can respond with greater nuance and sensitivity to our ecumenical partners like James Dunn (Reformed) and Kilian McDonnell (Catholic), whose work on Spirit baptism has been provocative for us in the past.[34]

There is no question but that Pentecostals have put the topic of Spirit baptism on the ecumenical table. Though the roots of the doctrine are in the Holiness movement, the Pentecostals made it their key doctrine and brought it to the attention of the global church. The two most significant and creative developments of the doctrine (by Dunn and McDonnell) were written in response to the Pentecostal challenge.[35] There are three issues that emerge from the Pentecostal challenge concerning Spirit baptism. First, the Pentecostals bring to the forefront the indwelling and overflowing presence of the Spirit as key to how one construes the work of the triune God in the world. The fact that we were made to be the dwelling place of the Spirit, that the Messiah came to impart the Spirit, and that the church exists to invoke the Spirit, all three, can have significant consequences for contemporary theology. Second, all early Pentecostals assumed that purity and power are ultimately inseparable and can be developed under a theology of divine love. Spirit baptism for them was "vocational sanctification," in the words of Singaporean pastor David Lim.[36] Pentecostals need to work to realize this idea on the practical level of personal and church life. Third, Pentecostals highlighted the fact that the Christian life lacks fullness without the outward moving (charismatic, social, missional) dimension of life empowered by the Spirit. One can refer to a dual conversion: first, from the world to God and, second, from God back to the world (out of love for the world and in service toward its renewal). There is in both movements a single conversion. This single insight holds great potential for spiritual renewal. Though there is significant diversity in Pentecostal understandings of Spirit baptism, there are also general implications from this root metaphor that offer challenges for Pentecostal and non-Pentecostal theology alike.

Healing and Eschatology

Next to Spirit baptism, healing is arguably the theological accent that has contributed more than anything else to the rapid spread of Pentecostalism globally. The practice of divine healing was waning in Holiness and Evangelical movements at the turn of the twentieth century, when Pentecostalism experienced its initial growth.[37]

Pentecostalism grew rapidly in part because it offered a haven for those who were dissatisfied with the waning of healing elsewhere. During the 1960s and '70s, Pentecostalism exploded in the Global South in part due to the massive divine healing campaigns of evangelists like T. L. Osborn, Benny Hinn, and Reinhard Bonnke. The healing doctrine was arguably part of the engine that drove the growth of the Pentecostal movement globally. Healing was all along one of the essential points of the Pentecostal fourfold gospel (Jesus as Savior, Spirit Baptizer, Healer, and Coming King). The "full" gospel includes healing because of the conviction that salvation is not only for the soul but also for one's embodied existence. Miroslav Volf thus refers to the "material" understanding of salvation that Pentecostals hold in common with liberation theology and others in the ecumenical movement.[38]

Part of the challenge involved in the Pentecostal healing doctrine is found in the supernatural understanding of healing prominent among Pentecostals. This understanding is due to the strongly Christological orientation to pneumatology among Pentecostals. Pneumatology tends to be read from the context of Christ's victorious death and resurrection, which transcends this world of natural processes and reaches for the world to come, granting us a foretaste of that world in the here and now. Pentecostals have been sensitive to the work of God in natural processes of healing, but their testimonies abound of miraculous cures that defy medical explanation. This hope cannot be simply brushed aside as irrelevant. Neatly dividing soul from body is hardly possible. Wholeness in one is bound to affect the other. Who is to say that the foretaste of the resurrection cannot cause dramatic results on occasion in the health of an individual or people in community?

However, one also has to avoid a dualism between the natural and the supernatural that promotes a "God in the gaps" theology in which God intrudes into the natural order to do something supernatural. God should rather be viewed as the "ground of all being," to use a phrase made famous by Paul Tillich, or the source of all hope and liberation, as Jürgen Moltmann has been known to say.

As Walter Hollenweger has reminded Pentecostals, the term *supernatural* is not in the Bible. God is the source of all life and light throughout all of nature. All that is natural already lives from God (Acts 17:28).[39] As personal, God is of course free to act through nature in ways that are extraordinary. But there is no divine action that intrudes or intervenes from that which is supernatural into that which is natural. As Amos Yong has noted, a noninterventionist understanding of the work of the Spirit (intruding supernaturally into the natural order) does not necessarily preclude experiences that are extraordinary and that reach eschatologically for greater fulfillment.[40]

The challenge of Pentecostalism's healing doctrine runs deep. Kimberly Alexander has shown us that it has deep roots in John Wesley's strong healing metaphor for salvation, a dimension of Wesley's thought developed by Howard Snyder.[41] Snyder shows us that a healing metaphor of salvation has greater potential for meeting our ecological crises theologically than the Reformation stress on juridical acquittal. Indeed, even the kingdom of God metaphor can be construed in strongly political terms, leaving out of the equation the Pentecostal groaning with the suffering creation for healing. If healing defines the "full" gospel, then even a juridical concept like justification by faith or a political metaphor like kingdom of God takes on a strongly cosmic dimension. Justification can be said to imply theosis or a transformative participation in God, as Veli-Matti Kärkkäinen shows us,[42] the just renewal and fellowship of all things, rooted not in any anthropocentric purpose but rather the purposes of God that confront all things as pure gift.[43] The kingdom of God bursts open as a metaphor to include the cosmic liberation of all things by the divine reign. All things are renewed and healed by becoming the dwelling place of God.

What all of this means is that eschatology for Pentecostalism cannot be an escape from the earth but rather a groaning and working for a new earth to come. This is not to say that we produce the new world coming, but neither do we wait passively for God to do it all without us. We also strive in prayer, dreaming and working to occasion signs of the coming world that will serve as "sacraments" God will use to usher in the final renewal of all things. As Murray Dempster noted, the prophetic tradition of Pentecostal witness assumes that there is a thread connecting this world with the one to come.[44] Extreme apocalypticism or supernaturalism that encourages escapist models of the future must be resisted if Pentecostalism is to capture its prophetic heritage and join others in challenging mainstream fundamentalist eschatology. The original vision of Azusa Street of a latter-day outpouring of the Spirit arises especially from the margins of society to challenge the powers of the age, subvert them, and cross boundaries to bear witness to God's just and liberating work in the world.

This eschatology "from below" cannot be used to dismiss an eschatology "from beyond." The resurrection of Jesus and the outpouring of the Spirit from the explosion of life that occurred at that event are enormously important to any movement of Christian affirmation. A biological vision of a world in the making through evolutionary process might offer hope for a vastly improved future for humanity and the earth, but such an end is not guaranteed. Even if it is achieved, what about all of the beings who were thrown into the ash heap of progress? What happens to them? How do they access hope? How are they remembered? Resurrection means that God has not forgotten them and will grant them a share in the rich fruit of the coming kingdom. When God indwells all things, all things will have a share in that indwelling. God will be all in all (1 Cor. 15:28). If there are losses, it will only be among those who permanently refuse God's gracious purposes for the world.

The Pentecostal vision of Spirit baptism, or a great outpouring of the Spirit upon all flesh, implies an eschatology that is oriented to universal divine indwelling and renewal of all things. The Christ who bore the Spirit descended on the cross into all that contradicts the Spirit (sin and death) in order to rise up and open a way into the Spirit of life for all of creation. Pentecost is the means by which resurrection fulfills its victory, for Christ rises as the life-giving Spirit (1 Cor. 15:45). It is there at Pentecost that creation is flooded with the Spirit of life, a tidal wave that seeks to move all things in the direction of the ultimate divine indwelling of all things. The end game? Revelation 21 states it nicely:

> I saw the Holy City, the new Jerusalem, coming down out of heaven from God, prepared as a bride beautifully dressed for her husband. And I heard a loud voice from the throne saying, "Look! God's dwelling place is now among the people, and he will dwell with them. They will be his people, and God himself will be with them and be their God. 'He will wipe every tear from their eyes. There will be no more death' or mourning or crying or pain, for the old order of things has passed away."
>
> —vv. 2–4, NIV

Conclusion

When I was a student at Union Theological Seminary, a professor of mine, Gerald T. Sheppard, had lamented in conversation with me more than once that significant numbers of Pentecostals in the United States left the margins in search of the mainstream. In the process, they sought to mimic fundamentalist hermeneutics, theology, and politics. They would have been so much better off, he speculated, if they had stayed at the margins and continued to think theologically from there.[45] There are Pentecostals still thinking theologically this way, and part of the challenge for the larger movement will be to pay special attention to those voices. Listening to those voices will bring Pentecostals back to the prophetic voices of the biblical canon in its witness to the way of Christ in the world and to the witnesses from their early past in constructive dialogue. From that process, Pentecostals will listen carefully to voices from the larger Christian family, as well as others who also speak from the Spirit. The tongues of Pentecost that sing praises to Christ cannot be confined to only one story. But rediscovering our own story will help us clarify the ongoing theological challenge that the Spirit has uniquely gifted us as a movement to pose both to ourselves and to the larger church world.

Chapter 23

Global Oneness Pentecostal Theology: Contributions and Challenges for the Twenty-First Century

David A. Reed

Oneness Pentecostalism (OP) is an enigma. How is it that a movement born within the womb of the Christocentric, finished-work-of-Calvary stream and the pneumatologically charged Pentecostal revival within two years be expelled from its native fellowship, the Assemblies of God (AG), as a "Sabellian" heresy? During the two years prior to its expulsion in 1916, the "New Issue" (as it was first called) was controversial but certainly not immediately discerned as a scorned heresy. In 1915, the Third General Council issued a plea for tolerance on both sides to contend for their views so long as they honored the views of their host when preaching in churches or camp meetings.

With the collapse of this experiment in hospitality, the 1916 Fourth General Council placed before the ministerial body for ratification a clearly worded Trinitarian document called the Statement of Fundamental Truths. It also took the uncharacteristic move of denouncing the new teaching as a recurrence of the ancient heresy of Sabellianism. Up to this point, the AG fellowship could be characterized as Biblicist and restorationist, with little theological investment in the authority of church tradition and creeds. The motion passed, but not before bequeathing to the departing minority a label that would haunt them for a century.[1] Now a century later, the global numerical strength of OP may be as high as twenty-five million, with most of the growth occurring in regions of the Global South.[2]

In this essay, I begin with a brief look at the first, North American, face of OP in light of the effect of the 1916 decision to permanently sever relations. I then select four faces of OP outside North America, briefly highlighting distinctive features that illustrate the diverse ways in which Oneness theology has contextualized—Mexico, the African Diaspora in Britain, Ethiopia, and China. I conclude by reflecting upon contributions and challenges for the future, including some methodological considerations.[3]

The Face of Western Classical Orthodoxy

OPs and the Trinitarian Pentecostals quickly drifted apart institutionally, but the legacy of a label lingers as the norm for defining each other's identity. The discourse in both solitudes has been framed along the orthodoxy-heresy axis. Most Oneness writings have been produced by leaders within the United Pentecostal Church International (UPCI), and Trinitarian writers have sometimes been Pentecostals but more recently fundamentalist-Evangelical apologists who hold a narrow, polemical view and lack appreciation for the theological complexity within the history of the doctrine of the Trinity.

The first major challenge to the Oneness doctrine following the 1916 schism came four decades later. Assemblies of God pastor Carl Brumback (1917–1987) published a vigorous refutation of the Oneness claims, sometimes recording a dialogue he was carrying on with Oneness proponents through personal correspondence. He was polemical throughout, claiming that Oneness theology was a "composite of the most heretical teachings that ever plagued the Church, ancient or modern."[4] In context, he was responding to exaggerated and uninformed Oneness charges that laid the doctrine of the Trinity at the feet of ancient paganism and the Roman Catholic Church. Admittedly not a scholarly work by current standards, yet many of his arguments were reasoned and deserve consideration. Brumback's polemic, however, may well have also reflected the growing drift within the Assemblies of God toward Evangelicalism and its preoccupation with orthodox doctrine and all heresies great and small.[5]

Following on the orthodox-heresy axis, occasionally Oneness writers attempt to trace their views historically along a path parallel to the orthodox Trinitarian tradition. Oneness historian Thomas Weisser published a popular study of Christian thinkers throughout history who held a variety of non-Trinitarian views, highlighting Modalists as those most closely approximating the Oneness doctrine of God. His purpose is twofold: to show that the doctrine of the Trinity "comes from man and not God" and to show that there has been a faithful line of Oneness believers throughout history, which he illustrates with a chart.[6]

Certainly the most prolific Oneness writer is David Bernard. While not an academic theologian at the time, he set out in a series of volumes to provide a clear and compelling articulation of the official doctrine of UPCI. He claims that OP is fundamentally the true biblical "Christian Monotheism," in contrast to the adulterated Trinitarian version.[7] Unfortunately, Oneness literature is replete with the misunderstanding that the doctrine of the Trinity teaches "three separate and distinct persons," defining *person* in the modern sense of a discrete, autonomous center of consciousness. Regrettably, there has still been no serious reevaluation of this error, although we recognize, as Barth and other theologians do, that the problematic term nearly dies the death of a thousand qualifications.

Bernard represents the mainstream Oneness view that God in transcendence is one center of consciousness, the unqualified One, but acts in history in a threefold manner. God in transcendence is Spirit (one center of consciousness with will and power to act) and in the incarnate state the person of Jesus. Since Jesus is divine, God must be personal. Although Oneness theology is primarily a biblical theology, it has not avoided the debates and labels which emerged in the postapostolic church and generally recognizes its own view as a form of Modalism.

One aspect of the defense of God's undifferentiated unity is the Oneness rejection of the eternal Sonship, since to do so would imply two eternal persons. Prior to the incarnation, Jesus was the Word of God as the expression or going forth of the mind of God, but in a nonhypostatic way. This is hinted at by David Norris, a leading UPCI biblical scholar. Regarding Christ's preexistence, Norris points out how God accomplished God's purpose by speaking the world into existence and speaking redemptively and prophetically of the coming of Christ: "It is only in this way, and precisely in this way, that Jesus Christ may be said to 'pre-exist.'"[8]

Others have been more adventuresome. Canadian Oneness writer John Paterson (1898–1998) believes there is a distinct status within the nature of God related to the Word as "the embodiment of the invisible God."[9] This "embodiment," however, refers to the pre-incarnate state, similar to a hypostatic distinction, but in a way that does not threaten the one nature of God. Paterson draws his insights from the "us" passages, Genesis 1:26 and 3:22.

The most complex figure is Andrew D. Urshan (1884–1967), Persian immigrant missionary, evangelist, and a founding contributor to Oneness doctrine. Although he was baptizing in the name of Jesus as early as 1910, he maintained until his death a unique understanding of the Trinitarian nature of the Godhead. Although he opposed what he considered to be a Trinity of "three separate and distinct persons," he never embraced the notion of God as undifferentiated Spirit. He sought to explain the doctrine, somewhat incorrectly, through the lens of his Syrian Christian roots and divine attributes of mind, wisdom, and power. The following statement reflects his conviction that the "three-ness" within the divine nature is a mystery, one which he continued to affirm until his death: "I personally cannot refrain from believing that there is a plurality in God's mysterious Being, and that this plurality is shown as a three-ness, not three separate, distinct Beings or Persons of God, but a mysterious, inexplicable, incomprehensible three-ness."[10] Urshan consistently used terms like *triune*, *Tri-one*, and *three-one* to affirm this mystery.[11]

The most distinctive but often overlooked aspect of Oneness theology is its theology of the name of Jesus. The New Issue "revelation" and controversy over the name to be invoked in baptism was more than a debate over baptismal formulas. The name of Jesus was nothing less than the divinely given name for salvation in the New Covenant. As the Evangelical and Pentecostal world was being saturated with language of Jesus and His power to save and heal, the New Issue invested the power of that name in baptism. As Norris puts it boldly, "When the first Jewish members of the audience were plunged into baptismal waters and the name of Jesus was invoked over them, what happened was nothing less than the birth of Christianity, for it was not Yahweh who was the covenant partner, but it was Jesus Christ."[12]

For our purpose, I propose that this semiontological status invested in the name of Jesus has the potential to bridge the Platonic divide in early Modalism that separates the transcendent deity from the temporal modes. Humans cannot know or experience the transcendent God in this cultural dualism. Unlike early Modalism, the believer is brought near not only through the Incarnation but in the name of the Incarnate one. The name of Jesus bridges that gap in Oneness—the Yahweh of the Old Covenant is the Jesus of the New. Indeed, it is *experientially* true for all Pentecostals. The ecumenical possibility might be a robust biblical theology of the name with the potential to achieve broad consensus within the wider Christian community.[13]

In sum, much of the discourse on both Oneness and Trinitarian sides has been framed by the 1916 charge of heresy. Oneness writers have also written on Christology and salvation, but the most animated discussions are still reserved for those teachings that stand outside Trinitarian orthodoxy.

Oneness With an Ecumenical Face

The ecumenical face of Oneness Pentecostalism belongs to a Mexican leader, Manuel J. Gaxiola-Gaxiola (1927–2014). He devoted his life and ministry to the Iglesia Apostólica de la Fe en Cristo Jesús (ACFCJ), the oldest Pentecostal denomination in Mexico. He held most offices in ACFCJ, including two terms as presiding bishop and thirty-two years on the national executive. This legacy demonstrates that he was not an ecclesiastical maverick but a respected representative for his Oneness faith and the Iglesia Apostólica.[14]

Gaxiola, however, had a remarkable ability to place his Oneness faith within the arena of the wider Christian community. He associated with and contributed to numerous Christian endeavors with the blessing of his church. His many ecumenical accomplishments included participating as an official observer for an international Roman Catholic-Pentecostal dialogue and as an observer at a World Council of Churches consultation (1973). In 1974 he was full partner in a Lausanne consultation.[15] He was one of the first Latin American leaders to complete doctoral studies.[16] More significant for Pentecostals, in 1990 Gaxiola served as president of the Society for Pentecostal Studies. A year later he was consultant for an issue of *Pneuma: The Journal of the Society for Pentecostal Studies* devoted to Latin American Pentecostalism, in which he also wrote the leading essay.[17]

In 1977 Gaxiola presented a paper at the first Apostolic Faith seminar held at the headquarters of UPCI in Hazelwood, Missouri. Its title, "The Unsettled Issue," reveals his concerns for the Oneness movement, both internally and ecumenically.[18] Externally, he proffered that patience should have ruled over excommunication of the New Issue in 1916. Sufficient time was not accorded to listen and settle the dispute over time. Although he acknowledges that the historic doctrine of the Trinity was at the time "an adequate way of settling a theological dispute," the doctrine is still not fully resolved, alluding here to the appearance of the twentieth-century Oneness movement. Specifically, he calls upon Trinitarians to do two things:

revise their doctrine to account for the presence of truth in Oneness theology and explore without prejudice the practice of baptism in the name of Jesus according to the Acts of the Apostles.

Gaxiola then challenges Oneness leaders on three fronts. One is a chastisement over internal divisions along the lines of race and regionalism (referring particularly to the racial split in 1924). Second, he appeals for a wider consensus on the doctrine of God, noting that the Oneness doctrine does not preclude affirming plurality within the Godhead. Here he refers to the writings of Andrew Urshan and Kenneth Reeves. Finally, he enjoins Oneness leaders to be open to scholarship and research without bias. Much has happened since 1977 that would encourage this ecumenical Oneness visionary. But as he would surely admit, progress on most of the issues remains "unsettled."

A Cultural-Contextual Face of Oneness Pentecostalism

Roswith Gerloff (1933–2013) is both gift and challenge to (Apostolic) Oneness Pentecostalism. She is gift because she introduces to the white Western Pentecostal culture the face of its own African roots that, although partly forgotten, is still present in its African American Pentecostal community. She is challenge in that she presents a way of being Pentecostal that confronts the rational, speculative, and propositional method of doing theology, an approach that denies aspects of the Pentecostal heritage. Her case study is the Oneness Pentecostals among the African Diaspora in Britain.[19]

Methodologically, all theology is embedded within a culture and is by definition contextual. Lest the point be missed, Gerloff clarifies: "Black majority churches necessarily know the connection between culture and identity. Culture is intrinsic to humanity, and if culture is not affirmed, they become dehumanized, as colonial history has demonstrated."[20]

Pentecostalism has been profoundly shaped by its African origins, culturally and theologically. Although an understanding of

African spirituality and ways of doing theology have nearly disappeared among white Pentecostals, the black majority Pentecostal churches have not forgotten, even through the process of hybridization that inevitably occurs when one culture encounters another. Gerloff's profile of an African-shaped Pentecostalism provides the context for understanding the difference between white and black Oneness Pentecostal theologizing, even while using the same words. Of first order is the priority given to *experiencing* God, especially in worship, from praise to preaching. Truth is dynamic, meaning that a doctrine that does not arise from and lead back into the experience of God is of little use.

Theologizing, then, is in *narrative* form rather than through abstract propositions. The Bible is the primary textbook, dynamic and accessible to an encounter with Jesus, the living Word. Because they believe in the spirit world, central to African-shaped Pentecostal praxis is calling upon the *power of the Spirit*, the primary means of confronting serious life obstacles and spiritual evil forces. The normal locus for experiencing spiritual power is worship; in Gerloff's words, worship is *empowerment*. In sum, that which serves to bring one into an empowering experience of God is honored; that which does not is not truth in the fullest sense of the term.[21]

This profile is particularly significant for Gerloff's case study of the Oneness movement. The primary Christocentric thrust of the new movement with emphasis on the name of Jesus in baptism reshapes the understanding and appropriation of the new "revelation." Black Oneness followers read the account of the new doctrine in a nonspeculative way, unlike the white constituency, which is preoccupied with rational orthodoxy. Rather, priority is given to the experience and power that resides in the name of Jesus. As Gerloff observes:

> The force behind the growth and far-reaching mission of the Black Oneness movement…has therefore not been the metaphysical-rationalistic or speculative debate about the "nature

> of the Godhead" as on the White side, but rather the experience of a dynamic truth, and the transmission of this truth or power, as both Christian and contextual.[22]

In other words, according to Gerloff, Oneness Christology is doxology and *dunamis*.

This link between the "revelation" and power in the name of Jesus was made by Frank Ewart, first architect of the New Issue. When he launched his new ministry with preaching and baptizing in Jesus's name, he reported that it was attended by a revival of conversions and healings.[23] Years later, Morris Golder, author and bishop in the Pentecostal Assemblies of the World, commented that the early Oneness were "completely immersed in the revelation of the mighty God in the man Jesus of Nazareth. This for them was 'Bible truth,' and as such entirely different from analytical theories."[24] Gerloff's summation is this:

> The issue these Pentecostals raised, and the answer they received, were not on the Trinity or the immanent nature of God; they rather asked the question: In whose power, or name, or authority, or presence do we preach, teach, heal, baptize and build the church?...they were given the answer: "in the name of Jesus only."[25]

The Face of Oneness Theological Innovation

The most comprehensive challenge to orthodox Oneness Christology comes from Teklemariam Gezahagne, founding bishop of the Apostolic Church of Ethiopia (ACE). Originally planted by UPCI missionaries in the early sixties, the ACE grew to become the largest global Oneness denomination, numbering three million.[26] Teklemariam was reared in a Coptic home in the northern Tigray region, eventually converted to the Protestant faith during the Pentecostal revival that was sweeping through Ethiopia, and after some education became a prominent evangelist. He met and was persuaded by UPCI missionaries Bobbye and Kenneth Wendell of the Oneness message and was baptized in 1969.[27]

In 1999, Teklemariam surprised many outside Ethiopia with the publication of *Bible Writers' Theology*, a major treatment of his distinctive Christology.[28] He retains most of his inherited Oneness doctrines, including the name, divine tri-unity in manifestation only, as well as near ubiquitous misunderstanding of the meaning of persons in the Godhead.[29]

Most controversial is Teklemariam's theology of the one nature, or "divine flesh," of Christ, faintly echoing the teaching of Christ's one nature in the ancient Ethiopian Orthodox Tewahedo (meaning "unified") Church. In brief, it is a controversial version of the doctrine of Christ's impeccability, the belief that Christ was unable to sin, a view held by certain conservative Reformed theologians.[30] Following the trajectory of some early fundamentalists, the essential element in the Atonement is the human purity of Christ, the sacrificial Lamb.

Whether or not Jesus was really tempted in His incarnate state is irrelevant. For fundamentalists, the corrupt biological line from Adam was bypassed by means of the Virgin Birth, wherein God provided the one thing necessary for redemption, an unblemished Lamb.

Teklemariam affirms the pure-blood theory but adds to it the redemptive need for unadulterated flesh. Since the Adamic flesh is worthless for redemption, God provided "divine" flesh. Teklemariam explains it this way: "God the Father has flesh, blood and bones. These three are inseparable for eternity."[31] Teklemariam is here affirming that God is by nature *incarnate-able*, in itself an orthodox position. The Word within the eternal Father is *potentially* flesh, blood, and bone. The Incarnation is that divine Word acting in history. The redemptive significance is that Jesus's sacrifice is efficacious to atone for sins precisely because he is the Word of God made flesh, blood, and bones.

It is not evident whether Teklemariam's "heavenly flesh" doctrine is at root a Docetic Christology or a novel but valid account of the Incarnation. It is premised upon an already widespread view of the need for a redemptively pure vessel and may be an idiosyncratic version of the impeccability Christology. There is another possibility. Teklemariam may have been introduced to the "divine flesh" teaching during two summer theological programs conducted by a Mennonite Bible academy.[32] A near-identical teaching circulated among certain early Anabaptists, including Menno Simons. In the end, Teklemariam's Christology was not able to be assimilated within UPCI Oneness doctrine. He was excommunicated from UPCI in 2003, immediately upon which the ACE followed him.[33]

A Oneness Face Outside the Camp

The True Jesus Church (TJC) is an indigenous Chinese church, started in 1917 in Beijing by a Christian bookseller, Paul Wei (1877–1919), a textile merchant, along with the ministries of two others, Barnabas Zhang (1895–1960) and Ling-Sheng Zhang (1863–1935). Motivated by a radical restoration theology and emerging at the beginning of an anti-Western movement in China, the TJC became an exclusive church, claiming that its core doctrines were delivered to these original workers by revelation.

Although it borrowed doctrines and practices from the missionary churches, they are referred to as "precursors" of TJC's foundational revelational truths.[34] For our purpose, I will focus briefly on the TJC core doctrine of the "one true God" as manifested in Jesus Christ, and salvation according to Acts 2:38—including repentance, water baptism in the name of Jesus Christ, and baptism of the Holy Spirit with speaking in tongues.[35]

Two contextual issues are of interest here. One is the status of the TJC understanding of the "one true God." Although the written description is similar to Western Oneness Modalism, it appears that, unlike the North American contentious orthodox-heresy debate, the doctrine is not given a particularly high profile. As one TJC seminary instructor explained to me, it is not strongly emphasized and is more similar to the historic view called the "economic Trinity."[36]

The second is the way in which the TJC has adapted Acts 2:38. Like UPCI, it teaches that repentance, baptism in the name of Jesus Christ, and the baptism of the Spirit with speaking in tongues together constitute the new birth. But it diverges in four important ways. The TJC teaches that baptism is a sacrament, which is the church's reasoning for why baptism is essential for salvation. It also practices infant baptism, which, like the Orthodox churches, is administered by full immersion. Third, all baptisms are conducted in natural or "living" water: lake, river, or ocean. This is an outworking of TJC theology that baptism is salvific, since in Scripture water is associated with salvation. Finally, the candidate is baptized face forward into the water, following the symbolism of identifying with Christ in His death (Rom. 6:4). As Christ on the cross "bowed his head and gave up his spirit" (John 19:30, NRSV), so the convert bows the head as an act of dying to self so that the resurrected life of Christ may be received. In the case of the TJC, the New Issue was transported globally by a magazine, read by a missionary, shared with a Chinese believer, and reconstituted in a new and exclusive church, incorporating elements that to the North American founders would be surprising at best and false teaching at worst.

Assessment and Prospect

Oneness theology's various global faces are a reminder that innovative ideas born on North American soil a century ago take on nuances and novelty as they move through time and space. This concluding section will briefly reflect on contributions and challenges of Oneness theology, including methodological considerations, as it enters its second century.

Contributions

To begin, Oneness theology must be credited with birthing a distinctive, nontraditional doctrine of God and salvation from the spiritual and theological materials inherited from Pietistic Evangelicalism and the earliest Pentecostal revival. With its component teachings considered together, it is arguably *sui generis*, perhaps earning the reputation of being the only original theology produced by the Pentecostal movement. However inadequate, the earliest writings attest that OP intended to be wholeheartedly Pentecostal and aimed to complete Pentecostalism's inherent Christocentrism and emphasis on the power of God by extending to baptism the already embedded experience of power in the name of Jesus.

Second, within the constellation of Oneness beliefs, OP makes a distinctive contribution to biblical theology through its theology of the name, especially with regard to how it applies to the doctrine of God. The name uniquely functions to ground the life of the triune God in its monotheistic foundation and provides the revelatory link between God's transcendence and the threefold manifestation in history, which is missing in traditional Modalism, overlooked in critiques of Oneness theology, and underdeveloped within Oneness theology until recently.[37]

Oneness theology, therefore, provides an opportunity for the wider theological world to reconsider alternate approaches to Modalism. It may well open up possibilities for enlarging the boundaries of acceptable diversity within the Christian tradition.[38]

Oneness theology may also encourage revision of orthodox judgments on figures in Christian history who were judged as heretics in their time. The person with whom most Oneness theologians identify is Michael Servetus, who was burned at the stake in John Calvin's Geneva for the heresy of supposedly denying the doctrine of the Trinity. He objected that he did not deny the Trinity, only its Hellenistic formulation. His intention was to develop a biblical approach that would make the Christian doctrine more accessible to Jews and Muslims. It is significant that the Unitarians apparently refuse to claim Servetus one of theirs, with one author describing him more suitably as a "highly unorthodox trinitarian."[39]

Finally, a mature Oneness theology of religions may well have a unique opportunity to engage in interfaith dialogue with Islam. Its commitment to biblical theology, especially the Jewish monotheistic tradition and divine encounter through the revelation of the name of God, could provide a bridge of understanding with Muslim theology, which is also an Abrahamic faith.[40]

As missiologist and historian Andrew Walls observes, there are limits to speaking about God in strictly Hellenistic categories. Within the apostolic period, as Christians passed from Jewish to Gentile communities, "the process threw up questions which only struck minds soaked in Greek tradition and required answers in categories drawn from that tradition."[41] Walls recommended a Oneness-Muslim dialogue on the basis that, since Islam primarily inhabits a Semitic culture, there is unique potential for Muslims to dialogue with a Christian theology that is less invested in Hellenistic categories than the Jewish strands of biblical theology.[42]

Challenges

First, the time is right for Oneness theology to explore the diversity within its own history as permission for future theological development. UPCI has devoted the past half-century in honing its own orthodoxy, often by neglecting its theological diversity, especially on such topics as complexity within the Godhead and the two streams of interpretations of Acts 2:38.[43] Since most Oneness publications are produced by UPCI, other Oneness voices, especially if divergent, are not considered.[44]

A related but crucial task for Oneness theologians is to revise its language for the threefold reference to God as Father, Son, and Holy Spirit, specifically the terms *persons* and *manifestations*. A way forward might involve asking these questions: Against what were the founding Oneness leaders reacting, and what did they hope to restore or preserve by their rejection of the doctrine of the Trinity? In light of the best historical and theological resources available, how do Oneness theologians understand the meaning of *persons*? In what ways, if any, does the term remain inadequate for them? How, if at all, would a revised Oneness alternative shift the boundaries of *koinonia* with Trinitarian Christians?

One can anticipate two directions, both compatible with Oneness possibilities. Oneness theology can move sufficiently toward a

Christocentric Trinitarian theology in ways that would, in effect, erase the doctrinal boundary with classical Trinitarian doctrine and restore *koinonia*.[45] It can also explore alternatives outside the traditional categories. Given the current awareness of the complex nature of language and culture, it may be advantageous for OPs to step outside the Western orthodoxy-heresy debate and seek out a distant theological cousin who is Trinitarian but models alternative language. By way of example, African Trinitarian theologian J. N. K. Mugambi rejects the language of "persons" as being "misleading, vague, and confusing" for the African mind.[46] All this of course assumes that such developments are most effective when carried out mutually in dialogue with Trinitarians, especially Pentecostals with whom *koinonia* has been broken.

There is also need from the Trinitarian community for a robust accounting of Christianity's monotheistic foundation. This concern is evident in the pre-Nicene church, which resisted speculations that did not adequately provide such structure. As Christianity moved further from its Jewish roots, its monotheistic priority was weakened. But as OP reminds us, there are still Christians for whom this accounting is still required.[47]

An accounting is also required from OP theologians for the status of Trinitarian Christians, specifically from those who adhere to the new-birth interpretation of Acts 2:38. They refuse to deny salvation to others but remain silent and agnostic and are often reluctant to share in worship with the wider community. The restorationism of a century ago, which pronounced judgment upon those who refused to "walk in the light," can no longer be sustained.

Prospect

This leads to a final methodological reflection. The future task is to formulate a process for the development of doctrine. As Gaxiola and Gerloff have pointed out, culture, language, and context call for change and adaptation over time and space. This is not compromising truth but making truth transferable to new contexts. Otherwise one may be transporting a cultural artifact rather than the gospel. As Australian Pentecostal scholar Shane Clifton points out, the task is "not just exegetical and doctrinal but examination of the experiences and texts which gave rise (over time) to the Pentecostal doctrine."[48] The constellation of ideas and experiences that produced the New Issue a century ago no longer exist and therefore cannot be sustained a century later. New insights and formulations are required.

For the future of Oneness Pentecostal theology, the original "revelation" of the name of Jesus is not to be jettisoned but reappropriated. A clue to the way forward may be found by revisiting the past, beginning with R. E. McAlister's baptismal sermon in 1913. His observation regarding the baptismal name "Lord Jesus Christ" holds important Christocentric implications for all Pentecostals and by which they can make common claim in two important ways.

One is the *Christocentric character of Pentecostal experience.* It reminds Pentecostals that their encounter with the living God is fervently Christocentric, that God is apprehended and contemplated only through their experience of Jesus Christ. There is no knowledge or experience of Father or Holy Spirit that does not have the person and face of Jesus Christ stamped upon it. For Pentecostals, Jesus is both means and object of their deepest devotion.

Second, *a theology of the name belongs to all Pentecostals and even to all Christians.* It should be no surprise that the New Issue message of the name of Jesus spread so rapidly. Ultimately, in Pentecostal and Christian experience, the name is the source of power, and Pentecostal and Christian power is embedded in the name.

Notes

Introduction
"Back" to the West: Possibilities and Challenges for Pentecostal Histories and Theologies in the Twenty-First Century

1. For elaboration and complication of these streams, see Vinson Synan, ed., *The Century of the Holy Spirit: 100 Years of Pentecostal and Charismatic Renewal* (Nashville: Thomas Nelson, 2001).
2. On Parham, see James R. Goff Jr., *Fields White Unto Harvest: Charles F. Parham and the Missionary Origins of Pentecostalism* (Fayetteville, AR: University of Arkansas Press, 1988).
3. See Cecil M. Robeck Jr., "William J. Seymour and 'The Bible Evidence,'" in *Initial Evidence: Historical and Biblical Perspectives on the Pentecostal Doctrine of Spirit Baptism*, ed. Gary B. McGee (Peabody, MA: Hendrickson Publishers, 1991), 72–95.
4. Cecil M. Robeck Jr., *The Azusa Street Mission and Revival: The Birth of the Global Pentecostal Movement* (Nashville: Thomas Nelson, 2006).
5. See also Dale T. Irvin, "'Drawing All Together in One Bond of Love': The Ecumenical Vision of William J. Seymour and the Azusa Street Revival," *Journal of Pentecostal Theology* 6 (1995): 25–53.
6. See Allan Heaton Anderson, *To the Ends of the Earth: Pentecostalism and the Transformation of World Christianity* (Oxford: Oxford University Press, 2013).
7. See also Vinson Synan, *An Eyewitness Remembers the Century of the Holy Spirit* (Grand Rapids, MI: Chosen Books, 2010).
8. See, for example, Walter J. Hollenweger, *The Pentecostals* (Minneapolis: Augsburg Fortress, 1972).
9. The story is told variously; see William K. Kay and Anne E. Dyer, eds., *European Pentecostalism*, Global Pentecostal and Charismatic Studies 7 (Leiden: Brill, 2011); and Paul Schmidgall, *European Pentecostalism: Its Origins, Development, and Future* (Cleveland, TN: CPT Press, 2013).
10. See Joshua R. Ziefle, *David du Plessis and the Assemblies of God: The Struggle for the Soul of a Movement*, Global Pentecostal and Charismatic Studies 13 (Leiden: Brill, 2013).

11. See, for example, David Bundy, *Visions of Apostolic Mission: Scandinavian Pentecostal Mission to 1935*, Studia Historico-Ecclesiastica Upsaliensia 45 (Uppsala, Sweden: Uppsala University, 2009).
12. Allan Anderson, *Spreading Fires: The Missionary Nature of Early Pentecostalism* (London: SCM Press, 2007).
13. On the North American side, see Kirk Dombrowski, *Against Culture: Development, Politics, and Religion in Indian Alaska* (Lincoln, NE: University of Nebraska Press, 2001); and Angela Tarango, *Choosing the Jesus Way: American Indian Pentecostals and the Fight for the Indigenous Principle* (Chapel Hill, NC: The University of North Carolina Press, 2014). On the European continent, see David Thurfjell, *Faith and Revivalism in a Nordic Romani Community: Pentecostalism Amongst the Kaale Roma of Sweden and Finland*, Library of Modern Religion 21 (London: I. B. Tauris, 2013); and David Thurfjell and Adrian Marsh, eds., *Romani Pentecostalism: Gypsies and Charismatic Christianity* (New York: Peter Lang, 2013).
14. Miroslav Atanasov's chapter in this book discusses the Roma Pentecostal movement. For more on North American Native Pentecostalism, see Corky Alexander, *Native American Pentecost: Praxis, Contextualization, Transformation* (Cleveland, TN: CPT Press, 2012).
15. Richard Riss, *The Latter Rain Movement of 1948 and the Mid-Twentieth-Century Evangelical Awakening* (Peabody, MA: Hendrickson Publishers, 1987).
16. For the role of healing, see Candy Gunther Brown, ed., *Global Pentecostal and Charismatic Healing* (Oxford: Oxford University Press, 2011).
17. See Vinson Synan, *Under His Banner: The History of the Full Gospel Business Men's Fellowship International* (Costa Mesa, CA: Gift Publications, 1992); and Matthew Tallman, *Demos Shakarian: The Life, Legacy, and Vision of a Full Gospel Businessman* (Wilmore, KY: Emeth Press, 2010).
18. See Stephen Hunt, *A History of the Charismatic Movement in Britain and the United States of America: The Pentecostal Transformation of Christianity*, 2 vols. (Lewiston, NY: Edwin Mellen Press, 2009).
19. Walter J. Hollenweger, *Pentecostalism: Origins and Developments Worldwide* (Peabody, MA: Hendrickson, 1997). Part 5 discusses what he calls the "ecumenical root" of Pentecostalism.
20. See Kevin and Dorothy Ranaghan, *Catholic Pentecostals* (Paramus, NJ: Paulist Press, 1969); and Edward O'Connor, *The Pentecostal Movement in the Catholic Church* (Notre Dame, IN: Ave Maria Press, 1971).

21. Susan A. Maurer, *The Spirit of Enthusiasm: A History of the Catholic Charismatic Renewal, 1967–2000* (Washington, DC: University Press of America, 2010).
22. See Leon Joseph Cardinal Suenens, *Ecumenism and Charismatic Renewal: Theological and Pastoral Orientations* (Ann Arbor, MI: Servant Books, 1978).
23. Kilian McDonnell, *Charismatic Renewal and the Churches* (New York: Seabury Press, 1976); and Kilian McDonnell, ed., *Presence, Power, Praise*, 3 vols. (Collegeville, MN: Liturgical Press, 1980).
24. This was especially vigorous in Latin America. See, for example, Edward L. Cleary, *The Rise of Charismatic Catholicism in Latin America* (Gainesville, FL: University Press of Florida, 2011).
25. See, for example, Cephan N. Omenyo, *Pentecost Outside Pentecostalism: A Study of the Development of Charismatic Renewal in the Mainline Church in Ghana* (Zoetermeer: Boekencentrum, 2002); and Jakob Egeris Thorsen, *Charismatic Practice and Catholic Parish Life: The Incipient Pentecostalization of the Church in Guatemala and Latin America*, Global Pentecostal and Charismatic Studies 17 (Leiden: Brill, 2015).
26. See, for instance, Donald E. Miller and Tetsunao Yamamori, *Global Pentecostalism: The New Face of Christian Social Engagement* (Berkeley, CA: University of California Press, 2007).
27. Guy Chevreau, *Catch the Fire: The Toronto Blessing—An Experience of Renewal and Revival* (Toronto: Marshall Pickering, 1994); and John Arnott, *The Father's Blessing* (Lake Mary, FL: Creation House, 1996). See also Margaret Poloma, *Main Street Mystics: The Toronto Blessing and Reviving Pentecostalism* (Walnut Creek, CA: AltaMira Press, 2003).
28. See Leo Sandon, "Pentecost in Pensacola: The Brownsville Revival," *The Christian Century* 114, no. 24 (1997): 748–49; and Steve Rabey, *Revival in Brownsville* (Nashville: Thomas Nelson, 1999).
29. The beginnings of the discussion of ours as a postdenominational time go back two decades. See Creighton Lacy, "Toward a Post-Denominational World Church," in *Beyond Establishment: Protestant Identity in a Post-Protestant Age*, eds. Jackson W. Carroll and Wade Roof Clark (Louisville, KY: Westminster John Knox Press, 1993), 327–42; and Mark G. Toulouse, "What Is the Role of a Denomination in a Post-Denominational Age?," *Lexington Theological Quarterly* 29, no. 4 (1994): 207–47.
30. See C. Peter Wagner, *Church Quake! The Explosive Power of the New Apostolic Reformation* (Ventura, CA: Regal, 1999). For a more scholarly

analysis, see William K. Kay, *Apostolic Networks in Britain: New Ways of Being Church* (Eugene, OR: Wipf & Stock, 2007).

31. See, for example, Mark Evans, *Open Up the Doors: Music in the Modern Church* (London: Equinox, 2006); and Monique M. Ingalls and Amos Yong, eds., *The Spirit of Praise: Music and Worship in Global Pentecostal-Charismatic Christianity* (University Park, PA: Penn State University Press, 2015).
32. See Simon Coleman, *The Globalization of Charismatic Christianity* (Cambridge: Cambridge University Press, 2000).
33. Ron Steele, *Plundering Hell to Populate Heaven: The Reinhard Bonnke Story* (Tulsa, OK: Harrison House, 1988); and Reinhard Bonnke, *Living a Life of Fire: An Autobiography* (Orlando, FL: E-R Productions, 2009). For a scholarly analysis, see Paul Gifford, "'Africa Shall Be Saved': An Appraisal of Reinhard Bonnke's Pan-African Crusade," *Journal of Religion in Africa* 17, no. 1 (1987): 63–92.
34. Sung-Hoon Myung and Young-Gi Hong, eds., *Charis and Charisma: David Yonggi Cho and the Growth of Yoido Full Gospel Church* (Oxford: Regnum, 2011).
35. Todd Johnson et al., "Christianity 2015: Religious Diversity and Personal Contact," *International Bulletin of Missionary Research* 39, no. 1 (2015): 29.
36. See David J. Courey, *What Has Wittenberg to Do with Azusa? Luther's Theology of the Cross and Pentecostal Triumphalism* (London and New York: Bloomsbury Academic, 2015).
37. See the discussion on Israel and Pentecostal eschatology in chapter 8 of Amos Yong, *In the Days of Caesar: Pentecostalism and Political Theology* (Grand Rapids, MI: Eerdmans, 2010).
38. Calvin L. Smith, ed., *The Jews, Modern Israel, and the New Supersessionism*, rev. ed. (London: Kings Divinity Press, 2013).
39. Leading the way courageously in this regard, even if controversially, is Paul N. Alexander, ed., *Christ at the Checkpoint: Theology in the Service of Justice and Peace*, Pentecostals, Peacemaking, and Social Justice Series (Eugene, OR: Wipf & Stock, 2012).
40. This question is confronted directly in chapter 7 of Amos Yong, *Renewing Christian Theology: Systematics for a Global Christianity*, images and commentary by Jonathan A. Anderson (Waco, TX: Baylor University Press, 2014).
41. Help is on the way. See, for example, Rickie D. Moore, *The Spirit of the Old Testament*, Journal of Pentecostal Theology Supplement Series 35

(Dorset, England: Deo Publishing, 2011); and Jacqueline Grey, *Three's a Crowd: Pentecostalism, Hermeneutics, and the Old Testament* (Eugene, OR: Wipf & Stock, 2011).

42. The theological issues are discussed in Veli-Matti Kärkkäinen, "Proselytism and Church Relations: Theological Issues Facing Older and Younger Churches," *The Ecumenical Review* 52, no. 3 (2000): 379–90.

43. A strong initiative for this conversation is Edmund J. Rybarczyk, *Beyond Salvation: Eastern Orthodoxy and Classical Pentecostalism on Becoming Like Christ* (Milton Keynes, England: Paternoster Press, 2006).

44. This is the project, for instance, of Daniela C. Augustine, *Pentecost, Hospitality, and Transfiguration: Toward a Spirit-Inspired Vision of Social Transformation* (Cleveland, TN: CPT Press, 2012).

45. One set of case studies is Mechteld Jansen and Hijme Stoffels, eds., *A Moving God: Immigrant Churches in the Netherlands*, International Practical Theology 8 (Berlin: LIT Verlag, 2008); see also Michael Wilkinson, ed., *Global Pentecostal Movements: Migration, Mission, and Public Religion*, International Studies in Religion and Society 14 (Leiden: Brill, 2012).

46. See, for example, Claudia Währisch-Oblau, *The Missionary Self-Perception of Pentecostal/Charismatic Church Leaders From the Global South in Europe: Bringing Back the Gospel*, Global Pentecostal and Charismatic Studies 2 (Leiden: Brill, 2012).

47. Philip Jenkins, *God's Continent: Christianity, Islam, and Europe's Religious Crisis* (Oxford: Oxford University Press, 2007).

48. See the special issue titled "Race and Global Renewal: Mulattic Tongues and Hybridic Imagination to the Ends of the Earth," *Pneuma: The Journal of the Society for Pentecostal Studies* 36, no. 3 (2014).

49. See, for example, Samuel Cruz, "A Post-Colonial Re-Reading of Puerto Rican Pentecostalism in the Diaspora," *Apuntes* 25, no. 4 (2005): 124–45; and Joshua Reichard, "Mutually Transformative Missions: A Postcolonial, Process-Relational Pentecostal Missiology," *Missiology* 43, no. 3 (2015): 245–57.

50. See, for instance, J. D. Y. Peel, "Postsocialism, Postcolonialism, Pentecostalism," in *Conversion After Socialism: Disruptions, Modernisms, and Technologies of Faith in the Former Soviet Union*, ed. Mathijs Pelkmans (New York and Oxford: Berghahn Books, 2009), 183–99.

51. For the beginnings of a Pentecostal epistemology, see James K. A. Smith, *Thinking in Tongues: Pentecostal Contributions to Christian Philosophy* (Grand Rapids, MI: Eerdmans, 2010), chapter 3.
52. See Dale M. Coulter and Amos Yong, eds., *The Spirit, the Affections, and the Christian Tradition* (Notre Dame, IN: University of Notre Dame Press, 2016).
53. As delineated by Harvey G. Cox, *Fire From Heaven: The Rise of Pentecostal Spirituality and the Reshaping of Religion in the Twenty-First Century* (Reading, MA: Addison-Wesley, 1995).
54. We use *American* in the rest of this chapter with some misgivings, since historically this term has by and large excluded First Nations and Native American populations. One of us has worked hard to register indigenous American perspectives on the Pentecostal theological register; see Amos Yong, "Conclusion: The Missiology of Jamestown: 1607–2007 and Beyond—Toward a Postcolonial Theology of Mission in North America," in *Remembering Jamestown: Hard Questions About Christian Mission*, eds. Amos Yong and Barbara Brown Zikmund (Eugene, OR: Pickwick Publications, 2010), 157–67. The following ought to be read with this in mind. See also Angela Tarango, "Jonathan Edwards, Early Pentecostals, and the Missionary Encounter With Native Americans," in *From Northampton to Azusa: Pentecostals and the Theology of Jonathan Edwards*, eds. Steven M. Studebaker and Amos Yong (Bloomington and Indianapolis: Indiana University Press, forthcoming).
55. Detailed by Paul Alexander, *Peace to War: Shifting Allegiances in the Assemblies of God* (Telford, PA: Cascadia, 2009).
56. See Amos Yong, "The Church and Mission Theology in a Post-Constantinian Era: Soundings From the Anglo-American Frontier," in *A New Day: Essays on World Christianity in Honor of Lamin Sanneh*, ed. Akintunde E. Akinade (New York: Peter Lang, 2010), 49–61. See also Steven M. Studebaker, *Citizens of the Cities: A Pentecostal Political Theology for American Renewal* (New York: Palgrave Macmillan, 2016).
57. Leading the way here is Nigerian Pentecostal social ethicist and theologian Nimi Wariboko. See Nimi Wariboko, *The Charismatic City and the Public Resurgence of Religion: A Pentecostal Social Ethics of Cosmopolitan Urban Life* (New York: Palgrave Macmillan, 2014).
58. Nimi Wariboko is also at the forefront of thinking about these matters from a Pentecostal perspective. See Nimi Wariboko, *Economics in*

Spirit and in Truth: A Moral Philosophy of Finance (New York: Palgrave Macmillan, 2014).

59. An exploratory foray into this nexus is found in Katherine Attanasi and Amos Yong, eds., *Pentecostalism and Prosperity: The Socioeconomics of the Global Charismatic Movement*, Christianities of the World 1 (New York: Palgrave Macmillan, 2012).
60. See, for example, Bradley Truman Noel, *Pentecostal and Postmodern Hermeneutics: Comparisons and Contemporary Impact* (Eugene, OR: Wipf & Stock, 2010).
61. About which topic, in any case, rapprochement may yet be possible; see Amos Yong, *The Spirit of Creation: Modern Science and Divine Action in the Pentecostal-Charismatic Imagination* (Grand Rapids, MI: Eerdmans, 2011), chapters 4–5.
62. See Samuel Zalanga and Amos Yong, "What Empire? Which Multitude? Pentecostalism and Social Liberation in North America and Sub-Saharan Africa," in *Evangelicals and Empire: Christian Alternatives to the Political Status Quo*, eds. Bruce Ellis Benson and Peter Goodwin Heltzel (Grand Rapids, MI: Brazos Press, 2008), 237–51; cf. David Tonghou Ngong, *The Holy Spirit and Salvation in African Christian Theology: Imagining a More Hopeful Future for Africa* (New York: Peter Lang, 2010).
63. As developed preliminarily in Veli-Matti Kärkkäinen, Amos Yong, and Kirsteen Kim, eds., *Interdisciplinary and Religio-Cultural Discourses on a Spirit-Filled World: Loosing the Spirits* (New York: Palgrave Macmillan, 2013).
64. This unhelpful bifurcation is addressed in Amos Yong, *The Spirit Poured Out on All Flesh: Pentecostalism and the Possibility of Global Theology* (Grand Rapids, MI: Baker Academic, 2005), chapter 7; see also Amos Yong, ed., *The Spirit Renews the Face of the Earth: Pentecostal Forays in Science and Theology of Creation* (Eugene, OR: Pickwick Publications, 2009); and James K. A. Smith and Amos Yong, eds., *Science and the Spirit: A Pentecostal Engagement With the Sciences* (Bloomington, IN: Indiana University Press, 2010).
65. See D. William Faupel, *The Everlasting Gospel: The Significance of Eschatology in the Development of Pentecostal Thought*, Journal of Pentecostal Theology Supplement Series 10 (Sheffield, UK: Sheffield Academic Press, 1996).
66. See, for example, Peter Althouse, *Spirit of the Last Days: Pentecostal Eschatology in Conversation with Jürgen Moltmann*, Journal of

Pentecostal Theology Supplement Series 25 (New York: Bloomsbury Academic, 2003); and Matthew K. Thompson, *Kingdom Come: Revisioning Pentecostal Eschatology*, Journal of Pentecostal Theology Supplement Series 37 (Blandford Forum, UK: Deo Publishing, 2010).

67. See, for instance, Amos Yong, *Spirit of Love: A Trinitarian Theology of Grace* (Waco, TX: Baylor University Press, 2012); see also Veli-Matti Kärkkäinen, *Toward a Pneumatological Theology: Pentecostal and Ecumenical Perspectives on Ecclesiology, Soteriology, and Theology of Mission*, ed. Amos Yong (New York: University Press of America, 2002).
68. Amos Yong argues this in his "The Spirit, Vocation, and the Life of the Mind: A Pentecostal Testimony," in *Pentecostals in the Academy: Testimonies of Call*, eds. Steven M. Fettke and Robby Waddell (Cleveland, TN: CPT Press, 2012), 203–20.
69. For instance, Talmadge L. French delineates the ecumenical relevance of the Oneness question in his *Early Interracial Oneness Pentecostalism: G. T. Haywood and the Pentecostal Assemblies of the World (1901–1931)* (Eugene, OR: Pickwick Publications, 2014).

Chapter 1
Diverse Contours of Pentecostalism in Israel/Palestine

1. Allan H. Anderson, *To the Ends of the Earth: Pentecostalism and the Transformation of World Christianity* (New York: Oxford University Press, 2013), 5, 8.
2. Cecil M. Robeck, "The Status of Global Pentecostalism: An Overview," 11, available at http://www.globalchristianforum.org/papers.html (accessed May 12, 2016).
3. Christians represent a mere 2 percent of the population of Israel. Christians in Israel amount to one hundred sixty-one thousand out of a total population of 8.345 million. Of these, one hundred twenty-seven thousand are Arab Christians. About 45 percent are Catholic, 40 percent are Orthodox, and 20 percent fall under the category of "other" (see Jewish Virtual Library, "Vital Statistics: Latest Population Statistics for Israel," 2015, at https://www.jewishvirtuallibrary.org/jsource/Society_&_Culture/newpop.html [accessed May 9, 2015]). It is estimated that between six thousand and fifteen thousand Israelis are adherents of Messianic Judaism, some of whom are Pentecostals (see Paul A Pomerville, *The New Testament Case Against Christian Zionism* [Seattle: CreateSpace, 2015], 150; and Maoz Israel, "Messianic Jews," accessed May 6, 2015, http://www.maozisrael.org/site/PageServer?pagename=messianic_jews).

In Palestine, there are about fifty thousand Christians in the West Bank and three thousand in Gaza out of a total population of approximately 4.5 million. Christians comprise approximately 2 percent of the population of the West Bank and 1 percent in Gaza. These estimates cannot be verified because the Palestinian Authority does not use a census to obtain population statistics. Christian groups in the West Bank and Gaza include Eastern Orthodox, Oriental Orthodox, Catholic (Eastern and Western rites), Anglican, Protestant, and Pentecostal, concentrated mainly in East Jerusalem, Ramallah, Nablus, and Bethlehem. (See also Institute for Middle East Understanding, "Palestinian Christians in the Holy Land," December 17, 2012, accessed May 9, 2015, http://imeu.org/article/palestinian-christians-in-the-holy-land.)

4. David Lazarus, "Celebrating Jesus and Israel's Restoration on Mount Zion," *Israel Today*, December 26, 2012, accessed May 9, 2015, http://www.israeltoday.co.il/NewsItem/tabid/178/nid/23590/Default.aspx?article=related_stories.
5. Ibid.
6. Nihad Salman was interviewed by Lynn Grassmeyer of Evanglicals for Social Action, who asked, "As a Christian living amidst constant military presence and the threat of violence, what does Christ as Prince of Peace mean to you?" See Lynn Grassmeyer, "In Thy Dark Streets Shineth…," EvangelicalsForSocialAction.org, December 30, 2014, accessed May 12, 2015, http://www.evangelicalsforsocialaction.org/prayers-for-peace/in-thy-dark-streets-shineth/, italics in original.
7. Don Seeman, "Pentecostal Judaism and Ethiopian Israelis," in *Religious Conversions in the Mediterranean World*, eds. Nadia Marzouki and Oliver Roy (New York: Palgrave Macmillan, 2013), 60–76.
8. Steven Kaplan and Hagar Salamon, "Ethiopian Jews in Israel: A Part of the People or Apart From the People?," in *Jews in Israel: Contemporary and Cultural Patterns*, eds. Uzi Rebhun and Chaim I. Waxman (Lebanon, NH: Brandeis University Press, 2004), 118.
9. Ibid., 60–61.
10. Ibid., 63.
11. Ibid.
12. For a full account of the Pentecostal mission in Palestine, see Eric N. Newberg, *The Pentecostal Mission in Palestine: The Legacy of Pentecostal Zionism* (Eugene, OR: Pickwick, 2012).

13. The Pentecostal movement began in 1901. Its trademark doctrine, known as "initial evidence," held that all Christians should seek a postconversion religious experience called baptism of the Holy Spirit, with the accompanying physical evidence of speaking in tongues. The Charismatic movement began in 1960. While gravitating toward the Pentecostal experience of Spirit baptism and speaking in tongues, the Charismatic movement differed from classical Pentecostalism in that its adherents eschewed the doctrine of initial evidence and remained in their mainline denominations rather than join Pentecostal denominations. Pentecostals and Charismatics both claim that the New Testament gifts of the Spirit are operative today. See David Barrett and Todd Johnson, "Global Statistics," in *New International Dictionary of Pentecostal and Charismatic Movements*, eds. Stanley M. Burgess and Eduard van der Maas (Grand Rapids, MI: Zondervan, 2002), 290–91.
14. Stephen Mansfield, *Derek Prince: A Biography* (Lake Mary, FL: Charisma House, 2005), 98.
15. A pseudonym for the Pentecostal missionary Laura Radford. See Lydia and Derek Prince, *Appointment in Jerusalem* (Charlotte, NC: Derek Prince Ministries International, 1975), 101.
16. Raymond Perkins, "Israel and Missions," private manuscript, 18.
17. S. D. Moore, "Shepherding Movement," in Burgess and van der Maas, *New International Dictionary*, 1060–2062.
18. Derek Prince Ministries, "Derek Prince: The Man and his Ministry," 13.
19. For autobiographical information, see Derek Prince, *Jubilee 1995 Celebration: Fiftieth Year in Ministry* (Fort Lauderdale, FL: Derek Prince Ministries International, 1995), 1–23. For biographical information on Derek Prince, see Linda Howard, "A New Beginning," *Charisma*, April 1984, 38–43; and Mansfield, *Derek Prince*.
20. Mansfield, *Derek Prince*, 270.
21. Ibid., 270–71.
22. Peter Hocken, *The Glory and the Shame: Reflections on the Twentieth-Century Outpouring of the Holy Spirit* (Surrey, UK: Eagle, 1994), 19–20.
23. Ibid., 38.
24. Kai Kjaer-Hansen and Bodil F. Skjott, *Facts and Myths About the Messianic Congregations in Israel* (Jerusalem: United Christian Council in Israel, 1999), 57–67.
25. Ibid., 51.

26. Ibid., 19.
27. Hocken, *The Glory and the Shame*, 38.
28. The account of the story of King of Kings Assembly is taken from its website. See http://www.kkcj.org/about/our-history.
29. Epicenter Conference, "Dr. Erez Soref," accessed May 11, 2015, http://www.epicenterconference.com/features/speakers/dr-erez-soref.
30. OneForIsrael.org, "Because the Best Way to Bless Israel Is With Yeshua," 2015 overview, available at http://www.oneforisrael.org/overview2015.pdf (accessed May 11, 2015).
31. D. B. Hatfield, "Palestine," *Church of God Evangel*, July 16, 1949, 5.
32. J. Herbert Walker, "Missionaries Return to Middle East," *Church of God Evangel*, April 22, 1950, 13.
33. "Rev. D. B. Hatfield, Mrs. Hatfield, Darryl, Lynn and Sheralyn," *Church of God Evangel*, July 22, 1950, 5.
34. Charles W. Conn, *Where the Saints Have Trod: A History of the Church of God* (Cleveland, TN: Pathway, 1977), 272–73.
35. DaoudKuttab.com, "Celebrating the Life of Rev. George M. Kuttab," accessed May 15, 2015, http://www.daoudkuttab.com/2006/george.htm.
36. Margaret Gaines, *Of Like Passions: Missionary to the Arabs* (Cleveland, TN: Pathway Press, 2000), 133.
37. Margaret Gaines, "Birth of a Church," *Church of God Evangel*, December 1, 1969, 7.
38. Gaines, *Of Like Passions*, 168–70.
39. Madiha Rashid al Madfai, *Jordan, the United States and the Middle East Peace Process, 1974–1991* (Cambridge: Cambridge University Press, 1993), 21.
40. Gaines, *Of Like Passions*, 148.
41. Ibid., 202.
42. The Church of God sent a missionary couple to Aboud in 1999, but they returned home in 2001 due to a medical emergency. See "Our Missionaries in the Holy Land," *Mission Line* 18, no. 3 (Summer 2002): n.p.
43. Gaines, *Of Like Passions*, 213.
44. Sarah S. Willen, ed., introduction to *Transnational Migration to Israel in Global Comparative Context* (New York: Macmillan Palgrave, 2013), 9.
45. Ibid., 11.
46. Ibid., 12.
47. Ibid.

48. Dafna Strauss, “The Black Diaspora in Israel, 1965 to 2011,” BlackPast.org, accessed April 30, 2015, http://www.blackpast.org/perspectives/black-diaspora-israel-1965-2011.
49. Galia Sabar, “African Christianity in the Jewish State: Adaptation, Accommodation and Legitimation of Migrant Workers’ Churches, 1990–2003,” *Journal of Religion in Africa* 34, no. 4 (2004): 419.
50. Galia Sabar, “The Rise and Fall of African Migrant Churches: Transformations in African Religious Discourse and Practice in Tel Aviv,” in Willen, *Transnational Migration to Israel*, 190–96.
51. According to the International Christian Embassy Jerusalem website, branches are located in Angola, Australia, Austria, Barbados, Belgium, Benin, Bolivia, Botswana, Brazil, Burkina Faso, Canada, China, Colombia, Democratic Republic of Congo, Costa Rica, Croatia, Czech Republic, Denmark, El Salvador, Estonia, Fiji, Finland, France, Gabon, Germany, Ghana, Guatemala, Honduras, Hong Kong, Hungary, Iceland, India, Ireland and Northern Ireland, Ivory Coast, Kenya, Latvia, Liberia, Lithuania, Malaysia, Mauritius, Mexico, Nepal, Netherlands, New Zealand, Niger, Nigeria, Norway, Panama, Papua New Guinea, Philippines, Portugal, Romania, Russia, Senegal, Sierra Leone, Singapore, Slovakia, Slovenia, Solomon Islands, South Africa, South Pacific Islands, Sri Lanka, Sweden, Switzerland, Taiwan, Tanzania, Togo, Ukraine, United Kingdom, Uruguay, United States, and Zimbabwe. See http://int.icej.org/about/worldwide-branches.
52. Donald E. Wagner, *Anxious for Armageddon: A Call to Partnership for Middle Eastern and Western Christians* (Scottsdale, PA: Herald Press, 1995), 105–7.
53. Tristan Sturm and Seth Frantzman, “Religious Geopolitics of Palestinian Christianity: Palestinian Christian Zionists, Palestinian Liberation Theologists, and American Missions to Palestine,” *Middle Eastern Studies* 51, no. 3 (2015): 433–51.
54. Janet Polen, “Margaret Gaines, Missionary in Israel,” *Church of God Evangel*, November 28, 1977, 18.
55. Gaines, *Of Like Passions*, 204.
56. See Ministry to Israel, http://ministrytoisrael.com/voice-to-the-nations/ (accessed July 21, 2016).
57. Sabar, “Rise and Fall of African Migrant Churches,” 196–201.

Chapter 2
Pentecostals and Charismatics in Russia, Ukraine, and Other Post-Soviet States: History and Future Prospects

1. Roman Poplavsky, "Pentecostal Churches in Russia: Changing Self-Images and Inculturation in Tyumen,'" *Religion, State & Society* 40 (2012): 117.
2. For example, through the International Assembly of Christians of Evangelical Faith (Международная ассемблея христиан веры евангельской), which provides a common forum for Pentecostals from Russia, Belarus, Ukraine, Lithuania, Moldavia, Armenia, Kyrgyzstan, and Uzbekistan and for Slavic Pentecostals living in the West.
3. William Fletcher, *Soviet Charismatics: The Pentecostals in the USSR* (Bern, Switzerland: Peter Lang, 1985), 28. Ibid., 44.
4. Albert Boiter, "Law and Religion in the Soviet Union," *The American Journal of Comparative Law* 35, no. 1 (1987): 102.
5. Catherine Wanner, *Communities of the Converted: Ukrainians and Global Evangelicalism* (Ithaca, NY: Cornell University Press, 2007), 49. The RSFSR law served as a model for the religious legislation in the other union republics (Fletcher, *Soviet Charismatics*, 45).
6. Vladimir Franchuk, *Просила Россия дождя у Господа* [Russia asked the Lord for rain], 3 vols. (Kiev: Svitankova Zoria, 2001–2003), 1.420–21.
7. Ibid., 1.430.
8. Ibid., 1.558.
9. Wanner, *Communities of the Converted*, 57.
10. Catherine Wanner, "Missionaries and Pluralism: How the Law Changed the Religious Landscape in Ukraine," in *Contemporary Ukraine on the Cultural Map of Europe*, eds. Larissa Z. Onyshkevych and Maria G. Rewakowicz (Armonk, NY: M. E. Sharpe, 2009), 91; see also Catherine Wanner, "Explaining the Appeal of Evangelicalism in Ukraine," in *Rebounding Identities: The Politics of Identity in Russia and Ukraine*, eds. Dominique Arel and Blair A. Ruble (Washington DC: Woodrow Wilson Press, 2006), 244.
11. Franchuk, *Просила Россия*, 3.908, 912; Roman Lunkin, "Пятидесятничество и харизматическое движение" [Pentecostalism and the Charismatic movement], in *Современная религиозная жизнь России* [Contemporary religious life in Russia], eds. M. Burdo (Bourdeaux) and S. Filatov, vol. 2. (Moscow: Logos, 2003), 267.

12. L. Uzzell, "Politics, Propriety, and Proselytism in Russia," *The Brandywine Review of Faith and International Affairs* 3, no. 2 (2005): 16.
13. Mark Elliott and Sharyl Corrado, "The Protestant Missionary Presence in the Former Soviet Union," *Religion, State & Society* 25 (1997): 335. For other statistics on foreign missionaries in Russia, see Mark Elliott and Anita Deyneka, "Protestant Missionaries in the Former Soviet Union," in *Proselytism and Orthodoxy in Russia*, eds. John Witte Jr. and Michael Bourdeaux (Maryknoll, NY: Orbis, 1999), 199.
14. Christopher Marsh and Artyom Tonoyan, "The Civic, Economic, and Political Consequences of Pentecostalism in Russia and Ukraine," *Society* 46 (2009): 516.
15. Wanner, "Missionaries and Pluralism," 93, writes, "As of 2001 there were 914 Ukrainian evangelical missionaries, mostly serving in Russia."
16. Central Intelligence Agency, *The World Factbook*, "People and Society," accessed May 17, 2016, https://www.cia.gov/library/publications/the-world-factbook/geos/rs.html.
17. Sergei Filatov and Roman Lunkin, "Statistics on Religion in Russia: The Reality Behind the Figures," *Religion, State & Society* 34 (2006): 46.
18. Roman Lunkin, "Российский протестантизм: евангелчские христиане кан новый социальный феномен" [Russian Protestantism: Evangelical Christians as a new social phenomenon], *Современная Европа* [Contemporary Europe] 3, no. 59 (2014): 136, 139.
19. Lunkin, "Российский протестантизм," 136. The Russian Church of Christians of Evangelical Faith (Российская Церковь христиан веры евангелской) (www.hve.ru) has fraternal relations with the Assemblies of God.
20. Lunkin, "Российский протестантизм," 136; Российский Объединённый Союз христиан веры еванглской (Пятидесятников) (www.cef.ru). In some publications, the name of the denomination is rendered Russian United Union of Christians of Evangelical Faith.
21. Объединённая Церковь христиан веры евангельской.
22. S. G. Safronov, "Territorial Structure of the Confessional Space in Russia and Other Post-Soviet States," *Regional Research of Russia* 3 (2013): 204–10; P. Goble, "Protestant Congregations Outnumber Orthodox in Russian Far East," *East-West Church & Ministry Report* 19, no. 2 (2011): 16; A. Krindatch, "Patterns of Religious Change in Postsoviet Russia: Major Trends From 1998 to 2003," *Religion, State & Society* 32, no. 2 (2004): 117, 131.

23. I. Naletova, book review, *Religion, State & Society* 38, no. 3 (2010): 312; Alexander Agadjanian, “Revising Pandora’s Gifts: Religious and National Identity in the Post-Soviet Societal Fabric,” *Europe-Asia Studies* 53 (2011): 481; “‘Orthodox’... is in most cases a marker of ethnic consciousness.”
24. Lunkin, “Российский протестантизм,” 138.
25. Central Intelligence Agency, *The World Factbook*, “People and Society,” accessed May 16, 2016, https://www.cia.gov/library/publications/the-world-factbook/geos/up.html.
26. Three Orthodox churches compete for the allegiance of Ukrainians: the Ukrainian Orthodox Church—Moscow Patriarchate, the Ukrainian Orthodox Church—Kiev Patriarchate, and the Ukrainian Autocephalous Orthodox Church; see Victor Yelensky, “Religious Freedom: The Case of Ukraine,” *Review of Faith and International Affairs* 6, no. 2 (2008): 67–71. In addition, there is a strong Greek-rite Catholic Church in Ukraine. According to Wanner, “Missionaries and Pluralism,” 89, over 90 percent of Ukrainians associate either with one of these Orthodox denominations or the Greek-rite Catholic Church.
27. Yelensky, “Religious Freedom.”
28. Wanner, “Missionaries and Pluralism,” 89.
29. Judging by a survey from 2006, they make up approximately 2.5 percent of the population of Ukraine; see Victor Yelensky, “Religiosity in Ukraine According to Sociological Surveys,” *Religion, State & Society* 38 (2010): 217. Catherine Wanner, “Up and Out: Movement and Mobility Among Pentecostals in Eurasia,” *PentecoStudies* 9 (2010): 205, notes that while he was mayor of Kiev, Leonid Chernovetskyi spoke openly about his activity in the Charismatic Embassy of God church. See also Nikolai Mitrokhin, “Aspects of the Religious Situation in Ukraine,” *Religion, State & Society* 29 (2001): 184–85.
30. Roman Lunkin, “The Ukrainian Revolution and Christian Churches,” *East-West Church and Ministry Report* 22, no. 3 (2014): 5. For statistics for 2011 and earlier, see Religious Information Service of Ukraine, “Religious Organizations in Ukraine as of 1 January, 2011,” accessed May 16, 2016, http://risu.org.ua/en/index/resourses/statistics/ukr2011/48586/.
31. Allan Anderson, *An Introduction to Pentecostalism: Global Charismatic Christianity* (Cambridge: Cambridge University Press, 2004), 100. It has been estimated that 80 percent of Pentecostal churches in the USSR were located in the Ukraine (Franchuk, *Просила Россия*, 3.903).

32. Церква Християн Віри Євангельскої України (www.chve.org.ua), headed by Mykhaylo Panochko, with approximately one hundred thousand members and approximately fifteen hundred churches in 2015; see http://www.chve.org.ua/aboutus/history. The group has fraternal relations with the Assemblies of God.
33. Союз свободных церквей христиан евангельской веры Украины, with 180 congregations 2011.
34. Central Intelligence Agency, *The World Factbook*, "People and Society," accessed May 16, 2016, https://www.cia.gov/library/publications/the-world-factbook/geos/bo.html.
35. Oleg Łatyszonek, "Belarusian Nationalism and the Clash of Civilizations," *International Journal of Sociology* 31, no. 3 (2001): 71.
36. Roman Catholic Church in Belarus, "Dioceses," accessed May 16, 2016, http://catholic.by/2/en/belarus/dioceses.html.
37. Łatyszonek, "Belarusian Nationalism," 69.
38. Объединенная Церковь христиан веры евангелской в Республике Беларусь (www.cxbe.by).
39. Łatyszonek, "Belarusian Nationalism," 71. A listing of many of the denomination's congregations is found on their homepage (www.cxbe.by).
40. Religious Information Service of Ukraine, "Number of Religious Organizations as of 1 January, 2004 Broken Down According to Regions of Ukraine," http://risu.org.ua/en/index/resourses/statistics/ukr-reg2004 (accessed May 16, 2016).
41. Institute for Religious Freedom, "Donbas and Crimea: New Challenges for Religious Freedom in 2014," February 3, 2015, accessed May 16, 2016, http://www.irf.in.ua/eng/index.php?option=com_content&view=article&id=424:1&catid=36:com&Itemid=55.
42. See further Alexandra Novitchkova, et al., *When God Becomes the Weapon: Persecution Based on Religious Beliefs in the Armed Conflict in Eastern Ukraine* (Kyiv: Center for Civil Liberties, and Brussels: International Partnership for Human Rights, 2015). Available online at http://iphronline.org/wp-content/uploads/2015/07/when_god_becomes_the_weapon_may2015.pdf (accessed July 21, 2016).
43. According to *Avainmedia* (February 2015): 4, there were fifteen Pentecostal congregations in Luhansk (eastern Ukraine) before the hostilities began; in February 2015, only two or three were left.
44. Yelensky, "Religiosity," 216–17, observed that while the Moscow Patriarchate had three times more parishes in Ukraine than the Kiev

Patriarchate in 2006, more Ukrainians considered themselves adherents of the Kiev Patriarchate; he concludes, "By declaring that he or she belongs to the Kiev and not the Moscow Patriarchate a person declares his or her identity with the Ukrainian nation" (217). It is likely that this tendency of shifting identities from the Moscow to the Kiev Patriarchate has become even more apparent today.

45. See further Catherine Wanner, "Fraternal Nations and Challenges to Sovereignty in Ukraine: The Politics of Linguistic and Religious Ties," *American Ethnologist* 41 (2014): 427–39.
46. The same is true for other Protestant denominations in Russia as well; cf. William Yoder, "Remembering How It Was When We Were Still Brothers: How Russian Evangelicals Are Responding to the Crisis in Ukraine," *Occasional Papers on Religion in Eastern Europe* 34, no. 2 (2014): 32.
47. On April 9–11, 2014, Russian and Ukrainian Protestant church leaders met on neutral ground in Jerusalem to discuss the tensions between their states; not much came of that meeting, as pastors on both sides refused to criticize the state in which their congregation was located (see Lunkin, "Ukrainian Revolution").
48. Mark R. Elliott, "The Impact of the Ukrainian Crisis on Religious Life in Ukraine and Russia," *East-West Church and Ministry Report* 22, no. 3 (2014): 12.
49. Wanner, "Explaining," 257; and Wanner, "Missionaries and Pluralism," 92.
50. Elliott, "Impact," 14.
51. Poplavsky, "Pentecostal Churches," 114–17.
52. *Ljus i öster* (November 2014): 8.
53. V. Lyubashchenko, "Protestantism in Ukraine: Achievements and Losses," *Religion, State & Society* 38, no. 3 (2010): 280; and Peter Kuzmič, "Pentecostal Theology and Communist Europe: Pentecostal Power Under Political Pressure," in *European Pentecostalism*, eds. William K. Kay and Anne E. Dyer (Leiden: Brill, 2011), 341.
54. See Lunkin, "Российский протестантизм," 140–41.
55. Sergei Filatov and Roman Lunkin, "'My Father's House Has Many Mansions': Ethnic Minorities in the Russian Orthodox Church," *Religion, State & Society* 38 (2010): 361–78.
56. The Russian Church of Christians of Evangelical Faith, "One Year for Jesus Project—Our Mission: To Provide God's Word to Every Person in

Russia," March 12, 2011, accessed May 16, 2016, http://russianpentecostal.org/one-year-for-jesus/one-year-for-jesus-news-a-reports/4213-one-year-for-jesus-project-our-mission-to-provide-gods-word-to-every-person-in-russia-.

57. Miriam Dobson, "Child Sacrifice in the Soviet Press: Sensationalism and the 'Sectarian' in the Post-Stalin Era," *The Russian Review* 73 (2014): 237–59.
58. Poplavsky, "Pentecostal Churches," 117.
59. Kuzmič, "Pentecostal Theology," 342.
60. Lyubashchenko, "Protestantism in Ukraine," 284.
61. Poplavsky, "Pentecostal Churches," 116.
62. Mark R. Elliott, "The Current Crisis in Protestant Theological Education in the Former Soviet Union," *Religion in Eastern Europe* 30, no. 4 (2010): 1–22.
63. Cf. Kuzmič, "Pentecostal Theology," 342.
64. Oksana Kuropatkina, "The 'New' Pentecostals and the Russian 'National Idea,'" *Religion, State & Society* 40 (2012): 135. The relatively recent systematic theology written by representatives of the Belarusian Pentecostal union helps fill this gap; see S. Khomich, ed., *Вероучение объединенной церкви христиан веры евангельской в Республике Беларусь* [Theology of the United Church of Christians of Evangelical Faith in the Republic of Belarus] (Minsk: Kovcheg Spaseniya, 2009).
65. See Joshua T. Searle, "From Christian Worldview to Kingdom Formation: Theological Education as Mission in the Former Soviet Union," *European Journal of Theology* 23 (2014): 104–15; D. Marsden, "Does Post-Soviet Theological Training Need to Be Revamped?" *East-West Church and Ministry Report* 14, no. 4 (2006): 3; and Lyubashchenko, "Protestantism in Ukraine," 279.

Chapter 3
The Pentecostal Church of Poland: A Historical Analysis and Current Missional Development

1. John D. Nagle and Alison Mahr, *Democracy and Democratization: Post-Communist Europe in Comparative Perspective* (London: SAGE Publications Ltd, 1999), 14.
2. Marek Kamiński, *Kościół świadomy powołania: Priorytety rozwoju Kościoła Zielonoświątkowego w Polsce* [The church aware of its calling: Priorities for growth of the Pentecostal Church of Poland] (Warszawa: WST, 2011), 9.

3. According to Polish government data in 2010, there were thirty different and officially registered church networks and associations that could be characterized as Charismatic and associated with Pentecostal spirituality. See A. Migda, *Mistycyzm pentekostalny w Polsce* [Pentecostal mysticism in Poland] (Kraków: Nomos, 2013), 9.
4. Wojciech Włoch points to the dynamic changes in the Charismatic movement since the fall of Communism in 1989 and the passing of new laws that allowed for new churches to register easily. See Włoch, "Współczesne protestanckie ruchy charyzmatyczne w Polsce: problemy klasyfikacji" [Contemporary Protestant Charismatic movements in Poland: problems with classification], *Nomos* 39/40 (2002): 41–53.
5. See, for instance, Zbigniew Pasek, *Ruch zielonoświątkowy: Próba monografii* [The Pentecostal movement: Attempted analysis] (Kraków: Instytut Wydawniczy Nomos, 1992).
6. The Catholic Charismatic Renewal movement continues to grow in Poland, and according to Dr. Darius Jeziorny, chairman of the European subcommittee of International Catholic Charismatic Renewal Services (ICCRS), there are around eight hundred prayer groups that meet regularly. The biggest Catholic Charismatic event was organized in Łódź and attracted two hundred fifty thousand people in attendance. See William K. Kay et al., "Pentecostal Theology and Catholic Europe," in *European Pentecostalism*, eds. William K. Kay and Anne E. Dyer (Leiden: Brill, 2011), 329–30.
7. For a concise history of the Pentecostal movement in Poland available in English, see Wojciech Gajewski and Krzysztof Wawrzeniuk, "A Historical and Theological Analysis of the Pentecostal Church of Poland," *JEPTA: The Journal of the European Pentecostal Theological Association* 20 (2000): 32–48; and Tim Case and Mark Kamiński, "The Development of Pentecostalism in Central European Countries; Poland, Bulgaria, Hungary, Czech Republic and Slovakia: Poland," in Kay and Dyer, *European Pentecostalism*, 225–29.
8. Zbigniew Pasek and Wojciech Włoch, "Historia ruchu zielonoświątkowego i odnowy charyzmatycznej na ziemiach polskich" [History of the Pentecostal movement and Charismatic Renewal in Poland], in *Historia ruchu zielonoświątkowego i odnowy charyzmatycznej: Stulecie Ducha Świętego 1901–2001* [The century of the Holy Spirit: One hundred years of Pentecostal and Charismatic Renewal, 1901–2001], ed. Vinson Synan (Kraków-Szczecin: Instytut Wydawniczy Compassion, 2006), 488–89.

9. Gajewski and Wawrzeniuk, "A Historical and Theological Analysis," 33.
10. Case and Kaminski, "The Development of Pentecostalism," 225; Gajewski and Wawrzeniuk translate the name of this alliance as the Fellowship for Resolute Christianity.
11. For a more detailed history and characteristics of the alliance, see Zbigniew Pasek, *Stanowczy Chrześcijanie: Studium historii idei religijnych* [The committed Christians: Study in the history of religious ideas] (Kraków: Instytut Religioznastwa UJ, 1993).
12. Case and Kaminski, "The Development of Pentecostalism," 226.
13. Pasek and Włoch, "Historia ruchu," 489.
14. Gajewski and Wawrzeniuk, "A Historical and Theological Analysis," 35–36.
15. Case and Kaminski, "The Development of Pentecostalism," 226.
16. Ibid., 227.
17. For a detailed account of historical and legal formation of the Pentecostal Church of Poland, see the monograph authored by the current bishop, Marek Kaminski, *Kościół Zielonoświątkowy w Polsce w latach 1988–2008: Studium historyczno-ustrojowe* [The Pentecostal Church of Poland in years 1988–2008: Historical and legal analysis] (Warszawa: WST, 2012).
18. Pasek and Włoch, "Historia ruchu," 494.
19. For more on this, see J. W. Derleth, *The Transition in Central and East European Politics* (London: Prentice Hall International, 2000).
20. Gajewski and Wawrzeniuk, "A Historical and Theological Analysis," 37–38.
21. Kamiński, *Kościół Zielonoświątkowy*, 197–99.
22. The full text of the Declaration of Faith was approved in 1997 by the church council with commentary and biblical references and is available on the official website of the Pentecostal Church of Poland at www.kz.pl.
23. Andrzej Siemieniewski, *Ochrzeczeni w jednym Duchu: Perspektywy integracji mistycyzmu pentekostalnego z duchowością katolicką* [Baptized in one Spirit: Perspectives of integration of Pentecostal mysticism with Catholic spirituality] (Wrocław: Papieski Wydział Teologiczny, 2002), 94; see also Migda, *Mistycyzm pentekostalny*, 185ff.
24. Gajewski and Wawrzeniuk, "A Historical and Theological Analysis," 41–42.

25. Edyta Bednarz and Romuald Tomaszewski, *Wprowadzenie do nauki o Biblii oraz doktryny i praktyki ruchu zielošwiątkowego* [Introduction to the study of Bible, doctrine, and practice of the Pentecostal movement] (Warszawa: WST, 2010), 250–64.
26. Kamiński, *Kościół świadomy*, 12; in this chapter, all translations from Polish works into English are my own unless otherwise noted.
27. Ibid., 15–16.
28. See Margaret M. Poloma, *The Assemblies of God at the Crossroads: Charisma and Institutional Dilemmas* (Knoxville, TN: The University of Tennessee Press, 1989); William K. Kay, *Pentecostals in Britain* (Carlisle, UK: Paternoster Press, 2000); William K. Kay, *Apostolic Networks in Britain: New Ways of Being Church* (Milton Keynes, UK: Paternoster, 2007); and Oliwier Cieślar, "The Study of the Correlation Between Charismatic Activity and Growth of the Pentecostal Church of Poland" (master's thesis, Glyndŵr University, 2012).
29. Ibid., 76–83.
30. Ibid., 85.
31. See, for instance, Włoch "Współczesne protestanckie."
32. Pasek and Włoch, "Historia ruchu," 500.
33. For more on this movement, see their official website at www.polskadlajezusa.org.
34. Wojciech Gajewski, "Dynamika ewangelikalizmu polskiego: Krytyczne spojrzenie z uwzględnieniem perspektywy pentekostalnej" [Dynamics of Polish Evangelicalism: A critical view from a Pentecostal perspective], in *Ewangelikalny protestantyzm w Polsce u progu XXI stulecia* [Evangelical Protestantism at the threshold of twenty-first century], ed. Tadeusz J. Zieliński (Warszawa-Katowice: WBST-Credo, 2004), 91.
35. Migda, *Mistycyzm pentekostalny.*
36. Ibid., 411–14.
37. Piotr Karaś, "Kościół w mocy Ducha: eklezjologia pentekostalna wobec współczesnych wyzwań ekumenicznych" [The church in power of the Spirit: Pentecostal ecclesiology in the light of ecumenical challenges] (unpublished lecture, Polish Ecumenical Council conference, Warsaw, Poland, November 27, 2012), 4–10.
38. See, for instance, Kamil Hałambiec, "Considering the Need for Apostles in the Twenty-First Century Church: A Pentecostal Perspective," *Theologica Wratislaviensia* 8 (2013): 135–46. See also Artur Śmieja, "Modele

przywództwa we wspólnotach typu charyzmatycznego" [Leadership models in Charismatic-type fellowships], *Theologica Wratislaviensia* 9 (2014): 61–70.

39. For more information on Wyższa Szkoła Teologiczno-Społeczna, see their website at www.wst.edu.pl. Another school that plays a significant role in theological education is Evangelical School of Theology, which is interdenominational and, as such, attracts a lot of Pentecostal students. For more information, see www.en.ewst.pl.
40. For more on this, see Wojciech Kowalewski, "Missiological Challenges in Polish Evangelical Theological Education," in *Theological Education as Mission*, ed. P. F. Penner (Schwarzenfeld: Neufeld Verlag, 2005), 331–41.
41. Wojciech Kowalewski, "Towards an Integrative Approach in Post-Communist Missiological Thinking: A Polish Study Case," *Acta Missiologiae* 1 (2008): 67–89.
42. Edward Czajko, "Misja Kościoła z perspektywy chrześcijaństwa entuzjastycznego" [Mission of the church from the perspective of enthusiastic Christianity], in *Misja w Polsce jako problem międzykościelny* [Mission in Poland as an interchurch issue], ed. Tadeusz J. Zieliński (Warszawa-Katowice: WBST-Credo, 2006), 21–29.
43. Ibid., 22–23.
44. See also Wojciech Kowalewski, "Jedność i różnorodność działalności ewangelizacyjnej a paradygmat misjologii trynitarnej" [Unity and diversity of evangelistic activity and the paradigm of Trinitarian missiology], in Zieliński, *Misja w Polsce*, 65–84.
45. Czajko, "Misja Kościoła," 23–28.
46. Ibid., 29.
47. Ibid., 25–26.
48. Ibid., 26–27.
49. Wojciech Kowalewski, "Evangelicals and Socio-Political Involvement in Post-Communist Poland," in *Dynamizing Evangelical Witness in Post-Communist Era*, ed. Pavel Prochazka (Praha: ECM, 2008), 63–77.
50. Tomasz Debowski, "Społeczne zaangażowanie chrześcijan ewangelikalnych w Polsce" [Social involvement of Evangelical Christians in Poland], in *Ewangelikalizm polski wobec wyzwań współczesności* [Polish Evangelicalism facing contemporary challenges], eds. Sebastian Smolarz, Sławomir Torbus, and Wojciech Kowalewski (Wroclaw: EWST, 2013), 247–55.

51. Piotr Karaś, *Działalność socjalna kościołów ewangelikalnych w Polsce* [Social activities of Evangelical churches in Poland] (Warszawa: WSTS, 2013).
52. Ibid., 277–328.
53. Czajko, "Misja Kościoła," 27–28.
54. Kaminski, *Kościół świadomy powołania*, 18–25.
55. See, for example, Mark 1:15; Matthew 4:23, 9:35, 24:14; and Luke 4:43, 8:1.

Chapter 4
"Not by Might, nor by Power, but by My Spirit": Pentecostalism in Romania

1. See, for example, Cecilia Moloce, "Eroi ai credinței" [Heroes of faith], *Cuvântul adevărului: Buletinul cultului Creștin Penticostal* [The word of truth: The bulletin of the Christian Pentecostal denomination], series 2, 19, no. 10 (2008): 5; Pavel Riviș-Tipei, "1922–2007: 85 de ani de la înființarea primei biserici penticostale din România" [1922–2007: Eighty-five years from the establishment of the first Pentecostal church in Romania], *Cuvântul adevărului*, series 2, 18, no. 12 (2007): 4; and Marcel Codreanu, "Romania," in *The New International Dictionary of Pentecostal and Charismatic Movements*, eds. Stanley M. Burgess and Eduard van der Maas (Grand Rapids: Zondervan, 2002), 212.
2. See Trandafir Sandru, *Biserica Penticostală în istoria Creștinismului* [The Pentecostal Church in the history of Christianity] (București: Editura Bisericii lui Dumnezeu Apostolice Penticostale din România, 1992), 130; Trandafir Sandru, *Trezirea spirituală Penticostală din România* [The Pentecostal spiritual awakening in Romania] (București: Editura Institutului Teologic Penticostal, 1997), 92–93; Vinson Synan and Valeriu Andreiescu, *Tradiția mișcării Penticostale* [The Pentecostal tradition] (Oradea: Betania, 2004), 300; and Ioan Ceuță, *Mișcarea Penticostală în evenimente și relatări ale secolului XX* [Pentecostal events and stories of the twentieth century] (București: Lumina Evangheliei, 2002), 132–35.
3. Pauliș is located in Arad county but at that time belonged to the district of Lipova, Timișoara region.
4. Gheorghe Bradin, "Istoricul Cultului Penticostal: Biserica lui Dumnezeu Apostolică din Republica Populară România" [The history of the Pentecostal denomination: The Apostolic Church of God of the Republic of Romania] (unpublished manuscript, 1960), 9–11; Sandru, *Trezirea*

spirituală, 67; Sandru, *Biserica Penticostală*, 125–27; Synan and Andreiescu, *Tradiţia*, 300–1.

5. Bradin, "Istoricul," 6, 10; Synan and Andreiescu, *Tradiţia*, 301; Sandru, *Biserica Penticostală*, 127.
6. Bradin, "Istoricul," 12–13; Bradin, "Pogorârea Duhului Sfânt în România" [Pentecost in Romania], *Cuvântul adevărului* 3, no. 5 (1931): 1–2.
7. Sandru, *Biserica Penticostală*, 129.
8. Gheorghe Bradin, "Mişcarea Penticostală în România" [The Pentecostal movement in Romania], *Vestitorul Evangheliei* [The herald of the gospel] 3, no. 11 (1947): 4–6.
9. "Proces verbal" [Minutes], *Cuvântul adevărului* 1, no. 10 (1929): 8.
10. Bradin, "Mişcarea Penticostală în România," 5. Ion Bododea, "Buletinul prigonirilor" [The bulletin of the perpetrators], *Cuvântul adevărului* 3, no. 8 (1931): 10.
11. Bradin, "Istoricul," 34.
12. Arcade Coroamă, Constantin Pătraş, and Pavel Coroamă, "În amintirea fratelui Cristian Gavrilă" [In remembrance of Brother Cristian Gavrila], *Buletinul Cultului Penticostal* [The bulletin of the Pentecostal denomination] 5–6 (May–June 1972): 15.
13. "Zi de post şi rugăciune" [Day of fasting and prayer], *Cuvântul adevărului* 9, no. 3 (1937): 12.
14. Gheorghe Bradin, "Persecuţiile religioase" [Religious persecutions], *Cuvântul adevărului* 3, no. 11 (1931): 2–3.
15. "Ştiri" [News], *Cuvântul adevărului* 3, no. 10 (1931): 8.
16. Constantin Cuciuc, *Religii care au fost interzise în România* [Religions forbidden in Romania] (Bucureşti: Gnosis, 2001), 81.
17. Bradin, "Istoricul," 18–19; Archive of National Council for the Study of Securitate Archives, Bucharest, folder R 6937, vol. 1, 10–12.
18. *Cuvântul adevărului* [The word of truth] and *Credinţa apostolică* [The apostolic faith].
19. Central Romanian National Archives, Bucharest, Fund Romanian Communist Party's Central Committee, Administrative and Political, folder 46/1950, 1; folder 113/1950, 1; State Secretariat for Religious Affairs Archive, Bucharest, folder 97/1951, 6.
20. See "Zi de post şi rugăciune," referenced above.
21. Bradin, "Istoricul," 21.

22. "Conferința din Luna de sus" [Conference in Luna de Sus], *De la Uniunea Baptiștilor Liberi (Independenți) din România* [From the Free (Independent) Baptist Union in Romania], undated leaflet, 1–3; Alexandru Szaday, *Circulară de la Uniunea Baptiștilor Liberi (Independenți) din România, către adunările* [Circular from the Free (Independent) Baptist Union in Romania by communities], leaflet, Purcăreni, January 5, 1939; same leaflet in Hungarian, Sandor Szaday, *Korlevel a Romaniai Szabad (Fugghetlen) Baptista Szovetsegtol a gyulekezetekhez*, Purkerec, January 5, 1939.
23. Bradin, "Istoricul," 21.
24. Bradin, "Mişcarea Penticostală în România," 6.
25. Gheorghe Bradin, "Lucrul acesta a fost cârmuit de Domnul" [This was ruled by the Lord], *Pacea* [Peace] 8, no. 10–11 (1940): 7–8; Bradin, "O clarificare" [A clarification], *Pacea* 8, no. 12–13 (1940): 11–12; Iosif Iacob and Simion Eva, "Lămuriri generale" [General clarifications], *Pacea* 8, no. 10–11 (1940): 10–12.
26. "Întristați dar nu descurajați" [Saddened but not deterred], *Mângăietorul* [Comforter] 2, no. 7 (1940): 7.
27. Alexa Popovici, *Istoria baptiștilor din România 1856–1989* [The history of Baptists in Romania 1856–1989] (Oradea: Făclia, 2007), 637–40.
28. Archive of National Council for the Study of Securitate Archives, folder D 15290, 1–30; Archive of National Council for the Study of Securitate Archives, folder D 6886, 251; Sandru, *Trezirea*, 78.
29. Ioan Mihălcescu, "Prefață" [Preface], in *Pentru neam și lege: Patruzeci cuvântări de învățătură împotriva adventiștilor și baptiștilor* [For the nation and law: Forty speeches against Adventists and Baptists], by Gheorghe Comşa (Caransebeş: Editura Librăriei Diecezane Caransebeş şi P. Suru, 1923), 5.
30. Sandru, *Trezirea*, 102–4.
31. Bradin, "Istoricul," 23; Sandru, *Trezirea*, 97–104; Sandru, *Biserica Penticostală*, 140–46; Synan and Andreiescu, *Tradiția mișcării Penticostale*, 317–20; Pavel Bochian, *Viața unui păstor din România* [The life of a pastor from Romania] (Bucureşti: Editura Privilegiu, 1997), 79–80.
32. Synan and Andreiescu, *Tradiția*, 318; cf. Sandru, *Trezirea*, 102–4.
33. Adrian Nicolae Petcu, "Securitatea şi cultele în 1949" [Security and denominations in 1949], in *Partidul, securitatea și cultele 1945–1989* [Party, security, and denominations 1945–1989], ed. Adrian Nicolae Petcu (Bucureşti: Nemira, 2005), 180; Elis Neagoe-Pleşaand Liviu Pleşa, "Cultele neoprotestante din România în perioada 1975–1989" [Protestant

denominations in Romania during 1975–1989], in Petcu, *Partidul, securitatea şi cultele*, 357; Bochian, *Viaţa unui păstor*, 67.

34. Petcu, "Securitatea şi cultele," 148.
35. *Statutul de organizare şi funcţionare al Cultului Penticostal: Biserica lui Dumnezeu Apostolică—din RPR* [Statutes of the organization and functioning of the Pentecostal church: The Church of God Apostolic, Popular Republic of Romania] (Bucharest, 1951), 7.
36. *Statutul de Organizare al Asociaţiei Religioase: Biserica lui Dumnezeu Apostolică-Penticostală din România* [Organizing statute of religious association: Apostolic-Pentecostal Church of God from Romania] (Arad, 1947), 3, 6–7.
37. *Statutul de organizare şi funcţionare al Cultului Penticostal*, 8–9.
38. Trandafir Sandru, *Îndrumătorul păstorului* [Pastoral guide] (Bucureşti: Editura Cultului Penticostal—Biserica lui Dumnezeu Apostolică din Republica Socialistă România, 1976), 11–18.
39. Archive of National Council for the Study of Securitate Archives, folder R 268371, 3, 27, 30, 34.
40. Vasilică Croitor, *Răscumpărarea memoriei: Cultul Penticostal în perioada comunistă* [The redemption of memory: The Pentecostal Church in the Communist period] (Medgidia: Succeed Publishing, 2010), 40–48.
41. Ibid., 138–48.
42. Sandru, *Biserica Penticostală*, 150; *Harfa Bisericilor lui Dumnezeu* [Churches of God hymnbook], 4th ed. (Timisoara: Editura "Vestitorul Evangheliei," 1946); *Harfa Bisericilor lui Dumnezeu* [Churches of God hymnbook], 5th ed. (Timisoara: Editura "Vestitorul Evangheliei," 1952).
43. State Secretariat for Religious Affairs Archive, folder 104/1951, 33–34.
44. Archive of National Council for the Study of Securitate Archives, folder R 309405, vol. 1, 140, 151.
45. Sandru, *Trezirea*, 107.
46. Ibid., 107–10.
47. Synan and Andreiescu, *Tradiţia*, 322.
48. Archive of National Council for the Study of Securitate Archives, folder SIE 11113, 3.
49. Archive of National Council for the Study of Securitate Archives, folder I 210110, vol. 1, 164, 167.
50. Vasilică Croitor, "Constantin Caraman în luptă cu ateismul comunist" [Constantin Caraman's battle with Communist atheism], in *Şi cerul s-a*

umplut de sfinți: Martiriul în antichitatea creștină și în secolul XX [And the heaven was filled with saints: martyrdom in Christian antiquity and the twentieth century], eds. Cristian Bădiliță and Emanuel Conțac (București: Curtea Veche, 2012), 206–14.

51. Marga şi Cornel Avram, *Adu-ţi aminte!* [Remember!] (n.p.: n.d.), 59–75.
52. Sergiu Grossu, *Calvarul României creştine* [The calvary of Christian Romania] (n.p.: Convorbiri Literare & ABC DAVA, 1992), 110.
53. Ibid., 113–14.
54. Croitor, "Constantin Caraman," 216–18.
55. Grossu, *Calvarul*, 157–58.
56. Ibid., 166.
57. Synan and Andreiescu, *Tradiţia*, 330.
58. Grossu, *Calvarul*, 186; Mărioara Măcelaru, *Însemnări pe uşorii casei* [Notes on the doorposts of the house] (Brasov: Casa Literaturii Creştine, 2007), 50–53.
59. Sandru, *Biserica Penticostală*, 153–56.
60. Elis Neagoe-Pleşa and Liviu Pleşa, "Cultele neoprotestante" [Neo-Protestant denominations], in Petcu, *Partidul, securitatea şi cultele*, 357–58.
61. Bochian, *Viaţa unui pastor*, 68, 110.
62. "Penticostalii din România" [Pentecostalism in Romania], *Cuvântul adevărului*, series 2, 14, no. 7–8 (2003): 25.
63. Institutul National de Statistica, "Populatia dupa etnie si," accessed September 1, 2015, http://www.insse.ro/cms/files/RPL2002INS/vol4/tabele/t5.pdf.
64. Institutul National de Statistica, "Volume 2: Population (Residents)—Ethnic and Confessional," see table 11, accessed September 1, 2015, http://www.recensamantromania.ro/rezultate-2/.
65. Peter Kuzmic, "Why Romania Has Become the Korea of Europe," *Global Church Growth Magazine* 20 (1983): 13.
66. Ghiţă Riţisan, APME presentation at the Consultation in Costa Rica, April 13–17, 2015.
67. See the vision, mission, and strategy, as well as other interesting facts and data, at www.apme.ro.
68. For a more detailed history plus the strategy and development of APME, see Gheorghe Ritisan, "APME: A Case Study in Cross-Cultural Mission Originating From Eastern Europe," in *Mission in Central and Eastern*

Europe: Realities, Perspectives, Trends, eds. Corneliu Constantineanu et al. (Oxford: Regnum Books, forthcoming).

69. Moise Ardelean et al., eds., *Monografia învățământului din Cultul Crestin Penticostal* [A monograph on education in the Christian Pentecostal denomination], Cultul Crestin Penticostal din România, Departementul de Învățământ (Timisoara: Editura Dalia, 2013), 33ff.
70. For a full picture of the Theological Institute in Bucharest, see www.itp-bucuresti.ro.
71. See www.mg-tec.ro.
72. See www.atp-exodus.com.
73. See www.marelbo.ro.
74. See the report of Sofia Marie-Pierre, the regional director of UNICEF, in "Quinze mille enfants abandonnés chaque année dans les pays post-communistes" [Fifteen thousand abandoned children each year in post-Communist countries], *Le Monde*, November 21, 2012, accessed September 10, 2015, http://www.lemonde.fr/europe/article/2012/11/21/quinze-mille-enfants-abandonnes-chaque-annee-dans-les-pays-post-communistes_1793535_3214.html.
75. For more details on this remarkable story, see http://romania-reborn.org/news/ (accessed September 1, 2015).
76. For an excellent and in-depth study about the situation of children at risk in Romania and how the various churches and NGOs have responded, see Bill Prevette, *Child, Church, and Compassion: Toward Child Theology in Romania* (Oxford: Regnum, 2012).
77. The financial national newspaper *Ziarul Finaciar* and the MEDIAFAX agency devoted an entire article to highlight several of the success stories of the Onesim Centre. See Pacala Dana and Christiana Sabau, "Un fost deținut de la penitenciarul Bistrița a ajuns patronul unei companii de transport în Irlanda" [A former prisoner from the Bistirita penitentiary becomes the owner of a transport company in Ireland], *Ziarul Finaciar*, October 19, 2012, accessed September 2, 2015, http://www.zf.ro/analiza/un-fost-detinut-de-la-penitenciarul-bistrita-a-ajuns-patronul-unei-companii-de-transport-in-irlanda-10244838.
78. For a complete description of the Christian democratic proposal to politics in Romania, see www.ucdr.ro.
79. For an academic study about the situation of Roma Christians in the neighboring Bulgaria, see Miroslav A. Atanasov, *Gypsy Pentecostals: The*

Growth of the Pentecostal Movement Among the Roma in Bulgaria and Its Revitalization of Their Communities (Wilmore, KY: Emeth Press, 2010).

80. For an excellent analysis of the larger phenomenon of Roma Christianity, see Melody J. Wachsmuth, "Roma Christianity in Central and Eastern Europe: Challenges, Opportunities for Mission, Modes of Appropriation, and Social Significance," in Constantineanu et al., *Mission in Central and Eastern Europe*, forthcoming.
81. B.J., "Romania's Evangelical Romanies," *The Economist*, January 17, 2011, accessed September 1, 2015, http://www.economist.com/blogs/easternapproaches/2011/01/religion_romania.
82. See www.elim.ro/filiale/.
83. See www.peniel.ro.
84. Valeriu Andreiescu, *Istoria Penticostalismului romanesc* [History of Romanian Pentecostalism], vol. 1 (Oradea: Casa Cărţii, 2011), 667. We found it significant that professor Andreiescu subtitled his two volumes of work "The Full Gospel and the Power of God" and "The Works of the Power of God."
85. There are already some efforts, even some advanced research that begins to address this lack of data; see, for example, the excellent study done by a Romanian Pentecostal at the doctoral level, Vasile Marchis, "A Theology of Mission for Romanian Pentecostals in a Post-Dictatorial Context: An Integrative Approach" (PhD thesis, University of Birmingham, United Kingdom, 2014).

Chapter 5
The Pentecostal Movement in Austria and Hungary: History of Migration, Wars, and Challenges

1. For this chapter, I have relied on two informants: Alan Ambrose for Austria, whom I interviewed via Skype on November 3, 2014, and Louis Lajos Simonfalvi for Hungary, whom I interviewed via Skype on January 31, 2015, and February 3, 2015. Ambrose is one of about ten American Assemblies of God missionaries working in Austria; he lives in Graz and does outreach to university students in the city. Simonfalvi (now retired) has been both a key leader and an instructor of leaders for the Hungarian Pentecostal movement for many years. Unless otherwise documented, details in the following pages derive from these interviews (or my own firsthand knowledge).

2. The influence of these missionaries spread as Germans from West Hungary came to attend Georg Steen's Bible Studies in Vienna in 1923. Steen's father-in-law, Benjamin Schilling, was later active in evangelizing the German-speaking communities in Hungary, and the spiritual fruits of his labor were evident there.
3. Paul Schmidgall, *European Pentecostalism: Its Origins, Development, and Future* (Cleveland, TN: CPT Press, 2013), 104.
4. Halbgasse was the name of the street where the church met for worship. It was customary at the time for churches to be named after the town or street where they were located.
5. Schmidgall, *European Pentecostalism*, 104. *Anschluss* refers to the incorporation of Austria into Nazi Germany in 1938.
6. Ibid., 105.
7. Those regions were formerly under the Austro-Hungarian Empire and were inhabited by many German-speaking Serbs.
8. Some of the details in this and the next few paragraphs come from Schmidgall, *European Pentecostalism*, 105.
9. Ibid.
10. About fifty of those congregations claim existence as a group back to the 1946 meeting mentioned earlier in the paper. In 2004–2005, two new networks of churches—the Charismatic branch and the Life Church branch—were added to the main group of Freie Christengemeinde-Pfingstgemeinde Oesterreich (FCPO); therefore, that organization came to about seventy-five local congregations. This statistic does not include the Romanian congregations that are part of the Church of God.
11. One major problem originally was that the Catholic Church counts as members all baptized persons, which begins normally at infancy. The FCPO does the same but does not baptize until they are fourteen. The government and the movement had to determine how to count adherents and children, not just baptized members. The final result amounted to a number above the quota.
12. One advantage of leaving them is that such a departure excuses Austrians from paying that tax.
13. Those fears are usually unfounded, according to Ambrose.
14. Exceptions to those are the Austrian Catholic churches that have strong social agendas and outreach programs; they are alive and well attended. The Polish Catholic churches in Austria are usually full, and many Poles attend them for the purpose of social networking.

15. The governing regent at the time was Calvinist, and there was a balance of power between the Catholics and the Reformed churches. This was actually a false Christian era. The persecution from the historical churches against the Pentecostals during this time even resulted in short-term imprisonment of some evangelists and was worse than the indirect one they experienced during the Communist regime later.
16. Information regarding this and the next three groups are summarized from Schmidgall, *European Pentecostalism*, 183.
17. Some sources claim that she was the main founder of the Pentecostal church in Hungary, but her evangelistic activities were only limited to a small area in the southwestern part of the country.
18. Schmidgall, *European Pentecostalism*, 183.
19. Ibid. They received support by the Russian Missionary Society, and their first fellowship was established under the covering of the Russian and East European Mission.
20. Ibid., 184.
21. Ibid., 183.
22. Czaba Tenkely, "Hungary," in *European Pentecostalism*, eds. William Kay and Anne Dyer (Leiden: Brill, 2011), 245. According to Simonfalvi, in 1931 Raroha and other Pentecostal evangelists started being persecuted for political reasons as the Lutherans, Catholics, and Calvinists brought false accusations against them to the local police. Raroha left the country and came back in 1934. In 1935, he had to leave permanently because of the ever-increasing pressures of the pro-Fascist government.
23. Tenkely, "Hungary," 245.
24. Barbara Lange, *Holy Brotherhood: Romani Music in a Hungarian Pentecostal Church* (Oxford: Oxford University Press, 2003), 40–42.
25. Ibid. Some Lutherans and Calvinists were also imprisoned, but the Catholics suffered the most.
26. This was quite relevant at the time, since most of the Pentecostal pastors were supporting their families by working secular jobs.
27. Schmidgall, *European Pentecostalism*, 185.
28. Tenkely, "Hungary," 247.
29. The Pentecostals survived that and are presently providing covering for many smaller groups.
30. Tenkely, "Hungary," 247. This last statement also includes the Hungarian Charismatics.

31. Interestingly enough, senator John McCain of Arizona caused a diplomatic scandal by calling prime minister Victor Orban a "neo-Fascist" from the floor of the United States Senate in December 2014.
32. Tenkely, "Hungary," 247; see also Church of God World Missions, "We Are Missionaries," October 10, 2014, accessed March 30, 2015, http://cogwm.org/we-are-missionaries/.
33. Schmidgall, *European Pentecostalism*, 185.
34. Egyhás és Társadalom, "The 2011 Census Data on Religion," April 4, 2013, accessed March 30, 2015, http://www.egyhazestarsadalom.hu/a-szemhataron-innen/egyeb-irasok/mate-toth-andras-nagy-gabor-daniel-a-2011-es-nepszamlalas-vallasi-adatairol/; the strong showing of the Faith Church, which claims between sixty thousand and seventy thousand members, is not accounted for in this statistic, while it is a notable phenomenon.
35. The term *Progressive Pentecostalism* is developed and thoroughly explained in the seminal work of Donald E. Miller and Tetsunao Yamamori, *Global Pentecostalism: The New Face of Christian Social Engagement* (Berkeley, CA: University of California Press, 2007).
36. Brother Fabian was the actual person who brought the Fellowship of Evangelical Pentecostals under the covering of the worldwide Assemblies of God on the basis of some unproven claims that the latter were in Hungary since 1928.
37. In recent years, the Hungarian Roma believers have been moving toward self-governing in their branch of the Pentecostal movement.

Chapter 6
Pentecostalism in Italy: Origins, Developments, and Future Challenges

1. Vinson Synan, *The Holiness-Pentecostal Movement in the United States* (Grand Rapids: Eerdmans, 1971), 147–48; Roberto Bracco, *Il risveglio Pentecostale in Italia* [The Pentecostal revival in Italy] (Roma: n.p., 1956), 7.
2. Emile G. Leonard, *Storia del Protestantesimo: Declino e rinascita* [History of Protestantism: Decline and revival], vol. 3, part 2 (Milano: Il Saggiatore, 1971), 197–98; Giorgio Spini, *Studi sull'evangelismo italiano tra otto e novecento* [Studies on Italian evangelism in the nineteenth and twentieth centuries] (Torino: Claudiana, 1994), 119–20.
3. Francesco Toppi, "Risveglio Pentecostale Italiano" [The Pentecostal revival in Italy], *Cristiani Oggi* 23 (1988): 2–4. *Cristiani Oggi* is a

fortnightly publication of the Assemblee di Dio in Italia (from now on ADI). It's likely that these members belonged to the group of the Favalesi, in whose ancestral doctrines could be found elements from the tradition of the Free Churches that in some elements accepted adult baptism; see Domenico Maselli, *Tra risveglio e millennio: Storia delle Chiese Cristiane dei Fratelli 1836–1886* [Between revival and millennium: History of the Brethren Christian Churches 1836–1886] (Torino: Claudiana, 1974), 84–120, 204–5.

4. Italian Pentecostalism, therefore, as the Anglo-American was born comprising several souls, whose only connection was the baptism with the Holy Spirit; see David Womack and Francesco Toppi, *Le radici del movimento Pentecostale* [The roots of the Pentecostal movement] (Roma: Adi Media, 1989), 123–24.
5. Bracco, *Il risveglio*, 7.
6. Francesco Toppi, "Risveglio Pentecostale Italiano" [The Pentecostal revival in Italy], *Cristiani Oggi* 17 (1991): 2–5. In Brazil was founded the Christian Congregation of Brazil, which in 1947 counted no fewer than 571 communities and 8,065 newly baptized believers. The members are defined "Pentecostal extremists of Italian origins"; see Leonard, *Storia del Protestantesimo*, 242.
7. Francesco Toppi, "Risveglio Pentecostale Italiano" [The Pentecostal revival in Italy], *Cristiani Oggi* 18/19 (1991): 2–4; Bracco, *Il risveglio*, 8–15. What was the exact dynamics of the events that led to the spread in these first twenty years we do not know, as we have an almost total absence of documents. The list was reliably compiled by Mario Piacentini, a senior evangelical magistrate. See Giorgio Rochat, "Le fonti della polizia fascista sulle chiese Pentecostali" [The sources of the Fascist police on the Pentecostal churches], *Bollettino della Società di Studi Valdesi* [Bulletin of the Society of Waldesian Studies] 169 (1991): 73. The fact, however, that out of one hundred fifty places there were only twenty-five places of worship open to the public suggests that in the list was reported the presence of individuals sometimes even occasional.
8. Bracco, *Il risveglio*, 24–26; Giorgio Peyrot, *La circolare Buffarini Guidi e i Pentecostali* [The Buffarini Guidi circular and the Pentecostals] (Roma: Associazione per la Libertà Religiosa, 1955); Giorgio Rochat, *Regime Fascista e chiese Evangeliche* [The Fascist regime and the Evangelical churches] (Torino: Claudiana, 1990), 113–26.
9. Of course, the Pentecostals were not the only ones to suffer from Fascist hostility; very harassed were also the Jehovah's Witnesses, the Salvation

Army, and the Baptists, but the Pentecostals suffered more real persecution. See Rochat, *Regime Fascista e chiese Evangeliche*, 257–330; *Annuario Evangelico* 1983–1984 (Torino: Claudiana, 1983), 76.

10. Rochat, *Regime Fascista e chiese Evangeliche*, 241–56; Bracco, *Il risveglio*, 12.
11. Roberto Bracco, *Persecuzione in Italia* [Persecution in Italy] (Roma: n.p., 1954). This is an autobiographical booklet that describes with apologetic tone the events of those years and the harassment to which Pentecostal churches were subjected. It was also released in a second edition in 1964.
12. Rochat, *Regime Fascista e chiese Evangeliche*, 257–73; Rochat, "Le fonti della polizia," 71–77; Peyrot, *La circolare*, 14–20; Spini, *Studi sull'evangelismo italiano*, 233–50. In the debate for the abolition of this circular intervened several established men of culture and lawyers as Leopoldo Picardi, Carlo Arturo Jemolo, Gaetano Salvemini, and Giorgio Spini, but certainly from a technical and legal perspective particular credit is due to Giorgio Peyrot. See Mario Affuso, "Il movimento Pentecostale" [The Pentecostal movement], *Fedeltà* 122 (1985): 406–7.
13. Bracco, *Il risveglio*, 27.
14. It's almost impossible to obtain reliable information about this wing of the Pentecostal movement in Italy. Not much is known of its leading exponent, Domenico Zaccardi (1900–1978), who seemed to have had good relations with the Chicago church led by Francescon and from whom probably he had borrowed many of his ideas. Also known as *zaccardiani*, these Pentecostals have lived in a semiclandestine state almost without any relationship with the outside world and have maintained a strong sense of local autonomy that, in fact, was annulled by the enormous power of the "elders" of the church of Rome. They are distributed in seventy locations all over Italy, even if the majority is concentrated in central and south Italy. Most of these communities are small in number, except the one in Rome, which numbers up to half of the approximately two thousand members nationwide.
15. See Sarah Eekhoff Zylstra, "Pope Francis Apologizes for Pentecostal Persecution, but Italy's Evangelicals Remain Wary," *Christianity Today*, July 30, 2014, accessed May 5, 2015,). http://www.christianitytoday.com/gleanings/2014/july/pope-francis-apologizes-for-pentecostal-persecution-italy.html.
16. Bracco, *Il risveglio*, 28–29; *Raccolta degli Atti*, 15.
17. Bracco, *Il risveglio*, 14 (translation ours).

18. There was also an attempt to affiliate with the Christian Churches of North America, but it was a wrong move, as they did not have the legal recognition and therefore would not have brought any benefit to the legal position of churches in Italy; Bracco, *Il risveglio*, 33.
19. In our chapter, we have not included discussion of the Apostolic Church in Italy of Pentecostal inspiration, which differs from Italian Pentecostalism as to ecclesiastical structures and historical origins; in fact, it represents the Italian branch of the English Apostolic Church, which came forth after the Welsh awakening (1904) and has been present in Italy since 1927, when the English mission replaced the Danish one. See Mario Affuso, "L'esperienza nello Spirito" [The experience of the Spirit], *Fedeltà* 107 (1984): 287–88; Roberto Mazzeschi, "Apostolici" [The apostolics], in *Dizionario di teologia Evangelica* [Dictionary of Evangelical theology], eds. Pietro Bolognesi et al. (Marchirolo: EUN, 2007), 54–55.
20. *Atti dei convegni nazionali dal 1958 al 1978* [Proceedings of national conferences from 1958 to 1978] (1979), 13.
21. This is what was established in the November 24–26, 1959, conference held in Benevento; see *Atti dei convegni nazionali dal 1958 al 1978*, 15. (This conference, by the way, affirmed women in ministry so long as such was subordinate to male ministry.) Indeed, the confession of faith of the Pentecostal congregations (which can be read at the end of their hymnal) adds to that of 1927 the article of collegiality, stated: "We believe in the collective form, manifested in the joint function of the elders who meet together voluntarily, with same sentiments and equality between them, before God, to solve problems relating to His work. At the end of each meeting, the elders return to their communities equal among themselves (1 Tim. 4:14; Acts 20:17, 1 Tim. 5:1)." For many years, moreover, the congregations have also maintained the practice of having pastors with no salary.
22. Romolo Ricciardiello, ed., *Sulle orme di un servo di Dio: Alle sorgenti del Sele* [Following the footsteps of a servant of God: At the sources of the River Sele] (Battipaglia: n.p., 1980), 5. Petrelli emigrated to the United States in 1905 and exercised his ministry among the Italian Baptist Churches until 1916. In 1915, he became Pentecostal and developed an itinerant ministry among the Italian Pentecostal churches. He wrote many books and published several magazines. See Carmine Napolitano, "Il pensiero di Giuseppe Petrelli: Per una storia del movimento Pentecostale Italiano" [The thought of Giuseppe Petrelli: For a history of the Italian Pentecostal movement] in *Movimenti Evangelici popolari nei*

secoli XIX e XX [Popular Evangelical movements in the nineteenth and twentieth centuries], ed. Domenico Maselli (Firenze: Fedeltà Edizioni, 1999), 94–153; and Carmine Napolitano, *Giuseppe Petrelli: Teologo Pentecostale delle origini* [Giuseppe Petrelli: A theologian of the early Pentecostal movement] (Aversa: Fondazione Chàrisma Edizioni, 2015).

23. As for the statistics and descriptions of the various movements, you can profitably consult Massimo Introvigne and Pierluigi Zoccatelli, eds., *Enciclopedia delle religioni in Italia* [Encyclopedia of religions] (Leumann: Elledici, 2006), 217–320. If you add up the Charismatics, the numbers are much higher; cf. William K. Kay and Anne Dyer, eds., *European Pentecostalism* (Leiden: Brill, 2011), appendix.
24. This is in line with what is happening in the countries of origin of these immigrants where Pentecostalism is rapidly growing. See Paolo Naso, "La sfida pentecostale" [The Pentecostal challenge], *Limes*, 2 supplement (2005): 127–34. See also the careful research carried out on the city of Rome by Carmelo Russo and Marta Bernardini, "L'immigrazione Pentecostale a Roma" [The Pentecostal immigration to Rome], in *Fratelli e sorelle di Jerry Masslo* [Jerry Masslo's brothers and sisters], ed. Paolo Naso (Torino: Claudiana, 2014), 107–64.
25. See Pino Lucà Trombetta, *Cristianesimi senza frontiere* [Christianities without borders] (Roma: Borla, 2013), 177; Riccardo Burigana, *Una straordinaria avventura: Storia del movimento ecumenico in Italia (1910–1920)* [An extraordinary adventure: History of the ecumenical movement in Italy (1910–1920)] (Bologna: Edizioni Dehoniane, 2013), 182–83; and Paolo Naso, *Cristianesimo: Pentecostali* [Christianity: the Pentecostals] (Bologna: EMI, 2013), 118.
26. In Campania (a southern region of Italy), for instance, a Pentecostal outreach was founded twenty-five years ago as the first Evangelical community for the rehabilitation of drug addicts that deploys scientific programs; see www.nuova-vita.org.
27. Gianfranco Giuni, "L'impegno sociale nel mondo Pentecostale" [The social commitment in the Pentecostal world], *Odos: The Journal of the Pentecostal Faculty of Theology and Religious Studies* (2011): 117–25, in which is also contained an initial list of the most significant organizations.
28. A sign that in this direction something was changing in the Pentecostal mentality; see *Raccolta degli Atti dei convegni nazionali e delle Assemblee Generali 1928–1969*, 9, translation ours.

29. Walter J. Hollenweger, *Pentecostalism: Origins and Developments in Worldwide* (Peabody, MA: Hendrickson, 1997), 216. It is likely that one of the reasons for the nonadherence of the Pentecostals to the constitution of the Federation of Evangelical Churches in Italy (FCEI) is due to their different conception of political commitment; see Carmine Napolitano, "The Pentecostals and FCEI," in *Uniti per l'Evangelo*, eds. Gianni Long and Renato Maiocchi (Torino: Claudiana, 2008), 96–106. Another instance to keep in mind was the political orientation of the Pentecostal churches of southeastern Sicily that in the 1960s saw many of their members involved in the organization of farmers' cooperatives.
30. Carmine Napolitano, "Il patto e la spiritualità Pentecostale" [The pact and Pentecostal spirituality] in *Un patto per il futuro: Teologia, società e politica* [A pact for the future: theology, society, and politics], ed. Paolo Naso (Torino: Claudiana, 2012), 137–42; and Naso, *Cristianesimo*, 124–28.
31. Ecumenical relations are developing within an informal circuit known as the Global Christian Forum with a very large participation of Pentecostal churches. Its activities began in 1998, and for several years this network has worked with discretion until the meeting in Nairobi in 2007 confirmed that the work had produced significant results. In this context, Pentecostal churches feel more at ease than what they had been able to discern in the World Council of Churches. The Italian Federation of Pentecostal Churches has participated regularly in the meetings of the Global Christian Forum since 2006.
32. The Claudiana, an important Evangelical publishing house in Turin, has published two books (one in 2002 and one in 2010) of the documents relating to this dialogue: *Valdesi Metodisti e Pentecostali in dialogo: Testi dei documenti* [Waldensians, Methodists, and Pentecostals in dialogue: Texts of the documents].
33. Napolitano, *I Pentecostali e la FCEI.*
34. Napolitano, "I Pentecostali e l'ecumenismo," 127–39; and Carmine Napolitano, "Italian Pentecostalism and Ecumenism," *JEPTA: The Journal of the European Pentecostal Theological Association* 35, no. 1 (2015): 69–77.
35. Remo Cristallo, "La visita del papa al Pastore Traettino: un'intervista al Past. Remo Cristallo presidente della Federazione delle Chiese Pentecostali" [The visit of the pope to Pastor Traettino: An interview with Remo Cristallo, president of the Federation of Pentecostal Churches], August 4, 2014, accessed May 5, 2015, http://www.fcpitalia.org/wp-content/uploads/2014/08/Leggi-lintervista2.pdf.

Chapter 7
Swiss Pentecostals: A Journey Between Corporate Identity and Christian Unity

1. The presence of women missionaries like Elisabeth Cooke-Collins, Baroness M. von Brasch, Eleanor Patrick, and Anna Maria Gerber indicate that the early Pentecostal witness in Europe was not limited to the male gender as some group photographs of early Pentecostal conferences would suggest. As a matter of fact, the ladies attending the Sunderland conferences in England (1908–1914) were photographed separately and even outnumbered the male participation. Cf. photographs from *The Works of Alexander A. Boddy 1854–1930* (Waltham: Revival Library, 2010), DVD.
2. The earliest congregations could be found in Nyon, Lausanne, and Gland (near Geneva).
3. Early references are made to contacts with Italian Pentecostals in Italy in the British magazine *Confidence* in 1908. A Signora Guilielmina Malan from Torre Pellice, the center of the Valdensian Christians in northern Italy, shared in the July issue of *Confidence* in 1908 how she experienced healing and received the baptism in the Holy Spirit. Swiss pastor Anton Reuss, returning from a missionary visit in India, met with church leaders in Italy in 1910. He probably met Oreste Coppini, who was later a conference speaker in Zurich in 1915 and probably visited on earlier occasions, as well.
4. Little is known of that conference except that C. E. D. de Labillière and Alexander Niblock (both England), T. B. Barratt (Norway), Jonathan Paul and Eugen Edel (both Germany), and Gerrit Polman and his wife, Wilhelmina (the Netherlands), were its speakers.
5. Declaration by Richard P. Ruff and Anton Reuss in *Die Verheissung des Vaters* [The promise of the Father] (November 1913): 1–2.
6. The same year, the Schweizerische Pfingstmissions-Gesellschaft sent its first missionary, Reinhard Gschwend, to Basutoland (later to be Lesotho) and supported missionaries in Eastern Europe and on other continents.
7. Jean-Daniel Plüss, *Vom Geist bewegt: Die Geschichte der Schweizerischen Pfingstmission* [Moved by the Spirit: The history of the Swiss Pentecostal Mission] (Asaph: Keuzlingen, 2015), 60.
8. The magazine was called *Die Verheissung des Vaters* and stayed in print until 1967. Its twelve-point statement of faith includes a reference to the

baptism in the Holy Spirit and its signs in accordance to the Scriptures, but it does not state an initial evidence theory.

9. In 1933, another group of Pentecostals churches, mainly situated in the Bernese Oberland, constituted themselves as Gemeinde für Urchristentum. And in 1936, the French-speaking revival churches founded the association of Eglises Evangéliques du Réveil.
10. Donald Gee, "The Basel Church and Relief Work in Europe," *Pentecost* (September 1947): 4.
11. Donald Gee, "Zurich: Review of Reviews," *Pentecost* (September 1947): 1.
12. Donald Gee, *Pentecost* (September 1947): 18. This was the first issue of that magazine.
13. Christian Krust, *50 Jahre Deutsche Pfingstbewegung* [Fifty years of Pentecostal movement in Germany] (Nürnberg: Missionsbuchhandlung und Verlag Altdorf bei, 1959?), 188.
14. The Schweizerische Pfingstmission was more established, mainly due to the fact that it was the oldest Pentecostal group in Switzerland. Due to pressures from some Evangelical churches that upheld the Berlin Declaration published in 1909 that proclaimed the Pentecostal movement to be "from below," they had adopted a somewhat sober form of Pentecostalism. The Gemeinde für Urchristentum was more apostolic in outlook, and its members were not afraid to emphasize the use of prophetic speech and exorcisms. The Eglises Evangéliques de Réveil had some links to Reformed churches in western Switzerland and had a more open attitude. The Freie Christengemeinden, which had been started through the missionary activities of Georg Steen, a Swede, developed in the rural part of eastern Switzerland under the supervision of its mother church.
15. *Verheissung des Vaters* (June 1959): 14.
16. Plüss, *Vom Geist bewegt*, 132–34.
17. *Wort und Geist* [Word and Spirit] (July 1972): 5.
18. *Wort und Geist* (September 1973): 12–13.
19. The term *neo-Pentecostal* is chosen a) because of the more or less open Charismatic teaching and practices of these churches, although they would not necessarily call themselves by that name and b) in order to emphasize that their existence is in ideological competition with classical Pentecostals.
20. *Wort und Geist* (September 1975), in *Missions-Beilage* 1–4; and *Wort und Geist* (July 1993): 12–13.

21. In 1959, the Gemeinde für Urchristentum bought the Park Hotel in Gunten. The Swiss Pentecostal Mission opened a national center in Emmetten in 1972. The Freie Christengemeinden built a conference hotel in the late 1980s in Ebnat-Kappel.
22. For a discussion on the function of these aspects, see Jean-Daniel Plüss, "Pfingstler Perspektiven 2" [Pentecostal perspectives 2], in *Religion als Wahrnehmung: Konzepte und Praxis in unterschiedlichen Kulturen und Kirchen* [Religion as perception: Concepts and practice in various cultures and churches], ed. Engelbert Gross, Forum Religionspädagogik interkulturell 8 (Berlin: Lit Verlag, 2006), 187–210.
23. During that conference, the issue of unity among Pentecostals was much discussed, and Leonhard Steiner took up that concern in the reports on the conference he published in the periodical *Die Verheissung des Vaters* in every issue from July to December 1939.
24. See the Swiss Evangelical Alliance at www.each.ch and the Federation of Free Churches in Switzerland at www.freikirchen.ch.
25. In a study commissioned by the Pew Forum in 2011, the Center for the Study of Global Christianity at Gordon Conwell Theological Seminary estimated the number of Christian denominations to number about 41,000. See Pew Forum, "Appendix B: Methodology for Estimating Christian Movements," in *Global Christianity*, available at http://www.pewforum.org/files/2011/12/ChristianityAppendixB.pdf (accessed March 27, 2015). See also George Weigel, "Christian Number-Crunching," *First Things*, February 9, 2011, accessed March 27, 2015, http://www.firstthings.com/web-exclusives/2011/02/christian-number-crunching.
26. The notion itself has repeatedly surfaced since the Second Vatican Council. A practical introduction to this notion has been provided by Cardinal Walter Kasper, *A Handbook of Spiritual Ecumenism* (Hyde Park, NY: New City Press, 2007).
27. The Lutheran World Federation considers itself primarily to be a communion of churches and secondarily a church of Lutheran confession (cf. https://www.lutheranworld.org/content/about-lwf). Similar views are expressed in the Baptist World Alliance, the World Communion of Reformed Churches, and other bodies.

Chapter 8
Pentecostalism in Germany: Historical and Theological Perspectives

1. See Paul Fleisch, *Geschichte der Pfingstbewegung in Deutschland von 1900 bis 1950* [History of the Pentecostal movement in Germany, 1900–1950] (Marburg an der Lahn: Verlag der Francke-Buchhandlung GmbH, 1983), 88; in this chapter, all translations from German sources are my own unless otherwise noted.
2. Dates for named persons will be given when available in the remainder of this chapter.
3. Fleisch, *Geschichte der Pfingstbewegung*, 77f.
4. Dominik P. Reinmund, "The Berlin Declaration: Germany's Uneasiness With the Pentecostal and Charismatic Movement" (unpublished paper, 2003), 8, available at http://lesbar.down-to-earth.de/media/Reinmund%20-%20Berlin%20Declaration.pdf (accessed October 26, 2015).
5. Ernst Giese, *Und flicken die netze: Dokumente zur erweckungsgeschichte des 20. jahrhunderts* [And mend the nets: Documents from the history of revivals in the twentieth century] (Metzingen/Württ: Ernst Franz Verlag, 1988), 65–91.
6. Christian Krust, *50 Jahre Deutsche Pfingstbewegung Mülheimer richtung* [Fifty years of the German Pentecostal Mülheim movement] (Altdorf bei Nürnberg: Missionsbuchhandlung und Verlag, 1958), 48.
7. Cited in Giese, *Und flicken die netze*, 70.
8. Reinmund, "The Berlin Declaration," 7.
9. Heinrich Dallmeyer, *Die zungenbewegung: Ein beitrag zu ihrer geschichte und eine kennzeichnung ihres geistes* [The tongues movement: A historical and critical analysis] (Lindhorst: Adastra-Verlag, 1924), 21.
10. Ekkehart Vetter, *Jahrhundertbilanz—erweckungsfasziniert und durststreckenerprobt: 100 jahre Mülheimer Verband Freikirchlich-Evangelischer gemeinden* [A century of revival and renewal movements assessed: One hundred years of the Mülheim Association Free Church Protestant communities] (Bremen: Missionsverlag des Mülheimer Verbandes Freikirchlich-Evangelischer Gemeinden GmbH, 2009), 107–17.
11. Giese, *Und flicken die netze*, 134.
12. Summarized in Reinmund, "The Berlin Declaration," 10.

13. This document is available at http://www.glopent.net/iak-pfingstbewegung/Members/GerhardBially/berliner-erklaerung#mek (accessed October 25, 2015); see also Giese, *Und flicken die netze*, 129–33.
14. Walter J. Hollenweger, *The Pentecostals: The Charismatic Movement in the Churches* (Minneapolis: Augsburg Publishing House, 1972), 231.
15. Walter J. Hollenweger, *Pentecostalism: Origins and Developments Worldwide* (Peabody, MA: Hendrickson Publishers, 1997), 338.
16. Vetter, *Jahrhundertbilanz*, 197.
17. Krust, *50 jahre*, 144.
18. Fleisch, *Geschichte der Pfingstbewegung*, 161.
19. Krust, *50 jahre*, 64.
20. Jonathan Paul, *Die taufe in ihrem vollsinn: ein zeugnis für die einheit der kinder Gottes zur erbauung des leibes Christi* [The full meaning of the baptism: A witness to the unity of the children of God for the edification of the body of Christ] (Mühlheim: Missionsgesellschaft, 1930).
21. Wilhelm Kowalski, "Bericht über die freie Pfingstbewegung in Ost-Deutschland" [Report on the free Pentecostal movement in Eastern Germany] (unpublished typescript, Edmonton, 1969), 1.
22. Ludwig Eisenlöffel, *Ein feuer auf erden* [A fire on the earth] (Erzhausen: Leuchter-Verlag, 1965), 102.
23. Martin Kielwein, "Wichtige daten der Gemeinde Gottes" [Important data on the Church of God], in *Die geschichte der Pfingstbewegung* [The history of the Pentecostal movement] (unpublished typescript presented at Rudersberg, now Kniebis, European Theological Seminary, n.d.), 40.
24. H. J. G., "Heimat für heimatlose 1934–1945" [Home for the homeless 1934–1945], in *60 jahre Volksmission Berlin* [Sixty years of the Berlin People's Mission] (Berlin: Volksmission entschiedener Christen e.V., 1994), 12.
25. Rosa Munzinger, "Augenzeugenbericht über die entstehung der Weckhofgemeinde" [Eyewitness reports on the origins of the Weckhof community] (unpublished typescript, Künzelsau, 1998), 1.
26. Joseph Colletti, "Russian and Eastern European Mission," in *International Dictionary of Pentecostal and Charismatic Movements*, eds. Stanley M. Burgess and Eduard M. van der Maas (Grand Rapids: Zondervan Publishing House, 2003), 1031–32.
27. Gary B. McGee, "Schmidt, Gustav Herbert," in Burgess and van der Maas, *International Dictionary of Pentecostal and Charismatic Movements*, 1042–43.

28. Gerhard Krüger, *Erlebte Gottesgnade* [Experiencing God's grace], 5th ed. (Aachen: Missionsverlag Horst Krüger, 1969), 52.
29. Fleisch, *Geschichte der Pfingstbewegung*, 284.
30. Dallmeyer, *Die zungenbewegung*, 137.
31. Kowalski, "Bericht," 2.
32. Valtter Veikko Luoto, "Skandinavien," in *Die Pfingstkirchen: Selbstdarstellungen, dokumente, kommentare* [The Pentecostal church: Self-understanding, documentation, and commentary], ed. Walter J. Hollenweger, Die Kirchen der Welt 7 (Stuttgart: Evangelisches Verlagswerk, 1971), 44.
33. Hermann Dittert, "Elim-Chronik: Bericht eines zeitzeugen" [Elim chronicles: Report of an eyewitness], *Elim-Gruß: Journal of Christengemeinde Elim* [Elim-greetings: Journal of the Elim Christian community] (1980–1985): 7.
34. Ibid., 27.
35. Reinhold Hildebrandt, *Protokoll der "erweiterten Pfingstbrüderkonferenz" am 13. und 14.5.47 in Stuttgart—Zuffenhausen* [Papers of the "Advancing Pentecostal Churches Conference" on May 13–14, 1947, in Stuttgart Zuffenhausen] (Erzhausen: BFP-Archiv, 1947), 1.
36. Gottfried Sommer, "'Alle Juden nach Ägypten!': Heilsgeschichte als alibi im 'Dritten Reich'—Beispiele aus der Pfingstbewegung" ["All the Jews to Egypt!": Salvation history as an alibi in the Third Reich—examples from the Pentecostal movement], in *Freikirchen und Juden im "Dritten Reich": Instrumentalisierte heilsgeschichte, antisemitische vorurteile und verdrängte schuld* [Free churches and Jews in the Third Reich: Instrumentalizing salvation history, anti-Semitic prejudices, and repressed guilt], ed. Daniel Heinz (Göttingen: V&R Unipress, 2011), 148.
37. Paul Schmidgall, *Hundert jahre Deutsche Pfingstbewegung 1907–2007* [One hundred years of the German Pentecostal movement 1907–2007] (Nordhausen: Verlag Traugott Bautz GmbH, 2007), 323–24.
38. Hermann Lauster, *Vom pflug zur kanzel* [From the plough to the pulpit] (Urbach: Stiwa Druck und Verlag, 1985), 74–77.
39. Emil Meyer, *Alle Juden nach Ägypten!* [All the Jews to Egypt!] (Brockstedt: Selbstverlag, 1939), 28.
40. For further discussion of this issue, see Sommer, "Alle Juden nach Ägypten!," 149.
41. Ibid., 148.

42. Fritz Voll, "Night of the Broken Glass" (November 8, 1998), accessed October 25, 2015, http://www.jcrelations.net/Night+of+the+Broken+Glass+%28Reichskristallnacht%29.2354.0.html?L=3.
43. From Sommer, "Alle Juden nach Ägypten!," 139–40.
44. Vetter, *Jahrhundertbilanz*, 294.
45. Fleisch, *Geschichte der Pfingstbewegung*, 360.
46. Mina Christine Arnold, "Re-education Germany," *The Pentecostal Evangel*, May 26, 1945, 5.
47. Anonymous, "An Open Door in Germany," *The Pentecostal Evangel*, June 23, 1945, 3.
48. Erwin Lorenz, "Daheim!," *Der leuchter* [The chandelier] 12 (1969): 10.
49. Walter Hollenweger, "Hermann [sic], Harold," in his "Handbuch der Pfingstbewegung" [Handbook of Pentecostalism] (PhD thesis, University of Zürich, 1965–1967), vol. 7, 618.001 (reference number, without page number).
50. Edith L. Blumhofer, "Waldvogel, Hans R.," in Burgess and van der Maas, *International Dictionary of Pentecostal and Charismatic Movements*, 1182–82; the reference to Billy Graham derives from an oral interview with Kurt Redlin, June 1999.
51. Willard Cantelon, "Grußwort" [Foreword], in *Missionarisch in die zukunft: 50 Jjahre volksmission entschiedener Christen* [A missionary in the future: Fifty years of committed Christian missions], ed. Gottlob Ling (Stuttgart: Selbstverlag Volksmission, 1995), 41.
52. Karl Fix, *Preiset mit mir den Herrn: 30 jahre volksmisssion entschiedener Christen Berlin* [Praise the Lord with me: Thirty years of committed Berlin Christian missions] (Schorndorf: Verlag Deutsche Volksmission entschiedener Christen, 1964), 54.
53. Erwin Lorenz, "…Gehe ein zu deines Herrn freude" [Go to thy Lord with joy], *Wort + Geist* [Word + Spirit] 8 (1977): 2.
54. Reimer Dietze, "Schwimmgnade, nicht knöchelgnade" [Liberating, not burdensome, grace] (unpublished ordination paper, BFP-Archiv, Erzhausen, 1993), 37.
55. Gustav Kinderman, "Pentecostal Unity in Germany," *The Pentecostal Evangel*, November 6, 1948, 14-15.
56. Reinhold Hildebrandt, *Bericht von der einheitskonferenz der Freien Pfingstgemeinden in Deutschland vom 21. –23.9.1948 in Hamburg* [Report

of the conference on the Free Pentecostal Churches in Germany, September 21–23, 1948, in Hamburg] (Erzhausen: BFP-Archiv, 1948), 8.

57. Proofed by the circular letter of the Arbeitsgemeinschaft der Christengemeinden in Deutschland from April 1, 1952, from the BFP-Archiv in Erzhausen, 1.

58. Arthur Bergholz, *Die konferenz der arbeitsgemeinschaft der Freien Pfingstgemeinden Deutschlands vom 8. -12. Oktober 1951 in Hamburg: Kurzbericht* [The short report of the working group of the Free Pentecostal Churches in Germany, October 8–12, 1951, in Hamburg] (Erzhausen: BFP-Archiv, 1951), 1.

59. Report of the Secod Einheits-Konferenz (Hauptkonferenz) in Mülheim, in the BFP-Archiv, Erzhausen, 21–22.

60. Krust, *50 Jahre*, 195.

61. Kurt Lukas, interview with author, July 27, 1999.

62. Gerhard Wessler, ed., *Beschlüsse der bruderschaft der arbeitsgemeinschaft der Christengemeinden e. V. von 1951 bis 1971* [Decisions of the brotherhood of the working group of the Christian churches 1951–1971] (Frankfurt am Main: Sekretariat der ACD, 1971), 12.

63. Gustav Kinderman, *Rundschreiben* [Circular] (Stuttgart: General Council Assemblies of God, Abt. Bibelschule, Oktober 1951).

64. Gustav Kinderman, *Konstitution des theologischen instituts* [Constitution of the theological institute] (Stuttgart: General Council Assemblies of God, Abt. Bibelschule, n.d.), 1.

65. Arnold Hitzer, "Protokoll über unterredung mit dem vorstand des Mülheimer gemeinschaftsverbandes" [Report of the Mülheim community board meeting] (Stuttgart, April 29, 1953), 22.

66. Dieter Hampel, Richard Krüger, and Gerhard Oertel, *Der auftrag bleibt: Der Bund Freikirchlicher Pfingstgemeinden auf dem weg ins dritte jahrtausend: Innenansichten ab 1980 bis 2000, Teil B: Zuflüsse durch gemeindeverbände verbreitern den strom* [The work that remains: The Free Pentecostal Churches on the way to the third millennium—insider views from 1980–2000, part B: inflows and widening currents] (Erzhausen: Bund Freikirchlicher Pfingstgemeinden KdöR, 2009), 107–329.

67. Ibid., 128–33.

68. Ibid., 261–329.

69. Ibid., 167–260.

70. Ibid., *Teil A: Quellflüsse und zuflüsse warden zum strom* [Part A: Sources and tributories of power], 91–92.
71. Kurt Redlin, interview with author.
72. The declaration is available at http://www.glopent.net/iak-pfingstbewegung/Members/GerhardBially/berliner-erklaerung (accessed October 26, 2015).
73. See Die Evangelische Allianz in Deutschland, "Gemeinsame Erklärung des Evangelischen Gnadauer Gemeinschaftsverbandes und des Mülheimer Verbandes Freikirchlich-Evangelischer Gemeinden zur 'Berliner Erklärund' von 1909," January 2009, accessed October 26, 2015, http://www.ead.de/nachrichten/nachrichten/einzelansicht/article/gemeinsame-erklaerung-des-evangelischen-gnadauer-gemeinschaftsverbandes-und-des-muelheimer-verbandes.html.
74. For instance, besides other pieces already referenced, Ludwig David Eisenlöffel, *Freikirchliche Pfingstbewegung in Deutschland: Innenansichten 1945–1985* [The Free Pentecostal Churches in Germany: Insider views 1945–1985] (Göttingen: Vandenhoeck & Ruprecht, 2006); Paul Schmidgall, *Hundert jahre Deutsche Pfingstbewegung 1907–2007* [A century of Pentecostalism in Germany 1907–2007] (Nordhausen: Verlag Traugot Bautz, 2007); Horst Krüger, *Pentekostale Gemeindegründungen in Osteuropa zwischen den Weltkriegen: Gustav Herbert Schmidt—Pionier unter Deutschen und Slawen* [Foundations of Pentecostalism in Eastern Europe between the World Wars: Gustav Herbert Schmidt—pioneer among Germans and Slavs] (Adelheidsdorf: self-published, 2011); and Bernhard Olpen, *Gekämpft mit Gott und menschen: Das leben Heinrich Vietheers* [Wrestling with God and humanity: The life of Heinrich Vietheers] (Erzhausen: Leuchter Edition, 2007).
75. See Gottfried Sommer, "Die Belowianer in Hinterpommern und ihr weg vom enthusiastischen aufbruch zur bildung einer freikirche" [The Belowianer in Hinterpommern: From enthusiastic awakenings to the formation of the free churches] (PhD thesis, University of Leuven, 2010).
76. Paul Clark, *Die gründung von Pfingstgemeinden in Deutschland 1945–2005: Implikationen für intentionale mission im 21. jahrhundert* [The foundation of Pentecostal churches in Germany 1945–2005: Implications for intentional mission in the twenty-first century] (Priority Publishing, 2011).
77. Hartmut Knorr, *Leitbild und praxis des pastoralen dienstes: Eine empirische untersuchung zum verständnis und der gestaltung des pastoralen berufs im Bund Freikirchlicher Pfingstgemeinden (BFP)* [Guiding

principles and practice of pastoral service: An empirical investigation to understand and shape pastoral work in the Free Pentecostal Churches] (self-published, 2014).

Chapter 9

Dutch Pentecostalism and Eschatology: Consequences of Tapping into an Eschatologically Charged Religious Matrix

1. Cees van der Laan, *De spade regen; Geboorte en groei van de Pinksterbeweging in Nederland 1907–1930* (Kampen: Kok, 1989). Translated in English as *Sectarian Against His Will: Gerrit Polman and the Birth of Pentecostalism in the Netherlands* (Metuchen: Scarecrow Press, 1991).
2. Van der Laan, *Spade*, 54–73. See also Huib Zegwaart, *Pinksterkerken: Geschiedenis en verschijningsvormen van het Pentecostalisme* [Pentecostal churches: History and manifestations of Pentecostalism], Serie Wegwijs (Kampen: Kok, 2003), 41–97.
3. Van der Laan, *Spade*, 15–41.
4. This part is based on Huib Zegwaart, "Het eschatologische accent in de Pinksterbeweging" [The eschatological accent in the Pentecostal movement], in George Harinck, ed., *"Steek elke pastorie in brand!": Honderd jaar dwarsverbindingen tussen Pinkstergemeenten en Protestantse kerken* ["Put the fire into every parsonage!": One hundred years of connections between Pentecostal and Protestant churches] (Amsterdam: Historisch Documentatiecentrum voor het Nederlands protestantisme [1800–heden] and Vrije Universiteit, 2008), 42–48.
5. Van der Laan, *Spade*, 15–23.
6. Verzuiling (pillarization) is one way of coping with religious and cultural diversity. Since its beginnings in the sixteenth century (it broke away from Spain in a war that lasted from 1568 until 1648), Dutch society has known an ethnic and cultural diversity and has adopted a policy of tolerance toward minorities of different persuasions.
7. Van der Laan, *Spade*, 24–41.
8. Cf. Donald W. Dayton, *Theological Roots of Pentecostalism* (Peabody, MA: Hendrickson, 1991), passim.
9. The "kingdom of God" debate raged in the former half of the twentieth century. See Wendell Willis, ed., *The Kingdom of God in Twentieth-Century Interpretation* (Peabody, MA: Hendrickson, 1987).
10. This came to be known as inaugurated eschatology.

11. The de-apocalyptization of the Kerugma was a gradual process, having moreover a nonlinear character. See Brian E. Daley, *The Hope of the Early Church: A Handbook of Patristic Eschatology* (Cambridge: Cambridge University Press, 1991).
12. The putative apocalyptic character of Jesus's preaching leads to vigorous disagreement. John Collins therefore included two contributions in *The Encyclopedia of Apocalypticism*, vol. 1 (New York: Continuum, 1998). Dale C. Allison Jr., "The Eschatology of Jesus," 276 –302, argues that Jesus preached an apocalyptic form of eschatology, whereas Richard A. Horsley, "The Kingdom of God and the Renewal of Israel: Synoptic Gospels, Jesus Movements, and Apocalypticism," 303–44, makes the opposite case. Having extensively studied apocalypticism, I side with exegetes who consider Jesus's message thoroughly apocalyptic.
13. Personal eschatology stands over against cosmological eschatology. The former asks questions about the final state of the individual, the latter concerning itself with creation as a whole. In many apocalypses the two are fused, but in later Christian apocalypses, such as the Apocalypse of Peter and the Apocalypse of Paul, personal eschatology dominates.
14. See, for example, Bernard McGinn, *Apocalyptic Spirituality* (Mahwah, NJ: Paulist Press, 1979); and Norman Cohn, *The Pursuit of the Millennium; Revolutionary Millenarians and Mystical Anarchists of the Middle Ages* (1957; reprint, London: Paladin, 1970).
15. On the interpretation of an apocalyptic text like John's Apocalypse, see Arthur W. Wainwright, *Mysterious Apocalypse: Interpreting the Book of Revelation* (Nashville: Abingdon, 1993).
16. This specifically German form of liberal theology was in vogue in the latter half of the nineteenth century. See Theopedia, "Theological Liberalism," accessed April 6, 2015, http://www.theopedia.com/Theological_liberalism; and James Richmond, "Liberal Protestantism," in *A New Dictionary of Christian Theology*, eds. A. Richardson and J. Bowden (London: SCM Press, 1983), 325–28. For a different view, see R. S. Goizueta, "Liberalism," in *Global Dictionary of Theology*, eds. W. A. Dyrness and V-M. Kärkkäinen (Downers Grove, IL: IVP Academic, 2008), 485–86.
17. See Huib Zegwaart, *Denken over God in veranderende tijden: Theologie sinds 1900* [Thinking about God in times of change: Theology since 1900], chapter 4, forthcoming.

18. See Cees J. den Heyer, *Jesus Matters: 150 Years of Research* (London: SCM Press, 1996).
19. See Klaus Koch, *The Rediscovery of Apocalyptic: A Polemical Work on a Neglected Area of Biblical Studies and Its Damaging Effects on Theology and Philosophy* (London: SCM Press, 1972).
20. Darby's influence on the American Holiness Movement is documented by Ernest R. Sandeen, *The Roots of Fundamentalism: British and American Millenarianism, 1800–1930* (Chicago and London: The University of Chicago Press, 1970). For the connection between the Holiness Movement and Pentecostalism (especially in America), see, for example, Robert M. Anderson, *Vision of the Disinherited: The Making of American Pentecostalism* (Peabody, MA: Hendrickson, 1992).
21. Van der Laan, *Spade*, 36–38.
22. The book was fully revised in 1917 by Cyrus I. Scofield (1843–1921) himself. Later revisions followed, and in 1990 the title was changed to the *Scofield Study Bible*. Both dispensationalism and fundamentalism are key to its handling of biblical materials and the theology espoused in it. The work is still in print and, judging by the many entries on the Internet, still widely popular in conservative circles.
23. See Sandeen, *Roots*. Postmillennialism was deeply ingrained in American consciousness, as it was this particular view that motivated the Pilgrim Fathers to set sail for North America in order to create a New World. The eschatological ring of this term is no coincidence. The new society they founded was to be a "shining city on a hill," a light not to be hidden.
24. Other possibilities: it will take place during the Great Tribulation, at the end of it, or not at all.
25. This was, of course, also the view espoused by Hal Lindsey in the 1970s and more recently by Tim LaHaye and Jerry B. Jenkins in the Left Behind series.
26. He was quite charmed by the early reports about Pentecostalism, but then fellow preachers from Germany pointed him at the Berlin Declaration (1909). From then on, he spoke out against the new movement that in so many ways was so akin to his own eschatological and revivalist movement.
27. In the Netherlands there used to be a lot of antagonism between the original movement that can trace its history back to the beginning of the twentieth century and the movements that originated after 1950:

Stromen van Kracht and Kracht van Omhoog. This antagonism only abated in the late 1980s and 1990s.

28. See Van der Laan, *Spade*, 54–64, and the autobiography of Margaretha A. Alt, *Herinneringen uit mijn leven* [Memories from my life] (Velp: Vereniging De Pinksterzending, 1971).
29. This term, peculiar to Dutch Pentecostalism, designates the Pentecostal churches that trace their origin to the turn of the twentieth century, whereas the churches that were founded in the late 1950s and 1960s called themselves New Pentecostalism.
30. See Cees van der Laan and Paul van der Laan, *Toen de kracht Gods op mij viel: 100 jaar Pinksterbeweging in Nederland, 1907–2007* [When God's power came over me: One hundred years of Pentecostalism in the Netherlands] (Kampen: Kok, 2007), 79–84.
31. See Alt, *Herinneringen*, 36–40. At present, Cees van der Laan is writing a study on the life of this remarkable woman and pioneer of Pentecostalism in Indonesia and Holland.
32. Which is, of course, not to say that individual pastors did not fall into that trap or that splits like the Ephraim Society (around AD 2000) did not develop into eschatological sects.
33. However, he also publishes an article in which Darby's dispensationalism is criticized (Laan, *Spade*, 157).
34. Gerrit R. Polman, "Gekomen ... komende 'naar de Schriften'" [Has come ... is coming "according to the Scriptures"], *Spade regen* 32 (January 1913): 1.
35. Van der Laan, *Spade*, 157.
36. Margaretha A. Alt, *Bijbelstudie voor zelfonderricht* [Bible study for at home] (1951; reprint, Velp: Vereniging De Pinksterzending, 1968); see Gouden Schoven, accessed July 21, 2016, http://www.goudenschoven.nl/werk/boeken/.
37. The letters together do not, in the first place, represent the Christian church of all ages.
38. On exegetical grounds, the identification of the martyrs of Revelation 20:4 with the believers is highly problematic. The whole of chapter 20 has spurred theological controversy. For a discussion of some of these, see Huibert H. Zegwaart, "Apocalyptic Eschatology and Pentecostalism: The Relevance of John's Millennium for Today," *Pneuma: The Journal of the Society for Pentecostal Studies* 10, no. 1 (1988): 3–25, 18–22.

39. This is one of the denominations out of which the Verenigde Pinkster- en Evangeliegemeenten was formed in 2002. The denomination with which it merged was the Volle Evangelie Gemeenten Nederland, which itself was a merger between two smaller Full Gospel denominations. See Zegwaart, *Pinksterkerken*, 66–68.
40. K. van Balen, R. L. Leach, and G. van Polen, *Het zal zijn in de laatste dagen* [It shall be in the last days] (Den Haag: Broederschap van Pinkstergemeenten, 1967).
41. It should be noted that the Statement of Fundamental Truths of the Assemblies of God (USA) were formulated in 1916; that is at a time when eschatological expectations ran high.
42. The American format also has four statements dealing with eschatology, but since it only has sixteen articles and a preamble, it appears to be slightly more balanced. For the text of these sixteen articles, see http://ag.org/top/Beliefs/Statement_of_fundamental_truths/sft_short.cfm (accessed March 11, 2015).
43. J. W. Embregts, *Geen uitstel meer* [No more delay] (Rotterdam: Gramma, 1978).
44. In 2005, he published a theological study in which he repudiated the endeavor to set a date for end-time events; J. W. Embregts, *Dag noch uur: De vergeefse zoektocht naar een einddatum* [Neither day nor hour: The vain search for an end date] (Nieuwleusen: Elia stichting, 2005).
45. See Van der Laan and Van der Laan, *Toen*, 97–100; and Zegwaart, *Pinksterkerken*, 57–60.
46. Elisabeth Hoekendijk-La Rivière, *Ja, ik kom spoedig* [Yes, I am coming soon] (Baarn: Stromen van Kracht, n.d.).
47. See Zegwaart, *Pinksterkerken*, 60–63; and Van der Laan and Van der Laan, *Toen*, 97–100.
48. J. E. van den Brink, *De gemeente in de eindtijd* [The church in the end times] (Gorinchem: Kracht van Omhoog, 1968), 5.
49. Ibid., 6.
50. Ibid., 87–88. The author's language contains many expressions that in the New Testament have their home in eschatological passages. Thus, he calls the "preaching of the gospel" the "proclamation of the Kingdom" and refers to preachers as "Sons of God."
51. This is, of course, quite common in Christian apocalypses of ancient times. This can also be said of the Book of Revelation, that though it is primarily an eschatological apocalypse, it also contains heavenly

journeys. For a typology of apocalypses, see John J. Collins, "Introduction: Towards the Morphology of a Genre," *SEMEIA* 14 (1979): 1–20. The double dualism (temporal and spatial) is incorporated in his definition of apocalyptic literature, which is "a genre of revelatory literature with a narrative framework, in which a revelation is mediated by an otherworldly being to a human recipient, disclosing a transcendent reality which is both temporal, insofar as it envisages eschatological salvation, and spatial insofar as it involves another, supernatural world" (4).

52. Van den Brink, *Gemeente*, 81, 94.
53. Ibid., 83.
54. Ibid., 82.
55. Ibid., 88.
56. Ibid., 91.
57. Ibid., 33, cf. 72.
58. Ibid., 122–23.
59. Ibid., 110, 111.
60. Zegwaart, "Apocalyptic Eschatology."
61. Paul N. van der Laan, "What Is Left Behind? A Pentecostal Response to Eschatological Fiction," *JEPTA: The Journal of the European Pentecostal Theological Association* 24 (2006): 49–70—translated in Dutch as "Wat Is Left Behind?" *Parakleet* 95 (2007): 3–11—wrote in reaction of the publication of this series of novels, in which he, too, calls for serious theological reevaluation of Pentecostalism's dispensationalist heritage.
62. Jean-Jacques Suurmond, *Het spel van Woord en Geest: Aanzet tot een charismatische theologie* (Baarn: Ten Have, 1994)—translated in English as *Word and Spirit at Play* (Grand Rapids: Eerdmans, 1994), 19—notes that to the degree to which (white) Pentecostals rose on the social ladder, eschatological fervor declined.
63. D. William Faupel, *The Everlasting Gospel: The Significance of Eschatology in the Development of Pentecostal Thought*, Journal of Pentecostal Theology Supplement Series 10 (Sheffield: Sheffield Academic Press, 1996).
64. George O. Wood, "Onze hoop en hulp: Vervulling van de Grote Opdracht in het licht van Zijn komst" [Our blessed hope and help: Fulfilling the Great Commission in light of His return], *Parakleet* 48 (1993): 3–10, which is a Dutch translation of his address to the Pentecostal World Assemblies of God Fellowship held in Oslo, Norway, September 14, 1992. Something similar was attempted in 2007 with the Dutch

translation of a theological book with a decisively eschatological orientation by the South-African author Lemmer du Plessis, *De komst van Christus: Perspectief op Gods eeuwige plan* [The coming of Christ: A perspective on God's eternal plan] (Pretoria: Aktua Pers, 2007).

65. This happened to certain strands of Jewish apocalypticism; cf. Ithamar Gruenwald, *Apocalyptic and Merkavah Mysticism* (Leiden: Brill, 1980).

66. As does Amos Yong; see Yong's recent *Renewing Christian Theology: Systematics for a Global Christianity*, images and commentary by Jonathan A. Anderson (Waco, TX: Baylor University Press, 2014), 29–56.

Chapter 10
Pentecostalism in France: A Multiform and Ecumenical Movement of the Spirit?

1. The word *Pentecostalism* is used in this chapter as a generic concept for various modern (dis)similar Christian movements of the Spirit. A more extensive treatment of the subject is found in several chapters the author has published in *European Pentecostalism*, eds. William K. Kay and Anne E. Dyer (Leiden: Brill, 2011).
2. As found, for example, in the writings of François de Sales, Lawrence of the Resurrection, François Fénelon, and Madame de Guyon.
3. Carter Lindberg, *The Third Reformation: Charismatic Movements and the Lutheran Tradition* (Macon, GA: Mercer University Press, 1983), 131–39, 144.
4. Donald Dayton, *Theological Roots of Pentecostalism* (Grand Rapids: Zondervan, 1987), 35–60. The expression *baptism in the Holy Spirit* is also linked with Swiss-born Jean-Guillaume de la Fléchère, alias John Fletcher of Madely (1729–1785) and close collaborator of John Wesley (1703–1791). Fletcher believed in experiencing Christ in the power of the Holy Spirit, both as a punctual experience and as a continuing and dynamic operation in the Christian life. Cf. Daniel Brandt-Bessire, *Aux sources de la spiritualité pentecôtiste* [At the roots of Pentecostal spirituality] (Genève: Labor et Fides, 1986), 63–72.
5. Due to its distinct ethnocultural identity and language, the province of Alsace is probably the most important exception with the ministry of local pastor Paul Siefer (1903–1973) and through longtime links with Pentecostal movements in Switzerland and Germany.
6. Alexander A. Boddy, "Across the Channel: Days in France," *Confidence* 2, no. 11 (November 1909): 263–64.

7. All figures pertaining to the total number of local churches found in the various Pentecostal-Charismatic denominations in France are taken from the website www.eglises.org (accessed April 1, 2015).
8. Pentecostal statistics in general are not always reliable, and statistical estimation for French Pentecostalism in particular remains approximate. Some figures on French Pentecostalism are listed on the website of the French Protestant Federation, "Le Pentecôtisme," http://www.protestants.org/index.php?id=32527 (accessed April 21, 2015).
9. This figure would include children and youth as well as regular adult visitors.
10. In the French language, an interesting, subtle distinction has been introduced between *pentecôtiste* (Pentecostal) and *pentecôtisant* (Pentecostal-like).
11. By *ethnic Pentecostalism* is meant a sizable group of Pentecostal believers sharing a common and distinctive culture, lifestyle, and language.
12. In Romani language, a *gadjo* is a person who is not a Gypsy.
13. René Zanellato, "L'action Mondiale Tzigane," 2006, accessed April 12, 2015, http://www.queditlabible.com/laction-tzigane-mondiale.php.
14. In August 2008, the annual convention organized by the MET (Mission Vie et Lumière) gathered around twenty-five thousand people. Cf. Céline Schmink, "Tziganes: la vague Pentecôtiste—Entretiens avec deux témoins de l'évangélisation chez les Roms" [Interviews with two witnesses of evangelism among Roma people], *Religioscope*, September 24, 2008, accessed April 2, 2015, http://religion.info/french/entretiens/article_395.shtml#.VRv2gfmsV8G.
15. Christophe Bernard, e-mail message to author, April 20, 2015.
16. Daniel Lucero, e-mail message to author, April 9, 2015.
17. Walter Hollenweger, "Some Aspects of European Charismatics," in *Perspectives on the New Pentecostalism*, ed. Russell P. Spittler (Grand Rapids: Baker, 1976), 50–54.
18. There is no link between this denomination and the Full Gospel Business Men's Fellowship International (FGBMFI) also to be found in France.
19. These are some of the smaller Pentecostal-like denominations or networks found in France: Fédération des Églises et Communautés Baptistes Charismatiques; Union des Églises Pentecôtisantes Indépendantes; Confédération Évangélique Protestante Francophone d'Expression Pentecôtiste; Fédération des Églises Agapé; Union d'Églises Missionnaires; Fédération des Eglises Chrétiennes Evangéliques; Newfrontiers.

20. Interview with Jean-Paul Willaime by Marie Lemonnier, "Le Réveil des Protestants" [Revival among Protestants], *L'Observateur* 2354 (December 17, 2009).
21. Fédération Des Eglises Pentecôtistes Unies De France, accessed July 21, 2016, http://epufrance.org.
22. Olivier Landron, *Les communautés nouvelles* [New ecclesial communities] (Paris: Les Edition du Cerf, 2004), 202.
23. As seen on the cover page of *Documents "Expériences"* 8 (1972).
24. Clément Le Cossec, "Une indispensable mise au point" [A necessary clarification], *Document "Expériences"* 8 (1972): 64–73.
25. This translates the French word *récupération.*
26. René Laurentin, *Pentecôtisme chez les Catholiques* (Paris: Beauchesne, 1974), translated by Matthew J. O'Connellas, *Catholic Pentecostalism* (New York: Doubleday, 1977).
27. Landron, *Les communautés nouvelles*, 461.
28. Daniel Juster and Peter Hocken, *The Messianic Jewish Movement: An Introduction* (Toward Jerusalem Council II, 2004), 26–27.
29. Beth Yeshua Assemblée Messianique, accessed June 28, 2016, http://www.bethyeshoua.org/index.php/les-responsables/566-temoin-p-ghennassia.
30. France's Jewish population represents, however, only 3.3 percent of Jewry, following Israel (42.9 percent) and the United States (40.1 percent); Jewish Virtual Library, "Vital Statistics: Jewish Population of the World (1882–Present)," accessed April 8, 2015, https://www.jewishvirtuallibrary.org/jsource/Judaism/jewpop.html.
31. Alliance Francophone des Juifs Messianiques, accessed June 28, 2016, http://www.yechoua.com/afjm.html.
32. Peter Hocken, *The Challenges of the Pentecostal, Charismatic, and Messianic Jewish Movements: The Tensions of the Spirit* (Farnham: Ashgate, 2009), 104–10.
33. Bernard Boutter, "Pentecôtisme et ethnicité en France" [Pentecostalism and ethnicity in France], in *La recomposition des Protestantismes en Europe latine: Entre émotion et tradition* [The reconfiguration of Protestantism in southern Europe: Between emotion and tradition], ed. Jean-Pierre Bastian (Genève: Labor et Fides, 2004), 286.
34. Council of the Fédération Protestante de France, "Les Eglises issues de l'immigration" [Churches of immigrant background], available at http://www.protestants.org/uploads/media/

Les_Eglises_issues_de_l_immigration_de_quoi_parlons-nous_version_finale_PDF_BDF.pdf (accessed April 21, 2015).

35. For example, 90 percent of the member churches of the Communauté des Eglises d'expression Africaine en France have a Pentecostal orientation; this African network of churches has, however, adopted a creed that is not particularly Pentecostal or Charismatic in its formulation. Cf. Ilhame Taoufiqi, "Eglise Pentecôtiste: Entreprises spirituelles en concurrence" [Pentecostal church: Spiritually competing companies], *Regards*, February 1, 2006, accessed June 18, 2015, http://www.regards.fr/acces-payant/archives-web/eglise-pentecotiste-entreprises,2275.
36. Depending on the sources, between five thousand and ten thousand (external estimations) and seven thousand (my own estimations). See www.charisma.fr.
37. "Le mouvement Evangelique," Charisma Eglise Chretienne, accessed July 21, 2016, http://www.charisma.fr/fr/presentation/le_mouvement_evangelique.php.
38. In 2011, it became associated with the Fédération Protestante de France through its affiliation with the Communauté des Eglises d'Expression Africaines de France.
39. Sébastien Fath, "Selvaraj Rajiah (1952–2011), *Blog de Sébastien Fath*, accessed April 9, 2015, http://blogdesebastienfath.hautetfort.com/apps/search?s=Selvaraj+Rajiah.
40. Sandra Fancello, "Réveil de l'ethnicité akan et Pentecôtisme 'indigène' en Europe" [Awakening of Akan ethnicity and 'indigenous' Pentecostalism in Europe], *Diversité urbaine* 7, no. 1 (2007): 51–67.
41. Marion Aubrée, "Un néo-Pentecôtisme brésilien parmi les populations immigrées en Europe de l'Ouest" [Brazilian neo-Pentecostalism among immigrant populations in Western Europe], *Anthropologie et Sociétés* 27, no. 1 (2003): 65–84. Cf. André Corten, Jean-Pierre Dozon, and Ari-Pedro Oro, *Les nouveaux conquérants de la foi: l'église universelle du royaume de Dieu (Brésil)* [The new conquerors of the faith: The universal church of the kingdom of God (Brazil)] (Paris: Karthala, 2003), 128–29.
42. Founded by Samuel Bilehou Joseph Oshoffa (1909–1985).
43. The Yeruba people are an ethnic group of southwestern Nigeria and southern Benin.
44. Due to limited space, global Pentecostal-Charismatic organizations established in France, such as the Full Gospel Business Men's Fellowship

International, Youth With A Mission, or the Alpha Course, cannot be presented in this chapter.

45. Particularly disturbing has been what is perceived as a display of charismatic authority by lay leaders who seemed to be ruling by "divine right." Cf. Sébastien Fath, *Du ghetto au réseau: Le Protestantisme Évangélique en France (1800–2005)* [From ghetto to network: Evangelical Protestantism in France (1800–2005)] (Genève: Labor et Fides, 2005), 184–85, 256.
46. Founded in 1905, the French Protestant Federation is an ecumenical organization representing member bodies with a shared Protestant identity that is expressed in a charter that outlines their common Protestant heritage and values and their declared will to demonstrate mutual respect. See The French Protestant Federation, accessed August 31, 2016, http://www.protestants.org/index.php?id=33339.
47. "Nous sommes tous Évangéliques à tendance Pentecôtiste" ["We all are Evangelicals with a Pentecostal inclination"], as quoted in Schmink, "Tziganes."
48. Fath, *Du ghetto au réseau*, 215, 234. His 2005 figures mention 350,000 French Evangelicals, out of which 200,000 are Pentecostal-Charismatics.
49. Yves Congar, *I Believe in the Holy Spirit* (1983; three vols. in one, New York: Crossroad Herder, 2005).
50. Seven Pentecostal denominations are not affiliated with the CNEF or with the FPF.

Chapter 11
History, Nature, and Challenges of Spanish Pentecostalism

1. Calvin L. Smith, "Latin American Pentecostalism and the Academy," in *Pentecostal Power: Expressions, Impact, and Faith of Latin American Pentecostalism*, ed. Calvin L. Smith (Leiden: Brill, 2010), 1–5.
2. Raised the son of Pentecostal pioneer missionaries to Andalucía during the latter years of the dictatorship of Francisco Franco (my parents began their ministry there in 1969), I recall these as difficult times. I will include recollections of my parents in the endnotes of this chapter, where appropriate.
3. Máximo García Ruiz, "Corrientes teológicas y sociológicas que han influido en el Protestantismo Español" [Theological and sociological currents that have influenced Spanish Protestantism], *Anales de Historia Contemporánea* 17 (2001): 100–1.
4. George Borrow, *The Bible in Spain* (1843).

5. García Ruiz, "Corrientes teológicas," 109–12.
6. Allan Anderson, *An Introduction to Pentecostalism: Global Charismatic Christianity* (Cambridge: Cambridge University Press, 2004), 97; and Martin Arroyo and Paulo Branco, "The Development of the Pentecostal Movement in Iberia," in *European Pentecostalism*, eds. William K. Kay and Anne Dyer (Leiden: Brill, 2011), 165. A Spanish Protestant historian dates that plant to 1922; Manuel de León de la Vega, *Historia del Protestantismo en Asturias: 150 años de la segunda Reforma Protestante en España* [History of Protestantism in Asturias: 150 years of the second Protestant Reformation in Spain] (unpublished manuscript, 2010), 213; available at https://manueldeleon.wordpress.com/2010/10/31/historia-del-protestantismo-en-asturias/ (accessed November 2, 2015).
7. Arroyo and Branco, "Pentecostal Movement in Iberia," 165; also see de la Vega, *Historia del Protestantismo*, 216.
8. Arroyo and Branco, "Pentecostal Movement in Iberia," 165.
9. De la Vega, *Historia del Protestantismo*, 216.
10. Ibid., 214.
11. Ibid.
12. Arroyo and Branco, "Pentecostal Movement in Iberia," 165.
13. Peter Smith, *Global Warming—The Fire of Pentecost in World Evangelism: An Anecdotal History of the Work of Elim Missions, 1919–1989* (Antrim: Elim Pentecostal Irish Churches, 2006), chapter 10 (volume does not include page numbers).
14. De la Vega, *Historia del Protestantismo*, 216 (footnote).
15. Asambleas de Dios Islas Canarias, "Información," accessed November 2, 2015, http://www.adcanarias.es.
16. Clifton L. Holland, *A Chronology of Protestant Beginnings: Spain* (San José, Costa Rica: PROLADES, 2003); this short document is available at the PROLADES website at http://www.prolades.com/historical/spn-chron.pdf (accessed November 2, 2015).
17. Arroyo and Branco, "Pentecostal Movement in Iberia," 166.
18. Smith, *Global Warming*, chapter 10.
19. De la Vega, *Historia del Protestantismo*, 318.
20. Vinson Synan, *In the Latter Days: The Outpouring of the Holy Spirit in the Twentieth Century* (Ann Arbor, MI: Servant Publications, 1991; reprint, Maitland, FL: Xulon Press, 2001), 57.
21. Arroyo and Branco, "Pentecostal Movement in Iberia," 165.

22. De la Vega, *Historia del Protestantismo*, 308, 317. Justo worked with my father for many years.
23. Christopher and Christine Smith (my parents), interview with the author, Birchington, Kent, United Kingdom, May 16, 2014. My father met Correll, who studied under Aimee Semple McPherson, through a pastor friend in Indiana whose ministry included Correll as a board member; see Missions Morningstar/CMM, "Dr. Sidney and Helen Correll," accessed November 2, 2015, http://eaglemissions.org/about/cmm-history.
24. H. A. (Hank) Roso, "Helen Elliot Correll: A True General in God's Army Goes Home," *The Evangel* 45, no. 3 (2004): 3.
25. Garcia Ruiz, "Corrientes teológicas," 115.
26. Arroyo and Branco, "Pentecostal Movement in Iberia," 166–67.
27. Ibid., 167.
28. Christopher and Christine Smith, interview with the author. My great-uncle attended one of del Vecchio's churches.
29. Ibid.
30. Gordon Burgess, interview with the author, Mutxalmel, Alicante, June 18, 2015. Well-known among the Spanish Assemblies of God, Burgess was my parents' first contact when they first traveled to Spain in 1969.
31. Colin Warner, *The Call to Spain* (unpublished memoirs, 2015), 23.
32. It was to this region, specifically the then-considerably-underdeveloped province of Almería, that our family moved to work among the Gypsy people at that time when Spain's Gypsies were regarded with disdain as outcasts and were often poverty-stricken, some of them living in caves (indeed, my parents focused much of their efforts in the village of Cuevas del Almanzora, literally the Caves of the Almanzora).
33. Raymond Pfister, "Pentecostalism in Francophone Countries," in Kay and Dyer, *European Pentecostalism*, 122–24.
34. A video of Osborn preaching to Gypsies in Lille, France, in 1960 is available on YouTube at https://www.youtube.com/watch?v=wvVd5GzS4sc (accessed October 29, 2015).
35. Gordon Burgess, interview with author.
36. P. D. Hocken, "European Pentecostalism," in *Dictionary of Pentecostal and Charismatic Movements*, eds. Stanley Burgess and Gary B. McGee (Grand Rapids: Zondervan, 1988), 277.
37. Synon, *In the Latter Days*, 57; also discussed by Christopher and Christine Smith, interview with author.

38. Anderson, *An Introduction to Pentecostalism*, 97.
39. Hocken, "European Pentecostalism," 278.
40. *ProtestanteDigital.com*, "Fallece el fundador de la iglesia Gitana Evangélica en España" [Death of the founder of the Evangelical Gypsy church in Spain], August 24, 2011, accessed September 8, 2015, http://protestante digital.com/espana/26376/Fallece_el_fundador_de_la_Iglesia_gitana_evangelica_en_Espantildea.
41. Arroyo and Branco, "Pentecostal Movement in Iberia," 166–67.
42. Garcia Ruiz, "Corrientes teológicas," 115.
43. De la Vega, *Historia del Protestantismo*, 217.
44. Garcia Ruiz, "Corrientes teológicas," 113.
45. Clifton L. Holland, *Religion in Spain* (San José, Costa Rica: PROLADES, 2003), 15, available at the PROLADES website at http://www.prolades.com/cra/regions/ibero/spain-eng/Religion-in-Spain-clh-2003.pdf (accessed November 2, 2015).
46. Felipe Betim, "El número iglesias Evangélicas en España se duplica en 10 años" [The number of Evangelical churches in Spain doubled in ten years], *El Pais*, June 12, 2014, accessed November 2, 2015. http://sociedad .elpais.com/sociedad/2014/06/12/actualidad/1402606692_853823.html.
47. Gordon Burgess, interview with author.
48. William K. Kay, *Pentecostalism* (London: SCM, 2009), 190.
49. Felipe Betim, "El número iglesias Evangélicas en España."
50. For a detailed discussion, see de la Vega, *Historia del Protestantismo*, 236–77.
51. Warner, *The Call to Spain*; and Gordon Burgess, interview with author. My parents, Christopher and Christine Smith (interview), recall that our family was assigned a secret policeman to watch and record our activities (the local mayor introduced my father to him some years after Franco's death). There was always a policeman by our house who would jot down every time we left the house.
52. In 1973, a group of nuns visited our state school, singling me out and publicly warning the other children to stay away from me because I was *protestante*.
53. Gordon Burgess, interview with author; and Christopher and Christine Smith, interview with author. Once, one woman publicly spat in my mother's face for being an *evangélico* (the woman apologised years later, explaining that it was done out of fear and the need to be seen to oppose

evangelicós). On another occasion, when our family opened a new fellowship in the village of Cuevas, it was attended one evening by a member of the Guardia Civil with a carbine slung over his shoulder who listened carefully to my father's rather nervously delivered sermon. The incident caused grave fear for our oldest convert, Hermano Reverte, a former Republican in the Civil War who was later imprisoned by the Spanish Fascists. Opposition even extended to many Catholics being unwilling to sell land to Protestants (our family had to purchase land from a Frenchman to build a church).

54. For example, see *ProtestanteDigital.com*, "El PP se reúne con Evangélicos Gitanos y Asambleas de Dios" [The PP meets with Evangelical Gypsies and the Assemblies of God], April 7, 2014, accessed November 2, 2015, http://protestantedigital.com/espana/30872/El_PP_se_reune_con_evangelicos_gitanos_y_Asambleas_de_Dios.
55. Gordon Burgess, interview with author.
56. Ibid.
57. Garcia Ruiz, "Corrientes teológicas," 116; see also an interesting volume exploring Romani Pentecostalism: David Thurfjell and Adrian Marsh, eds., *Romani Pentecostalism: Gypsies and Charismatic Christianity* (Frankfurt: Peter Lang, 2014).
58. My father recalls how, after we moved to Spain and established a Gypsy work in the province of Almería, Le Cossec (who was in the Alicante region) visited unexpectedly and insisted that the new mission could only continue to minister to the Gypsies under the Filadelfia banner. My parents, who had already established the first pioneer works in that area, where no Filadelfia presence existed, declined, later observing how it was all quite political at the time; Christopher and Christine Smith, interview with author.
59. Anderson, *Introduction to Pentecostalism*, 79, 97. Gordon Burgess also discusses an influx of Latin American missionaries (interview).
60. Felipe Betim, "El número iglesias Evangélicas en España."
61. Evangelismo a Fondo España (Evangelism in Depth Spain), "Latinos: Factor clave en el crecimiento de iglesia Española" [Latinos: A key factor in the growth of Spanish church], March 26, 2015, accessed November 2, 2015, https://evaf.org.es/2015/03/26/latinos-factor-clave-en-el-crecimiento-de-iglesia-espanola/ ().
62. Gordon Burgess, interview with author.

63. As explained to me by Rafael Restrepo, a non-Charismatic American missionary with Colombian roots who pastors the International Christian Assembly, Torrevieja. Gordon Burgess also discusses this phenomenon (interview). Note also that my father recently spoke at a church in Murcia he had not visited for some years and noted considerable growth since his last visit, owed mainly to new Latin American members. Introducing my father, the Spanish pastor observed, "You'll notice the accents have changed around here; we all speak South American now"; Christopher and Christine Smith, interview with author.
64. Paola Garcia, "Integración y migración: Las iglesias Pentecostales en España" [Integration and migration: Pentecostalism in Spain], *Les Cahiers ALHIM* 20 (2010), accessed November 2, 2015, http://alhim.revues.org/3691.
65. Gordon Burgess, interview with author.
66. Hocken, "European Pentecostalism," 277.
67. Christopher and Christine Smith, interview with author.
68. Anderson, *Introduction to Pentecostalism*, 97.
69. See Jessica Martinez, "Spain Is a Cemetery for Preachers, Evangelists, Missionaries, Says Assemblies of God Pastor," *Christian Post*, August 9, 2014, accessed November 2, 2015, http://www.christianpost.com/news/spain-is-a-cemetery-for-preachers-evangelists-missionaries-says-assemblies-of-god-pastor-124557/.
70. Ibid.

Chapter 12
Pentecostalism in Sweden and Finland

1. Bloch Hoell, *Pinsebevegelsen: En undersøkelse av Pinsebevegelsens tilblivelse, utvikling og særpreg med særlig henblikk på bevegelsens utforming i Norge* [Pentecostal movement: A study of the Pentecostal movement's origin, development, and distinctives with focus on the development in Norway] (Oslo: Universitetsforlaget, 1958), 289. The original text reads, "Sverige står som det mest 'pinsebetonte' land i verden. Det er nesten 13 promille p.venner i Sverige."
2. Olof Palme was prime minister of Sweden and an actor on the international political scene for decades; he was murdered in 1986. Raoul Wallenberg saved the lives of thousands of Jews during the Second World War but died in a Soviet prison in 1947; he has been awarded the title

Righteous Among the Nations by Israel and is an honorary citizen of Israel, Hungary, the United States, Canada, and Australia.

3. Bundy writes, "Scandinavian Pentecostal Missionaries were active around the world. The converts of these early missionaries have created major segments of 21st century Pentecostalism"; see David Bundy, *Visions of Apostolic Mission: Scandinavian Pentecostal Mission to 1935*, Studia Historico-Ecclesiastica Upsaliensia 45 (Uppsala: Uppsala University Library, 2009), 1.
4. Finnish is the majority language in Finland and an official minority language in Sweden. Swedish is the majority language in Sweden and the only official minority language in Finland.
5. See, for example, the Swedish Baptist periodical *Swedish Tribune* [*Svenska tribunen*] that in 1906 featured many references to "Spirit baptism" and "baptism in the Holy Spirit" as well as to a book on that very subject by John Paul "Pastor in Ravenstein" (e.g., October 10, 1906).
6. Bundy, *Apostolic Missions*, 31ff. Add to this the influences from, for example, the Evangelical Alliance World Conference in Denmark 1884, reports from and visits to the Keswick meetings, as well as abundant reports from the Welsh revival.
7. Jan-Åke Alvarsson, "Pingstväckelsens etablering i Sverige: Från Azusa Street till Skövde på sju månader" [The establishment of Pentecostalism in Sweden: From Azuza Street to Skövde in seven months], in *Pingströrelsen: Händelser och utveckling under 1900-talet* [Pentecostal movement: Events and development during the twentieth century], vol. 1, eds. Claes Waern et al. (Örebro: Libris, 2007), 11, 16–17. The predominantly African American prayer group behind the Azusa Street revival first met at South Union Avenue in February 1906 and later at 214 North Bonnie Brae Street before moving to 312 Azusa Street on April 14, 1906. For further information about the Azusa Street movement, see Cecil M. Robeck Jr., *The Azusa Street Mission and Revival: The Birth of the Global Pentecostal Movement* (Nashville, TN: Nelson Reference & Electronic, 2006).
8. Johnson was born in Skövde, Sweden, in 1878 as Anders Gustaf Johansson but anglicized his name to Andrew G. Johnson when he emigrated to the United States. This was the name he himself always used when he signed his reports or articles. When he returned to Sweden in 1906, a journalist retranslated his name as Jansson—something that stuck with him as he became famous. Tired of this, he again changed his last name to 'Ek' around 1917, and from the 1920s he is known only as Andrew Ek.

9. Andrew Johnson-Ek, *Då elden föll: Av ett ögonvittne* [When the fire fell: From an eyewitness] (Mariestad: Eget förlag, 1933), 10–11.
10. The report says, "I would like to be in California, but the Spirit says that I have some more work on the other side of the sea. I hope you are praying for me. This is not Azusa Street Mission here, but I am praying that the Lord would grant us fire from heaven and give life to half-dead Christians"; *The Apostolic Faith* 1, no. 5 (1906): 3.
11. The other Baptist seminary at the time, Betelseminariet in Stockholm, was at the time only open to men.
12. This movement is now known as Fria Missionsförbundet; Nils G. Holm, *Pingströrelsen: En religionsvetenskaplig studie av Pingströrelsen i Svenskfinland* [The Pentecostal movement: A scientific study of the Pentecostal movement in Swedish-speaking Finland], Meddelanden från Stiftelsen för Åbo Akademi Forskningsinstitut 31 (Åbo: Tidningsbokhandeln, 1978), 21.
13. Pekka Brofeldt is called Pietaari Brofeldt by Holm, *Pingströrelsen*, 23.
14. The Assambléias de Deus do Brasil is today the single-largest Pentecostal movement of the world, reporting more than fourteen million members.
15. Geir Lie, ed., *Norsk Pinsekristendom og Karismatisk fornyelse: Ettbinds oppslagsverk* [Norwegian Pentecostalism and Charismatic Renewal: A one-volume dictionary], REFLEKS-serien 8 (Oslo: Refleks Publishing, 2008), 3; Bundy, *Apostolic Missions*, 255–57. This was an offshoot of the Oakland branch of the Apostolic Faith Mission.
16. Eric Emil Valdemar Olsson (1881–1959) studied at Ongman's Bible school in Örebro and became an evangelist in 1906. He later moved to the United States and continued his studies at the Northern Baptist Theological Seminary in Chicago.
17. Lewi Pethrus (1884–1974) was born Petrus L. Johansson but changed his name to Levi Petrus when he entered the army. After some time in Stockholm, he embellished his name to Lewi Pethrus, the spelling that will be used throughout the article. Pethrus came to Stockholm from the Baptist congregation in Lidköping.
18. Gunnar Westin, *Den Kristna Friförsamlingen i Norden: Frikyrklighetens uppkomst och utveckling* [The Christian Free Church in the Nordic countries: Free Church origins and developments] (Stockholm: Westerbergs, 1956), 360; Holm, *Pingströrelsen*, 21–22.
19. It is interesting to note that even though the Finnish Pentecostal movement was inspired by Barratt, the wave of rebaptism was evident long

before Barratt's own believer's baptism, which did not take place until 1913; Alvarsson, "Pingstväckelsens," 17.

20. This journal was a translation of the Norwegian *Korsets seier* (precisely "Victory of the cross"), edited by Barratt.
21. In Tampere in 1913, for the first time in Finland, the term *Pentecostal revival* was used to denote what was now conceived of as a separate revivalist movement.
22. Smidt returned to Norway and worked in Oslo as Barratt's coworker. Thereafter, he visited the United States in 1916–1917.
23. *Evangelii härold* was the unofficial journal of the Swedish Pentecostal movement from 1915 until 1993. Among the editors was Swedish poet and writer Sven Lidman (editor in chief from 1922–1948).
24. Lauri Ahonen claims that Smidt "played a part in the split"; see Lauri Ahonen, "Finland," in *New International Dictionary of Pentecostal and Charismatic Movements*, eds. Stanley M. Burgess and Eduard van der Maas (Grand Rapids: Zondervan, 2002), 103.
25. The Pentecostal Friends ceased to function in the 1990s; Ahonen, "Finland," 103.
26. Westin, *Den kristna friförsamlingen i Norden*, 365.
27. Bundy, *Apostolic Missions*, 335.
28. The public dimension was something new in the movement. It was also something that was clearly disputed. Rev. Georg Gustafsson, one of the leading pastors of the Swedish Pentecostal movement, was clearly against healing in public and remained so for the rest of his life; Nils-Eije Stävare, *Georg Gustafsson: Församlingsledare, predikant och förebedjare inom den Svenska Pingströrelsen* [Georg Gustafsson: Leader, preacher, and healer within the Swedish Pentecostal movement], Studia Historico-Ecclesiastica Upsaliensia 43 (Uppsala: Uppsala University Library, 2008), 134ff.
29. Juhani Kuosmanen, Herätyksen historia [History of the revival] (Tikkurila: Ristin Voitto, 1979), 354.
30. William Freeman visited Stockholm in January and February 1950, and William Branham was first in Finland and later in Sweden in May 1950; see Olof Djurfeldt, "Missionsintresset växte i förnyelseväckelsen" [Mission engagement grew in renewal], in Waern et al., *Pingströrelsen*, 178.
31. Lauri K. Ahonen, *Suomen helluntaiherätyksen historia* [History of the Finnish Pentecostal revival] (Hämeenlinna: Päivä oy, 1994), 147–48.

32. Ahonen, *Suomen*, 186–87; Jan-Åke Alvarsson, "Från kaffeplantage till tv-studio: Några huvuddrag i Svensk Pingstmission" [From coffee plantation to TV studio: Main features in Swedish Pentecostal mission], in *Pingströrelsen: Verksamheter och särdrag under 1900-talet* [Pentecostal movement: Activities and distinctives during the twentieth century], vol. 2, eds. Claes Waern et al. (Örebro: Libris, 2007), 163.
33. Gunilla Nyberg Oskarsson, "Fler än 340 församlingar bildade under tio år" [More than 340 congregations founded in ten years], in Waern et al., Pingströrelsen, 1.63.
34. Westin, Den kristna friförsamlingen i Norden, 365; Oddvar Nilsen,... *og Herren virket med: Pinsebevegelsen gjennom 75 år* [...And the Lord acted: The Pentecostal movement through seventy-five years] (Oslo: Filadelfiaforlaget A/S, 1981), 129.
35. Ahonen, "Finland," 104.
36. See *Evangelii härold* [The gospel herald] (June 22, 1944): 593–94.
37. Parallel to the spiritual renewal in Sweden, new commercial grounds were covered. In 1951, the Allmänna Spar-och Kreditkassan (Pentecostal Bank) was founded after an initiative by Lewi Pethrus.
38. IBRA read International Broadcasting Radio Association, but nowadays the acronym has become a trademark in its own right: Ibra Radio.
39. The name in Swedish was Lewi Pethrus stiftelse för filantropisk verksamhet and came into use in 1961, as Pethrus first refused to have his name associated with the foundation. But leader Erik Edin insisted and eventually succeeded.
40. Kuosmanen, *Herätyksen*, 358.
41. The original name was Pingstmissionens U-landshjälp (roughly Development Aid of the Pentecostal Mission), but later this was changed to Pingstmissionens utvecklingssamarbete (roughly Development Cooperation of the Pentecostal Mission), still abbreviated PMU, and in English PMU InterLife.
42. Kuosmanen, *Herätyksen*, 360.
43. See the uncredited column of data in Waern et al., *Pingströrelsen*, 2.447.
44. The Swedish name was Trossamfundet Pingst—Fria församlingar i samverkan.
45. Thomas Ball Barratt was excluded from the Methodist movement in 1909, and this had repercussions in Norway, as well as in Sweden and probably Finland.

46. The first congregation to be founded as a distinctly Pentecostal (i.e., non-Baptist) congregation in Sweden was that of Skövde in 1912. All previous ones were identified as Baptist churches. See Alvarsson, "Pingstväckelsens," 36–38.
47. Nilsen, *Herren virket*, 14–15; Göran Janzon, *'Den andra omvändelsen': Från Svensk mission till Afrikanska samfund på Örebromissionens arbetsfält i Centralafrika 1914–1962* [The second conversion: From Swedish mission to African denominations in the Örebromissionen in Central Africa 1914–1964], Studia Missionalia Svecana 62 (Örebro: Libris, 2008), 87ff.; Artur Sundstedt, *Pingstväckelsen: en världsväckelse* [The Pentecostal movement: A worldwide revival], vol. 5 (Stockholm: Normans Förlag, 1973), 62.
48. The author and volume editors are grateful to Ulrik Josefsson for his help with reformatting the references into endnotes and providing English translations of the sources.

Chapter 13
Pentecostal Movements in Norway

1. Barratt was of English origin; he had received training in music and art from Norway's finest artisans, but he decided to become a Methodist pastor. From 1892–1898, he was the presiding elder in the denomination. He was also a member of the municipal board of Oslo for the Temperance Party. See Nils Bloch-Hoell, *Pentecostal Movement: Its Origin, Development, and Distinctive Characters* (Oxford: Oxford Univ Press, 1964), 179. See also Jan-Åke Alvarsson, "En komparativ översikt av Pentekostalismens historia i Norden från 1906 till i dag" [A comparative overview of Pentecostal histories in the Nordic countries from 1906 to the present], in *Pentekostale perspektiver* [Pentecostal perspectives], eds. Knut-Willy Sæther and Karl Inge Tangen (Oslo: Fagbokforlaget, 2015), 31–60; note that this chapter is also based on interviews with eyewitnesses.
2. Bloch-Hoell, *Penecostal Movement*, 67.
3. See Paul Schmidgall, *European Pentecostalism: Its Origins, Development, and Future* (Cleveland, TN: CPT Press, 2013), chapter 5.
4. Allan Heaton Anderson, *An Introduction to Pentecostalism: Global Charismatic Christianity*, 2nd ed. (New York: Cambridge University Press, 2013), 93–95.

5. Ida Bertea Seehuus, *Erindringer* [Memories] (Oslo: Filadelfiaforlaget 1935), 63–68.
6. See also Terje Hegertun, *Det brodersind som Pinseaanden nødvendigvis maa føde: analyse av økumeniske posisjoner i Norsk Pinsebevegelse med henblikk på utviklingen av en Pentekostal økumenikk og fornyelse av økumeniske arbeidsformer* [The mind of brotherhood to which the Spirit of Pentecost with necessity must give birth: An analysis of ecumenical positions in the Pentecostal movement of Norway, regarding generating a Pentecostal ecumenism and a renewal of ecumenical methods] (Trondheim: Tapir, 2009).
7. Several preachers among the Free Friends continued to preach about baptism in the Holy Spirit and operated in charismatic gifts like healing, prophecy, and tongues and interpretation also after this; see Asbjørn Froholt, "Erik Andersen Nordquelle" (master's thesis, University of Oslo, 1981).
8. Bloch-Hoell, *Pentecostal Movement*, 74, says that there were thirty thousand Pentecostal believers in 1950.
9. Tor Edvin Dahl and John-Willy Rudolph, *Fra seier til nederlag: Pinsebevegelsen i Norge* [From victory to defeat: The Pentecostal movement in Norway] (Oslo: Land og Kirke/Gyldendal, 1978).
10. Note that some of the classic hymns actually were edited by Barratt to fit with Pentecostal theology; see *Nils Bloch-Hoell, Pinsebevegelsen: En undersøkelse av pinsebevegelsens tilblivelse, utvikling og særpreg med særlig henblikk på bevegelsens utforming i Norge* [The Pentecostal movement: Its origin, development, and distinctive character with particular emphasis on the formation of the movement in Norway] (Oslo: Universitetsforlaget, 1956), 388–89.
11. This included a remake of "Daisy Bell" with Barratt's own texts. See Dagmar Engstrøm, *Ha tro til Gud: Alt er mulig for den som tror* [Have faith in God: Everything is possible for one who believes] (Oslo: Filadelfiaforlaget, 1980), 15.
12. See Bloch-Hoell, *Pentecostal Movement*, 73.
13. Here I loosely follow Ulrik Josefsson, *Liv och övernog* [Life and abundance] (Skellefteå: Artos & Norma, 2005). Yet see my comment on the doctrine of sanctification.
14. More research needs to be done in order to confirm this hypothesis that nevertheless has been well received as I have discussed it with Scandinavian church historians.

15. See Stiftelsen Betania Alta, "Alma Halse," accessed May 25, 2015, http://www.betania-alta.no/wwwroot/htm_filer/Alma%20Halse.html.
16. In Norway, the missionary society was gradually scaled down and dissolved from 1929 to 1932. See Oddvar Nilsen, *Og Herren virket med* [The Lord worked with them] (Oslo: Filadefiaforlaget, 1981).
17. See Nilsen, *Og Herren virket med.*
18. See Martin Ski, Egil Strand, and Erling Strøm, eds., *Frem til urkristendommen* [Forward to the early church], vol. 2 (Oslo: Filadelfiaforlaget, 1955).
19. In *Korsets seier* in 1939, Barratt is actually arguing against those who call for a freer Pentecostalism; see Nilsen, *Og Herren virket med.*
20. Bloch-Hoell, *Pentecostal Movement*, 74.
21. Ibid., 73.
22. Martin Ski and his co-editors note that Oscar Halvorsen's Evangelisalen in Oslo in the 1920s was concentrating more on Spirit baptism, spiritual gifts, and healing, whereas Barratt had come to focus more on teaching; see Ski, Strand, and Strøm, *Frem til Urkristendommen*, 46.
23. See Margaret Poloma and John C. Green, *The Assemblies of God: Godly Love and the Revitalization of American Pentecostalism* (New York: New York University Press, 2010).
24. See Nilsen, *Og Herren virket med*, 270–74.
25. The problem for his friends, like Maranata pastor Peter Gylver, who tried to lead the sensitive evangelist, was that the same person who cried and asked for forgiveness in private conversations gave them a storm of hostile polemics as he entered the pulpit. See Rudolph and Dahl, *Fra seier til nederlag*, 137.
26. The following presentation draws from a number of sources, including Rudoph and Dahl, *Fra seier til nederlag*; Madelene Harris, *Drømmer blir virkeligehet: Den autentiske biografien om Aril Edvardsen* [Dreams become reality: The authentic biography of Aril Edvardsen] (Kvinnesdal: Logos Forlag 1986); and Aril Edvardsen's own books, the most important being *Meg har Gud vist* [God has shown me] (Kvinnesdal: Logos Forlag, 1974).
27. It is, for instance, well recognized that Edvardsen played an important part in the peace process in Burundi; see Erik Solheim, "Gud er tillbake i moderne storpolitikk" [God is back in international politics], in *Gud er tilbake* [God is back], eds. Silje K. Bjørndal and Karl Inge Tangen (Oslo: Frekk forlag, 2013), 114–27.

28. These churches include both Kristen Tjeneste and Kristent Felleskap; see Geir Lie, "Norsk fellesskapsbevegelse med fokus på tidlige år" [The Norwegian Fellowship movement, with focus on the early years], *Refleks* 6, no. 1 (2007): 16–45.
29. See Geir Lie, "Trosbevegelsen i Norge—en historisk gjennomgang" [The faith movement in Norway: A historic review], *Refleks* 7, no. 1 (2008): 72–104.
30. There were public meetings, but also theological dialogues with the church's pastors (Morgan Kornmo, Magne Tangen, and Tore Deila) but also older pastors, like Osvald Orlien.
31. This includes the Pentecostal World Conference in Oslo in 1992, the church growth conference in 1994, and, more importantly, the Scandinavian Revival conference in 1998 (initiated by Johannes Engeli), which also marked a public reconciliation between Aril Edvardsen and Toralf Gilbrant. See also Geir Lie, "Fra Pinsevenn eller Karismatiker til Pinsekarismatiker: Norsk Pinsekristendom og Karismatisk Fornyelse fra 1980-årene og fram til i dag" [From Pentecostal to Pentacharismatics: Norwegian Pentecostal Christianity and the Charismatic Renewal from the 1980s to the present], *Refleks* 8, no. 1 (2009): 48–63.
32. In 1995, Egil Svartdahl was elected senior pastor in Filadelfia, Oslo. He declared that the church lacked strength to be the leading church in the Pentecostal movement. As a result, the movement established an advisory committee of leaders that would represent the movement in relation to its environment and coordinate common resources. The present leader is Sigmund Kristoffersen.
33. The church still believes in and practices believer's baptism.
34. Note, however, that the Apostolic Faith churches, which were established in Norway in 1912, might be regarded as a third stream. It still has two churches in the country (Stavanger and Tromsø).
35. As Geir Lie observes, there were already charismatic elements in established free churches like the Covenant church, the Salvation Army, and among Baptists and Methodists. Moreover, there were also individual Lutheran Charismatics, like Tore Lende and Reidar Paulsen. See Geir Lie, "Norsk Karismatisk Fornyelse: en kortfattet oversikt" [The Norwegian Charismatic Renewal: A short overview], *Refleks* 7, no. 1 (2008): 35–56.
36. The Norwegian branch was fully integrated in the international organization in 1984; see Lie, "Norsk Karismatisk Fornyelse," 69.

37. See Asbjørn Simoness, "Særtrekk ved helgings: og Pinserørsla og kva betydning dei har hatt for framveksten av den Lutherske Karismatiske rørsla" [The distinctive character of the Holiness and Pentecostal movement, and their impact on the formation of the Lutheran Pentecostal movement], in Sæther and Tangen, *Pentekostale Perspektiver*, 130–31.
38. Tove Rustan Skaar, "Lovsang forener: Moderne lovsang som økumenisk spiritualitet i vår tid" [Worship unites: Modern worship music as ecumenical spirituality in our time], in *Kristen spiritualitet: Perpsektiver, tradisjoner, utrykksformer* [Christian spirituality: Perspectives, traditions, and forms of expression], ed. Knut-Willy Sæther (Trondhei: Akademika, 2013), 167–88.
39. The movement has, since its beginning, been criticized by conservative Lutherans; see Simoness, "Særtrekk ved helgings."
40. Here I follow Lie, "Fra Pinsevenn eller Karismatiker til Pinsekarismatiker," 70.
41. Migrantmeneigheter.no estimates 250, and the Dawn Report 2010 suggests 80–100 churches in the Oslo areas. However, a PhD study in progress undertaken by Stian Eriksen will show that these numbers are too low.
42. Roald Synnes, *Kristne migrantmenigheter i Oslo* [Christian migrant churches in Oslo], KIFO Report 2012.1 (Oslo: KIFO Stiftelsen Kirkeforskning, 2012), 40.
43. Stian Eriksen, personal communication with the author, based on data from Eriksen's dissertation in progress, April 2, 2015; note that Charismatic Catholics are not included in the estimation.
44. This can be seen in Barratt's work as editor in *Korset seier*, but also in his books, like *Verdens midtpunkt: Jesus Kristus* [The center of the world: Jesus Christ] (Oslo: Filadelfiaforlaget, 1926), which establishes a front against the "new" liberal theology.
45. For cultural Protestantism, see H. Richard Niebuhr, *Christ and Culture*, reprint ed. (San Francisco: Harper & Row, 1975); on the Norwegian knowledge regime (here called integration theology), see Slagstad Rune, *De nasjonale strategier* [The national strategies] (Oslo: Pax forlag, 2001), 466–75.
46. Dahl and Rudolph, *Fra seier til nederlag.*
47. As noted above, Barratt also attracted middle-class people; still he served as an apologetic leader for a working-class movement. See Rakel Ystebø Alegre, "Thomas Ball Barratt: Pinsebevegelsens apologet" [Thomas Ball

Barratt: Apologist of the Pentecostal movement], in Sæther and Tangen, *Pentekostale perspektiver*, 73–90.

48. See the chapter on Denmark by Tangen and Jacobsen in this volume.
49. James William McClendon Jr., *Systematic Theology, Volume 1: Ethics* (Abingdon Press, 2002), chapter 1, §1.
50. See David Bundy, *Visions of Apostolic Mission: Scandinavian Pentecostal Mission to 1935*, Studia Historico-Ecclesiastica Upsaliensia 45 (Uppsala: Uppsala University Library, 2009).
51. I agree with Terje Hegertun, *Det brodersind som pinseaanden nødvendigvis maa føde*, who sees Norwegian Pentecostal ecumenism in terms of a wave movement. From the formation of enthusiastic ecumenical alliances in the beginning, the movement fell into to a sort of protectionism during the Edvardsen debate in the 1970s, yet it has recently risen toward a more mature ecumenical position.
52. See Poloma and Green, *The Assemblies of God.*
53. Max Weber, *The Theory of Social And Economic Organization* (reprint; New York: The Free Press, 2009); see also Karl Inge Tangen, "Et teologisk perspektiv på Karismatisk lederskap" [A theological perspective on Charismatic leadership], in Sæther and Tangen, *Pentekostale perspektiver*, 221–40.
54. Thomas Ball Barratt, *Erindringer* [Memories] (Oslo: Filadelfiaforlaget, 1941), 95.
55. See Max Weber, "The Protestant Sects and the Spirit of Capitalism," in *From Max Weber: Essays in Sociology*, eds. Hans H. Gerth and C. Wright Mills (London: Routledge, 1991), 302–22.
56. The conversion of Swedish faith movement leader Ulf Ekman to the Roman Catholic Church has also received much attention in Norway.
57. For the fluidity of late modernity, see Zygmunt Bauman, *Liquid Modernity* (Stafford, UK: Polity, 2000).
58. Steven Jack Land, *Pentecostal Spirituality: A Passion for the Kingdom* (reprint; Cleveland, TN: CPT Press, 2010).
59. For an overview of such approaches, see Christopher A. Stephenson, *Types of Pentecostal Theology: Method, System, Spirit* (New York: Oxford University Press, 2012). One should also consider Veli-Matti Kärkkäinen, *Christ and Reconciliation: A Constructive Christian Theology for the Pluralistic World*, vol. 1 (Grand Rapids: Eerdmans, 2013).

60. This observation was recently made by the Norwegian minister of education and research, Torbjørn Røe Isaksen. See Torbjørn Røe Isaksen, "Morgenbladet: Politisk (u)korrekt," February 6, 2015, accessed May 28, 2015, http://konservativ.no/2015/02/morgenbladet-politisk-ukorrekt/.
61. For an interesting contribution to such fundamental questions, see James K. A. Smith, *Desiring the Kingdom: Worship, Worldview, and Cultural Formation* (Grand Rapids: Baker Academic, 2009).
62. Different alternatives may be found in Amos Yong, *Spirit—Word—Community: Theological Hermeneutics in Trinitarian Perspective* (Burlington, VT: Ashgate, 2002); and Mark J. Cartledge, *Practical Theology: Charismatic and Empirical Perspectives* (Eugene, OR: Wipf & Stock, 2012).
63. The perhaps most burning question in the area of sexual ethics is: Who are "least of these brothers and sisters" of mine? Is it practicing homosexuals or transsexual people, who undoubtedly have been marginalized as sinners in the history of Pentecostal churches? Or is it people with homosexual orientation who, due to their consciousness, choose to live in celibacy or even seek "reorientation" and who are perceived as "traitors" by the gay community and often are disregarded and marginalized by those who otherwise use the rhetoric of an inclusive church?
64. For such an alternative social imaginary, see Judith Butler, *Undoing Gender* (London: Routledge, 2004). For internal debates in queer theology, see Susannah Cornwall and Lisa Isherwood, *Controversies in Queer Theology* (London: SCM Press, 2011).
65. Amos Yong, *Hospitality and the Other: Pentecost, Christian Practices, and the Neighbor* (Maryknoll, NY: Orbis Books, 2008); see also Luke Bretherton, *Hospitality as Holiness* (Aldershot, UK: Ashgate, 2010).
66. Philip Jenkins, *The Next Christendom: The Coming of Global Christianity*, 3rd ed. (Oxford: Oxford University Press, 2011).

Chapter 14
Pentecostal and Charismatic Movements in Denmark and Iceland

1. Nils Bloch-Hoell, *Pentecostal Movement: Its Origin, Development, and Distinctive Characters* (Oxford: Oxford University Press, 1964).
2. Håkon Hansen, *Anna Larssen Bjørnar* (Oslo: Filadelfiaforlaget, 1950).
3. See Jan-Åke Alvarsson, "En komparativ översikt av Pentekostalismens historia i Norden från 1906 til i dag" [A comparative overview of Pentecostal histories in the Nordic countries from 1906 to the present], in

Pentekostale perspektiver [Pentecostal perspectives], eds. Knut-Willy Sæther and Karl Inge Tangen (Oslo: Fagbokforlaget, 2015), 36.

4. Pinsekirken says in their historical self-presentation that the church was established in 1926 (http://www.kirkenikulturcenteret.dk, accessed April 1, 2015).
5. Jan-Åke Alvarsson, "En komparativ översikt," 40.
6. Later theological accounts, such as those of Lorenzen and Hansen, seem to fall in with a fourfold pattern; see Alfred Lorenzen, *Veien til Åndens kraft* [The way to the power of the Spirit] (Oslo: Filadelfiaforlaget, 1987); and Johannes Hansen, "Apostolisk Kirke" [The Apostolic Church], in *Kristne kirkesamfund i Danmark* [Christian denominations in Denmark], eds. Birgitte Larsen and Peter Lodberg (Århus: Anis, 1997), 145–53. Barratt's key role in the early movement may indicate that there may have been some influence of the fivefold gospel in the early days (including sanctification as a distinct experience). The somewhat surprising absence of any strong doctrinal conflict on the issue of sanctification in Scandinavia in general calls for further research but may probably be explained by the strong personal alliance between Pethrus and Barratt.
7. See T. Jacobsen, J. E. Jacobsen, and L. Ahonen, "Denmark," in *New International Dictionary of Pentecostal Charismatic Movements*, eds. Stanley M. Burgess and Eduard M. van der Maas (Grand Rapids: Zondervan, 2002), 80.
8. Thomas Ball Barratt, "Om den 'Apostoliska Kyrkan' i Danmark" [The "Apostolic Church" in Denmark], *Evangelii härold* [Herald of the gospel] 40 (October 1, 1931): 674; see also Geir Lie, "Apostler og apostletjeneste i internasjonal pinsekirstendom" [Apostles and apostolic ministry in international Pentecostalism], *Refleks* 1, no. 1 (2002): 3–11.
9. See Jacobsen, Jacobsen, and Ahonen, "Denmark," 80.
10. Traditionally, decisions could not be made before the prophet had confirmed it. See Apostolsk Kirke: Danmark, "Om Netværket," accessed April 6, 2015, http://apostolskkirke.dk/index.php?id=10.
11. Ibid. The five ministries that lead the movement are elected every second year, though most decisions are made locally.
12. Jacobsen, Jacobsen, and Ahonen, "Denmark," 80.
13. Here and the rest of this paragraph derive from Jacobsen, Jacobsen, and Ahonen, "Denmark."
14. See www.kirkenikulturcenteret.dk.

15. See Alfred Lorenzen, *Forbønnens hensikt og makt* [The purpose and power of intercession] (Oslo: Filaelfiaforlaget, 1982).
16. See Lorenzen, *Veien til Åndens kraft*, 46.
17. Ibid., 56.
18. Ibid., 81–82.
19. See Phil Zuckerman, "Why Are Danes and Swedes So Irreligious?" *Nordic Journal of Religion and Society* 22, no. 1 (2009): 55–69.
20. See Karl Inge Tangen, *Ecclesial Identification Beyond Late Modern Individualism?* (Leiden: Brill, 2012).
21. For example, in Ib Sørensen, "Leg med ilden: Pentekostale trosfællesskaber og problematiske omverdensrelationer" [Playing with fire: Pentecostal faith communities and problematic social relations] (PhD dissertation, Syddansk Universitet, 2010), two of three case churches were not members.
22. This happened in a Holiness meeting in Germany with R. A. Torrey. See Hans Kristian Neerskov, "Karismatisk Fornyelse i Danmark" [The Charismatic Renewal in Denmark], in *Karismatisk Fornyelese i Danmark* [The Charismatic Renewal in Denmark], ed. Hans K. Neerskov (Aarhus: ProRex Foralg, 2008), 9.
23. Stig Torben Christensen, "Dansk Oase" [Danish Oase], in Neerskov, *Karismatisk Fornyelese i Danmark*, 127.
24. Ibid., 129.
25. Helge Pahus, "Løftet om Helligånden" [The promise of the Holy Spirit], in Neerskov, *Karismatisk Fornyelese i Danmark*, 41–56.
26. This included Give, Sønderborg, Karlslunde, and Silkeborg; see Hakon Bojsen, "Fornyelsen i Silkeborg kirke" [The renewal in the church of Silkeborg], in Neerskov, *Karismatisk Fornyelese i Danmark*, 57–62.
27. Christensen, "Dansk Oase," 132; see also Levi E. Dørken, "Dansk Oase: den grimme ælling blandt vækkelseskristne?" [Danish Oase: The ugly duckling among revival Christians?] (BA thesis, Det Danske menighedsfakultet, 2009), 7.
28. Dørken, "Dansk Oase," 26; cf. Levi Dørken, "Dansk Oase: den grimme ælling blandt vækkelsesbevægelserne?" [Danish Oase: The ugly duckling among revival Christians?], *Dansk tidsskrift for teologi og kirke* [Danish journal for theology and church] 37, no. 4 (2010): 37–48.

29. Filadelfia.fo, "Um Filadelfia," October 27, 2008, accessed April 7, 2015, http://filadelfia.fo/index.php?option=com_content&view=article&id=54&Itemid=74.
30. Jogvan Lamhauge, personal communication with the author.
31. See Alvarsson, "En komparativ översikt," 40. The decline of the emerging movement may have caused moral failures associated with the first leaders that discredited the movement; pastor Helgi Gudnason, personal communication with the author.
32. I. Ahonen with T. Birgisson, "Iceland," in Burgess and van der Maas, *New International Dictionary of Pentecostal and Charismatic Movements*, 117.
33. A group of believers was actually established in 1921, but it became a formal church in 1924; Helgi Gudnason, personal communication with the author.
34. In 2004, it was the third largest movment, but at the moment is the fourth largest; Helgi Gudnason, personal communication with the author.
35. For an elaboration of these claims, see Tonny Jacobsen, "The Process of Christian Conversion and Discipleship Within a Post-Christendom, Postmodern Context With Special Reference to Evangelical-Charismatic, Free Churches in Denmark" (PhD thesis, University of Wales, Trinity St. David, 2010).
36. Kirkeministeriet, "Kirkestatistik," accessed May 20, 2015, http://www.km.dk/kirke/kirkestatistik. The numbers of churchgoers are not counted, with estimates oscillating between 2 to 4 percent on a given Sunday; see Trine Bille et al., *Danskernes kultur- og fritidsaktiviteter 2004: med udviklingslinjer tilbage til 1964* [Danish culture and leisure activities 2004: With historical lines back to 1964] (København: AFK-Forlaget, 2005), 232–36.
37. For a contemporary introduction to the apostolic tradition, see Alan Kreider, ed., *The Origins of Christendom in the West* (Edinburgh: T&T Clark, 2001).

Chapter 15
Pentecostalism in the United Kingdom: Retrospect and Prospect

1. See, for instance, John Stevenson, *The Pelican Social History of Britain: British Society 1914–45* (Harmondsworth: Penguin Books, 1984); David Thomson, *England in the Twentieth Century*, 2nd ed. by Geoffrey Warner

(Harmondsworth: Penguin, 1981); Arthur Marwick, *A History of the Modern British Isles, 1914–1999* (London: John Wiley & Sons, 2000).

2. The best book in English on the Welsh revival is R. Tudur Jones, *Faith and the Crisis of a Nation: Wales 1890–1914* (Cardiff: University of Wales Press, 2004). This is a book that was originally written in Welsh and makes extensive use of Welsh sources.
3. *Confidence* 7, no. 11 (November 1914): 208, 209, 212–14.
4. These can be found scattered in *Confidence* magazine, which was edited by Alexander Boddy. The magazine has been digitized and is available at www.revival-library.org.
5. Gavin Wakefield, *Alexander Boddy: Pentecostal Anglican Pioneer* (London: Paternoster, 2007). Additional information is given in the entry on Alexander Boddy in the Oxford Dictionary of National Biography at www.oxforddnb.com.
6. *Confidence* is still the best source for understanding Pentecostalism in Britain in the years before 1914. There were no other magazines with a similar range and reach because Boddy ensured that *Confidence* contained reports from all over the country as well as internationally. The contribution of women is shown by the number of articles (often printed versions of sermons) by female preachers as well as by occasional allusions to the biblical justification for female ministry.
7. See James Robinson, *Divine Healing: The Years of Expansion, 1906–1930* (Eugene, OR: Pickwick Publications, 2014).
8. A. S. Booth-Clibborn, *Blood Against Blood*, 3rd ed. (1907; reprint, New York: Charles Cook, 1914).
9. Leigh Goodwin, "The Response of Early British Pentecostals to National Conscription During the Great War (1914–1918)," *JEPTA: The Journal of the European Pentecostal Theological Association* 34 (2014): 77–92.
10. A brief history with bibliography of the Apostolic Church is given by W. K. Kay, "Apostolic Church," in *The New International Dictionary of Pentecostal and Charismatic Movements*, eds. Stanley M. Burgess and Eduard M. van der Maas (Grand Rapids: Eerdmans, 2002), 322, 323.
11. Doncaster Pentecostal Church's own identity became clearer after 1924 when Assemblies of God was formed, and it was less frequently dubbed Christian Scientist or confused with the spiritualists. See, more generally, W. R. Inge, *Lay Thoughts of a Dean* (London: Puttenham's Sons, 1926).
12. In the January 1939 issue of *Redemption Tidings* (the official journal of Assemblies of God in Britain), John Carter wrote on "The Christian's

Attitude to War," and he stoutly defended the position of the conscientious objector and argued that "in the last war voices were confused, some religious leaders maintaining that it was the duty of all young men to enlist in the fighting ranks," but, so far as he was concerned, "the soul's allegiance to God must ever take precedence over our obligation to the State."

13. Billy Graham, *Just as I Am* (London: HarperCollins, 1998), 208.
14. William K. Kay, *Inside Story* (Mattersey Hall, UK: Mattersey Hall Publishing, 1990).
15. See also the entry on George Jeffreys in the Oxford Dictionary of National Biography at www.oxforddnb.com. No full life story of Jeffreys has yet been written, although the present author has started on the task. For an insightful chapter, see Neil Hudson and Andrew Walker, "George Jeffreys, Revivalist and Reformer: A Revaluation," in *On Revival: A Critical Examination*, eds. Andrew Walker and Kristin Aune (Carlisle, UK: Paternoster, 2003), 137–56.
16. William K. Kay, "Pentecostalism and Fundamentalism," in *Evangelicalism and Fundamentalism*, eds. David Bebbington and David Ceri Jones (Oxford: Oxford University Press, 2013), 309–27.
17. *Elim Evangel* 6, no. 1 (January 1, 1925): 14.
18. George Jeffreys, *Healing Rays* (London: Elim Publishing Company, 1932), 154.
19. Gordon Weeks, *Chapter Thirty-Two: Part of the History of the Apostolic Church, 1900–2000* (Barnsley, UK: Prontaprint, 2003), 62.
20. Gee's first book, *Concerning Spiritual Gifts,* was published in 1928; *The Ministry Gifts of Christ* followed in 1930 and *Concerning Shepherds and Sheepfolds* in the same year. They were published by various publishers. A biography of Gee by someone who knew him can be found in Richard Massey, *Another Springtime: Donald Gee, Pentecostal Pioneer—A Biography* (Guildford, UK: Highland Books, 1992).
21. Various Church of God groupings belong to the Evangelical Alliance in the United Kingdom.
22. See the European Values Study at www.europeanvaluesstudy.eu.
23. For a general account of the Charismatic movement in Britain, see Peter Hocken, *Streams of Renewal: Origins and Early Development of the Charismatic Movement in Great Britain* (Carlisle, UK: Paternoster, 1997). See also Michael Harper, *As at the Beginning* (London: Hodder & Stoughton, 1974).

24. William K. Kay, *Apostolic Networks in Britain* (Carlisle, UK: Paternoster, 2007).
25. In 1971, the African population of Britain stood at about 75,000, but by 2001 this had risen to around 500,000. See D. Coleman, "The Demographic Consequences of Immigration to the United Kingdom," in *Work in Progress: Migration, Integration, and the European Labour Market*, ed. H. Disney (London: Institute for the Study of Civil Society, 2003), 9–40.
26. See, for instance, Richard Burgess, "African Pentecostal Spirituality and Civic Engagement: The Case of the Redeemed Christian Church of God in Britain," *Journal of Beliefs and Values* 30, no. 3 (2009): 255–73.
27. H. Womersley, *Wm F.W. Burton: Congo Pioneer* (London: Victory Press, 1973). See also David Maxwell, "Photography and the Religious Encounter: Ambiguity and Aesthetics in Missionary Representations of the Luba of South East Belgian Congo," *Comparative Studies in Society and History* 53, no. 1 (2011): 38–74; David Maxwell "Freed Slaves, Missionaries, and Respectability: The Expansion of the Christian Frontier From Angola to Belgian Congo," *Journal of African History* 54 (2013): 79–102.
28. S. David Moore, *The Shepherding Movement: Controversy and Charismatic Ecclesiology* (London: T & T Clark, 2003).
29. Malcolm R Hathaway, "The Elim Pentecostal Church: Origins, Development, and Distinctives," in *Pentecostal Perspectives*, ed. Keith Warrington (Carlisle, UK: Paternoster, 1998), 1–39.
30. William K. Kay, "British Assemblies of God in the 1930s," *Paraclete* 22, no. 4 (1988): 22–26. As further evidence, note the hymn "Hold the Fort, for I Am Coming" contains the line "See the mighty host advancing, Satan leading on."
31. Andrew Walker, *Restoring the Kingdom: The Radical Christianity of the House Church Movement* (Guildford, UK: Eagle, 1998), is relevant here.
32. See Callum G. Brown, *The Death of Christian Britain* (London: Routledge, 2001); or Steve Bruce, *God Is Dead: Secularization in the West* (Oxford: Blackwell, 2002).
33. Babatunde Adedibu, "Migration, Identity, and Marginalisation: The Case of Britain's Black Majority Churches," *Journal of Africana Religions* 2 no. 1 (2014): 110–17.
34. For a theological unpacking of the work of the Spirit, see Graham Tomlin, *The Prodigal Spirit* (London: St Paul's Theological Centre, 2011). Tomlin is dean of St. Mellitus College, which has connections with Holy

Trinity Brompton, a leading Anglican Charismatic church in London and the organizing center of the Alpha Course.

Chapter 16
The Origins and Development of the Assemblies of God in the Republic of Ireland: Exploring the Opportunities and Challenges That Pentecostalism Faces in the Island of "Saints and Scholars" in the Twenty-First Century

1. Tom Inglis, *Moral Monopoly* (Dublin: University College Dublin Press, 1998), 15.
2. Ibid., 17.
3. Ibid., 205.
4. M. O'Connell, *Changed Utterly: Ireland and the New Irish Psyche* (Dublin: The Liffey Press, 2001), 72.
5. Central Statistics Office, *Profile 7: Religion, Ethnicity, and Irish Travellers* (Dublin: Government of Ireland, October 2012).
6. Central Statistics Office, 2012.
7. Other studies in the Irish context that focus in part on the Pentecostal community are as follows: David Carnduff, *Ireland's Lost Heritage* (Ireland: IPBC, 2003); Robert Dunlop, ed., *Evangelicals in Ireland: An Introduction* (Dublin: The Columba Press, 2004); James Robinson, *Pentecostal Origins: Early Pentecostalism in the Context of the British Isles* (Eugene, OR: Wipf & Stock, 2005); and Abel Ugba, *Shades of Belonging: African Pentecostals in Twenty-First-Century Ireland* (Trenton, NJ: Africa World Press, 2009).
8. Stanley Burgess and Eduard van der Maas, eds., *The New International Dictionary of Pentecostal and Charismatic Movements* (Grand Rapids: Zondervan, 2002), xx; see also Assemblies of God Great Britain, "How It All Started," accessed November 15, 2014, http://www.aog.org.uk/about-us/how-it-all-started.
9. Statistics retrieved from *Irish Christian Handbook* (London: Marc Europe, 1992), 37. Statistics are revised annually in the January issue of *International Bulletin of Missionary Research* 12 (July 1988), with detailed calculations from David Barrett and Todd Johnson; see also Burgess and van der Maas, *New International Dictionary*, 284–90.
10. Respondent 34, interview with author.

11. Respondents 34, 45, 46, 49, and 50, interviews with author. Data gathered from recorded speeches from the official launch of the Assemblies of God Ireland at University College Dublin (November 2005).
12. Carnduff, *Ireland's Lost Heritage*, 3.
13. Respondents 10, 11, 12, 15, 17, 20, 33, 34, 36, 37, 45, 46, 47, 48, 49, and 50, interviews with author.
14. The work of IBI began in 1982, and its vision is to see vibrant, gospel-centered churches making an impact for Christ across Ireland. Its mission is to serve the Irish church through commitment to excellence in biblical education and leadership development. IBI is an accredited third-level college that has validation from York St. John's University in England, and it offers a range of validated courses, from certificate level up to master's awards. It is the only nondenominational Christian college in the Republic of Ireland that offers BA and MA degrees in applied theology, along with degrees in transformational leadership and youth ministry. The rich diversity of the students and the staff contributes to the core ethos of IBI—that of educating people "head, hands and heart": informing the head while nourishing the heart that leads to applying the gospel in everyday life.
15. Notes adapted from Thomas Flynn, *The Charismatic Renewal and the Irish Experience* (London: Hodder and Stoughton, 1974), 31–50.
16. Fergus Ryan, "Re-staging Ireland's Christian Drama," in *Evangelicals in Ireland: An Introduction*, ed. Robert Dunlop (Dublin: The Columba Press, 2004), 25–28.
17. Dermot Keogh, *Twentieth-Century Ireland* (Ireland: Gill & Macmillan, 1994), 340.
18. Kevin and Dorothy Ranaghan, *Catholic Pentecostals* (New York: Paulist Press, 1969). See Charles B. Lamb, *Path of Hope in Ireland* (Dublin: CBL Services, 1983).
19. For further information on the CCR, see www.charismaticrenewal.ie; www.catholicireland.net; www.irishcatholic.ie; and the website of the Irish school of evangelism, http://www.esatclear.ie/~isoe/.
20. The Irish Centre for Immigration Studies and the University College Cork. See also https://www.ucc.ie/en/iss21/clusters/migration/ (accessed July 21, 2016). The mapping project at the Trinity Immigration Initiative, Trinity College Dublin (see http://www.tcd.ie/immigration/css/downloads/Mapping_final12.08.09.pdf), is similar to an earlier project completed by the Migrant Rights Centre of Ireland, the Immigrant Council of Ireland, and

the All-Ireland Churches Consultative Committee on Racism (AICCMR), the Directory of Migrant-Led Churches 2009. The research conducted by Dr. Livingstone Thompson and Dr. Alan Bruce led to the publication of AICCMR Directory of Migrant-Led Churches 2008.

21. See William H. Marnell, *Light From the West: The Irish Mission and the Emergence of Modern Europe* (New York: Seabury Press, 1978); Thomas Cahill, *How the Irish Saved Civilization: The Untold Story of Ireland's Heroic Role From the Fall of Rome to the Rise of Medieval Europe* (New York: Doubleday, 1995); and Philip Freeman, *The World of St. Patrick* (Oxford: Oxford University Press, 2014).

Chapter 17
Women in Pentecostalism in Europe

1. Lisa P. Stephenson, *Dismantling the Dualisms for American Pentecostal Women in Ministry: A Feminist-Pneumatological Approach* (Leiden: Brill, 2011), 60. Stephenson mentions the research of scholars such as Charles H. Barfoot and Gerald T. Sheppard, as well as Margaret Poloma and David Roebuck, as examples of this approach. See also Estrelda Alexander, "The Future of Women in Ministry," in Vinson Synan, ed., *Spirit-Empowered Christianity in the Twenty-First Century* (Lake Mary, FL: Charisma House, 2011), 375–78.
2. Stephenson, *Dismantling the Dualisms*, 64. Stephenson mentions the research of scholars Edith L. Blumhofer and Grant Wacker as examples of this approach.
3. See, for example, Alexander, "The Future of Women in Ministry," 375–99.
4. See Grant Wacker, "Are the Golden Oldies Still Worth Playing? Reflections on History Writing Among Early Pentecostals," *Pneuma: The Journal of the Society for Pentecostal Studies* 8, no. 2 (1986): 95.
5. Allan Anderson, *To the Ends of the Earth: Pentecostalism and the Transformation of World Christianity* (New York: Oxford University Press, 2013), 98.
6. See, for example, Estrelda Alexander, *Limited Liberty: The Legacy of Four Pentecostal Women Pioneers* (Cleveland, OH: Pilgrim Press, 2008); Estrelda Alexander and Amos Yong, eds. *Philip's Daughters: Women in Pentecostal-Charismatic Leadership* (Eugene, OR: Pickwick Publications, 2009); and Jennifer A. Miskov, *Life on Wings: The Forgotten Life and Theology of Carrie Judd Montgomery (1858–1946)* (Cleveland, TN: CPT Press, 2012).

7. Nils Bloch-Hoell, *Pinsebevegelsen* [The Pentecostal movement] (Oslo: Universitetsforlaget, 1956), 267; Vinson Synan, *Century of the Holy Spirit: Charismatic Movements in the Twentieth Century* (Nashville: Thomas Nelson, 2001), 75–76; Allan Anderson, *An Introduction to Pentecostalism: Global Charismatic Christianity* (New York: Cambridge University Press, 2004), 84–92; Anne E. Dyer, introduction to *European Pentecostalism*, eds. William K. Kay and Anne E. Dyer (Leiden: Brill, 2011), 9.
8. Thomas Ball Barratt, *When the Fire Fell, and an Outline of My Life* (Oslo: Alfons Hansen & Sønner, 1927), 103–9; and David Bundy, "Spiritual Advice to a Seeker: Letters to T. B. Barratt From Azusa Street, 1906," *Pneuma: The Journal of the Society for Pentecostal Studies* 14 (1992): 164. Significantly, the first person he corresponded with at Azusa Street was a woman, Mrs. I. May Throop.
9. Barratt, *When the Fire Fell, and an Outline*, 128.
10. Thomas Ball Barratt, *When the Fire Fell: Or God's Dealings With One of His Children* (Sunderland: n.p., 1907), 23. This comment indicating struggles with asking a woman for prayer only appears in his first account of the experience and is taken out in later editions. See, for example, Barratt, *When the Fire Fell, and an Outline*, 128.
11. Barratt, *When the Fire Fell, and an Outline*, 129–30.
12. See Martin Ski, *T. B. Barratt: Døpt i ånd og ild* [T. B. Barratt: Baptized in Spirit and fire] (Oslo: Filadelfiaforlaget, 1979), 44–45, 52, 57–58; Barratt, *When the Fire Fell, and an Outline*, 105, 202; David Bundy, *Visions of Apostolic Mission: Scandinavian Pentecostal Mission to 1935*, Studia Historico-Ecclesiastica Upsaliensia 45 (Uppsala: Uppsala Universitet, 2009), 154, 341; and Martin Ski, *Fram til Urkristendommen: Pinsevekkelsen gjennom 50 år* [Towards primitive Christianity: The Pentecostal revival through fifty years], vol. 2 (Oslo: Filadelfiaforlaget, 1957), 9–11.
13. Ski, *T. B. Barratt*, 152; and Laura Barratt, *Minner* [Memories] (Oslo: Filadelfiaforlaget, 1946), 18–19.
14. Ski, *Fram til Urkristendommen*, 9–11.
15. Bloch-Hoell, *Pinsebevegelsen*, 273–74; and Bundy, *Visions of Apostolic Mission*, 195–210.
16. Ralph Meier, "Fra Kristiania til Kassel: Pinsebevegelsens begynnelse i Tyskland og forholdet til Gemeinschaftsbevegelsen" [From Christiania to Kassel: The Pentecostal movement's beginning in Germany and its relation to the *Gemeinschaft* movement], in *Pentekostale perspektiver*

[Pentecostal perspectives], eds. Knut-Willy Sæther and Karl Inge Tangen (Bergen: Fagbokforlaget, 2015), 96–97.

17. Ibid., 98.
18. Ibid., 99.
19. Carl Simpson, "The Development of Pentecostal and Charismatic Movements in the Germanic Countries," in Kay and Dyer, *European Pentecostalism* (Leiden: Brill, 2011), 80–81.
20. Bundy, *Visions of Apostolic Mission*, 212.
21. *Confidence* (June 1908): 11, 16–17, 21–22.
22. Bloch-Hoell, *Pinsebevegelsen*, 204.
23. Diana Chapman, "The Rise and Demise of Women's Ministry in the Origins and Early Years of Pentecostalism in Britain," *Journal of Pentecostal Theology* 12, no. 2 (2004): 217–46; Diana Chapman, "The Role of Women in Early Pentecostalism, 1907–1914," *JEPTA: The Journal of the European Pentecostal Theological Association* 28, no. 2 (2008): 131–44.
24. Chapman "The Role of Women," 133.
25. Ibid., 134.
26. Gavin Wakefield, *Alexander Boddy: Pentecostal Anglican Pioneer*, Studies in Pentecostal and Charismatic Issues (London: Paternoster, 2007), 84.
27. Ibid., 87–89.
28. Chapman, "The Role of Women," 135–36.
29. Chapman, "The Rise and Demise of Women's Ministry," 226–28; and *Confidence* (June 1908): 4–22. Some of the women that ministered were, as we have seen, Dagmar Gregersen, Agnes Thelle, Laura Barratt, and Mary Boddy, but there were also others, such as Lydia Walshaw and Miss Elisabeth Sisson.
30. Chapman, "The Role of Women," 137–40.
31. Chapman, "The Rise and Demise of Women's Ministry," 219–24.
32. Anna Larssen Bjørner, *Teater og tempel: Livserindringer* [Theater and temple: Memoirs] (Copenhagen: H. Hirschsprungs Forlag, 1935), 94.
33. Ibid., 95–98.
34. Bloch-Hoell, *Pinsebevegelsen*, 271; Barratt, *When the Fire Fell, and an Outline*, 172.
35. Bjørner, *Teater og tempel*, 111–18.
36. Barratt, *When the Fire Fell, and an Outline*, 173; Bundy, *Visions of Apostolic Mission*, 197–98.

37. Barratt, *When the Fire Fell, and an Outline*, 184–85.
38. Bundy, *Visions of Apostolic Mission*, 197–98. When she married (in 1912), she changed her name to Anna Larssen Bjørner.
39. Cornelis van der Laan, "The Development of Pentecostalism in Dutch-Speaking Countries," in Kay and Dyer, *European Pentecostalism*, 85.
40. Ibid., 86.
41. Jan-Åke Alvarsson, "The Development of Pentecostalism in Scandinavian Countries," in Kay and Dyer, *European Pentecostalism*, 22.
42. van der Laan, "The Development of Pentecostalism," 109–10.
43. Anderson, *To the Ends of the Earth*, 101; Ski, *Fram til Urkristendommen*, 11–12.
44. Chapman, "The Role of Women," 131.
45. Bundy, *Visions of Apostolic Mission*, 211.
46. Kyu-Hyung Cho, "The Move to Independence From Anglican Leadership: An Examination of the Relationship between Alexander Alfred Boddy and the Early Leaders of the British Pentecostal Denominations (1907–1930)" (PhD dissertation, University of Birmingham, 2009), 70.
47. Bundy, *Visions of Apostolic Mission*, 418.
48. Chapman, "The Role of Women," 142; *Confidence* (November 1914): 208–14.
49. Chapman, "The Rise and Demise of Women's Ministry," 231–32.
50. Ibid., 233; see also *Confidence* (November 1914): 213.
51. Wakefield, *Alexander Boddy*, 125.
52. Thomas Ball Barratt, *Kvinnens stilling i menigheten* [Woman's position in the church], 2nd ed. (Oslo: Filadelfiaforlaget, 1980), 29.
53. Ibid., 9–19, 25.
54. Ibid., 18–19.
55. Ibid., 19–25, 38.
56. Ibid., 26, 30, 33–34, 39.
57. Ibid., 31–32, 40.
58. Ibid., 8–9, 29–31.
59. Ski, *Fram til Urkristendommen*, 9–11.
60. Alvarsson, "The Development of Pentecostalism in Scandinavian Countries," 37.
61. Ski, *Fram til Urkristendommen*, 8–11. Few other churches adopted this model, and most did not permit women on the board.
62. Ibid.

63. Kirsti Thuseth Gunnestad, "Kvinner i lederskap i Pinsebevegelsen i Norge: En undersøkelse av endringer i synet på kvinner i eldste-og forstandertjenesten i Pinsebevegelsen i Norge" [Women in leadership in the Pentecostal movement in Norway: An investigation into changes in the view of women as elders and pastors in the Pentecostal movement in Norway], in Sæther and Tangen, *Pentekostale perspektiver*, 210.
64. Nils-Olov Nilsson, "The Debate on Women's Ministry: Summary and Analysis," *Cyberjournal for Pentecostal-Charismatic Research* 5 (1999), available at http://www.pctii.org/cyberj/cyberj5/nilsson1.html (accessed March 25, 2015).
65. Alvarsson, "The Development of Pentecostalism in Scandinavian Countries," 34.
66. Nilsson, "The Debate on Women's Ministry."
67. Gunnestad, "Kvinner i lederskap," 212.
68. Nilsson, "The Debate on Women's Ministry"; see Ole-Georg Hoaas and Oddvar Tegnander, *Kvinnen—fri til tjeneste?* [Women—free to minister?] (Oslo: Filadelfiaforlaget, 1984).
69. Thoralf Gilbrant, *"Her er ikke mann og kvinne"* ["There is neither male or female"] (Oslo: Rex Forlag, 1995), 41–42, 167–79.
70. Alvarsson, "The Development of Pentecostalism in Scandinavian Countries," 34.
71. Gunnestad, "Kvinner i lederskap," 214.
72. Jenny Bergh and Anethe Carlson, "Jämställdhet i pingströrelsen: Informella och formella hinder för kvinnor" [Equality in the Pentecostal movement: informal and formal barriers for women] (2013); available online at: http://www.pingstung.se/91-nyheter/100927-las-pingst-ungs-rapport-om-jamstalldheten-i-pingstrorelsen (accessed June 29, 2016).
73. Torbjørg Oline Nyli, "Etterlysning kvinner" [Women wanted], *Korsets Seier* (February 7, 2014): 36.
74. Ingvild Ofte Arntsen, "Mannsdominert bevegelse" [Male-dominated movement], *Korsets Seier* (November 28, 2014): 26; William Fuglset, "Pinsefeministen" [The Pentecostal feminist], *Korsets Seier* (November 28, 2014): 4–6.
75. Anders Myklebust, "Krever kvinnekvote hos Pinsevenner" [Demands quota of women among Pentecostals], *Vårt land* [Our land] (November 29, 2014); William Fuglset, "Pinsepastorer vurderer kvotering" [Pentecostal pastors consider quotas], *Korsets seier* (January 16, 2015): 12–13.

76. Sigmund Kristoffersen and Andreas Hegertun, "Kvinner ønsket" [Women wanted], *Korsets seier* (December 19, 2014): 30; Lars Christian Gjerlaug, "'Jenteprat' med sjefen" ["Girl talk" with the boss], *Korsets seier* (December 19, 2014): 2; Karl Andreas Jahr "Kvinnebevegelsen" [The women's movement], *Korsets seier* (February 20, 2015): 18–21.
77. According to Jean-Daniel Plüss, most European Pentecostal denominations today have women in pastoral ministry, although their number is now relatively small; Jean-Daniel Plüss, "Pentecostal Theology and Protestant Europe," in Kay and Dyer, *European Pentecostalism*, 30; see also Stephenson, *Dismantling the Dualisms*, 56–57. Concerning other dynamics that currently limit Pentecostal women's ministry in the United States, see Kimberly Ervin Alexander and James P. Bowers, *What Women Want: Pentecostal Women Ministers Speak for Themselves* (Lanham, MD: The Seymour Press, 2013).
78. This diversity is demonstrated in Kay and Dyer, *European Pentecostalism*.
79. Gunnestad, "Kvinner i lederskap," 215–19.
80. Alexander, "The Future of Women in Ministry," 397–98.
81. See the analysis and discussion of these factors in Alexander and Bowers, *What Women Want*.

Chapter 18
Canadian Pentecostals: Between a "Rock" (United States) and a "Hard Place" (Britain) Versus "Come Out From Among Them"

1. Michael Gauvreau, "Protestantism Transformed: Personal Piety and the Evangelical Social Vision, 1815–1867," in *The Canadian Protestant Experience 1760–1990*, ed. George A. Rawlyk (Montreal: McGill-Queen's University Press, 1990), 87.
2. Phyllis D. Airhart, "Ordering a New Nation and Reordering Protestantism 1867–1914," in Rawlyk, *The Canadian Protestant Experience*, 113–114. That Pentecostalism took advantage of this enmeshment of Christianity with the state is evident from the establishment of a tax-funded Pentecostal separate school system in the new province of Newfoundland when this province was founded in 1949.
3. Kevin J. Christiano, "Church and State in Institutional Flux," in *Rethinking Church, State, and Modernity: Canada Between Europe and America*, eds. David Lyon and Marguerite Van Die (Toronto: University of Toronto Press, 2000), 71–72.
4. Ibid., 73.

5. Charles Taylor, "Can Canada Survive the Charter?," *Alberta Law Review* 30, no. 2 (1992): 445, as quoted by Christiano, "Church and State in Institutional Flux," 86.
6. Sam Reimer, "Evangelical Subcultures in Canada and the United States," in Lyon and Van Die, *Rethinking Church, State, and Modernity*, 228–248, 235, and 237.
7. Nancy Christie, "'In These Times of Democratic Rage and Delusion': Popular Religion and the Challenge to the Established Order, 1760–1815," in Rawlyk, *The Canadian Protestant Experience*, 16–17.
8. George Egerton, "Trudeau, God, and the Canadian Constitution: Religion, Human Rights, and Government Authority in the Making of the 1982 Constitution," in Lyon and Van Die, *Rethinking Church, State, and Modernity*, 92.
9. Roger O'Toole, "Canadian Religion: Heritage and Project," in Lyon and Van Die, *Rethinking Church, State, and Modernity*, 35–51, especially 41–42.
10. Ibid., 42–45.
11. Ibid., 44, quoting sociologist S. D. Clark, *The Developing Canadian Community* (Toronto: University of Toronto Press, 1968), 171.
12. Egerton, "Trudeau, God, and the Canadian Constitution," 109.
13. See *Report of the Royal Commission on Bilingualism and Biculturalism*, especially vol. 4: *The Cultural Contribution of the Other Ethnic Groups* (Ottawa: Queen's Printer, 1970).
14. Leo Driedger, *Multi-Ethnic Canada: Identities and Inequalities* (Toronto: Oxford University Press, 1996), 106–8.
15. Wil Kymlicka, "Canadian Multiculturalism in Historical and Comparative Perspective: Is Canada Unique?" *Constitutional Forum* 13, no. 1 (2003): 1–8.
16. Pamela E. Klassen and Courtney Bender, "Introduction: Habits of Pluralism," in *After Pluralism: Reimagining Religious Engagement*, eds. Courtney Bender and Pamela E. Klassen (New York: Columbia University Press, 2010), 10.
17. Egerton, "Trudeau, God, and the Canadian Constitution," 90.
18. Mark Noll, "Canadian Evangelicalism: A View From the United States," in *Aspects of the Canadian Evangelical Experience*, ed. George A. Rawlyk (Montreal: McGill-Queen's University Press, 1997), 3–20.

19. See Winnifred Fallers Sullivan, "Religion Naturalized," in Bender and Klassen, *After Pluralism*, 82–97, especially at 84.
20. O'Toole, "Canadian Religion," 45, quoting John H. Simpson, "Religion and the Churches," in *Understanding Canadian Society*, eds. James Curtis and Lorne Tepperman (Toronto: McGraw-Hill Ryerson, 1988), 351.
21. Benjamin L. Berger, "The Cultural Limits of Legal Tolerance," in Bender and Klassen, eds., *After Pluralism*, 99.
22. Janet R. Jakobsen, "Ethics After Pluralism," in Bender and Klassen, *After Pluralism*, 33.
23. Anver M. Emon, "Pluralizing Religion: Islamic Law and the Anxiety of Reasoned Deliberation," in Bender and Klassen, *After Pluralism*, 60.
24. Michael Di Giacomo, "Pentecostal and Charismatic Christianity in Canada: Its Origins, Development, and Distinct Culture," in *Canadian Pentecostalism: Transition and Transformation*, ed. Michael Wilkinson (Montreal: McGill-Queen's University Press, 2009), 31.
25. Thomas Miller, *Canadian Pentecostals: A History of the Pentecostal Assemblies of Canada* (Mississauga, Ontario: Full Gospel Publishing House, 1994), 39–40.
26. Ibid., 187.
27. Ibid., 62–67.
28. Ibid., 108.
29. Phyllis D. Airhart, "Ordering a New Nation and Reordering Protestantism 1867–1914," in Rawlyk, *The Canadian Protestant Experience*, 111.
30. David Lyon, introduction to *Rethinking Church, State, and Modernity*, eds. Lyon and Van Die, 7.
31. John G. Stackhouse Jr., *Canadian Evangelicalism in the Twentieth Century: An Introduction to Its Character* (Toronto: University of Toronto Press, 1993), 161, 167; see also Egerton, "Trudeau, God, and the Canadian Constitution," 102.
32. George Egerton, "Trudeau, God, and the Canadian Constitution," 106.
33. Stackhouse, *Canadian Evangelicalism in the Twentieth Century*, 169–70.
34. Ibid., 170.
35. Ibid., 171.
36. Pamela Holmes, "The Spirit Nature and Canadian Pentecostal Women: A Conversation With Critical Theory," in *Philip's Daughters: Women in Pentecostal-Charismatic Leadership*, eds. Estrelda Alexander and Amos Yong (Eugene, OR: Pickwick Publications, 2009), 185–202.

37. O'Toole, "Canadian Religion," 35–37.
38. Gerald T. Sheppard. "Biblical Interpretation After Gadamer," *Pneuma: The Journal of the Society for Pentecostal Studies* 16, no. 1 (1994): 121–41.
39. Ibid., 127.
40. See my essay "Paul Tillich, Pentecostalism, and the Early Frankfurt School: A Critical Constellation," in *Paul Tillich and Pentecostal Theology: Spiritual Presence and Spiritual Power*, eds. Nimi Wariboko and Amos Yong (Bloomington, IN: Indiana University Press, 2015), 185–89.
41. Gordon Atter, *The Third Force* (Peterborough, ON: College Press, 1962), x, 121, 303. Gordon Atter, an early Canadian Pentecostal historian, picking up on a theme from *Life* magazine in the summer of 1958, labeled the Pentecostal movement the "Third Force." In his book *The Third Force*, which traces the emergence of the Pentecostal movement, Atter argues that Pentecostalism, while a significant segment of the Christian churches, is a third camp in Christianity. No longer is Christianity primarily divided into two general camps—the Roman Catholic and the Protestant (he ignores Orthodox Christians, Mormons, Jehovah's Witnesses, etc.). Now there is a third camp, a "third force," which places a strong emphasis on the person and ministry of the Spirit rather than the first two persons of the Trinity and is primarily experiential rather than rational or sacramental.
42. Miller, *Canadian Pentecostals*, 101.
43. Pamela Holmes, "Ministering Women in the Pentecostal Assemblies of Canada: A Feminist Exploration," in Wilkinson, ed., *Canadian Pentecostalism*, 171–94, especially 180–84.
44. Pamela Holmes, "Acts 29 and Authority: Towards a Pentecostal Feminist Hermeneutic of Liberation," in *A Liberating Spirit: Pentecostals and Social Action in North America*, eds. Michael Wilkinson and Steven M. Studebaker (Eugene, OR: Pickwick Publications, 2010), 192.
45. Ibid., 193–97.
46. Adam Stewart, "Quenching the Spirit: The Transformation of Religious Identity and Experience in Three Canadian Pentecostal Churches" (PhD thesis, University of Waterloo, Ontario, Canada 2012), 118–37.
47. See Pamela Holmes, "A Never-Ending Canadian Pentecostal Challenge," in *The Many Faces of Global Pentecostalism*, eds. Harold D. Hunter and Neil Ormerod (Cleveland, TN: CPT Press, 2013), 264–85, especially 273–76 and 278–80.

48. See also Pamela Holmes, "Towards Useable Categories of 'Women's Experiences' and 'Power': A Canadian Feminist Pentecostal Considers the Work of Margaret Kamitsuka and Kwok Pui-lan," *Pneuma: The Journal of the Society for Pentecostal Studies* 35, no. 1 (2013): 9–23, specifically 13–14 and 21–22.
49. Sam Reimer, "A Generic Evangelicalism? Comparing Evangelical Subcultures in Canada and the United States," in Lyon and Van Die, *Rethinking Church, State, and Modernity*, 235.
50. Alistair MacIntyre, *Whose Justice? Whose Rationality?* (Notre Dame, IN: University of Notre Dame Press, 1988), 336–39. See also Winnifred Fallers Sullivan, "Religion Naturalized," in Bender and Klassen, *After Pluralism*, 82–97, for further discussion.
51. Kristen Deede Johnson, *Theology, Political Theory, and Pluralism: Beyond Tolerance and Difference* (Cambridge: Cambridge University Press, 2007), 2.
52. In Stackhouse, *Canadian Evangelicalism in the Twentieth Century*, 172.
53. Stewart, "Quenching the Spirit," 140.
54. Some of the newer works include Adam Stewart, *The New Canadian Pentecostals* (Waterloo, ON: Wilfred Laurier University Press), 2015; and Sam Reimer and Michael Wilkinson, *A Culture of Faith: Evangelical Congregations in Canada* (Toronto and Montreal: McGill-Queen's University Press, 2015).
55. Studies of Pentecostal immigration contribute toward this end; see Michael Wilkinson, *The Spirit Said Go: Pentecostal Immigrants in Canada* (New York: Peter Lang, 2006); cf. Wilkinson, "Charles W. Chawner and the Missionary Impulse of the Hebden Mission," in *Winds From the North: Canadian Contributions to the Pentecostal Movement*, eds. Michael Wilkinson and Peter Althouse (Leiden: Brill, 2010), 39–54.

Chapter 19
The Pentecostal Movement in Hawaii

1. "Resident Population of Islands: 1960 to 2010," in Hawaii State Data Book (Hawaii: Mutual Publishing, 2012), 4.
2. Ibid., 18.
3. David T. Olson, "Hawaii 2007 Population by Ethnicity," in "The State of the Church in Hawaii: 2000–2010," 16, available at http://www.theamericanchurch.org/state/HI0.htm (accessed April 13, 2013).

4. Olson, "Hawaii Church Attendance Percentage in 2009," in "The State of the Church in Hawaii," 22.
5. Daniel I. Kikawa, *Perpetuated in Righteousness: The Journey of the Hawaiian People From Eden (Kalana i Hauola) to the Present Time*, eds. Leon Siu and Tomas Watene Rosser, 4th ed. (Hawaii: Aloha Ke Akua Publishing, 1994), 56.
6. Henry K. Boshard, *The History of Mokuaikaua Church: The Oldest and First Founded Christian Church in the State of Hawaii* (Hawaii: James Roark Design, 1985), 9.
7. Kikawa, *Perpetuated in Righteousness*, 54.
8. Ibid., 196.
9. Ibid., 57.
10. Ibid.
11. Ibid., 53.
12. Ibid.
13. Ibid., 196.
14. Al Castro, certified Hawaiian teacher and Kupuna of His Highest Praise, interview with the author on the spiritual state of the early Hawaiian people, May 30, 2013.
15. See the discussion "Henry Opukahaia: First Hawaiian Christian," in Catherine Millard, *Great American Statesmen and Heroes* (Camp Hill, PA: Horizon Books, 1995), 198–206.
16. Kikawa, *Perpetuated in Righteousness*, 156.
17. Boshard, *The History of Mokuaikaua Church*, 14.
18. Millard, *Great American Statesmen and Heroes*, 199.
19. Kikawa, *Perpetuated in Righteousness*, 156.
20. Ibid., 157.
21. Boshard, *The History of Mokuaikaua Church*, 28.
22. Glen Grant and Bennet Hymer, *Hawaii Looking Back: An Illustrated History of the Islands*, 5th printing (Hawaii: Mutual Publishing, 2007), 168.
23. Kikawa, *Perpetuated in Righteousness*, 168–169.
24. Ibid., 171.
25. Titus Coan, *Life in Hawaii: An Autobiographical Sketch of Mission Life and Labors (1835–1881)* (New York: Anson D. F. Randolph & Company, 1882), 49–50.
26. Ibid., 54–55.

27. Al Castro, interview with the author.
28. Eddie L. Hyatt, *2000 Years of Charismatic Christianity: A 21st-Century Look at Church History From a Pentecostal/Charismatic Perspective* (Lake Mary, FL: Charisma House, 2002), 166.
29. Vinson Synan, *The Century of the Holy Spirit: 100 Years of Pentecostal and Charismatic Renewal* (Nashville: Thomas Nelson, 2001).
30. Hawaii Assemblies of God, "Dedication," in *Light on the Past: Ka Malamalama No Ka Makahiki Ihala* (Hawaii: Pacific Printers, 1975), 13.
31. Ibid., 12.
32. Ibid., 14.
33. Dr. George Nagato, district superintendent for the Assemblies of God, Hawaii, interview with the author on the history, successes, and challenges of the Assemblies of God, April 11, 2013.
34. Ibid.
35. Hawaii Assemblies of God, "Attaining District Status," 17.
36. Ibid., 27.
37. Robert Donovan, *Her Door of Faith: The Life Story of Mildred Johnson Brostek, Hawaii's Miracle Missionary* (Hawaii: Orovan Books, 1971), 63.
38. H. Presley, general secretary, "General Board Minutes," in *The Pentecostal Holiness Advocate*, June 5, 1940.
39. Barbara Tengan, senior pastor of the Wailuku Door of Faith Church, Maui, interview with the author on the history of the Door of Faith ministry and her work with Dr. Mildred Brostek, May 31, 2013.
40. Cited in Donovan, *Her Door of Faith*, 102.
41. Charles W. Conn, *Where the Saints Have Trod: A History of Church of God Missions* (Cleveland, TN: Pathway Press, 1959), 206.
42. Ibid., 208.
43. Fred Abbott, state bishop for Church of God for the state of Hawaii, interview with the author, June 5, 2013.
44. Gary Langley, e-mail message to the author, May 15, 2013.
45. Byron D. Klaus, "Reflection on Pentecostal Mission for the Twenty-First Century," in *Spirit-Empowered Christianity in the 21st Century: Insights, Analysis, and Future Trends*, ed. Vinson Synan (Lake Mary, FL: Charisma House, 2011), 131; see also 129–40 and 549–51.
46. Calvary Chapel Association, "History of Calvary Chapel," http://www.calvarychapelassociation.com/general-information/history/ ().

47. Chuck Smith, "The Philosophy of Ministry of Calvary Chapel," accessed April 15, 2013, http://web.ccbce.com/multimedia/Chuck_Smith_Books/tpomocc.htm, from which are taken also the other quotations that follow.
48. Calvary Chapel Honolulu, "Pastor Bill's Story," accessed May 19, 2016, https://www.calvarychapelhonolulu.com/about-us/.
49. Wayne Cordeiro, *Doing Church as a Team* (Ventura, CA: Regal Books, 2001), 46.
50. Vinson Synan, *The Holiness-Pentecostal Traditions: Charismatic Movements in the Twentieth Century*, 2nd ed. (Grand Rapids: Eerdmans, 1997), 272–90.
51. Ibid., 291.
52. Ibid. Synan refers to Newbigin's *The Household of God: Lectures on the Nature of the Church* (New York: Friendship Press, 1953).

Chapter 20
The Emergence of Prosperity and Blessing Theology: Black Pentecostalism in North America, 1980–2010

1. See Martha Simmons, "Trends in the African American Church," *The African American Pulpit* (Spring 2007): 9–16; Robert M. Franklin, *Another Day's Journey: Black Churches Confronting the American Crisis* (Minneapolis: Fortress Press, 1997), 29–82; and Larry Mamiya, *River of Struggle, River of Freedom: Trends Among Black Churches and Black Pastoral Leadership*, Pulpit and Pew Research Reports (Durham, NC: Duke Divinity School, 2006).
2. Eugene Robinson, *Disintegration: The Splintering of Black America* (New York: Doubleday, 2010), 5.
3. Kenneth E. Hagin, *Redeemed From Poverty, Sickness, and Spiritual Death* (Tulsa, OK: Faith Library Publications, 1983); Frederick K. C. Price, *Is Healing for All?* (Los Angeles: Faith One Publishing, 1976); Frederick K. C. Price, *The Purpose of Prosperity* (Los Angeles: Faith One Publishing, 2001); Creflo Dollar, *No More Debt* (College Park, GA: Creflo Dollar Ministries, 2000); and Kenneth Copeland, "Live in the Blessing," in *Believers Voice of Victory* (September 2007): 4–8.
4. Eddie Long, *Taking Over* (Lake Mary, FL: Charisma House, 1999); Eddie Long, *It's Your Time* (New Kensington, PA: Whitaker House, 2003); T. D. Jakes, *Maximize the Moment* (New York: Berkeley Books, 1999); T. D. Jakes, *The Great Investment* (New York: G. P. Putnam and Sons, 2000);

and T. D. Jakes, *Reposition Yourself* (New York: Africa Books, 2007). See also Debra Mumford, *Exploring Prosperity Preaching* (Valley Forge, PA: Judson Press, 2012).

5. Research in this section derives from Lewis Brogdon, *The New Pentecostal Message?* (Eugene, OR: Cascade Books, 2015), 101–22, and is used by permission of Wipf and Stock Publishers (www.wipfandstock.com).
6. For a discussion of reasons why African Americans chose Methodist, Holiness, and Pentecostal churches, see Amos Yong and Lewis Brogdon, "The Decline of African American Theology? A Critical Response to Thabiti Anyabwile," *Journal of Reformed Theology* 4, no. 2 (2010): 129–44.
7. "America's Black Churches Debate Role in Society," Voice of America, at http://www.voanews.com/content/a-13-2005-08-17-voa22/302987.html (accessed June 22, 2016).
8. Scott Billingsley, *It's a New Day* (Tuscaloosa, AL: University of Alabama, 2008).
9. Creflo Dollar, *Total Life Prosperity* (Nashville: Thomas Nelson Publishers, 1999), x.
10. For a study examining rural Pentecostalism, see Marla Frederick, *Between Sundays: Black Women and Everyday Struggles of Faith* (Berkeley, CA: University of California, 2003).
11. As a historical theologian, black religious scholar, and ministry practitioner, I turn to the discipline of practical theology to give meaning and language to the contours of prosperity teaching in West Virginia. Edward Farley's *Practicing Gospel* (Louisville, KY: Westminster John Knox, 2003) and Patricia O'Connell Killen and John de Beer's *The Act of Theological Reflection* (New York: Crossroad, 1999) are models of how to reflect theologically on one's experience and tradition. These works serve as a guide for my attempt to critically reflect on this experience, as have follow-up interviews with Fred Brown, the pastor of the congregation I discuss in the next section. With permission to use his name, the name of this congregation, and to report my findings in this study, I draw on practical theological methods to understand a rural church in West Virginia.
12. United States Census Bureau, "Quick Facts: West Virginia," accessed July 9, 2014, http://quickfacts.census.gov/qfd/states/54000.html.
13. Health Statistics Center for the West Virginia Department of Health and Human Resources, "Frequently Requested Statistics," accessed July 9, 2014, http://www.wvdhhr.org/bph/hsc/Statserv/Stat_Triv.asp.

14. For a study of the United Holy Church, an African American Pentecostal denomination, see William C. Turner Jr., *The United Holy Church of America: A Study in Black Holiness-Pentecostalism* (Piscataway, NJ: Gorgias Press, 2006).
15. For an examination of pneumatology and prosperity teaching, see Amos Yong, *In the Days of Caesar: Pentecostalism and Political Theology* (Grand Rapids: Eerdmans, 2010), 257–315.
16. For studies of Word of Faith teaching, see Bruce Barron, *The Health and Wealth Gospel* (Downers Grove, IL: InterVarsity, 1987); Robert Bowman, *The Word of Faith Controversy* (Grand Rapids: Eerdmans, 2001); and Andrew Perriman, *Faith, Health, and Prosperity* (Carlisle, UK: Paternoster, 2003).
17. See Robert Franklin, *Crisis in the Village: Restoring Hope in African American Communities* (Minneapolis: Fortress Press, 2007); Shayne Lee, *T. D. Jakes: America's New Preacher* (New York: New York University Press, 2005); Milmon F. Harrison, *Righteous Riches: The Word Faith Movement in Contemporary African American Religion* (New York: Oxford Press, 2005); and Stephanie Y. Mitchem, *Name It and Claim It: Prosperity Preaching in the Black Church* (Cleveland, TN: The Pilgrim Press, 2007).

Chapter 21
"I Will Pour Out of My Spirit Upon All Flesh": A Historical and Theological Meditation on Pentecostal Origins

1. Allan Heaton Anderson, *To the Ends of the Earth: Pentecostalism and the Transformation of World Christianity* (New York: Oxford University Press, 2013), 18–25. A different version of this essay appeared previously as "'I Will Pour Out My Spirit Upon All Flesh': An Historical and Theological Meditation on Pentecostal Origins," *Pneuma: The Journal of the Society for Pentecostal Studies* 37 (2015) 356–74. My thanks are due to Brill Publishers and to the editors of *Pneuma* for permission to republish some of the content that was first published there.
2. James R. Coggins and Paul G. Hiebert, eds., *Wonders and the Word: An Examination of Issues Raised by John Wimber and the Vineyard Movement* (Winnipeg: Kindred Press, 1989); and John Wimber, *Power Evangelism* (San Francisco: Harper & Row, 1986).
3. Edward Irving, "Missionaries After the Apostolical School," in *The Collected Writings of Edward Irving*, ed. G. Carlyle, 5 vols. (London: Alexander Strahan, 1864), 1.427–523. Cf. Arnold Dallimore, *The Life of*

Edward Irving: Fore-Runner of the Charismatic Movement (Edinburgh: Banner of Truth, 1983). Some later evangelicals, such as C. H. Spurgeon and J. Hudson Taylor, who did not adopt Irving's view regarding charismatic gifts, did agree that missionaries should go forth without pre-arranged financial provision, as Irving had argued. See Brian Stanley, "C. H. Spurgeon and the Baptist Missionary Society, 1863–66," *Baptist Quarterly* (1980): 319–28; Gary B. McGee, "The Dilemma Over the Apostolic Nature of Mission in Modern Missions," *Encounter* (Winter 2005), accessed March 3, 2015, https://agts.edu/encounter/articles/2005_winter/mcgee.htm.

4. Jouko Ruohomäki, "The Call of Charisma: Charismatic Phenomena During the 18th and 19th Centuries in Finland," *JEPTA: The Journal of the European Pentecostal Theological Association* 29 (2009): 25–40.
5. In Africa, there is abundant evidence for charismatic phenomena and prophetic movements occurring without any connection to global Pentecostalism. Cf. Ogbu Kalu, *African Pentecostalism* (New York: Oxford University Press, 2008). For nineteenth-century Australia, see Peter Elliott, "Nineteenth-Century Australian Charismata: Edward Irving's Legacy," *Pneuma: The Journal of the Society for Pentecostal Studies* 34 (2012): 26–36.
6. My thanks are due to those who invited me to speak at the session on Pentecostal origins at the Society for Pentecostal Studies conference on March 12, 2015, on the campus of Southeastern University, Lakeland, Florida. I also wish to thank Dr. Estrelda Alexander, of William Seymour College, for her incisive comments.
7. Some have used the terms monocentric and polycentric. Yet mono/polygenesis clearly pertain to the question of origins that is the focus in this discussion. Theoretically, one could combine polygenesis and monocentrism (if a single center came to dominate) or monogenesis and polycentrism (if a singly centered origin gave way to multiple centers).
8. Clay Banks and Jessie Ottolini, *The Asuza Street Project*, directed by Clay Banks (Hollywood: Global Media GodWorks Productions, April 2006), 44:20, posted by Mariusz Jurga on YouTube as "Azusa Street Revival Documentary," December 6, 2011, accessed March 3, 2015, http://www.youtube.com/watch?v=iqROdLQQvz8.
9. Cecil Robeck, "Pentecostal Origins From a Global Perspective," in *All Together in One Place*, eds. Harold D. Hunter and Peter Hocken (Sheffield, UK; Sheffield Academic Press, 1993), 170, quoted in Michael Bergunder, "The Cultural Turn," in *Studying Global Pentecostalism: Theories*

and Methods, eds. Allan Anderson et al. (Berkeley, CA: University of California Press, 2010), 57.

10. Cecil Robeck, "Launching a Global Movement: The Role of Azusa Street in Launching Pentecostalism's Growth and Expansion," in *Spirit and Power: The Growth and Global Impact of Pentecostalism*, eds. Donald Miller et al. (New York: Oxford University Press, 2013), 47.
11. Allan H. Anderson, *Spreading Fires: The Missionary Nature of Early Pentecostalism* (Maryknoll, NY: Orbis Books, 2007), 288.
12. Adam Stewart, "From Monogenesis to Polygenesis in Pentecostal Origins: A Survey of the Evidence from the Azusa Street, Hebden, and Mukti Missions," *PentecoStudies* 13 (2014): 160–61.
13. Ibid., 168–70.
14. Bartlemen, *How Pentecost Came to Los Angeles*, cited in Anderson, *To the Ends of the Earth*, 32.
15. Noel Gibbard, *On the Wings of the Dove: The International Effects of the 1904–1905 Revival* (Bridgend, Wales: Brytirion Press, 2002).
16. Willis Collins Hoover, *History of the Pentecostal Revival in Chile*, trans. Mario G. Hoover (Santiago: Imprenta Eben-Ezer, 2000).
17. Allan Anderson, "The Emergence of a Multidimensional Global Missionary Movements: Trends, Patterns, and Expressions," in Miller et al., *Spirit and Power*, 25–41.
18. Anderson, "Emergence," 31. Anderson adds, "Ramabai was a woman who resisted patriarchal oppression in India and western domination in Christianity and was attracted to what a biographer calls 'the gender-egalitarian impulse of Christianity,'" citing Meera Kosambi, ed. and trans., *Pandita Ramabai Through Her Own Words: Selected Words* (New Delhi: Oxford University Press, 2000), 18.
19. Néstor Medina, "Latina/o Pentecostalism, a dónde vamos?," unpublished essay presented at the Society for Pentecostal Studies meeting, March 13, 2015. Thanks are due to Dr. Medina for supplying a copy.
20. Everett A Wilson, "Sanguine Saints: Pentecostalism in El Salvador," *Church History* 52 (1983): 189. Cf. Ronald Wilfredo Luna, "Transforming Espacios Culturales Into Cultural Spaces: How the Salvadoran Community Is Establishing Evangelical Protestant Churches" (PhD dissertation, University of Maryland at College Park, 2008).
21. Virginia Garrard-Burnett, *Living in the New Jerusalem: Protestantism in Guatemala* (Austin: University of Texas Press, 1998), 37–38.

22. Juana Berges Curbelo, *Pentecostalismo en Cuba: ¿Alienación o compromiso social?* (Mexico: Publicaciones para el Estudio Científico de las Religiones, 2008).
23. I am quoting remarks made by Dr. Paulo Ayres Mattos of the Methodist University of São Paulo at the Society for Pentecostal Studies conference on March 12, 2015, Southeastern University, Lakeland, Florida.
24. Aimee Semple McPherson was also linked to the Hebden Mission in Toronto via her first husband, Robert Semple, who died on the mission field shortly after they had arrived as Hebden missionaries.
25. These reflections are based on Michael Bergunder's essay "The Cultural Turn," 51–73.
26. Stan Ingersol, "Church of the Nazarene," in *Encyclopedia of Religious Revivals in America*, 2 vols., ed. Michael J. McClymond (Westport, CT: Greenwood Press, 2007), I.116–17.
27. Peter Althouse informs me that Catholic Charismatic scholars—Kilian McDonnell, Peter Hocken, or both—may have introduced the term classical Pentecostal. Following a Bergundian approach, though, it matters less who introduced a term and more that a term has stuck and become a common self-designation.
28. This idea regarding a connection between churches is reminiscent of second-century Catholic debates. As global Pentecostalism enters its second century, "Charismatic succession" becomes an issue like the earlier apostolic succession.
29. Frank Bartleman, *How Pentecost Came to Los Angeles*, cited in Anderson, *To the Ends of the Earth*, 45.
30. Gastón Espinosa, *Latino Pentecostals in America: Faith and Politics in Action* (Cambridge: Harvard University Press, 2014), 24, 32.
31. Espinosa, *Latino Pentecostals*, 55–56, citing William Seymour. The emphasis on Christian love and holy practice as marks of genuine spiritual experience brought Seymour's thinking in line with that of Jonathan Edwards. Cf. Michael J. McClymond and Gerald R. McDermott, *The Theology of Jonathan Edwards* (New York: Oxford University Press, 2012), especially 311–20 and 424–47.
32. Gastón Espinosa discusses the Mexican laborer who experienced the Holy Spirit on April 13, 1906—a day before the Azusa Street Mission opened its doors—and the Mexican man healed in "'The Holy Ghost Is Here on Earth': The Latino Contributions to the Azusa Street Revival," *Enrichment* (Spring 2006): 118–25. On the seeming marginalization of

Latinos as Azusa Street, see Espinosa, "Holy Ghost," 122–23, especially 125n25; and Espinosa, *Latino Pentecostals*, 51–53.

33. Richard Owen Roberts, ed., *Scotland Saw His Glory: A History of Revivals in Scotland* (Wheaton, IL: International Awakening Press, 1995).
34. Leigh Eric Schmidt, *Holy Fairs: Scotland and the Making of American Revivalism* (Grand Rapids: Eerdmans, 2001).
35. W. R. Ward, *The Protestant Evangelical Awakening* (Cambridge: Cambridge University Press, 1992).
36. On the far-reaching importance of Paul's mission to the Gentiles and the emergence of a multicultural and multilinguistic Christian movement, see the brilliant analysis of Lamin Sanneh, *Translating the Message: The Missionary Impact on Culture*, 2nd rev. and expanded ed. (Maryknoll, NY: Orbis Books, 2009).

Chapter 22
God's Indwelling Spirit: Reflecting on the Theological Challenges of Pentecostalism

1. William Seymour, "The Same Old Way," *Apostolic Faith* 1, no. 1 (September 1906): 3. Though Seymour does not place his name at the bottom of this entry (as he sometimes does) it bears his typical theme and terminology.
2. Notice what he says about the "black oral roots" of Pentecostalism; Walter J. Hollenweger, *Pentecostalism: Origins and Developments Worldwide* (Peabody, MA: Hendrickson, 1997), 18–80.
3. See Dale T. Irvin, "Pentecostal Historiography," *Pneuma: Journal of the Society for Pentecostal Studies* 27, no. 1 (2005): 35–50. He balances well the "multiple origins" view of Pentecostalism with evidence for the vast influence of the Azusa Street revival globally. One may say with Douglas Jacobsen that Azusa Street was the Grand Central Station of global Pentecostalism; see Jacobsen, *Thinking in the Spirit: Theologies of the Early Pentecostal Movement* (Bloomington, IN: Indiana University Press, 2003), 10.
4. Both Walter Hollenweger and Cecil M. Robeck Jr. have pointed in similar directions in describing the ethos of Pentecostalism. See Walter J. Hollenweger, "After Twenty Years of Research on Pentecostalism," *International Review of Mission* 75 (1986): 6; and Cecil M. Robeck Jr., "Taking Stock of Pentecostalism: The Personal Reflections of a Retiring Editor," *Pneuma: The Journal of the Society for Pentecostal Studies* 15, no. 1 (1993): 35–60.

5. Seymour, "The Same Old Way," 3.
6. Terry Cross, "The Rich Feast of Theology: Can Pentecostals Bring the Main Course or Only the Relish?" *Journal of Pentecostal Theology* 16 (2000): 27–47.
7. P. C. Nelson, *Bible Doctrines* (reprint; Springfield, MO: Gospel Publishing House, 2009).
8. Jürgen Moltmann, *The Spirit of Life: A Universal Affirmation*, trans. Margaret Kohl (Minneapolis: Fortress, 2001), 5–7.
9. Gerald T. Sheppard, "Biblical Interpretation after Gadamer," *Pneuma: The Journal of the Society for Pentecostal Studies* 16 (1984): 121–41, at 127.
10. Kenneth Archer, *A Pentecostal Hermeneutic: Spirit, Scripture, and Community* (reprint; Cleveland, TN: CPT Press, 2009), especially 1–9.
11. Karl Barth, *Church Dogmatics*, vol. 1, part 1 (Edinburgh: T & T Clark, 1975), 139.
12. Hans Küng, *The Church* (New York: Sheed & Ward, 1967), 184.
13. Veli-Matti Kärkkäinen, "Pentecostalism and the Claim for Apostolicity: An Essay in Ecumenical Ecclesiology," *Ecumenical Review of Theology* 25 (2001): 323–26.
14. So says James D. G. Dunn, "Challenge to Traditional Ecclesiology," in *Charismatic Experiences in History*, ed. Cecil M. Robeck (Peabody, MA: Hendrickson, 1985), 81–95.
15. Peter D. Neumann, *Pentecostal Experience: An Ecumenical Encounter* (Eugene, OR: Pickwick, 2012), 100–61.
16. Lisa Stephensen, *Dismantling the Dualisms for American Pentecostal Women in Ministry: A Feminist-Pneumatological Approach* (Leiden: Brill, 2011). I used the same method earlier in my work on justification, except my concern was with more dogmatic issues. See Frank D. Macchia, *Justified in the Spirit: Redemption, Creation, and the Triune God* (Grand Rapids: Eerdmans, 2010).
17. John Christopher Thomas, "Women, Pentecostals, and the Bible: An Experiment in Pentecostal Hermeneutics," *Journal of Pentecostal Theology* 5 (1994): 41–56.
18. David D. Daniels, "Everybody Bids You Welcome: A Multicultural Approach to North American Pentecostalism," in *Globalization of Pentecostalism: A Religion Made to Travel*, eds. Murray W. Dempster, Byron Klaus, and Douglas Peterson (Oxford: Regnum, 1999), 222–58.

19. Amos Yong, *Spirit-Word-Community: Theological Hermeneutics in Trinitarian Perspective* (Burlington, VT: Ashgate, 2002).
20. Daniela Augustine, *Pentecost, Hospitality, and Transfiguration: Toward a Spirit-Inspired Vision of Social Transformation* (Cleveland, TN: CPT Press, 2012).
21. More than any other theologian, Amos Yong has impressed this thought upon me.
22. Charles Mason, no title, *Apostolic Faith* (February–March 1907): 7.
23. Frank D. Macchia, "Tongues as a Sign: Towards a Sacramental Understanding of Pentecostal Experience," *Pneuma: The Journal of the Society for Pentecostal Studies* 15, no. 1 (1993): 61–76.
24. See Frank D. Macchia, *Baptized in the Spirit: A Global Pentecostal Theology* (Grand Rapids: Zondervan, 2006); and, Macchia, *Justified in the Spirit.*
25. William Seymour, "The Way Into the Holiest," *The Apostolic Faith* 1, no. 2 (October 1906): 4.
26. "The Feast of Pentecost," *The Apostolic Faith* 1, no. 9 (September 1907): 2.
27. *The Apostolic Faith* 1, no. 11 (January 1908): 2.
28. T. Hezmalhalch, "Among the Indians at Needles California," *The Apostolic Faith* 1, no. 5 (January 1907): 3.
29. *The Apostolic Faith* 1, no. 11 (January 1908): 4.
30. D. William Faupel, *The Everlasting Gospel: The Significance of Eschatology in the Development of Pentecostal Thought* (Sheffield, UK: Sheffield Academic Press, 1993), esp. chapter 6.
31. Simon Chan, *Pentecostal Ecclesiology: An Essay on the Development of Doctrine* (Dorncaster, UK: Deo, 2011).
32. Chris E. W. Green, *Toward a Pentecostal Theology of the Lord's Supper: Foretasting the Kingdom* (Cleveland, TN: CPT Press, 2012).
33. Roger Stronstad, *The Charismatic Theology of St. Luke* (Peabody, MA: Hendrickson, 1988); Robert Menzies, *Empowered for Witness: The Spirit in Luke-Acts* (New York: T & T Clark, 2004).
34. See James D. G. Dunn, *Baptism in the Holy Spirit* (Philadelphia: Westminster John Knox Press, 1977); Kilian McDonnell and George Montague, *Christian Initiation and Baptism in the Holy Spirit: Evidence From the First Eight Centuries* (Collegeville, MN: Liturgical Press, 2004).
35. I refer here to the work of Dunn and McDonnell; see the previous endnote.
36. As shared with the author.

37. Raymond J. Cunningham, "From Holiness to Healing: The Faith Cure in America, 1874–1892," *Church History* 43 (1974): 449–513.
38. Miroslav Volf, "Materiality of Salvation: An Investigation Into the Soteriologies of Pentecostal and Liberation Theologies," *Journal of Ecumenical Studies* 26 (1989): 447–67.
39. Walter J. Hollenweger, "Creator Spiritus: The Challenge of Pentecostal Experience to Pentecostal Theology," *Theology* 81, no. 679 (1978): 32–40.
40. Amos Yong, *The Spirit of Creation: Modern Science and Divine Action in the Pentecostal-Charismatic Imagination* (Grand Rapids: Eerdmans, 2011), 96–99.
41. Kimberly Alexander, *Pentecostal Healing: Models in Theology and Practice* (Dorchester, UK: Deo, 2006); Howard Snyder, *Salvation Means Creation Healed: The Ecology of Sin and Grace: Overcoming the Divorce Between Heaven and Earth* (Eugene, OR: Wipf & Stock, 2011).
42. Veli-Matti Kärkkäinen, *One With God: Salvation as Deification and Justification* (Collegeville, MN: Liturgical Press, 2004).
43. See Macchia, *Justified in the Spirit.*
44. Murray W. Dempster, "Christian Social Concern in Pentecostal Perspective: Reformulating Pentecostal Eschatology," *Journal of Pentecostal Theology 2* (1993): 51–64.
45. I've heard Veli-Matti Kärkkäinen make much the same point.

Chapter 23
Global Oneness Pentecostal Theology: Contributions and Challenges for the Twenty-First Century

1. For a summary of the birth of the Oneness movement, see David Reed, *'In Jesus' Name': The History and Beliefs of Oneness Pentecostals* (Dorset, UK: Deo Publishing, 2008), chapters 6–7.
2. David S. Norris, *I AM: A Oneness Pentecostal Theology* (Hazelwood, MO: Word Aflame Press, 2009), 3.
3. On a personal note, I am a child of these two solitudes—reared in a devout Oneness home for a quarter-century, one in which I spiritually came to know the same Jesus proclaimed by all Pentecostals. Consequently, the spirit of this essay is both existential and theological.
4. Carl Brumback, *God in Three Persons: A Trinitarian Answer to the Oneness or "Jesus Only" Doctrine Concerning the Godhead and Water Baptism* (Cleveland, TN: Pathway Press, 1959), 22. Brumback was not always well enough informed regarding the diversity within Oneness teaching

to sift marginal views from mainstream Oneness teaching. See especially his extensive critique of C. Haskell Yadon's unrepresentative, near-Arian Christology, a reprint of Robert D. Weeks's *Jehovah-Jesus: The Oneness of God; The True Trinity* (New York: Dodd, Mead and Co., 1876), republished as *Jehovah-Jesus—The Supreme God: Son of God, Son of Man*, ed. C. Haskell Yadon (Twin Falls, ID: by the editor, 1952).

5. For a list of Evangelical publications that label Oneness theology as a heresy, including Oneness defense against the charge, see Talmadge L. French, *Our God Is One: The Story of Oneness Pentecostals* (Indianapolis: Voice and Vision Publications, 1999), 21–25. See also Edward L. Dalcour, *A Definitive Look at Oneness Theology: Defending the Tri-Unity of God* (New York: University Press of America, 2005). The charge that Oneness is a Sabellian heresy appeared recently in an article by Justin S. Holcomb, "Why You Shouldn't Call That False Teaching a Heresy," *Christianity Today*, October 6, 2015, 38.
6. Thomas Weisser, preface to *After the Way Called Heresy* (privately published, 1981), 115.
7. See chapter 1 in David Bernard, *Oneness of God*, Series in Pentecostal Theology 1 (Hazelwood, MO: Word Aflame Press, 1983). For a more detailed summary, see Reed, *In Jesus' Name*, chapter 12. Resistance by Jewish-oriented Christians in the second and third centuries to the emerging Hellenistic Logos theology reflects a weakening in the methodology that as first order gives account of Christianity's biblical monotheism; see also J. N. D. Kelly, *Early Christian Doctrines,* 2nd ed. (New York: Harper & Row, 1960), 125.
8. Norris, *I AM*, 63.
9. John Paterson, *God in Christ Jesus* (Montreal: by the author, 1964), 39.
10. Andrew D. Urshan, *The Almighty God in the Lord Jesus Christ* (Los Angeles: by the author, 1919), 77.
11. Daniel Segraves, "Andrew D. Urshan: A Theological Biography" (PhD dissertation, Regent University, 2011), 363. Segraves's thesis is an excellent account of the life and theology of Urshan. The book version is published and available as *Andrew D. Urshan: A Theological Biography*, Asbury Theological Seminary's Series on Christian Revitalization (Lexington, KY: Emeth Press, 2017).
12. Norris, *I AM*, 143.
13. See Reed, *In Jesus' Name*, chapters 11 and 16.

14. For a detailed account of the beginnings of Apostolic (Oneness) Pentecostalism in Mexico, see Daniel Ramirez, *Migrating Faith: Pentecostalism in the United States and Mexico in the Twentieth Century* (Chapel Hill, NC: University of North Carolina Press, 2015), 62–72; also Kenneth D. Gill, *Toward a Contextualized Theology for the Third World: The Emergence and Development of Jesus' Name Pentecostalism in Mexico*, Studies in the Intercultural History of Christianity 90 (New York: Peter Lang, 1994), 43–46. For a history of the Iglesia Apostólica de la Fe en Cristo Jesús, see Gaxiola-Gaxiola, "The Serpent and the Dove: A History of the Apostolic Church of the Faith in Christ Jesus in Mexico: 1914-1974" (master's thesis, Fuller Theological Seminary, School of World Mission, 1977).

    Oneness historian Talmadge French, *Our God Is One*, 133–36, details the close link between the Azusa Street revival and the early Oneness movement, especially through the African American Oneness leader Garfield Haywood and the Pentecostal Assemblies of the World (PAW). Romanita Valenzuela, a Mexican immigrant Pentecostal convert in Los Angeles, was the first person to take the Oneness message back to Mexico. She had been part of a small house church that, according to Gill, was likely under the oversight of the early Pentecostal Assemblies of the World, which in turn was intimately associated at that time with the Azusa Street revival. Gaxiola-Gaxiola, "Latin American Pentecostalism: A Mosaic Within a Mosaic," *Pneuma: The Journal of the Society for Pentecostal Studies* 13, no. 1 (1991): 115, states that most of the early Mexican Oneness converts had originally been associated with the Azusa Street revival.

15. In a personal conversation with me, Gaxiola told the story of how his involvement occurred as a Oneness Pentecostal. When invited to participate, he pointed out that he was unable to agree to the Trinitarian Statement of Faith. When asked what would need to be changed in order to make it acceptable to him, he responded, "Remove the word *persons*." They did.

16. Manuel J. Gaxiola-Gaxiola, "Mexican Protestantism: The Search for Identity and Relevance in a Pluralistic Society" (PhD dissertation, University of Birmingham, 1990).

17. Manuel J. Gaxiola-Gaxiola, "Latin American Pentecostalism," 107–29.

18. Manuel J. Gaxiola-Gaxiola, "The Unsettled Issue" (unpublished paper, in the possession of the author, 1977).

19. Gerloff, an ordained German pastor, carried out her research on the Christian Diaspora in Europe as part of her doctoral program at Birmingham University, following which she became professor at Leeds University until her retirement. She developed an extensive case study of the black Oneness Pentecostal immigrant churches in Britain.
20. Roswith Gerloff, "The African Christian Diaspora in Europe: Religious and Cultural Aspects" (paper delivered at the International Association of Mission Studies Assembly, Malaysia, 2004), 3, 8.
21. Roswith Gerloff, *A Plea for British Black Theologies: The Black Church Movement in Britain and Its Transatlantic Cultural and Theological Interaction,* Studies in the Intercultural History of Christianity 77, 2 vols. (Frankfurt: Peter Lang, 1991), 1.61–65.
22. Ibid., 1.85. Gerloff recounts the case in which the black Church of God in Christ (COGIC) denomination had been for years tolerant of Oneness ministers and churches within its fellowship. But during a period of increased cooperation with the AG, the latter pressed COGIC to change its policy, which resulted in expulsion and formation of new Oneness organizations; ibid., 88.
23. Frank Ewart, *The Phenomenon of Pentecost: A History of the Latter Rain* (St. Louis, MO: Pentecostal Publishing House, 1947), 52.
24. Cited in Gerloff, *Plea*, 1.94.
25. Ibid., 90.
26. Bishop Degu Kebede, national head of ACE, interview with the author, Addis Ababa, Ethiopia, May 10, 2011.
27. Nona Freeman, *Unseen Hands: The Story of Revival in Ethiopia* (Hazelwood, MO: Word Aflame Press, 1987), 79–87.
28. Teklemariam Gezahagne, *Bible Writers' Theology*, rev. ed. (Hazelwood, MO: Apostolic Experience Publishing, 2007).
29. Teklemariam Gezahagne, *The Identity of Jesus Christ*, rev. ed. (Addis Ababa: privately published, 2010), 45.
30. Representatives are Arthur Pink and recently Oliver Crisp, *Divinity and Humanity: The Incarnation Reconsidered* (Cambridge: Cambridge University Press, 2007).
31. Teklemarian, *Theology*, 128.
32. Freeman, *Unseen Hands*, 23.
33. See also David A. Reed, "Then and Now: The Many Faces of Global Oneness Pentecostalism," in *The Cambridge Companion to Pentecostalism*,

eds. Cecil M. Robeck Jr., and Amos Yong (Cambridge, UK: Cambridge University Press, 2014), 52–70, especially 61–64.

34. For an historical analysis of this period and influence of revivalism on new indigenous movements like the TJC, see Daniel H. Bays, "Christian Revival in China, 1900–1937," in *Modern Christian Revivals*, eds. Edith L. Blumhofer and Randall Balmer (Chicago: University of Illinois Press, 1993), chapter 9. For the TJC allusion to Pentecostal movements as "precursors," see *History of the True Jesus Church* (1979).

35. It was Bernt Bernsten, a Norwegian-American missionary, who embraced the New Issue in 1915 and through whom Paul Wei learned of it and received it as a revelation from Scripture. Other distinctive TJC doctrines include: Sabbath-keeping, foot-washing as the third sacrament with baptism and Holy Communion, and the church as the "latter rain," end-times-restored Apostolic Church to take the gospel from the East to the West.

36. Personal conversation with TJC seminary teacher, Taichung, Taiwan, April 9, 2008. He commented that many are not aware of the TJC view because its preachers frequently speak of "Father, Son, and Spirit."

37. A major critique of Modalism, as noted, is that in the world of Platonic dualism, there is no assurance that one truly meets the real God behind the three "masks" revealed in history. Note this conclusion by Lutheran theologian Robert Jenson: "Beyond denying distinctions, modalism fails by locating God above time"; quoted in Veli-Matti Kärkkäinen, *The Trinity: Global Perspectives* (Louisville, KY: Westminster John Knox Press, 2007), 165. Kärkkäinen likewise concludes that Modalism makes the Incarnation only a "passing moment" (299). Neither of these represents the Oneness position.

38. I propose only that this configuration of a name theology is one valid approach to the doctrine of God, not the only alternative. Nor does it resolve the question of distinctions within the Godhead.

39. Peter Hughes, "Michael Servetus," *Dictionary of Unitarian and Universalist Biography,* accessed November 2, 2015, http://uudb.org/articles/michaelservetus.html.

40. This interfaith possibility has already been observed by Amos Yong, *The Spirit Poured Out on All Flesh: Pentecostalism and the Possibility of Global Theology* (Grand Rapids: Baker Academic, 2005), 230–31.

41. Andrew Walls, editorial, *Journal of African Christian Thought* 3, no. 1 (June 2000): 4.

42. Andrew Walls, interview with the author, Overseas Mission Study Center, New Haven, Connecticut, November 12, 2014.
43. Segraves, "Andrew Urshan," 439–40, acknowledges that Urshan's view of God "did not survive to become normative" for Oneness doctrine and refers to UPCI historian Robin Johnston's study—*Howard A. Goss: A Pentecostal Life* (Hazelwood, MO: Word Aflame Press, 2010), 153–55—on the two interpretations of Acts 2:38. The UPCI does allow difference of opinion. But it tends to treat alternative interpretations in the tradition as historical artifacts rather than part of the normative living theology of UPCI.
44. Three examples come to mind. Historian Thomas A. Fudge's *Christianity Without the Cross: A History of Salvation in Oneness Pentecostalism* (Parkland, FL: Universal Publishers, 2003), is a study of the conversionist interpretation of Acts 2:38 within the UPCI tradition and is critical of what he argues has been an intentional suppression of interpretation in favor of the new birth interpretation. Another distinct conversionist voice comes from a small Oneness organization, Associated Brotherhood of Christians, which has an open policy on fellowshipping with Trinitarian Christians. The Canadian-based Apostolic Church of Pentecost (ACOP) was founded by Franklin Small, one of the original architects of Oneness theology. In 1958, ACOP took in a small Trinitarian organization, requiring a reformulation of its faith statement on belief in God. It now reads, "We believe in the eternal existence of one true God who is Father, Son, and Holy Spirit"; http://www.acop.ca/acop_faith.php (accessed November 2, 2015).
45. For example, Andrew Urshan's quoted affirmatively and without qualification from the writings of Presbyterian theologian J. Monro Gibson, clearly a Christocentic Trinitarian; Urshan, *Almighty God*, 38, 79–83). See also a recent blog post by Segraves in which he quotes a Trinitarian statement by Alister McGrath, an Evangelical Trinitarian, with the heading "A Good Oneness Statement," at http://danielsegraves.blogspot.com.tr/2012/01/good-oneness-statement.html (accessed May 19, 2016).
46. J. N. K. Mugambi, *The African Heritage and Contemporary Christianity* (Nairobi: Longman, 1989), 75, 77, quoted in James Kombo, "The Trinity in Africa," *Journal of Reformed Theology* 3 (2009): 125–43.
47. Kelly, *Early Christian Doctrines*, 109. Harold O. J. Brown, *Heresies: Heresy and Orthodoxy in the History of the Church* (Peabody, MA: Hendrickson, 1988), 138, likewise observes the shift that occurred between the Council of Nicea (325) and Council of Constantinople (381), in which the former was monotheistic in a Trinitarian way, and in the

latter the language of "consubstantiality of persons" eclipsed the monotheistic foundation. See also Joseph T. Lienhard, *Contra Marcellum: Marcellus of Ancyra and Fourth-Century Theology* (Washington DC: The Catholic University of America Press, 1999), 41, 135, which is a study of the diahypostatic approach to the doctrine of the Trinity and how it fails to give a proper accounting of Christianity's monotheistic foundations.

48. Shane Clifton, "The Spirit and Doctrinal Development: A Functional Analysis of the Traditional Pentecostal Doctrine of the Baptism in the Holy Spirit," *Pneuma: The Journal of the Society for Pentecostal Studies* 29 (2007): 11. In many ways, Clifton's method for doctrinal development of the Pentecostal doctrine of baptism in the Holy Spirit applies to Oneness doctrine.

Index

B

C

D

E

F

G

H

L

M

N

O

P

R

S

T

U

V

W